MW01049592

# MUSIC INDUSTRY CONTRACTS

ASPEN SELECT SERIES

# MUSIC INDUSTRY CONTRACTS
## CASES AND FORMS

**ATTORNEY RICKY ANDERSON**
**WALT CHAMPION**

To contact Customer Service, e-mail customer.service@wolterskluwer.com, call 1-800-234-1660, fax 1-800-901-9075, or mail correspondence to:

Wolters Kluwer
Attn: Order Department
PO Box 990
Frederick, MD 21705

Printed in the United States of America.

1 2 3 4 5 6 7 8 9 0

ISBN 978-1-4548-7753-0

# About Wolters Kluwer Legal & Regulatory Solutions U.S.

Wolters Kluwer Legal & Regulatory Solutions U.S. delivers expert content and solutions in the areas of law, corporate compliance, health compliance, reimbursement, and legal education. Its practical solutions help customers successfully navigate the demands of a changing environment to drive their daily activities, enhance decision quality and inspire confident outcomes.

Serving customers worldwide, its legal and regulatory solutions portfolio includes products under the Aspen Publishers, CCH Incorporated, Kluwer Law International, ftwilliam.com and MediRegs names. They are regarded as exceptional and trusted resources for general legal and practice-specific knowledge, compliance and risk management, dynamic workflow solutions, and expert commentary.

This book is dedicated to my wife Toi, our Daughter Alysia,
and our Son Ricky II, for their continued support.
Watching our children mature in the Entertainment Industry is
PRICELESS.
That's right, Team Anderson always working!!!

# Summary of Contents

# Table of Contents

# Acknowledgments

First, I must thank GOD, for Your guidance and allowing me to do Your work daily.

Thank you to Prairie View A&M University and Thurgood Marshall School of Law for the exceptional education that these two great HBCUs have provided me. You both are right, "**Knowledge Is Power**." Special thanks to Texas Southern University President Dr. John Rudley; Texas Southern University President and Law School Dean James Douglas; Law School Dean Dannye Holley; Law School Dean McKen Carrington; Assistant Dean of Student Development Virgie Mouton, Assistant Dean of External Affairs Prudence Smith; and my Adjunct Administrator, Ms. JoAnne Alridge.

Thank you Steve Harvey, Rushion McDonald, Yolanda Adams, Mo'Nique Hicks, Sidney Hicks, Adele Givens, Judge Greg Mathis, Isaiah Washington, Cassi Davis, Earthquake, Rickey Smiley, Sinbad, Mary Mary, Bishop Hezekiah Walker, Dwayne Wiggins (and the "Tony Toni Tone" Team), Mali Music, Attorney Benjamin Crump, Sybrina Fulton, Tracy Martin, Preston Middleton—and I know that I am missing some names (so please, forgive me) that I will include in my Entertainment Law Book, Second Edition. Also, the publisher asked me to limit the character count.

Thank you Attorney Wendle Van Smith. It's been a joy working with you for the past 28 years, my Omega Psi Phi Fraternity Brother. Also, thank you Attorney Walter Strickland, Attorney Ray Shackleford, Attorney "Nick" Pittman, and Dr. Harris Bell, in the True Spirit of Omega.

David Villarreal (my Paralegal), you are a one of a kind and the best in the business. Your best just keeps getting better. Thank you for your tireless efforts and sacrifices. You have been absolutely PRICELESS with your supportive deliverables. Keep making your Sons proud.

Again, Professor Walter Champion, thank you for your friendship (since my law school days) and your support with this second book.

To my many, many family members, Omega Psi Phi Fraternity Brothers, and friends, who are too many to include or the publisher will terminate my Publishing Agreement, please know that you are loved and appreciated.

Attorney Ricky Anderson
www.AttorneyRickyAnderson.com

# Chapter 1
# Introduction

In our other book, *Entertainment Law: Cases, Documents, and Materials*, the authors looked at entertainment law through the unique eyes of the entertainment industry. Here, we have entitled our book *Music Industry Contracts: Cases and Forms*, and we now look at music industry contracts with the caveat that, essential to all aspects of music production and performance, there must be a mechanism for payment to the artist. There is no free lunch. Art for Art's sake, money for God's sake! The forms are vitally important to that payment scheme—why spend thousands of hours perfecting your talents and spending likewise thousands of dollars to make your performances marketable and commercial if there is no remuneration? Another aspect of this scheme is the "handlers" of the creative people (the talent—performers, producers, etc.); e.g., management, booking agents, roadies, etc.

Paid musicians have been a part of our society since the hunters and gatherers learned to grow crops, domesticate animals, and congregate in towns. This led to leisure time (a concept Rae Dawn Chong did not know in *Quest for Fire*), which necessitated that music could now be a paid vocation. Why toil in the fields when you can make more money playing the lute?

The case of *Lumley v. Wagner* involves the famous mezzo-soprano, Johanna Wagner (niece of composer Richard Wagner) who was the DIVA of her age, who sought the right to terminate her performance with Benjamin Lumley to sing exclusively at Her Majesty's Theatre on Haymarket from April 1, 1852, for three months, two nights a week. Frederick Gye, who ran Convent Gardens, wanted to break the contract with Her Majesty's Theatre. Gye acted maliciously. Lumley sought and was granted an injunction to stop Wagner from performing at the Convent Gardens.

Johanna Wagner appealed the granting of the injunction—the crux of the problem was whether the injunction constituted indirect specific performance. The order prohibited her from performing in any place other than at Her Majesty's Theatre during the contractual period. The judge stated that you cannot "suffer them to depart from contracts at their pleasure." "It is true that I have not the means of compelling her to sing . . . . The jurisdiction which I now exercise is wholly within the power of the court." *Lumley v. Gye* 118 E.R. 749 (1854, QB, Crompton, J.) asserts that one may claim damages from a third person who interferes in the performance of a contract by another. This is a nascent example of the tort of tortious interference of a business relationship, when the interference is malicious and causes great and immediate damages.

Recording contracts are usually the first step in the direction of a musical career. "We in the music industry depend on our contracts. They are the one thing that gives our industry some order. We need that (contractual) guarantee so the artists that are successful will continue making records for us, and we can reinvest those profits in new artists. It's important that everyone respect the sanctity of the contracts, otherwise there would be chaos." (Terry Ellis, Imago Records, suing DreamWorks Records for $40,000,000, quoted in Daily Variety, June 12, 1996, reprinted in Richard Schulenburg, Legal Aspects of the Music Industry 10 (1999)). Usually, the recording company will offer a contract to the would-be entertainer that is one-sided but adds a clause saying that it is a legal document and should be reviewed by an attorney. Like they say in boxing, protect yourself at all times.

All music industry contracts are legal documents and should be reviewed by an attorney. There should be a clause at the end of each contract that reminds you that this is a legal, binding contract and legal advice might be necessary. If there is no such clause, then you should really seek legal advice. There are many types of "music industry contracts," such as publisher agreements, management contracts, production agreements, recording contracts, distribution agreements, foreign distribution agreements, ASCAP and BMI agreements, booking agent contracts, performance contracts (including riders), promotion contracts, merchandising contracts, touring agreements, film and TV music contracts, video game music agreements, and internet and/or phone-based music agreements.

With apologies to the memory of Professor Williston; the first stage of the contracting process is the formation of a contract which can be divided into offer and acceptance. After formation, there might be an interpretation of the contract, which could include an analysis of terminations, assignments, defenses, or remedies that might accompany an alleged breach of contract. It is readily admitted that there is no entirely satisfactory definition of the term "contract." One definition is that "[a] contract is a promise, or set of promises, for breach of which the law gives a remedy, of the performance of which the law in some way recognizes as a duty" (1 Williston, Contracts Section 1:1 (4th ed. 1990), as quoted in Joseph Perillo, Calamari and Perillo on Contracts 1 (5th ed., 2003)).

"The whole point of a contract is to create legal consequences." (Thomas Haggard, Contract Law from a Drafting Perspective 55 (West, 2003)). The clauses that can create legal consequences are duties, rights, privileges, conditions, and/or warranties. For example, when there is a "Duties" clause, look to see if the duty is anteceded by a *shall* or a *will*. "A contract duty is something the non-performance of which will be considered a breach. Contract duties can be created by using either *shall* or *will*." "Duties to refrain from acting are created with the words of shall not or will not. Negations of, exceptions to, and quantifications upon previously created duties are expressed by saying it is not required to." (Haggard Contract Law from a Drafting Perspective 55).

A valid contract is formed if both parties intended the act of signing to be the last act in the formation of a binding contract. In this contractual discussion, identify the offeror and the offeree, and then ascertain if there was a proper response. There must be an offer and acceptance. If there's a problem, the party who now has a better offer alleges that the contract is breached. Here, interpretation of the contract comes into play. "In determining, the meaning of an indefinite or ambiguous term in a contract, the language should be read in light of all the surrounding circumstances. The interpretation that is placed on a contract by the parties prior to the time that it becomes a matter of controversy is entitled to great, if not controlling influence in ascertaining the intent and understanding of the parties," (Walter Champion, Sports Law in a Nutshell (West, 4th ed., 2009)).

In *Ketchum v. Hall Syndicate, Inc.*, 37 Misc. 2d 693, 236 N.Y.S. 2d 206 (1962), which follows, the court did not allow a contract to be terminated on the grounds that there was a lack of mutuality as the terms of the contract were indefinite.

Henry K. Ketcham, Plaintiff,
v.
Hall Syndicate, Inc., Defendant
Supreme Court, Special and Trial Term, New York County
December 19, 1962
236 N.Y.S. 2d 206

On January 24, 1951 the plaintiff (the creator of the cartoon panel entitled "Dennis The Menace") and the defendant, then known as the Post-Hall Syndicate, Inc., entered into an agreement for the syndication by Hall of the cartoon panels.

The contract provided that the panels were to be delivered to Hall's office in the City of New York at least six weeks prior to the scheduled date or release.

The agreement further provided that its duration should be for the period of one year with automatic renewals from year to year without notice unless the plaintiff's share from syndication did not equal certain minimum stipulated weekly payments, in which event either party had the right to terminate it.

There is no claim that the minimum returns have not been met. In fact, the evidence is quite to the contrary, and it is uncontradicted that the payments are now over five times the required minimum.

The parties performed under the contract from the date thereof until December 18, 1961 when the plaintiff wrote a letter to the defendant in which he purported to cancel and terminate the contract as of March 11, 1962. However, the plaintiff is still performing under the contract by reason of the provision in the aforesaid letter of December 18, 1961, that if the cancellation were not recognized then the plaintiff would continue to perform until such right of cancellation and termination should be established by litigation.

In answer to the plaintiff's letter, on March 8, 1962, the defendant advised the plaintiff that by reason of the payment of the minimum provided by the terms of the contract that it would deem the contract renewed for the further period of one year and that it would also deem it renewed from year to year thereafter provided the stipulated payments had been made.

The plaintiff's complaint seeks a declaratory judgment determining whether the plaintiff has the legal right to terminate the contract on the grounds (a) that it is for an indefinite term and that there is no mutuality; (b) that section 2855 of the Labor Code of the State of California provides that such a contract may not be enforced beyond seven years from the commencement of the services; and (c) that if the contract is governed by the laws of the State of California it may be cancelled and terminated since it is no longer enforceable under the aforesaid section of the Labor Code.

The questions of law are clearly defined and are (1) is the contract governed by the laws of the State of New York or of the State of California; (2) if the contract is governed by the laws of California, is it terminable by reason of section 2855 of the Labor Code; and (3) is the contract, which calls for automatic renewals upon the payment of certain minimums, voidable either by reason of indefiniteness or lack of mutuality.The California statute (Labor Code, § 2855) provides as follows: "§ 2855. Enforcement of contract to render personal service; time limit. A contract to render personal service, other than a contract of apprenticeship as provided in Chapter 4 of this division, may not be enforced against the employee beyond seven years from the commencement of service under it. Any contract, otherwise valid, to perform or render service of a special, unique, unusual, extraordinary, or intellectual character, which gives it peculiar value and the loss of which can not be reasonably or adequately compensated in damages in an action at law, may nevertheless be enforced against the person contracting to render such service, for a term not to exceed seven years from the commencement of service under it. If the employee voluntarily continues his service under it beyond that time, the contract may be referred to as affording a presumptive measure of the compensation."

There is no decision of the California courts which has determined whether a contract such as the one in question is governed by the above-quoted statute. Defendant contends that the contract in question established a relationship not of employer-employee but one of the status of an independent contractor and that therefore the section relied on does not apply.

Section 2750 of said code defines a contract of employment as one "by which one, who is called the employer, engages another, who is called the employee to do something for the benefit of the employer or a third person."

Edwin S. Pillsbury, Esq., plaintiff's expert on California law, testified on cross-examination that the contract in question "does not establish, in my opinion, the relationship of employer and employee in the strict sense"; and further testified that this contract would fall within the category of "an independent contractor relationship", and that Mr. Ketcham was an independent contractor by reason of the fact that there was no "right of supervision, direction and control."

Mr. Pillsbury, however, testified that section 2855 of the California Labor Code applied to independent contractors. That the second sentence of section 2855 relating to contracts to "render service of a special, unique, unusual, extraordinary, or intellectual character, which gives it peculiar value" had reference to independent contractors and that Mr. Ketcham's contract was of this type. However, he never stated the basis for his opinion, except that there was a strong public policy (in California) "to the effect that an employee should be protected by law against improvidently contracting his services away for a longer period than seven years."

Reliance is also placed by plaintiff on *De Haviland v. Warner Bros.* (67 Cal. App. 2d 225). However, in that case the acting was performed by the employee at the direction of her employer at places designated by her employer. In this case, however, plaintiff's performance was delivery by him at the defendant's New York office of six daily cartoon panels per week. There was no supervision, plaintiff worked where he pleased. The provision regarding the quality of the panels is usual in certain types of sales or building contracts and does not imply supervision.

Sidney Justin, Esq., defendant's expert witness on California law, testified that he was "very intensively" acquainted with the provisions of section 2855 by reason of his employment in the legal department of Paramount Pictures Corp. because the section involved all of the employment contracts of the studio. He testified that the contract was one "to furnish materials" and similar to contracts between motion picture producers and distributors, whereas the contract in the *De Haviland* case (*supra*) was "a typical employment contract." He testified that the sole purpose of section 2855 "was to protect employees" and that there were no provisions of the Labor Code which he could find which govern independent contractors. He testified that although the word "employee" was not used in the second sentence of section 2855 (relating to unique services) it must be read into it. Since the third sentence commences: "If the employee voluntarily continues his service under it", the conclusion is inescapable that the word employee must be read into the second sentence.

Furthermore, it should be noted that the first sentence of section 2855 refers to "employee". "Employee" is defined by the same Labor Code in subdivision (b) of section 350 as follows: "(b) 'Employee' means every person including aliens and minors, rendering actual service in any business for an employer, whether gratuitously or for wages or pay and whether such wages or pay are measured by the standard of time, piece, task, commission, or other method of calculation and whether such service is rendered on a commission, concessionaire, or other basis."

It should also be noted that the defendant is not an "employer" as defined by subdivision (a) of section 350 of the Labor Code as follows: "(a) 'Employer' means every person engaged in any business or enterprise in this State, which has one or more persons in service under any appointment, contract of hire, or apprenticeship, express or implied, oral or written, irrespective of whether such person is the owner of the business or is operating on a concessionaire or other basis."

The above definitions add additional weight to the conclusion of the defendant's expert, whose opinion seems more compelling. The court adopts his interpretation of the statute that the sentence is only intended to include employees and would exclude independent contractors.

It is obvious that under the usual rules of statutory interpretation the provisions of section 2855 would apply only to the normal employer-employee relationship and not to situations where one of the parties was an independent contractor.

Since the second sentence was not interpreted by the California courts, I believe that we can accept our own definition of an independent contractor as laid down by our Court of Appeals in *Hexamer v. Webb* (101 N. Y. 377, 385): "The test to determine whether one who renders service to another does so as a contractor or not is to ascertain whether he renders the service in the course of an independent occupation, representing the will of his employer only as to the result of his work, and not as to the means by which it is accomplished. (Shearm. & Redf. on Neg., § 76.) In *Blake v. Ferris* (5 N. Y. 48, 58), within the rule last stated it is held that when a man is employed in doing a job or piece of work with his own means, and his own men, and employs others to help him, or to execute the work for him, and under his control, he is the superior who is responsible for their conduct, no matter for whom he is doing the work. To attempt to make the primary principal or employer responsible in such cases would be an attempt to push the doctrine of *respondeat superior* beyond the reason on which it is founded". (See, also, 56 C. J. S., Master and Servant, § 3, subd. (1), p. 41.)

The evidence also establishes that the parties by their own conduct never considered the relationship to be that of employer-employee. There was never a withholding by the defendant for income taxes or social security; the plaintiff paid all the expenses of producing the cartoons; and the plaintiff in filing his Federal income tax return paid the "self employment tax" which was measured by the income received from the defendant.

The contract provides that: "Should Ketcham become incapacitated or unable to deliver the material ... or in the event of the decease of Ketcham, he or his executors shall have the privilege of employing substitute services to prepare the materials" or that the defendant "shall have the privilege of securing substitute services."

In either event Ketcham (or his estate) was still to receive the benefits of the contract (less the cost of the substitute).

Ketcham was not an employee and the contract is at best one for his services as an independent contractor. Indeed in most of its aspects it is more a contract of sale or a contract to supply a product rather than services.

There is yet another reason for holding the California Statute inapplicable. The New York conflict of laws rules require a finding that the contract is governed by New York law, under the theory of "center of gravity" or the "grouping of contacts". Defendant's office is and was in New York, all of its operations (other than traveling salesmen) are conducted in New York, including the mat makers, the editorial work, financial work, photoengravers, etc. Performance of the contract by plaintiff was to be by delivery of the panels at defendant's New York office. The contract was signed in New York by defendant and by "Kennedy Associates, Inc. By *John J. Kennedy*as agents for Hank Ketcham." The verified complaint sets forth that Kennedy Associates, Inc. "executed the contract as agent for the plaintiff". Plaintiff prepared the panels at various residences during the years following the execution thereof. Indeed the place where plaintiff or his substitute was to prepare the panels was of absolutely no significance. The most important contact was the place of delivery, the fixed place where all of defendant's work had to be performed. New York was the place of most significant contact when the contract was signed, was so during the intervening years and is today, and therefore New York law governs (*Haag v. Barnes*, 9 N Y 2d 554, 559; *Auten v. Auten*, 308 N. Y. 155).

The first, second and third affirmative defenses have been proven and therefore the Californian statute will not be applied.

Since we have decided that the California law is inapplicable, the remaining questions to be determined are whether the contract is indefinite and does it lack mutuality.

The issue of mutuality poses no problem. Plaintiff's argument that the contract lacks mutuality of obligation is adequately answered by a comparison of the facts in this case and those in *Wood v. Duff-Gordon* (222 N. Y. 88). In this case, the defendant was expressly obligated to produce certain minimum payments to keep the contract in force, whereas in the *Wood* case (*supra*) the court merely implied an obligation on plaintiff's part to use its best efforts. There is thus certainly more basis for finding mutuality than existed in*Wood*, where the Court of Appeals found mutuality.

Whether or not the contract is indefinite presents a more difficult question and is probably the most important problem to be resolved in this case. The question, however, is not whether the contract is for an *indefinite term*, it is whether the contract, by its terms, *is indefinite as to its duration*. If it is, then judicial construction is necessary and thus plaintiff should prevail because it is well settled in New York, that a contract will not be construed to require perpetual performance where another construction is available (*Cronk v. Vogt's Ice Cream*, 15 N. Y. S. 2d 649, 654 [1939]; *Mitler v. Friedeberg*, 32 Misc 2d 78 [1961].) Absent a fixed or *determinable duration* or an express provision that the duration is perpetual, the contract is one terminable at will (*A. S. Rampell, Inc. v. Hyster Co.*, 3 N Y 2d 369, 382).

The contract in the case at bar is not indefinite as to duration. Paragraphs 4, 5 and 6 provide specifically for termination by either party upon the happening of certain events. The contract provides that it "shall be for a period of one year ... and shall renew itself automatically from year to year for additional periods of one year each without the giving of notice by either party to the other, except that each of the parties shall have the right to terminate this agreement at the end of any one year period hereof ... in the event" that plaintiff's share fall below the stipulated amount and the defendant at its sole discretion, to avoid a termination of this agreement, failed to advance the difference in the minimum stipulated amount.

The plaintiff asserts that these provisions render the contract indefinite because they include no specific date for the termination of the contract. This, however, is not the kind of indefiniteness which renders the contract voidable, since specific provision is made for termination. It is this specificity which destroys the plaintiff's case. The contract is for one year and renewable from year to year, but this, from the terms of the contract itself, appears to have been the intention of the parties. The paragraphs regarding termination clearly provide for automatic renewal and just as clearly give the defendant the right to keep the contract alive in the event certain requirements for automatic renewal are not met. It was the intention of the parties that the contract should run so long as the minimum receipts were realized and that during such period that neither party should be able to desert the other. The strip started as an idea and both parties were to be integral parts of its development, the plaintiff by his creative ability and the defendant by his promotion and salesmanship. The terms of the contract are clear and unambiguous and freely signed by the plaintiff and his agent.

That contracts providing for perpetual performance are not invalid is undoubtedly the law of New York, although no precise holding on this point can be found among the New York cases. For judicial language to this effect, see *Cronk v. Vogt's Ice Cream* (*supra*, p. 654) and *Mitler v. Friedeberg* (*supra*).

For contracts which had no calendar fixed date of termination but were held as contracts for a definite term, see *Matter of Exercycle Corp.* (*Maratta*) (11 A D 2d 677, affd. 9 N Y 2d 329); *Ehrenworth v. Stuhmer & Co.* (229 N. Y. 210, 214, 215); *Deucht v. Storper* (44 N. Y. S. 2d 350, 351). In *Exercycle*, the contract provided for continuation until the employee voluntarily leaves the employ of Exercycle. In *Ehrenworth*, the contract was for "as long as the plaintiff ... remained in business." In *Deucht*, the employment was to be for so long a time as defendant "continued to employ workers, trained, developed and gathered by plaintiff". (See *Warner-Lambert Pharmaceutical Co. v. John J. Reynolds, Inc.*, 178 F. Supp. 655, 661 [U. S. Dist. Ct., S. D. N. Y., 1959].)

A square holding on facts virtually identical with those presented herein is *Liberty Ind. Sales v. Marshall Steel Co.* (272 F. 2d 605 [C. C. A. 7th, 1959]) which the plaintiff takes great pains to distinguish. In that case, as here, the parties considered the duration of the contract. They provided for termination in the event certain quotas were not met. There, as here, the contract did not state specifically the outer limits of the duration of the contract. In finding against the party desiring termination on terms other than those specifically provided for in the contract the court said at page 606, citing *Noble v. Reid-Avery Co.* (89 Cal. App. 75): "'Such provisions for the duration of the contract are sufficiently certain and valid. As a general proposition the failure of an executory contract to state a time presently definite for its termination does not render it void for uncertainty.'"

The parties have been unable to find other citations dealing with this identical situation. Our independent research indicates that they made an exhaustive search of the authorities.

The defendant, therefore, must prevail. Contracts which are vague as to their duration generally will not be construed to provide for perpetual performance, but where, such as the case here, the contract is not vague, no judicial construction is necessary.

## Cal. Civ. Code § 3423

An injunction may not be granted:

(a) To stay a judicial proceeding pending at the commencement of the action in which the injunction is demanded, unless this restraint is necessary to prevent a multiplicity of proceedings.

(b) To stay proceedings in a court of the United States.

(c) To stay proceedings in another state upon a judgment of a court of that state.

(d) To prevent the execution of a public statute, by officers of the law, for the public benefit.

(e) To prevent the breach of a contract the performance of which would not be specifically enforced, other than a contract in writing for the rendition of personal services from one to another where the promised service is of a special, unique, unusual, extraordinary, or intellectual character, which gives it peculiar value, the loss of which cannot be reasonably or adequately compensated in damages in an action at law, and where the compensation for the personal services is as follows:

(1) As to contracts entered into on or before December 31, 1993, the minimum compensation provided in the contract for the personal services shall be at the rate of six thousand dollars ($6,000) per annum.

(2) As to contracts entered into on or after January 1, 1994, the criteria of subparagraph (A) or (B), as follows, are satisfied:

(A) The compensation is as follows:

(i) The minimum compensation provided in the contract shall be at the rate of nine thousand dollars ($9,000) per annum for the first year of the contract, twelve thousand dollars ($12,000) per annum for the second year of the contract, and fifteen thousand dollars ($15,000) per annum for the third to seventh years, inclusive, of the contract.

(ii) In addition, after the third year of the contract, there shall actually have been paid for the services through and including the contract year during which the injunctive relief is sought, over and above the minimum contractual compensation specified in clause (i), the amount of fifteen thousand dollars ($15,000) per annum during the fourth and fifth years of the contract, and thirty thousand dollars ($30,000) per annum during the sixth and seventh years of the contract. As a condition to petitioning for an injunction, amounts payable under this clause may be paid at any time prior to seeking injunctive relief.

(B) The aggregate compensation actually received for the services provided under a contract that does not meet the criteria of subparagraph (A), is at least 10 times the applicable aggregate minimum amount specified in clauses (i) and (ii) of subparagraph (A) through and including the contract year during which the injunctive relief is sought. As a condition to petitioning for an injunction, amounts payable under this subparagraph may be paid at any time prior to seeking injunctive relief.

(3) Compensation paid in any contract year in excess of the minimums specified in subparagraphs (A) and (B) of paragraph (2) shall apply to reduce the compensation otherwise required to be paid under those provisions in any subsequent contract years.

However, an injunction may be granted to prevent the breach of a contract entered into between any nonprofit cooperative corporation or association and a member or stockholder thereof in respect to any provision regarding the sale or delivery to the corporation or association of the products produced or acquired by the member or stockholder.

(f) To prevent the exercise of a public or private office, in a lawful manner, by the person in possession.

(g) To prevent a legislative act by a municipal corporation.

California and New York set the standard for enforcement of music contracts. The previous section, Cal. Civ. Code § 3423, "When Injunction may not be granted," stipulates again at (E), "To prevent the breach of a contract which would not be specifically enforced, other than a contract in writing for the rendition of personal services from one to another where the promised service is of a special, unique, extraordinary, or intellectual character, which gives it peculiar value, the loss which cannot be adequately compensated in damage in an action in law . . . "

Like with baseball superstar Napoleon Lajoie (c. 1902), an injunction was issued since his services were unique (see Philadelphia Ball Club v. Lajoie, 51 A. 973 (Pa. 1902)). The following California Code section (Cal. Fam. Code § 6710), deals with the contracts of minors (e.g., the young Michael Jackson), which allows the disaffirmance of the contract by a minor.

Cal Fam Code § 6710. Right of disaffirmance

Except as otherwise provided by statute, a contract of a minor may be disaffirmed by the minor before majority or within a reasonable time afterwards or, in case of the minor's death within that period, by the minor's heirs or personal representative.

Cal Fam Code § 6750. Application of chapter

(a) This chapter applies to the following contracts entered into between an unemancipated minor and any third party or parties on or after January 1, 2000:

(1) A contract pursuant to which a minor is employed or agrees to render artistic or creative services, either directly or through a third party, including, but not limited to, a personal services corporation (loan-out company), or through a casting agency. "Artistic or creative services" includes, but is not limited to, services as an actor, actress, dancer, musician, comedian, singer, stunt-person, voice-over artist, or other performer or entertainer, or as a songwriter, musical producer or arranger, writer, director, producer, production executive, choreographer, composer, conductor, or designer.

(2) A contract pursuant to which a minor agrees to purchase, or otherwise secure, sell, lease, license, or otherwise dispose of literary, musical, or dramatic properties, or use of a person's likeness, voice recording, performance, or story of or incidents in his or her life, either tangible or intangible, or any rights therein for use in motion pictures, television, the production of sound recordings in any format now known or hereafter devised, the legitimate or living stage, or otherwise in the entertainment field.

(3) A contract pursuant to which a minor is employed or agrees to render services as a participant or player in a sport.

(b)(1) If a minor is employed or agrees to render services directly for any person or entity, that person or entity shall be considered the minor's employer for purposes of this chapter.

(2) If a minor's services are being rendered through a third-party individual or personal services corporation (loan-out company), the person to whom or entity to which that third party is providing the minor's services shall be considered the minor's employer for purposes of this chapter.

(3) If a minor renders services as an extra, background performer, or in a similar capacity through an agency or service that provides one or more of those performers for a fee (casting agency), the agency or service shall be considered the minor's employer for the purposes of this chapter.

(c)(1) For purposes of this chapter, the minor's "gross earnings" shall mean the total compensation payable to the minor under the contract or, if the minor's services are being rendered through a third-party individual or personal services corporation (loan-out company), the total compensation payable to that third party for the services of the minor.

(2) Notwithstanding paragraph (1), with respect to contracts pursuant to which a minor is employed or agrees to render services as a musician, singer, songwriter, musical producer, or arranger only, for purposes of this chapter, the minor's "gross earnings" shall mean the total amount paid to the minor pursuant to the contract, including the payment of any advances to the minor pursuant to the contract, but excluding deductions to offset those advances or other expenses incurred by the employer pursuant to the contract, or, if the minor's services are being rendered through a third-party individual or personal services corporation (loan-out company), the total amount payable to that third party for the services of the minor.

Cal Fam Code § 6751. Disaffirmance of contracts approved by court

(a) A contract, otherwise valid, of a type described in Section 6750, entered into during minority, cannot be disaffirmed on that ground either during the minority of the person entering into the contract, or at any time thereafter, if the contract has been approved by the superior court in any county in which the minor resides or is employed or in which any party to the contract has its principal office in this state for the transaction of business.

(b) Approval of the court may be given on petition of any party to the contract, after such reasonable notice to all other parties to the contract as is fixed by the court, with opportunity to such other parties to appear and be heard.

(c) Approval of the court given under this section extends to the whole of the contract and all of its terms and provisions, including, but not limited to, any optional or conditional provisions contained in the contract for extension, prolongation, or termination of the term of the contract.

(d) For the purposes of any proceeding under this chapter, a parent or legal guardian, as the case may be, entitled to the physical custody, care, and control of the minor at the time of the proceeding shall be considered the minor's guardian ad litem for the proceeding, unless the court shall determine that appointment of a different individual as guardian ad litem is required in the best interests of the minor.

In the Matter of Twentieth Century Fox Film Corp.
190 A.D.2d 483
Supreme Court, Appellate Division, First Department, New York
June 3, 1993

The issue on this appeal, which has been jointly brought by petitioner and respondents, involves the applicability of section 216.1 of the Uniform Rules for Trial Courts (22 NYCRR 216.1), which deals with the sealing of court records, to the documents offered by the parties to the Surrogate's Court in order to obtain approval of a contract under section 35.03 of the Arts and Cultural Affairs Law.

This proceeding was commenced in order to gain the Surrogate's approval of certain contracts (hereinafter referred to as the contract) entered into by petitioner Twentieth Century Fox with then-11-year-old respondent Macaulay Culkin in connection with the sequel to the motion picture "Home Alone." Such approval was sought pursuant to section 35.03 of the Arts and Cultural Affairs Law, which establishes a detailed procedure for the review of performing contracts entered into by infants. Under this statute, if the court determines that the submitted contract is "reasonable and provident and for the best interests of the infant" (§ 35.03 [5] [k]), the infant will be precluded from later disaffirming the contract on the ground of infancy or on the ground that his or her parent or guardian lacked authority to make the contract. Included in the review are not only the terms of the contract itself but the proportion of the infant's earnings which are to be set aside in trust for the future and the proportion which should be made available to the infant's family for current use (§ 35.03 [3] [b]).

In order to allow the court to properly perform its review, it must have access to extensive information regarding the parties. Thus, review of the propriety of the motion picture contracts in this case will necessarily involve an inquiry not only into the contracts themselves, which include a certificate of employment, a performing agreement, a commercial tie-in agreement and a merchandising contract, but also, in addition, the screenplay, a schedule of the infant's gross earnings, estimated outlays and net earnings, and information concerning the financial status of the infant, his parents, and his siblings.

The parties moved to seal the records in the proceeding so as to prevent public disclosure of the underlying information. This motion was brought pursuant to 22 NYCRR 216.1 (a), which provides: "Except where otherwise provided by statute or rule, a court shall not enter an order in any action or proceeding sealing the court records, whether in whole or in part, except upon a written finding of good cause, which shall specify the grounds thereof. In determining whether good cause has been shown, the court shall consider the interests of the public as well as the parties."

The Surrogate found that, in this case, the public interest in disclosure outweighed the stated reasons of the parties for requesting confidentiality and that, with the exception of the screenplay, the records should therefore not be sealed.

On this appeal, the parties seek to overturn the Surrogate's order. Petitioner argues that its individual performance contracts are confidential business information which could give competitors an advantage and could disadvantage petitioner in future negotiations with other artists. Furthermore, respondents have offered proof that substantial efforts have been made to preserve the privacy of the Culkin family, and it is argued that disclosure of the details of the contract would invite harassment and annoyance from investment advisors and could subject the infant to potential dangers.

We find that the Surrogate failed to take into account certain factors militating against disclosure of the particular contracts involved herein, and upon taking those factors into account, we conclude that the records should be sealed.

Although the subject of some controversy, the enactment of 22 NYCRR 216.1 (a) did not effect a change in the law, which has always favored public disclosure of court records. The rule was enacted largely in response to a concern that, in cases in which the parties were in agreement to seal the records, courts were not sufficiently taking into account the public interest and exercising their discretion to override the parties wishes *(see,* Hoenig, Products Liability, *New York's Rule on Sealing of Court Records,* NYLJ, Mar. 1, 1991, at 3, col 1; Carpinello, *Public Access to Court Records in Civil Proceedings: The New York Approach,* 54 Alb L Rev 93, 98-100). In particular, concern had been widely expressed about the practice of sealing records of settlements in product liability and other tort actions where the information might alert other consumers to potential defects *(id.,* at 100-101; *see generally,* Herman, *No more Dirty Little Secrets in the Courts,* Washington Post, Sept. 15, 1989, at A31, col 6).

Clearly, the public has no similar interest in the particular information involved in the instant proceeding. The Surrogate, however, found that the necessary focus in making a determination under section 216.1 (a) was not merely the public's interest in the particular information sought to be sealed, but in the presumed benefit to the administration of justice if court records remain open to the public except in certain exceptional circumstances. In particular, the Surrogate noted that, in a matter involving an infant, the court acts as a representative of the public in protecting the infant, and the public therefore has a particular interest in overseeing the court's handling of this important duty.

There is no question that there is a general public interest in disclosure of court records *(see, Nixon v Warner Communications,* 435 US 589, 597; *see also, Matter of Newsday, Inc. v Sise,* 71 NY2d 146, 153, n 4, *cert denied* 486 US 1056; *Matter of Brownstone,* 191 AD2d 167), or that that interest is a factor which should be taken into account when a court is deciding whether to grant a motion to seal pursuant to section 216.1. On the other hand, confidentiality is, in certain circumstances, necessary in order to protect the litigants or encourage a fair resolution of the matter in controversy. As one commentator has noted, "Courts must have discretion to balance the competing interests of the parties, the public, and the justice systems. When the balance favors confidentiality, confidentiality should be provided". (Miller, *The Private Costs of Public Justice,* 63 NY St B J 12, 13 [July/Aug. 1991].) In this case, while we agree with the Surrogate that the public has a strong interest in overseeing the conduct of the courts in matters involving the protection of an infant, we find that that interest is not sufficient to overcome the compelling arguments made in favor of preserving the privacy of the parties, particularly the infant. To conclude, as did the Surrogate, that the public's interest must always predominate would make disclosure virtually automatic in any proceeding brought pursuant to Arts and Cultural Affairs Law § 35.03, and would create a substantial risk of undermining the very purpose of that section.

By virtue of section 35.03, the court may insulate an infant from deleterious practical effects which arise by reason of the intended protection of the common law in rendering voidable any contract entered into by an infant *(see, Joseph v Schatzkin,* 259 NY 241; *Casey v Kastel,* 237 NY 305) or entered into by another on an infant's behalf *(see, Lee v Silver,* 262 App Div 149, *affd* 287 NY 575). The statute affords a means of overcoming the natural reluctance on the part of a party who might otherwise contract with an infant to enter into an agreement which does not bind the other party. Thus, the purpose of the statute is to bestow upon the infant an advantage of which he or she would otherwise be deprived by law, i.e., the ability to be bound by contract. Its goal is to permit the party contracting with an infant to be as confident of the survival of the contract as if the infant had reached majority *(see, Shields v Gross,* 58 NY2d 338, 345-346), and thereby encourage parties to enter into contracts beneficial to the infant which they would otherwise forego because of the uncertainty of voidability. Toward this end, infants involved in the performing arts have been singled out by law, albeit for their benefit, as a special class who must reveal to the court very private information concerning their finances and business arrangements, and compel parties who wish to contract with them to do the same, in order to be able to effectively contract. If such information were to be made public as a matter of course in order to permit a contract to receive the benefits of section 35.03, the prospect of such disclosure would undoubtedly have a chilling effect on the willingness of those who would otherwise wish to contract with infants. This is precisely the result which the statute was designed to ameliorate.

This is not to say that the records in such proceedings should automatically be sealed in every case. It means only that the type of proceeding, in and of itself, is an important factor which the court should take into account in determining whether the parties have established sufficient good cause to seal the records to overcome any public interest in their disclosure. In this case, we find that the parties have offered sufficient additional reasons to demonstrate that the essentially confidential nature of such a proceeding should be preserved. In addition to the arguments relevant to the best interests of the infant and his family, we also take note of petitioner's argument that its relationship with its competitors, as well as with other artists in its employ, could be compromised by the disclosure of the details of the contracts, which include information as to how it has marketed the subject motion picture. *(See, Matter of Crain Communications v Hughes,* 135 AD2d 351, 352, *affd* 74 NY2d 626.)

Under all of the circumstances here present, we find that the records should be sealed and the order of the Surrogate denying sealing should be reversed.

Accordingly, the order of the Surrogate's Court, New York County (Eve Preminger, S.), entered June 11, 1992, which denied petitioner's motion pursuant to 22 NYCRR 216.1 to seal court records, including the contracts and financial schedules required to be submitted to the court in relation to the within petition brought pursuant to section 35.03 of the Arts and Cultural Affairs Law, should be unanimously reversed, on the law, the facts, and in the exercise of discretion, the motion granted, and the records sealed, without costs.

Sullivan, J. P., Ellerin, Wallach, Kupferman and Ross, JJ., concur.

Order, Surrogate's Court, New York County, entered June 11, 1992, unanimously reversed, on the law, the facts, and in the exercise of discretion, without costs, the motion granted, and the records sealed.

---

Home Alone star Macaulay Culkin made millions as a minor; he hopes to keep the terms of his contracts confidential and asks the surrogate's court to obtain approval of his motion picture contracts for an infant under N.Y. Arts & Cultural Affairs Law Section 35.03 (including commercial tie-in and merchandising contracts) to be sealed under 22 NYCRR 216.1. On appeal, the court held that the purpose of Section 35.03 was to effectuate and protect the rights of minors in the entertainment business; therefore, sealing the records would allow Macaulay to enjoy the benefits of Section 35.03.

Matter of Skutch Publ., Inc., 2012 N.Y. Misc. LEXIS 6575
Surrogate's Court of New York, New York County
July 28, 2012, Decided
2012 N.Y. Misc. LEXIS 6575

ANDERSON, S.

In these two miscellaneous proceedings brought pursuant to Arts and Cultural Affairs Law §35.03, Skutch Publishing, Inc., and Skutch Entertainment, Inc., referred to collectively as "Skutch" or "petitioner," seeks judicial approval of two contracts, a music publishing agreement and an exclusive recording agreement, for the services of a 15 year old infant. If the contracts are approved, the infant may not, either during her minority or upon reaching majority, disaffirm the agreements on the ground of infancy (Arts and Cultural Affairs Law §35.03[1]).

Petitioner also asks the court to appoint the infant's parents as limited guardians to receive and hold one-fourth of the infant's net earnings pursuant to Arts and Cultural Affairs Law § 35.03(3), and to seal the entire record of these proceedings.

A hearing was held before a court attorney/referee on June 24, 2014. Testimony was rendered by: an attorney for Skutch; the attorney who represented the infant and her parents in the negotiation of the contracts; the infant's father, who, along with her mother, has been managing the infant's song-writing and recording activities; and the infant herself. The guardian ad litem appointed for the infant, who is familiar with entertainment law and the entertainment business, actively participated in the hearing.

The guardian ad litem recommended certain changes to the contracts which Skutch has accepted. She recommends that the contracts as amended be approved.

The record indicates that the terms of the contracts as amended are typical of these types of contracts or, in some respects, are more favorable to the infant than is typical; that the infant understands her obligations under the contracts, is desirous of pursuing a career in music and is ready and willing to meet those obligations; that the financial terms of the contract are fair to the infant and her family and are otherwise in accord with the infant's interests; and that the contracts meet the statutory requirements of Arts and Cultural Affairs Law § 35.03. The infant and her parents were represented by an experienced entertainment lawyer during the contract negotiations.

Based on the evidence presented and the report of the guardian ad litem, the court finds that the contracts are fair and consistent with industry practices, and that they adequately protect the infant's professional and pecuniary rights. Accordingly, the contracts are approved as being in the infant's best interests.

The infant's parents are appointed as limited guardians to receive and hold one-fourth of the infant's net earnings pursuant to Arts and Cultural Affairs Law §35.03(3) and (7).

Petitioner also requests the permanent sealing of the court record in this matter pursuant to Uniform Rules for Trial Courts (22 NYCRR 216.1). Case law favors the disclosure of court files in order to satisfy the public interest in knowing what transpires in court proceedings (Mosallem v Berenson, 76 AD3d 345, 905 N.Y.S.2d 575 [1st Dept 2010]). Deviation from the usual rule favoring open court records accordingly requires a weighing of the public right to know against special circumstances which establish that such disclosure would be harmful to the parties (Mancheski v Gabelli Group Capital Partners, 39 AD 3d 499, 502, 835 N.Y.S.2d 595 [2d Dept 2007]). Such special circumstances include the protection of children (Matter of Twentieth Century Fox Film Corp., 190 AD2d 483, 601 N.Y.S.2d 267 [1st Dept 1993]) and the risk of personal or economic harm (see, e.g.,  Mancheski v Gabelli Group Capital Partners, supra; Danco Lab, v Chemical Works of Gedeon Richter, 274 AD2d 1, 711 N.Y.S.2d 419 (1st Dept 2000]). Both of these special circumstances are present here, since the court must review personal and financial information about the infant and her family and the financial details of the proposed agreements (Matter of Twentieth Century Fox Film Corp., supra, 190 AD2d at 487). This mandated disclosure, if publically revealed, not only carries the risk of subjecting the child and her family to unwanted and undeserved public attention, but could also harm the infant's competitive standing in the music industry. The court thus approves a limited sealing of the portions of the record which contain the infant's home address and social security number and the financial and business details contained in the contracts.

Decrees signed.

Dated: July 28, 2012

/s/ Nora S. Anderson

SURROGATE

Richcar Music Co. v. Towns, 53 A.D.2d 501
Supreme Court of New York, Appellate Division, First Department
July 20, 1976
53 A.D.2d 501; 385 N.Y.S.2d 778

We are here concerned with the rights in the musical composition "You've Got To Change Your Evil Ways", also known as "Evil Ways", and with the proceeds derived therefrom.

The author of the song is Clarence A. Henry, also known as Sonny Henry. He wrote it in or about 1957, appropriately enough while serving a prison sentence for second degree murder. After his release from jail (he was incarcerated at the age of 15), he worked with a band as a guitarist and music arranger. The band was under the leadership of one William Correa, professionally known as Willie Bobo. In 1967, having learned that Bobo proposed to record "Evil Ways", Henry registered a claim to statutory copyright for an unpublished musical composition and received from the Register of Copyrights a certificate dated April 13, 1967.

The defendant Chris Towns is a half brother of Henry's and had his own music company and familiarity with the music business, and he claims that he obtained for Henry the copyright office "E" application (see Rules and Regulations of the Copyright Office, 37 CFR 202.8), and that he instructed Henry how to complete this relatively simple form. Thereafter, in June, 1967, Bobo recorded "Evil Ways" and another of Henry's compositions on the MGM Verve phonograph record label. Henry participated in the recording thereof as a musician and as an arranger of the music. It is from this that the unfounded claim of the defendant Gilsan Music Corp. is derived. Bobo, along with others, was a principal in Gilsan, and the label on this record showed Gilsan Music Corp. as the publisher of the song. The trial court properly gave short shrift to this claim, and there has been no appeal from it.

The Bobo record achieved no success. However, when Henry learned that Gilsan was wrongfully claiming to be the publisher of the song and of others of Henry's works which Bobo had recorded, he sought advice from his brother Towns as to how to protect himself against Gilsan's claim. Towns advised Henry to file a notice of use (see US Code, tit 17, § 101, subd [e]) and furnished to him and assisted him in completing this relatively simple copyright office "U" form (Copyright Office Rules and Regulations 37 CFR 202.18).

Towns counselled Henry to form his own company for the publication of his song and made the necessary arrangements for the formation of Sah Music Company early in 1968, Sah being the acronym of Sonny A. Henry's name. Henry then signed publishing contracts with Sah for "Evil Ways" and the other musical compositions which Bobo had recorded, and Towns became a partner in Sah, for which company a business certificate was filed in the New York County Clerk's office.

Shortly after the Bobo recording in June, 1967 and before the formation of Sah, Henry met Richard Carpenter, an officer of Richcar Music Co., the plaintiff, at a bar frequented by musicians, and it is contended, and the trial court so found, that at that time he sang "Evil Ways" as well as another musical composition to Carpenter and then went to Carpenter's office where he executed a publishing contract, assigning the rights in both songs to Richcar under a royalty arrangement with a cash advance of $ 100, for which Henry gave a receipt. Henry did not tell Carpenter about his previous copyright of the unpublished work nor of the Bobo record nor did he give him any written music or lyrics.

It is claimed that Carpenter of Richcar on several occasions requested of Henry a "lead sheet" (a written representation of the melodic line and words of a song), but received none and for that reason did not record his assignment in the Copyright Office (US Code, tit 17, § 30) or do anything to exploit the music.

Towns took care of whatever business arrangements were necessary for Sah, including having Sah affiliate with Broadcast Music, Inc. (BMI) for the purpose of obtaining royalties for public performance, if any, of the music. BMI paid an advance of $ 5,000, of which Towns received $ 2,500. However, because of conflicting claims to the song, there was a problem as to collecting public performing rights royalties at BMI. Towns was not told by Henry, his partner and half brother, of his assignment to Richcar.

None of the foregoing would be of any real interest, except for the fact that in 1969 a musical group known as Santana recorded the song on the Columbia Record label under the title "Evil Ways", and it was a tremendous success. Here again, the original jacket for the record with the song and the label credited someone else as the author and publisher. It seems that a different song, also entitled "Evil Ways", written a number of years before, was mistakenly believed to be the one recorded.

In 1970, with "Evil Ways" a success, Towns recommended to Henry that an arrangement be entered into with the defendant Ensign Music Corporation (a subsidiary of Gulf & Western). A two-year contract, retroactive to January 1, 1970, was entered into in March, 1970 between Sah and Ensign, confirmed by Henry, for Ensign to handle world rights in five musical compositions listed in a schedule to have been authored by Henry, all registered as unpublished works in the Copyright Office. The ownership of the rights was warranted by Sah and Henry, and Ensign had no knowledge of Richcar's claim. Ensign, among other things, was to receive 15% of the United States and Canada income, and 50% of the income abroad. It advanced $ 1,500 to Sah and $ 1,500 to Henry as author, against the accumulated royalties that would be due to them. However, Towns took $ 1,500 and Henry $ 1,500 because of their understanding that they would split advances from whatever source derived. Of course, the only song of consequence in the agreement was "Evil Ways", already an established hit.

In November, 1970, Henry played the Santana recording for Carpenter who recognized it. Henry then gave Carpenter a lead sheet, and Carpenter then filed a copyright registration. Supposedly, the following year, 1971, Carpenter learned of Henry's original copyright registration in April, 1967 for an unpublished musical composition, and filed an assignment claim to that 1967 copyright and a notice of use.

The 1967 royalty agreement and copyright assignment between Richcar and Henry is challenged as specious by Towns and Ensign. Although Henry confirms it, there are several disturbing aspects. It was entered into in cavalier fashion without the assignee of the rights obtaining any copy, by any means preserved, audible or visual, of the property conveyed. Further, the agreement signed by both parties (Mrs. Carpenter signed for Richcar) given to Henry was not produced in court, allegedly lost by fire or theft. Only the Richcar copy was received into evidence and that one, although stated to be signed by Henry in 1967, was not signed for Richcar until 1971. Nonetheless, we adopt the finding of the trial court which, after a nonjury trial, meticulously reviewed the evidence and found as a fact that the 1967 agreement had indeed been executed.

Henry does not challenge the rights of Richcar. Under the June, 1967 royalty agreement, there was the possibility for Henry to seek to renounce that agreement for failure of Richcar to exploit the musical composition, but Henry never raised that. (See Vidor v Serlin, 7 NY2d 502; cf. Dolfi Music v Drake, 76 LRRM 2313 [Sup Ct, Spec Term, Part I, NY County, 1970].) In fact, his legal and factual position is in complete support of the Richcar claim, seemingly to his own detriment.

The trial court determined that Richcar by virtue of its prior assignment is the holder of the copyright in "Evil Ways" and subject to its royalty agreement with Henry, and we affirm. There is no obligation to register such an assignment. (See Kupferman, Copyright and Judges, 19 Bull Copyright Soc. 343, 351 [June, 1972].) It is only between a subsequent bona fide purchaser (without notice who has given consideration) who has recorded within three months of the assignment, and a prior assignee who has failed to record "within three calendar months after its execution" (US Code, tit 17, § 30) that it becomes of moment. (Marks Music Corp. v Harris Music Pub. Co., 255 F2d 518 [2d Cir, 1958].)

Richcar did not record, but neither did Sah. Further, Sah gave no consideration. (Venus Music Corp. v Mills Music, 261 F2d 577 [2d Cir, 1958].)

While Sah, therefore, has no right in the composition, Towns has cross-claimed against Henry for the misrepresentation that he was the copyright owner of "Evil Ways". The trial court awarded Towns as against Richcar 25% of the income of "Evil Ways" less advances, and Richcar appeals. Richcar has no obligation to Sah or Towns. Towns' claim is on behalf of and as a partner in Sah as against Henry as author who breached his warranty. Towns has already received $ 4,000 in advances from BMI and Ensign, which would cover normal services. If Sah received the full payment that would be due to a publisher (see Menzel v List, 24 NY2d 91) from that amount there would first be paid the royalty due from Sah to Henry under his songwriter's agreement with it, and then from the remainder Towns would share in the income after expenditures of this business entity, Sah. As to this, the matter should be remanded for further hearing, including, in the discretion of the Trial Judge, if necessary, a partnership accounting.

To the same extent, but limited to the two-year period of the term of its agreement, Ensign has a claim against Sah and against Henry for breach of warranty. It has also sought and been awarded $ 10,000 as a counsel fee as a result of this litigation for which provision is made in the agreement. It seeks, however, $ 24,000 in counsel fee admittedly expended. The counsel fee awarded was fair and reasonable, but it is a claim only as against Sah and Henry.

The trial court directed the appointment of a receiver to collect all sums from any source derived from "Evil Ways" and to disburse in accordance with the judgment. In our view of the case, the direction to that effect is vacated.

The judgment of the Supreme Court, New York County (Stecher, J.), entered July 29, 1975, declaring the respective rights of the parties in and to the musical composition entitled "Evil Ways" and the proceeds thereof, should be modified, on the law and the facts, without costs and without disbursements, to remand as to the amount of damage with respect to breach of warranty in the claim of Towns as a partner in Sah as against Henry, including a partnership accounting, if the Trial Judge be so advised, and as to the amount of damage with respect to breach of warranty in the claim of Ensign against Sah and Henry, the direction for appointment of a receiver vacated, and the judgment amended to state that the amount heretofore received by Towns from advances is $ 4,000 rather than $ 5,250, and, as so modified, should be otherwise affirmed.

Judgment, Supreme Court, New York County, entered on July 29, 1975, unanimously modified, on the law and the facts, without costs and without disbursements, to remand as to the amount of damage with respect to breach of warranty in the claim of Towns as a partner in Sah as against Henry, including a partnership accounting, if the Trial Judge be so advised, and as to the amount of damage with respect to breach of warranty in the claim of Ensign against Sah and Henry, the direction for appointment of a receiver vacated, and the judgment amended to state that the amount heretofore received by Towns from advances is $ 4,000 rather than $ 5,250, and, as so modified, the judgment is otherwise affirmed.

———————

In *Richcar Music Co. v. Towns* 385 N.Y.S. 2d 778 (1976), music composer was counseled by his partner to form his own music company, but the composer executed a contract with another company. The partner and the subsequent assignee challenged the new agreement as specious, but the composer confirmed it. The court held that the second agreement was done in a cavalier manner, but concluded that the royalty payments should be paid first to the composer under the songwriter's agreement, and then the partner would share after the music company's expenditures. The court remanded for an accounting. In the following case, *A&M Records, Inc. v. Gen. Audio Video Cassettes*, 948 F. Supp. 1449 (1996), it was alleged that defendant defrauded a major record company by selling empty cassette cartridges and time-loaded audio tapes of 156 sound recordings for which A&M Records owned the copyrights and trademarks.

A&M Records, Inc. v. Gen. Audio Video Cassettes, Inc.
District of California
March 21, 1996, Decided; November 18, 1996, FILED
948 F. Supp. 1449

## I. BACKGROUND

On February 24, 1994, twenty-six major record companies sued numerous corporations and individuals, including Mohammad Abdallah, who were allegedly engaging in copyright and trademark infringement. The other defendants either failed to respond to the complaint or settled, but the case against Mr. Abdallah proceeded to trial. Mr. Abdallah is the president and sole owner of defendant General Audio Video Cassettes, Inc. ("GAVC"), a California corporation that sells blank audiotapes and duplicating equipment.

Soon after the lawsuit began, Mr. Abdallah retained attorneys for himself and for GAVC, believing that his legal expenses would be reimbursed from an insurance policy that he owned. On June 15, 1995, one of his two attorneys of record requested to withdraw from the case, stating that Mr. Abdallah could no longer pay their fee according to the fee agreement due to "a change in circumstances." It was later revealed that Mr. Abdallah's insurance company had determined that the claims against Mr. Abdallah were not covered by his policy, and so refused to reimburse Mr. Abdallah for his fees.

Prior to making the motion to withdraw, Mr. Abdallah's first attorney sent a letter to Mr. Abdallah explaining that the motion for withdrawal would be made and advising Mr. Abdallah to retain new counsel. On July 11, 1995, this Court granted the motion for withdrawal, and warned Mr. Abdallah in its order that "failure to take appropriate action may result in serious legal consequences and you might want to seek legal assistance." At this point trial was still eight months away, and Mr. Abdallah was fully aware of the need to retain new counsel.

On September 6, 1995, Mr. Abdallah's other attorney of record also withdrew from the case for the same reason. At this point, Mr. Abdallah and his corporation, GAVC, were unrepresented by counsel. However, nearly all of the discovery in the case had already been completed at that time.

Trial was set in the case for January 22, 1996, and so Mr. Abdallah had over five months to find and retain another attorney. However, his efforts were less than diligent, and he did not retain another attorney until January 9, 1996, less than two weeks before trial. This third attorney prepared Mr. Abdallah's pre-trial memoranda and trial documents, but was fired by Mr. Abdallah on January

15, 1996. The attorney stated that Mr. Abdallah had failed to cooperate with his attorney, refused to supply his attorney with essential information, and refused to follow his attorney's advice. Consequently, the third attorney moved to withdraw, and the Court granted that motion, again warning Mr. Abdallah that trial was only one week away and there would be no extension of the trial date.

On January 22, the morning of the trial, Mr. Abdallah showed up with a fourth attorney, who told the Court that he had just been retained and therefore required an extra week to examine the files and prepare for trial. The Court noted that the plaintiffs were prepared for trial and had expended resources to have all their witnesses ready that morning, and thus agreed to extend the trial date for a week if Mr. Abdallah reimbursed the plaintiffs for the expenses they had incurred in bringing their witnesses to court that day. Mr. Abdallah decided to proceed with the trial without an attorney.

Although it is unfortunate that Mr. Abdallah ended up representing himself at trial, he had been given numerous warnings of the dangers of self-representation and ample time in which to locate an attorney. Moreover, although Mr. Abdallah's case would probably have been presented more efficiently had he been represented by an attorney, his self-representation did not affect the final result of the case. As detailed below, the plaintiffs presented overwhelming evidence of Mr. Abdallah's illegal conduct, both through testimony and documentary evidence. Mr. Abdallah's legal arguments were ably set out by his third attorney in pre-trial memoranda that were submitted just before that attorney was dismissed. Thus, there is no doubt that the outcome of the case would have remained the same even if Mr. Abdallah had been represented by an attorney at trial.

## II. FINDINGS OF FACT

A. The following facts are undisputed by the parties and are thus accepted by this Court as true:

Plaintiffs are twenty-six major record companies in the United States, doing business in Los Angeles, California. Together they own the copyrights and trademarks for the 156 sound recordings and 24 trade names that are listed in Appendices A and B attached hereto.

Defendant Mohammad Abdallah is the president and sole owner of GAVC. GAVC is a California corporation doing business in California, with a branch office in New Jersey. GAVC sells empty cassette cartridges, spools of blank recording tape, audio duplicating equipment, and "time-loaded" audio tapes. A "time-loaded" audio tape is a tape that runs for a certain time period that is specified by the customer. For example, a customer would order 10,000 tapes with a playing time of 27 minutes and 45 seconds, and GAVC would then assemble 10,000 cassette tapes of that length out of blank recording tape and empty cassette cartridges using tape loading machines.

Between 1990 and 1992, GAVC sold time-loaded audio tapes to defendants Rizik Muslet, Mohammed Issa Halisi, and Mohammed Alabed. These individuals used the time-loaded audio tapes to illegally counterfeit the plaintiffs' copyrighted works, including the 156 titles listed in Appendix A. These individuals also packaged these counterfeit tapes in cassette cartridges using insert cards with the plaintiffs' trademarks. The counterfeiters were never licensed to use the plaintiffs' copyrights or trademarks.

B. The Court finds the following facts to be true by a preponderance of the evidence, primarily from the testimony of Rizik Muslet and Asmar Chabbo, whom this Court found to give credible testimony:

Audiocassette counterfeiters such as Mr. Muslet, Mr. Halisi, and Mr. Alabed must have blank cassettes timed to specific lengths in order to produce marketable counterfeit tapes. Tapes of standard lengths (e.g., 30 or 60 minutes) are unacceptable because they either cut off the music of the sound recording or leave large amounts of silent time on each side of the tape. Therefore, counterfeiters are dependent on suppliers such as GAVC to acquire blank tapes that are timed to the specific length of the sound recording that they wish to counterfeit.

In September of 1991, Mr. Muslet was searching for a new supplier of time-loaded tapes for his counterfeiting operation. He met with Mr. Abdallah and informed him about the nature of the counterfeit operation, and the two agreed on a price for blank time-loaded cassettes. Mr. Muslet also needed a new supplier for insert cards for the counterfeit tapes, and asked Mr. Abdallah to assist him in that regard. Mr. Abdallah said that he would have somebody contact Mr. Muslet, and a few days later a supplier called Mr. Muslet having been referred by Mr. Abdallah.

Throughout their business relationship, Mr. Muslet sent Mr. Abdallah numerous "legitimate" tapes (i.e., non-counterfeit tapes of sound recordings) to time. Mr. Abdallah would time these cassettes and send them back to Mr. Muslet with the time of the cassette written on it. Mr. Muslet would then use these times when ordering blank tapes from Mr. Abdallah.

From September of 1991 to October of 1992, Mr. Muslet purchased over 300,000 blank cassettes and a tape duplicating machine from GAVC. In October of 1992, Mr. Muslet's counterfeiting operation was raided by the police and he was arrested.

Mr. Abdallah's knowledge of his customer's counterfeiting activities was also demonstrated by his conversations with his employee, Asmar Chabbo. Mr. Chabbo worked for GAVC from July 1990 until July 1992. During that period, he became Mr. Abdallah's office manager in GAVC's branch office in New Jersey. Mr. Chabbo testified that Mr. Abdallah explained to him that some of GAVC's customers used the blank time-loaded tapes to counterfeit legitimate sound recordings, and also explained the methods that his customers used to counterfeit tapes.

Mr. Chabbo further testified as to Mr. Abdallah's relationship with Mohammed Halisi, GAVC's largest customer. At one point Mr. Abdallah mentioned that he was worried about the credit he had extended to Mr. Halisi, because Mr. Halisi had been raided by the police for counterfeiting activities and all his merchandise had been seized. On another occasion, Mr. Halisi complained to Mr. Abdallah that the time-loaded cassettes he had purchased from GAVC were too short for the "Michael Jackson cassette." These and other episodes related by Mr. Chabbo made it clear that Mr. Abdallah was aware of Mr. Halisi's illegal counterfeiting activities and yet still continued to supply him with time-loaded audio cassettes.

Mr. Chabbo also testified that Mr. Abdallah frequently timed new legitimate cassettes for his customers. Sometimes, as Mr. Muslet had previously explained, the customer would send in the legitimate cassette and Mr. Abdallah would time it, write the time on the cassette, and send the cassette back to the customer. On other occasions, the customer would send Mr. Abdallah the legitimate cassette and an order for time-loaded cassettes. Mr. Abdallah would then time the legitimate cassette and manufacture thousands of blank time-loaded cassettes based on the time of the legitimate cassette. The blank time-loaded cassettes were sent back to the customer along with the original legitimate cassette.

To support this contention, plaintiffs introduced numerous legitimate cassettes that had been seized from a raid on Mr. Muslet's warehouse. These cassettes had their time written on them in Mr. Abdallah's handwriting, as identified by both Mr. Chabbo and an independent handwriting expert. Thus, there was credible evidence from three different sources that Mr. Abdallah had timed legitimate cassettes for his customers. This fact strongly indicates that Mr. Abdallah knew what his counterfeiting customers were doing with the tapes that he sold them.

In conclusion, this Court finds that at least three of Mr. Abdallah's customers engaged in a substantial amount of counterfeiting and trademark infringement, including the 156 copyrighted sound recordings and 24 trade names listed in Appendices A and B, respectively. This Court further finds that the time-loaded cassettes which Mr. Abdallah sold to these customers was a material contribution to their counterfeiting activities, since audiotape counterfeiters must have blank tapes timed to specific lengths. Finally, and most critically, this Court concludes that Mr. Abdallah had actual knowledge of the counterfeiting and trademark infringement being done by his customers, and that, notwithstanding that knowledge, he continued to supply these customers with the time-loaded audiocassettes necessary to continue their counterfeiting activities.

There was no evidence that Mr. Abdallah or anyone at GAVC ever copied any sound recordings themselves.

### III. CONCLUSIONS OF LAW

A. Copyright infringement

Since it is undisputed that Mr. Abdallah did not participate in any copyright or trademark violations directly, the plaintiff's only basis for liability rests on a theory of contributory liability. This theory was outlined in Gershwin Publishing Corp. v. Columbia Artists Management, 443 F.2d 1159, 1162 (2d Cir. 1971), which stated that "one who, with knowledge of the infringing activity, induces, causes or materially contributes to the infringing conduct of another" is "equally liable with the direct infringer." This theory of liability was adopted in the Ninth Circuit by Universal City Studios v. Sony Corp. of America, 659 F.2d 963, 975 (9th Cir. 1981), rev'd on other grounds, 464 U.S. 417, 78 L. Ed. 2d 574, 104 S. Ct. 774 (1984). Under Gershwin, a plaintiff must prove two elements in order to establish a case of contributory liability: 1) the underlying copyright violation; and 2) the defendant knowingly induced, caused or materially contributed to that violation.

The Ninth Circuit's most recent analysis of contributory copyright infringement is found in Fonovisa v. Cherry Auction, 76 F.3d 259 (9th Cir. 1996). Fonovisa involved a swap meet where numerous vendors were selling counterfeit sound recordings. The owner of the infringed copyrights sued the company that organized the swap meet, claiming that the company was liable for contributory infringement. After the district court granted a motion by the defendants for failure to state a claim, Fonovisa appealed. The Ninth Circuit applied the Gershwin test, noting that both the underlying violation and the defendant's knowledge of that violation were properly pled. The only question was whether or not the defendant had "induced, caused, or materially contributed to" the copyright violation. Id. at 264 (citing Gershwin). The Ninth Circuit held that merely "providing the site and facilities for known infringing activity is sufficient to establish contributory liability," Id., and thus allowed the plaintiff's case to go to trial.

In the present case, the plaintiffs have established every element set out by Gershwin. As in Fonovisa, the underlying counterfeit activity is undisputed. This Court has concluded that Mr. Abdallah had actual knowledge of his customer's counterfeit activity and continued to provide them with time-loaded cassettes. And finally, the Court has found that Mr. Abdallah's provision of time-loaded cassettes was a material contribution to his customers' counterfeiting activities.

Mr. Abdallah's contribution to the underlying counterfeiting activity seems at least as significant as the contribution made by the swap meet in Fonovisa. Therefore, the plaintiffs have successfully demonstrated that Mr. Abdallah is liable for contributory copyright infringement.

The defendant argues that the Supreme Court's decision in Sony Corp. of America v. Universal City Studios, 464 U.S. 417, 78 L. Ed. 2d 574, 104 S. Ct. 774 (1984) has altered the Gershwin test. In Sony, the plaintiffs argued that the sale of video cassette recorders ("VCR's") constituted contributory copyright infringement because the sellers had at least constructive knowledge that the VCR's were being used to illegally copy movies broadcast on television. The Supreme Court ruled against the plaintiffs, holding that "the sale of copying equipment, like the sale of other articles of commerce, does not constitute contributory infringement if the product is widely used for legitimate, unobjectionable purposes. Indeed, it need merely be capable of substantial noninfringing uses." Id. at 442. In the present case, Mr. Abdallah argues that, just as VCR's have legitimate, noninfringing uses, the time-loaded cassettes that he sold also have legitimate, noninfringing uses.

This Court rejects the defendant's argument for three reasons. First, the Supreme Court developed the Sony doctrine by borrowing a concept from patent law, which provides that the sale of a "staple article or commodity of commerce suitable for substantial noninfringing use" cannot constitute contributory infringement." See 35 U.S.C. § 271(c) (1984); Sony at 439-40). Arguably, the Sony doctrine only applies to "staple articles or commodities of commerce," such as VCR's, photocopiers, and blank, standard-length cassette tapes. Its protection would not extend to products specifically manufactured for counterfeiting activity, even if such products have substantial noninfringing uses. Second, even if the Sony doctrine does apply to items specifically designed for counterfeit use, Sony requires that the product being sold have a "substantial" noninfringing use, and although time-loaded cassettes can be used for legitimate purposes, these purposes are insubstantial given the number of Mr. Abdallah's customers that were using them for counterfeiting purposes.

Finally, even if Sony protected the defendant's sale of a product specifically designed for counterfeiters to a known counterfeiter, the evidence in this case indicated that Mr. Abdallah's actions went far beyond merely selling blank, time-loaded tapes. He acted as a contact between his customers and suppliers of other material necessary for counterfeiting, such as counterfeit insert cards; he sold duplicating machines to help his customers start up a counterfeiting operation or expand an existing one; he timed legitimate cassettes for his customers to assist them in ordering time-loaded cassettes; and he helped to finance some of his customers when they were starting out or needed assistance after a police raid. Therefore, even if Sony were to exonerate Mr. Abdallah for his selling of blank, time-loaded cassettes, this Court would conclude that Mr. Abdallah knowingly and materially contributed to the underlying counterfeiting activity.

### B. Trademark infringement

Again, the plaintiff's only possible theory of liability is one of contributory trademark infringement, since Mr. Abdallah himself never directly violated any of the plaintiffs' trademarks. The test for contributory trademark infringement is similar to that for contributory copyright infringement: a defendant is guilty of contributory trademark infringement if he or she (1) intentionally induces another to infringe on a trademark or (2) continues to supply a product knowing that the recipient is using the product to engage in trademark infringement. Inwood Laboratories v. Ives Laboratories, 456 U.S. 844, 854-55, 72 L. Ed. 2d 606, 102 S. Ct. 2182 (1982); Fonovisa, 76 F.3d at 264. As noted above, the plaintiffs effectively demonstrated that Mr. Abdallah continued to supply blank, time-loaded cassettes to his customers even though he knew that they used the cassettes to engage in trademark infringement, and therefore Mr. Abdallah is liable for contributory trademark infringement.

## IV. DAMAGES

### A. Copyright infringement

Section 504 of the Copyright Act allows the plaintiffs to elect either statutory damages or actual damages for copyright infringement, and the plaintiffs in this case have elected statutory damages. 17 U.S.C. § 504(c)(1). The plaintiffs have also attempted to prove that Mr. Abdallah committed the infringement willfully, thus increasing the potential statutory damage award. 17 U.S.C. § 504(c)(2)

For the purposes of § 504(c)(2), a defendant acts willfully if he or she knew, had reason to know, or recklessly disregarded the fact that his or her conduct constituted copyright infringement. See, e.g., Peer Int'l Corp. v. Pausa Records, Inc., 909 F.2d 1332, 1335-36 (9th Cir. 1990). Given the fact that Mr. Abdallah continued in his business for a number of years with the knowledge that his customers were using his product to counterfeit sound recordings, combined with the fact that he continued selling to these counterfeiters even after his own business was raided at least three times by police, this Court concludes that at the very least Mr. Abdallah had a reckless disregard for whether or not his conduct violated copyright laws. Therefore, this Court finds that Mr. Abdallah is liable for willful infringement.

Section 504(c)(2) states that the Court may award statutory damages of up to $ 100,000 for each instance of willful infringement. The legislative history of the Copyright Act indicates that for the purposes of calculating damages, "[a] single infringer of a single work is liable for a single [award of statutory damages], no matter how many acts of infringement are involved in the action . . . ." House Report No. 94-1476, at 162, quoted in 1976 U.S. Code Cong. & Admin. News 565, 577. Therefore, in calculating statutory damages, this Court must first determine the number of different works that Mr. Abdallah infringed upon, and multiply that number by the amount to be awarded for each infringement.

The plaintiffs have provided a list of 156 different sound recordings that Mr. Abdallah's customers had counterfeited. Although there is no direct evidence that Mr. Abdallah knew he was contributing to the illegal copying of each of these 156 different sound recordings, the testimony at trial indicated that Mr. Abdallah was aware that he was contributing to the counterfeiting of many different sound recordings. Mr. Abdallah was aware that each legitimate sound recording that his customers were counterfeiting had its own unique length, and therefore every different length of time that was requested for his time-loaded cassettes represented a different copyrighted work that would be illegally counterfeited. Therefore, it would be impossible for Mr. Abdallah's customers to copy 156 different sound recordings, each with its own unique length, without Mr. Abdallah—or somebody at GAVC—knowing that 156 different sound recordings were being copied. Given this inference, the Court finds that Mr. Abdallah knowingly contributed to the copyright infringement of at least 156 different works.

This Court finds that a statutory award of $ 1,000 is appropriate for each infringement, totaling $ 156,000 for all 156 copyright infringements established by the plaintiffs. Although this is a relatively small amount of statutory damages for each infringement, the total award is sufficiently substantial to fulfill the purposes of the statutory damages. Furthermore, as noted below, Mr. Abdallah is liable under the Lanham Act for triple the amount of his counterfeiting profits, so there is no danger of his profiting from his illegal activity.

B. Trademark infringement

As a preliminary matter, the Court notes that the Ninth Circuit has held that if a defendant infringes upon a plaintiff's copyright and its trademark, the plaintiff can recover both statutory damages under the Copyright Act and actual damages under the Lanham Act. Nintendo of America v. Dragon Pacific Int'l, 40 F.3d 1007, 1011 (9th Cir. 1994). As the Ninth Circuit pointed out, the purpose of the statutory damages, particularly when the infringement was willful, is to penalize the infringer and deter similar conduct in the future. Actual damages under the Lanham Act are designed to compensate the trademark owner for its lost profit and prevent the defendant from unjust enrichment. Therefore, this

Court will award actual damages under the Lanham Act for Mr. Abdallah's trademark violations.

The Lanham Act states that the plaintiff shall recover defendant's profits and any damages sustained by the plaintiff. The plaintiffs in this case produced no evidence of actual damages that they sustained, and therefore their damages for trademark infringement derive solely from Mr. Abdallah's profits from his illegal activity.

In determining the defendant's profits, the plaintiff bears the burden of proving the defendant's sales; the defendant must then prove any costs or deductions from the gross sales figure. The Act also states that the trial court "may enter judgment, according to the circumstances of the case, for any sum above the amount found as actual damages, not exceeding three times such amount." Thus, the Court has the discretion to award up to treble damages for a Lanham Act violation. 15 U.S.C. § 1117(a). If the violation is found to be willful, the trial court should award treble damages unless it finds "extenuating circumstances."

The plaintiffs did not receive full cooperation from the defendants regarding GAVC's financial records, so they were forced to offer GAVC's bank statements as proof of GAVC's gross sales for the period in question. According to these bank statements, GAVC received approximately $ 7.7 million for the period from 1991 to 1992. This large figure is supported by other testimony of Mr. Chabbo, who stated that during certain periods of time, GAVC's California office would sell 150,000 cassettes a week to a single customer, as well as tape duplicating machines. When Mr. Chabbo was transferred to GAVC's New Jersey office, he testified to selling between 120,000 and 140,000 tapes a week. Testimony from one of Mr. Abdallah's customers indicated that each tape cost the buyer between 26 and 34 cents, depending on its length. These figures indicate that GAVC was grossing roughly $ 60,000 to $ 90,000 a week, which could easily account for over seven million dollars over two years.

Mr. Abdallah offered no proof as to how much of these receipts were used for operating costs and expenses. Clearly GAVC had expenses, such as the raw materials required to construct the tapes, and the salaries of its various employees. However, the Court was not provided with any information as to the amount of these expenses, and GAVC was unwilling to disclose such information to the plaintiffs during discovery. In the absence of any details regarding GAVC's expenses, this Court is forced to estimate that 50% of GAVC's gross sales went to pay various expenses. Thus 50% of the $ 7.7 million, or $ 3.35 million, represents GAVC's total profit for the years in question.

The plaintiffs propose that 70% of this profit came from sales to illegitimate customers, based on Mr. Chabbo's estimate that 70% of GAVC's customers were engaged in counterfeiting activity. Since there was no other evidence on this point, this Court finds that 70% of these gross receipts were directly attributable to Mr. Abdallah's contributory trademark violations. GAVC's profit from its contributory counterfeiting activities for these two years was therefore approximately $ 2.34 million.

As noted above, the Lanham Act states that the trial court should award treble damages if the infringement was intentional unless "extenuating circumstances" exist. The Court finds no extenuating circumstances, and therefore triples the damages for trademark infringement, for a total of $ 7,000,000.

### C. Attorneys' fees and costs

Under section 505 of the Copyright Act, this Court may award costs to either party in a copyright infringement action. Traditionally, a trial court will award costs to a party if the court determines that the opposing party acted in bad faith during the litigation. See, e.g., Sanford v. Columbia Broadcasting Sys., 108 F.R.D. 42, 43 (N.D. Ill. 1985). It is clear that Mr. Abdallah created undue difficulties for the plaintiffs by failing to respond to interrogatories in a timely fashion and refusing to turn over his own financial records.

However, there were more serious allegations of misconduct on the part of Mr. Abdallah. Mr. Chabbo, the plaintiffs' key witness, testified that Abdallah attempted to intimidate him into changing his story through threats of violence against him and his family. Mr. Chabbo claims that these threats did in fact lead him to change his story, causing him to relate a different set of facts in a second deposition. The intimidation was ultimately unsuccessful, since Mr. Chabbo subsequently changed his story back in time for a third deposition and the trial. Certainly if these allegations are true, Mr. Abdallah is guilty of bad faith during the litigation, and since this Court accepted the plaintiffs' version of Mr. Chabbo's story, it must conclude by a preponderance of the evidence that Mr. Abdallah engaged in some form of witness tampering. This serious misconduct alone warrants the impositions of costs against Mr. Abdallah.

This Court has the discretion to award reasonable attorneys' fees to the prevailing party in a copyright infringement case. See 17 U.S.C. § 505. According to Fogerty v. Fantasy, 510 U.S. 517, 114 S. Ct. 1023, 127 L. Ed. 2d 455 (1994), attorneys' fees should be awarded in such a case "only as a matter of the court's discretion." Id. at 1033. The Supreme Court noted that the trial court should consider, inter alia, the losing party's "frivolousness, motivation, objective unreasonableness (both in the factual and in the legal components of the case) and the need in particular circumstances to advance considerations of compensation and deterrence." Id. at 1033, n.19. This Court has concluded that Mr. Abdallah intentionally contributed to the copyright infringement, and thus the Court imposes attorney's fees in order to deter others from such flagrant violations of the Copyright Act.

Furthermore, the Lanham Act also provides attorney's fees to a prevailing plaintiff if the infringement was intentional. 15 U.S.C. § 1117(b). Thus, the Lanham Act violations provide an independent reason for awarding the attorney's fees to the plaintiffs.

D. Injunction

Under both the Copyright Act and the Lanham Act, prevailing plaintiffs are entitled to an injunction prohibiting the defendant from any further infringement of the plaintiffs' trademarks or copyrighted material. See 17 U.S.C. § 502 (a); 15 U.S.C. § 1116. This Court finds that such an injunction is appropriate in this case.

## V. CONCLUSION

For the foregoing reasons, this Court finds that defendant Mohammad Abdallah is liable for willful contributory copyright infringement in violation of the Copyright Act, and or contributory trademark infringement in violation of the Lanham Act. Accordingly, this Court awards statutory damages of $ 156,000 for 156 separate violations of the Copyright Act, and actual damages of $ 7,000,000 for violating the Lanham Act. The defendant is also enjoined from infringing or knowingly contributing to another's infringement of any of the plaintiffs' copyrights or trademarks.

Furthermore, Mr. Abdallah is responsible for the costs and reasonable attorneys' fees incurred by the plaintiffs during the course of this litigation. Plaintiffs are directed to submit to the Court an accounting of their attorneys' fees to determine the exact amount of the attorneys' fees award.

The above memorandum constitutes the Court's amended Findings of Fact and Conclusions of Law.

IT IS SO ORDERED.

Dated: 18 Nov, 1996.

Nunc Pro Tunc as of

21 Mar 96

LAUGHLIN E. WATERS

Senior United States District Judge

AMENDED JUDGMENT - November 21, 1996, ENTERED

TO ALL PARTIES AND THEIR ATTORNEYS OF RECORD:

Pursuant to the memorandum of decision and order filed herewith, the court hereby enters judgment in favor of plaintiffs and against defendant Mohammad Abdallah, and awards damages of $ 7,156,000, plus attorneys' fees and costs. Defendant Abdallah is also enjoined from infringing or knowingly contributing to another's infringement of any of the plaintiffs' copyrights or trademarks.

IT IS SO ORDERED.

DATED: 18 Nov, 1996

———————

In the preceding case, *A&M Records, Inc. v. Gen. Audio Video Cassettes, Inc.*, 948 F. Supp. 1949 (1996), the defendant was the only one of many defendants who proceeded to trial, and he did so without counsel. Defendant sold time-loaded cassettes to individuals who used the tapes to illegally counterfeit works, and defendant knew this. Defendant was liable for willful contributory copyright and trademark infringement. The court awarded attorney fees and costs to plaintiffs and enjoined defendant from further infringement. The Master Recording and Synchronization Rights Agreement, which follows, allows the licensing of an artist's music for a film. Artist/licensor must warrant that he or she is the owner of a valid copyright in the listed musical compositions.

### Master Recording and Synchronization Rights Agreement

This Agreement is between **Musical Artist,** hereafter referred to as "Licensor", and **Production Company**, hereafter referred to as "Licensee".

1. Licensor warrants and represents that Licens
or is the owner of valid United States copyrights in the musical compositions listed in Attachment A. Licensor acknowledges that Licensor is the sole writer of each of the original musical compositions listed in Attachment A. Licensor warrants and represents that Licensor has the right to allow Licensee to use the master recordings of the same musical compositions in the manner specified in this Agreement. Licensor further warrants and represents that Licensor has the right to grant the license and all rights covered in this Agreement.

2. Licensor grants to Licensee the nonexclusive, irrevocable right, privilege and license, to use the master recordings of the above named and copyrighted musical compositions in synchronism or timed-relation with the following video, television program, motion picture or film (hereafter referred to as the "visual image"):

### *Name of the Film*

The method of usage and transmission of the visual image shall be: in all forms of motion picture, film, television broadcast of any kind, videocassette and any other formats or transmissions of said visual image whether currently in existence or later created or discovered, including advertising and promotion of the visual image.

3. This license is granted upon the express condition that the recording is to be used solely in synchronism or timed-relation with the above listed visual image. No sound recordings produced or licensed under this license are to be manufactured, sold, licensed or used separately or apart from the visual image. The visual image shall not be used, transmitted or exhibited except as specifically noted in this Agreement.

4. If the method of usage and transmission of the visual image is one that is not subject to performing rights granted to any performing rights society, then this Agreement shall constitute a valid performing rights license from the Licensor to the Licensee.

If the method of usage and transmission of the visual image is one that is subject to performing rights granted to any performing rights society, then the exercise of recording rights granted in this license are subject to the broadcaster having a valid performing rights license. Licensee shall have no claim against Licensor if the broadcaster which Licensee intends to broadcast through does not have, or is unable to obtain a valid performing rights license.

5. This license is granted for the geographic territory of the World.

6. The term of this license shall be for as long as the copyrights in the musical compositions remain valid and in force. At the end of this period, all rights given from the Licensor to the Licensee shall terminate, including the right to make or authorize any use or distribution whatsoever of said recordings of the musical composition, subject to those rights which the Licensee may then be able to obtain with regard to public domain compositions.

7. For the rights granted in this Agreement, Licensee shall pay compensation to Licensor at the rate of 1% of the film's net per musical composition for compositions, up to a total of $5000 US per song used in the completed project. This total compensation shall be paid entirely as deferred compensation. Such deferred compensation shall be payable only if all expenses and costs of any kind incurred in connection with the Picture are first recovered in full by Licensee. If Licensee never receives full reimbursement of all expenses and costs incurred in connection with the Picture, then Licensor shall never receive the stated deferred compensation. Licensor understands that the possibility exists that Licensor may never receive any portion of the stated deferred

compensation, and Licensor expressly agrees to these terms. If Licensee receives full reimbursement for all expenses and costs incurred in connection with the Picture, Licensor shall receive the stated deferred compensation in a manner proportionate to all other persons who are entitled to deferred compensation. While Licensee shall be obligated to pay such deferred compensation once all expenses and costs incurred by Licensee in connection with the Picture have been fully reimbursed, the actual frequency of the payment of such deferred compensation shall be at the discretion of Licensee. The failure of Licensor to receive compensation because Licensee has not been fully reimbursed for its expenses and costs shall not be grounds to terminate or revoke the rights granted by Licensor to Licensee in this Agreement.

8. Licensee shall inform Licensor of the necessary format and technical requirements for the master recordings. Should Licensor fail to deliver master recordings that are satisfactory to Licensee, Licensee may either require Licensor to supply new master recordings that are satisfactory, or Licensee may cancel a portion of this Agreement and adjust fees due to Licensor accordingly, whichever Licensee so chooses.

9. Licensor indemnifies and shall hold Licensee harmless from all loss, damage or expense (including legal expenses and attorney's fees) arising out of, or connected with any claim by a third party which is inconsistent with any of Licensor's promises or warranties in this Agreement, or by reason of any adjudication invalidating the copyright in the musical compositions.

10. Licensee may assign this Agreement without the written consent of the Licensor, but only to the extent necessary or advisable to properly effect the distribution, exhibition or transmission of the visual image. This Agreement shall be binding upon the heirs, legal representatives, successors and assigns of the parties. The execution of this Agreement by Licensee shall constitute and is accepted by Licensor as full compliance with all obligations of Licensee to Licensor, statutory and otherwise, which arise from or are connected with Licensee's use of the musical compositions as stated in this Agreement.

11. Licensee shall give Licensor credit in the credit section of the visual image. While Licensee shall endeavor to give such credit in the form noted in Attachment A, Licensee reserves the right to edit such credit as may be necessary due to space limitations or other production constraints.

12. The persons signing below guarantee that they are authorized to sign this Agreement on behalf of the parties, and bind the parties to all terms of this Agreement.

ALL TERMS ACCEPTED AND AGREED

LICENSEE                                    LICENSOR


_____        _____
Print Name                                  Print Name

By _____        By _____



Date: _____        Date _____

# ATTACHMENT A

Album Title: _____

Songs for Consideration: _____

_____

_____

_____

Performed by: _____

Courtesy of: _____

From the album: _____

Written by: _____

Publishing company: _____

Other: _____


**Name of Production Company**
**Contact Person**
**Address**
**Email**
**Phone**

Questions and Discussion

1. *Ketchum v. Hall Syndicate, Inc.*, 236 N.Y.S. 2d (1962) involved popular cartoonist, Hal Ketchum, and his attempt to terminate his contract. He argues that since the contract was for an indefinite term, there was no mutuality. "The theory of mutuality of obligation is commonly expressed in the phrase that in a bilateral contract 'both parties must be bound or neither is bound.'" (Calamari & Perillo 205, footnotes omitted). However, in *Ketchum,* the court held that Cal. Lab. Code Section 2855, which provides that a contract cannot be enforced after seven years, is inapplicable because the alleged employee was an independent contractor. Also, New York law applied, not California.

Do you see where this is going? Draft your contracts so that the most favorable law (potentially) applies. Music industry contracts should be based on the win-win philosophy. DO NOT KICK YOUR MULE. Draft your own contracts with the goal of subtle advocacy (see Thomas Haggard, Contract Law from a Drafting Perspective—An Introduction to Contract Drafting for Law Students (West 2003)). Sure, start with forms, but then personalize them. Offer your forms when there is a potential contract; gain the advantage—it's like playing chess. But do not humiliate your "opponent." Remember, the enemy of my enemy is my friend.

2. Minors! How should the law deal with the young Doogie Howsers of this world? How should we deal with their entertainment contracts that were written while they were still infants? Macauly Culkin in *In re Twentieth Century Fox Film Corp.*, 601 N.Y.S. 2d. 267 (1993), was able to seal court records. The courts view minors, as well as those of us who are mentally infirm, as possessing limited contractual capacity. "Their agreements are either void, or more often, voidable" (Calamari & Perillo 285).

3. In *Matter of Skutch Publ. Inc.*, 2012 N.Y. Misc. LEXIS 6575, the petitioner seeks judicial approval of two contracts, a music publishing agreement and an exclusive recording agreement, for the services of a 15-year-old infant. "If the contracts are approved, the infant may not, either during her minority or upon reaching majority, disaffirm the agreements on the ground of infancy (Arts and Cultural Affairs Law Section 35.03(3)), and to seal the entire record of these proceedings." The court agreed based at least partially on the fact that "[t]he infant and her parents were represented by an experienced entertainment lawyer during the contract negotiations." In these situations, the major recording companies will not throw the baby out with the bathwater. It is in their best interest to form an ongoing relationship with these young prodigies. This is not always the case with independent production companies and record labels. Note that, again, the court seals the record (which is somewhat unusual under ordinary circumstances) so as to protect the minor

and her family from "unwarranted and undeserved public attention" that could "harm the infant's competitive standing in the music industry."

# Chapter 2
# Publisher Agreements

Music publishing is a major source of income for singer-songwriter types. The deal is between the publisher and the songwriter. The record company ordinarily does the marketing and promotion of the song. There are four general streams of income from music publishing: public performance, mechanical rights, print music, and synchronization. Since compensation must be conveyed to the copyright owners for the public performance of their music, performing rights organizations have developed so as to license the right of public performances. Music users are licensed by their organizations and pay money to them, which is then eventually redistributed to the copyright owners. The three performing rights organizations are: ASCAP (American Society of Composers, Authors, and Publishers), BMI (Broadcast Music Incorporated), and SESAC (formerly Society of European Stage Authors and Composers). "Mechanical income is earned from the manufacture and sale of sound recordings." "Synchronization income is the money paid by motion picture and television production companies and advertising agencies for the right to use compositions in motion pictures or in dramatic presentations on television" ("Music Publishing," by Neville Johnson in Mark Halloran, The Musician's Business & Legal Guide 130-132 (Prentice Hall, 2001)).

In *Mellencamp v. Riva Music, Ltd.*, 698 F. Supp. 1154 (S.D.N.Y 1988), which follows, famous musician John Couger Mellencomp is in a dispute with his music publishers, who hold the copyright to his work.

Mellencamp v. Riva Music, Ltd., 698 F. Supp. 1154
United States District Court for the Southern District of New York
November 2, 1988, Decided
698 F. Supp. 1154

Plaintiff John J. Mellencamp, professionally known as John Cougar Mellencamp, is a songwriter, performer, and recording artist who has enjoyed enormous success in recent years. Defendants (collectively "the Riva companies") are affiliated corporations owned and/or controlled by William A. Gaff. On May 12, 1977, Mellencamp entered into a written publishing agreement with defendant G.H. Music, Ltd. Pursuant to the 1977 agreement, Mellencamp assigned to G.H. Music the worldwide copyrights in and to the compositions to be authored by him during the term of the agreement. The 1977 agreement was modified by a written agreement, dated February 28, 1979, and by letter agreement, dated February 21, 1980. On June 15, 1981, John Cougar, Inc. entered into a written publishing agreement with defendant Riva Music, Ltd. whereby John Cougar, Inc. assigned Mellencamp's songwriting and composing services and copyrights to Riva. On June 1, 1983, Mellencamp entered into a third publishing agreement with defendant Riva Music, Inc. Finally, by written agreement dated July 26, 1985, among Riva Music, Inc., Riva Music, Ltd., G.H. Music, Ltd, Mellencamp, and John Cougar Inc., each of the prior publishing agreements was amended in certain respects. In exchange for the assignment of the copyrights, Mellencamp received a percentage of the royalties earned from the exploitation of his music.

By virtue of the publishing agreements, according to the complaint, the Riva companies became fiduciaries for Mellencamp's interests. In his first and second claims, Mellencamp alleges that defendants breached their fiduciary duties by failing to actively promote his songs and to use their best efforts to obtain all the monies rightfully due him from third parties. In his third claim, Mellencamp contends that the Riva companies breached the various publishing agreements controlling their relationship by consistently underreporting royalties due him and by failing to timely render royalty statements and payments. In his fourth and final claim, Mellencamp contends that he entered into a binding agreement with the Riva companies pursuant to which the defendants agreed to release him from all obligations under the publishing contracts and to return all the rights to and in his musical compositions in exchange for $ 3 million dollars. This agreement was reached, according to plaintiff, at a luncheon meeting in a New York City restaurant among Sigmund Balaban, Mellencamp's accountant and advisor, William Gaff, and Milton Marks,

Gaff's attorney. Both sides agree that the sale of the Riva companies' rights in Mellencamp's compositions was discussed, at least in general terms, at this meeting. The parties are in sharp dispute, however, over the legal consequences of their discussions.

Defendants now move pursuant to Rule 12(b)(6) to dismiss the complaint on the ground that it fails to state any valid claim for relief. Specifically, defendants contend 1) that the first two claims fail as a matter of law because no fiduciary duties are owed by a publisher to an author under a publishing agreement 2) that the third claim fails to specify which of the publishing agreements were breached, who the parties to the agreements were, and which provisions of the agreements were breached, and also fails to include a necessary party, and 3) that the fourth claim must be dismissed because the enforcement of an oral agreement to transfer copyrights is barred by § 204(a) of the Copyright Act and/or the New York Uniform Commercial Code statute of frauds § 1-206(1). In the alternative, defendants argue that they are entitled to summary judgment dismissing the fourth claim on the ground that the parties did not intend the alleged oral agreement to be binding.

## ANALYSIS
## I. FIDUCIARY DUTIES

Under New York law, the existence of fiduciary obligations in a particular relationship cannot be determined by recourse to fixed formulas or precedents:

Broadly stated, a fiduciary relationship is one founded upon trust or confidence reposed by one person in the integrity and fidelity of another. It is said that the relationship exists in all cases in which influence has been reposed and betrayed. The rule embraces both technical fiduciary relations and those informal relations which exist whenever one man trusts in, and relies upon, another (see Mobil Oil Corp. v. Rubenfeld, 72 Misc. 2d 392, 399-400, 339 N.Y.S.2d 623, aff'd. 77 Misc. 2d 962, 357 N.Y.S.2d 589, revs. on other grounds 48 A.D.2d 428, 370 N.Y.S.2d 943). Such a relationship might be found to exist, in appropriate circumstances between close friends (see Cody v. Gallow, 28 Misc. 2d 373, 214 N.Y.S.2d 127) or even where confidence is based upon prior business dealings (see Levine v. Chussid, 31 Misc. 2d 412, 221 N.Y.S.2d 311).

Penato v. George, 52 A.D.2d 939, 942, 383 N.Y.S.2d 900, 904-05 (2d Dep't 1976). Notwithstanding this broad rule, defendants, relying on Van Valkenburgh, Nooger & Neville, Inc. v. Hayden Publishing Co., 30 N.Y.2d 34, 330 N.Y.S.2d 329, 281 N.E.2d 142 (1972), cert. denied, 409 U.S. 875, 34 L. Ed. 2d 128, 93 S. Ct. 125 (1972), argue that the relationship between an author and a publisher can never be a fiduciary relationship. Van Valkenburgh does not support this proposition.

There, a publisher and an author entered into a written agreement which provided, inter alia, that the publisher was obligated to use its best efforts to promote the author's books. Id., 30 N.Y.2d at 43, 330 N.Y.S.2d at 331. The agreement also provided that the author would receive a 15% royalty on all books sold. Id. The trial court found that the publisher did not use its best efforts to promote the books, the publisher occupied a fiduciary relationship to the author, and the publisher failed to act in good faith in that relationship. Id. at 44, 330 N.Y.S.2d at 332. On appeal, the Appellate Division determined that no fiduciary relationship existed between the parties. Id. Instead, the court concluded, the relationship between the parties was one of ordinary contract. Id. The court also concluded that the publisher did not breach its duty of good faith but found that the publisher did breach its contractual obligation to use its best efforts to promote the author's books. Id. The New York Court of Appeals affirmed, concluding that "it could be found, as a matter of law, on the record, that there was no fiduciary relationship." Id. at 46, 330 N.Y.S.2d at 334 (emphasis added). See also Lane v. Mercury Record Corp., 21 A.D.2d 602, 252 N.Y.S.2d 1011 (1st Dep't 1964) (a royalty or percentage arrangement would not in and of itself establish a fiduciary relationship), aff'd, 18 N.Y.2d 889, 276 N.Y.S.2d 626, 223 N.E.2d 35 (1966). The Court did not hold that fiduciary obligations could never arise in a relationship based at least in part on publishing agreements.

The complaint as drafted, however, goes further than this, suggesting that fiduciary obligations attach to the publisher-author relationship as a matter of law and, consequently, that the Riva companies' alleged failure to meet their express or implied contract obligations amounts to a breach of trust. In addition, there is language in several older state cases, as well as in federal cases interpreting New York state law, that arguably supports the view that a publisher-author contract creates a "technical fiduciary relation." If these cases can be so interpreted, they are directly at odds with the greater weight of authority which teaches that the conventional publisher-author arrangement is not a per se fiduciary relationship. Commenting on the ambiguities in the caselaw, Judge Haight observed that "the legal responsibilities attendant upon this status . . . are far from clear." Warfield v. Jerry Vogel Music Co., Inc., Copyright L. Rep. (CCH) para. 25,005, at 15,033 (S.D.N.Y. Mar. 21, 1978). These cases warrant discussion.

Under New York law, every contract includes an implied covenant of good faith and fair dealing which precludes a party from engaging in conduct that will deprive the other contracting party of his benefits under their agreement. Filner v. Shapiro, 633 F.2d 139, 143 (2d Cir. 1980). A contract is also deemed to include any promise which a reasonable person in the position of the promisee would be justified in believing was included. Rowe v. Great Atlantic & Pacific Tea Co., Inc., 46 N.Y.2d 62, 69, 412 N.Y.S.2d 827, 831, 385 N.E.2d 566 (1978). When the essence of a contract is the assignment or grant of an exclusive license in exchange for a share of the assignee's profits in exploiting the license, these principles imply an obligation on the part of the assignee to make reasonable efforts to exploit the license. Havel v. Kelsey-Hayes, 83 A.D.2d 380, 382, 445 N.Y.S.2d 333, 335 (4th Dep't 1981). See also Zilg v. Prentice-Hall, Inc., 717 F.2d 671 (2d Cir. 1983) (promise of publisher to publish book which it has obtained exclusive rights to implies good faith effort to promote the book). The critical point here is that a publisher's obligation to promote an author's work is one founded in contract rather than on trust principles.

While it is true that several of the cases cited by plaintiff discuss certain "trust elements that are part of the relationship between a writer and a publisher," Nolan v. Sam Fox Publishing Company, Inc., 499 F.2d 1394, 1400, 182 U.S.P.Q. (BNA) 513 (2d Cir. 1974), it is apparent that the courts were in fact discussing a publisher's implied-in-law contract obligations or were relying on trust principles in situations where the publisher tolerated or participated in tortious conduct against the author. For example, in Schisgall v. Fairchild Publications, 207 Misc. 224, 137 N.Y.S.2d 312 (Sup. Ct. N.Y. Cty. 1955), the plaintiff-author alleged that his publisher refused to fill existing orders for his book, withdrew his book from sale, and refused to transfer the rights to the book back to the author, all for "the single purpose to abort or destroy . . . the defendant's interests." Id. 207 Misc. at 232, 137 N.Y.S.2d at 319. In determining whether the alleged conduct created tort liability in addition to liability in contract, the court observed that "the intentional infliction of injury without just cause is prima facie tortious." Id. at 230, 137 N.Y.S.2d at 317.

As a preliminary matter, however, the court had to determine whether the plaintiff could be deemed to have suffered any injury in the absence of express contractual obligations or rights governing the complained of conduct. In response to defendants' assertion that the plaintiff retained no protectible interest in his literary product because he assigned all his rights to the defendant, the court stated:

As I read the contract, even though there be an absolute assignment, there was such an assignment on the basis of the business to be done — such a transfer of rights and property to the defendant as did not denude the plaintiffs of a certain right and interest, and that arrangement resulted in that kind of relationship that fair dealing was required between the parties. It is not the express contractual reservation of rights per se on which plaintiffs rely, but upon the defendant's breach of the special relationship thus created — plus the defendant's intentional purpose to destroy. It is not necessary to use the magic words of "fiduciary relationship", or to hold that a "relationship of trust and confidence" was created by the contract, or to find that defendant became a "trustee" of the copyright for the benefit of the plaintiffs (as well as of the defendant). As Chief Judge Cardozo put it in Wood v. Lucy, Lady Duff-Gordon,

222 N.Y. 88, 91, 118 N.E. 214: "The law has outgrown its primitive stage of formalism when the precise word was the sovereign talisman, and every slip was fatal. It takes a broader view today. A promise may be lacking and yet the whole writing may be 'instinct with an obligation,' imperfectly expressed." Similarly, the special relationship here may not be specifically expressed, and yet the whole factual situation may be instinct with a duty which should be imposed by law upon the publisher.

The law implies a promise on the defendant's part to endeavor to make the book and copyright productive, since that is the very purpose of the assignment of literary rights and the correlative obligation to pay royalties, In re Waterson, Berlin & Snyder Co. v. Irving Trust Co., 48 F.2d 704.

Id. 207 Misc. at 230-31, 137 N.Y.S.2d at 317-18 (emphasis added). Despite the reference to "fiduciary relationship" and "relationship of trust," it is clear, in context, that the court was talking about a publisher's implied-in-law contract obligation to use its best efforts to promote an author's work, where the publisher has exclusive rights in the work. The single case cited in the court's discussion of the "special relationship" between author and publisher, Wood v. Lucy, Lady Duff-Gordon, 222 N.Y. 88, 91, 118 N.E. 214 (1917) (Cardozo, C.J.), is the seminal authority on an exclusive licensee's implied promise to use reasonable efforts to generate profits from the license. The court's reliance on contract principles is confirmed later in the opinion:

If the defendant acted merely as a contracting party (at legal liberty perhaps to breach its agreement on payment of damages), that is one thing. But if the defendant went further, and acted with intent to inflict injury beyond that contemplated as a result of the mere breach of contract, I would hold that the contract does not grant the defaulter immunity from tort liability. Even though the act would not be actionable in tort if the defendant "elected" to breach its contract in furtherance of its legitimate business interests, it is tortious (as well as a breach of contract) if there be no self-interest involved, but rather the sole purpose be that of injury to another.

Id., 207 Misc. at 232, 137 N.Y.S.2d at 319 (emphasis added). The holding of Schisgall is that a publisher who breaches his implied contract obligation to exploit an author's work with no motive other than to injure the author, is liable for prima facie tort. See Nifty Foods Corp. v. Great Atlantic & Pacific Tea Co., 614 F.2d 832, 838 n.7 (2d Cir. 1980) ("Schisgall . . . involved the deliberate and unjustified destruction of a property right entrusted under a contract").

Relying on the two paragraphs from pages 230-31, 317-18 of Schisgall quoted above, the court in Manning v. Miller Music Corp., 174 F. Supp. 192, 195-96 (S.D.N.Y. 1959), characterized the relationship between publisher and author as one involving fiduciary obligations. But as in Schisgall, the court did not hold that the publisher's breach of contract obligations gave rise to liability as a fiduciary, nor was such liability even at issue. The question in Manning was whether the plaintiffs, composers of a song who assigned their copyrights to a publisher, had standing to maintain a suit for infringement against a third party. Id. at 194. The court concluded that the "peculiar relationship between the author and his publisher," id. at 195, gives the authors standing to bring suit against a third party infringer when the publisher fails to do so. "It is this fiduciary relationship imposing equitable obligations upon the publisher beyond those ordinarily imposed by law upon those dealing fully at arms' length, which gives the plaintiffs standing to sue here." Id. at 196. Analogizing the situation to a stockholder's derivative action, id. at 196, the court reasoned that plaintiffs could maintain the infringement action as long as the publisher was joined as a nominal defendant. Id. Notably, the court concluded that it would be inappropriate to force plaintiffs to institute "a separate action in contract against the publisher" to achieve the same end. Id. at 197 (emphasis added). See also Cortner v. Israel, 732 F.2d 267, 271 (2d Cir. 1984) (when a composer assigns a copyright title to a publisher in exchange for the payment of royalties, an equitable trust relationship is established between the two parties which gives the composer standing to sue for infringement of the copyright). In a similar vein, the court in Nelson v. Mills, 278 A.D. 311, 104 N.Y.S.2d 605, 89 U.S.P.Q. (BNA) 554 (1951), aff'd, 304 N.Y. 966, 110 N.E.2d 892 (1953), held that a publisher's actual promotion of a song which infringed the author's was a "breach of contract or trust." Id. 278 A.D. at 312, 104 N.Y.S.2d at 606. But the court also asserted, echoing Schisgall, that "the defendant was not obligated to promote the sale of plaintiff's song." Id. at 312, 104 N.Y.S.2d at 607.

To the extent the cases discussed above intended to posit a per se rule that a publisher with exclusive rights in a work is a fiduciary for the author's interests, they must be rejected as inconsistent with Van Valkenburgh. The better view, and the one consistent with Van Valkenburgh, is that the "trust elements" in a publisher-author relationship come into play when the publisher tolerates infringing conduct, Manning, Cortner, or participates in it, Nelson v. Mills. Ordinarily, however, the express and implied obligations assumed by a publisher in an exclusive licensing contract are not, as a matter of law, fiduciary duties. See Sobol v. E.P. Dutton, Inc., 112 F.R.D. 99, 104 [1160] (S.D.N.Y. 1986) (Weinfeld, J.); Ekern v. Sew/Fit Company, Inc., 622 F. Supp. 367, 373 (N.D. Ill. 1985) (citing Van Valkenburgh). Cf. Beneficial Commercial Corp. v. Murray Glick Datsun, 601 F. Supp. 770, 772 (S.D.N.Y. 1985) (absent assumption of control or responsibility and corresponding repose of trust, arm's length business transaction does not give rise to fiduciary relationship). Accordingly, since plaintiff's first two claims are predicated solely upon the professional relationship between the parties and do not plead any specific conduct or circumstances upon which trust elements are implicated, they are dismissed. In the unlikely event that plaintiff can repair his pleadings in this regard, he is given leave to replead within twenty days of the date of this order.

## II. BREACH OF CONTRACT.

Defendants contend that the third claim for breach of contract should be dismissed because it fails to specify the contracts and specific contract provisions at issue in the lawsuit. The Court disagrees. It is now axiomatic that a complaint need only provide "'a short and plain statement of the claim' that will give the defendant fair notice of what the plaintiff's claim is and the grounds upon which it rests." 2A J. Moore, Moore's Federal Practice para. 8.13 at 8-62 (2d ed. 1987). The present complaint clearly satisfies this minimal requirement. Defendants' motion to dismiss demonstrates their awareness of the contracts at issue in this case, and the alleged breach — defendants' failure to fully and timely report royalties — is more than sufficient to put defendants on notice of the claims against them. The two cases relied on by defendants on this leg of their motion are wholly inapposite to the case at bar.

In Nordic Bank P.L.C. v. Trend Group, 619 F. Supp. 542 (S.D.N.Y. 1985), the complaint alleged only that certain agreements between the parties had been breached. Id. at 562. The pleadings were bereft of any reference to a specific promise or the nature of defendant's failure to meet its obligations. Id. The court ruled, quite reasonably, that such a "conclusory allegation provide[d] insufficient notice of the facts underlying the breach of contract claim." Id. at 562. In Murphy v. White Hen Pantry Co., 691 F.2d 350, 353 (7th Cir. 1982), the complaint lacked even the conclusory allegation of a breach found in Nordic Bank. Id. at 351. Instead the plaintiffs argued, in response to defendant's motion to dismiss, that such a claim was "implicitly alleged in the complaint." Id. Even under those circumstances, the court did not dismiss plaintiff's argument out of hand but concluded that the complaint did not plead facts sufficient to notify defendants of a contract claim. Id. at 352. The instant complaint is simply not comparable to the inscrutable pleadings in Nordic Bank and Murphy.

The Court does, however, agree that defendants Avir Music, Inc. and H.G. Music, Inc. must be dismissed from the complaint. Mellencamp alleges that he entered into agreements with defendants G.H. Music Ltd., Riva Music, Ltd., and Riva Music Inc. "Before [a] defendant may be held accountable for the breach of a contract, it must be demonstrated that he was a party thereto." Stratton Group, Ltd. v. Sprayregen, 458 F. Supp. 1216, 1218 (S.D.N.Y. 1978). Avir Music, Inc. and H.G. Music, Inc. are not alleged to be parties to the publishing agreements and thus the pleadings do not provide any basis upon which relief could be granted against these defendants. See id.; Franklin v. Carpinello, 84 A.D.2d 613, 613, 444 N.Y.S.2d 248, 249 (3d Dep't 1981). The Court is unaware of any authority, and plaintiff has not offered any, to support plaintiff's assertion that these two defendants may be liable for the breach of a contract which they are strangers to simply because they share the same director and/or owner as the other corporate defendants or because they assisted the other corporate defendants in the "administration of the Mellencamp publishing agreements." Plaintiff's Memorandum at 11. Plaintiff's third claim is dismissed as against Avir Music, Inc. and H.G. Music, Inc. with leave to replead within twenty days of the date of this order.

Defendants contend that the third claim is defective, at least with respect to the publishing agreement dated June 15, 1981, because John Cougar Inc. and not Mellencamp is the party to that contract. As Judge Stanton has observed, "in order to state a contract claim a plaintiff must at least allege either that he was a party to a valid contract . . . or that he was an intended beneficiary of a contract between the defendant and a third party." Tampa Chain Company of Providence, Inc. v. Odena Marketing International Corp., No. 84 Civ. 0707, slip op. at 2 (S.D.N.Y. April 3, 1986) (Lexis Genfed Library, Dist. File). Although under New York law, an agent can maintain an action in his own name on behalf of his principal, he can only do so if he is a party to the contract, a transferee, or a holder of an interest in the contract. Colonial Securities, Inc. v. Merrill Lynch, Pierce, Fenner & Smith, Inc., 461 F. Supp. 1159, 1165 (S.D.N.Y. 1978); In re Best Film v. Video Corp., 46 Bankr. 861, 876 (E.D.N.Y. 1985). While Mellencamp may in fact have no rights under the 1981 agreement, this issue cannot be resolved on the face of the pleadings since the complaint, construed broadly, asserts that Mellencamp is a party to or an intended beneficiary of all relevant publishing agreements. Because defendants have submitted matters outside of the pleadings, specifically the 1981 contract, it is appropriate to treat this leg of the motion as one for partial summary judgment. Fed. R. Civ. P. 12(b)(6). Plaintiff shall, within twenty days of the entry of this order, submit evidence on the issue of his rights under the 1981 agreement.

### III. STATUTE OF FRAUDS.

The Statute of Frauds provision of the Copyright Act, 17 U.S.C. § 204(a), provides:

A transfer of copyright ownership, other than by operation of law, is not valid unless an instrument of conveyance, or a note or memorandum of the transfer, is in writing and signed by the owner of the rights conveyed or such owner's duly authorized agent.

According to defendants, § 204(a) bars plaintiff's fourth claim which, they argue, alleges the existence of an oral agreement to transfer to him the copyrights in his compositions. Defendants also rely, in the alternative, on § 1-206(1) of the New York Uniform Commercial Code which provides:

[A] contract for the sale of personal property is not enforceable by way of action or defense beyond five thousand dollars in amount or value of remedy unless there is some writing which indicates that a contract for sale has been made between the parties at a defined or stated price, reasonably identifies the subject matter, and is signed by the party against whom enforcement is sought or his authorized agent.

With respect to the Copyright Act, Mellencamp attempts to draw a distinction between cases where the validity of a purported oral transfer is at issue and cases where, as here, an oral agreement to transfer a copyright is sought to be enforced. The Copyright Statute of Frauds only applies to the former, according to Mellencamp. He also makes the unrefuted observation that the writing confirming the transfer of a copyright license can be executed after the transfer. See Eden Toys, Inc. v. Florelee Undergarment Co., Inc., 697 F.2d 27, 38 (2d Cir. 1982).

Turning first to the applicability of the statute of frauds, the cases do not support Mellencamp's restrictive reading of § 204(a). In Library Publications, Inc. v. Medical Economics Co., 548 F. Supp. 1231 (E.D. Pa. 1982), aff'd, 714 F.2d 123 (3d Cir. 1983), a trade book publisher sued another publisher charging, inter alia, that the defendant breached an oral contract to grant plaintiff the right to distribute a certain book. Id. at 1232. Because § 204(a) requires such agreements to be in writing, the court granted summary judgment dismissing the complaint. Id. at 1234. See also 3 Nimmer, On Copyright § 10.03[a] at 10-34 n. 5.1 (1988) (the writing requirement of § 204(a) is significant in actions for breach of contract as well as in actions for copyright infringement). Moreover, Mellencamp's cramped interpretation of § 204 is inconsistent with the underlying purpose of the statute of frauds which is "to protect copyright holders from persons mistakenly or fraudulently claiming oral licenses." Eden Toys, Inc., 697 F.2d at 36. Thus there is no merit to plaintiff's contention that a contract to transfer a copyright can be enforced without a writing.

Plaintiff attempts to avoid the U.C.C. statute of frauds by arguing that the principal asset to be transferred pursuant the oral agreement was Mellencamp's services as a songwriter rather than the copyrights and thus the agreement "cannot be characterized as merely a 'sale' of copyrights." Plaintiff's Memorandum at 16. Though not stated, it is implied that the statute of frauds is inapplicable to a contract which subject matter falls, in part, outside the scope of the statute. Plaintiff's Memorandum at 15. Plaintiff also contends that § 1-206 is inapplicable to a sale of copyrights. Neither assertion is correct.

First, the single case relied on by plaintiff for the partial-sale argument is inapposite to the present facts. In Lee v. Joseph E. Seagram & Sons, Inc., 413 F. Supp. 693 (S.D.N.Y. 1976), the alleged oral contract did not involve the sale of personal property at all. Id. at 704. Although no authority is presented on the point by either side, plaintiff's partial-sale argument does beg the question of whether a contract is unenforceable in its entirety where certain terms of the agreement fall within the statute of frauds and others without. The general rule in New York is:

if part of an entire contract is void under the Statute of Frauds, the whole of such contract is void ( De Beerski v. Paige, 36 N.Y. 537, 539). Where however, a parol contract is a severable one, i.e., susceptible of division and apportionment, having two or more parts not necessarily dependent upon each other, those which, if standing alone, are not required to be in writing, may be enforced (see, Markey v. Kelly, 10 A.D.2d 650, 651, 197 N.Y.S.2d 891; 56 N.Y.Jur., Statute of Frauds, §§ 322-325, 329).

Dickenson v. Dickenson Agency, Inc., 127 A.D.2d 983, 984, 512 N.Y.S.2d 952, 953 (4th Dep't 1987). In Dickenson, the plaintiff was employed by the defendant as an insurance salesman. The complaint alleged the existence of an oral agreement containing three distinct parts. First, that plaintiff was entitled to commissions on initial policy sales and subsequent renewals. Second, that he was entitled to renewal commissions even when the renewal took place after his termination. And third, that he was entitled to bonus payments. Id. 127 A.D.2d at 983-84, 512 N.Y.S.2d at 952-53. The court found that the provision granting plaintiff the right to commissions on sales and renewals occurring before his termination were severable, and thus enforceable, from the provision granting post-termination rights which was void under the statute of frauds. Id. at 984, 512 N.Y.S.2d at 953. Here the package of rights to be transferred to Mellencamp under the alleged oral agreement was to be exchanged for the single lump sum of $ 3 million dollars. Although plaintiff has argued that the non-copyright aspects of the agreement are worth a great deal more to him than the copyrights themselves, plaintiff has not attempted apportionment of the $ 3 million dollars to the various rights in the agreement nor does the contract contain separate parts susceptible to severance.

Finally, with respect to the U.C.C. statute of frauds, Mellencamp reasons that copyright sales must be excluded from the purview of § 1-206 because a) the section governs the sale of general intangibles b) the Official Comment to the section refers to Article 9 for the definition of general intangibles and c) Article 9 is supposedly pre-empted by the Copyright Act. The Official Comment to § 1-206 indicates that the section governs the sale of "general intangibles" as defined in U.C.C. § 9-106, and the Official Comment to § 9-106 in turn lists rights to performance and copyrights as examples of "general intangibles." Article 9, which governs secured transactions, by its terms does not apply to:

a security interest subject to any statute of the United States to the extent that such statute governs the rights of parties to and third parties affected by transactions in particular types of property.

§ 9-104(a). Assuming that this provision excludes security interests in copyrights from Article 9, it does not follow that a copyright is not a "general intangible" the sale of which is governed by the U.C.C. statute of frauds. The Official Comment to § 1-206 provides that it applies to "general intangibles" as defined in Article 9 and to transactions excluded from Article 9 by § 9-104. In other words, exclusion under § 9-104 means inclusion under § 1-206.

Notwithstanding the application of the statute of frauds to the alleged contract, it is impossible to determine from the face of the pleadings whether Mellencamp can prove no set of facts in support of his claim that would entitle him to relief. See E. Farnsworth, Contracts § 6.10 at 427 (1982) (plaintiff need not allege facts showing that statute was satisfied). The complaint would be subject to a motion to dismiss if it showed on its face that the contract sued upon is within the statute and that the statute has not been satisfied, id., but the complaint does not reveal whether the agreement to transfer the rights under the publishing agreements was oral or otherwise lacking a confirmatory memorandum. Although the statute of frauds issue overlaps, to some extent, the arguments advanced by defendants in their motion for summary judgment, and defendants have established that no written agreements were entered into for the sale to Mellencamp of the Riva copyrights, they have not addressed the possibility that a note or memorandum executed after the luncheon meeting satisfies the statute of frauds.

To satisfy the statute, a memorandum or note signed by the party to be charged need only:

(1) identify the parties to the contract and show that a contract has been made by them or offered by the signatory to the other; (2) indicate the nature of the contract and its subject matter; (3) state the essential terms of the promises to be performed under the contract.

E. Farnsworth, Contracts § 6.7 at 409 (1982). Although a dispositive ruling on the statute of frauds question is thus inappropriate, and unnecessary for reasons discussed below, one observation is in order. In response to defendant's summary judgment motion, Mellencamp has submitted certain letters that allegedly evince the Riva companies' acknowledgement of a binding agreement on all material terms. One letter, dated April 10, 1987, was written by Richard Parrington of Riva to Gaff's attorney, Gary Baker. Commenting on a document request received from Mellencamp's attorney, Henry Goldstein, in connection with his due diligence investigation for the deal, Parrington asserts that most of the requested documents had already been supplied to Mellencamp's representatives or were not relevant. A copy of this letter was sent to Balaban with a cover note from Parrington urging Balaban to "keep the legal bills down." To the extent that these letters have been offered or would be offered to satisfy the statute of frauds, they do more harm than good for Mellencamp's position.

For one thing, Parrington refers to the copyright sale as a "proposed deal" in his letter to Baker. Parrington also opines that certain documents requested by Goldstein "are irrelevant to the current negotiations" and specifically asserts that earnings on unrecouped balances from sub-publishers "would have to be

[the] subject of negotiation." In addition, none of the documents submitted are alleged to state the essential terms of the agreement. Where the memorandum offered to satisfy the statute of frauds contains a provision or understanding that a more formal contract is to be executed later and leaves material terms to be negotiated or omits them, the memorandum is insufficient. Read v. Henzel, 67 A.D.2d 186, 189, 415 N.Y.S.2d 520, 523 (4th Dep't 1979). These letters are thus consistent with defendants' position that a binding agreement would come into existence only upon the execution of a formal contract.

### IV. ABSENCE OF A BINDING AGREEMENT.

Lastly, defendants argue that summary judgment should be entered dismissing Mellencamp's fourth claim on the ground that the parties did not enter into a binding agreement for the sale of Mellencamp's copyrights and his songwriting services. Plaintiff, of course, resists that argument, and contends that the issue is one of fact, turning largely on determinations of credibility, which precludes summary judgment "as a matter of judicial policy." Plaintiff's Memorandum at 21. The Court disagrees with plaintiff on both points. While the intent of the parties to be bound is a question of fact, the issue is not immune from disposition on summary judgment, and summary judgment is appropriate in this case.

In Scheck v. Francis, 26 N.Y.2d 466, 311 N.Y.S.2d 841, 260 N.E.2d 493 (1970), the former personal business manager of the popular singer Connie Francis brought suit against her and her three business corporations alleging that defendants breached certain written employment agreements governing their relationship. The contracts sued upon were drafted following negotiations between plaintiff and Francis' attorney, Marvin Levin. During the course of negotiations, Levin submitted several drafts of proposed contracts to plaintiff all of which were rejected. Id. 26 N.Y.2d at 469, 311 N.Y.S.2d at 842. After the final negotiating session, Levin sent plaintiff four unsigned agreements in quadruplicate. The agreements were accompanied by the following cover letter:

Dear George:

Enclosed . . . are the employment agreements between you and GGC Productions Corp., Connie Francis, Antigony Music Ltd., and Brookings Music Inc. Please sign all copies, have Connie sign all copies and distribute the copies as follows:

One set to me
One set for the office
One set for you
One set for Sol Granett [Plaintiff's attorney]
If you have any questions or comments, please call me.

Id. at 469 n.1, 311 N.Y.S.2d at 842 n.1. Plaintiff signed the agreements but Francis did not. Nonetheless, plaintiff continued to work for Francis for almost a year, after which he was informed that no contract existed between himself and Francis. Id. at 469, 311 N.Y.S.2d at 842-43.

In reviewing the trial court's dismissal of the complaint, the Court of Appeals observed that "if the parties to an agreement do not intend it to be binding upon them until it is reduced to writing and signed by both of them, they are not bound and may not be held liable until it has been written out and signed." Id. at 469-70, 311 N.Y.S.2d at 843. Applying this principle, the Court found it to be:

quite clear, from Mr. Levin's letter alone, that the agreements were to take effect only after both parties had signed them. Thus, he had instructed the plaintiff that he was to sign them and "have Connie sign" them, expressly advising to call if there were "any questions or comments". Although the agreements themselves were not required to be delivered to the plaintiff's attorney . . . before the parties had signed, a copy of the covering letter was sent to him. This combination of circumstances unquestionably gave the plaintiff an opportunity to decline to go through with the deal before he signed. Certainly, the defendant Francis enjoyed the same privilege, and she never did sign. In short, both parties must plainly have understood that the agreements were to take effect only after they had signed them and, until that time, the matter was still in the stage of negotiations.

Id. at 470, 311 N.Y.S.2d at 843. See also Schwartz v. Greenberg, 304 N.Y. 250, 107 N.E.2d 65 (1952).

The mutual lack of intent to be bound absent an executed contract is, if anything, clearer here than it was in Francis. On or about April 1, 1987, Gary Baker received a letter from Henry Goldstein requesting certain documents in connection with his due diligence investigation of the proposed sale. The letter provided as follows:

I enclose a preliminary Document Request List in connection with our preparation of an agreement pursuant to which, among other things, John Mellencamp will effect the cancellation of his songwriter agreements with Riva Music, et al.

Please note that the Document Request List is designed for our due diligence investigation and evaluation and accordingly, is intended to be illustrative rather than exhaustive. It is expected that, during the course of our review of the materials and our preparation of the agreement, we will make requests for additional information.

(emphasis added). On April 27, Baker received a draft agreement from Goldstein accompanied by a letter which stated:

I enclose a draft of the proposed agreement between John J. Mellencamp and Riva Music pursuant to which, among other things, John Mellencamp will effect the cancellation of his songwriter agreements with Riva Music, et al.

Under separate cover, I will shortly be sending you the various Exhibits to the proposed agreement. I would appreciate it if, while you are reviewing the proposed agreement, you prepare the Schedules to the proposed agreement and forward same to me.

As soon as you have reviewed the proposed agreement, please call me.

Please note that I am simultaneously sending a copy of the proposed agreement to our client for review; therefore, I must reserve the right to make any changes which it may require.

(emphasis added). Finally, in a letter sent to Mellencamp by Balaban on April 21, 1987, more than a month after the allegedly binding luncheon agreement, Balaban states:

I have been in frequent communication with Hank Goldstein regarding the proposed contract with Riva Music Ltd. and its associated entities.

In that connection Hank forwarded to me a preliminary draft dated April 16, 1987 for my comments. I suggested to Hank that he delete certain words on page 1 of the draft because they do not appear to me to be necessary, and may result in a hostile reaction from Gaff. . . .

I have also indicated to Hank that while Gaff and his companies should release you from all obligations under the prior agreements, there does not appear to me to be any reason for you to release Gaff et al from anything, except acting as your publisher. This is of course the lawyer's domain.

(emphasis added). As a general observation, the evidence of the tentative nature of the agreement can only be described as manifest, especially in comparison to Francis. This conclusion is further confirmed by analyzing the evidence under the four factor test set forth in two recent decisions by the Second Circuit. The factors are 1) whether there has been an express reservation of the right not to be bound absent a writing 2) whether there has been partial performance of the alleged contract 3) whether all of the terms of the contract have been agreed upon, and 4) whether the contract concerns complex and substantial business matters that would not ordinarily be the subject of an oral agreement. Winston v. Mediafare Entertainment Corp., 777 F.2d 78, 80 (2d Cir. 1985); R.G. Group, Inc., 751 F.2d at 75-76. The evidence on each of the four factors weighs conclusively in defendants' favor.

a) Express Reservation

As already noted, Goldstein informed Baker that he reserved the right to make any changes in the contract following Mellencamp's review of the first draft and without exception referred to the draft as a proposed agreement. Cf. Winston, 777 F.2d at 81 (although neither party expressly reserved right not to be bound, reference in correspondence of parties to the "proposed settlement" and to "consummation of proposed settlement" revealed such an intent). In addition to the Goldstein letter, the proposed agreement itself, which was drafted by Mellencamp's lawyer, confirms that the agreement would only be binding upon execution:

NOW THEREFORE, the parties hereto hereby agree as follows:

FIRST: Release, Transfer and Payment. Contemporaneously with the execution and delivery of this Agreement on this   day of  , 1987 (the "Closing Date") and in full consideration of the releases, transfers, assignments and agreements provided in this Article FIRST and the remainder of this Agreement, Mellencamp is herewith delivering to the Publishers . . . THREE MILLION DOLLARS . . . receipt of which is hereby acknowledged by the Publishers, and in consideration thereof:

A. The Publishers, jointly and severally, agree that (i) the term of the Publishing Agreement and each other Prior Agreement that has not expired and has not been terminated prior to the Closing Date shall be terminated as of the closing date. . . .

B. All prior or contemporaneous agreements, contracts, promises, representations and statements, if any, between the parties hereto, or their representatives, as to the subject matter hereof, are merged into this Agreement . . . and this Agreement and the Schedules and Exhibits hereto shall constitute the entire agreement between them. This Agreement . . . constitutes the entire understanding between the parties and no waiver or modification of the terms hereof shall be valid unless in writing signed by the party to be charged and only to the extent therein set forth.

(emphasis supplied emphasis added). In addition to the payment of the purchase price, other key provisions in the draft agreement, including the termination of the existing publishing agreements, assignment of the copyrights, assignment of third-party contracts, termination of defendants' rights in Mellencamp's likeness, voice, and sound, appointment of Mellencamp as attorney-in-fact over the rights transferred, and the payment to Mellencamp of royalties received after a specified date, are triggered only by the execution of a final agreement. The tenor of the draft agreement is wholly inconsistent with the notion that it would constitute a mere memorialization of a prior binding oral agreement. Cf. R.G. Group, Inc., 751 F.2d at 76 (where contract on its face declared that it would set forth the parties rights and obligations "when duly executed" and that there was no other agreements between the parties, the parties were not bound until such execution took place).

Further confirming the absence of a binding agreement under this factor, as well as providing an independent basis for dismissal of the fourth claim, is the presence, in 3 of the 4 publishing agreements, of "no oral modification" clauses, "no oral cancellation" clauses, or both. New York General Obligations Law § 15-301 gives effect to contract provisions that prohibit oral modification or termination. Section 15-301 can be avoided where there has been part performance of or substantial reliance on the oral modification if either action is "unequivocally referable to the oral modification," Rose v. Spa Realty Assoc., 42 N.Y.2d 338, 343-44, 397 N.Y.S.2d 922, 926-27, 366 N.E.2d 1279 (1977), but neither circumstance is alleged to be present here.

b) Partial Performance.

Mellencamp has not alleged that performance, partial or otherwise, has taken place on either side.

c) Terms Left to be Agreed Upon.

According to Balaban, it was agreed at the luncheon meeting that the copyrights to be transferred were free of financial encumbrances; that Mellencamp was the sole composer of most of the musical compositions covered by the copyrights; that all mutual outstanding obligations between Mellencamp and defendants would survive the closing; and that a closing date of no later than June 30, 1987 was anticipated. These, Balaban asserts, were all the material terms of the agreement. The draft agreement, however, which defendants accurately describe as a "17 page, highly dense, and technical contract," Baker Affidavit at 10, is much broader in scope. For one thing, defendants' rights to Mellencamp's services as a songwriter is not mentioned by Balaban as a specific agreed upon term although elsewhere in his affidavit he describes such rights as representing the lion's share of the value of the publishing contracts. Yet those rights are addressed at length in the draft agreement. Also present in the draft agreement, but conspicuously absent from Balaban's affidavit, are sweeping warranties and indemnifications running from defendants to Mellencamp and covenants giving Mellencamp the sole discretion to assume or terminate agreements which defendants had with third parties. Under the circumstances, it can hardly be said that "there was literally nothing left to negotiate or settle, so that all that remained to be done was to sign what had already been fully agreed to." R.G. Group, Inc., 751 F.2d at 76.

d) Scope and Complexity of the Alleged Oral Agreement.

Here again, the draft agreement speaks for itself, consisting of 17 single typed pages containing numerous representations, guarantees, warranties and covenants. One can also infer, from the non-exclusive list of documents sought by Goldstein from Baker in connection with his due diligence investigation more than two weeks after the allegedly binding handshake agreement, that significant information, upon which Mellencamp would undoubtedly base his decision to be bound, was not known at the time of the luncheon meeting. Goldstein sought, among other things, a list of all Mellencamp compositions subject to agreements between Mellencamp and the Riva companies; all agreements, contracts, and licenses for the exploitation of Mellencamp's compositions, including sublicenses, mechanical licenses, performing rights and administrative contracts; a summary of all pending litigation relating to the compositions; copies of all royalty statements; and all contracts that could have an effect on the publishers' rights in and to the compositions. In addition to indicating that material facts were not known at the time of the luncheon meeting, the nature of the inquiry, a due diligence investigation, is inexplicably inconsistent with the pre-existence of a binding deal. If Mellencamp could not withdraw from the deal or alter it in any material way based on information discovered through the due diligence investigation, it is not clear why such an investigation would go forward. Finally, the fact that the proposed purchase price was $ 3 million dollars strongly supports the inference that a written agreement was contemplated. Cf. R.G. Group, Inc., 751 F.2d at 77 (where contract covered detailed business matters, parties discussed initial investment of $ 2 million, and plaintiff alleged damages of at least $ 80 million, agreement was not one which would ordinarily be relied upon without a writing); Winston, 777 F.2d at 83 (although agreement was only 4 pages parties thought terms and language used were complex enough to require substantial redrafting, and $ 62 thousand at issue in lawsuit was not a trifling amount). The Court concludes that the overwhelming and uncontradicted evidence demonstrates that the parties never entered into a binding agreement.

I note, as a final matter, that Mr. Balaban devotes 2 sentences in his 6 page affidavit to the question of the parties intent to be bound by the agreement reached at the luncheon meeting:

At the conclusion of the meeting Milton Marks, William Gaff and I joined hands and Milton Marks solemnly stated the Hebrew words "Mazel Bracha" which literally means "good fortune and blessing" and which are customarily said in some circles to evidence a firm agreement. I am also aware that in the entertainment business handshake agreements, particularly where there have been extensive negotiations prior to the agreement, are honored and binding.

These wholly ephemeral assertions are inadequate as a matter of law. First and foremost, even if Marks was a member of one of the unidentified "circles," his statement does not provide a basis to avoid N.Y. Gen. Oblig. L. § 15-301. Second, while on summary judgment "doubts must be resolved in favor of the party opposing the motion, the opposing party must provide 'concrete particulars' showing that a trial is needed, and 'it is not sufficient merely to assert a conclusion without supplying supporting arguments or facts in opposition to that motion.'" R.G. Group, Inc., 751 F.2d at 77. The plaintiff in R.G. Group asserted that defendant's representative assured him that they had "a handshake deal today and right now." Id. at 76. Although the Court concluded that the evidence "might, in a different context, have indicated some doubt about the writing requirement," the reference to a handshake deal could not overcome the parties' repeated expressions of the need for a writing and the absence of any express waiver of the writing requirement. Id. The statement relied on by plaintiff here is far less concrete than the admission of a "handshake deal" in R.G. Group, Inc., and the evident need for a writing is at least as compelling here.

Accordingly, plaintiff's fourth claim is dismissed. Plaintiff's third claim as against defendants Avir Music, Inc. and H.G. Music, Inc. is dismissed with leave to replead within twenty days of the date of this order. Plaintiff's first and second claims are also dismissed with leave to replead within twenty days of the date of this order. Plaintiff shall, within twenty days of the date of this order, submit materials in opposition to defendants' motion for partial summary judgment dismissing that part of the third claim predicated upon the 1981 publishing agreement.

SO ORDERED

Dated: New York, New York, November 2, 1988

———————

In *Mellencamp*, plaintiff sues alleging breach of fiduciary duty, breach of contract, and breach of an oral agreement to transfer the copyright to plaintiff. The outcome was that John Cougar Mellencamp was allowed to amend his complaint to allege that plaintiff was an intended beneficiary of the contract. *Woods v. Bourne Co.*, 60 F.3d 978 (2d Cir. 1995), which follows, looks into plaintiffs' claim as heirs of the author of the popular song, "When the Red, Red, Robin, Comes Bob, Bob, Bobbin' Along."

Woods v. Bourne Co.
United States Court of Appeals for the Second Circuit
February 3, 1995, Argued; July 25, 1995, Decided
60 F.3d 978

FEINBERG, Circuit Judge:

This appeal requires us to address conflicting claims to royalties generated by various uses of the song "When the Red, Red, Robin Comes Bob, Bob, Bobbin' Along" (the Song) during what is known in copyright law as an extended renewal term. Plaintiffs, heirs of song composer Harry Woods, and defendant Bourne, Inc., Woods's music publisher, both claim the right to receive certain royalties generated during this period. Essentially, plaintiffs claim that they are entitled to the royalties because they have exercised their statutory right to terminate the publisher's interests in the Song pursuant to 17 U.S.C. § 304(c). Bourne maintains that the royalties belong to it because all the disputed post-termination uses of the Song are attributable to so-called derivative works, which were prepared under its authority prior to termination and which therefore do not revert to the author. 17 U.S.C. § 304(c)(6)(A).

The royalties at issue were generated by several different uses of the Song following termination. These uses include (1) television performances of movies and television programs that incorporate the Song (hereafter sometimes referred to collectively as "audiovisual works"); (2) radio performances of sound recordings of the Song; and (3) sales of reprints of published arrangements. Following a bench trial before Judge Richard Owen in the United States District Court for the Southern District of New York, judgment was entered in March 1994 granting all the disputed royalties to plaintiffs-appellees. The opinion of the district court is reported at 841 F. Supp. 118.

The district court essentially reached its determination by analyzing whether any of the musical arrangements of the Song contained in the movies, television shows, sound recordings and printed arrangements were sufficiently original to qualify as derivative works. Finding that, with one minor exception, no version of the Song was sufficiently original, the district court granted judgment for the plaintiffs. The district court did not consider it relevant that some of the disputed royalties were generated by performances of audiovisual works, such as movies containing the Song, which are conceded to be original enough to qualify as derivative works.

For reasons set forth below, we hold that when a musical arrangement is contained within an audiovisual work produced under license from a publisher prior to termination, the publisher is entitled to receive royalties from post-termination performances of the audiovisual work under the terms of pre-termination licenses governing performance rights. It is irrelevant to disposition of those royalties whether the musical arrangement in the audiovisual work would qualify independently as a derivative work. We reverse the ruling of the district court in this respect and direct payment of royalties to Bourne for these performances in accordance with the terms of the licenses governing performance of the Song immediately prior to termination.

Whether a particular musical arrangement prepared under the authority of the publisher is a derivative work is relevant, however, to most other disputed categories of royalties before us. We essentially affirm the judgment with respect to those categories. For reasons set forth below, we affirm in part, reverse in part and remand for further proceedings consistent with this opinion.

## I. Background

### A. The Grant

Harry Woods (Woods) wrote the words and music to "When The Red, Red, Robin Comes Bob, Bob, Bobbin' Along" in 1926. That same year, Woods entered into a Songwriter's Agreement with the publishing company of Irving Berlin, Inc. (Berlin). The heirs of Woods, doing business as Callicoon Music (Callicoon), are plaintiffs-appellees in this matter. At some point in the 1940s, the Bourne Company (Bourne), defendant-appellant herein, succeeded to Berlin's interests in the Song.

By the Songwriter's Agreement, Woods transferred to Berlin

the original musical composition . . . including the publishing rights, the performing rights, the rights to use the same for mechanical reproduction, the right to make, publish and perform any arrangement or adaptation of the same, and all copyrights and the rights to secure copyrights and extensions and renewals of copyrights in the same, or in any arrangements or adaptations thereof.

In April 1926, Berlin obtained a certificate of registration of copyright for the original unpublished musical composition. The copyright certificate indicates that Woods is the author of the words and music. Berlin also published a piano-vocal arrangement, and Berlin obtained a certificate of copyright for that arrangement one month after registering the unpublished Song. The copyright certificate for the piano-vocal arrangement also names Woods as the author of the words and music. Berlin is listed as the copyright owner on both certificates. The certificates do not indicate that anyone other than Woods acted as arranger.

B. The Extended Renewal Term

Under the Copyright Act of 1909, in effect at the time of Woods's grant to Berlin, the original term of a copyright was 28 years, followed by a renewal term of another 28 years. Pub. L. No. 349, 35 Stat. 1075, § 23 (1909). Thus, the grant from Woods to Berlin in the Songwriter's Agreement, which included renewal rights, was to endure for up to 56 years, ending in 1982.

The reason for including a renewal term in the Copyright Act was to permit an author who sold the rights in his work for little consideration, when measured against the work's subsequent success, to enjoy a second opportunity with more bargaining power to reap the full value of the work. See 2 Melville B. Nimmer & David Nimmer, Nimmer on Copyright § 9.02 at 9-28 to 9-29 (1994). Thus, Congress attempted to alleviate the problem of the inability of authors to know the true monetary value of their works prior to commercial exploitation. Id. at 9-30. That purpose, however, was largely eroded by a subsequent Supreme Court decision holding that renewal rights were assignable along with original term rights in a work. Fisher Music Co. v. M. Witmark & Sons, 318 U.S. 643, 87 L. Ed. 1055, 63 S. Ct. 773 (1943); see 2 Nimmer § 9.06[B][1] at 9-108.

When the Copyright Act was thoroughly revised in 1976, Pub. L. No. 94-553, 90 Stat. 2541 (1976), Congress attempted to restore a second chance to authors or their heirs. Among other changes, Congress prolonged the duration of copyrights then in the renewal term so that they would continue for an additional 19 years. 17 U.S.C. § 304(b). At the end of the 28th year of the renewal term, the author (if alive) or the author's surviving spouse or children may terminate the rights of a grantee, usually a publisher, to whom the author had transferred rights in the original work. 17 U.S.C. § 304(c)(1)-(3). During the 19-year extended renewal term, a copyrighted work does not enter the public domain but continues to generate royalties. If the author or heirs elect to terminate the publisher's rights, royalties become payable to them rather than to the publisher. 17 U.S.C. § 304(c)(6). The author or heirs thus "recapture" rights in the copyrighted work and may thereby be relieved "of the consequences of ill-advised and unremunerative grants that had been made before the author had a fair opportunity to appreciate the [work's] true value." Mills Music, Inc. v. Snyder, 469 U.S. 153, 172-73, 83 L. Ed. 2d 556, 105 S. Ct. 638 (1985).

There is an important exception to the reversion rights of the author or heirs for derivative works produced by an authorized party during the original and renewal copyright terms. The Copyright Act of 1976 provides that

[a] derivative work prepared under authority of the grant before its termination may continue to be utilized under the terms of the grant after its termination, but this privilege does not extend to the preparation after the

termination of other derivative works based upon the copyrighted work covered by the terminated grant.

17 U.S.C. § 304(c)(6)(A) (referred to hereafter as "the Derivative Works Exception" or simply "the Exception"). The Act defines a derivative work as a work based upon one or more preexisting works, such as a translation, musical arrangement, dramatization, fictionalization, motion picture version, sound recording, art reproduction, abridgment, condensation, or any other form in which a work may be recast, transformed, or adapted. A work consisting of editorial revisions, annotations, elaborations, or other modifications which, as a whole, represent an original work of authorship, is a "derivative work."

17 U.S.C. § 101.

The renewal term for Bourne's copyright in the Song came to an end in April 1982, and Callicoon terminated Bourne's rights immediately thereafter.

C. Registration and Commercial Exploitation of the Song

During the original and renewal copyright terms, Berlin, and then its successor Bourne, successfully exploited the Song for its commercial value. As already noted, Berlin published a piano-vocal arrangement of the Song in 1926, shortly after receiving the grant from Woods. Berlin registered the piano-vocal arrangement with the Copyright Office, naming Woods as the author. Berlin or Bourne eventually prepared and published approximately 19 other arrangements of the Song for various combinations of voices and musical instruments. Bourne obtained 16 different registrations of copyright for different arrangements of the Song. The copyright registrations for these arrangements indicate that Woods is the author of the words and music. Other people are listed as arrangers or authors of new material. Bourne authorized the Hal Leonard Publishing Company (Leonard) to reprint arrangements of the Song in assorted sheet music compilations. Bourne also issued numerous licenses (known as mechanical licenses), often through its agent, the Harry Fox Agency, to record companies to make sound recordings of the Song as performed by popular artists. Bourne also issued licenses (known as synchronization licenses or synch licenses), frequently through the Harry Fox Agency, to motion picture and television studios to incorporate the Song in movies and in television programs.

After terminating Bourne's rights in the Song, Callicoon began to commercially exploit the Song. Bourne claims, and Callicoon does not dispute, that Callicoon licensed Leonard to reprint published arrangements of the Song formerly licensed by Bourne, simply changing the copyright notice to read "Callicoon" instead of "Bourne." When Leonard announced that it would continue to pay Bourne the royalties for these reprints, Callicoon licensed Warner Brothers Publications instead to reprint arrangements of the Song.

Callicoon (or the Harry Fox Agency as Callicoon's agent) also issued synch licenses for use of the Song in various new television programs. Callicoon also granted new synch licenses, similar to an expired license originally issued by Bourne prior to termination, for use of the Song in an episode of "The Lucy Show." Further, Callicoon licensed use of the Song in a television advertisement for Delta Faucet.

### D. Performance Rights

The principal issues in this case concern rights to perform the Song publicly. Under the Copyright Act, "to 'perform' a work means to recite, render, play, dance, or act it, either directly or by means of any device or process . . . ." 17 U.S.C. § 101. As relevant here, performances include television broadcasts of the Song as captured in movies and television programs and radio broadcasts of the Song as captured in sound recordings.

The right to perform a work publicly has been described as "one of the greatest sources of revenue in the music industry." Sidney Shemel & M. William Krasilovsky, This Business of Music 196 (1990); see also 2 Nimmer § 8.19 at 8-264. However, given the ephemeral nature of performance, it is difficult for the owners of this right to monitor and enforce it. To facilitate these functions, authors and publishers early in this century established a performing rights society, the American Society of Composers, Authors and Publishers (ASCAP). Currently, two other societies, Broadcast Music, Inc. (BMI) and the Society of European State Authors and Composers (SESAC), carry out similar functions. See generally 2 Nimmer at 8-264 to 8-273. Both Bourne and Callicoon are members of ASCAP.

By becoming members of ASCAP, authors and publishers may transfer to it the public performance rights in their works. ASCAP in turn issues licenses to radio stations, television stations, restaurants, stores and other entities that "perform" music publicly. Television stations generally obtain blanket licenses from ASCAP that entitle them to perform any musical composition in ASCAP's extensive catalogue. In exchange, the stations pay ASCAP a percentage of their annual gross receipts. Shemel & Krasilovsky, at 197.

ASCAP surveys all forms of public performance of members' musical compositions in order to determine allocation of licensing fees. As between the composer and publisher of a particular composition, ASCAP distributes half of the collected fees to each, unless the author and publisher indicate otherwise in their contract with each other. Al Kohn & Bob Kohn, The Art of Music Licensing 635-36 (1992).

During the original and renewal terms, Bourne received royalties from ASCAP for television broadcasts of movies and television programs containing the Song and radio broadcasts of the Song. A typical synch license issued by

Bourne for the production of an audiovisual work required a producer to pay a flat fee but provided that any broadcast entity performing the Song as contained in the audiovisual work must obtain a performance license from ASCAP or Bourne. Thus, for each pre-recorded audiovisual work incorporating the Song, Bourne had two sources of income: royalties from the producer for the right to incorporate the Song in the audiovisual work and royalties from television stations, via ASCAP, for each performance of the Song contained in the work. Similarly, Bourne received income from both record producers and, via ASCAP, radio stations performing recordings of the Song. However, the licenses Bourne issued to the record producers do not address performance rights, as the audiovisual synch licenses do.

E. The Parties' Dispute

Public performances of the Song as contained in movies, television programs and sound recordings continue to generate substantial royalties. Since Callicoon exercised its termination right in April 1982, Callicoon has continued to receive from ASCAP the author's 50% share of performance royalties, which share is not disputed.

What is disputed is the publisher's share of royalties for several categories of post-termination public performances of the Song. The first category concerns post-termination television broadcasts of audiovisual works produced under licenses issued by Bourne before termination. The second category concerns radio performances during the extended renewal term of the Song through sound recordings that were produced before termination under licenses issued by Bourne. Another category concerns post-termination television and radio broadcasts of the Song for which source material is not identified in ASCAP records. In a fourth category by itself is a television commercial for Delta Faucet licensed by Callicoon after termination; according to Bourne, the commercial contains a 1981 Bourne-authorized arrangement of the Song that is a derivative work.

Prior to Callicoon's termination of Bourne's rights, Bourne notified ASCAP of Bourne's contention that it "'continued to be possessed of the right to receive income from all derivative works retained by it.'" ASCAP then deemed that a dispute existed between the parties as to rights to publisher's royalties from post-termination performances of the Song. In accordance with ASCAP policy, such royalties have been held in escrow pending resolution of the dispute. The parties have stipulated that the publisher's share of post-termination royalties withheld by ASCAP from the fourth quarter of 1982 to the first quarter of 1992 is $ 85,042.69. This share is comprised of the following components: (1) $ 27,157.78 from television performances of audiovisual works created before termination; (2) $ 1,058.56 from radio performances of the Song in sound recordings created before termination; (3) $ 17,985.28 from television and radio performances for which source materials were not identified in ASCAP records; and (4) $ 38,841.07 from television performances of audiovisual works created after termination (including $ 13,365.78 from the Delta Faucet advertisement). As of October 1, 1992, an additional $ 32,181 in the escrow account was attributable to accrued interest and miscellaneous special distributions.

In addition to performance royalties, the parties dispute rights to royalties from sales of reprints of published arrangements of the Song in sheet music compilations produced and distributed by Leonard and Warner Brothers during the extended renewal term.

In September 1989, Callicoon filed an amended complaint against Bourne and ASCAP in the district court seeking principally a declaration that Callicoon is entitled to the publisher's royalties withheld by ASCAP. Callicoon also sought a determination of rights to reprint royalties. The district court held a bench trial in November 1992, and rendered its decision in January 1994. Judgment in favor of Callicoon was entered in March 1994.

### F. The Decision Below

The district court determined that Callicoon was entitled to all of the royalties generated by post-termination performances of the Song, including performances contained in pre-termination derivative audiovisual works. The court acknowledged, and the parties do not dispute, that the works in which the Song was incorporated — for example, movies -were by definition derivative. Nevertheless, the court found the controlling issue, as to all categories of performance, to be whether the underlying arrangement of the Song itself is a derivative work. Only then would performance royalties continue to go to Bourne during the extended renewal term. 841 F. Supp. at 120. The court then considered whether any of the printed or performed arrangements of the Song were derivative works. It found, first, that the original piano-vocal arrangement published by Berlin (Bourne's predecessor in interest) was not a Berlin-created derivative work. The court then found that none of the printed or performed arrangements of the Song, with the exception of one arrangement performed by Fred Waring, could be called a derivative work. Id. at 123.

Since Bourne claimed an exception to the general rule in the 1976 Act permitting termination of the publisher's rights, the court placed the burden on Bourne to identify performances of derivative arrangements. Since Bourne offered no evidence of performances of the Fred Waring arrangement, the court held that all of the withheld ASCAP royalties should be paid to Callicoon. Id. The district court also found that none of the printed arrangements made after the piano-vocal arrangement were derivative works. Accordingly, it ordered all reprint royalties to be paid to Callicoon. Id.

This appeal by Bourne followed.

## II. Discussion

The appeal poses two principal issues. The first is the basis for determining whether a publisher is entitled to receive royalties for post-termination performances of the Song in pre-termination audiovisual works, such as movies, that are concededly derivative works. As already indicated, the district court found the relevant inquiry to be whether the arrangement of the Song within a derivative work is itself a derivative work. We disagree with the district court in this respect. Whether the arrangement of the Song is itself a derivative work is not relevant to this category of royalties.

The derivative work status of an arrangement of the Song, however, is relevant to several other kinds of royalties at issue in this suit. These include royalties from performances of pre-termination sound recordings, performances of post-termination audiovisual works and sales of sheet music reprints. The second principal issue in this appeal can be broken into two parts: whether the district court invoked the correct standard for determining whether arrangements of the Song are sufficiently original to be derivative works and, if so, whether the court correctly applied that standard to the facts before it.

A. Royalties from Television Performances

We consider first the basis for determining entitlement to royalties from post-termination performances of the Song as contained in pre-termination movies and television programs.

The Derivative Works Exception preserves the right of owners of derivative works to continue to exploit their works during the extended renewal term under previously negotiated terms. Without such an exception, authors might use their reversion rights to extract prohibitive fees from owners of successful derivative works or to bring infringement actions against them. See Mills Music, 469 U.S. at 172-74 (discussing legislative history of termination right and Derivative Works Exception); id. at 183-84 n.8 (White, J., dissenting) (explaining that under the 1909 Act, films had been removed from public circulation during renewal periods for fear of infringement actions).

The goal of keeping derivative works in public circulation does not require that publishers rather than authors receive royalties for their use. As long as the royalties paid by a derivative work user remain unchanged, the user should be indifferent as to whether an author or publisher receives the payment. See Mills

Music, 469 U.S. at 177. The royalties generated during the extended renewal term will be a windfall to either authors (and their heirs) or publishers since, at the time the rights at issue were originally established, neither group expected to get royalties for more than 56 years. The question, therefore, is: Who is the beneficiary of this windfall?

### 1. The Mills Music Decision

The answer, according to the decision of the Supreme Court in Mills Music, Inc. v. Snyder, is found in the phrase "under the terms of the grant," as used in the Derivative Works Exception. We quote its text again for convenience:

A derivative work prepared under authority of the grant before its termination may continue to be utilized under the terms of the grant after its termination, but this privilege does not extend to the preparation after the termination of other derivative works based upon the copyrighted work covered by the terminated grant.

17 U.S.C. § 304(c)(6)(A) (emphasis supplied); see Mills Music, 469 U.S. at 156.

Mills Music posed circumstances similar to those of the instant case. Snyder, treated for purposes of that case as the sole author of the song "Who's Sorry Now," had assigned renewal rights in the song to a publisher, Mills, in 1940 in exchange for, among other things, a 50% share in mechanical royalties, that is, royalties from sales of copies of sound recordings. Mills in turn licensed record companies to produce copies of sound recordings of the song. Upon termination of the grant from Snyder to Mills, Snyder's heirs claimed the right to 100%, rather than just 50%, of future mechanical royalties. Harry Fox Agency, Inc. v. Mills Music, Inc., 543 F. Supp. 844, 850 (S.D.N.Y. 1982), rev'd, 720 F.2d 733 (2d Cir. 1983), rev'd sub nom. Mills Music, Inc. v. Snyder, 469 U.S. 153, 83 L. Ed. 2d 556, 105 S. Ct. 638 (1985). Mills claimed that the sound recordings at issue were derivative works created under the terms of the grant from Snyder to Mills and that, therefore, Mills should continue to share in mechanical royalties according to the terms of that grant. 543 F. Supp. at 850.

In the district court, Judge Edward Weinfeld held that the sound recordings produced before termination were derivative works and that the terms of the grant required payment of mechanical royalties to Mills. Id. at 852. This court reversed, holding that upon termination only the grant from Mills to the record companies remained in effect. Since the basis for Mills's retention of half the mechanical royalties was the grant from Snyder, and since that grant was now terminated, all mechanical royalties should revert to Snyder's heirs. 720 F.2d at 739.

The Supreme Court reversed. It found that the phrase "terminated grant," the last two words in the Derivative Works Exception, must refer to the original grant from author to publisher. The Court reasoned that the other two uses of the word "grant" in the single sentence of the Derivative Works Exception must logically refer to the same grant. 469 U.S. at 164-65. The court noted that "the 1940 grant from Snyder to Mills expressly gave Mills the authority to license others to make derivative works." Id. at 165. It then concluded that "a fair construction of the phrase 'under the terms of the grant' as applied to any particular licensee would necessarily encompass both the [original] grant [from author to publisher] and the individual license [to record producers] executed pursuant thereto." Id. at 166-67. Because the combination of the two grants directed record companies to pay royalties to Mills, and Mills in turn to pay 50% of the amount collected to Snyder, the Court held that Mills was entitled to retain its 50% share of mechanical royalties on sales of records produced before termination but sold during the extended renewal term. Id. at 178.

Mills Music is, of course, binding upon us. Mills Music appears to require that where multiple levels of licenses govern use of a derivative work, the "terms of the grant" encompass the original grant from author to publisher and each subsequent grant necessary to enable the particular use at issue. See Howard B. Abrams, Who's Sorry Now? Termination Rights and the Derivative Works Exception, 62 U. Det. L. Rev. 181, 234-35 (1985) (describing holding in Mills Music as "preserving the entire paper chain that defines the entire transaction"). If one of those grants requires payment of royalties by licensees to an intermediary, such as a publisher, then continued utilization of derivative works "under the terms of the grant" requires continued payments to the intermediary. See Mills Music, 469 U.S. at 167. The effect of Mills Music, then, is to preserve during the post-termination period the panoply of contractual obligations that governed pre-termination uses of derivative works by derivative work owners or their licensees.

2. Applying the Mills Music Decision

The derivative works involved in Mills Music were sound recordings, and the use there was the sale of copies. The concededly derivative works we now address are audiovisual works and the use in question is public performance. We believe that the reasoning of Mills Music also applies in this situation.

There is no question that the owners of the copyrights in audiovisual works have the right to perform the works publicly. They typically exercise this right by licensing television stations to broadcast their works. In this case, the terms of the synch licenses issued by Bourne to the producers required the television stations performing the audiovisual works to obtain a second grant from either Bourne or ASCAP, licensing the stations to perform the Song contained in the audiovisual works. In practice, this license is always obtained from ASCAP, which then remits the publisher's share of fees to Bourne pursuant to the agreement between Bourne and ASCAP. Under our reading of Mills Music, the "terms of the grant" include the provisions of the grants from Bourne to ASCAP and from ASCAP to television stations. This pair of licenses is contemplated in the grant of the synch licenses from Bourne to film and television producers.

Callicoon contends that neither the terms of the grants from Bourne to audiovisual work producers nor the terms of the grant from Bourne to ASCAP identify Bourne as the payee of performance royalties. By contrast, Callicoon points out that the mechanical licenses to record companies in Mills Music explicitly named Mills as payee, and the Supreme Court viewed this fact as dispositive. Therefore, Callicoon argues, termination in this case "simply subjects distribution of the royalties to ASCAP's usual procedures, under which, absent any specific direction to the contrary, royalties are distributed to current copyright owners."

We do not agree. The fact that the performance right in the Song is conveyed separately through ASCAP is simply an accomodation dictated by the practical problem of enforcing performance rights and should not control analysis of the distribution of performance royalties. It may be true that no license specifically identifying audiovisual works containing "Red, Red, Robin" requires payment of performance royalties to Bourne. However, as explained above, performance royalties are generally traded "in bulk," with a publisher granting ASCAP non-exclusive performance rights in all of its songs, whether contained in derivative works or not. Television broadcast stations in turn obtain blanket licenses from ASCAP. Thus, even if the terms of a grant to perform any single work may be somewhat obscured by the bulk trading of performance rights, the terms are necessarily contained within the overarching grants (from Bourne to ASCAP and from ASCAP to the television broadcast stations) and may be reconstructed by reference to them. The relevant terms, according to Mills Music, would be those that were in place "at the time of termination." 469 U.S. at 174.

We therefore reverse the decision of the district court as to royalties from post-termination performances of pre-termination audiovisual works. On remand, the court should enter judgment ordering defendant ASCAP to pay these royalties to Bourne in accordance with the terms of the grants in effect immediately prior to the effective date of Callicoon's termination.

### B. Royalties from Sound Recordings and Other Works

The analysis in Part A above, which applies to post-termination performances of pre-termination movies and television programs, does not apply to certain other post-termination uses of the Song. The various post-termination uses which we now consider have little in common except that for each, the question whether the arrangement of the Song itself is a derivative work is relevant to the allocation of post-termination royalties.

The first category to which we turn is post-termination radio performances of pre-termination sound recordings. At first blush, it may seem anomalous that sound recordings should be subject to a different analysis than the audiovisual works considered above. Like audiovisual works, sound recordings are clearly derivative works, which at least for some purposes fall within the Derivative Works Exception. See generally Mills Music, 469 U.S. 153, 83 L. Ed. 2d 556, 105 S. Ct. 638 (addressing sales of copies of sound recordings). However, while the Act confers a right of public performance on the owner of a copyright in an audiovisual work, it specifically denies such a right to the owner of a copyright in a sound recording. 17 U.S.C. § 114(a); see generally Agee v. Paramount Communications, Inc., 59 F.3d 317, 1995 U.S. App. LEXIS 15862 (2d Cir. 1995). Instead, the right to perform a song contained in a sound recording belongs to the owner of the copyright in the song. 17 U.S.C. § 106(4); see Abrams at 235.

The Derivative Works Exception provides for continued utilization of a derivative work. As the Supreme Court noted in Mills Music, "The purpose of the Exception was 'to preserve the right of the owner of a derivative work to exploit it, notwithstanding reversion.'" 469 U.S. at 173 (quoting statement of Barbara Ringer in Further Discussions and Comments on Preliminary Draft for Revised U.S. Copyright Law 39, 88th Cong., 2d Sess., Copyright Law Revision, Part 4 (H. Judiciary Comm. Print 1964)) (emphasis supplied). Thus, the Exception protects only authorized uses made by derivative work copyright owners, or their licensees.

Therefore, even though a sound recording is concededly a derivative work, that fact alone does not justify application of the Derivative Works Exception to performances of sound recordings — as it did with the performances of audiovisual works discussed in part A above. We must still consider, however, whether a different analysis requires application of the Exception. Since the owner of the copyright in the Song holds the public performance right for sound recordings, that right would ordinarily revert to Callicoon during the extended renewal term. However, if the particular Song arrangements contained in the sound recordings are themselves Bourne-authorized derivative works, as Bourne contends, then Bourne should retain the performance right under the Derivative Works Exception and receive the royalties therefrom.

The same analysis applies to the royalties from the remaining post-termination uses of the Song, since Bourne argues with respect to all of them that they utilize arrangements of the Song that are Bourne-authorized derivative works. These categories of uses are the reprinting and selling of sheet music of pre-termination arrangements, the performance of a television commercial for Delta Faucet, which was produced after termination, and post-termination radio and television performances for which ASCAP records do not identify source material.

In the district court and again on appeal, Bourne has argued that all of the pre-termination arrangements prepared under its authority qualify as derivative works. This argument stems from the premise that the first published piano-vocal arrangement of the Song was itself a Bourne-authorized derivative work.

The original grant from Woods to Berlin, according to Bourne, was just a "lead sheet" — a very simple, hand-written rendering of the lyrics and melody of the composition without harmonies or other embellishments. Bourne argues that Berlin modified the lead sheet by adding harmonies and other elements to create a commercially exploitable piano-vocal arrangement that qualifies as a derivative work. Bourne also argues that the 1981 arrangement allegedly used in the Delta Faucet commercial, as well as all other Bourne-authorized arrangements, were derivative works. Because only the first piano-vocal arrangement, the 1981 arrangement and other Bourne-authorized arrangements were ever commercially exploited, Bourne concludes that any given performance of the Song is "more likely than not" a performance of a Bourne-authorized derivative work.

The district court rejected both aspects of this argument — that the piano-vocal or any other Bourne-authorized arrangements were derivative works and that all relevant performances were in fact performances of Bourne-authorized arrangements. In finding that the piano-vocal arrangement is not a derivative work, the court relied on a close reading of the statutory definition of a derivative work and inferences regarding industry practice. 841 F. Supp. at 121. For convenience, we repeat the Copyright Act's definition of a derivative work as a work based upon one or more preexisting works, such as a . . . musical arrangement . . . motion picture version, sound recording . . . or any other form in which a work may be recast, transformed, or adapted. A work consisting of editorial revisions, annotations, elaborations, or other modifications which, as a whole, represent an original work of authorship, is a "derivative work."

17 U.S.C. § 101.

The district court found that the first sentence of that definition, which plainly identifies a "musical arrangement" as one type of derivative work, must be read in conjunction with the second sentence's requirement of "modifications which, as a whole, represent an original work of authorship." 841 F. Supp. at 121. Therefore, according to the district court, not every musical arrangement is entitled to derivative work status. The arrangement must be an original work of authorship. The court then asserted that Bourne's claim that Berlin's arrangers somehow exercised authorship by turning the lead sheet into a commercially exploitable piano-vocal arrangement was "contrary to the ways of the trade." Id. The court inferred that Woods "doubtless played the song for Berlin when he brought it into the firm," id., and that, at the very least, he must have approved the piano-vocal arrangement before it was published and made available to the public. The court concluded that, "accordingly, the very first piano and voice version that was sold could not possibly be a 'musical arrangement' making it a 'derivative work' of the lead sheet." Id. The court went on to find that none of the printed or (with one minor exception) performed arrangements were derivative works. Id. at 122-23.

1. The Standard of Originality

In order for a work to qualify as a derivative work it must be independently copyrightable. Weissmann v. Freeman, 868 F.2d 1313, 1320-21 (2d Cir.), cert. denied, 493 U.S. 883, 107 L. Ed. 2d 172, 110 S. Ct. 219 (1989). The basis for copyright protection contained in both the constitution and the Copyright Act is originality of authorship. L. Batlin & Son, Inc. v. Snyder, 536 F.2d 486, 490 (2d Cir.) (in banc), cert. denied, 429 U.S. 857, 50 L. Ed. 2d 135, 97 S. Ct. 156 (1976). While a certificate of copyright registration, such as the one that Berlin obtained for the piano-vocal arrangement, creates a presumption of copyrightability, the existence of a registration certificate is not dispositive. Weissmann, 868 F.2d at 1320.

We thoroughly discussed the standard of originality in a derivative work in our in banc decision in Batlin. There we held that "there must be at least some substantial variation [from the underlying work], not merely a trivial variation." Batlin, 536 F.2d at 491; accord Durham Indus., Inc. v. Tomy Corp., 630 F.2d 905, 909 (2d Cir. 1980) ("To support a copyright the original aspects of a derivative work must be more than trivial."). Further, "the requirement of originality [cannot] be satisfied simply by the demonstration of 'physical skill' or 'special training' . . . ." Batlin, 536 F.2d at 491; see also Tempo Music, Inc. v. Famous Music Corp., 838 F. Supp. 162, 170 (S.D.N.Y. 1993) (discussing Batlin). Our discussions of the originality standard in recent decisions, such as Weissmann, 868 F.2d at 1321, and Gaste v. Kaiserman, 863 F.2d 1061, 1066 (2d Cir. 1988), upon which Bourne relies, do not render the Batlin standard inapplicable. See Waldman Publishing Corp. v. Landoll, Inc., 43 F.3d 775, 782 (2d Cir. 1994) (relying on Batlin as authoritative statement of originality requirement).

In Batlin we warned that "to extend copyrightability to minuscule variations would simply put a weapon for harassment in the hands of mischievous copiers intent on appropriating and monopolizing public domain work." 536 F.2d at 492. At least one other circuit, relying on this court's opinion in Batlin, has advised special caution in analyzing originality in derivative works, since too low a threshold will "give the first [derivative work] creator a considerable power to interfere with the creation of subsequent derivative works from the same underlying work." Gracen v. Bradford Exchange, 698 F.2d 300, 305 (7th Cir. 1983). As the Gracen court explained in discussing the originality requirement for a painting derived from a photograph, there must be "sufficiently gross difference between the underlying and the derivative work to avoid entangling subsequent artists depicting the underlying work in copyright problems." 698 F.2d at 305. This observation may be particularly relevant in the musical context. While it is easy enough to describe the threshold of originality as being low, it is difficult to translate this standard from one medium to another. See Tempo Music, 838 F. Supp. at 170 ("The risk of copyright confusion seems particularly significant in music cases given that finders of fact often lack musical expertise."); 1 Nimmer § 2.05[C] at 2-57 (noting "tendency to require a somewhat greater degree of originality in order to accord copyright in a musical arrangement"). But see 1 William F. Patry, Copyright Law and Practice 237 (1994).

Bourne argues that the district court overstated the degree of originality required for an arrangement of a song to merit derivative work status. Bourne focuses on the court's statement that "there must be such things as unusual vocal treatment, additional lyrics of consequence, unusual altered harmonies, novel sequential uses of themes . . . ." 841 F. Supp. at 121. We agree that the sentence that Bourne quotes does overstate the standard for derivative work originality. As we have observed on several occasions, the requirement of originality is not the same as the requirement of novelty, the higher standard usually applied to patents. E.g., Batlin, 536 F.2d at 490 ("There must be independent creation, but it need not be invention in the sense of striking uniqueness, ingeniousness, or novelty . . . ."); Alfred Bell & Co. v. Catalda Fine Arts, Inc., 191 F.2d 99, 102-03 (2d Cir. 1951). However, we read the district court's statement as brief dictum within a discussion that otherwise does identify the correct standard.

Earlier in its opinion, the district court correctly cited the statutory definition of a derivative work, which the court said required "the 'modification' to the composition to be an original work of authorship." 841 F. Supp. at 121. Following its apparent exaggeration of the standard for derivative work originality, the court explained that

[there must be] something of substance added making the piece to some extent a new work with the old song embedded in it but from which the new has developed. It is not merely a stylized version of the original song where a major artist may take liberties with the lyrics or the tempo, the listener hearing basically the original tune. It is, in short, the addition of such new material as would entitle the creator to a copyright on the new material.

Id.

This, we believe, is a correct statement of the originality standard as set out in Batlin. The first and third sentences simply reiterate Batlin's "substantial variation" requirement. The second sentence, disqualifying "stylized versions of the original song," as well as the district court's earlier dismissal of "cocktail pianist variations of the piece that are standard fare in the music trade by any competent musician," id., merely express, in terms relevant to the musical context, our explanation in Batlin that "the demonstration of 'physical skill' or 'special training,'" 536 F.2d at 491, is insufficient to satisfy the requirement of originality. Because we conclude that the district court articulated the correct standard of originality, we turn to consider the application of the standard to the facts of this case.

2. Application of the Originality Standard

To determine whether a work is sufficiently original to be a derivative work, the judge in a bench trial must make findings of fact based upon a comparison of two works. The judge must then apply the legal standard of originality to the facts to determine whether the standard has been met. Although this seems at first blush to be a two-step process, with review of the factual findings governed by a clearly erroneous standard and the legal conclusion subject to de novo review, most courts, including this one, apparently view the process as purely a factual inquiry, reviewable for clear error alone. E.g., Folio Impressions, Inc. v. Byer California, 937 F.2d 759, 763 (2d Cir. 1991); Weissmann v. Freeman, 868 F.2d 1313, 1322 (2d Cir. 1989) (citing Fed.R.Civ.P. 52(a)); Financial Information, Inc. v. Moody's Investors Serv., Inc., 808 F.2d 204, 207 (2d Cir. 1986), cert. denied, 484 U.S. 820, 98 L. Ed. 2d 42, 108 S. Ct. 79 (1987); cf. American Geophysical Union v. Texaco, Inc., 37 F.3d 881, 886 (2d Cir. 1994), as amended on denial of reh'g (analyzing fair use), petition for cert. filed, 63 U.S.L.W. 3788 (U.S. Apr. 24, 1995) (No. 94-1726); 1 Patry, Copyright Law and Practice 145 n.106 (cataloguing cases). Regardless of the applicable standard of review, in the instant case we believe that there is adequate support in the record for Judge Owen's determinations. In other words, on this aspect of the case we find that the district court did not err — period. Obviously, therefore, it did not clearly err.

a. The piano-vocal arrangement

Harry Woods is the sole person identified as author of the words and music on copyright certificates for both the lead sheet and the piano-vocal arrangement that Berlin obtained in 1926. No one else is listed as the arranger of either of these works, but later Bourne-authorized derivative works do list different arrangers. Although the district court did not rely heavily on these uncontested facts, we view them as evidence supporting the district court's conclusion that Woods, not Berlin, composed the Song represented by both the lead sheet and the piano-vocal arrangement or at least that at the time of the grant, Berlin credited Woods with such authorship. A reasonable inference could be made that the piano-vocal arrangement closely approximated the composition conveyed from Woods to Berlin in 1926. Thus, regardless of whether the piano-vocal arrangement may be considered original as compared with the lead sheet, any original creativity that went into producing it was the result of Woods's effort and occurred before the rights in the composition were granted to Berlin.

This theory, apparently adopted by the district court, is supported by the trial testimony of Beebe Bourne, the current president of Bourne, Inc. and the daughter of one of Berlin's founders. She testified to the operating procedure at Berlin in 1926, stating:

a Harry Woods would come in then and in subsequent years and bring in what we call a lead sheet. . . . And they would often work at the piano. Some of the musicians . . . could not even read and write music as we know it, but had a tremendous ear for sound. They would come in and it would be reviewed . . . to determine the merits of it insofar as the commercial salability for those times.

Later she explained that in-house editors, whom she referred to as "technicians," would "actually write the piano vocal . . . ."

These statements, that the Berlin employees who physically wrote out the musical notes were "technicians," and that the composers "would often work at the piano" when they came in to sell a song, certainly lend additional support to the district court's view that any act of independent creation distinguishing the lead sheet from the piano-vocal arrangement was attributable to Woods before he sold the Song to Berlin. 841 F. Supp. at 121 (noting that Woods "doubtless played the song for Berlin when he brought it into the firm.").

The scant record evidence thus suggests that the lead sheet and the piano-vocal arrangement were simply two different renderings of a single composition, the rights in which Woods granted to Berlin. Upon termination, the heirs recovered rights in the composition, rendered in both forms, and any subsequent Bourne arrangements that were not sufficiently original to be considered derivative works.

In addition to finding that the piano-vocal arrangement essentially represents the composition granted from Woods to Berlin, the district court found that the piano-vocal arrangement is not sufficiently original compared with the lead sheet to be considered a derivative work. A side-by-side comparison of the two printed documents quickly reveals that they are not literally identical. But it is not readily apparent whether the differences between the two documents are "substantial." At trial, both Callicoon and Bourne presented expert testimony on whether the differences were "substantial variations" reflecting deliberate aesthetic choices or merely "trivial" changes dictated, for instance, by applying conventional rules of harmony to the melody in the lead sheet. The district court was ultimately persuaded by Callicoon's expert, Thomas Shepard, that the variations in the piano-vocal arrangement were insubstantial.

We have considered the record before the district court, and we cannot say that on the particular facts before it the court erred in making this determination. Accordingly, even if all the disputed performances were based upon the piano-vocal arrangement, as Bourne contends, this would not compel judgment for Bourne.

Moreover, even if the piano-vocal arrangement could fairly be described as a derivative work, there is little if any evidence in the record to suggest that the versions of the Song in sound recordings and audiovisual works were based upon the piano-vocal arrangement. To the contrary, Callicoon's expert testified that each performance he had listened to was different. The only common elements were the words and melody contained in the lead sheet. He also stated that arrangers do not always use piano-vocal arrangements in developing subsequent arrangements; they often work from memory or from lead sheets. Therefore, even if the district judge had agreed with Bourne that the piano-vocal arrangement was a derivative work, the judge need not have concluded that the performances of the Song were ultimately performances of the piano-vocal arrangement.

b. The 1981 arrangement

A new arrangement of the Song was made under license from Bourne in 1981. This arrangement is potentially significant because, according to Bourne, it is this arrangement that is performed in the post-termination Delta Faucet commercial, which has earned approximately $ 13,000 in performance royalties. The district court found that the 1981 arrangement "in no way exhibits the degree of creativity required to make it a derivative work." Id. at 123.

According to both parties' experts, the principal variation in the 1981 arrangement as compared with the piano-vocal arrangement concerns the bass line in the piano part. While the bass line in the first piano-vocal arrangement consists primarily of quarter notes on the first and third beat of each measure, there is a so-called "moving bass line" in the 1981 arrangement.

As with the piano-vocal arrangement, we have considered the record before the district court, and we are unable to conclude that the court erred in finding the 1981 arrangement, which Bourne contends was used in the Delta Faucet commercial, insufficiently original to be called a derivative work. Accordingly, Bourne is not entitled to post-termination royalties from the Delta Faucet commercial. The judgment of the district court is affirmed to the extent that it awards royalties from the Delta Faucet commercial to Callicoon.

c. Other printed and performed arrangements

We have reviewed the evidence concerning other recorded and printed arrangements and find that the district court did not err in its determinations regarding the originality of any of these arrangements.

As we stated above, Bourne would not be entitled to royalties generated by post-termination radio performances of pre-termination sound recordings unless the arrangements in those recordings were themselves Bourne-authorized derivative works. Since we are unable to conclude that the district court erred in finding none of the Bourne-authorized arrangements (with the exception of one performance by Fred Waring) to be derivative works, we affirm the judgment of the district court to the extent that it awards Callicoon royalties from post-termination performances of pre-termination sound recordings. We also affirm the court's judgment to the extent that it orders Bourne to remit to Callicoon reprint royalties that Bourne continued to receive after termination.

C. Royalties from Performances Where Source Material was not Identified

We are left with the category of royalties, worth about $ 18,000, pertaining to radio and television performances monitored by ASCAP for which source materials were not sufficiently identified. The district court placed the burden on Bourne, as the party claiming an exception to the heirs' right of termination to prove that any post-termination performances were based upon pre-termination derivative arrangements of the Song. 841 F. Supp. at 122 (citing United States v. Allen, 163 U.S. 499, 41 L. Ed. 242, 16 S. Ct. 1071 (1896)). Finding that Bourne failed to meet this burden, the court awarded the royalties to Callicoon.

On appeal, Bourne claims that the recapture right and the Derivative Works Exception are two parts of a legislative compromise, and that the two parts should be placed "on a level playing field." On that view, Bourne contends that the usual rule, requiring a party claiming an exception to bear the burden of proof, does not apply. Bourne then argues that because it is "more likely than not" that post-termination performances are performances of Bourne-authorized derivative works, the burden of proof should in fact be on Callicoon. In the alternative, Bourne suggests that royalties from unidentified performances be allocated in proportion to royalties for all identified performances.

We are unpersuaded by Bourne's argument that the Derivative Works Exception should not be treated like any other exception to a statutory rule. It is clear from the statutory scheme that it is indeed an exception to the general rule of reversion of rights to the author's heirs upon termination, and it was thus described by the Supreme Court in Mills Music, 469 U.S. at 162. Therefore, we hold that the district court properly placed the burden on Bourne to prove that particular performances were based upon Bourne-authorized derivative works.

Because, as the parties stipulated, the "source materials" for these performances were unidentified, it is impossible to determine from the record whether the works performed were created before or after termination. As to the unidentified television performances, Bourne has introduced no evidence that any of these disputed performances were of pre-termination audiovisual works, which would entitle it to royalties under the analysis of Part A above. In addition, in light of our affirmance of the district court's ruling that virtually none of the Bourne-authorized arrangements are derivative works, it is not more likely than not that unidentified performances are performances of Bourne-authorized derivative works. Thus, the district court did not err in finding that Bourne had failed to satisfy its burden of proof. Accordingly, we affirm the judgment to the extent that it awarded Callicoon approximately $ 18,000 attributable to post-termination performances of unidentified material.

### D. Miscellaneous Issues

The briefs raise two additional issues that should be decided on remand. First, the parties dispute entitlement to certain royalties from a musical work, "Freckles," that allegedly infringed the copyright in the Song. During the renewal term, Bourne entered into a settlement agreement with the publisher of "Freckles." The district court apparently determined that Callicoon is entitled to receive royalties from "Freckles" during the extended renewal term, but the basis of the ruling is not clear in the opinion. Second, Bourne raises a question concerning an episode of "The Lucy Show" for which Bourne had issued a synch license in 1973. The synch license had a five-year term, and Bourne apparently never renewed the license. However, during the extended renewal term, in 1988 and again in 1990, Callicoon issued renewal licenses for the same "Lucy Show" episode, for which it received a total of $ 1,700. Bourne now contends that by issuing these renewal licenses Callicoon was encroaching on Bourne's right to utilize during the extended renewal term derivative works prepared before termination. In its opinion, the district court did not address Bourne's contention. We remand to the district court to decide both the "Freckles" and "Lucy Show" issues in accordance with the principles set forth in this opinion.

### III. Conclusion

To summarize, we hold as follows: (1) As to performance royalties attributable to pre-termination movies and television programs, the judgment of the district court is reversed. The royalties withheld by ASCAP from those performances should be paid in accordance with the terms of the grant of performance rights from Bourne to ASCAP and from ASCAP to television stations that existed immediately before termination; (2) The judgment of the district court is affirmed as to (a) royalties attributable to radio performances of pre-termination sound recordings, (b) reprint royalties, (c) the Delta Faucet commercial, and (d) unidentified television and radio performances; (3) On remand, the district court should address the "Freckles" and "Lucy Show" issues and enter judgment consistent with this opinion.

The problem is that the song was used for various purposes during an extended renewal term. It is question of who is entitled to what royalties.

———————

SINGLE SONG PUBLISHING AGREEMENT

THIS AGREEMENT, made and entered into as of this ____day of _____, 2015, by and between John Doe Publishing Inc., (hereinafter "Publisher"), whose address is 3333 Tulip Lane, Houton, Texas 77777, and Joshua Doe whose address is 5555 Granite Blvd., Houston, Texas 77777 (hereinafter "Writer"), with respect to the following original work:

Title of Song: "I Love Joshua Doe" composed in the following undivided percentages ("Writer's Share") by the following Writer:

Joshua Doe 80%

John Doe Publishing, Inc. 20%

(hereinafter sometimes referred to as the "Composition"), creation of which was completed by Writer in the year 2015.

NOW THEREFORE, for good and valuable consideration, the receipt of which is hereby acknowledged, Publisher and Writer agree as follows:

1. <u>Musical Works</u>. Writer hereby sells, assigns and delivers to Publisher, its successors and assigns, his/her entire undivided right and interest in and to the Composition above-referenced as his/her Writer's Share, including the title, words and music thereof, all worldwide rights therein, all copyrights therein and thereto, all registrations with respect thereto, and the exclusive right to secure copyrights and any extensions of copyrights in the same and in any arrangements and adaptions thereof, all throughout the world. Writer affirms that, for purposes of translations, adaptions and arrangements, Publisher may change the title of the Composition, and that Publisher, by Writer's execution of this Agreement as well as the Assignment of Copyright (attached hereto as Schedule 1 to this Agreement as if fully set forth herein) has acquired the words and music of the Composition, and all rights therein, and all copyrights and rights to secure copyright throughout the world, including the aforesaid as to any arrangements, adaptions, or translations of the original Composition, and to have and to hold said copyright and all rights presently or in the future existing thereunder, subject to the terms of this Agreement.

2. <u>Writer's Warranty</u>. Writer hereby warrants, covenants and represents that the Composition is Writer's original unpublished work and that no part thereof infringes upon the title, the literary or musical property or the copyright in any work or the statutory, common law or other rights (including rights of privacy

and publicity) of any person, firm or corporation, nor unfairly competes with any person or entity; that with respect to the Composition, Writer is author and Writer and owner thereof and of all the rights therein, and that prior to executing this Agreement, Writer has not sold, assigned, transferred, pledged or mortgaged any right, title or interest in the Composition, the copyright therein, or in any of the rights herein conveyed; that there are no other authors or coauthors other than those listed above, that Writer has not made or entered into any copyrights or rights therein, and that no person, firm or corporation other than Writer claims, or has claimed any right, title, power and authority to enter this Agreement and make all of the grants, promises and covenants herein contained.

3. Assignment of Copyright. Simultaneously with the execution of this Agreement, Writer shall execute a short form assignment of his/her entire share of the copyright in the Composition attached hereto and incorporated herein as Schedule 1 to this Agreement as additional evidence of this transfer of rights. Writer does hereby appoint Publisher and its successor and its assigns as Writer's attorney-in-fact to take such action and to make, sign, execute, acknowledge and deliver such documents, in Writer's name or its own name, as may from time to time be necessary to secure, transfer, assign (to itself or others), register a claim to, record or otherwise evidence Publisher's rights to the copyright in the Composition and all other rights herein granted; said power shall be irrevocable and coupled with an interest.

4. Public Performance Rights. Publisher and Writer mutually acknowledge that they have heretofore entered into or will hereinafter enter into contracts with a performing rights society, which contracts provide the Publisher and Writer shall receive their respective shares of public performance royalties throughout the world directly from their own affiliated performing rights society, and that one shall have no claim whatsoever against the other for any royalties received by either from any performing rights society which makes distribution directly to Publisher and/or Writer. Publisher agrees that it will execute all documents and accomplish all acts necessary to secure proper registration and clearance of the musical work with the appropriate performing rights society. Writer acknowledges that Writer is currently affiliated for performing rights with ASCAP.

5. Grant of Rights. Writer agrees that with respect to the Composition, that all rights in the Composition as enumerated and defined in Title 17 of the United States Code, the Copyright Law of the United States, are hereby granted to Publisher subject to the terms and conditions of this Agreement, as same

pertains to the termination of transfers provisions of Section 203 of said Copyright Law.

6. <u>Consideration</u>. In consideration of this Agreement, the Publisher agrees to pay the Writer herein the following royalties, as follows:

(a) Fifty percent (50%) of any and all net sums actually received by Publisher for all pianoforte and/or vocal copies thereof sold and paid for in the United States;

(b) Fifty percent (50%) of any and all net sums actually received by Publisher for use of the Composition in all choral parts, instrumental parts, or orchestrations thereof sold and paid for in the United States;

(c) Fifty percent (50%) of any and all net sums actually received by Publisher for use of the Composition in folios or collections sold and paid for in the United States;

(d) Fifty percent (50%) of any and all net sums actually received by Publisher or its agent in the United States (after deduction of collection fees, if any, charged by any such agent or other collecting organization) from the manufacture and distribution of phonorecords in the United States and from the exercise of rights and from other sources in the United States not otherwise specified in this paragraph, provided that the Writer shall not be entitled to share in any sums received by Publisher as the so-called publisher's share of public performance of the Composition from any performing rights organizations which pays a share of performance fees directly to writers or composers; and

(e) Fifty percent (50%) of any and all net sums actually received by Publisher from print, mechanical and all other uses of the Composition originating in countries other than the United States, provided that Writer shall not be entitled to share in Publisher's share of any sums received by Publisher as the so-called publisher's share of public performance of the Composition from any performing rights organization which pays a share of performance fee directly to writers or composers.

(f) In the event the Composition is cowritten by Writer and another person or persons, Publisher shall pay to Writer a share of the foregoing sums corresponding to Writer's ownership interest in the Composition.

(g) It is agreed that Publisher shall not be required to pay any royalties on professional or complimentary copies or any copies or phonorecords which are distributed or sold by or under Publisher's authority at or below Publisher's cost or for promotional or similar purposes for which Publisher receives no payment.

(h) Notwithstanding the foregoing, however, the extent of the exploitation of the Composition, including the publication of sheet music or other printed editions or the decision to refrain therefrom, shall be entirely within the discretion of Publisher.

(l) Publisher may, with approval of the authors, retitle, arrange and otherwise edit, revise and adapt any Composition. In the event that Publisher shall cause the Composition to be translated into a language other than English, Writer agrees that Publisher may deduct from the royalties payable to Writer with respect to the translated Composition a sum equal to any compensation paid to the translator, including, without limitation, that portion of royalties otherwise payable hereunder required by contract or the regulations of the applicable mechanical rights or performance rights organization.

(j) As used herein, the term "net sums" shall mean the gross sums actually received by Publisher or its agent in the United States, or credited against an advance actually received, reduced by collection fees charged by any collection agent or organization; reasonable legal fees and court costs incurred by Publisher in the collection of such sums; reasonable auditor's and accountant's fees; and any other costs related to the Composition.

7. <u>Copyright Law</u>. (a) Unless otherwise provided herein, all terms used herein shall, to the extent applicable, have the meaning set forth in Title 17, United States Code, §101, et seq. (Public Law 94-553), as amended. For purposes of registering the copyright to the Composition, the term "Writer" as used herein shall include all the persons who are an author of the Composition, as listed above, as well as the Writer who executed this Agreement including legal heirs and representatives, and the covenants herein contained shall be deemed to be both joint and several by each of such persons.

(b) Writer acknowledges that Publisher may retitle, arrange and otherwise edit, translate, revise and adapt the words and music of the Composition. In the event that Publisher shall create or cause to be created a separately copyrightable arrangement, adaption or translation, Writer agrees that Publisher may pay to the Writer of said arrangement, adaption or translation, a portion, but not exceeding one-half (½), of the sums that would otherwise be or become due to Writer pursuant to Paragraph 6 above.

8. <u>Accounting</u>. (a) Publisher agrees that it will render to Writer semiannually within ninety (90) days after the last day of December and June of each calendar

year during which royalties are accrued hereunder, a statement showing all sales and royalties and the sources thereof earned by Writer during such accounting period, and Publisher will pay at the same time all sums shown to be due to Writer less the amounts of any advances, if any, which had been previously incurred by or paid to Writer by Publisher and any other sums owed to Publisher by Writer; provided that Publisher shall be obligated to pay royalties hereunder only with respect to sums actually received by Publisher or credited to Publisher's account.

(b) All royalty statements and other accounts rendered to Writer hereunder will be binding upon Writer unless specific objection in writing stating the basis thereof sent by registered or certified mail, return receipt requested, is received by Publisher within two (2) years from the date such statement was rendered in which event such statement shall be binding in all respects except for those specifically stated in such written objection. Writer shall be barred from instituting or maintaining any action, audit or proceedings of any kind or nature with respect to any statements rendered hereunder unless such is commenced within one (1) year after delivery of such written objection by Writer to Publisher. Writer and any attorney or certified public accountant designated by Writer shall have the right to examine and inspect Publisher's books and records with respect to the Composition at Publisher's principal office upon at least thirty (30) days written notice during normal business hours, and at Writer's sole expense. Any audit shall be limited to the then two (2) most current accounting periods, and no statement, including the books and records pertaining thereto, shall be reviewed and/or audited more than once, and Writer shall only have the right to examine Publisher's books and records once during each calendar year.

9. Infringement Actions.

(a) Any legal action brought by the Publisher against any alleged infringer of the Composition shall be initiated and prosecuted at its sole expense, and any recovery made by Publisher as a result thereof, after deduction of litigation expenses, including attorneys' fees, a sum equal to fifty percent (50%) shall be paid to Writer.

(b) If a claim is presented against Publisher alleging that the Composition is an infringement upon some other composition and because thereof Publisher is jeopardized, it shall thereupon serve written notice upon Writer and thereafter, until the claim has been adjudicated or settled, Publisher may withhold such sums as Publisher in its sole discretion deems sufficient to protect Publisher from any and all liability, including all costs and attorneys' fees, out of any monies coming due Writer hereunder to be held pending the outcome of such claim.

(c) From and after the service of a summons in a suit for infringement against Publisher in respect of the Composition, out of all payments hereunder thereafter coming due to Writer, Publishing may withhold such sum as Publisher in its sole discretion deems sufficient to protect Publisher from any and all liability, including all costs and attorneys' fees, unless Writer shall elect to file an acceptable bond in the sum of such payments, in which event the sums due shall be paid to Writer. Writer agrees to reimburse Publisher for court costs and reasonable counsel fees incurred by Publisher in defending the suit.

10. Name and Likeness. Publisher shall have the right to use Writer's name, likeness and biographical material concerning him, in connection with Publisher's business in general and with the use, promotion and exploitation of the Composition in particular.

11. Publisher's Right of Assignment. The Writer hereby grants to Publisher the right to assign this Agreement or any of its rights hereunder, or the Composition, or copyright, to any other person, firm or corporation subject, however, to the payment of royalties herein specified.

12. Publisher's Default. Publisher shall not be deemed to be in default hereunder unless Writer shall notify Publisher thereof and Publisher shall fail to remedy same within thirty (30) days thereafter, or if the alleged default is of such a nature that it cannot be remedied within such thirty-day period, Publisher shall fail to commence the remedying of such alleged default within such thirty-day period and to proceed to complete the same within a reasonable time thereafter.

13. Notices. All notices, hereunder shall be in writing and shall be given by personal delivery, registered or certified mail (return receipt requested) or overnight courier (such as Federal Express) prepaid, at the address shown above, or such other address or addresses as may be designated by either party. Notice shall be deemed given when mailed, except that notice of change of address shall be deemed effective only from the date of its receipt.

14. Independent Counsel. The Writer hereby certifies that Writer has read this Agreement in its entirety and understands all the provisions in this Agreement and that Writer had the opportunity to review same with legal counsel of Writer's choice.

15. <u>Choice of Law and Venue</u>. This Agreement shall be deemed to be executed in the State of Tennessee, County of Davidson and shall be construed in accordance with Tennessee law.

16. <u>Miscellaneous</u>. In the event any provision of this Agreement shall be illegal or unenforceable, such provision shall not affect the validity of the remaining portions and provisions hereof. The waiver by Publisher of any breach of this Agreement shall not in any way be construed as a waiver by Publisher of any subsequent breach, whether similar or not, of this Agreement by Writer. This Agreement sets forth the entire understanding and agreement of the parties hereto and may not be altered, modified, canceled or terminated in any way except by written agreement of the parties hereto in writing. The headings contained in this Agreement are inserted for reference purposes only and shall not affect the meaning or interpretation of this Agreement.

17. <u>Reversion Right</u>. Notwithstanding anything to the contrary contained with respect to the copyright ownership and exclusive administration of the Composition assigned herein, if Publisher is unable to (a) secure a commercial recording of the Composition by recording artist, which is signed to a record company with national distribution (b) issue a mechanical license or a synchronization license with respect to the Composition, or (c) secure a hold and have the Composition exploited within twenty-four (24) months after the date the hold, by a recording artist, a producer, or record company A&R personnel or personal manager with respect to the Composition (as the term "hold" is customarily understood in the music publishing business), on or before the earlier of thirty six (36) months from the date of this Agreement, then Writer may, upon written notice to Publisher within sixty (60) days from the expiration or termination of this Agreement, demand that Publisher reassign the copyright and all rights therein and such rights shall simultaneously be assigned to Writer, and Publisher agrees to execute any and all Assignment of Copyright, direction letters and other documents that may be necessary to effectuate the foregoing intent. And further, if the reversion right is exercised under this Agreement, Publisher appoints Writer, its successors and assigns as Publisher's attourney-in-fact to effectuate such reversion.

18. <u>Entire Agreement</u>. This Agreement supersedes any and all prior negotiations, understanding and agreements between the parties with respect to the subject matter hereof. Each of the parties acknowledges and agrees that neither party has made any representations or promises in connection with this Agreement of the subject matter hereof which are not contained herein.

IN WITNESS WHEREOF, the parties hereto have executed this Agreement the day and year first written above.

_____, and its publishing designee _____

By:

_____

FOR WRITER

_____

_____

DOB:

— — — — — — — — — — — — — — — — — — — — — — — — — — — — — — — —

SCHEDULE 1

ASSIGNMENT OF COPYRIGHT

FOR AND IN CONSIDERATION of the mutual covenants, promises and undertakings set forth in the Agreement For Purchase of Copyrights between the undersigned and the assignee of even date herewith, with respect to the composition (hereinafter "Composition") listed below, the undersigned writer, _____ (hereinafter "Writer") individually and/or on behalf of Writer's publishing designee, hereby assigns, transfers, sets over and conveys to _____ _____ and its publishing designee _____, Writer's entire undivided one hundred percent (100%) share of all right, title, and interest, in the percentage listed below as Writer's Share, in and to the following Composition held by Writer individually and/or on behalf of any publishing designee, as follows:

TITLE WRITER'S SHARE YR OF CREATION REGIS. NO.

_____ _____%

The within assignment, transfer and conveyance includes, without limitation, the lyrics, music and title of said Composition, any and all works derived therefrom, the United States and worldwide copyright therein, and any renewals or extensions thereof, and any and all other rights that Writer now has or to which Writer may become entitled under existing or subsequently enacted federal, state or foreign laws, including, without limitation, the following rights: to prepare derivative works based upon the Composition, to distribute copies or phonorecords of the Composition, and to perform and display the Composition publicly. The within grant further includes any and all causes of action or infringement of the Composition, past, present and future, and all the proceeds from the foregoing accrued and unpaid and hereafter accruing.

EXECUTED this _____ day of _____, 200_.


By:_____


_____


ACKNOWLEDGMENT

STATE OF _____ )

) ss.:

COUNTY OF _____ )

On the _____ day of _____, 200__, before my personally came _____, to me known to be the individual described in and who executed the foregoing instrument and acknowledged to me he/she executed it.


_____


NOTARY PUBLIC

My Commission Expires:_____

Questions and Discussion

1. There are three different types of contracts that pertain to songwriters; there are songwriter agreements, co-publishing agreements, and administration agreements. Songwriter agreements are either single-song agreements or long-term agreements. With these agreements, the income is usually split between mechanical income, performance income, print income, synchronization income, and foreign income (*see* Neville Johnson, "Music Publishing," in Musician's Business and Legal Guide 132-133).

2. "In a single-song deal, the publisher owns the copyright in the composition for the term of its copyright, "subject to the possibility of reversion to the composer 35 years after publication (the first commercial distribution) or 40 years after its assignment (transfer), whichever is earlier (*Id.*, at 133)."

# Chapter 3
# Representing Artists

Alfred Schlesinger suggests that the need for artist representation stems from the need to promote and market your artist's compositions. "The manager, whether an individual or a company, must have honesty and integrity, knowledge and capability" (Alfred Schlesinger, "What a Manager Does," in Hallorann, The Musician's Business and Legal Guide 254 (2001)). "Your manager represents, advises and works for you. This person or organization handles all of your day-to-day business while you create, and for that receives a percentage of your earnings. If you make money, your manager makes money. If not, your manager will have spent an awful lot of time and effort for nothing" (*Id.*).

The following case, *ABKCO Music, Inc. v. Harrisongs Music, Ltd.*, 722 F.2d 988 (2d Cir. 1983), is the famous infringement case where the beloved George Harrison was successfully sued for illegally copying The Chiffons' "He's So Fine" in his spiritual composition, "My Sweet Lord." But, there is a back story here, as there often is in music contracts, between George Harrison's former manager, who essentially purchased the rights to "He's So Fine" once the negotiations to settle the infringement case progressed to the point that an eventual lucrative settlement was assured. In fact, the former manager was involved in these negotiations!

ABKCO Music, Inc. v. Harrisongs Music, Ltd.
United States Court of Appeals for the Second Circuit
November 24, 1982, Argued; November 3, 1983
722 F.2d 988

PIERCE, Circuit Judge:

## I. BACKGROUND

A. Events Leading to Liability Trial

On February 10, 1971, Bright Tunes Music Corporation (Bright Tunes), then copyright holder of the song "He's So Fine," composed by Ronald Mack, brought this copyright infringement action in the United States District Court for the Southern District of New York against former member of the musical group "The Beatles" George Harrison, and also against related entities (hereinafter referred to collectively as "Harrison Interests"), alleging that the Harrison composition, "My Sweet Lord," (hereinafter referred to alternatively as "MSL") infringed the Ronald Mack composition, "He's So Fine," (hereinafter referred to alternatively as "HSF").

When this action was commenced, the business affairs of The Beatles, including Harrison Interests, were handled by ABKCO Music, Inc. (ABKCO) and Allen B. Klein, its President and "moving spirit." *ABKCO Music, Inc. v. Harrisongs Music, Ltd.*, 508 F. Supp. 798, 799 (S.D.N.Y.1981). ABKCO was Harrison's business manager during the initial stages of the copyright liability action herein, at which time the litigation was handled for Harrison by ABKCO's General Counsel.

The following events preceded the instant appeal. Shortly after this action was commenced in February, 1971, Klein (representing Harrisongs Music, Inc. and George Harrison) met with Seymour Barash (President and major stockholder of Bright Tunes) to discuss possible settlement of this lawsuit. Although Klein, at trial, denied having specific knowledge of the details of this discussion, he testified that he had suggested to Barash, around February of 1971, a purchase of the entire stock of Bright Tunes as a way to dispose of this lawsuit. Thus, in 1971, Klein was acting on behalf of Harrison Interests in an effort to settle this copyright infringement claim brought by Bright Tunes, although no settlement resulted.

Subsequent to the Klein-Barash meeting, Bright Tunes went into "judicial dissolution proceedings." This infringement action was placed on the district court's suspense calendar on March 3, 1972, and was resumed by Bright Tunes (in receivership) in early 1973. Also in early 1973 (March 31), ABKCO's management contract with The Beatles expired. Bitter and protracted litigation ensued between The Beatles and ABKCO over the winding down of management affairs — a dispute that ended in 1977 with The Beatles paying ABKCO $ 4.2 million in settlement.

There is some disagreement as to whether further settlement negotiations took place between Harrison Interests and Bright Tunes between 1973 and mid-1975. It appears undisputed, however, that Harrison Interests' attorney at least initiated settlement talks in the late summer of 1975; that in the period October 1975 through February 1976, settlement discussions took place between Bright Tunes' counsel and counsel for Harrison Interests regarding settlement of this infringement action (an offer by Harrison Interests based on United States royalties); and that those discussions were in the 50%/50% or 60%/40% range. These discussions culminated in a $ 148,000 offer by Harrison Interests in January of 1976 (representing 40% of the United States royalties).

At about the same time (1975), apparently unknown to George Harrison, Klein had been negotiating with Bright Tunes to purchase all of Bright Tunes' stock. That such negotiations were taking place was confirmed as early as October 30, 1975, in a letter from Seymour Barash (Bright Tunes' former President) to Howard Sheldon (Bright Tunes' Receiver), in which Barash reported that there had been an offer from Klein for a substantial sum of money. The same letter observed that "[Klein] would not be interested in purchasing all of the stock of Bright Tunes . . . if there was any doubt as to the outcome of this litigation."

In late November 1975, Klein (on behalf of ABKCO) offered to pay Bright Tunes $ 100,000 for a call on all Bright Tunes' stock, exercisable for an additional $ 160,000 upon a judicial determination as to copyright infringement. In connection with this offer, Klein furnished to Bright Tunes three schedules summarizing the following financial information concerning "My Sweet Lord" (1) domestic royalty income of Harrisongs Music, Inc. on MSL; (2) an updated version of that first schedule; and (3) Klein's own estimated value of the copyright, including an estimate of foreign royalties (performance and mechanical) and his assessment of the total worldwide future earnings.

Barash considered the Klein offer only a starting point. He thought that a value of $600,000 was more accurate and recommended a $200,000 call, based on a $600,000 gross sales price. Also in December 1975, Barash noted, in a letter to counsel for the Peter Maurice Co., that Harrison Interests' counsel had never furnished a certified statement of worldwide royalties of MSL, but that from conversations between Stephen Tenenbaum (accountant for several Bright Tunes stockholders) and Klein, Bright Tunes had been given that information by Klein.

Shortly thereafter, on January 19, 1976, Barash informed Howard Sheldon (Bright Tunes' Receiver) of the Klein offer and of the Bright Tunes stockholders' unanimous decision to reject it. Barash noted that "since Mr. Klein is in a position to know the true earnings of "My Sweet Lord", his offer should give all of us an indication of the true value of this copyright and litigation." Sheldon responded in a letter dated January 21, 1976, noting, *inter alia*, that Harrison's attorneys were informed that no settlement would be considered by Bright Tunes until total sales of MSL were determined after appropriate figures were checked.

On January 30, 1976, the eve of the liability trial, a meeting was held by Bright Tunes' attorney for all of Bright Tunes' stockholders (or their counsel) and representatives of Ronald Mack. The purpose of the meeting was to present Bright Tunes with an offer by Harrison Interests of $ 148,000, representing 40% of the writers' and publishers' royalties earned in the United States (but without relinquishment by Harrison of the MSL copyright). At the time, Bright Tunes' attorney regarded the offer as "a good one." 508 F. Supp. at 802. The Harrison offer was not accepted, however. Bright Tunes raised its demand from 50% of the United States royalties, to 75% worldwide, plus surrender of the MSL copyright. The parties were unable to reach agreement and the matter proceeded to trial.

B. Liability Trial and Events Thereafter

A three-day bench trial on liability was held before Judge Owen on February 23-25, 1976. On August 31, 1976 (amended September 1, 1976), the district judge rendered a decision for the plaintiff as to liability, based on his finding that "My Sweet Lord" was substantially similar to "He's So Fine" and that Harrison had had access to the latter. *Bright Tunes Music Corp. v. Harrisongs Music, Ltd.*, 420 F. Supp. 177 (S.D.N.Y. 1976).The issue of damages and other relief was scheduled for trial at a later date.

Following the liability trial, Klein, still acting for ABKCO, continued to discuss with Bright Tunes the purchase of the rights to HSF. During 1977, no serious settlement discussions were held between Bright Tunes and Harrison Interests. Indeed, the record indicates that throughout 1977 Bright Tunes did not authorize its attorneys to give Harrison a specific settlement figure. By November 30, 1977, Bright Tunes' counsel noted that Klein had made an offer on behalf of ABKCO that "far exceeds any proposal that has been made by the defendants."

On February 8, 1978, another settlement meeting took place, but no agreement was reached at that meeting. Although it appears that everyone present felt that the case should be settled, it also appears that there were no further settlement discussions between Harrison Interests and Bright Tunes subsequent to that date. The Bright tunes negotiations with ABKCO, however, culminated on April 13, 1978, in a purchase of ABKCO of the HSF copyright, the United States infringement claim herein, and the worldwide rights to HSF, for $587,000, an amount more than twice the original Klein (ABKCO) offer. This purchase was made known to George Harrison by Klein himself in April or May of 1978. Harrison "was a bit amazed to find out" about the purchase.

C. Damages Proceedings and Foreign Settlements

On July 17, 1978, ABKCO adopted Bright Tunes' complaint and was substituted as the sole party plaintiff in this action. In May 1979, Harrison Interests obtained leave to assert affirmative defenses and counterclaims against Klein and ABKCO for alleged breaches of fiduciary duty relating to the negotiation for and purchase of the Bright Tunes properties. An eight-day bench trial was held on damages and counterclaims between August 27 and October 15, 1979.

While the matter was still *sub judice*, Harrison Interests, on April 3, 1980, entered into an agreement with Essex Music International, Ltd. (Essex), authorizing Essex to negotiate and enter into settlement agreements, on a 60%/40% basis, on behalf of Harrison Interests throughout the world (except the United Kingdom, the United States and Canada) with any party owning an interest in HSF. These terms were consistent with those of the Maurice-Harrison settlement of the United Kingdom claim, whereby the parties were to use "best endeavours" to obtain 60%/40% settlements throughout the world. ABKCO then settled foreign claims with Essex, also on April 3, 1980.

The damages decision was filed on February 19, 1981. *ABKCO Music, Inc. v. Harrisongs Music, Ltd.*, 508 F. Supp. 798 (S.D.N.Y.1981). Having determined that the damages amounted to $ 1,599,987, the district judge held that ABKCO's conduct over the 1975-78 period limited its recovery, substantially because of the manner in which ABKCO had become a plaintiff in this case. Particularly "troublesome" to the court was "Klein's covert intrusion into the settlement negotiation picture in late 1975 and early 1976 immediately preceding the trial on the merits." *Id.* at 802. He found, *inter alia*, that Klein's status as Harrison's former business manager gave special credence to ABKCO's offers to Bright Tunes and made Bright Tunes less willing to settle with Harrison Interests either before or after the liability trial. Moreover, the court found that in the course of negotiating with Bright Tunes in 1975-76, Klein "covertly furnished" Bright Tunes with certain financial information about MSL which he obtained while in Harrison's employ as business manager. The foregoing conduct, in the court's view, amounted to a breach of ABKCO's fiduciary duty to Harrison. The court held that although it was not clear that "but for" ABKCO's conduct Harrison Interests and Bright Tunes would have settled, he found that good faith negotiations had been in progress between the parties and Klein's intrusion made their success less likely, since ABKCO's offer in January 1976 was viewed by Bright Tunes as an "insider's disclosure of the value of the case." *Id.* at 803. Consequently, the district judge directed that ABKCO hold the "fruits of its acquisition" from Bright Tunes in trust for Harrison Interests, to be transferred to Harrison Interests by ABKCO upon payment by Harrison Interests of $ 587,000 plus interest from the date of acquisition.

## II. ABKCO'S ARGUMENTS ON APPEAL

ABKCO presents two principal arguments on appeal. First, it is argued that ABKCO did not breach its fiduciary duty to Harrison because (a) no confidential information was improperly passed from ABKCO to Bright Tunes during the negotiations to purchase HSF, and (b) there was no causal relationship between ABKCO's actions and Harrison Interests' failure to obtain settlement. Second, appellant argues that the scope of the constructive trust imposed by Judge Owen is too broad because it covers foreign rights. ABKCO contends that the remedy thus jeopardizes the post-liability-trial settlements of the foreign infringement claims between ABKCO and Harrison Interests (through Essex). As to the first contention, we reject appellant's arguments and affirm the decision of the district judge. With respect to appellant's objection to the scope of the remedy, however, we modify the judgment and remand the case for further consideration in light of this opinion.

### A. Breach of Fiduciary Duty

There is no doubt that the relationship between Harrison and ABKCO prior to the termination of the management agreement in 1973 was that of principal and agent, and that the relationship was fiduciary in nature. *See Meese v. Miller*, 79 A.D.2d 237, 241, 436 N.Y.S.2d 496, 499 (4th Dept. 1981). The rule applicable to our present inquiry is that an agent has a duty "not to use confidential knowledge acquired in his employment in competition with his principal." *Byrne v. Barrett*, 268 N.Y. 199, 206, 197 N.E. 217, 218 (1935). This duty "exists as well after the employment is terminated as during its continuance." *Id.; see also Restatement (Second) of Agency* § 396 (1958). On the other hand, use of information based on general business knowledge or gleaned from general business experience is not covered by the rule, and the former agent is permitted to compete with his former principal in reliance on such general publically available information. *Byrne v. Barrett*, 268 N.Y. at 206, 197 N.E. at 218; *Restatement (Second) of Agency* § 395 comment b (1958). The principal issue before us in the instant case, then, is whether the district court committed clear error in concluding that Klein (hence, ABKCO) improperly used confidential information, gained as Harrison's former agent, in negotiating for the purchase of Bright Tunes' stock (including HSF) in 1975-76.

One aspect of this inquiry concerns the nature of three documents — schedules of MSL earnings — which Klein furnished to Bright Tunes in connection with the 1975-76 negotiations. Although the district judge did not make a specific finding as to whether each of these schedules was confidential, he determined that Bright Tunes at that time was not entitled to the information. 508 F. Supp. at 803. It appears that the first of the three schedules may have been previously turned over to Bright Tunes by Harrison. The two additional schedules which Klein gave to Bright Tunes (the detailed updating of royalty information and Klein's personal estimate of the value of MSL and future earnings) appear not to have been made available to Bright Tunes by Harrison. Moreover, it appears that at least some of the past royalty information was confidential. The evidence presented herein is not at all convincing that the information imparted to Bright Tunes by Klein was publicly available. *Cf. Franke v. Wiltschek*, 209 F.2d 493, 495 (2d Cir.1953) (former fiduciary precluded from using confidential information in competition with former principal even if the information is readily available from third parties or by other means). Furthermore, the district judge was in a better position to assess the credibility aspects of evidence bearing on this question than we are.

Another aspect of the breach of duty issue concerns the timing and nature of Klein's entry into the negotiation picture and the manner in which he became a plaintiff in this action. In our view, the record supports the position that Bright Tunes very likely gave special credence to Klein's position as an offeror because of his status as Harrison's former business manager and prior coordinator of the defense of this lawsuit. *See e.g.*, letter from Barash to Sheldon, dated January 19, 1976 ("Since Mr. Klein is in a position to know the true earnings of My Sweet Lord, his offer should give all of us an indication of the true value of this copyright and litigation ."). To a significant extent, that favorable bargaining position necessarily was achieved because Klein, as business manager, had intimate knowledge of the financial affairs of his client. Klein himself acknowledged at trial that his offers to Bright Tunes were based, at least in part, on knowledge he had acquired as Harrison's business manager.

Under the circumstances of this case, where there was sufficient evidence to support the district judge's finding that confidential information passed hands, or, at least was utilized in a manner inconsistent with the duty of a former fiduciary at a time when this litigation was still pending, we conclude that the district judge did not err in holding that ABKCO had breached its duty to Harrison.

We find this case analogous to those "where an employee, with the use of information acquired through his former employment relationship, completes, for his own benefit, a transaction originally undertaken on the former employer's behalf." *Group Association Plans, Inc. v. Colquhoun*, 151 U.S. App. D.C. 298, 466 F.2d 469, 474 (D.C.Cir.1972); *cf. Renz v. Beeman*, 589 F.2d 735, 746 (2d Cir.1978) (opportunity for purchase that comes to [trustee] while in fiduciary capacity compels trustee to give right of first refusal to trust estate), *cert. denied*, 444 U.S. 834, 62 L. Ed. 2d 43, 100 S. Ct. 65 (1979); *Meinhard v. Salmon*, 249 N.Y. 458, 467, 164 N.E. 545, 548 (1928) ("There may be no abuse of special opportunities growing out of a special trust as manager or agent."). In this case, Klein had commenced a purchase transaction with Bright Tunes in 1971 on behalf of Harrison, which he pursued on his own account after the termination of his fiduciary relationship with Harrison. While the initial attempt to purchase Bright Tunes' catalogue was several years removed from the eventual purchase on ABKCO's own account, we are not of the view that such a fact rendered ABKCO unfettered in the later negotiations. Indeed, Klein pursued the later discussions armed with the intimate knowledge not only of Harrison's business affairs, but of the value of this lawsuit — and at a time when this action was still pending. Taking all of these circumstances together, we agree that appellant's conduct during the period 1975-78 did not meet the standard required of him as a former fiduciary.

In so concluding, we do not purport to establish a general "appearance of impropriety" rule with respect to artist/manager relationship. That strict standard — reserved principally for the legal profession — would probably not suit the realities of the business world. The facts of this case otherwise permit the conclusion reached herein. Indeed, as Judge Owen noted in his Memorandum and Order of May 7, 1979 (permitting Harrison Interests to assert counterclaims), "The fact situation presented is novel in the extreme. Restated in simplest form, it amounts to the purchase by a business manager of a known claim against his former client where, the right to the claim having been established, all that remains to be done is to assess the monetary award." We find these facts not only novel, but unique. Indeed, the purchase, which rendered Harrison and ABKCO adversaries, occurred in the context of a lawsuit in which ABKCO had been the prior protector of Harrison's interests. Thus, although not wholly analogous to the side-switching cases involving attorneys and their former clients, this fact situation creates clear questions of impropriety. On the unique facts presented herein, we certainly cannot say that Judge Owen's findings and conclusions were clearly erroneous or not in accord with applicable law.

Appellant ABKCO also contends that even if there was a breech of duty, such breach should not limit ABKCO's recovery for copyright infringement because ABKCO's conduct did not cause the Bright Tunes/Harrison settlement negotiations to fail. *See* 508 F. Supp. at 803 & n.15. Appellant urges, in essence, that a finding of breach of fiduciary duty by an agent, to be actionable, must be found to have been the proximate cause of injury to the principal. We do not accept appellant's proffered causation standard. An action for breach of fiduciary duty is a prophylactic rule intended to remove all incentive to breach — not simply to compensate for damages in the event of a breach. *See Diamond v. Oreamuno*, 24 N.Y.2d 494, 498, 248 N.E.2d 910, 912, 301 N.Y.S.2d 78, 81 (1969) ("The function of [an action founded on breach of fiduciary duty] . . . is not merely to compensate the plaintiff for wrongs committed by the defendant but . . . 'to *prevent* them, by removing from agents and trustees all inducement to attempt dealing for their own benefit in matters which they have undertaken for others, or to which their agency or trust relates.'") (emphasis in original). Having found that ABKCO's conduct constituted a breach of fiduciary duty, the district judge was not required to find a "but for" relationship between ABKCO's conduct and lack of success of Harrison Interests' settlement efforts.

ABKCO argues further that the offer to sell substantially what had been gained in the purchase from Bright Tunes to Harrison for $ 700,000, and Harrison's rejection of that offer, *see supra* note 7, bars Harrison Interests from obtaining a constructive trust in this action, *per Turner v. American Metal Co.*, 268 A.D. 239, 50 N.Y.S.2d 800 (1st Dept. 1944) (where former fiduciary offers former employer what he obtained in violation of fiduciary duty at price equivalent to his cost of acquisition and former employer refuses offer, fiduciary not held liable for breach of duty), *appeal dismissed*, 295 N.Y. 822, 66 N.E.2d 591 (1946). We find this argument unpersuasive. First, in *Turner*, unlike the case at bar, there was no finding of breach of fiduciary duty. Moreover, we find somewhat disingenuous ABKCO's claim that a $ 700,000 offer was a "price equivalent to his cost of acquisition," which had been $ 587,000. In any event, it is unclear whether that which ABKCO offered Harrison Interests was equivalent to that which ABKCO had brought from Bright Tunes.

Finally, on the facts herein, we agree that a constructive trust on the "fruits" of ABKCO's acquisition was a proper remedy. *See Meinhard v. Salmon*, 249 N.Y. at 467, 164 N.E. at 548 ("A constructive trust is then the remedial device through which preference of self is made subordinate to loyalty to others."); *In re: McCrory Stores Corp.*, 12 F. Supp. 267, 269 (S.D.N.Y 1935) (agent prohibited from making profit by acquiring claims against principal (debtor) at discount immediately after resignation and enforcing them at great amount); *see also Restatement of Restitution* § 200 (1937) (where fiduciary in violation of duty to beneficiary acquires property through use of confidential information, he holds the property so acquired in constructive trust for beneficiary); *Restatement (Second) of Agency* § 403 (1958) comment (d) (agent employed to settle claim who purchases the claim for himself holds such claim as a constructive trustee of the principal).

## B. Scope of Constructive Trust: Foreign Settlements

Finally, appellant asserts that if this court is to affirm the district judge's finding of breach and its imposition of a constructive trust, the scope of that constructive trust should be limited to the American infringement claim. Appellant's argument is two-fold. First, appellant contends that because Harrison insisted on settling only the American infringement claim throughout the negotiations, and because the complaint in this case related only to the American claim, the remedy should be limited to that claim. Second, appellant argues that because the constructive trust encompasses foreign rights, the remedy serves to disturb settlement agreements that have already been achieved as to the foreign infringement claims against Harrison. As to appellant's first contention, in our view the district judge was not constrained by the scope of the settlement negotiations in fashioning this equitable relief. Moreover, it was within the discretion of the district court to provide a remedy not simply as to appellant's claims, but also as to appellee's counterclaims. *See Alexander v. Hillman*, 296 U.S. 222, 242, 56 S. Ct. 204, 80 L. Ed. 192 (1935) ("Courts of equity . . . will decide all matters in dispute and decree complete relief.").

The second point raised by appellant, however, in our view, warrants modification of the judgment and remand to the district court for reassessment of the scope of the constructive trust. On April 3, 1980, after the damages trial, but before Judge Owen rendered his opinion, Harrison Interests, through its agent, Essex Music International, with full knowledge that its counterclaim was pending before Judge Owen, voluntarily entered into agreements with ABKCO, settling MSL infringement claims in various foreign territories as between HSF subpublishers and MSL subpublishers. As a general matter, we note first that courts favor the policy of encouraging voluntary settlement of disputes. *See, e.g., Williams v. First National Bank*, 216 U.S. 582, 595, 54 L. Ed. 625, 30 S. Ct. 441 (1910); *In re: Penn Central Transportation Co.*, 455 F.2d 811, 814 n. 6 (3d Cir.), *cert. denied*, 407 U.S. 915, 92 S. Ct. 2440, 32 L. Ed. 2d 690 (1972); *D.H. Overmyer Co. v. Loflin*, 440 F.2d 1213, 1215 (5th Cir.), *cert. denied*, 404 U.S. 851, 30 L. Ed. 2d 90, 92 S. Ct. 87 (1971); *Petty v. General Accident Fire and Life Assurance Corp.*, 365 F.2d 419, 421 (3d Cir. 1966). Bearing this principle in mind, we conclude that, since the parties or their agents entered into settlement agreements as to certain foreign infringement claims while the damages issues were *sub judice*, the trust should not include that portion of ABKCO's acquisition constituting a purchase of the foreign rights involved in those settlements. We remand the case to the district court to determine what portion of the $ 587,000 paid by ABKCO to Bright Tunes is attributable to the foreign rights involved in the April 3, 1980 settlement. That sum should be subtracted from the $ 587,000 to determine the amount the

Harrison Interests must pay to acquire only the rights not affected by the April 3, 1980 settlement.

### III. CROSS-APPEAL: COPYRIGHT INFRINGEMENT

"It is well settled that copying may be inferred where a plaintiff establishes that the defendant had access to the copyrighted work and that the two works are substantially similar." *Warner Brothers v. American Broadcasting Companies*, 654 F.2d 204, 207 (2d Cir.1981). In this case Judge Owen determined that "My Sweet Lord is the very same song as He's So Fine with different words, and Harrison had access to He's So Fine." *Bright Tunes Music Corp. v. Harrisongs Music, Ltd.*, 420 F. Supp. at 180-81. He concluded that the substantial similarity coupled with access constituted copyright infringement, even though subconsciously accomplished. *See id.* at 180, 181 (citing *Sheldon v. Metro-Goldwyn Pictures Corp.*, 81 F.2d 49, 54 (2d Cir.1936); *Northern Music Corp. v. Pacemaker Music Co.*, 147 U.S.P.Q. 358, 359 (S.D.N.Y.1965)).

Appellees argue on cross-appeal that the instant case differs significantly from those cases relied upon by the district court to support its conclusion of subconscious infringement, and from the only other case in this circuit which held that subconscious copying can constitute infringement, *i.e., Fred Fisher, Inc. v. Dillingham*, 298 F. 145 (S.D.N.Y. 1924). In addition, they urge upon this court the position that it is unsound policy to permit a finding of copyright infringement on the basis of subconscious copying. We reject both arguments and affirm the decision of the district judge.

First, we do not find dispositive appellees' distinction between the instant case and *Sheldon* and *Fisher* cases. Appellees point out that in those two cases, the infringing work was created very shortly after the infringer had had access to the infringed work. Here, in contrast, appellees note. Harrison's access to HSF occurred in 1963, some six years before he composed MSL. We disagree with appellees' position that such temporal remoteness precludes a finding of access. First, Harrison himself admitted at trial that he remembered hearing HSF in the early sixties when it was popular. Moreover, even if there had not been such direct evidence of access, access still may have been found because of the wide dissemination of HSF at that time. *See Arnstein v. Porter*, 154 F.2d 464, 469 (2d Cir.1946); 3 M. Nimmer, *Nimmer on Copyright* § 13.02[A] (1983). Indeed, in 1963, the year of Harrison's admitted access to HSF, the song was "Number One on the *Billboard* charts" in the United States for five weeks, and it was one of the "Top Thirty Hits" in England for seven weeks that same year. Thus, even if the evidence, standing alone, "by no means compels the conclusion that there was access . . . it does not compel the conclusion that there was not." *Heim v. Universal Pictures Co.*, 154 F.2d 480, 487 (2d Cir.1946).

As to the requisite finding of substantial similarity, we affirm the determinations of the district judge, since we do not find them to be clearly erroneous, *Bright Tunes Music Corp. v. Harrisongs Music, Ltd.*, 420 F. Supp. at 178-80. Even Harrison conceded at trial that the two songs were "strikingly similar" as played by a pianist during the liability trial.

This case is unlike *Darrell v. Joe Morris Music Co.*, 113 F.2d 80 (2d Cir. 1940), cited by appellees. In *Darrell*, the Court of Appeals affirmed the district court's finding of no plagiarism, when there had been "substantial identity" between the songs at issue. The *Darrell* court found of particular significance that the songs' themes were trite and access had occurred some seven and a half years before the defendant's song was composed. The court noted:

Such simple, trite themes as these are likely to recur spontaneously; . . . It must be remembered that, while there are an enormous number of possible permutations of the musical notes of the scale, only a few are pleasing; and much fewer still suit the infantile demands of the popular ear. Recurrence is not therefore an inevitable badge of plagiarism.

*Id.* at 80. We find this case distinguishable. Indeed, on the facts herein, the district judge did not find repetition of "trite themes," but rather, "a highly unique pattern," 420 F. Supp. at 178. Moreover, in Darrell, the court found that the allegedly infringed song "had had very scant publicity" and credited the defendant's denial of ever having heard it. This is unlike the case at bar where HSF had had very substantial dissemination and where Harrison acknowledged that he had heard HSF at least a few times. We accept the *Darrell* court's observation that "recurrence is not . . . an inevitable badge of plagiarism." However, on the facts presented herein, where the similarity was so striking and where access was found, the remoteness of that access provides no basis for reversal.

Appellees argue next that it is unsound policy to permit a finding of infringement for subconscious copying, particularly on the facts of this case. They assert that allowing for subconscious infringement brings the law of copyright improperly close to patent law, which imposes a requirement of novelty. *See Alfred Bell & Co. v. Catalda Fine Arts, Inc.*, 191 F.2d 99, 103 (2d Cir.1951) ("'independent reproduction of a copyrighted . . . work is not infringement', whereas it is *vis a vis* a patent") (quoting *Arnstein v. Edward B. Marks Music Corp.*, 82 F.2d 275, 275 (2d Cir.1936)). We do not accept this argument.

It is not new law in this circuit that when a defendant's work is copied from the plaintiff's, but the defendant in good faith has forgotten that the plaintiff's work was the source of his own, such "innocent copying" can nevertheless constitute an infringement. *See Sheldon v. Metro-Goldwyn Pictures Corp.*, 81 F.2d at 54; *see also* 3 M. Nimmer, *Nimmer on Copyright* § 13.08 (1983). We do not find this stance in conflict with the rule permitting independent creation of copyrighted material. It is settled that "intention to infringe is not essential under the [Copyright] Act," *Buck v. Jewell-LaSalle Realty Co.*, 283 U.S. 191, 198, 51 S. Ct. 410, 75 L. Ed. 971 (1931); *see also Plymouth Music Co. v. Magnus Organ Corp.*, 456 F. Supp. 676, 680 (S.D.N.Y.1978); 3 M. Nimmer, *Nimmer on Copyright*, § 13.08 (1983) ("Innocent intent should no more constitute a defense in an infringement action than in the case of conversion of tangible personalty."). Moreover, as a practical matter, the problems of proof inherent in a rule that would permit innocent intent as a defense to copyright infringement could substantially undermine the protections Congress intended to afford to copyright holders. We therefore see no reason to retreat from this circuit's prior position that copyright infringement can be subconscious.

Because there was sufficient evidence of record to support the district judge's findings of substantial similarity and access, we affirm the finding of copyright infringement.

## IV. CONCLUSION

Having considered all of the parties' arguments on appeal and cross-appeal, we affirm, with modification, the decisions of the district court and remand to the district judge for reassessment of the scope of the remedy, consistent with this opinion. Each party is to bear its own fees and costs.

Park v. Deftones
Court of Appeal of California, Second Appellate District, Division Two
May 11, 1999, Decided
No. B124598.
71 Cal. App. 4th 1465

NOTT, Acting P. J.

Dave Park appeals from the summary judgment entered against him in his action for breach of contract and intentional interference with contractual relations. His action arises from the termination of his personal manager contract by the Deftones, a music act whose members are Camillo Wong Moreno, Stephen Carpenter, Abe Cunningham, and Chi Ling Cheng (referred to collectively as the Deftones), without paying him commissions which he asserts are due him. In addition, Park alleges that after he secured a recording contract for the Deftones with Maverick Records (Maverick), the record company and one of its agents, Guy Oseary, purposefully interfered with Park's contractual relationship with the Deftones. The trial court granted summary judgment on the ground that the management contract between the Deftones and Park was void, Park having violated the Talent Agencies Act (the Act) by securing performance engagements for the Deftones without being licensed as a talent agency. (Lab. Code, § 1700 et seq.) We affirm on that ground.

## PROCEDURAL AND FACTUAL BACKGROUND

Park filed this action in October 1996, alleging breach of certain management agreements against the Deftones and the individual band members and intentional interference with contractual relations against Maverick and Oseary. He attached to his complaint his written agreements with the Deftones entered into in February 1992, February 1993, and January 1994. In February 1997, the Deftones filed a petition before the Labor Commissioner, seeking to void the management agreements. Park unsuccessfully sought dismissal of the petition as untimely filed. The Labor Commissioner determined that Park had violated the Act by obtaining performance engagements for the Deftones on 84 occasions without a license. He issued an order stating that the personal management agreements entered into in 1992, 1993, and 1994 were "null, void and unenforceable." Park demanded a trial de novo in the administrative proceeding.

Maverick and Oseary filed a motion for summary judgment on the grounds that the undisputed facts showed that (1) Park and the Deftones entered into a written contract for management services dated January 18, 1994, (2) between September 1991 and September 1994, Park procured numerous performances for the Deftones, and (3) Park was not a licensed talent agency during that period. Maverick and Oseary relied in part upon the transcript of the Labor Commission proceeding to establish the facts. The Deftones filed a similar motion.

Park opposed the motions. He objected to use of the Labor Commission hearing transcript, but admitted that he had obtained more than 80 engagements for the Deftones. He asserted that the Deftones' petition before the Labor Commission was untimely filed and that his services did not require a talent agency license because they were rendered without a commission and were undertaken in order to obtain a recording agreement. The trial court entered summary judgment in favor of all defendants.

## DISCUSSION
### I. TIMELINESS

Park contends that the Deftones' petition before the Labor Commissioner and the defense based upon the Act are barred by the one-year statute of limitations: "No action or proceeding shall be brought pursuant to this chapter with respect to any violation which is alleged to have occurred more than one year prior to commencement of the action or proceeding." (§ 1700.44, subd. (c).)

In declaration testimony, Park stated that the last time he booked a concert for the Deftones was in August 1994. He urges that the Deftones' petition, filed in February 1997, was therefore not timely. Park concludes that the Deftones may not rely upon the Act as a defense because Park's own action was filed more than one year after he last booked a concert for the Deftones.

The Labor Commissioner, who is statutorily charged with enforcing the Act (§ 1700.44, subd. (a)), found that the Deftones' petition was timely because it was brought within one year of Park's filing an action to collect commissions under the challenged contract. The Commissioner stated that the attempt to collect commissions allegedly due under the agreements was itself a violation of the Act. (Moreno v. Park (Jan. 20, 1998, Lab. Comr.) No. 9-97, p. 4.)

In construing a statute, the court gives considerable weight to the interpretation placed on the statute by the administrative agency charged with enforcing it. (Robinson v. Fair Employment & Housing Com. (1992) 2 Cal. 4th 226, 234 [5 Cal. Rptr. 2d 782, 825 P.2d 767].) The Labor Commissioner's interpretation avoids the encouragement of preemptive proceedings before it. It also assures that the party who has engaged in illegal activity may not avoid its consequences through the timing of his own collection action. We conclude that the Labor Commissioner's interpretation is reasonable, and that the Deftones' petition was timely filed.

## II. INCIDENTAL PROCUREMENT OF EMPLOYMENT

The Act provides that "No person shall engage in or carry on the occupation of a talent agency without first procuring a license therefor from the Labor Commissioner." (§ 1700.5.) A talent agency is "a person or corporation who engages in the occupation of procuring, offering, promising, or attempting to procure employment or engagements for an artist or artists, except that the activities of procuring, offering, or promising to procure recording contracts for an artist or artists shall not of itself subject a person or corporation to regulation and licensing under this chapter. . . ." (§ 1700.4, subd. (a).)

(3) Unlike talent agents, personal managers are not covered by the Act. Personal managers primarily advise, counsel, direct, and coordinate the development of the artist's career. They advise in both business and personal matters, frequently lend money to young artists, and serve as spokespersons for the artists. (See Waisbren v. Peppercorn Productions, Inc. (1995) 41 Cal. App. 4th 246, 252-253 [48 Cal. Rptr. 2d 437] (Waisbren).)

Park argues that as a personal manager his goal in procuring engagements for the Deftones was to obtain a recording agreement. He contends that his actions were therefore exempt from regulation. That position was rejected in Waisbren, supra, 41 Cal. App. 4th at page 259. In Waisbren, a promoter brought an action for breach of contract against a company engaged in designing and creating puppets. The defendant moved for summary judgment on the ground the parties' agreement for the plaintiff's services was void because he had performed the duties of a talent agent without obtaining a license. The plaintiff asserted that a license was unnecessary because his procurement activities were minimal and incidental. He had also assisted in project development, managed certain business affairs, supervised client relations and publicity, performed casting duties, coordinated production, and handled office functions. In return, he was to receive 15 percent of the company's profits. Waisbren holds that even incidental activity in procuring employment for an artist is subject to regulation under the Act.

The reasoning of Waisbren is convincing. It relies upon the remedial purpose of the Act and the statutory goal of protecting artists from long recognized abuses. The decision is also based upon the Labor Commissioner's long-held position that a license is required for incidental procurement activities. The court in Waisbren found the Labor Commissioner's position to be supported by legislative history and, in particular, by the recommendations contained in the Report of the California Entertainment Commission, which were adopted by the Legislature in amending the Act in 1986.

Wachs v. Curry (1993) 13 Cal. App. 4th 616 [16 Cal. Rptr. 2d 496], relied upon by Park, does not further his cause. In Wachs, the personal manager plaintiffs brought a declaratory relief action challenging the constitutionality of the Act on its face. They took the position that the Act's exemption for procurement activities involving recording contracts violated the equal protection clause and that the Act's use of the term "procure" was so vague as to violate due process. Wachs rejected both of those positions. It also interpreted the Act, which applies to persons engaged in the occupation of procuring employment for artists, as applying only where a person's procurement activities constitute a significant part of his business. ( Id. at pp. 627-628.) The court did not define "significant part." The court acknowledged that ". . . the only question before us is whether the word 'procure' in the context of the Act is so lacking in objective content that it provides no standard at all by which to measure an agent's conduct" ( id. at p. 628, italics omitted). We agree with Waisbren that the interpretation stated in Wachs is dictum and that even incidental procurement is regulated.

### III. ABSENCE OF A COMMISSION

Park also contends that his procuring employment for the Deftones is not regulated by the Act because he was not compensated for that work. We disagree.

Park's 1993 and 1994 agreements with the Deftones expressly provided that Park was to receive a 20 percent commission on all income earned from employment that Park secured. Although Park stated in declaration testimony that he received no commission for procuring engagements for the Deftones, the contracts appear to provide for compensation. In addition, Park would receive compensation for his services ultimately from commissions for obtaining a recording contract for the Deftones. Thus, it is not clear that Park should be treated as one who was not compensated for his services.

Park's position, moreover, is not supported by the language of the Act. The Act regulates those who engage in the occupation of procuring engagements for artists. (§ 1700.4, subd. (a).) The Act does not expressly include or exempt procurement where no compensation is made. Waisbren states at footnote 6: "By using [the term 'occupation'], the Legislature intended to cover those who are compensated for their procurement efforts." (41 Cal. App. 4th at p. 254, fn. 6.) The issue of compensation, however, was not before the court in Waisbren. The language in footnote 6 is dictum which we conclude is not supported by the purpose and legislative history of the Act. One may engage in an occupation which includes procuring engagements without receiving direct compensation for that activity.

As explained in Waisbren, the purpose of the Act is remedial, and its aim goes beyond regulating the amount of fees which can be charged for booking acts. For example, an agent must have his form of contract approved by the Labor Commissioner, maintain his client's funds in a trust fund account, record and retain certain information about his client, and refrain from giving false information to an artist concerning potential employment. (See § 1700.23, 1700.25, 1700.26, 1700.32, and 1700.41.) Because the Act is remedial, it should be liberally construed to promote its general object. (See Buchwald v. Superior Court (1967) 254 Cal. App. 2d 347, 354 [1472] [62 Cal. Rptr. 364].) The abuses at which these requirements are aimed apply equally where the personal manager procures work for the artist without a commission, but rather for the deferred benefits from obtaining a recording contract.

In 1982, the Legislature created the California Entertainment Commission (the Commission) to study the laws and practices of this and other states relating to the licensing of agents and representatives of artists in the entertainment industry in order to recommend to the Legislature a model bill regarding licensing. (See Waisbren, supra, 41 Cal. App. 4th at p. 256.) In 1985, the Commission submitted its report to the Governor and the Legislature (the Report). The Legislature followed the Commission's recommendations in enacting the 1986 amendments to the Act. (See Waisbren, supra, 41 Cal. App. 4th at p. 258.)

The Report states that the Commission reviewed and rejected a proposal which would have exempted from the Act anyone who does not charge a fee or commission for procuring employment for an artist. The Commission concluded: "It is the majority view of the Commission that personal managers or anyone not licensed as a talent agent should not, under any condition or circumstances, be allowed to procure employment for an artist without being licensed as a talent agent, except in accordance with the present provisions of the Act." (Rep., supra, at p. 6.)

The Legislature accepted the Report and codified the Commission's recommendations, approving the Commission's view that no exemption should be created for those who do not charge a fee for procuring employment for an artist. We conclude that the Act requires a license to engage in procurement activities even if no commission is received for the service.

DISPOSITION

The judgment appealed from is affirmed.

Zebrowski, J. and Mallano, J.

---

This case involves the contractual duties of an agent for the musical group, the Deftones, under the Talent Agencies Act, Cal. Lab. Code Section 1700 et seq. The Deftones terminated the contract of their former personal manager. The manager sued for breach of contract and intentional interference with a contractual relationship by the Deftones' recording company. The court held that the manager's contract was void and violated Section 1700 et seq. by securing performance agreements for the Deftones without being licensed as a talent agency. The court further held that even incidental activity associated with procuring employment for an artist is subject to regulation under the Talent Agencies Act.

**JANE DOE FIRM**
**EXCLUSIVE PERSONAL MANAGEMENT AGREEMENT**
**JOHN DOE**

**1.**     <u>**Acceptance**</u>

This Agreement shall not be binding until it is executed by all parties to this Agreement.

**2.**     <u>**Amendment or Modification**</u>

This Agreement shall represent the entire Agreement by and between the parties hereto, except as otherwise provided herein and it may not be changed except by written Agreement duly executed by all of the parties hereto.

**3.**     <u>**Assignment**</u>

Manager shall have the right to transfer or assign their interest in this Agreement without the prior written consent of the other Party hereto, of which notice shall forward to Artist within Thirty (30) Days.

**4.**     <u>**Complete Understanding and Cancellation of Prior Undertakings**</u>

By execution of this Agreement, the parties hereto acknowledge that they have read and understand each provision, term and obligation contained in this Agreement.  This Agreement although drawn by one Party, shall be construed fairly and reasonably and not more strictly against the drafting Party than the non-drafting Party.

Upon execution of this Agreement by all parties, all previous Management Agreements, Management Contracts, Management Arrangements, or Management Undertakings of any kind relative to the matters contained herein are hereby cancelled and all claims and demands not contained in this Agreement are deemed fully completed and satisfied, with the exception of the Term of this Contract. The effective date January 1, 2013, and expiration date of January 1, 2018, are agreed and clearly understood as the Five (5) year term as referenced within this Contract.

## 5.   Confidential Information

The parties hereto agree that the information and data at each other's disposal during the term of the negotiation of this Agreement, operation and enforcement of this Agreement is considered proprietary information and confidential. Such information if disseminated to third parties would be detrimental to the owner of said proprietary data. Accordingly, each Party hereto agrees to take any and all reasonable precautions to restrict the dissemination of such information by its Employees, Agents or Sub-Contractors.

This obligation shall continue notwithstanding the termination of this Agreement for a period of Five (5) years from the effective date of January 1, 2013, of this Agreement.

During the term of this Agreement or any extension thereto, neither Party shall permit access by any non-affiliated employees or person to said proprietary information, without the other Party's written permission thereto.

## 6.   Corporate Authority

If any Party hereto is a legal entity, including but not limited to, an association, corporation, joint venture, limited partnership, partnership, or trust, such Party represents to the other that this Agreement and the transactions contemplated herein and the execution and delivery hereof have been dully authorized by all necessary corporate partnership or trust proceedings and actions including but without limitation to the action on the part of the directors, officers and agents of said entity. Furthermore, said Party represents that appropriate corporate meetings were held to authorize the aforementioned obligations and certified copies of such corporate minutes and corporate resolutions authorizing this transaction have been delivered to all Parties to this Agreement prior to or at the time of execution of this Agreement.

## 7.   Date of Effectiveness

This Agreement shall become effective upon its execution by all of the parties hereto. Thereafter, all obligations contained herein shall be conclusive and binding upon all of the parties hereto. Accordingly, this Agreement shall no longer be considered executory as of the date that all parties have affixed their signatures to it.

## 8.     Defense, Hold Harmless and Indemnity Clause

It is the specific and express intent and the Agreement of the parties hereto that in the event one Party hereto should cause, either directly or indirectly, damage, loss, destruction, liability or claims against the other Party as a result of intentional conduct, negligence or otherwise, said offending Party shall hold harmless and indemnify the other Party from any and all obligations, liabilities, causes of action, lawsuits, damages, assessments, including legal fees, etc., as a result of said offending Party's intentional actions or negligence.

This indemnification clause shall survive this Agreement and be enforceable as a separate Agreement in the event the same becomes necessary.

## 9.     Term

I do hereby engage you as my sole and exclusive worldwide Personal Manager in all areas of the Entertainment Industry for an initial period of Five (5) years, with the ("effective Date") January 1, 2013, commencing as of the date first above written.  I hereby irrevocably grant to you the option to extend the initial period for a further consecutive renewal period of one (1) year, with the written consent of Jane Doe Firm, and executed with a notarized verification by both parties unless written notice is delivered to the contrary at any time prior to the end of the initial period.  Jane Doe Firm, has the irrevocable right to terminate this Contract, at any time prior to the expiration of the initial five (5) year term.   The initial period and any renewals are hereinafter called the "Term".  Nothing contained herein is intended to cause the Term to extend for a period in excess of the period permitted by applicable law, if any, for the enforcement of personal services Agreements, but in the event the Term shall be deemed by a Court of competent jurisdiction to extend for such excess period, then the Term shall be automatically deemed modified only to the extent necessary to conform the Term to that permitted by law, and as modified this Contract shall remain in full force and effect.

## 10.     Authority

(a) During the Term and any extensions, renewals, substitutions or modifications thereof, you are irrevocable authorized and empowered by me to act on my behalf as my Attorney-in-Fact, in your discretion, to do the following: (a) approve and permit any and all publicity and advertising:  (b) approve and permit the use of my name, photograph, likeness, voice, sound effects, caricatures and literary, artistic and musical materials for purposes of advertising and publicity, and in the promotion and advertising of any and all products and services: (c) to accept payments for my Professional Services, have the compensation made payable to Attraction Management Group, Inc, negotiate and deposit the Compensation into Jane Doe Firm, Corporate Bank Account, retaining, their twenty percent 20% Management, commission then issue the remaining Eighty percent 80% to John Doe.

Continue to promote John Doe as a Star Talent, with open communication with John Doe on a daily, weekly, or monthly as needed basis for the maximum proficiency in marketing and managing the career of John Doe.

## 11.    Service

As and when requested by me during and throughout the Term, Management agrees to advise and counsel Artist:    (a) in the selection of Artist/Producer and Audio Visual, Television Broadcast, and Ancillary Opportunities: (b) concerning publicity, public relations and advertising: (c) with respect to the adoption of proper format for presentation of my Artist/Producer talents and in the determination of proper style, mood, setting and characterization in keeping with my talents: (d) in the selection of Artist/Producer talent to assist, accompany or embellish my Artist/Producer talents in the entertainment industries: and (f) with respect to matters of which you may have knowledge concerning compensation and privileges extended for similar Artist/Producer values.

## 12.    Further Assurances

Each Party hereto further agrees that it shall take any and all necessary steps, sign and execute any and all necessary documents or Agreements which are required to implement the terms of the Agreement of the parties contained in this Contract, and each Party shall refrain from taking any action, either expressly or impliedly, which would have the effect of prohibiting or hindering the performance of the other Party to this Agreement.  This Agreement and exhibits attached hereto and incorporated herein, contain the entire Agreement of the parties, and there are no representations, inducements, promises, Agreements, arrangements, undertakings, oral or written, between the parties hereto other than those expressly set forth hereinabove, and duly executed in writing.  No Agreement of any kind shall be binding upon either Party until the same has been made in writing and duly executed by both parties hereto.

## 13.    Force Majeure

Neither Party shall be liable or responsible to the other Party for any delay, damage, loss, failure, or inability to perform caused by "force majeure."

The term "force majeure", as used in this Agreement, shall include the following:  an act of God, strike, act of the public enemy, war, mines or other items of ordinance, blockage, public rioting, lightning, fire, storm, flood, explosions, inability to obtain materials, supplies, labor permits, servitudes, rights or way, acts or restraints of any governmental authority, epidemics, landslides, lightning storms, earthquakes, flood, storms, washouts, arrests, restraints of rulers and peoples, civil disturbances, explosions, breakage or accident to machinery or lines of equipment, temporary failure of equipment, freezing of equipment and any other cause whether of the kinds specifically enumerated above or otherwise which are not reasonably within the control of the Parties hereto and which by the exercise of due diligence could not be reasonably prevented or overcome.

Such causes or contingencies effecting the performance of this Agreement by any Party hereto, shall not relieve such Party of liability in the event of its concurring negligence or in the event of its failure to remedy this situation if it is within its reasonable control, or it could have reasonably removed the cause which has prevented its performance.

The Parties shall use all reasonable dispatch to remove all contingencies effecting the performance of this Agreement.  This clause shall not relieve any Party from its obligations to make payments of amounts then due for previous work obligations contemplated and performed hereunder.

Furthermore, the Party asserting this privilege shall give a full and complete notice of the facts, which it considers to excuse its performance under this "force majeure" clause.

In the event time limits are not met under this Agreement as a result of "force majeure", the Parties hereto agree to an extension of said time limit or deadline for the number of days for which the "force majeure" condition existed and after said force majeure condition has expired, the contract shall continue under the same operations and circumstances as existed prior to the "force majeure" event.

## 14.    Independent Status

It is agreed and understood that any work requested by the parties hereto shall be performed under the terms of the Agreement and that all parties hereto are considered independent Contractors. Each Party is interested only in the results obtained hereunder and has the general right of inspection and supervision in order to secure the satisfactory completion of such work.

Neither Party shall have control over the other Party with respect to its hours, times, employment, etc.

Under no circumstances, shall either Party hereto be deemed an employee of the other, nor shall either Party act as an Agent of the other Party.

Furthermore, the parties hereto warrant that all obligations imposed on them by this Agreement shall be performed with due diligence in a safe, competent, workmanlike manner and in compliance with any and all applicable statutes, rules and regulations.

Any and all joint venture or partnership status is hereby expressly denied and the parties expressly state that they have not formed, either expressly or impliedly, a joint venture or partnership.

## 15.    Loans and Advances

You are not required to make any loans or advances to me for my account, but in the event you do so, I shall repay them promptly upon demand, and I hereby authorize you to deduct the amount of any such loans or advances from any sums you may receive for my account under this Contract. My failure or delay in repaying any such loans, however, shall not be deemed a breach of this Contract, but nothing herein contained shall prevent you from seeking legal and equitable remedies you would otherwise have against me to collect such debt, including your rights pursuant to the immediately preceding sentence. I acknowledge that Management has advanced to me directly, or for my benefit to Third Parties, cash in the amount of not less than, approximately Ten Thousand Dollars ($10,000.00), of which I authorize Management to recover this amount, and in addition to this amount, any amount expended on my behalf, or approved by me, from my portion, of any compensation, due for my Professional Services.

16.     **Artist's Career**

        I, John Doe, agree at all times to devote myself to my career and to do all things reasonably necessary and desirable to promote my career and earnings therefrom. I shall at all times utilize proper Booking Agents, or other employment agencies to obtain engagements and employment for me. I shall not sign any Agreements concerning my services or business affairs without first consulting you for your advice.

17.     **Not An Employment Agent**

        You have advised me that you are not licensed as a "talent agent' Under the Labor Code of the State of California, or as a theatrical employment agency under the General Business Law of the State of New York. It is understood that you are not a booking, theatrical or employment agent, but rather shall represent me in my dealings with such agents. You are not obligated to and shall not be expected to render any services, which would require you to be licensed as an employment agent in any jurisdiction.

18.     **Scope:  Breach**

        This Contract shall not be construed to create a partnership between us. I understand that you are acting hereunder as an independent Contractor and you may appoint or engage any and all other persons, firms and corporations through the world in your discretion to assist you in performing any or all of the services which you have agreed to perform hereunder. Your services hereunder are not exclusive. You may at all times render the same or similar services for others, and you may engage in any and all other business activities. You shall only be required to render reasonable services, which are called for by this Contract as a when reasonably requested by me. In no event shall you or I be deemed to be in default hereunder unless and until you or I, as the case may be, shall first have given to the other a written notice by certified mail, describing the exact default which is alleged hereunder, and then, a default shall only occur in the event that you or I, as the case may be, shall thereafter fail, for a period of thirty (30) consecutive days, you or I, as the case may be, shall only be required to initiate such steps within said thirty (30) day period as are necessary to remedy such default, provided such default is remedied in due course thereafter.

## 19.   Compensation

(a)      I agreed to pay to you, as and when received by me, or on my behalf and during and through the Term, a sum equal to twenty percent (20%) of any and all gross monies or other considerations which I may hereafter during the term earn (whether received during or after the Term), receive, or acquire, or become entitled to, directly or indirectly, as a result of my activities in an throughout the worldwide entertainment industries, including such activities pursuant to engagements, employment and Agreements now in existence. Any commissions that may be payable to another manager(s) previously utilized by me are solely my responsibility and shall become 100% from my share of such gross monies or other considerations. Following the expiration or termination of the Term, I agree to pay you a commission as more particularly described herein.

(b).      As used herein the term "entertainment industries" shall include, without limitation, or any and all aspects of the entertainment's, amusement, music, recording, publishing, television, motion picture, nightclub, concert, radio, literary and theatrical industries, and shall include and or all forms of advertising, endorsements, merchandising, or other exploitations using my name, photograph, voice, sound effects, likeness, caricatures, talents, or materials.  The term "activities": shall include, without limitation, my activities in as a live performer, recording artist, producer, author, composer, director, consultant or otherwise, and shall also include the use of my name, voice likeness, etc. As aforesaid. The term "gross monies or other considerations" shall include, without limitation, salaries, earnings, fees, advances against royalties, royalties, residuals, repeat and/;or re-run fees, non-bonafide gifts (i.e., a disguised payment for services rendered in the entertainment industries), bonuses, shares of profit, shares of stock, partnership interest, percentages, all sums resulting from my activities in the entertainment industries and uses of the results and proceeds thereof, payments for termination of my activities, payments to refrain from any such activities and payments in connection with the settlement or other disposition of any dispute concerning said activities, after first deducting legal fees incurred in connection therewith, which are earned or received directly or indirectly by me or my heirs, executors, administrators or assigns, or by any other person, firm, or corporation on my behalf, without deduction or any nature or sort.  Notwithstanding the foregoing:

(i)      you shall not be entitled to a commission hereunder, on any gross monies or other considerations paid or credited to me or on my behalf, and used to pay record or video production costs (including producer's and engineer's fees, advances and royalties), nor shall you be entitled to a commission hereunder on so-called "deficit tour support" advances.

(c)     As to the proceeds of any motion picture, phonorecord, film, tape, wire transcription, recording or other reproduction or result of my activities in the commission with respect thereto shall continue for so long as any of same are issued, sold, leased or otherwise exploited, whether during or after the Term.  In the event I receive, as all or part of my compensation for activities hereunder, stock or the right to buy stock or my right to become the packager or any entertainment property or programs, you and I shall Mutually agree, in good faith, upon what portion of the total package price your commission hereunder shall be based.

(d)     Following the termination or expiration of the Term and notwithstanding anything to the contrary herein before contained, with respect to gross monies or other considerations thereafter earned by me, you shall only be entitled to a commission hereunder from the following sources, at the following rates and during the following period of time:

(1)     Television Activities.  I shall pay to you, as and when received by me or on my behalf, a sum equal to twenty percent (20%) of any and all gross monies or other considerations which I may earn as a performer in television programs recorded during the term, and the two (2) years following the expiration of this Contract, in perpetuity, provided such performances were rendered pursuant to Agreements entered into, or substantially negotiated for, during the Term.

(2)     Motion Picture Activities.  I shall pay to you, as when received by me or on my behalf, a sum equal to twenty percent (20%) of any and all gross monies or other considerations which I may earn as a performer in motion picture sound tracks, in perpetuity from performances rendered pursuant to Agreements entered into, or substantially negotiated for, during the Term.

(3)     Recording and Music Publishing Activities.  I shall pay you, as and when received by me or on my behalf, a sum equal to twenty percent (20%) of any and all gross monies or other considerations which I may earn as a recording artist, songwriter and music publisher, in perpetuity, from the exploitation of all master recordings embodying my performance which were recorded during the Term and from the exploitation of musical compositions which were commercially exploited during the Term. You shall not be entitled to any commissions hereunder after the Term on any other master

recordings embodying my performances or any other musical compositions. A master recording shall be deemed "recorded" during a particular period of time if it was substantially completed during such period.

(4)    Concert Activities.  I shall pay to you, as an when received by me or on my behalf, a sum equal to twenty percent (20%) of any and all gross monies or other considerations which I may earn as a "live" performer, in perpetuity, from engagements performed pursuant to Agreements entered into, or substantially negotiated for, during the Term.

(5)    Books/Literary Works Activities.  I shall pay to you, as and when received by me or on my behalf, a sum equal to twenty percent (20%) of any and all gross monies or other considerations which may earn as an author, in perpetuity, from the exploitation of literary works pursuant to Agreements therefore entered into, or substantially negotiated for, during the Term.

(6)    Subsidiary Rights.  I shall pay to you, as and when received by me or on my behalf, a sum equal to twenty percent (20%) of any and all gross monies or other considerations which I may earn, in perpetuity, from subsidiary rights in and to commissionable motion pictures, television programs, and books in connection with which you are otherwise entitled to a commission pursuant to this Contract (other than by reason of this subparagraph (d), provided and only to the extent that such subsidiary rights are granted and/or licensed during that one (1) year period following the expiration of the Term (e.g., and Agreement granting motion picture rights in a commissionable book, which Agreement is entered into during such one (1) year period).

(7)    Merchandising Rights.  I shall pay to you, as and when received by me or on my behalf, a sum equal to twenty percent (20%) of any and all gross monies or other considerations which I may earn, in perpetuity, from the exploitation of so-called  "merchandising rights" in my name and likeness pursuant to Agreements therefore entered into, or substantially negotiated for, during the Term.

(e)    Notwithstanding the foregoing, (i) should the financial terms of any engagements, Contracts or Agreements, in connection with which you are otherwise entitled to a commission hereunder, be augmented after the Term, you shall only be entitled to your commission hereunder based upon such terms as they existed prior to such augmentation and (ii) all references in the preceding subparagraphs to "Agreements...substantially negotiated for during the term" shall only refer to and include Agreements actually signed or the subject of an oral Agreement reached within nine (9) months after the expiration hereof (with the understanding, however, that the fact that an Agreement is signed or the subject of an Agreement reached during said nine (9) month period shall not in and of itself create a presumption that it was "substantially negotiated for during the Term"). If an "Agreement" is otherwise commissionable pursuant to above referenced paragraphs any extensions, renewals, or substitutions of such Agreement shall likewise be commissionable at the same applicable rate.

(8)     Booking Agency. In the event a Booking Agency is used, the Booking Agency's commission shall be paid from the Gross Booking fee as designated in this Agreement.

## 20.  Expenses

All reasonable direct expenses, other than your normal office operating expenses (i.e., rents, salaries, etc.) actually incurred by you, including, without limitation, long distance telephone calls, postage on all items which exceed one dollar ($1.00), messenger fees, travel expenses, and other disbursements contributable to me shall be paid by me. In the event your presence is required outside of the metropolitan area of Houston, Texas, I agree that I will pay for the travel expenses incurred by you which are directly attributable to the services rendered on my behalf. All of the foregoing expenses incurred on my behalf are to be paid immediately by me upon the presentation on an itemized expense sheet. All such expenses shall be itemized in the semi-annual accounting statements required to be sent to me pursuant to this Agreement, (but shall be reimbursed to you on a monthly basis).

## 21.  Publicity

You shall have the unrestricted right to advertise and publicize yourself as my personal Manager and Representative, in perpetuity.

## 22.  Conflicting Interest-Waiver of Commission When Employed By You

(a)     From time to time during the Term, other persons or entities owned and/or controlled, directly or indirectly by you, or your partners, shareholders, officers, directors, and employees, whether acting alone or in association with others, may package an entertainment program in which I am employed as an entrepreneur or promoter of an entertainment program in which I am employed as an artist, or may employ me in connection with the production of phonograph records, or as a songwriter, composer, arranger or otherwise in connection with the creation of literary or musical works. Such activity on your part shall not be or be deemed to be a breach of this Contractor of your fiduciary obligations and duties to me and shall not in any way affect your right to commissions hereunder in all instances not covered by the following exceptions. However, you shall not be entitled to commissions from me in connection with any gross monies or other considerations derived by me (i) from any employment other Agreements whereunder I am employed by you or by any of your partners, shareholders, officers, directors or employees, as (A) the package agent for the entertainment program in which I am so employed (B) or a music or literary publisher, or otherwise, or (ii) from the sale, license, or grant of any literary or musical rights by me to you or any person, firm or corporation owned or controlled by you, further, you shall not render nor shall you be obligated to render the personal management services contemplated in this Contract with respect to the aforesaid non-commissionable employment, Agreements, sales, licenses, and grants, in connection with which I shall have the right to seek and retain independent legal and management advice. Moreover, I shall be absolutely free to enter into any such employment, Agreements, sales, licenses or grants, or to refrain therefrom, as I in my sole discretion may elect.

(b)    Nothing contained in subparagraph (a) hereof shall be construed to excuse me from the payment of commissions upon gross monies or other considerations derived by me from any employment or any sale, license or grant of rights in connection with any entertainment program, phonograph record, or other matter merely because you or any of your partners, shareholders, officers, directors, or employees are also employed in connection therewith as a producer, director, conductor, or in some other management or supervisorial capacity, but not as my employer, grantee or licensee.

## 23.    Litigation

In the event of litigation hereunder, the prevailing Party shall be entitled to recover any and all reasonable Attorney's fees and other costs incurred in the enforcement of the terms of this Contract or for the breach thereof.

## 24.    Assignment/Benefits/Obligations

Manager shall have the right to assign this Contract to a partnership at least one of whose partners are you, or to a corporation which acquires all or substantially all of your assets. This Agreement shall be binding upon and inure to the benefit of you and me, our heirs, executors, administrators and assigns.

## 25. Life Insurance

Management shall have the right during the Term to obtain life insurance on Artist's life at your sole cost and expense, with you being the sole beneficiary thereof. I agree to fully cooperate in connection with the obtaining of same and to submit to a physical examination and complete any and all documents reasonably necessary or desirable in respect thereof. I hereby acknowledge that neither my estate nor I shall have the right to claim the benefits of any such policy obtained by Management.

## 26. Parties Bound Clause

This Agreement shall be binding upon and inure to the benefit to the parties hereto, their respective heirs, executors, administrators, legal representatives, successors and assigns.

## 27. Representations

No representations, promise, guarantees or warranties were made to induce either Party to execute this Agreement other than those stated in the Agreement.

## 28. Termination

This Agreement shall be effective from the effective date of November 1, 2015, and shall extend to October 30, 2016, and shall remain in force from year to year thereafter until terminated as mutually agreed by each Party hereto upon at least thirty (30) days prior written notice by return, receipt requested mail to the non-terminating Party.

This Agreement may be cancelled prior to the execution of the above stated term due to the following events:

a)      by mutual written agreement;

b)      in the event either party files for relief under federal bankruptcy proceedings;

c)      in the event involuntary bankruptcy proceedings are initiated against either party hereto;

d)      in the event of death, liquidation, physical or mental incapacity of either party hereto; and,

e)      in the event of any material breach by one of the

parties that detrimentally effects the success of the career of John Doe;

f)     in the event of fraud or misrepresentation by one of the parties hereto.

## 29.   Time Limit

Time is of the essence in this Agreement and, accordingly, all time limits shall be strictly construed and strictly enforced.

Failure of one Party to this Agreement to meet a deadline imposed hereunder shall be considered a material and significant breach of this Agreement and shall entitle the non-breaching Party to any and all rights of default as stated hereinabove.

## 30.   Signatory Clause

This Agreement is signed, accepted and agreed to by all parties hereto by and through the parties or their agents or authorized representatives.  All parties hereto hereby acknowledge, that they have read and understand this Agreement and the attachments and/or exhibits hereto, and have allowed the Attorney of their choice, to review this document, and explain the Legal Obligations contained herein, or had the opportunity, to have the Attorney of their choice, review and explain the Legal Obligations, contained herein, prior to the execution by each Party.  All parties further acknowledge that they have executed this legal document voluntarily, and of their own free will.

## 31.   Applicable Law

This Contract shall be deemed to be executed in the State of Texas, and shall be construed in accordance with the laws of the State of Texas.  The parties agree, however, the Courts located in the jurisdiction of Harris County, Texas shall have exclusive jurisdiction of any dispute arising out of this Contract. In the event any provision hereof shall for any reason be invalid, illegal or unenforceable and in any such event, the same provisions hereof; however, if any such invalidity illegality or unenforceability materially affects your right to compensation hereunder, you may at any time thereafter terminate the Term.

## 32.   Notices

All notices hereunder shall be prepaid telegram or cablegram, or by certified or registered mail, return receipt requested, postage prepaid, and if to me, shall be sent to the address set forth below, and if to you shall be sent to the address on page one, unless we notify each other as provided herein that notices shall be sent to a difference address.

Jane Doe Firm              John Doe
Attn: Ms. Jane Doe
1234 Smith Street       _____
Houston, Texas 77777   _____

_____

**33.**    <u>Miscellaneous</u>

This Contract constitutes the entire Agreement between Management and Artist relating to the subject hereof, all previous understandings, whether oral or written, having been emerged herein. The headings of the paragraphs hereof are for convenience only and shall not be deemed to limit or in any way affect the scope, meaning of or intent of this Contractor any portion thereof. This Contract may not be changed or modified, or any convenant or provision hereof waived, except by an Agreement in writing, signed by the Party against whom enforcement of the change, modifications or waiver is sought.

If the foregoing meets with your approval, please indicate your acceptance and Agreement by signing in the space herein below provided and returning to me.

AGREED AND ACCEPTED:

BEFORE ME, the undersigned, a Notary Public in and for said County and State, on this day personally appeared Kathy Sapp, Authorized Agent for Jane Doe Firm, known to me to be the person whose name is subscribed to the foregoing instrument, and acknowledged to me that he executed the same for the purposes and consideration therein expressed.

_____     _____

Ms. Jane Doe, Authorized Agent for     Date
Jane Doe Firm

SUBSCRIBED AND SWORN TO BEFORE ME on this the _____ day of _____, 2015, to certify which witness my hand and official seal.

[SEAL]

_____

Notary Public

BEFORE ME, the undersigned, a Notary Public in and for said County and State, on this day personally appeared John Doe, known to me to be the person whose name is subscribed to the foregoing instrument, and acknowledged to me that he executed the same for the purposes and consideration therein expressed.

_____        _____

By: John Doe                                                    Date

       SUBSCRIBED AND SWORN TO BEFORE ME on this the _____ day of _____, 2015, to certify which witness my hand and official seal.
[SEAL]


_____

Notary Public


In *Lindey*, under a form, "Agreement between a personal manager and a 'new artist,'" clause 2(a) stipulates that a "manager is not required to render exclusive services to Artist or to devote the entire time of manager or the entire time of any of manager's employees to the affairs of Artist. Nothing herein shall be construed as limiting Manager's right to represent other persons whose talents may be similar to or who may be in competition with Artist or to have and pursue business interests which may be similar to or may compete with those of Artist." (*See* Alexander Lindey and Michael Landau, 4 Lindsey on Entertainment Publ. & the Arts Section 9:55 (3d ed.) (database updated Dec. 2012)).

Other sections of note in an artist-manager contract might include Commissions, Non-exclusivity, Advertising, Entire Agreement, Conflicting Interest, Scope, Assignment, Artist's Warranties, and Arbitration. The agent is a fiduciary of the artist, and thus is in a relationship of special trust: the best interest of the artist must always come first. In other words, there must be a complete disclosure of all information that can affect the artist's career—that is, no side deals, no secret profits, etc. Agents should also urge the artist to seek independent advice when necessary if a conflict of interest arises.

Questions and Discussion

1. In *Abkco Music, Inc. v. Harrisongs Music, Ltd.*, 722 F.2d 988 (2d Cir. 1983), it was claimed that George Harrison's song "My Sweet Lord" infringed on "He's So Fine." If the alleged infringement was accidental, should George Harrison bear the consequences of basic musical themes that are a part of every musician's sensibilities?

2. *Abkco* also deciphers the intricacies of artist representation and the possibility of conflicts of interest. "There is no doubt that the relationship between Harrison and ABKCO prior to the termination of the management agreement in 1973 was that of principal and agent and that the relationship was fiduciary in nature" (at 994). ABKCO was Harrison's former manager, with a former fudiciary obgligation to Harrison, and ABKCO handled Harrison's business affairs through the liability stage of the litigations; ABKCO then began negotiation to acquire the rights to the allegedly infringed song, and after infringement was determined, bought the song's rights and were substituted as sole plaintiffs. The court affirmed both infringement and the imposition of a constructive trust, holding that innocent intent is as unacceptable as a defense to infringement as it is to a conversion of tangible property by ex-fiduciaries. That is, the imposition of a constructive trust was affirmed because ABKCO acquired the rights to "He's So Fine" through the use of confidential information.

# Chapter 4
# Production Agreements

"Production agreements are really a hybrid between an artist's recording agreement and an independent producer's agreement that combines most, if not all, of the elements of both. Production agreements are sometimes referred to as 'all-in' agreements" (Richard Schulenberg, Legal Aspects of the Music Industry 206 (1999)). Production agreements "are agreements whereby a production entity, which can be the artist, the producer, a company, or whatever, supplies all the production elements for a specific project to the record company" (Id.). "Production agreements between the record company and the production entity should always contain an inducement letter or provision" (Id., at 207).

In *Mattel, Inc. v. MCA Records*, 296 F. 3d 894 (9th Cir. 2002), Mattel tries to protect its trademark for the Barbie doll from a musical parody. The problem is, of course, that Barbie is already a parody. And, one might think any PR is good PR. This is actually (usually) determined to be a First Amendment-type case, but it sheds a great deal of light onto the somewhat murky machinations of music production, distribution, and the "creative genius" behind record production. "Mattel brought this lawsuit against the music companies who produced, marketed and sold Barbie Girl: MCA Records, Inc., Universal Music International Ltd., Universal Music A/S, Universal Music & Video Distribution Inc. and MCA Music Scandidinavia AB" (at 899).

Mattel, Inc. v. MCA Records,
United States Court of Appeals for the Ninth Circuit
December 5, 2000; July 24, 2002, Filed
No. 98-56453, No. 98-56577
296 F.3d 894

KOZINSKI, Circuit Judge:

If this were a sci-fi melodrama, it might be called Speech-Zilla meets Trademark Kong.

## I.

Barbie was born in Germany in the 1950s as an adult collector's item. Over the years, Mattel transformed her from a doll that resembled a "German street walker," as she originally appeared, into a glamorous, long-legged blonde. Barbie has been labeled both the ideal American woman and a bimbo. She has survived attacks both psychic (from feminists critical of her fictitious figure) and physical (more than 500 professional makeovers). She remains a symbol of American girlhood, a public figure who graces the aisles of toy stores throughout the country and beyond. With Barbie, Mattel created not just a toy but a cultural icon.

With fame often comes unwanted attention. Aqua is a Danish band that has, as yet, only dreamed of attaining Barbie-like status. In 1997, Aqua produced the song Barbie Girl on the album Aquarium. In the song, one bandmember impersonates Barbie, singing in a high-pitched, doll-like voice; another bandmember, calling himself Ken, entices Barbie to "go party." (The lyrics are in the Appendix.) Barbie Girl singles sold well and, to Mattel's dismay, the song made it onto Top 40 music charts.

Mattel brought this lawsuit against the music companies who produced, marketed and sold Barbie Girl: MCA Records, Inc., Universal Music International Ltd., Universal Music A/S, Universal Music & Video Distribution, Inc. and MCA Music Scandinavia AB (collectively, "MCA"). MCA in turn challenged the district court's jurisdiction under the Lanham Act and its personal jurisdiction over the foreign defendants, Universal Music International Ltd., Universal Music A/S and MCA Music Scandinavia AB (hereinafter "foreign defendants"); MCA also brought a defamation claim against Mattel for statements Mattel made about MCA while this lawsuit was pending. The district court concluded it had jurisdiction over the foreign defendants and under the Lanham Act, and granted MCA's motion for summary judgment on Mattel's federal and state-law claims for trademark infringement and dilution. The district court also granted Mattel's motion for summary judgment on MCA's defamation claim.

Mattel appeals the district court's ruling that Barbie Girl is a parody of Barbie and a nominative fair use; that MCA's use of the term Barbie is not likely to confuse consumers as to Mattel's affiliation with Barbie Girl or dilute the Barbie mark; and that Mattel cannot assert an unfair competition claim under the Paris Convention for the Protection of Industrial Property. MCA cross-appeals the grant of summary judgment on its defamation claim as well as the district court's jurisdictional holdings.

## II.

A. All three foreign defendants are affiliated members of Universal Music Group and have an active relationship with each other and with domestic members of the Group. Defendants entered into cross-licensing agreements and developed a coordinated plan to distribute the Barbie Girl song in the United States (including California), and sent promotional copies of the Barbie Girl single and the Aquarium album to the United States (including California). This conduct was expressly aimed at, and allegedly caused harm in, California, Mattel's principal place of business. See Panavision Int'l, L.P. v. Toeppen, 141 F.3d 1316, 1321 (9th Cir. 1998). Mattel's trademark claims would not have arisen "but for" the conduct foreign defendants purposefully directed toward California, and jurisdiction over the foreign defendants, who are represented by the same counsel and closely associated with the domestic defendants, is reasonable. See id. at 1321-22. The district court did not err in asserting specific personal jurisdiction over the foreign defendants.

B. Sales of the Aquarium album worldwide had a sufficient effect on American foreign commerce, and Mattel suffered monetary injury in the United States from those sales. See Ocean Garden, Inc. v. Marktrade Co., 953 F.2d 500, 503 (9th Cir. 1991). Moreover, Mattel's claim is more closely tied to interests of American foreign commerce than it is to the commercial interests of other nations: Mattel's principal place of business is in California, the foreign defendants are closely related to the domestic defendants, and Mattel sought relief only for defendants' sales in the United States. See Star-Kist Foods, Inc. v. P.J. Rhodes & Co., 769 F.2d 1393, 1395-96 (9th Cir. 1985). The district court properly exercised extraterritorial jurisdiction under the Lanham Act.

## III.

A. A trademark is a word, phrase or symbol that is used to identify a manufacturer or sponsor of a good or the provider of a service. See New Kids on the Block v. News Am. Publ'g, Inc., 971 F.2d 302, 305 (9th Cir. 1992). It's the owner's way of preventing others from duping consumers into buying a product they mistakenly believe is sponsored by the trademark owner. A trademark "informs people that trademarked products come from the same source." Id. at 305 n.2. Limited to this core purpose — avoiding confusion in the marketplace — a trademark owner's property rights play well with the First Amendment. "Whatever first amendment rights you may have in calling the brew you make in your bathtub 'Pepsi' are easily outweighed by the buyer's interest in not being fooled into buying it." Trademarks Unplugged, 68 N.Y.U.L. Rev. 960, 973 (1993).

The problem arises when trademarks transcend their identifying purpose. Some trademarks enter our public discourse and become an integral part of our vocabulary. How else do you say that something's "the Rolls Royce of its class?" What else is a quick fix, but a Band-Aid? Does the average consumer know to ask for aspirin as "acetyl salicylic acid?" See Bayer Co. v. United Drug Co., 272 F. 505, 510 (S.D.N.Y. 1921). Trademarks often fill in gaps in our vocabulary and add a contemporary flavor to our expressions. Once imbued with such expressive value, the trademark becomes a word in our language and assumes a role outside the bounds of trademark law.

Our likelihood-of-confusion test, see AMF Inc. v. Sleekcraft Boats, 599 F.2d 341, 348-49 (9th Cir. 1979), generally strikes a comfortable balance between the trademark owner's property rights and the public's expressive interests. But when a trademark owner asserts a right to control how we express ourselves — when we'd find it difficult to describe the product any other way (as in the case of aspirin), or when the mark (like Rolls Royce) has taken on an expressive meaning apart from its source-identifying function — applying the traditional test fails to account for the full weight of the public's interest in free expression.

The First Amendment may offer little protection for a competitor who labels its commercial good with a confusingly similar mark, but "trademark rights do not entitle the owner to quash an unauthorized use of the mark by another who is communicating ideas or expressing points of view." L.L. Bean, Inc. v. Drake Publishers, Inc., 811 F.2d 26, 29 (1st Cir. 1987). Were we to ignore the expressive value that some marks assume, trademark rights would grow to encroach upon the zone protected by the First Amendment. See Yankee Publ'g, Inc. v. News Am. Publ'g, Inc., 809 F. Supp. 267, 276 (S.D.N.Y. 1992) ("When unauthorized use of another's mark is part of a communicative message and not a source identifier, the First Amendment is implicated in opposition to the trademark right."). Simply put, the trademark owner does not have the right to control public discourse whenever the public imbues his mark with a meaning beyond its source-identifying function. See Anti-Monopoly, Inc. v. Gen. Mills Fun Group, 611 F.2d 296, 301 (9th Cir. 1979) ("It is the source-denoting function which trademark laws protect, and nothing more.").

B. There is no doubt that MCA uses Mattel's mark: Barbie is one half of Barbie Girl. But Barbie Girl is the title of a song about Barbie and Ken, a reference that — at least today — can only be to Mattel's famous couple. We expect a title to describe the underlying work, not to identify the producer, and Barbie Girl does just that.

The Barbie Girl title presages a song about Barbie, or at least a girl like Barbie. The title conveys a message to consumers about what they can expect to discover in the song itself; it's a quick glimpse of Aqua's take on their own song. The lyrics confirm this: The female singer, who calls herself Barbie, is "a Barbie girl, in [her] Barbie world." She tells her male counterpart (named Ken), "Life in plastic, it's fantastic. You can brush my hair, undress me everywhere/Imagination, life is your creation." And off they go to "party." The song pokes fun at Barbie and the values that Aqua contends she represents. See Cliffs Notes, Inc. v. Bantam Doubleday Dell Publ'g Group, 886 F.2d 490, 495-96 (2d Cir. 1989). The female singer explains, "I'm a blond bimbo girl, in a fantasy world/Dress me up, make it tight, I'm your dolly."

The song does not rely on the Barbie mark to poke fun at another subject but targets Barbie herself. See Campbell v. Acuff-Rose Music, Inc., 510 U.S. 569, 580, 127 L. Ed. 2d 500, 114 S. Ct. 1164 (1994); see also Dr. Seuss Ents., L.P. v. Penguin Books USA, Inc., 109 F.3d 1394, 1400 (9th Cir. 1997). This case is therefore distinguishable from Dr. Seuss, where we held that the book The Cat NOT in the Hat! borrowed Dr. Seuss's trademarks and lyrics to get attention rather than to mock The Cat in the Hat! The defendant's use of the Dr. Seuss trademarks and copyrighted works had "no critical bearing on the substance or style of" The Cat in the Hat!, and therefore could not claim First Amendment protection. Id. at 1401. Dr. Seuss recognized that, where an artistic work targets the original and does not merely borrow another's property to get attention, First Amendment interests weigh more heavily in the balance. See id. at 1400-02; see also Harley-Davidson, Inc. v. Grottanelli, 164 F.3d 806, 812-13 (2d Cir. 1999) (a parodist whose expressive work aims its parodic commentary at a trademark is given considerable leeway, but a claimed parodic use that makes no comment on the mark is not a permitted trademark parody use).

The Second Circuit has held that "in general the [Lanham] Act should be construed to apply to artistic works only where the public interest in avoiding consumer confusion outweighs the public interest in free expression." Rogers v. Grimaldi, 875 F.2d 994, 999 (2d Cir. 1989); see also Cliffs Notes, 886 F.2d at 494 (quoting Rogers, 875 F.2d at 999). Rogers considered a challenge by the actress Ginger Rogers to the film Ginger and Fred. The movie told the story of two Italian cabaret performers who made a living by imitating Ginger Rogers and Fred Astaire. Rogers argued that the film's title created the false impression that she was associated with it.

At first glance, Rogers certainly had a point. Ginger was her name, and Fred was her dancing partner. If a pair of dancing shoes had been labeled Ginger and Fred, a dancer might have suspected that Rogers was associated with the shoes (or at least one of them), just as Michael Jordan has endorsed Nike sneakers that claim to make you fly through the air. But Ginger and Fred was not a brand of shoe; it was the title of a movie and, for the reasons explained by the Second Circuit, deserved to be treated differently.

A title is designed to catch the eye and to promote the value of the underlying work. Consumers expect a title to communicate a message about the book or movie, but they do not expect it to identify the publisher or producer. See Application of Cooper, 45 C.C.P.A. 923, 254 F.2d 611, 615-16 (C.C.P.A. 1958) (A "title …identifies a specific literary work, …and is not associated in the public mind with the …manufacturer." (internal quotation marks omitted)). If we see a painting titled "Campbell's Chicken Noodle Soup," we're unlikely to believe that Campbell's has branched into the art business. Nor, upon hearing Janis Joplin croon "Oh Lord, won't you buy me a Mercedes-Benz?," would we suspect that she and the carmaker had entered into a joint venture. A title tells us something about the underlying work but seldom speaks to its origin:

Though consumers frequently look to the title of a work to determine what it is about, they do not regard titles of artistic works in the same way as the names of ordinary commercial products. Since consumers expect an ordinary product to be what the name says it is, we apply the Lanham Act with some rigor to prohibit names that misdescribe such goods. But most consumers are well aware that they cannot judge a book solely by its title any more than by its cover.

Rogers, 875 F.2d at 1000 (citations omitted).

Rogers concluded that literary titles do not violate the Lanham Act "unless the title has no artistic relevance to the underlying work whatsoever, or, if it has some artistic relevance, unless the title explicitly misleads as to the source or the content of the work." Id. at 999 (footnote omitted). We agree with the Second Circuit's analysis and adopt the Rogers standard as our own.

Applying Rogers to our case, we conclude that MCA's use of Barbie is not an infringement of Mattel's trademark. Under the first prong of Rogers, the use of Barbie in the song title clearly is relevant to the underlying work, namely, the song itself. As noted, the song is about Barbie and the values Aqua claims she represents. The song title does not explicitly mislead as to the source of the work; it does not, explicitly or otherwise, suggest that it was produced by Mattel. The only indication that Mattel might be associated with the song is the use of Barbie in the title; if this were enough to satisfy this prong of the Rogers test, it would render Rogers a nullity. We therefore agree with the district court that MCA was entitled to summary judgment on this ground. We need not consider whether the district court was correct in holding that MCA was also entitled to summary judgment because its use of Barbie was a nominative fair use.

**IV.**

Mattel separately argues that, under the Federal Trademark Dilution Act ("FTDA"), MCA's song dilutes the Barbie mark in two ways: It diminishes the mark's capacity to identify and distinguish Mattel products, and tarnishes the mark because the song is inappropriate for young girls. See 15 U.S.C. § 1125(c); see also Panavision Int'l, L.P. v. Toeppen, 141 F.3d 1316, 1324 (9th Cir. 1998).

"Dilution" refers to the "whittling away of the value of a trademark" when it's used to identify different products. 4 J. Thomas McCarthy, McCarthy on Trademarks and Unfair Competition § 24.67 at 24-120; § 24.70 at 24-122 (2001). For example, Tylenol snowboards, Netscape sex shops and Harry Potter dry cleaners would all weaken the "commercial magnetism" of these marks and diminish their ability to evoke their original associations. Ralph S. Brown, Jr., Advertising and the Public Interest: Legal Protection of Trade Symbols, 57 Yale L.J. 1165, 1187 (1948), reprinted in 108 Yale L.J. 1619 (1999). These uses dilute the selling power of these trademarks by blurring their "uniqueness and singularity," Frank I. Schechter, The Rational Basis of Trademark Protection, 40 Harv. L. Rev. 813, 831 (1927), and/or by tarnishing them with negative associations.

By contrast to trademark infringement, the injury from dilution usually occurs when consumers aren't confused about the source of a product: Even if no one suspects that the maker of analgesics has entered into the snowboard business, the Tylenol mark will now bring to mind two products, not one. Whereas trademark law targets "interference with the source signaling function" of trademarks, dilution protects owners "from an appropriation of or free riding on" the substantial investment that they have made in their marks. I.P. Lund Trading ApS v. Kohler Co., 163 F.3d 27, 50 (1st Cir. 1998).

Originally a creature of state law, dilution received nationwide recognition in 1996 when Congress amended the Lanham Act by enacting the FTDA. The statute protects "the owner of a famous mark ...against another person's commercial use in commerce of a mark or trade name, if such use begins after the mark has become famous and causes dilution of the distinctive quality of the mark." 15 U.S.C. § 1125(c). Dilutive uses are prohibited unless they fall within one of the three statutory exemptions discussed below. See pp. 10495-96 infra. For a lucid and scholarly discussion of the statutory terms, as well as the purposes of the federal dilution statute, we refer the reader to Judge Leval's opinion in Nabisco, Inc. v. PF Brands, Inc., 191 F.3d 208, 214-17 (2d Cir. 1999). Barbie easily qualifies under the FTDA as a famous and distinctive mark, and reached this status long before MCA began to market the Barbie Girl song. The commercial success of Barbie Girl establishes beyond dispute that the Barbie mark satisfies each of these elements.

We are also satisfied that the song amounts to a "commercial use in commerce." Although this statutory language is ungainly, its meaning seems clear: It refers to a use of a famous and distinctive mark to sell goods other than those produced or authorized by the mark's owner. Panavision, 141 F.3d at 1324-25. That is precisely what MCA did with the Barbie mark: It created and sold to consumers in the marketplace commercial products (the Barbie Girl single and the Aquarium album) that bear the Barbie mark.

MCA's use of the mark is dilutive. MCA does not dispute that, while a reference to Barbie would previously have brought to mind only Mattel's doll, after the song's popular success, some consumers hearing Barbie's name will think of both the doll and the song, or perhaps of the song only. This is a classic blurring injury and is in no way diminished by the fact that the song itself refers back to Barbie the doll. To be dilutive, use of the mark need not bring to mind the junior user alone. The distinctiveness of the mark is diminished if the mark no longer brings to mind the senior user alone.

We consider next the applicability of the FTDA's three statutory exemptions. These are uses that, though potentially dilutive, are nevertheless permitted: comparative advertising; news reporting and commentary; and noncommercial use. 15 U.S.C. § 1125(c)(4)(B). The first two exemptions clearly do not apply; only the exemption for noncommercial use need detain us.

A "noncommercial use" exemption, on its face, presents a bit of a conundrum because it seems at odds with the earlier requirement that the junior use be a "commercial use in commerce." If a use has to be commercial in order to be dilutive, how then can it also be noncommercial so as to satisfy the exception of section 1125(c)(4)(B)? If the term "commercial use" had the same meaning in both provisions, this would eliminate one of the three statutory exemptions defined by this subsection, because any use found to be dilutive would, of necessity, not be noncommercial.

Such a reading of the statute would also create a constitutional problem, because it would leave the FTDA with no First Amendment protection for dilutive speech other than comparative advertising and news reporting. This would be a serious problem because the primary (usually exclusive) remedy for dilution is an injunction. As noted above, tension with the First Amendment also exists in the trademark context, especially where the mark has assumed an expressive function beyond mere identification of a product or service. See pp. 10487-89 supra; New Kids on the Block v. News Am. Publ'g, Inc., 971 F.2d 302, 306-08 (9th Cir. 1992). These concerns apply with greater force in the dilution context because dilution lacks two very significant limitations that reduce the tension between trademark law and the First Amendment.

First, depending on the strength and distinctiveness of the mark, trademark law grants relief only against uses that are likely to confuse. See 5 McCarthy § 30:3 at 30-8 to 30-11; Restatement § 35 cmt. c at 370. A trademark injunction is usually limited to uses within one industry or several related industries. Dilution law is the antithesis of trademark law in this respect, because it seeks to protect the mark from association in the public's mind with wholly unrelated goods and services. The more remote the good or service associated with the junior use, the more likely it is to cause dilution rather than trademark infringement. A dilution injunction, by contrast to a trademark injunction, will generally sweep across broad vistas of the economy.

Second, a trademark injunction, even a very broad one, is premised on the need to prevent consumer confusion. This consumer protection rationale — averting what is essentially a fraud on the consuming public — is wholly consistent with the theory of the First Amendment, which does not protect commercial fraud. Cent. Hudson Gas & Elec. v. Pub. Serv. Comm'n, 447 U.S. 557, 566, 65 L. Ed. 2d 341, 100 S. Ct. 2343 (1980); see Thompson v. W. States Med. Ctr., 535 U.S. 357, 152 L. Ed. 2d 563, 122 S. Ct. 1497 (2002) (applying Central Hudson). Moreover, avoiding harm to consumers is an important interest that is independent of the senior user's interest in protecting its business.

Dilution, by contrast, does not require a showing of consumer confusion, 15 U.S.C. § 1127, and dilution injunctions therefore lack the built-in First Amendment compass of trademark injunctions. In addition, dilution law protects only the distinctiveness of the mark, which is inherently less weighty than the dual interest of protecting trademark owners and avoiding harm to consumers that is at the heart of every trademark claim.

Fortunately, the legislative history of the FTDA suggests an interpretation of the "noncommercial use" exemption that both solves our interpretive dilemma and diminishes some First Amendment concerns: "Noncommercial use" refers to a use that consists entirely of noncommercial, or fully constitutionally protected, speech. See 2 Jerome Gilson et al., Trademark Protection and Practice § 5.12[1][c][vi] at 5-240 (this exemption "is intended to prevent the courts from enjoining speech that has been recognized to be [fully] constitutionally protected," "such as parodies"). Where, as here, a statute's plain meaning "produces an absurd, and perhaps unconstitutional, result[, it is] entirely appropriate to consult all public materials, including the background of [the statute] and the legislative history of its adoption." Green v. Bock Laundry Mach. Co., 490 U.S. 504, 527, 104 L. Ed. 2d 557, 109 S. Ct. 1981 (1989) (Scalia, J., concurring).

The legislative history bearing on this issue is particularly persuasive. First, the FTDA's sponsors in both the House and the Senate were aware of the potential collision with the First Amendment if the statute authorized injunctions against protected speech. Upon introducing the counterpart bills, sponsors in each house explained that the proposed law "will not prohibit or threaten noncommercial expression, such as parody, satire, editorial and other forms of expression that are not a part of a commercial transaction." 141 Cong. Rec. S19306-10, S19310 (daily ed. Dec. 29, 1995) (statement of Sen. Hatch); 141 Cong. Rec. H14317-01, H14318 (daily ed. Dec. 12, 1995) (statement of Rep. Moorhead). The House Judiciary Committee agreed in its report on the FTDA. H.R. Rep. No. 104-374, at 4 (1995), reprinted in 1995 U.S.C.C.A.N. 1029, 1031 ("The bill will not prohibit or threaten 'noncommercial' expression, as that term has been defined by the courts.").

The FTDA's section-by-section analysis presented in the House and Senate suggests that the bill's sponsors relied on the "noncommercial use" exemption to allay First Amendment concerns. H.R. Rep. No. 104-374, at 8, reprinted in 1995 U.S.C.C.A.N. 1029, 1035 (the exemption "expressly incorporates the concept of 'commercial' speech from the 'commercial speech' doctrine, and proscribes dilution actions that seek to enjoin use of famous marks in 'non-commercial' uses (such as consumer product reviews)"); 141 Cong. Rec. S19306-10, S19311 (daily ed. Dec. 29, 1995) (the exemption "is consistent with existing case law[, which] recognizes that the use of marks in certain forms of artistic and expressive speech is protected by the First Amendment"). At the request of one of the bill's sponsors, the section-by-section analysis was printed in the Congressional Record. 141 Cong. Rec. S19306-10, S19311 (daily ed. Dec. 29, 1995). Thus, we know that this interpretation of the exemption was before the Senate when the FTDA was passed, and that no senator rose to dispute it.

To determine whether Barbie Girl falls within this exemption, we look to our definition of commercial speech under our First Amendment caselaw. See H.R. Rep. No. 104-374, at 8, reprinted in 1995 U.S.C.C.A.N. 1029, 1035 (the exemption "expressly incorporates the concept of 'commercial' speech from the 'commercial speech' doctrine"); 141 Cong. Rec. S19306-10, S19311 (daily ed. Dec. 29, 1995) (the exemption "is consistent with existing [First Amendment] case law"). "Although the boundary between commercial and noncommercial speech has yet to be clearly delineated, the 'core notion of commercial speech' is that it 'does no more than propose a commercial transaction.'" Hoffman v. Capital Cities/ABC, Inc., 255 F.3d 1180, 1184 (9th Cir. 2001) (quoting Bolger v. Youngs Drug Prods Corp., 463 U.S. 60, 66, 77 L. Ed. 2d 469, 103 S. Ct. 2875 (1983)). If speech is not "purely commercial" — that is, if it does more than propose a commercial transaction — then it is entitled to full First Amendment protection. 255 F.3d at 1185-86 (internal quotation marks omitted).

In Hoffman, a magazine published an article featuring digitally altered images from famous films. Computer artists modified shots of Dustin Hoffman, Cary Grant, Marilyn Monroe and others to put the actors in famous designers' spring fashions; a still of Hoffman from the movie "Tootsie" was altered so that he appeared to be wearing a Richard Tyler evening gown and Ralph Lauren heels. Hoffman, who had not given permission, sued under the Lanham Act and for violation of his right to publicity. Id. at 1183.

The article featuring the altered image clearly served a commercial purpose: "to draw attention to the for-profit magazine in which it appeared" and to sell more copies. Id. at 1186. Nevertheless, we held that the article was fully protected under the First Amendment because it included protected expression: "humor" and "visual and verbal editorial comment on classic films and famous actors." Id. at 1185 (internal quotation marks omitted). Because its commercial purpose was "inextricably entwined with [these] expressive elements," the article and accompanying photographs enjoyed full First Amendment protection. Id.

Hoffman controls: Barbie Girl is not purely commercial speech, and is therefore fully protected. To be sure, MCA used Barbie's name to sell copies of the song. However, as we've already observed, see pp. 10489-90 supra, the song also lampoons the Barbie image and comments humorously on the cultural values Aqua claims she represents. Use of the Barbie mark in the song Barbie Girl therefore falls within the noncommercial use exemption to the FTDA. For precisely the same reasons, use of the mark in the song's title is also exempted.

## V.

Mattel next argues that the district court erred in granting summary judgment for the foreign defendants on its unfair competition claim under the Paris Convention for the Protection of Industrial Property, Mar. 20, 1883, as revised at Stockholm, July 14, 1967, art. 10bis, 21 U.S.T. 1583, 1648, 828 U.N.T.S. 305, 337 (hereinafter Paris Convention). Mattel grounds its claim on Article 10bis, which provides that "the countries of the Union are bound to assure to nationals of such countries effective protection against unfair competition." Paris Convention, art. 10bis, 21 U.S.T. at 1648, 828 U.N.T.S. at 337. Mattel asserts that Article 10bis creates a federal cause of action for unfair competition in international disputes, and that section 44 of the Lanham Act, 15 U.S.C. § 1126, makes the substantive provisions of the Paris Convention available to United States nationals.

In Toho Co. v. Sears, Roebuck & Co., 645 F.2d 788, 790-92 (9th Cir. 1981), the Japanese producer and distributor of "Godzilla" asserted a claim against the manufacturer of "Bagzilla" garbage bags based on a "federal law of unfair competition." Subsection 44(b) gives to "persons whose country of origin is a party to any [trademark] convention or treaty … to which the United States is also a party" the benefits of section 44 to the extent necessary to give effect to the provisions of those treaties. 15 U.S.C. § 1126(b). These benefits include "effective protection against unfair competition." 15 U.S.C. § 1126(h). Thus, a foreign national is granted protection against unfair competition consistent with the protections of applicable trademark treaties.

However, we made clear in Toho that subsection 44(h) does not create a general federal law of unfair competition. See 645 F.2d at 792; see also Int'l Order of Job's Daughters v. Lindeburg & Co., 633 F.2d 912, 915-16, 916 n.5 (9th Cir. 1980). Rather, "the grant in subsection (h) of effective protection against unfair competition is tailored to the provisions of the unfair competition treaties by subsection (b), which extends the benefits of section 44 only to the extent necessary to give effect to the treaties." Toho, 645 F.2d at 792. Subsection 44(h) creates a federal right that is coextensive with the substantive provisions of the treaty involved. See id. Because the treaty involved in Toho required that Japanese corporations be treated as favorably as domestic companies with respect to unfair competition claims, we held that subsection 44(h) provided Toho with a federal forum in which to bring its state unfair competition claims. See id.

Subsection 44(i) goes no farther. It does not create a federal cause of action where subsection 44(h) would not, because it provides only that United States citizens "shall have the same benefits as are granted by this section to persons described in subsection (b) of this section." 15 U.S.C. § 1126(i). And, "so far as concerns 'unfair competition,' those 'benefits' are limited to such as may be found in some 'convention or treaty relating to ...the repression of unfair competition.' The purpose of [subsection 44(i)], [908] quite clearly, is no more than to extend to citizens and residents those 'benefits' that any 'convention or treaty' gives to aliens, including the same remedies for 'protection against unfair competition' that subsection (h) gives to aliens." Am. Auto. Ass'n v. Spiegel, 205 F.2d 771, 775 (2d Cir. 1953). The only protection against unfair competition that subsection 44(h) grants to foreign nationals, and that subsection 44(i) therefore grants to American citizens, is that "necessary to give effect to any provisions of [trademark treaties]." 15 U.S.C. § 1126(b). Therefore, Mattel's federal unfair competition claim depends on the extent to which the substantive provisions of the Paris Convention create one.

However, we've also held that "the Paris Convention was not intended to define the substantive law in the area of 'unfair competition' of the signatory countries." Kemart Corp. v. Printing Arts Research Labs., Inc., 269 F.2d 375, 389 (9th Cir. 1959). The Paris Convention does not provide substantive rights but ensures "national treatment." 4 McCarthy § 29:25. That is, it requires that "foreign nationals ...be given the same treatment in each of the member countries as that country makes available to its own citizens." Vanity Fair Mills v. T. Eaton, 234 F.2d 633, 640 (2d Cir. 1956).

Section 44 and the Paris Convention therefore interact as follows: A foreign national is entitled to the same "effective protection against unfair competition" to which an American is entitled, Paris Convention, art. 10bis, and in turn, the

American gets the same right that the foreign national gets. We treat Mattel like a foreign national, who is treated like an American under the Paris Convention. Accordingly, Mattel is entitled to assert a cause of action under the Lanham Act for trademark infringement, 15 U.S.C. § 1114, or for false designation of origin, 15 U.S.C. § 1125, or it may assert state law claims for unfair competition, as it did. See n.1 supra. But Mattel has no claim to a nonexistent federal cause of action for unfair competition. As said, the Paris Convention provides for national treatment, and does not define the substantive law of unfair competition. We therefore reject Mattel's argument that a treaty provision providing for "national treatment" gives it more protections against foreign nationals than it has against U.S. nationals.

## VI.

After Mattel filed suit, Mattel and MCA employees traded barbs in the press. When an MCA spokeswoman noted that each album included a disclaimer saying that Barbie Girl was a "social commentary [that was] not created or approved by the makers of the doll," a Mattel representative responded by saying, "That's unacceptable. ...It's akin to a bank robber handing a note of apology to a teller during a heist. [It ] neither diminishes the severity of the crime, nor does it make it legal." He later characterized the song as a "theft" of "another company's property."

MCA filed a counterclaim for defamation based on the Mattel representative's use of the words "bank robber," "heist," "crime" and "theft." But all of these are variants of the invective most often hurled at accused infringers, namely "piracy." No one hearing this accusation understands intellectual property owners to be saying that infringers are nautical cutthroats with eyepatches and peg legs who board galleons to plunder cargo. In context, all these terms are nonactionable "rhetorical hyperbole," Gilbrook v. City of Westminster, 177 F.3d 839, 863 (9th Cir. 1999). The parties are advised to chill.

AFFIRMED.

---

The circuit opinion was written by Kuzinski, C.J.; the plaintiff is a famous toy company that is attempting to protect the trademark of its equally famous doll, Barbie, by a musical parody, "Barbie Girl," by the Danish rock and roll band, Aqua. The Barbie doll has, of course, become a legitimate cultural icon. Mattel brought suit against the foreign and domestic musical companies that produced, marketed, and sold the song. The court of appeals found against Mattel since the song's title was relevant to the underlying work and the song did not suggest that the song was created by the toy company. Since the song was not purely commercial speech, it was fully protected by the First Amendment. The song's use of the doll's mark fell within the noncommercial use exception to the Federal Trademark Dilution Act. The "offensive" lyrics?—"I'm a Barbie girl, in my Barbie world. Life in plastic, it's fantastic. You can brush my hair, undress me anywhere. . . I'm a blonde bimbo girl in a fantasy world. . ."

McCollum v. CBS
Copy Citation
Court of Appeal of California, Second Appellate District, Division Three
July 12, 1988
No. B025565
202 Cal. App. 3d 989

Plaintiffs, Jack McCollum, Geraldine Lugenbuehl, Estate of John Daniel McCollum, Jack McCollum, administrator (hereinafter plaintiffs) appeal from an order of dismissal following the sustaining of a demurrer without leave to amend. The defendants John "Ozzy" Osbourne (Osbourne), CBS Records and CBS, Incorporated (hereinafter collectively CBS), Jet Records, Bob Daisley, Randy Rhoads, Essex Music International, Ltd., and Essex Music International Incorporated, composed, performed, produced and distributed certain recorded music which plaintiffs claim proximately resulted in the suicide of their decedent.

(See fn. 2.) As we conclude that plaintiffs' pleading (1) fails to allege any basis for overcoming the bar of the First Amendment's guarantee of free speech and expression and, in any event, (2) fails to allege sufficient facts to show any intentional or negligent invasion of plaintiffs' rights, we affirm.

## Factual and Procedural Background

On October 26, 1984, the plaintiffs' decedent, John Daniel McCollum (John), shot and killed himself while lying on his bed listening to Osbourne's recorded music. John was 19 years old at the time, and had a problem with alcohol abuse as well as serious emotional problems. Alleging that Osbourne's music was a proximate cause of John's suicide, plaintiffs filed suit against all of the named defendants.

The original complaint was filed on October 25, 1985, and, before an appearance by any defendant, was followed by the first amended complaint on December 4, 1985. Plaintiffs alleged claims which were based on theories of negligence, product liability and intentional misconduct. On August 7, 1986, the court sustained general demurrers to all causes of action without leave to amend, but granted plaintiffs permission to file, within 60 days, a motion for leave to file a second amended complaint. That motion was made and, on December 19, 1986, was denied. On the same date, the court signed the order of dismissal (based on its ruling of Aug. 7, 1986) from which the plaintiffs now appeal.

In the trial court's view, the First Amendment was an absolute bar to plaintiffs' claims. Nonetheless, the court did invite plaintiffs to seek leave to file a further pleading to see if that hurdle could be overcome. A proposed second amended complaint was submitted and the court made its final decision based on those allegations. For that reason, we here treat such proposed pleading as the operative one before us and assume that it states plaintiffs' case in its strongest light. In accordance with well-settled principles, we likewise assume those allegations to be true. (Baldwin v. Zoradi (1981) 123 Cal.App.3d 275, 278 [176 Cal.Rptr. 809]; Droz v. Pacific National Ins. Co. (1982) 138 Cal.App.3d 181, 182 [188 Cal.Rptr. 10].) They reflect the following facts.

On Friday night, October 26, 1984, John listened over and over again to certain music recorded by Osbourne. He listened repeatedly to side one of an album called, "Blizzard of Oz" and side two of an album called, "Diary of a Madman." These albums were found the next morning stacked on the turntable of the family stereo in the living room. John preferred to listen there because the sound was more intense. However, he had gone into his bedroom and was using a set of headphones to listen to the final side of the two-record album, "Speak of the Devil" when he placed a .22-caliber handgun next to his right temple and took his own life. When he was found the next morning he was still wearing his headphones and the stereo was still running with the arm and needle riding in the center of the revolving record.

Plaintiffs allege that Osbourne is well known as the "mad man" of rock and roll and has become a cult figure. The words and music of his songs and even the album covers for his records seem to demonstrate a preoccupation with unusual, antisocial and even bizarre attitudes and beliefs often emphasizing such things as satanic worship or emulation, the mocking of religious beliefs and death. The message he has often conveyed is that life is filled with nothing but despair and hopelessness and suicide is not only acceptable, but desirable. Plaintiffs further allege that all of the defendants, through their efforts with the media, press releases and the promotion of Osbourne's records, have sought to cultivate this image and to profit from it.

Osbourne in his music sought to appeal to an audience which included troubled adolescents and young adults who were having a difficult time during this transition period of their life; plaintiffs allege that this specific target group was extremely susceptible to the external influence and directions from a cult figure such as Osbourne who had become a role model and leader for many of them. Osbourne and CBS knew that many of the members of such group were trying to cope with issues involving self-identity, alienation, spiritual confusion and even substance abuse.

Plaintiffs allege that a "special relationship" of kinship existed between Osbourne and his avid fans. This relationship was underscored and characterized by the personal manner in which the lyrics were directed and disseminated to the listeners. He often sings in the first person about himself and about what may be some of the listener's problems, directly addressing the listener as "you." That is, a listener could feel that Osbourne was talking directly to him as he listened to the music.

One of the songs which John had been listening to on the family stereo before he went to his bedroom was called "Suicide Solution" which, plaintiffs allege, preaches that "suicide is the only way out." Included in a 28-second instrumental break in the song are some "masked" lyrics (which are not included in the lyrics printed on the album cover):

"Ah know people
You really know where it's at
You got it
Why try, why try
Get the gun and try it
Shoot, shoot, shoot" (this line
was repeated for about 10 seconds).

These lyrics are sung at one and one-half times the normal rate of speech and (in the words of plaintiffs' allegations) "are not immediately intelligible. They are perceptible enough to be heard and understood when the listener concentrates on the music and lyrics being played during this 28-second interval." In addition to the lyrics, plaintiffs also allege that Osbourne's music utilizes a strong, pounding and driving rhythm and, in at least one instance, a "hemisync" process of sound waves which impact the listener's mental state.

Following these general allegations, plaintiffs allege that the defendants knew, or should have known, that it was foreseeable that the music, lyrics and hemisync tones of Osbourne's music would influence the emotions and behavior of individual listeners such as John who, because of their emotional instability, were peculiarly susceptible to such music, lyrics and tones and that such individuals might be influenced to act in a manner destructive to their person or body. Plaintiffs further allege that defendants negligently disseminated Osbourne's music to the public and thereby (1) aided, advised or encouraged John to commit suicide (count I) or (2) created "an uncontrollable impulse" in him to commit suicide (count II); and that John, as a proximate result of listening to such music did commit suicide on October 26, 1984.

In the remaining two counts, plaintiffs allege, respectively, that defendants' conduct constituted (1) an incitement of John to commit suicide (count III) and (2) an intentional aiding, advising or encouraging of suicide in violation of Penal Code section 401 (count IV). In all four counts plaintiffs allege that defendants acted maliciously and oppressively and thus are liable for punitive damages.

## Contentions of the Parties

Plaintiffs argue that Osbourne's music and lyrics were the proximate cause of John's suicide and are not entitled to protection under the First Amendment. They seek recovery here on three separate theories. They claim that Osbourne and CBS (1) were negligent in the dissemination of Osbourne's recorded music, (2) intentionally disseminated that music with knowledge that it would produce an uncontrollable impulse to self-destruction in persons like John and (3) intentionally aided, advised or encouraged John's suicide in violation of Penal Code section 401, thus giving plaintiffs, as members of a group intended to be protected by that statute, a right of action for civil damages.

Defendants' initial and primary response is that plaintiffs' entire action, irrespective of the theory of recovery, is barred by the First Amendment's guarantee of free speech. In addition, they argue that the public dissemination of Osbourne's recorded music did not, as a matter of law, negligently or intentionally invade any right of plaintiffs or constitute a violation of Penal Code section 401.

## Discussion

### 1. The First Amendment Bars Plaintiffs' Action

Our consideration of plaintiffs' novel attempt to seek postpublication damages for the general public dissemination of recorded music and lyrics must commence "with [the] recognition of the overriding constitutional principle that material communicated by the public media . . . [including artistic expressions such as the music and lyrics here involved], is generally to be accorded protection under the First Amendment to the Constitution of the United States. ( Joseph Burstyn, Inc. v. Wilson (1952) 343 U.S. 495, 501 [96 L.Ed. 1098, 72 S.Ct. 777] []; Winters v. New York Co. (1948) 333 U.S. 507, 510 [92 L.Ed. 840, 68 S.Ct. 665] [].)" ( Olivia N. v. National Broadcasting Co. (1977) 74 Cal.App.3d 383, 387 [141 Cal.Rptr. 511] [Olivia I].) "First Amendment rights are accorded a preferred place in our democratic society. ( Thomas v. Collins (1945) 323 U.S. 516, 530 [89 L.Ed. 430, 440, 65 S.Ct. 315].) First Amendment protection extends to a communication, to its source and to its recipients. ( Va. Pharmacy Bd. v. Va. Consumer Council (1976) 425 U.S. 748, 756 [48 L.Ed.2d 346, 354, 96 S.Ct. 1817].) '[Above] all else, the First Amendment means that government has no power to restrict expression because of its message, its ideas, its subject matter, or its content.' ( Police Department of Chicago v. Mosley (1972) 408 U.S. 92, 95 [33 L.Ed.2d 212, 216, 92 S.Ct. 2286]; see Consolidated Edison v. Public Serv. Comm'n (1980) 447 U.S. 530, 538-539 [65 L.Ed.2d 319, 328-329, 100 S.Ct. 2326]; Carey v. Brown (1980) 447 U.S. 455, 462-463 [65 L.Ed.2d 263, 270-271, 100 S.Ct. 2286];

Cohen v. California (1971) 403 U.S. 15, 24 [29 L.Ed.2d 284, 293, 91 S.Ct. 1780]; New York Times Co. v. Sullivan (1964) 376 U.S. 254, 269-270 [11 L.Ed.2d 686, 700-701, 84 S.Ct. 710, 95 A.L.R.2d 1412].) Applied to the electronic media, the First Amendment means that it is the broadcaster that has authority to make programming decisions.     (Writers Guild of America, West, Inc. v. F. C. C. (C.D.Cal. 1976) 423 F.Supp. 1064, 1154.)" ( Olivia N. v. National Broadcasting Co. (1981) 126 Cal.App.3d 488, 492-493 [178 Cal.Rptr. 888] [Olivia II].)

First Amendment guaranties of freedom of speech and expression extend to all artistic and literary expression, whether in music, concerts, plays, pictures or books. (Schad v. Mount Ephraim (1981) 452 U.S. 61, 65 [68 L.Ed.2d 671, 101 S.Ct. 2176] (nonobscene nude dancing).) As the court in Schad noted, "Entertainment, as well as political and ideological speech, is protected; motion pictures, programs broadcast by radio and television, and live entertainment, such as musical and dramatic works, fall within the First Amendment guarantee." (Ibid.) "[Music] is a form of expression that is protected by the first amendment." (Cinevision Corp. v. City of Burbank (9th Cir. 1984) 745 F.2d 560, 567, cert. denied, 471 U.S. 1054 [85 L.Ed.2d 480, 105 S.Ct. 2115].)

"'[The] life of the imagination and intellect is of comparable import to the presentation of the political process; the First Amendment reaches beyond protection of citizen participation in, and ultimate control over, governmental affairs and protects in addition the interest in free interchange of ideas and impressions for their own sake, for whatever benefit the individual may gain.'" (Spiritual Psychic Science Church v. City of Azusa (1985) 39 Cal.3d 501, 512 [217 Cal.Rptr. 225, 703 P.2d 1119].) The rights protected are not only those of the artist to give free rein to his creative expression, but also those of the listener to receive that expression. (See Va. Pharmacy Bd. v. Va. Consumer Council (1976) 425 U.S. 748, 756 [48 L.Ed.2d 346, 354-355, 96 S.Ct. 1817].) "[The] central concern of the First Amendment . . . is that there be a free flow from creator to audience of whatever message a film or book might convey. . . . [The] central First Amendment concern remains the need to maintain free access of the public to the expression." (Young v. American Mini Theatres (1976) 427 U.S. 50, 77 [49 L.Ed.2d 310, 96 S.Ct. 2440], conc. opn. of Powell, J.)

However, the freedom of speech guaranteed by the First Amendment is not absolute. There are certain limited classes of speech which may be prevented or punished by the state consistent with the principles of the First Amendment: (1) obscene speech is not protected by the First Amendment. (Miller v. California (1973) 413 U.S. 15, 23, 34-35 [37 L.Ed.2d 419, 430, 436-437, 93 S.Ct. 2607], rehg. den., 414 U.S. 881 [38 L.Ed.2d 128, 94 S.Ct. 26]); (2) "libel, slander, misrepresentation, obscenity, perjury, false advertising, solicitation of crime, complicity by encouragement, conspiracy, and the like" are also outside the scope of constitutional protection. (Konigsberg v. State Bar (1961) 366 U.S. 36, 49, fn. 10 [6 L.Ed.2d 105, 116, 81 S.Ct. 997]); (3) the constitutional freedom for speech and press does not immunize "speech or writing used as an integral part of conduct in violation of a valid criminal statute." (Giboney v. Empire Storage Co. (1949) 336 U.S. 490, 498 [93 L.Ed. 834, 841, 69 S.Ct. 684]); and finally, (4) speech which is directed to inciting or producing imminent lawless action, and which is likely to incite or produce such action, is outside the scope of First Amendment protection. (Brandenburg v. Ohio (1969) 395 U.S. 444, 447-448 [23 L.Ed.2d 430, 433-434, 89 S.Ct. 1827].)

Plaintiffs argue that it is the last of these exceptions, relating to culpable incitement, which removes Osbourne's music from the protection of the First Amendment.

This issue is properly addressed on demurrer since the question of whether his music falls within the category of unprotected speech is one of law where, as is the case here, the facts are undisputed. (L. A. Teachers Union v. L. A. City Bd. of Ed. (1969) 71 Cal.2d 551, 556 [78 Cal.Rptr. 723, 455 P.2d 827]; Johnson v. County of Santa Clara (1973) 31 Cal.App.3d 26, 32 [106 Cal.Rptr. 862].)

It is settled that ". . . the constitutional guarantees of free speech and free press do not permit a State to forbid or proscribe advocacy of the use of force or of law violation except where such advocacy is directed to inciting or producing imminent lawless action and is likely to incite or produce such action." (Brandenburg v. Ohio, supra, 395 U.S. 444, 447 [23 L.Ed.2d 430, 434, 89 S.Ct. 1827]. Thus, to justify a claim that speech should be restrained or punished because it is (or was) an incitement to lawless action, the court must be satisfied that the speech (1) was directed or intended toward the goal of producing imminent lawless conduct and (2) was likely to produce such imminent conduct. Speech directed to action at some indefinite time in the future will not satisfy this test. (Hess v. Indiana (1973) 414 U.S. 105, 108 [38 L.Ed.2d 303, 94 S.Ct. 326].)

In the context of this case we must conclude, in order to find a culpable incitement, (1) that Osbourne's music was directed and intended toward the goal of bringing about the imminent suicide of listeners and (2) that it was likely to produce such a result. It is not enough that John's suicide may have been the result of an unreasonable reaction to the music; it must have been a specifically intended consequence. (Braxton v. Municipal Court (1973) 10 Cal.3d 138, 148 [109 Cal.Rptr. 897, 514 P.2d 697].)

We can find no such intent or likelihood here. Apart from the "unintelligible" lyrics quoted above from "Suicide Solution," to which John admittedly was not even listening at the time of his death, there is nothing in any of Osbourne's songs which could be characterized as a command to an immediate suicidal act. None of the lyrics relied upon by plaintiffs, even accepting their literal interpretation of the words, purport to order or command anyone to any concrete action at any specific time, much less immediately. Moreover, as defendants point out, the lyrics of the song on which plaintiffs focus their primary objection can as easily be viewed as a poetic device, such as a play on words, to convey meanings entirely contrary to those asserted by plaintiffs. We note this here not to suggest a reliance upon a construction which is contrary to plaintiffs' allegations, but to illuminate the very serious problems which can arise when litigants seek to cast judges in the role of censor.

Merely because art may evoke a mood of depression as it figuratively depicts the darker side of human nature does not mean that it constitutes a direct "incitement to imminent violence." The lyrics sung by Osbourne may well express a philosophical view that suicide is an acceptable alternative to a life that has become unendurable — an idea which, however unorthodox, has a long intellectual tradition. If that is the view expressed, as plaintiffs apparently contend, then defendants are constitutionally free to advocate it. Plaintiffs' argument that speech may be punished on the ground it has a tendency to lead to suicide or other violence is precisely the doctrine rejected by the Supreme Court in Hess v. Indiana, supra, 414 U.S. at pp. 107-109 [38 L.Ed.2d at pp. 306-307] (the words "We'll take the f   g street again (or later)," shouted to a crowd at an antiwar demonstration, amounted to "nothing more than advocacy of illegal action at some indefinite future time"; words could not be punished as "incitement" on the ground that they had a ""'"tendency to lead to violence"'"").

Moreover, musical lyrics and poetry cannot be construed to contain the requisite "call to action" for the elementary reason that they simply are not intended to be and should not be read literally on their face, nor judged by a standard of prose oratory. Reasonable persons understand musical lyrics and poetic conventions as the figurative expressions which they are. No rational person would or could believe otherwise nor would they mistake musical lyrics and poetry for literal commands or directives to immediate action. To do so would indulge a fiction which neither common sense nor the First Amendment will permit.

While we have found no California case dealing directly with recorded music and lyrics, the claim that certain fictional depictions in the film or electronic media have incited unlawful conduct, and should result in the imposition of tort liability, is by no means novel. However, all such claims have been rejected on First Amendment grounds. (See Olivia I and Olivia II (plaintiff was attacked and "artificially raped" with a bottle by persons who had recently seen and discussed similar scenes in the television film, "Born Innocent"); Bill v. Superior Court, supra 137 Cal.App.3d 1002 (plaintiff shot outside a theater showing a violent movie made by defendants which allegedly attracted violence-prone individuals who were likely to injure members of the general public at or near the theater); DeFilippo v. National Broadcasting Co. Inc. (R.I. 1982) 446 A.2d 1036 (plaintiffs' son died attempting to imitate a "hanging stunt" which he saw on television); Walt Disney Productions Inc. v. Shannon (1981) 247 Ga. 402 [276 S.E.2d. 580, 20 A.L.R.4th 321] (plaintiff partially blinded when he attempted to reproduce some sound effects demonstrated on television by rotating a lead pellet around in an inflated balloon); Zamora v. Columbia Broadcasting System (S.D.Fla. 1979) 480 F.Supp. 199 (minor plaintiff had become so addicted to and desensitized by television violence that he developed a sociopathic personality and as a result shot and killed an 83-year-old neighbor).

Plaintiffs, recognizing the dearth of case authority which would support their incitement theory, make essentially a procedural argument. They contend that the court cannot determine the question of whether Osbourne's music and lyrics constituted an incitement but rather the issue should be left to a jury. They rely on Olivia I, 74 Cal.App.3d 383, 389-390, where the court, in the first of two appellate decisions dealing with the film "Born Innocent," held that the trial judge, on the day assigned for jury trial and without any summary judgment motion pending, should not have viewed the film himself and made fact findings that the film did not advocate or encourage violent or depraved acts. The plaintiff had requested a trial by jury and was entitled to one.

However, plaintiffs' reliance on this case is misplaced. We view it as strictly a procedural decision dealing with the technical rights of a party after a proper request for a jury trial has been made. The First Amendment issue was never reached and the appellate opinion itself acknowledged that the court could have accomplished the same result if a properly noticed summary judgment motion had been before it. To the extent that any broader interpretation is given to Olivia I, we respectfully decline to follow it in this case.

In our view, the plaintiffs have fully pleaded the facts which will be presented on the issue of incitement and we conclude that, as a matter of law, they fail to meet the Brandenburg standard for incitement and that therefore Osbourne's music is speech protected by the First Amendment.

The scope of such protection is not limited to merely serving as a bar to the prior restraint of such speech, but also prevents the assertion of a claim for civil damages. "[The] fear of damage awards . . . may be markedly more inhibiting than the fear of prosecution under a criminal statute." (New York Times Co. v. Sullivan (1964) 376 U.S. 254, 277 [11 L.Ed.2d 686, 705, 84 S.Ct. 710].) Musical composers and performers, as well as record producers and distributors, would become significantly more inhibited in the selection of controversial materials if liability for civil damages were a risk to be endured for publication of protected speech. The deterrent effect of subjecting the music and recording industry to such liability because of their programming choices would lead to a self-censorship which would dampen the vigor and limit the variety of artistic expression. Thus, the imposition here of postpublication civil damages, in the absence of an incitement to imminent lawless action, would be just as violative of the First Amendment as a prior restraint.

2. The First Amendment Bar Aside, Plaintiffs Have Alleged No Basis for Recovery of Damages

a. Defendants Cannot Be Liable in Negligence as They Owed No Duty to Plaintiffs

The threshold and, in this case, dispositive question with respect to the assertion of a claim for negligence is whether any duty was owed to the plaintiffs. This is primarily a question of law (Weirum v. RKO General, Inc. (1975) 15 Cal.3d 40, 46 [123 Cal.Rptr. 468, 539 P.2d 36]) which is determined by an examination of several factors. Those factors include "the foreseeability of harm to the plaintiff, the degree of certainty that plaintiff suffered injury, the closeness of the connection between the defendant's conduct and the injury suffered, the moral blame attached to the defendant's conduct, the policy of preventing future harm, the extent of the burden to the defendant and the consequences to the community of imposing a duty to exercise care with resulting liability for breach, and the availability, cost, and prevalence of insurance for the risk involved." (Rowland v. Christian (1968) 69 Cal.2d 108, 113 [70 Cal.Rptr. 97, 443 P.2d 561, 32 A.L.R.3d 496]; Peterson v. San Francisco Community College Dist. (1984) 36 Cal.3d 799, 806 [205 Cal.Rptr. 842, 685 P.2d 1193].)

Foreseeability is one of several factors to be weighed in determining whether a duty is owed in a particular case. (Isaacs v. Huntington Memorial Hospital (1985) 38 Cal.3d 112, 125 [211 Cal.Rptr. 356, 695 P.2d 653].) "'In this balancing process, foreseeability is an elastic factor. [Citation.] The degree of foreseeability necessary to warrant the finding of a duty will thus vary from case to case. For example, in cases where the burden of preventing future harm is great, a high degree of foreseeability may be required. [Citation.] On the other hand, in cases where there are strong policy reasons for preventing the harm, or the harm can be prevented by simple means, a lesser degree of foreseeability may be required. [Citation.]'" ( Id., at p. 125.) Here, a very high degree of foreseeability would be required because of the great burden on society of preventing the kind of "harm" of which plaintiffs complain by restraining or punishing artistic expression. The "countervailing policies" which arise out of the First Amendment "have substantial bearing upon the issue whether there should be imposed upon [defendants] the exposure to liability of the kind for which plaintiffs contend." (Bill v. Superior Court, supra 137 Cal.App.3d 1002, 1013.)

Plaintiffs rely on Weirum for the proposition that harm to John from listening to Osbourne's music was foreseeable. In that case, a radio station was held liable for the wrongful death of a motorist killed by two speeding teenagers participating in the station's promotional giveaway contest. In live periodic announcements the station advised its mobile listeners that one of its disc jockeys, "the Real Don Steele," was traveling from location to location in a conspicuous red automobile and advised the audience of his intended destinations. The first listener to meet Steele at each location would get a prize. While following Steele's car, the two teenagers forced a motorist into the center divider where his car overturned resulting in his death. (Weirum v. RKO General Inc., supra, 15 Cal.3d at pp. 44-45.)

In our view, plaintiffs' reliance on Weirum is not justified. As the court there noted, the issue was "civil accountability for the foreseeable results of a broadcast which created an undue risk of harm to decedent. The First Amendment does not sanction the infliction of physical injury merely because achieved by word, rather than act." (Id., at p. 48.) Indeed, it would not be inappropriate to view the reckless importuning in Weirum as a specie of incitement to imminent lawless conduct for which no First Amendment protection is justified. What the conduct in Weirum and culpable incitement have in common, when viewed from the perspective of a duty analysis, is a very high degree of foreseeability of undue risk of harm to others. Under such circumstances, imposition of negligence liability does not offend the First Amendment.

The court, in Olivia II, placed Weirum in its proper perspective when it stated, in language equally applicable here, "[although] the language utilized by the Supreme Court was broad, it must be understood in light of the particular facts of that case. The radio station's broadcast was designed to encourage its youthful listeners to be the first to arrive at a particular location in order to win a prize and gain momentary glory. The Weirum broadcasts actively and repeatedly encouraged listeners to speed to announced locations. Liability was imposed on the broadcaster for urging listeners to act in an inherently dangerous manner." (Id., at p. 496.) That they were very likely to do so was clearly foreseeable. Not so here. Osbourne's music and lyrics had been recorded and produced years before. There was not a "real time" urging of listeners to act in a particular manner. There was no dynamic interaction with, or live importuning of, particular listeners.

While it is true that foreseeability is ordinarily a question of fact (Bigbee v. Pacific Tel. & Tel. Co. (1983) 34 Cal.3d 49, 56 [192 Cal.Rptr. 857, 665 P.2d 947]), it may be decided as a question of law if "'under the disputed facts there is no room for a reasonable difference of opinion.'" (Id., at p. 56.) This is such a case. John's tragic self-destruction, while listening to Osbourne's music, was not a reasonably foreseeable risk or consequence of defendants' remote artistic activities.

Plaintiffs' case is not aided by an examination of the other factors which are a part of the duty analysis. It cannot be said that there was a close connection between John's death and defendants' composition, performance, production and distribution years earlier of recorded artistic musical expressions. Likewise, no moral blame for that tragedy may be laid at defendants' door. John's suicide, an admittedly irrational response to Osbourne's music, was not something which any of the defendants intended, planned or had any reason to anticipate. Finally, and perhaps most significantly, it is simply not acceptable to a free and democratic society to impose a duty upon performing artists to limit and restrict their creativity in order to avoid the dissemination of ideas in artistic speech which may adversely affect emotionally troubled individuals. Such a burden would quickly have the effect of reducing and limiting artistic expression to only the broadest standard of taste and acceptance and the lowest level of offense, provocation and controversy. No case has ever gone so far. We find no basis in law or public policy for doing so here.

b. There Are No Allegations That Defendants Intended to Cause John's Suicide

The third and fourth alleged causes of action are essentially identical. They each rely upon the proposition that defendants incur intentional tort liability for John's suicide because of their intentional dissemination of Osbourne's recorded music with the alleged knowledge that it would result in self-destructive reactions among certain individuals. The third count characterizes this as an intentional incitement to suicide. We have already discussed in some detail why Osbourne's music and lyrics cannot be condemned as an incitement to imminent lawless action. It is also clear that plaintiffs have not adequately alleged a culpable intent. For example, there are no allegations that defendants actually intended any harm to John or any other listener.

It is not sufficient simply to allege that defendants intentionally did a particular act. It must also be shown that such act was done with the intent to cause injury. (Tate v. Canonica (1960) 180 Cal.App.2d 898, 909 [5 Cal.Rptr. 28].) In other words, plaintiffs would have to allege that defendants intended to cause John's (or some other listener's) suicide and made the subject recorded music available for that purpose. It is clear that no such allegation can be made in this case. What plaintiffs have alleged does not demonstrate the requisite intent.

The same analysis applies to plaintiffs' allegations (in count IV) regarding the violation of Penal Code section 401. Our Supreme Court has construed that section as proscribing the direct aiding and abetting of a specific suicidal act. The statute "contemplates some participation in the events leading up to the commission of the final overt act, such as furnishing the means for bringing about the death — the gun, the knife, the poison, or providing the water, for the person who himself commits the act of self-murder." (In re Joseph G. (1983) 34 Cal.3d 429, 436 [194 Cal. Rptr. 163, 667 P.2d 1176, 40 A.L.R.4th 690].) While this decision was rendered in the context of distinguishing those circumstances when a criminal defendant should be charged with murder instead of the lesser crime of aiding and abetting a suicide, we see no reason to give less weight here to the court's analysis. Some active and intentional participation in the events leading to the suicide are required in order to establish a violation.

To satisfy the burden of section 401, defendants would have to (1) have specifically intended John's suicide and (2) have had a direct participation in bringing it about. Plaintiffs' allegations that defendants intentionally produced and distributed Osbourne's music do not demonstrate that they intentionally aided or encouraged John's suicide. It is not sufficient to allege, as plaintiffs do here, that defendants "intentionally disseminated" Osbourne's music to the general public although they knew, or should have known, that there were emotionally fragile people who could have an adverse reaction to it.

In the absence of evidence of the requisite intent and participation, Penal Code section 401 cannot be applied to composers, performers, producers and distributors of recorded works of artistic expression disseminated to the general public which allegedly have an adverse emotional impact on some listeners or viewers who thereafter take their own lives.

### Conclusion

Absent an incitement, which meets the standards of Brandenburg v. Ohio, supra, 395 U.S. 444, 447 [23 L.Ed.2d 430, 433-434], the courts have been universally reluctant to impose tort liability upon any public media for self-destructive or tortious acts alleged to have resulted from a publication or broadcast (see, e.g., Olivia II, supra, 126 Cal.App.3d 488; Bill v. Superior Court, supra, 137 Cal.App.3d 1002; DeFilippo v. National Broadcasting Co. Inc., supra, 446 A.2d 1036; Walt Disney Productions Inc. v. Shannon, supra, 276 S.E.2d 580; Zamora v. Columbia Broadcasting System Inc., supra, 480 F.Supp. 199.) We share that reluctance and, for all of the reasons discussed above, conclude that the defendants, as a matter of law, have no liability for John's suicide.

The trial court was thus correct in bringing this action to a prompt end. "[Because] unnecessarily protracted litigation would have a chilling effect upon the exercise of First Amendment rights, speedy resolution of cases involving free speech is desirable. [Citation.]" (Good Government Group of Seal Beach, Inc. v. Superior Court (1978) 22 Cal.3d 672, 685 [150 Cal.Rptr. 258, 586 P.2d 572].)

The trial court's order of dismissal is affirmed. The defendants shall recover their costs on appeal.

The court could find no proximate cause between certain song lyrics and the suicide of a teenager. Under the First Amendment, plaintiffs were banned from bringing any cause of action based on the musician's speech on expression. The teenager's suicide was not reasonably foreseeable by defendants; there was no close connection between the teenager's death and defendant's composition, performance, production, and distribution of the music.

John Doe Entertainment
f/s/o John Doe
5524 Kruger Lane
Houston, Texas 77777

June 10, 2015

Joshua Doe Productions LLC
f/s/o Joshua Doe
9999 Bluebonnet Street
Houston, Texas 77777

Joshua Doe:

This letter, when signed by an authorized representative of John Doe Entertainment f/s/o John Doe ("Artist") and Joshua Doe (hereinafter collectively referred to as "Producer" or "you"), will constitute our agreement with respect to your furnishing the services of Producer to produce five (5) master recording(s) (the "Master(s)") embodying Artist's performance of the musical composition provisionally entitled "I Am John Doe", "John Doe Knows You", "John-Doe-licious", "Mighty John Doe", and "Amazing John Doe". Said Master(s) are being recorded in connection with the forthcoming record album (the "Album") to be delivered by Artist to Distributor pursuant to the exclusive recording agreement between Artist: and Distributor, as modified (the "Recording Agreement") and other uses thereof.

1.      **Services**

(a)      The term of this Agreement (the "Term") shall commence as of the date hereof and shall continue until the satisfactory completion of all your obligations hereunder. During the term, Producer shall render services to produce the Master pursuant to a production schedule designated by Artist after consultation with Producer.

(b)      All elements of the creation and production of the Master, including, without limitation, the compositions to be recorded and other individuals rendering services in connection with the Master(s) shall be selected by Artist, after consultation with Producer. Each Master shall be subject to the approval of Artist and Distributor as technically and commercially satisfactory for the manufacture and sale of phonograph records. At Artist's request, Producer shall re-record, re-edit, and or re-mix the master recording until a Master satisfactory to Artist and Distributor shall have been obtained. Producer shall perform such services as are customarily performed by producers in the recording industry, including, without limitation, engaging musicians, vocalists, conductors, contractors, arrangers and copyists, and arranging for the use of recording studios and other necessary technical facilities and personnel. Producer's services shall be rendered in a first-class, diligent and professional manner. With respect to recording sessions conducted by Producer and/or a person engaged and/or furnished by Producer, Producer shall be responsible for the preparation and submission of union forms and session reports to enable Artist and Distributor, as the case may be, to timely and properly complete and file all such documentation. Artist shall have the right to terminate your engagement hereunder in the event that Artist or the Distributor anticipate that the recording costs for the Master(s) will materially exceed the approved budget or that the Master(s) will not be technically and commercially satisfactory. Artist hereby acknowledges the Mater(s) as technically and commercially satisfactorily delivered.

2. **Recording Procedure**

(a) You shall cause Producer to:

(i)     Produce and record the Master;

(ii)     Deliver to Artist fully an edited and leadered stereophonic version of each Master technically and commercially satisfactory to Artist and the Distributor for the manufacture and sale of phonograph records. Upon Artist's request, Producer shall deliver to Artist and Distributor versions of each master which are edited for use on singles (other than so-called "specialty mixes"). All original session tapes and any derivatives, duplicates or reproductions thereof shall also be delivered to Distributor, or any other location designated by Distributor.

(iii)     With respect to Producer's contributions to the Master, deliver to Artist or Distributor all necessary licenses, approvals, consents, and permissions (excluding so called label waivers and/or side artist agreements). Notwithstanding the foregoing, mechanical licenses shall be delivered following commercial release upon Artist's and/or Distributor's request. Your submission of the Master(s) to Artist and Distributor shall constitute your representation that you have obtained all such materials; and

(iv)     With respect to recording sessions conducted by Producer and/or a person engaged and/or furnished by

Producer, obtain prior to each applicable recording session and deliver to Artist and/or Distributor within seventy-two (72) hours following each such recording session, a duly completed and executed Form 1-9 (or such similar or other forms as may be prescribed by the United States Immigration and Naturalization Service or other government agency regarding citizenship, permanent residency or so-called "documented worker" status) in respect of each individual employed to render recording services hereunder. Producer shall simultaneously obtain and deliver to Artist and/or Distributor true and complete copies of all evidentiary documents relating to the contents or subject matter of said forms. In the event you fail to comply with any of the foregoing requirements, Artist may deduct any resulting penalty payments from all monies payable to Producer under this Agreement.

(b)      Producer shall not enter into any agreements on Artist's or Distributor's behalf or incur, directly or indirectly, any liability or expense of any kind for which Artist or Distributor may be held liable, in connection with any recording session hereunder or otherwise, without having first obtained our written approval as to the nature, extent and limit thereof.

3.      **Recording Budget/Advances**

(a)      As full consideration for all of Producer's production services hereunder with respect to the Master(s) and all rights granted by Producer hereunder and conditioned upon your full performance of all of the material terms and conditions hereof, Artist will pay or cause to be paid to Producer a recoupable advance (the "Advance") of One Thousand Dollars ($1,000) per Master for a total Advance of Five Thousand Dollars ($5,000), of which full payment is due July 31, 2015.

(b)      All amounts paid to Producer pursuant to paragraph 3(a) hereof, as well as all monies paid by Artist to Producer, or on Producer's behalf with Producer's consent, during the term of this Agreement (other than royalties paid to Producer pursuant to paragraphs 4 and 7 hereof), shall constitute Advances hereunder and shall be recoupable from all royalties (excluding publishing royalties) payable to Producer under this Agreement.

4.      **Royalty**

(a)      As full and complete consideration for all of Producer's production services hereunder and all rights granted by Producer hereunder and conditioned upon Producer's full and faithful performance of all of the material terms and conditions hereof, Producer shall be entitled to a pro-rata royalty (pro-rated as provided below) of three percent (3%) wholesale (or the retail equivalent) for net sales through normal retail channels in the United States of Albums embodying the Master (as computed pursuant to the Recording Agreement).

(b)     The royalty rate payable to Producer shall be prorated and reduced (but not escalated unless otherwise provided herein) with respect to configurations, sales, exploitations and other uses of the Masters for which Artist is paid a prorated and/or reduced royalty rate under the Recording Agreement (e.g., singles, EP's, CD's, foreign sales, mid-line and budget records, records embodying the Master along with recordings other than the Master, etc.).

(c)     The royalty payable to Producer shall be calculated and computed on the same basis and in the same manner (e.g., definitions and applications of retail list price, percentage of sales on which royalties are payable, packaging deductions, "free goods", reserves, etc.) as Artist's royalty is calculated and computed under the Recording Agreement with Distributor; provided that with respect to sales or uses of the Master for which Artist receives a royalty which is computed as a percentage of Distributors net receipts, net monies, or the like, Producer's royalty hereunder in respect of such sale or use shall be equal to my royalty therefore multiplied by a fraction (the "Fraction"), the numerator of which is equal to your royalty rate as set forth in this paragraph, and the denominator of which is equal to Artist's basic "all-in" royalty rate for United States Normal Retail Channels Net Sales of top line albums ("USNRC"). The relevant provisions of the Recording Agreement are attached hereto as Exhibit B.

(d)     With respect to so-called audiovisual recordings embodying a Master produced hereunder ("Videos"), Producer shall be entitled to a royalty with respect to the commercial exploitation of the applicable Videos equal to one-half (1/2) of the amount determined by multiplying the total royalty payable to Artist with respect to such commercial exploitation of the applicable Video multiplied by the Fraction. Producer shall not be credited with any royalty in respect of a Video, unless and until the royalty credited to our account by Distributor in respect of such Video shall have exceeded all costs incurred in the production or acquisition of rights in respect of such Video, and following that point, your royalty for such Video shall be credited to your account on a prospective basis only.

(e)     As to records not consisting entirely of the Master produced hereunder, the royalty rate otherwise payable to Producer hereunder with respect to sales of any such record shall be prorated by multiplying such royalty rate by a fraction, the numerator of which is the number of Master(s) produced hereunder and embodied thereon and the denominator of which is the total number of royalty bearing masters embodied thereon (including the Master).

(f)     In the event the Master is produced by Producer with another producer to whom Distributor or Artist shall be obligated to pay a royalty, or in the event any other producer or mixer to whom Distributor or Artist shall be obligated to pay a royalty shall perform additional services with respect to the Master produced by Producer hereunder, then the royalty payable to Producer hereunder with respect to such Master shall be reduced by the royalty payable by Artist or Distributor, as applicable, to such other producer. Notwithstanding the foregoing, the Producer's Royalty shall not be reduced following the Delivery of the applicable Master unless such person was engaged and/or furnished by Producer.

(g)     Notwithstanding anything to the contrary contained in this Agreement, it is specifically understood and agreed that no royalties shall be payable to Producer hereunder unless and until Distributor has recouped all Recording Costs (excluding any in-pocket Advance to Artist or Artist's furnishing entity) incurred in connection with the Album from the "net artist" royalties (i.e., those royalties payable by Distributor to Artist excluding the royalties payable to all producers, engineers, mixers, and all other royalty participants including you) payable in respect of all of the masters recorded in respect of such Album. After recoupment of such Recording Costs **in** accordance with the preceding sentence, royalties shall be payable to Producer hereunder for all records sold for which royalties are payable, retroactively from the first such record sold, subject to recoupment from such royalties of all advances paid to Producer hereunder. For the avoidance of doubt, the producer advance shall be recouped once and that recoupment shall be as provided in this Paragraph 4(g).

5.    **Accountings**

(a)     Artist shall, pursuant to a letter of direction in our customary form (a copy of which is attached hereto as Exhibit "A"), use reasonable efforts to request that Distributor or its affiliate account and pay royalties directly to Producer. if Distributor fails or refuses so to account to Producer, then Artist shall render accountings, and pay any royalties due Producer, within thirty (30) days after Artist receives the applicable statement and payment from Distributor. All royalty statements and all other accounts rendered by Artist to you shall be binding upon Producer and not subject to any objection by Producer for any reason unless specific objection is in writing, stating the basis thereof, is given to Artist within thirty (30) months from the date such statement or accounting is due. Producer shall be foreclosed from maintaining any action, claim or proceeding against Artist in any forum or tribunal with respect to any statement or accounting due hereunder unless such action, claim or proceeding is commenced against Artist in a court of competent jurisdiction within one year (l ) after that thirty (30) month period. Producer shall have the right to appoint a Certified Public Accountant or attorney, who is not then currently engaged in an outstanding audit of Artist, to examine Artist's books and records relating to the sale of records hereunder provided that such examination shall take place at Artist's offices during normal business hours, on reasonable written notice, at your sole cost and expense. Such examination may be conducted only once with respect to any particular statement, and not more frequently than once in any calendar year. You shall cause your accountant to deliver a copy of the audit report to Artist within one (I) month after the completion of said accountant's examination of Artist's books and records. The rights granted herein to you constitute your sole right to examine Artist's books and records. For purposes of this paragraph 5(a), Artist shall be deemed conclusively to have rendered you each statement on the date prescribed in this paragraph 5(a) unless you notify Artist otherwise with respect to any particular statement within sixty (60) days after the date that Artist has failed to render that statement.

(b)     No royalties shall be payable to Producer on sales of phonograph records by any of Artist's or Distributor's licensees until payment on those sales has been received or credited against an advance previously received by Distributor (if Distributor is accounting to you directly) or by Artist (if Artist is accounting to you) in the United States. Sales by a licensee shall be deemed to have occurred in the semi-annual accounting period during which that licensee shall have rendered to Distributor (if applicable) or Artist accounting statements and payments for those sales. If Artist (or Distributor, if applicable) is unable, for reasons beyond its control, to receive payment for such sales in United States Dollars in the United States, royalties therefore shall not be credited to your account during the continuance of such inability; if any accounting rendered to you hereunder during the continuance of such inability requires the payment of royalties to you, Artist (or Distributor, if applicable) will, at your request and if Artist (or Distributor) is able to do so, deposit such royalties to your credit in such foreign currency in a foreign depository, at your direction and expense.

(c)     You hereby authorize and direct Artist to withhold from any monies due you hereunder any portion thereof required to he withheld by the United States Internal Revenue Service and/or any other governmental authority, if any, and to pay same to the United States Internal Revenue Service and/or such other authority, if required.

6. **Credit**

(a) Subject to your compliance with your material obligations hereunder, Artist shall use reasonable efforts to instruct Distributor to accord Producer an appropriate credit as to your producer services in connection with the Masters in substantially the following form:

(b)

"I Am John Doe" and "John Doe Knows You"
"Produced by Joshua Doe for Joshua Doe Productions."

Provided that with respect to the Masters currently entitled I Am John Doe", "John Doe Knows You", "John-Doe-licious", "Mighty John Doe", and "Amazing John Doe" the credit shall be in substantially the following form:

"Produced by Joshua Doe for Joshua Doe Productions"

Such credit shall appear on the liner notes and/or back cover of all reproductions of the Master(s) (to the extent same comports with Distributor's then customary practices and policies to do so), and all one-half (1/2) page or larger trade ads placed by Artist or under our or Artist's control, including without limitation, in so-called <u>Billboard</u> strip ads, which solely relate to the Master(s).

(c) Artist's inadvertent non-repetitive failure to comply with our obligations under this paragraph 6(a) shall not be deemed a breach hereof. The failure of Distributor to comply with Artist's instructions pursuant to this paragraph 6(a) shall not be deemed a breach hereof. Upon written notice from Producer, Artist shall use reasonable efforts to have any such failure corrected on a prospective basis.

7. **Mechanical Licenses**

(a) Producer hereby warrants and represents that the composition to be recorded hereunder is written, owned or controlled, in whole or in part, by Producer or an entity owned or controlled by, or affiliated with, you. The composition recorded hereunder shall be referred to herein as the "Controlled Composition."

(b) Producer hereby grants to Distributor and its designees in perpetuity an irrevocable license under copyright to use the Controlled Composition on the same terms and conditions and at the same rates, including, without limitation, aggregate mechanical "caps" and reduced rates for non-full priced Album sales, as are applicable pursuant to the relevant portions of the Recording Agreement attached hereto as Exhibit B.

(c)     Producer also grants to Distributor and its designees in perpetuity an irrevocable license under copyright to reproduce the Controlled Compositions in audiovisual works, to reproduce those audiovisual works, distribute them, and perform them in any manner, to manufacture and distribute audiovisual records and other copies of them, and to exploit them otherwise, by any method and in any form known now or in the future, throughout the world, and to authorize others to do so, all upon the same terms and conditions and at the same rates as are applicable pursuant to the Recording Agreement to compositions written solely by Artist.

(d)     With respect to your contributions to the Controlled Composition(s) and the Master(s), if any composition is recorded which is not a Controlled Composition you warrant and represent that Artist or Distributor shall be able to obtain mechanical licenses therefor for the United States at rates and on terms no less favorable to Artist than those contained in the then-current standard license form then being utilized by The Harry Fox Agency, Inc.

The signatories hereto, each for themselves, acknowledge that they (or their respective publishing designees), shall each have the separate right to administer and exploit their respective interests and shares in the compositions recorded hereunder on their own behalf and/or on behalf of their affiliated writers.

(e)     Upon our request, you shall execute or cause your publishing designee to execute and deliver to Artist all documents required by Artist to effectuate the purposes of this paragraph 7.

8.     **Embodied Copyrighted Materials**

(a)     With respect to Producer's contributions to the Mater(s) and those of persons and/or entities engaged and/or furnished by Producer, Producer represents and warrants that Producer shall not "interpolate", "quote from", "borrow" or otherwise adapt any (i) copyrighted words or copyrighted selections owned or controlled by third parties (hereinafter, "Copyrighted Compositions"), and/or (ii) copyrighted sound recordings (including, without limitation, any sounds accompanying copyrighted audiovisual works) owned or controlled by third parties (hereinafter, "Copyrighted Recordings"; Copyrighted Compositions and Copyrighted Recordings are sometimes hereinafter collectively referred to as "Embodied Copyrighted Materials") in connection with the Master(s) without Artist having requested in writing or consented in writing to the inclusion of the particular Embodied Copyrighted Material.

(b)    Without limiting any of Producer's obligations or Artist's rights hereunder, the Master (s) shall not be deemed to have been satisfactorily delivered prior to Producer obtaining all necessary clearances in respect of any Embodied Copyrighted Materials embodied on the Master(s), which clearances shall be in writing and in a form satisfactory to Artist and Distributor from all necessary parties in a timely manner on terms which provide that Artist and our designees shall have the sole and exclusive right to control and administer the exploitation of the Master in any manner and/or media as we shall determine, in our sole and absolute discretion. Notwithstanding anything to the contrary contained herein, if Producer is unable to obtain the necessary clearances with respect to any Embodied Copyrighted Material upon terms that Artist and Distributor consider reasonable in Artist's and Distributor's good-faith business judgment, then the applicable Master shall not be deemed Delivered hereunder unless and until such Embodied Copyrighted Material is either replaced and/or removed from the applicable Master, at our election and at your sole cost and expense.

(c)    If the Master(s) incorporates any Embodied Copyrighted Materials included by Producer and/or a person or entity engaged and/or furnished by Producer, Producer shall be responsible for paying one hundred percent (100%) of any and all expenses incurred by Artist, Artist and/or Distributor in arranging for the "clearance" of such Embodied Copyrighted Materials ("Clearance Fees"). In addition, you shall be responsible for any fees, advances and royalties or other continuing obligations to persons or entities from who clearances must be or are obtained (e.g., record companies, artists, publishers, writers) ("Sample Compensation"), and any Sample Compensation paid by Artist or Distributor shall be deductible from any and all sums due you hereunder. In the event you include Embodied Copyrighted Materials in a Master and we are required to transfer an interest in the copyright ( "Sample Copyright Interest") to such owner of the Embodied Copyrighted Materials, then 100% of the Sample Copyright Interest shall be solely deducted from your ownership in the underlying composition. Notwithstanding the foregoing, with respect to Embodied Copyrighted Materials that have been disclosed by Producer and approved in writing by Artist and Distributor prior to inclusion in the Master ("Approved Embodied Copyrighted Material"), Artist shall assist you in arranging for the clearance of such; the Clearance Fees associated with such shall be treated as additional recording costs; you shall be responsible for your prorated share of the Sample Compensation associated with such based on a fraction, the numerator of which is equal to your royalty rate as set forth in paragraph 4 of this Agreement, and the denominator of which is equal to Artist's basic "all-in" royalty rate for USNRC Net Sales of top line albums; and the Sample Copyright Interest associated with such shall come "off the top" and be borne equally by all co-writers. Producer hereby warrants and represents that Producer has not included any Embodied Copyrighted Materials in the Master.

9.      **Ownership of Master**

(a)      Each Master produced hereunder shall, from the inception of its creation, be considered a "work made for hire" for Artist or Distributor within the meaning of United States Copyright Law. If it is determined that the Master does not so qualify, then the Master, together with all rights, title and interest in and to it (including the sound recording copyright and all renewals and extensions thereof, but not including the copyright in the underlying musical composition), shall be deemed transferred to Artist or Distributor by this Agreement. Each Master shall, from the inception of its creation, be entirely the property of Artist or Distributor in perpetuity, throughout the Territory, free of any claim whatsoever by you or any persons deriving any rights or interests from you. Without limiting its rights, Artist or Distributor shall have the sole and exclusive right in perpetuity and throughout any media now known or hereinafter devised and throughout the Territory:

(i)      To manufacture, advertise, sell, license, exploit or otherwise dispose of the Master and phonograph records derived therefrom upon such terms, and under such trademarks, service marks or trade names as Artist or Distributor or its licensees elect, or, in its sole discretion, to refrain therefrom;

(ii)      To perform the Masters publicly and to permit the public performance thereof by any method and by any medium now or hereafter known; and

(iii)      To use and publish your name and likeness (including all current professional, group and assumed or fictitious names), approved photographs and approved biographical material in connection with the promotion, exploitation and sale of derivatives of the Master.

10.      **Warranties and Representations**

(a)      You represent, warrant, covenant and agree as follows:

(i)      You are free to enter into and perform this Agreement with Artist, and you are not and will not be under any disability, restriction or prohibition, contractual or otherwise, with respect to (1) your right to execute this Agreement, (2) your right to grant all of the rights granted to Artist and Distributor hereunder, and (3) your right to perform fully each and every material term and provision hereof. You agree not to do or attempt to do, or suffer to be done, during or after the term hereof, any act in derogation of or inconsistent with Artist's or Distributor's rights hereunder.

(ii)     With respect to your contributions and those of persons or entities engaged and/or furnished by you, neither the Master produced hereunder nor any of the contents thereof, nor the manufacture or sale of records made from the Master, nor any other exploitation or use thereof, and no materials or other properties furnished by Producer or any third party engaged by Producer and embodied or contained in or used in connection with the Master or the packaging or advertising for phonograph records hereunder, shall violate any law or infringe upon any common law or statutory rights of any other entity, person, corporation, or including without limitation, contractual rights, copyrights, trademarks and rights of privacy or publicity. Without limiting the generality of the foregoing, you specifically represent and warrant that no selections recorded or to be recorded hereunder are subject to any re-recording restriction under any previous recording contract to which you or any party engaged by you may have been a party. Neither you nor any person rendering services in connection with the Master recorded hereunder is or will be a party to any contract which would in any way impair or interfere with the rights granted Artist and Distributor hereunder.

(iii)     During the five (5) year period following delivery of the Master to Distributor in accordance herewith, you will not produce phonograph records of any artist embodying the musical compositions embodied in such Master(s).

(iv)     Intentionally Deleted

(v)     With respect to your contributions and those of persons or entities engaged and/or furnished by you, the Master delivered hereunder shall be free of all liens and encumbrances, and there shall be no claims, demands or actions of any nature pending, threatened in writing or known to you with respect thereto which are not released prior to the delivery of the Masters involved.

(vi) The Master produced pursuant to this Agreement shall be produced under and in conformity with any union agreements to which the Master or the recording and/or production thereof may at any time be or become subject.

(vii) Intentionally Deleted.

(viii) All of your representations and warranties shall be true and correct upon execution hereof and upon Delivery of the Masters hereunder, and shall remain in effect for so long as Artist, Distributor, their licensees, assignees, transferees or successors in interest have any rights in or to the Masters. Artist's or Distributor's acceptance of the Master or other materials hereunder shall not constitute a waiver of any of your representations, warranties or agreements in respect thereof.

(ix) Neither Distributor nor Artist shall he required to make any payments of any nature for or in connection with the acquisition, exercise or exploitation of any rights granted to Artist or Distributor hereunder, except as specifically provided in this Agreement.

(b) Artist hereby warrants, represents, covenants and agrees as follows:

(i) With respect to Artist's contributions and those of persons or entities engaged and/or furnished by Artist, neither the Master(s) hereunder nor any of the contents thereof, nor the manufacture or sale of records made from the Master(s), nor any other exploitation or use thereof, and no materials or other properties furnished by Artist or any third party engaged or furnished by Artist and embodied or contained in or used in connection with the Master or the packaging or advertising for phonograph records hereunder, shall violate any law or infringe upon any common law or statutory rights of any other entity, person, corporation, or including without limitation, contractual rights, copyrights, trademarks and rights of privacy or publicity.

11. **Indemnification**

(a) You agree to indemnify and hold Artist, Distributor and their respective successors, assigns, agents, distributors, licensees, past and present officers, directors and employees harmless against any claim, liability, cost and expense (including reasonable outside attorneys' fees and legal costs) in connection with any third-party claim which is inconsistent with any agreement, covenant, representation, or warranty made by you herein. You will reimburse Artist or Distributor upon demand for any payment made by Artist or Distributor at any time after the date hereof (including after the term of this Agreement terminates) in respect of any claim, liability, damage or expense to which the foregoing indemnity relates which claim is reduced to a final (i.e. non-interlocutory) non- appealable judgment or has been settled with your prior written approval, not to be unreasonably withheld (it being understood that you shall be deemed to have approved any settlement not in excess of Five Thousand ($5,000) Dollars). Upon the making or filing of any such claim, action or demand, Artist or Distributor shall be entitled to withhold from any amounts payable under this Agreement such amounts as are reasonably related to the potential liability in issue; provided, Artist or Distributor shall not withhold such sums if you post a bond in a form and with a bonding company reasonably acceptable to Artist or Distributor. You shall be notified of any such claim, action or demand and shall have the right, at your own expense, to participate in the defense thereof with counsel of your own choosing. Monies withheld from you by Artist or Distributor pursuant to the foregoing provisions of this paragraph 11 in connection with any claim, demand or action shall be credited to your royalty account hereunder for payment, if any, if and to the extent that litigation of that claim, demand or action is not commenced and active settlement discussions are not then taking place as of the date one (1) year after the end of the semi-annual accounting period during which those monies arc initially withheld unless Artist, in its reasonable business judgment, believes an action will be filed. Notwithstanding the foregoing, if after such release by Artist of sums withheld in connection with a particular claim, such claim is reasserted, then Artist's rights under this paragraph 11 will apply ab initio, in full force and effect.

(b)      Artist hereby indemnifies, saves and holds Producer and Producer's respective licensees, employees and agents harmless from any and all loss, damage, liability and other expense (including anticipated and actual court costs, expenses and reasonable outside attorneys' fees) arising out of, connected with, or as a result of any inconsistency with, failure of, or breach or threatened breach by Artist of any warranty, representation, agreement, undertaking or covenant contained in this Agreement resulting in a final (i.e. non-interlocutory) judgment or settled with Artist's prior written consent.

12.    **Force Majeure**

(a)      Artist shall not be deemed in default hereunder if performance of any of its obligations hereunder is delayed or becomes impossible or commercially impractical, or if Artist (or Distributor) is hampered in the recording, manufacture, distribution or sale of phonograph records or Artist's (or Distributor's) normal business operations become commercially impractical, by reason of any force majeure event not reasonably within Artist's (or Distributor's) control or which Artist (or Distributor) could not by reasonable diligence have avoided. Upon the happening of any such event, Artist, in addition to any other rights or remedies it may have hereunder or otherwise, may elect, by notice to you, to suspend Artist's obligations under this Agreement for the period of time that the effects of any such force majeure event continue. Any such suspension due to a force majeure event affecting Artist or Distributor shall not exceed six (6) months, unless such force majeure event also affects the majority of other record companies in the United States. You shall not be deemed in default hereunder if performance of your obligations hereunder is delayed or becomes impossible as a result of any such force majeure event not reasonably within your control.

(b)     Subject to paragraph 13 below, if at any time you fail to fulfill any of your material obligations herein, then, without limiting Artist's or Distributor's rights, Artist or Distributor, as applicable, shall have the option, exercisable at any time by notice to you, (i) to suspend Artist's and Distributor's obligations to you hereunder during the period of such default and/or (ii) to terminate this Agreement without any further obligation to you hereunder.

**13.     Default and Cure**

The failure by either party to perform any of its obligations hereunder shall not be deemed a breach of this Agreement unless the party alleging such breach gives written notice of such failure to the alleged breaching party to perform and such failure is not corrected within thirty (30) days from and after receipt of such notice.

**14.     Miscellaneous**

(a)     You acknowledge that your services hereunder, as well as the Master recorded and the rights and privileges granted to Artist under the terms of this agreement, are of a special, unique, unusual, extraordinary and intellectual character which gives them a peculiar value, and that, in the event of a breach by you of any material term, condition, representation, warranty, covenant or undertaking contained herein, Artist may be caused irreparable injury and damage. You expressly consent to be bound, in a court of equity or in any other forum, by the above characterization of Producer's services (as well as of the Masters recorded hereunder and the rights and privileges granted to Artist hereunder), and agree that Artist shall be entitled to seek remedies of injunction and other equitable relief to prevent or remedy a breach of this Agreement, which relief shall be in addition to any other rights or remedies, for damages or otherwise, which Artist may have. Nothing contained herein or otherwise shall prevent Producer from opposing such action for relief.

(b)     The respective addresses of Artist and you for all purposes of this Agreement shall be as set forth above until notice of a new address shall be duly given. Any notice desired or required to be given by either party to the other shall be in writing and shall be delivered by hand, or sent by United States certified mail, postage prepaid, return receipt requested, or sent by telex or telegraph with all charges prepaid, provided that any royalty statement may be sent by regular mail. Properly addressed notices delivered or sent as provided herein shall be deemed given when delivered by hand with signed confirmation of receipt, or when postmarked if delivered by mail. All payments and royalty statements hereunder shall be sent to Producer c/o Joshua Doe Productions.

(c)     This Agreement and the exhibits attached thereto constitute the entire agreement between the parties and shall not be modified, except by an instrument in writing, signed by each of the parties duly authorized to execute such modification. This Agreement has been entered into in the State of Texas, and the validity, interpretation and legal effect of this Agreement shall be governed by the laws of the State of Texas applicable to contracts entered into and performed entirely within the State of Texas, with respect to the determination of any claim, dispute or disagreement which may arise out of the interpretation, performance or breach of this Agreement.

If the foregoing accurately reflects our agreement, please indicate so by signing below.

_____

Joshua Doe Productions LLC

## Inducement

In order to induce John Doe Entertainment f/s/o John Doe ("Artist") to enter into the foregoing agreement ("Agreement") with Joshua Doe Productions LLC ( "Producer") the undersigned hereby:

    (a)    acknowledges that he has read and is familiar with all the terms and conditions of the Agreement;

    (b)    assents to the execution of the Agreement and agrees to be bound by the terms and conditions thereof, including but not limited to each and every provision of the Agreement that relates to the undersigned in any way, directly or indirectly, the services to be rendered thereunder by the undersigned and restrictions imposed upon the undersigned in accordance with the provisions of the Agreement, and hereby guarantees to Artist the fill and faithful performance of all the terms and conditions of the Agreement by the undersigned and by Productions.

    (c)    acknowledges and agrees that Artist shall be under no obligation to make any payments to the undersigned or otherwise, for or in connection with this inducement and for or in connection with the services rendered by the undersigned or in connection with the rights granted to Artist thereunder and the fulfillment of the undersigned's obligations pursuant to the Agreement.

_____

Joshua Doe

## EXHIBIT A

As of March 31, 2015

Joshua Doe

**Re:    Our Client    John Doe Entertainment f/s/o John Doe**

1.     We have engaged Joshua Doe ("Producer") as the Producer in connection with sound recordings constituting twelve five (5) master recording(s) (the "Master(s)") embodying Artist's performance of the musical composition provisionally entitled ""I Am John Doe", "John Doe Knows You", "John-Doe-licious", "Mighty John Doe", and "Amazing John Doe" containing the performance of the recording artist John Doe made pursuant to the agreement between John Doe and Joshua Doe, as amended (the "Recording Agreement").

2.     Although the Recording Agreement requires us to pay for the services of Producer, we hereby request and irrevocably authorize you to make payments to Producer for Producer's services on our behalf as follows:

(a) (1) An advance of One Thousand Dollars ($1,000) per Master for a total advance of Five Thousand Dollars and 00/100 Cents ($5,000.00) ("Advance"), payable as follows: one-half (1/2) upon the later of (i) commencement of recording or (ii) execution of a certificate of employment for the Masters or execution of a the producer agreement pertaining to the services of Producer, and the balance payable upon delivery to and acceptance by Distributor and Artist of the Masters and full execution of the producer agreement pertaining to the services of Producer. Those Advances will be recoupable by you from all monies (excluding publishing monies) becoming payable to the Producer under paragraph 2(b) below or otherwise. To the extent not so recouped, the Advances may be recouped by you from any monies becoming payable to us, but all amounts so recouped from monies payable to us will be credited to our royalty account if subsequently recouped from monies payable to you. Each such Advance will also be applied against the recording budget applicable to the Master under the Agreement.

(a)(2) Two Thousand Five Hundred Dollars ($2,500.00) of the Advance, with respect to the Masters entitled "I Am John Doe", "John Doe Knows You", "John-Doe-licious", "Mighty John Doe", shall be paid to Joshua Doe upon full execution of a Distribution Agreement for Joshua Doe Production Services on the aforementioned Masters and shall be an advance recoupable against any monies (excluding mechanical royalties) payable to John Doe Entertainment f/s/o John Doe for the aforementioned Master(s) and shall reduce the Advance otherwise payable to Joshua Doe. However, if a Distribution Agreement is not fully executed within ninety (90) days, Artist shall pay Producer an Advance in the amount of Two Thousand Five Hundred Dollars and 00/100 Cents ($2,500.00). Two Thousand Five Hundred Dollars ($2,500.00) of the Advance payable with respect to the Masters entitled "I Am John Doe", "John Doe Knows You", "John-Doe-licious", "Mighty John Doe", and "Amazing John Doe" for a total of Fifteen Thousand Dollars and 00/100 Cents ($5,000.00) shall be paid to Joshua Doe Productions upon delivery of the aforementioned Masters, to John Doe Entertainment f/s/o John Doe.

(b) (1) (i) A royalty (the "Royalty") on net sales of phonograph records derived from the Master, computed and paid in the same manner as the royalty payable to us under the Agreement (excluding escalations unless otherwise provided herein), at the same times, and subject to the same conditions, but at a basic rate of three percent (3%) of wholesale (or the retail equivalent) instead of the rate fixed in the Recording Agreement with proportionate reductions on all sales for which reduced royalties are payable under the Recording Agreement. The amount of the Royalty will be deducted from all monies payable or becoming payable to Artist under Artist's exclusive recording agreement.

3. The Royalty will not be payable until you have recouped an Recording Costs (excluding any in-pocket advances payable to Artist or Artist's furnishing entity) attributable to the Album under the Recording Agreement. After such recoupment, the Royalty will be computed and paid on all such records sold thereafter retroactively from the first record sold subject to recoupment of the Advance. Such recoupment will be computed at Artist's net royalty rate (i.e., those royalties payable by Distributor to Artist excluding the royalties payable to all producers, engineers, mixers, and all other royalty participants including Producer). For the avoidance of doubt, the Producer Advance shall only be recouped once.

4. Your compliance with this authorization will constitute an accommodation to us alone; Producer is not a beneficiary of it. All payments to Producer under this authorization will constitute payment to its and you will have no liability by reason of any erroneous payment or failure to comply with this authorization. We will indemnify and hold you harmless against any claims asserted against you and any damages, losses or expenses you incur by reason of any such payment or otherwise in connection herewith.

5. We hereby request that you accord an appropriate credit on jackets, labels of records and the liner notes of all records (in all configurations) derived from the Masters produced hereunder, and in national trade ads of one-half (112) page or larger (including Billboard strip ads) concerning (i) records solely embodying the Master; or (ii) other records embodying the Masters if all producers are mentioned) in substantially the following form:

"Produced by Joshua Doe Provided that with respect to the Master currently entitled "I Am John Doe", "John Doe Knows You", "John-Doe-licious", "Mighty John Doe", and "Amazing John Doe" the credit shall be in substantially the following form:
"Produced by Joshua Doe of Joshua Doe Production"

The failure of Distributor or any licensee of Distributor to comply with this instruction shall not be deemed a breach of the producer agreement pertaining to the Master(s).

6. (a) Subject paragraphs 5(b) and 5(c) below, all monies becoming payable under this authorization will be remitted to Producer at the following address or otherwise as Producer directs you in writing:

> Joshua Doe Productions LLC
> f/s/o Joshua Doe
> 9999 Bluebonnet Street
> Houston, Texas 77777

and will be accompanied by statements with respect to those payments. We understand that royalty payment instructions of this nature are usually placed in effect with respect to the accounting period in which you receive them if they are delivered to you within the first three (3) months of that period, and with respect to the next accounting period if delivered after that time, although administrative factors may result in variations from that procedure.

_____

Joshua Doe f/s/o Joshua Doe Productions, LLC


_____

John Doe, as the
Authorized Agent for
John Doe Entertainment

**EXHIBIT B**
Recording Agreement Extracts

John Doe Entertainment
f/s/o John Doe
5524 Kruger Lane
Houston, Texas 77777

Dated: March 31, 2015

Joshua Doe Productions LLC
f/s/o Joshua Doe
9999 Bluebonnet Street
Houston, Texas 77777

The following shall confirm the writer/publisher splits with respect to the compositions currently entitled ""I Am John Doe", "John Doe Knows You", "John-Doe-licious", "Mighty John Doe", and "Amazing John Doe" (the "Controlled Composition(s)") performed by John Doe (the "Artist").

| TITLE | AUTHOR | SHARE |
|---|---|---|
| "I Am John Doe" | John Doe | 25% |
| | Joshua Doe | 75% |
| "John Doe Knows You" | John Doe | 25% |
| | Joshua Doe | 75% |
| "John-Doe-licious" | John Doe | 25% |
| | Joshua Doe | 75% |
| "Mighty John Doe" | John Doe | 25% |
| | Joshua Doe | 75% |
| "Amazing John Doe" | John Doe | 25% |
| | Joshua Doe | 75% |

Joshua Doe hereby grants to John Doe Entertainment and its designees in perpetuity an irrevocable license under copyright to use the same terms and conditions and at the same rates, including, without mechanical "caps" and reduced rates for non-full priced Album sales.

_____
Joshua Doe

Questions and Discussion

1. In the Storyteller Entertainment production agreement, the most important aspect of the agreement is to produce five master recordings. Is that all that the artist must accomplish?

2. In the previous production agreement, clause five calls for "Accountings." How important is that?

3. Clause 6 mentions Credit—is that as important as royalties?

4. Each master is to be considered a "work made for hire." Is that an important distinction?

5. The Force Majeure provision allows the artist a way out of default if the performance of any of the obligations are delayed or becomes impossible or commercially impractical. What would constitute a commercial impracticability?

# Chapter 5
# Artist Recording Agreements

It is said that the journey to making money as a musician begins with the Artist Recording Contract. This is the written document between a recording artist and record company (or production company), which establishes the rights, obligations, and promises of all parties to the agreement. If this contract is supplied by the recording company, it will certainly be one-sided. It is not unusual for a new group to be ecstatic about a "million dollar deal" only to discover that the contract calls for five albums in one year, or some such nonsense, which is impossible. Not to mention, that most (if not all) of the money is proffered in the form of an advance (for studio time, toilet paper, etc.). These contracts can be a classic example of an adhesion contract—all the terms of the contract stick to you like glue. If it sounds too good to be true, it usually is. Richard Schulenburg says, "Depending upon your outlook, you may see the recording agreement as the pot of gold at the end of the rainbow or the rainbow itself. Unfortunately, it can also be like the pretty apple the wicked queen fed to Snow White" (Schulenburg, Legal Aspects of the Music Industry 10 (1999)).

Each provision of the recording agreement has the potential to cause difficulty to the artist; so, each clause must be studied and reviewed individually. As Richard Schulenburg notes, there is no standard contract, and when the record company states, "here is the standard contract," what they're really saying is "this is 'our' standard contract" (Schulenburg, Legal Aspects of the Music Industry 11). Note the number of years—do not sell your soul to the devil! Remember, "Sixteen Tons," "I owe my soul to the company store."

The next case is *Isley v. Motown Recording*, 69 F.R.D. 12 (S.D.N.Y. 1975), which involves the fabulous Isley Brothers and their activities after being released from their contract with Motown. The Brothers then published and pressed records of their hit song, "It's Your Thing" under their own label. Of course, the Isleys made more money this way, and the song sold 1,750,000 copies. "It's your thing, do what you want to do, I can't tell you who to sock it to." Good advice. . . . for Motown; take that Berry Gordy. Here, apparently the

Isley Brothers were not good witnesses in the jury trial and contradicted themselves, so, the judge set aside the jury's verdict and ordered a new trial.

Isley v. Motown Record Corp.
United States District Court for the Southern District of New York
November 18, 1975
No. 69 Civ. 2556
69 F.R.D. 12

OWEN, District Judge.

Plaintiffs, three brothers, are "pop" singers and recording artists. A jury found facts in their favor establishing their right to the income from a "hit" song they recorded with instruments and voices called "It's Your Thing". This favorable verdict was based solely upon their own testimony in the course of which they repudiated their own earlier sworn testimony which clearly supported a contrary conclusion, characterizing such earlier conflicting testimony variously as a lie and false. Given this basis for the verdict, and there being persuasive documentary and testimonial evidence to the contrary, the plaintiffs' favorable verdict cannot stand. It is set aside and a new trial is ordered.

In the mercurial field of popular music, the plaintiffs, brothers Ronald, Rudolph and O'Kelly Isley, singers and recording artists under the name Isley Brothers, had had their ups and downs. In 1968 they had been under contract to defendant Motown Record Corporation for several years and were not doing well. Under that contract from time-to-time they would record new songs, sometimes composed by themselves, sometimes by others. The tapes of those recording sessions were then delivered to Motown to press into records and distribute and the Isleys were paid royalties thereon. In December 1968, the Isleys applied for and obtained a release from the Motown contract. Thereafter, using two wholly-owned companies, Triple Three for the sheet music and T-Neck for the records, the Isleys published and pressed records of "It's Your Thing" using defendant Buddah Records, an independent firm, merely as a distributor. There is no question that the Isleys' income was greatly enhanced by marketing "It's Your Thing" under their own label rather than on the Motown label, for "It's Your Thing" was a hit and sold 1,750,000 copies.

The basic issue on the trial was the date on which "It's Your Thing" was first recorded.

Motown offered substantial documentary and testimonial proof to the effect that "It's Your Thing" was first recorded at the A & R Studios in New York on November 6, 1968 at a session for which Motown had advanced the money on condition the Isleys record original tunes; that at that time the Isleys were under contract to it, and that it was therefore entitled to the income from "It's

Your Thing" less the Isleys' royalties. The Isleys, to the contrary, testified that "It's Your Thing" was composed in late December 1968, shortly after they got the release from their Motown contract, was first recorded on January 3, 1969, and that Motown had no rights in it at all.

The jury answered three written questions as follows:

1. Have Motown and Jobete proved by a preponderance of the evidence that O'Kelly Isley on behalf of the Isley Brothers agreed on or about November 1, 1968 with Ralph Seltzer of Motown to obtain and furnish him with songwriter agreements on the forthcoming recording session as part of Seltzer's agreement to advance the money for the session?

"No"

2. Do you find that Motown and Jobete had proved by a preponderance of the evidence that "It's Your Thing" and "Turn On, Tune In, Drop Out" were recorded on November 6, 1968 at the A & R Studios in New York?

"No"

3. Do you find that the Isleys have proved by a preponderance of the evidence that "It's Your Thing" and "Turn On, Tune In, Drop Out" were recorded for the first time on January 3, 1969 at the Town Sound Studios in Englewood, New Jersey?

"Yes"

The infirmity in the Isleys' collective testimony, which was the sole support for the jury's several conclusions, is clearly demonstrated by a comparison of their 1969-70 testimony in depositions or before Judge Lasker with their 1975 testimony given on the trial.

The 1969-70 testimony was to the effect that after actually having auditioned another band, they engaged a band called the Midnight Movers as a second choice to do a couple of "ideas" they (the Isleys) had; that they thereafter wrote Motown on November 1 that they were going to do a session with the Midnight Movers and asked for money for the session and agreed to deliver the tape after the session; that they received from Motown songwriters agreements to be executed for original tunes; that in preparation for the recording session they had a 3-4 hour rehearsal on the night of November 5; that Ronald and O'Kelly Isley composed the music the Midnight Movers rehearsed; that O'Kelly Isley arranged for the recording studio for November 6, and told A & R how to set it up; that the Midnight Movers were paid $850 for the recording session; that although the Isleys were supposed to send the tape of the session to Motown, they did not, and the tape was still [as of 1969-70] somewhere at O'Kelly's home.

Thus, in 1969-70, while the Isleys maintained that they had not recorded "It's Your Thing" at the November 6 session, they clearly acknowledged that on that date they had made the various customary arrangements for a substantial recording session of music of their own, and absent the production of the tape, a trier of the fact could well conclude, given other evidence, that what they recorded was in fact "It's Your Thing".

However, on the trial in 1975 they presented a new story as follows: In the fall of 1968, they were broke and needed money for household expenses and Christmas presents; in order to get Motown to advance them some money, they decided to make up a story about doing a session; they told Motown of this stratagem to which Motown agreed, and wrote the November 1 letter to Motown about the "session" at Motown's suggestion so that there would be a basis for sending the money; that the name of the Midnight Movers was inserted in the letter just to have the name of a band, not having any real awareness of whether that band was available or not; that they had but a 45-60 minutes rehearsal; that they did no "ideas" of the Isleys, and no music composed by the Isleys was performed at either the rehearsal or the session at A & R the next night and in fact there was no vocal music at all; that the Midnight Movers were only paid $400 or $450 and the Isleys, pursuant to plan, pocketed the balance of the $850 they got from Motown for the band and finally, that the tape from the session was thrown out by the Isleys' mother in cleaning O'Kelly's basement in December 1968, the month following the session.

Motown's proof consisted first of contemporaneous writings of both parties which were strong circumstantial if not direct evidence that the Isleys intended to and did record new vocal music in the November 6 session. These writings included 1) the Isleys' letter of November 1, written five days before the session, 2) the records of the A & R Studios for the studio on November 6, showing two things, first that the studio had been set up for a solo vocal with a group vocal to be "overdubbed", (see n. 21 infra) and second, that during the recording session itself, a change was made as to which microphone was assigned to the "vocal"; 3) the Motown letter sent prior to the session after discussion with the Isleys enclosing songwriters agreements to be executed for the original tunes to be recorded, and 4) the letters exchanged a few weeks later when the Isleys demanded releases, at which time Motown wrote insisting on repayment of the entire cost of the session since the Isleys had sent no tapes, to which the Isleys agreed, and repayment was made.

Motown's second area of proof was the testimony of one of the Midnight Movers, George Chillious, a trombone player who played at the November 6, 1968 but not at the January 3, 1969 session. He testified that he played the music for "It's Your Thing" in the November 6 session from a written trombone part bearing the title "It's Your Thing", and after the end of the instrumental session heard Ronald Isley record the vocal part.

While I would not on this record, permit this verdict to stand in any event, this is an especially appropriate case for the granting of a new trial since much direct proof is available on a new trial that was not heretofore presented.

Frequently, in directing a new trial, a court is faced with the fact that a second jury can do no more than reappraise the same evidence heard on the first trial. Here, however, there are perhaps as many as ten other "Midnight Movers" available who could give testimony as to what was recorded on November 6, 1968, as could the sound engineer of the A & R Studio that night.

On such disinterested testimony, a second jury could obviously better determine the issues.

The law is well established that it is the duty of the trial judge to set aside a verdict and grant a new trial if, in his opinion, the verdict is based upon evidence which is false or the verdict results in a miscarriage of justice The trial court is empowered to do this even though there may be substantial evidence which would prevent the direction of a verdict. Aetna Cas. & Surety Co. v. Yeatts, 122 F.2d 350 (4th Cir. 1941); Reyes v. Grace Line, Inc., 334 F. Supp. 1104 (S.D.N.Y.1971). In my judgment, this verdict, on this record, results in a miscarriage of justice and was in part, if not in whole, based upon evidence which was false. I deem it fundamental that a party may not do a testimonial about-face, concede prior testimony to be false or a lie and then prevail solely upon the basis of that altered self-serving testimony.

For the foregoing reasons and pursuant to Rule 59 Fed.R.Civ.P., the conclusions of the jury as to all issues raised by the three questions submitted to it are set aside and a new trial is ordered. The action is placed on the calendar for trial on January 19, 1976.

---

The basic issue in the new trial of *Isley v. Motown*, 69 FRD 12 (1975), was the date on which "It's Your Thing" was first recorded. The two following statute selections are from the California Code and adds some insight to what can occur if a recording agreement goes south (Section 2855—arbitration; and Section 3423—injunctions).

### California Civil Code § 2855

Section 2855. Arbitration award against principal not award against surety

An arbitration award rendered against a principal alone shall not be, be deemed to be, or be utilized as, an award against his surety.

The intent of this legislation is to apply existing law to arbitration awards.

### California Civil Code § 3423

§ 3423. When injunction may not be granted

An injunction may not be granted:

(a) To stay a judicial proceeding pending at the commencement of the action in which the injunction is demanded, unless this restraint is necessary to prevent a multiplicity of proceedings.

(b) To stay proceedings in a court of the United States.

(c) To stay proceedings in another state upon a judgment of a court of that state.

(d) To prevent the execution of a public statute, by officers of the law, for the public benefit.

(e) To prevent the breach of a contract the performance of which would not be specifically enforced, other than a contract in writing for the rendition of personal services from one to another where the promised service is of a special, unique, unusual, extraordinary, or intellectual character, which gives it peculiar value, the loss of which cannot be reasonably or adequately compensated in damages in an action at law, and where the compensation for the personal services is as follows:

(1) As to contracts entered into on or before December 31, 1993, the minimum compensation provided in the contract for the personal services shall be at the rate of six thousand dollars ($6,000) per annum.

(2) As to contracts entered into on or after January 1, 1994, the criteria of subparagraph (A) or (B), as follows, are satisfied:

(A) The compensation is as follows:

(i) The minimum compensation provided in the contract shall be at the rate of nine thousand dollars ($9,000) per annum for the first year of the contract, twelve thousand dollars ($12,000) per annum for the second year of the contract, and fifteen thousand dollars ($15,000) per annum for the third to seventh years, inclusive, of the contract.

(ii) In addition, after the third year of the contract, there shall actually have been paid for the services through and including the contract year during which the injunctive relief is sought, over and above the minimum contractual compensation specified in clause (i), the amount of fifteen thousand dollars ($15,000) per annum during the fourth and fifth years of the contract, and thirty thousand dollars ($30,000) per annum during the sixth and seventh years of the contract. As a condition to petitioning for an injunction, amounts payable under this clause may be paid at any time prior to seeking injunctive relief.

(B) The aggregate compensation actually received for the services provided under a contract that does not meet the criteria of subparagraph (A), is at least 10 times the applicable aggregate minimum amount specified in clauses (i) and (ii) of subparagraph (A) through and including the contract year during which the injunctive relief is sought. As a condition to petitioning for an injunction, amounts payable under this subparagraph may be paid at any time prior to seeking injunctive relief.

(3) Compensation paid in any contract year in excess of the minimums specified in subparagraphs (A) and (B) of paragraph (2) shall apply to reduce the compensation otherwise required to be paid under those provisions in any subsequent contract years.

However, an injunction may be granted to prevent the breach of a contract entered into between any nonprofit cooperative corporation or association and a member or stockholder thereof in respect to any provision regarding the sale or delivery to the corporation or association of the products produced or acquired by the member or stockholder.

(f) To prevent the exercise of a public or private office, in a lawful manner, by the person in possession.

(g) To prevent a legislative act by a municipal corporation.

———————————

The use, or threat, of an injunction is a valuable tool in enforcing, or threatening to enforce, your version of a recording contract. In the following case, *ABC-Paramount, Inc. v. Topps Record Distributing Co.*, 374 F.2d 455 (5th Cir. 1967), the court looks at the question of what remedies are available for alleged breach of contracts in the music business.

ABC-Paramount Records, Inc. v. Topps Record Distributing Co.,
United States Court of Appeals for the Fifth Circuit
March 22, 1967
No. 23038
374 F.2d 455

GOLDBERG, Circuit Judge:

This case comes from the raucous, fast-moving, competitive world of American popular music, where nothing is more alive than the hope of success, nothing commoner than failure, nothing more ephemeral than fame, and nothing more fundamental than a smile and a shoeshine.

Ray Curran, one of the plaintiffs and a fledgling enterpriser in entertainment, was the manager of a country club in Jacksonville, Florida. Curran's first venture as a promoter was a large show in the Jacksonville Coliseum, scheduled for an evening in January or February of 1963. The plane carrying the entertainers was delayed, owing to fog, and Curran had eight or ten thousand people in his audience with no performers. Suddenly a small young man, unknown to Curran, appeared and asked if he could perform until the regulars arrived. Curran paused only to ask if the stranger had a union card, and on an affirmative answer he allowed the youngster to perform. After the show the youngster was paid and disappeared. Curran forgot him, but a few weeks later he walked into Curran's country club office, told Curran he wanted to make a recording, and convinced Curran to be a partner in the enterprise. The young man's name was James Tennant, but his stage name was Jimmy Velvit.

Velvit and Curran agreed that each would put up half the money for the recording session, but Velvit later told Curran that he could not afford to put up anything. So Curran paid the total cost, about $2,000.00, of making the recordings in Nashville. Velvit put up the talent, and they agreed that each owned half of the enterprise.

The session took place in Nashville on April 9, 1963, and Velvit recorded four songs on tape: "We Belong Together", "I'm Gonna Try", "History of Love", and "Mr. Lonely." The first two of these songs were pressed on 1,000 records, using the "Velvet" label (this label was used to give the word "velvet" as much exposure as possible).

These recordings on the Velvet label were not an end in themselves. Velvit and Curran wanted to sell the performances to a large recording company, which would sell the record nationally, pay a royalty to the owners, and make a reputation for Velvit.

Velvit and Curran were both neophytes, and both knew that they needed an experienced promoter to distribute the record and get it played on the air. Only success here would lead a large record company to purchase the record. Velvit therefore approached Gwynn M. (Babe) Elias, another plaintiff. Elias was at that time president of the Topps Record Company (another plaintiff), a record distributor. Elias's duties were "to get air play throughout Florida for new record releases, escort and introduce the artists, arranging interviews for them with the disc jockeys (DJs), columnists, accounts, set up displays in retail outlets, etc. His success depended on making and keeping excellent relations with all DJs, columnists and accounts, who controlled the extent of exposure a record would receive." He appeared to be just the man for the job, and he contracted in late April with Curran to attempt to sell the recording to a large company, in return for a half interest in the proceeds.

Elias then embarked upon an intensive campaign, including trips around Florida, phone calls, mailings, a trip to New York to arrange for national distribution, and other "promotional gimmicks and bonuses."

When Elias started to negotiate with several large companies who seemed interested, he found it hard to stay in contact with Curran, who was not knowledgeable in such matters. For these reasons Curran, on July 8, gave Elias full authority to make a deal on his own.

Finally, on August 14, Elias sold the record to Cortland Records, Inc., for distribution on Cortland's "Witch" label. While Cortland was not a large firm, it was young and pushing hard, and Elias testified that he thought it was willing to stake its new and hard fought reputation on the Velvit record, where a well-established but larger company might not. Since a great deal of the success or failure of a record depends upon the skill and persistence of its owners in promoting and selling it, this choice was extremely important.

Cortland paid Elias a $500 bonus promised to pay a royalty of 7 1/2 cents per record to Elias, and promised to pay the copyright royalties of 1 1/2 cents on "We Belong Together" and 2 cents on "I'm Gonna Try" to their respective owners (who are not a part of this litigation).

Cortland then immediately embarked upon intensive promotion of the Velvit record on the national market.

Apparently in ignorance of the deal which Elias had made with Cortland, Velvit, through an acquaintance, arranged to meet in Nashville with Felton Jarvis in late August in the offices of the defendant ABC-Paramount. Jarvis was in charge of ABC's artists and repertoire for the southeast United States.

Velvit testified that at the time he was dissatisfied because he thought the record had not been sold. He played all four songs which had been recorded in the April session in Nashville to Jarvis and to Gene Goodman, a member of a music publishing firm. Jarvis liked Velvit's recordings, and mentioned that ABC would be interested in buying the performances and in putting Velvit under contract.

Velvit then showed Jarvis and Goodman copies of his contract with Curran for the April recording session and Curran's contract with Elias for the promotion and sale of the record. Jarvis and Goodman read the contracts and declared them one-sided and not binding. Jarvis advised Velvit to "forget" Curran and his contract, and said that only Curran, and not Velvit, was bound to Elias, and therefore there was nothing to worry about from either Elias or Curran.

Velvit was then taken to New York by Goodman, and there, on August 23, Velvit met Larry Newton, then vice-president of ABC, and signed a contract selling the performances to ABC.

After his return to Nashville, on about September 4, Velvit read in a trade magazine that Elias had sold the performances to Cortland's Witch label. Very worried, Velvit went to see Jarvis at ABC and showed him the article. Jarvis, also worried, said that Velvit had better get things straightened out.

Velvit then called Cortland Records, and spoke to Earl Glicken and William Erman, the owners. Velvit told them in strong language and at length, that Elias had stolen the performances and had no right to sell them, and that ABC had bought them and was going to issue a record.

Glicken and Erman were concerned. They had staked Cortland's reputation on Velvit's record, and they felt that ABC, a large and well-advised company, would not have bought the record unless Velvit had had the right to sell it.

Erman immediately called Elias to ask him to explain. Elias answered that he would have Velvit call Cortland and explain, and Elias tried to reach Velvit at ABC in Nashville, but Jarvis instructed Velvit not to answer the phone or speak to Elias, and ABC's employees answered Elias's calls by saying Velvit was out. Glicken and Erman were still able to reach Velvit on the phone, and to them Velvit repeated his statements that Elias had had no right to sell the record.

Cortland, confronted with its own conversations with Velvit, and Elias's inability to reach Velvit, became convinced that Elias was in the wrong. Cortland cancelled its contract with Elias, and stopped production, promotion, and sales of the record. It called all of its distributors and the disc jockeys with whom it had influence and told them that it had had no right to make the record. To save embarrassment Erman testified,

"I tried to shift the blame [to Elias]; * * * we were innocent bystanders * * * and Babe Elias had taken advantage of us. That's why I cancelled the contract with him."

ABC began its own promotion of the record, which ultimately sold 55,000 copies. ABC paid a total of $2,676.02 in royalties on the record to Velvit; and it earned a net profit of $2,45.92. The sale of 55,000 was not good for the record business at that time. Newton testified that a successful record in 1963 would have sold 700,000 or 800,000 copies.

The plaintiffs, Curran, Elias and Topps (all Florida citizens) sued ABC-Paramount, a New York corporation, claiming damages for unfair competition, interference with contractual relations, and defamation. The case was tried to a jury. At the close of the evidence the trial judge ruled out all claims except that for interference with contractual relations.

The jury returned verdicts of $7,500 for Curran, and $15,000 for Topps. The trial court enjoined ABC from using the Velvit recordings and ordered their return to Topps.

ABC here appeals, contesting only the damages awarded. The plaintiffs cross-appeal, arguing that their claim of slander was wrongfully excluded, and that the trial judge should have charged the jury on the question of punitive damages.

We affirm in all respects, except that we hold that plaintiffs are entitled to a retrial on the issue of punitive damages only.

## I.

ABC contends that the compensatory damages awarded by the jury were unwarranted by the evidence and merely speculative.

Preliminarily we note that both parties argue the question of sufficiency of the evidence as if it were a question of Florida law. We disagree. It is true that

"cases following Erie [R. Co. v. Tompkins, 1938, 304 U.S. 64, 58 S. Ct. 817, 82 L. Ed. 1188] have evinced a broader policy to the effect that the federal courts should conform as near as may be — in the absence of other considerations — to state rules even of form and mode where the state rules may bear substantially on the question whether the litigation would come out one way in the federal court and another way in the state court if the federal court failed to apply a particular local rule. E.g., Guaranty Trust Co. [of New York] v. York, supra (326 U.S. 99, 65 S. Ct. 1464, 89 L. Ed. 2079); Bernhardt v. Polygraphic Co. [of America, Inc.], 350 U.S. 198 [76 S. Ct. 273, 100 L. Ed. 199]. Concededly the nature of the tribunal which tries issues may be important in the enforcement of the parcel of rights making up a cause of action or defense, and bear significantly upon achievement of uniform enforcement of the right. It may well be that in the instant personal-injury case the outcome would be substantially affected by whether the issue of immunity is decided by a judge or a jury. Therefore, were 'outcome' the only consideration, a strong case might appear for saying that the federal court should follow the state practice.

"But there are affirmative countervailing considerations at work here. The federal system is an independent system for administering justice to litigants who properly invoke its jurisdiction. An essential characteristic of that system is the manner in which, in civil common-law actions, it distributes trial functions between judge and jury and, under the influence — if not the command — of the Seventh Amendment, assigns the decisions of disputed questions of fact to the jury. Jacob v. [City of] New York, 315 U.S. 752 [62 S. Ct. 854, 86 L. Ed. 1166]. The policy of uniform enforcement of state-created rights and obligations, see, e.g., Guaranty Trust Co. [of New York] v. York (US), supra, cannot in every case exact compliance with a state rule — not bound up with rights and obligations — which disrupts the federal system of allocating functions between judge and jury. Herron v. Southern Pacific Co., 283 U.S. 91 [51 S. Ct. 383, 75 L. Ed. 857]. Thus the inquiry here is whether the federal policy favoring jury decisions of disputed fact questions should yield to the state rule in the interest of furthering the objective that the litigation should not come out one way in the federal court and another way in the state court." 78 S. Ct. at 900-901, 2 L. Ed. 2d at 962-963.

Byrd v. Blue Ridge Rural Electric Cooperative, 1958, 356 U.S. 525, 536-538, 78 S. Ct. 893, 900-901, 2 L. Ed. 2d 953, 962-963, reh. den. 357 U.S. 933, 78 S. Ct. 1366, 2 L. Ed. 2d 1375 (1958).

In Byrd, the Supreme Court held that Erie did not prevent the issue of whether Byrd was covered by workmen's compensation, which would be tried to a judge in a state trial, from being tried to a jury in a federal diversity case. The Court continued:

"It cannot be gainsaid that there is a strong federal policy against allowing state rules to disrupt the judge-jury relationship in the federal courts."

356 U.S. at 538, 78 S. Ct. at 901, 2 L. Ed. 2d at 963.

In the present case, the federal courts' judge-jury relationship would suffer a similar disruption if the trial judge had to apply the Florida rather than the federal standard of sufficiency of evidence in determining whether to take away from the jury certain fact issues concerning damages. This Court has held repeatedly that "* * * in a diversity case, state law controls as to the substantive elements of plaintiff's case and of defendant's defense, but the sufficiency of the evidence to raise a question of fact for the jury is controlled by federal law." Shirey v. Louisville & Nashville R. Co., 5 Cir. 1964, 327 F.2d 549, 552; Melton v. Greyhound Corp., 5 Cir., 1965, 354 F.2d 970; Kirby Lumber Corp. v. White, 5 Cir. 1961, 288 F.2d 566; Revlon, Inc. v. Buchanan, 5 Cir. 1959, 271 F.2d 795, 81 A.L.R.2d 222; Reuter v. Eastern Air Lines, 5 Cir. 1955, 226 F.2d 443.

We proceed to ABC's claim that the damages found were speculative. ABC asserts that the plaintiffs did not show how many of the Cortland records would be sold, and argues that damages should therefore be limited to the combined out-of-pocket expenses of Curran, Elias, and Topps, plus the $500 credit which Cortland retracted from the Topps account.

ABC admits liability. It admits that it knew Velvit was bound to Curran and Elias when it induced Velvit to ignore that contract and sign its own. ABC is the tortfeasor; its own act prevented anyone from determining how many copies of the record Cortland could have sold. Now ABC tries to use the uncertainty which it caused as a shield to any more than a pin prick of liability.

A successful attempt of this sort would be unjust and unbearable for our system. Such a result "* * * would enable the wrongdoer to profit by his wrongdoing at the expense of his victim. It would be an inducement to make wrongdoing so effective and complete in every case as to preclude any recovery, by rendering the measure of damages uncertain. [This result] * * * would mean that the more grievous the wrong done, the less likelihood there would be of a recovery." Bigelow v. RKO Radio Pictures, Inc., 1946, 327 U.S. 251, 264-265, 66 S. Ct. 574, 579-580, 90 L. Ed. 652, 660.

For these reasons, the rule which demands proof of damages (see Restatement, Torts, § 912 (1939)), is relaxed somewhat in cases where exact loss is unascertainable because of the tort.

"Although in such cases, the burden is on the injured person to prove with a fair degree of certainty that the business or transaction was or could have been profitable, it is not fatal to the recovery of substantial damages that he is unable to prove with definiteness the amount of profits he would have made or the amount of harm which the defendant has caused. It is only essential that he present such evidence as might reasonably be expected to be available under the circumstances * * *." Restatement, Torts § 912, Comment d (1939) [emphasis added].

The Supreme Court, in Bigelow, supra, 327 U.S. at 264, 66 S. Ct. at 580, 90 L. Ed. at 660, recognized this rule.

"But the jury may make a just and reasonable estimate of the damage based on relevant data, and render its verdict accordingly. In such circumstances 'juries are allowed to act on probable and inferential as well as [upon] direct and positive proof.' [citing Story Parchment Co. v. Paterson Parchment Paper Co., supra, 282 U.S. 555, at 564, 51 S. Ct. 248, at 250, 251, 75 L. Ed. 544, at 549, and Eastman Kodak Co. v. Southern Photo Materials Co., 273 U.S. 359, 47 S. Ct. 400, 71 L. Ed. 684]."

We have followed that result in Robey v. Sun Record Co., 5 Cir. 1957, 242 F.2d 684. See Hartley & Parker, Inc. v. Florida Beverage Corp., 5 Cir. 1962, 307 F.2d 916; Kelite Products v. Binzel, 5 Cir. 1955, 224 F.2d 131.

The "relevant data" in evidence in the present case included the contract setting royalty payments to Topps and the Curran-Elias agreement. There was evidence (from ABC's vice president, Newton) of the expected sales of a successful record at that time and evidence that the right to reissue a successful record as part of an album was worth up to $10,000. Cortland was represented as a young and eager company with several hits to its credit. Evidence which the jury could believe showed that skill and persistence in promotion, distribution and sale of a record can make the difference between success and failure.

Indeed, in Robey v. Sun Record Co., supra, a case in which the defendant enticed a popular singer away from a contract with plaintiff, we said

"In determining the amount of damages for the interference with a contract for the personal services of a musical artist, and we will not deny those who had and those who sought the right to his services the privilege of regarding him as such, there is not any fixed yardstick by which the award of damages is to be measured. There was a heavy sale of the first record made by Parker for Sun. The sales of the second record started well but declined rapidly. This is urged by Robey as showing that Parker's career was coming to a close and the interference by Robey, if any there was, did not result in damages. But, as Sun contends, it may be that the heavy sale of the first record might have been attributable to the skillful guidance of Sun as much as to the talents of Parker." 242 F.2d at 689.

We hold that the evidence was sufficient to support the jury's verdict.

## II.

On the cross-appeal, plaintiffs claim that the trial judge erroneously took the issues of punitive damages and slander from the jury.

Under Florida law, punitive damages may be asserted for "malice, moral turpitude, wantonness, or the outrageousness of the tort." Dr. P. Phillips & Sons, Inc. v. Kilgore, 152 Fla. 578, 12 So.2d 465; Winn & Lovett Grocery Co. v. Archer, 1936, 126 Fla. 308, 171 So. 214. The Florida cases also make it clear that "malice" does not necessarily mean "anger or a malevolent or vindictive feeling toward the plaintiff" ( Farish v. Smoot, 1952, Fla., 58 So.2d 534, 538), but can be inferred from "entire want of care or attention to duty, or great indifference to the persons, property or rights of others." Griffith v. Shamrock Village, 1957, Fla., 94 So.2d 854. See also LaPorte v. Associated Independents, Inc., 1964, Fla., 163 So.2d 267; Webb's City, Inc. v. Hancur, Fla. App.1962, 144 So.2d 319. The facts of Griffith show that this rule means what it says: the plaintiff, who lived in the defendant's apartment house, recovered compensatory and punitive damages for the defendant's wanton failure to deliver a telephone message from plaintiff's family advising plaintiff of his brother's wedding date. The plaintiff did not prove actual malice between the defendant and himself, but rested on the gross want of care showed by defendant in failing to carry out a duty which it had assumed. The Florida Supreme Court upheld a jury verdict including punitive damages.

In the present case, the trial judge followed the commendable practice of holding a detailed charge conference, portions of which are in the printed record on appeal. During this conference the judge indicated that he would not charge on punitive damages because the evidence did not warrant a finding of "malice" or "reckless disregard" of plaintiffs' contract rights. Scrutiny of the record in light of the Florida cases forces us to disagree. Reasonable minds might differ over ABC's motive and attitude in advising Velvit to drop his association with Curran and Elias. Velvit testified that Jarvis told him repeatedly to "forget" Curran and Elias. He also testified that rather stronger language was used to give this advice. ABC might have believed that Velvit's contract with Curran was not binding, but we do not think that the evidence excludes the possibility that ABC wanted Velvit for itself and felt that it could get away with inducing Velvit to break an otherwise binding agreement, in complete disregard of the rights of Curran, Elias, and Topps. This issue should have been left to the jury. E.g., Geddes v. Daughters of Charity of St. Vincent De Paul, Inc., 5 Cir. 1965, 348 F.2d 144.

## III.

We agree with the trial judge, however, that plaintiffs made out no cause of action for defamation.

The plaintiffs' brief on this point refers to two instances to support its claim that the slander issue should not have been taken from the jury. The first is Velvit's characterization of Elias in the telephone conversation with Erman and Glicken from the ABC office. The second is the characterization of Elias which Erman and Glicken made to the industry generally when they embarrassedly withdrew the Velvit record. The fatal deficiency in these claims is immediately obvious: ABC did not make these statements, and in fact nowhere in the transcript does any witness say that ABC said or wrote anything defamatory about any of the plaintiffs. Whatever else ABC may have done, it kept its mouth shut doing it.

There must be a retrial limited to the issue of punitive damages, but in all other respects the judgment is affirmed.

Affirmed in part; reversed and remanded in part.

———————————

This opinion was written by Judge Goldberg and as he avers, this case emanates "from the raucous, fast-moving, competitive world of American popular music, where nothing is more alive than the hope of success, nothing more commoner than failure, nothing more ephemeral than fame, and nothing more fundamental than a smile and a shoeshine" (paraphrasing from Arthur Miller's "Death of a Salesman, at 138 (1949)). It's difficult to measure damages, especially for a new artist, for entertainment violations and because of their high failure rate of entertainment projects. In this case, plaintiff record company, its president, and a record promoter sued another record company, ABC- Paramount, for unfair competition, interference with contractual relations, and defamation. The question is which recording company owned the rights to certain recordings by Jimmy Velvit.

In the opinion, the court avers that "Jimmy Velvit" was a stage name for James Tennant—that's a mistake. His real names is James Mullins, and he was born on January 11, 1941, in Coalgate, Oklahoma; he has also recorded under the name "James Bell." "Jimmy Velvit" asked Ray Curran, who was a golf club manager and fledgling concert promoter, if he could perform until the fog-delayed entertainers arrived at the Jacksonville Coliseum to perform for an impatient crowd of 8,000 to 10,000 people. When Ray asked if "Velvit" had a union card, he said he did and performed. Two weeks later, "Velvit" appeared at Curran's country club. Both Curran and "Velvit" were neophytes in the music industry. A STAR IS BORN??? They sought advice from a more experienced record company. Eventually, "Velvit," feeling his oats, left his benefactor and the first record company and did a deal with ABC-Paramount Records. The record sold indifferently (55,000). "Velvit" received a total of $2,676.02 in royalties from his new friends at ABC.

In their lawsuit, the jury returned a verdict of $7,500 for Curran, $15,000 for Topps (the first recording company), and enjoined ABC from using the "Velvit" recordings and ordered them returned to Topps. ABC appealed, but tellingly didn't care about the returned records, and contested only the award of damages. Plaintiffs argued in their cross-appeal that the trial judge should have charged the jury on the question of punitive damages. The appeals court affirmed, but allowed the plaintiffs a retrial on the issue of punitive damages only.

On appeal, ABC contended that the jury's award of compensation damages was merely speculative; "Velvit" was a new, inexperienced talent—your guess is as good as mine as to how much the first recording company would have earned without the intentional subverting of the original recording contract.

ABC admitted liability. It admitted that it knew "Velvit" was bound to Curran and Elias of Topps when it induced "Velvit" to ignore the contract and sign its own. ABC is the tortfeasor; its own act prevented anyone from determining how many copies of the record the original team of Curran and Topps could have sold. Now, ABC tried to use the uncertainty which it caused "as a shield to anymore than a pinprick of liability." A successful attempt of this sort would be unjust and unbearable as it would let tortfeasors profit by their wrongdoing. The usual demand that damages be proved (see Restatement, Torts, Section 912 (1939)) is "relaxed somewhat in cases where exact loss is unascertainable because of the tort."

Lamothe v. Atl. Recording Corp.
United States Court of Appeals for the Ninth Circuit
May 6, 1988, Argued and Submitted; June 1, 1988, Filed
No. 87-5785
847 F.2d 1403

THOMPSON, Circuit Judge:

Robert M. Lamothe and Ronald D. Jones appeal from the district court's grant of summary judgment in favor of Robinson L. Crosby and Juan Croucier, and Atlantic Recording Corp., Marshall Berle, Time Coast Music, Ratt Music, Chappell Music Co., Rightsong Music, Inc., Stephen Pearcy, Warren de Martini, Robert Blotzer, and WEA International, Inc. The district court held that summary judgment was appropriate because Lamothe and Jones failed to establish that section 43(a) of the Lanham Act, 15 U.S.C. § 1125(a), provides relief to co-authors whose names have been omitted from a record album cover and sheet music featuring the co-authored compositions. Because the court concluded that no federal cause of action existed, the court also dismissed the plaintiffs' pendent state law claims for an accounting, defamation, and misattribution of authorship.

We have jurisdiction of this appeal under 28 U.S.C. § 1291, and we reverse.

## I.
## STANDARD OF REVIEW

We review a grant of summary judgment de novo. T. W. Elec. Serv., Inc. v. Pacific Elec. Contractors Ass'n, 809 F.2d 626, 629 (9th Cir. 1987). "Summary judgment is proper if, after viewing the evidence in the light most favorable to the party opposing the motion, the movant is clearly entitled to prevail as a matter of law." Deukmejian v. United States Postal Serv., 734 F.2d 460, 462 (9th Cir. 1984). "The moving party is 'entitled to judgment as a matter of law' [when] the nonmoving party has failed to make a sufficient showing on an essential element of her case with respect to which she has the burden of proof." Celotex Corp. v. Catrett, 477 U.S. 317, 323, 91 L. Ed. 2d 265, 106 S. Ct. 2548 (1986) (quoting Anderson v. Liberty Lobby, Inc., 477 U.S. 242, 250, 91 L. Ed. 2d 202, 106 S. Ct. 2505 (1986)).

## II.
## FACTS

Viewing the evidence in the light most favorable to Lamothe and Jones, the nonmoving parties, the facts pertinent to this appeal are that Lamothe, Jones and Crosby are coauthors of two songs entitled "Scene of the Crime," and "I'm Insane." These works were composed while Lamothe, Jones and Crosby were members of a band called Mac Meda. After Mac Meda disbanded, Crosby joined another musical group called RATT. While Crosby was a member of RATT, he and Juan Croucier licensed the songs at issue to Time Coast Music, which in turn sub-licensed the songs to other of the defendants in this case, including Atlantic Recording. In 1984, Atlantic released an album by the group RATT entitled "Out of the Cellar," which included the recordings of the songs "Scene of the Crime" and "I'm Insane." Because of the popularity of this album, the music and lyrics for all compositions on the album were released in sheet music form by the sub-licensee Chappell Music Co. In both versions (album and sheet music), authorship of the music and lyrics of "I'm Insane" was attributed solely to Robinson Crosby and the music and lyrics of "Scene of the Crime" were attributed to Robinson Crosby and Juan Croucier. Neither Robert Lamothe nor Ronald Jones received credit for their roles in the writing of these songs.

## III.
## ANALYSIS

The principal issue on appeal is whether Lamothe and Jones have stated a claim under section 43(a) of the Lanham Act, 15 U.S.C. § 1125(a), which provides in pertinent part:

Any person who shall affix, apply, or annex, or use in connection with any goods or services . . . a false designation of origin, or any false description or representation, including words or other symbols tending falsely to describe or represent the same, and shall cause such goods or services to enter into commerce, and any person who shall with knowledge of the falsity of such designation of origin or description or representation cause or procure the same to be transported or used in commerce . . . shall be liable to a civil action by any person . . . who believes that he is or is likely to be damaged by the use of such false description or representation.

Id. The Lanham Act's prohibition of false designations or representations reaches either goods or services sold in interstate commerce. Smith v. Montoro, 648 F.2d 602, 605 (9th Cir. 1981). It has been applied to motion picture representations, id., and the defendants cite no case holding that it does not similarly reach musical compositions. We also note that "to recover for a violation of [section 43(a)] it is not necessary that a mark or trade-mark be registered. The dispositive question is whether the party has a reasonable interest to be protected against false advertising." Id. (quoting New West Corp. v. NYM Co. of Cal., 595 F.2d 1194, 1198 (9th Cir. 1979)); see also Smith, 648 F.2d at 605 n.3 (collecting cases describing reach of section 43(a)). Finally, we recently have made clear that in cases involving false designation, the actionable "conduct must not only be unfair but must in some discernable way be competitive." Halicki v. United Artists Communications, Inc., 812 F.2d 1213, 1214 (9th Cir. 1987). In the present case, the plaintiffs clearly have a legitimate interest in protecting their work from being falsely designated as the creation of another. The defendants do not dispute that the plaintiffs and Crosby are competitors in the relevant market. Having determined that the plaintiffs have an interest protected by the Lanham Act, we turn our attention to whether the defendants' conduct in this case constitutes a violation of section 43(a).

1. Prohibited Conduct Under Section 43(a)

The Lanham Act applies to two different types of unfair competition in interstate commerce. The first is "palming off" or "passing off," which involves selling a good or service of one person's creation under the name or mark of another. Smith v. Montoro, 648 F.2d 602, 604 (9th Cir. 1981). Section 43(a) also reaches false advertising about the goods or services of the advertiser. U-Haul Int'l, Inc. v. Jartran, Inc., 681 F.2d 1159, 1160 (9th Cir. 1982). Because we conclude that Lamothe and Jones, for purposes of surviving a motion for summary judgment, have produced evidence satisfying the elements of a "reverse passing off" claim, we need not decide whether the defendants' actions also constitute false advertising.

2. Passing Off

The leading case in this circuit discussing the "passing off" doctrine embodied in section 43(a) is Smith v. Montoro, 648 F.2d 602 (9th Cir. 1981). In that case, an actor named Paul Smith had contracted to star in a film. Smith's contract provided that he would receive star billing in the screen credits and any advertising associated with the distribution of the film. A licensee of the production company subsequently removed Smith's name from the screen credits and advertising materials and substituted the name of another actor, "Bob Spencer." Id. at 603. Smith sued the production company and its licensee, alleging a violation of the Lanham Act. The district court dismissed the complaint because it did not allege a practice "in the nature of, or economically equivalent to, palming off . . . and/or misuse of trademarks and trade names." Id. at 604. We disagreed and reversed the case and remanded it to the district court to reinstate Smith's complaint.

We began our analysis in Smith by defining "passing off" as the practice of selling one person's product or service under the name or mark of another. Id. Passing off may be either "express" or "implied." Id. Express passing off occurs when a business labels its goods or services with a mark identical to that of another enterprise, or otherwise expressly misrepresents the origin of the goods or services. Id. Implied passing off involves the use of a competitor's advertising material, or a sample or photograph of the competitor's product, to impliedly represent that the product being sold is made by the competitor. Id.

In Smith, we further explained that section 43(a) also encompasses merchandising "practices or conduct 'economically equivalent' to palming off." Id. at 605. Among those practices is "reverse passing off," which may be either "express" or "implied." Express reverse passing off is "accomplished . . . when the wrongdoer removes the name or trademark on another party's product and sells that product under a name chosen by the wrongdoer." Id. Implied reverse passing off is accomplished simply by removing or obliterating the name of the source and then selling the product in an unbranded state. Id.

We concluded in Smith that by deleting Smith's name from the film and advertising materials and substituting the name "Bob Spencer," the defendants had engaged in express reverse passing off. We explained that as a matter of policy, such conduct, like traditional palming off, is wrongful because it involves an attempt to misappropriate or profit from another's talents and workmanship. Moreover, in reverse palming off cases, the originator of the misidentified product is involuntarily deprived of the advertising value of [his] name and the goodwill that otherwise would stem from public knowledge of the true source of the satisfactory product. The ultimate purchaser (or viewer) is also deprived of knowing the true source of the product and may even be deceived into believing that it comes from a different source.

Id. at 607 (citations omitted). In the present case, taking the allegations of the complaint as true, the defendants engaged in express reverse palming off, by which they deprived Lamothe and Jones of recognition and profits from the release of the two songs that were their due.

The defendants' argument on appeal, reduced to its simplest form, is that there can be no express reverse passing off when the designation of a product's source is partially correct. Defendants argue that the failure to attribute authorship to Lamothe and Jones is a "mere omission," which is not actionable under section 43(a). We disagree. We do not read the "falsity" requirement in origination cases so narrowly that a partially accurate designation of origin, which [Text Deleted by Court Emendation] obscures the contribution of another to the final product, is a permissible form of competition.

The defendants place great emphasis on Universal City Studios, Inc. v. Sony Corp. of America, 429 F. Supp. 407 (C.D. Cal. 1977), which stated that "it is hard to see how a simple failure to disclose can be brought within [section 43(a)'s] terms." Id. at 410. This statement, however, must be read in the context of that case, which involved a claim by two film studios against the manufacturer of a video recording machine. The film studios argued that Sony's failure to disclose to consumers that videotaping copyrighted works from television might violate federal copyright law constituted a section 43(a) claim. The district court disagreed because the advertising in that case was not false. See id. at 409. To the extent that the Sony opinion addresses passing off claims, its conclusions are dicta. Moreover, the ultimate conclusion reached in Sony was that "it cannot be said that as conceived or enacted [section 43(a)] was designed to make all failures to disclose actionable." Id. (emphasis added).

In the present case, the defendants unilaterally decided to attribute authorship to less than all of the joint authors of the musical compositions. Had the defendants decided to attribute authorship to a fictitious person, to the group "RATT," or to some other person, this would be a false designation of origin. It seems to us no less "false" to attribute authorship to only one of several co-authors. Cf. Gilliam v. American Broadcasting Co's., 538 F.2d 14, 24 (2d Cir. 1976) (stating in dicta that broadcasting heavily edited version of "Monty Python's Flying Circus" without appropriate disclaimer that authors had not approved editing amounted to violation of section 43(a)); id. at 26 (Gurfein, J., concurring) ("So long as it is made clear that the ABC version is not approved by the Monty Python group, there is no misdescription of origin."). The policies we identified in Smith, namely, ensuring that the producer of a good or service receives appropriate recognition and that the consuming public receives full information about the origin of the good, apply with equal force here. An incomplete designation of the source of the good or service is no less misleading because it is partially correct. Misbranding a product to only partially identify its source is the economic equivalent of passing off one person's product under the name or mark of another. And the Smith case makes clear that in assessing section 43(a) claims, courts are to consider whether the challenged "practices or conduct [are] 'economically equivalent' to palming off." Smith, 648 F.2d at 605.

3. Liability of Licensees

Atlantic Recording and the other licensees or sublicensees of Crosby and Croucier argue that even if Lamothe and Jones have stated a section 43(a) claim, they cannot be held liable because they are licensees. We disagree. Some of the licensees may have been involved in affixing an incomplete designation of authorship. These licensees would be liable under section 43(a) regardless of knowledge. See 15 U.S.C. § 1125(a). The express language of section 43(a) also imposes liability upon those who "with knowledge of the falsity of such designation of origin . . . cause or procure the same to be transported or used in commerce." Id. The licensees have cited no case holding that a licensee is exempt from the prohibitions of the Lanham Act. Whether the licensees affixed the incomplete authorship or had knowledge of the false designation of origin are matters best left to the trier of fact to resolve.

## IV.
## CONCLUSION

Because we conclude that summary judgment was inappropriate, we reverse the decision of the district court and remand the case with instructions to reinstate Lamothe's and Jones's federal causes of action. We also instruct the district court to consider reinstating the plaintiffs' pendent state claims, which the district court dismissed for lack of jurisdiction when it dismissed the Lanham Act claim. See Simon Oil Co. v. Norman, 789 F.2d 780, 782 (9th Cir. 1986).

REVERSED AND REMANDED.

Radioactive, J.V. v. Manson
United States District Court for the Southern District of New York
July 29, 2001, Decided; July 31, 2001, Filed
01 Civ. 1948 (SAS)
153 F. Supp. 2d 462

OPINION AND ORDER

SHIRA A. SCHEINDLIN, U.S.D.J.:

On March 7, 2001, Radioactive Records, J.V. ("Radioactive") filed this diversity action against Shirley Manson, a well-known singer and performer, alleging, inter alia, a claim for breach of contract. Manson now moves to dismiss this action in favor of parallel state court proceedings in California, arguing that the California Action was filed first and that this Court should abstain from exercising jurisdiction. Radioactive cross-moves for partial summary judgment on two issues: (1) that New York law governs the recording contract between Manson and Radioactive; and (2) because New York law governs, California Labor Code § 2855 ("section 2855") is inapplicable to that recording contract. For the reasons set forth below, both motions are granted.

## I. BACKGROUND

A. The Relevant Contracts

On February 23, 1993, Manson, a resident of Scotland, signed a recording contract with Radioactive, a joint venture between Radioactive, Inc. and MCA Records (now Universal Music Group ("UMG")) (the "Manson-Radioactive Agreement"). See Plaintiff's Statement Pursuant to Local Rule 56.1 ("Pl. 56.1") PP 1, 2, 10; 4/27/01 Declaration of Shirley Manson in Support of Motion to Dismiss ("Manson Decl. I") P 2. That contract obligates Manson to deliver at least one album and, at the sole option of Radioactive, up to six additional albums. See Complaint PP 7. The contract also designates New York as the forum of choice and New York law as the rule of decision in any future dispute over the contract. See Pl. 56. 1 P 3; 2/23/93 Manson-Radioactive Agreement, Ex. G to 4/25/01 Declaration of Elizabeth Barrowman Gibson, Manson's counsel ("Gibson Decl."), at 40. Later that year, Radioactive released an album titled "Angelfish" featuring Manson as the lead singer. See Pl. 56.1. P 12; Manson Decl. I P 2. Angelfish was unsuccessful; only 10,000 copies were sold. See Manson Decl. I P 2.

In late 1994, Butch Vig, Steve Marker, and Doug (Duke) Erikson formed the band Garbage in Madison, Wisconsin and signed a recording contract with Almo

Records ("Almo"). See 12/21/94 Agreement between Almo and Garbage ("Almo-Garbage Agreement"), Ex. A to 5/21/01 Declaration of William A. Berrol, counsel for defendant, in Opposition to Plaintiff's Motion for Partial Summary Judgment ("Berrol Decl. II"). As veteran music producers, Vig, Marker, and Erickson wanted to ensure that their endeavor would be directed by Jerry Moss, a legendary figure in the music industry. See First Amended Complaint ("FAC") in Garbage, Inc. v. Almo Sounds, Inc., No. BC244047 (Cal. Supp. filed Jan. 29, 2001) ("Garbage v. Almo"), Ex. A to Gibson Decl, P 2. To that end, Garbage negotiated the inclusion of a "Key Man" clause in its agreement. See Almo-Garbage Agreement at 78. Garbage would only be bound to Almo Records as long as Jerry Moss was Chairman. See id. The contract also designates California as the forum of choice and California law as the rule of decision. See id. at 62.

Having seen Manson in an Angelfish video on MTV, Garbage invited Manson to record with them as the band's lead singer. See 5/18/01 Declaration of Shirley Manson in Opposition to Motion for Partial Summary Judgment ("Manson Decl. II") P 11; see also Manson Decl. I P 4. On August 10, 1994, Manson entered into a written agreement with Garbage — an agreement which was negotiated and entered into in California ("Manson-Garbage Agreement"). See Manson's Response to Plaintiff's Statement Pursuant to Local Rule 56.1 ("Def. 56.1") P 23; Manson Decl. I P 10. On December 21, 1994, Manson and Radioactive executed an Inducement Letter as a material part of the Garbage-Almo Agreement ("Manson Inducement Letter"). See Def. 56. 1 P 24; Manson Decl. I P 9. The Manson Inducement Letter contains a California choice of forum and a California choice of law provision. See Def. 56. 1 P 14; Manson Inducement Letter, Ex. 5 to 5/23/01 Declaration of Marc Marmaro, Manson's counsel, in Opposition to Plaintiff's Motion for Partial Summary Judgment ("Marmaro Decl."), at 149.

Shortly thereafter, Radioactive was asked to allow Manson to record one song with Garbage. See Complaint P 9. Radioactive granted such permission and subsequently agreed to let Manson record an entire album with Garbage. See Pl. 56. 1 P 13; Complaint P 10. The album, eponymously named "Garbage," was very successful, selling over 4 million copies worldwide and garnering three Grammy nominations. See Complaint P 11; FAC in Garbage v. Almo P 1. By agreement dated September 1, 1997, Radioactive agreed to allow Manson to record a second album with Garbage in return for a portion of the royalties. See Pl. 56. 1 P 14; Def. 56. 1 P 25; see also 9/1/97 Agreement between Almo and Radioactive ("Almo-Radioactive Agreement"), Ex. 6 to Marmaro Decl.; FAC in Garbage v. Almo P 1. The Almo-Radioactive Agreement also contained California choice of forum and choice of law clauses. See Def. 56. 1 P 25; Almo-Radioactive Agreement at 166. Garbage's second album, titled "Garbage Version 2.0," was also successful, selling another 4 million copies. See FAC in Garbage v. Almo P 1.

By Garbage's estimation, Radioactive garnered more than $ 1,000,000 in royalties from the album's sales. See Def. 56. 1 P 55.

In 2000, Moss sold his publishing company, which included Almo, among other affiliates, to UMG, the successor to MCA Records. See Berrol Decl. P 10; see also Irv Lichtman, "Moss, Alpert Sell Rondor to Universal, Settle Lawsuit," Billboard, August 12, 2000, Ex. C. to Berrol Decl. II, at 395. Thereafter, invoking the Key Man clause, Garbage sought on October 25, 2000 to terminate its contract with Almo on the assumption, supported by press coverage, that Jerry Moss was no longer the Chairman of Almo. See Barrol Decl. P 11; FAC in Garbage v. Almo P 2. According to Garbage, the band met with representatives of UMG, who informed them that even if they could terminate their contract, UMG would still control Manson's original contract with Radioactive. See Berrol Decl. P 12; FAC in Garbage v. Almo P 2.

## B. The California Action

On January 29, 2001, Manson and Garbage filed suit in California state court essentially peeking to become "free agents" (the "California Action"). See Pl. 56. 1 P 15. Their complaint seeks a declaratory judgment that both the Almo-Garbage Agreement and the Almo-Radioactive Agreement are unenforceable and/or have terminated. See Complaint in Garbage v. Almo PP 25-28. On February 5, 2001, the plaintiffs in the California Action filed the FAC, adding a claim that the Manson-Radioactive Agreement, executed in February 1993, become unenforceable after February 23, 2000 pursuant to California Labor Code § 2855 ("section 2855"), which provides that personal service contracts "may not be enforced . . . beyond seven years from the commencement of service under" the contract. See FAC in Garbage v. Almo P 26.

On March 8, 2001, one day after filing the instant complaint, Radioactive moved to dismiss the declaratory judgment claim in the California Action asserting that any claim regarding the Manson-Radioactive Agreement must be brought in New York. See Gibson Decl. P 5. Then, on March 15, 2001, Radioactive filed a Cross-Complaint against Manson in the California Action. See id. at 3; see also Conditional Cross-Complaint of Radioactive J.V., Ex. E to Gibson Decl. The Cross-Complaint asserted the same claims and factual allegations brought in the instant action. See Gibson Decl. P 6.

Radioactive's motion to dismiss was denied on April 10. The California court noted that both of the relevant contracts — the Almo-Garbage Agreement and the Manson-Radioactive Agreement — were inextricably intertwined, that dismissal would lead to piecemeal litigation, and that it expected the New York federal court to respect its decision. See 4/10/01 Minute Order of the Honorable Marvin M. Lager ("California Order"), Ex. C to Gibson Declaration; 4/10/01 Transcript of Proceedings before the Honorable Marvin M. Lager

("California Tr."), Ex. D to Gibson Decl., at 4-6, 10, 22, 25. On June 25, the California Court of Appeal denied Radioactive's petition for writ of mandate seeking review of the California court's order. See Radioactive Records, J.V. v. Shirley Manson, No. B149619 (Cal. App. 4th June 25, 2001), Ex. A to 6/26/01 Letter from Elizabeth Barrowman Gibson.

### C. The Instant Action

Radioactive filed this action more than five weeks after the California Action was filed. In this action, Radioactive asserts three claims. In Claim I, plaintiff contends that Manson breached the Manson-Radioactive Agreement by repudiating her obligations in the recording contract and refusing to deliver the required additional six albums. See Complaint PP 18-23. In Claim II, plaintiff maintains that in the event that section 2855 is deemed to render the Manson-Radioactive Agreement unenforceable, Radioactive should still be awarded damages pursuant to California Labor Code § 2855(b)(3) for Manson's failure to deliver the remaining six albums. See id. PP 25-27. Finally, in Claim III, plaintiff seeks a declaration that the California Action violates the choice of law and choice of forum clauses in the Manson-Radioactive Agreement, and that the Manson-Radioactive Agreement is enforceable. See id. PP 29-31.

## II. PLAINTIFF'S SUMMARY JUDGMENT MOTION

### A. Legal Standard for Motion for Summary Judgment

A party is entitled to summary judgment when there is "no genuine issue of material fact" and the undisputed facts warrant judgment for the moving party as a matter of law. See Fed. R. Civ. P. 56(c); Celotex Corp. v. Catrett, 477 U.S. 317, 321-22, 91 L. Ed. 2d 265, 106 S. Ct. 2548 (1986). "While genuineness runs to whether disputed factual issues can reasonably be resolved in favor of either party,' materiality runs to whether the dispute matters, i.e., whether it concerns facts that can affect the outcome under the applicable substantive law." Mitchell v. Washingtonville Cent. Sch. Dist., 190 F.3d 1, 5 (2d Cir. 1999) (quoting Graham v. Henderson, 89 F.3d 75, 79 (2d Cir. 1996)).

The moving party "always bears" the burden of production or "the initial responsibility of informing the . . . court of the basis for its motion, and identifying those portions of 'the pleadings, the depositions, answers to interrogatories, and admissions on file, together with the affidavits, if any,' which it believes demonstrate the absence of a genuine issue of material fact." Celotex, 477 U.S. at 323 (quoting Fed. R. Civ. P. 56(c)); see also LaFond v. General Physics Servs. Corp., 50 F.3d 165, 171 (2d Cir. 1995). Once that burden is satisfied, the non-moving party must present "significant probative supporting evidence" that a factual dispute exists. Fed. R. Civ. P. 56(e); Anderson v. Liberty Lobby, Inc., 477 U.S. 242, 249, 91 L. Ed. 2d 202, 106 S. Ct. 2505 (1986).

The court's role is not to try issues of fact, but rather to determine whether issues exist to be tried. See Rule v. Brine, Inc., 85 F.3d 1002, 1011 (2d Cir. 1996). All ambiguities must be resolved in favor of the party against whom summary judgment is sought. See Anderson, 477 U.S. at 255; Rule, 85 F.3d at 1011. If there is any evidence in the record from which a reasonable inference could be drawn in favor of the non-moving party on a material issue of fact, summary judgment is improper. See Hetchkop v. Woodlawn at Grassmere, Inc., 116 F.3d 28, 33 (2d Cir. 1997).

### B. Choice of Law

"Federal courts sitting in diversity in New York must apply New York's choice-of-law rules when determining the law that governs the contract." Lehman Bros. Commercial Corp. v. Minmetals Int'l Non-Ferrous Metals Trading Co., 2000 U.S. Dist. LEXIS 16445, *33, No. 94 Civ. 8301, 2000 WL 1702039, at *11 (S.D.N.Y. Nov. 13, 2000); see also Lund's Inc. v. Chemical Bank, 870 F.2d 840, 845 (2d Cir. 1989). New York courts follow the test laid out in the Restatement (Second) of Conflicts of Laws § 187. Accordingly, a court may refuse enforcement of a choice-of-law clause only where (1) there is no reasonable basis for the parties' choice, or (2) the application of the chosen law would violate a fundamental public policy of another jurisdiction with materially greater interests in the dispute. See Lehman Bros. Commercial Corp., 2000 WL 1702039, at *12; see also Hartford Fire Ins. Co. v. Orient Overseas Containers Lines (UK) Ltd., 230 F.3d 549, 556 (2d Cir. 2000) ("New York law is clear in cases involving a contract with an express choice-of-law provision: Absent fraud or violation of public policy, a court is to apply the law selected in the contract as long as the state selected has sufficient contacts with the transaction."); International Minerals and Res., S.A. v. Pappas, 96 F.3d 586, 592 (2d Cir. 1996) (same).

Manson, however, argues that the enactment of New York General Obligation Law § 5-1401 ("section 5-1401") in 1984 created an exception to this general rule with respect to personal service contracts. See Manson's Memorandum of Points and Authorities in Opposition to Plaintiff Radioactive Records, J.V.'s Motion for Partial Summary Judgment ("Def. Sum. Jud. Opp.") at 6-10. Section 5-1401 provides that 'for certain commercial contracts of at least $ 250,000, but explicitly excluding contracts for personal services, the parties' selection of New York law in the contract is enforceable even if the transaction itself bears no reasonable relation to New York. According to Manson, section 5-1401 carved out an exception for personal service contracts — such contracts are governed by the law of the state with the most significant contacts to the contract and parties (the "center of gravity" test) even where there is a contractual choice of law provision. See id.

Manson appears to have badly misread section 5-1401. By enacting that statute, "New York sought to secure and augment its reputation as a center of international commerce." See Lehman Bros. Commercial Corp., 2000 WL 1702039, at *12. The exclusion of personal service contracts from that law's purview merely establishes that the older reasonable basis standard still applies to choice of law clauses in those contracts. See, e.g., Woodling v. Garrett Corp., 813 F.2d 543, 551 (2d Cir. 1987) (applying reasonable basis standard to choice of law provision in employment contract); Aramony v. United Way of Am., 1998 U.S. Dist. LEXIS 5885, No. 96 Civ. 3962, 1998 WL 205331, at *2 (S.D.N.Y. Apr. 27, 1998) (same); Don King Prods. v. Douglas, 742 F. Supp. 741, 756 (S.D.N.Y. 1990) (applying reasonable basis standard to choice of law provision in promotional contract). Indeed, the New York legislature made clear in section 5-1401(2) that "nothing contained in [section 5-1401] shall be construed to limit or deny the enforcement of any provision respecting choice of law in any other contract, agreement or undertaking." N.Y. Gen. Obli. Law § 5-1401(2).

The Manson-Radioactive Agreement expressly designates New York law as the rule of decision in any dispute over the contract. Thus, Radioactive need merely show that New York has a "substantial relationship to the parties or the transaction," or that there was a "reasonable basis for the parties' choice." Restatement (Second) of Conflicts of Laws § 187. Manson's contention that California has the most substantial contacts with the contract and parties, therefore, is simply irrelevant to the choice-of-law inquiry.

Each party has provided reams of materials to dispute the "facts" asserted by the other. Radioactive asserts that its principal place of business is New York; Manson asserts that it is California. Radioactive asserts that its President Gary Kurfirst is based in New York; Manson asserts that he is based in Los Angeles. Luckily, these disputed facts are immaterial to the choice of law inquiry. Even if one accepts Manson's version of the facts, Radioactive and Manson had a reasonable basis for choosing New York law. Manson is a resident of Scotland, and New York may have seemed the most convenient forum for both parties. At least some of Manson's negotiations with Radioactive took place in New York. See Manson Decl. II at 3. UMG regularly put New York choice of law provisions in recording contracts. See Plaintiff's Memorandum of Points and Authorities in Support of Radioactive Records, J.V.'s Motion for Partial Summary Judgment at 4 ("New York federal and state courts have significant experience with music industry contracts, and the parties wanted to avail themselves of that experience by selecting a New York forum and New York law."). Manson's first album, "Angelfish", was recorded in the New York metropolitan area under the supervision of New York-based employees of Radioactive. See Manson Decl. II at

2-3. The album was mastered in New York and delivered to Radioactive in New York. See id. at 2. At the time the contract was executed, a time before any relationship with Garbage was envisioned, New York had sufficient contacts with the Manson-Radioactive transaction and New York law was a perfectly reasonable choice for the parties.

Manson argues, however, that section 2855 reflects a powerful California interest in controlling California employers, thus requiring that the New York choice of law clause be ignored. See Def. Sum. Jud. Opp. at 1-2. This argument is unavailing. In the primary California decision concerning the scope of section 2855, De Haviland v. Warner Bros. Pictures, Inc., 67 Cal. App. 2d 225, 235-36, 153 P.2d 983 (1944), the court found that the California legislature enacted section 2855 in an effort to protect California employees. Manson does not contend that she is a California employee. See Def. Sum. Jud. Opp. at 20 ("regardless of whether Ms. Manson is or is not a California resident. . . ."). Only one New York case has addressed section 2855's applicability to non-California employees. See Ketcham v. Hall Syndicate, Inc., 37 Misc. 2d 693, 236 N.Y.S.2d 206 (Sup. Ct. N.Y. Co. 1962), aff'd, 19 A.D.2d 611, 242 N.Y.S.2d 182 (1st Dept. 1963). That court held that section 2855 does not trump a New York conflict of laws determination that New York law should apply. See 236 N.Y.S.2d at 211-12; see also Foxx v. Williams, 244 Cal. App. 2d 223, 242, 52 Cal. Rptr. 896 (1966) (noting that the court in Ketcham held that "section 2855 did not apply, both because plaintiff was not an employee, and because the law of New York, not California, governed"). No court, in any state including California, has reached a contrary result. Moreover, as Radioactive points out, a determination that section 2855 applies to non-California employees of California employers would be problematic. Foreign employees of California businesses would suddenly receive the benefits of California's "7-year rule," a result the California legislature could not have intended.

Much like the "dog that did not bark," the overwhelming silence concerning section 2855 is the strongest clue. See Arthur Conan Doyle, "Silver Blaze," in The Complete Sherlock Holmes 347, 349 (Doubleday 1922) (1892). Section 2855 was enacted in 1937. Application of the law to non-California employees of California employers would have wide-reaching consequences. The fact that only one court has addressed its applicability to non-California employees — and held that it does not apply — militates against a finding that the California legislature intended to cover non-California employees.

Accordingly, plaintiff's motion for partial summary judgment is granted. New York law governs the Manson-Radioactive Agreement. Because New York law applies, section 2855 is not applicable to the Manson-Radioactive Agreement.

### A. First to File

Manson asserts that Radioactive's New York action should be dismissed pursuant to the first-to-file doctrine because the California Action was filed first. See Def. Mem. at 13-18. Manson misapplies the doctrine. The first-to-file doctrine applies to concurrent federal litigation — not concurrent state/federal litigation. "It is a 'well-settled principle' in this circuit that where proceedings involving the same parties and issues are pending simultaneously in different federal courts the first-filed of the two takes priority absent 'special circumstances' or a balance of convenience in favor of the second." Citigroup Inc. v. City Holding Co., 97 F. Supp. 2d 549, 555 (S.D.N.Y. 2000) (citation omitted); cf. Meeropol v. Nizer, 505 F.2d 232, 235 (2d Cir. 1974) ("Where an action is brought in one federal district court and a later action embracing the same issue is brought in another federal court, the first court has jurisdiction to enjoin the prosecution of the second action."). All of the cases cited by Manson involve two (or more) federal district courts. See, e.g., First City Nat'l Bank and Trust Co. v. Simmons, 878 F.2d 76, 77 (2d Cir. 1989); William Gluckin & Co. v. International Playtex Corp., 407 F.2d 177, 178 (2d Cir. 1969); Citigroup Inc., 97 F. Supp. 2d at 555; 800- Flowers, Inc. v. Intercontinental Florist, Inc., 860 F. Supp. 128, 131 (S.D.N.Y. 1994).

The Supreme Court has delineated a standard by which federal courts can determine whether to defer to parallel state actions. That standard is set forth in Colorado River Water Conservation Dist. v. United States, 424 U.S. 800, 47 L. Ed. 2d 483, 96 S. Ct. 1236 (1976). "Order in which the actions were filed" is one prong in a six-prong test for abstention. FDIC v. Four Star Holding Co., 178 F.3d 97, 101 (2d Cir. 1999). If Manson's argument were correct, and "first-to-file" could by itself necessitate dismissal from federal court in favor of parallel state proceedings, the inclusion of order of filing as one factor in a careful abstention-balancing test would be meaningless. Accordingly, Manson's motion to dismiss this action under the first-to-file doctrine is denied.

### B. Abstention

Manson also seeks to have this action stayed or dismissed under the Colorado River abstention doctrine. See Def. Mem. at 20-25, 20 n.3. The Second Circuit recently summarized that doctrine as follows:

Abstention is an extraordinary and narrow exception to a federal court's duty to exercise its jurisdiction. The Supreme Court has recognized that courts should abstain from the exercise of jurisdiction only in the exceptional circumstances where the order to the parties to repair to state court would clearly serve a countervailing interest. The test for determining whether abstention is appropriate, first articulated in Colorado River, now requires examination of six factors: (1) assumption of jurisdiction over a res; (2) inconvenience of the forum; (3) avoidance of piecemeal litigation; (4) order in which the actions were filed; (5) the law that provides the rule of decision; and (6) protection of the federal plaintiff's rights. The test does not rest on a mechanical checklist, but on a careful balancing of the important factors as they apply in a given case, with the balance heavily weighted in favor of the exercise of jurisdiction.

FDIC, 178 F.3d at 101 (quotation marks and citations omitted). The underlying principles of the Colorado River doctrine rest on considerations of "wise judicial administration, giving regard to conservation of judicial resources and comprehensive disposition of litigation." Colorado River, 424 U.S. at 817 (quotation marks and citation omitted). These principles, however, must be balanced with the "virtually unflagging obligation of the federal courts to exercise the jurisdiction given them." Id. In order to prevail on their motion, the moving parties must shoulder a heavy burden, see King v. Hahn, 885 F. Supp. 95, 97 (S.D.N.Y. 1995), because "only the clearest of justifications will warrant [a] dismissal." Colorado River, 424 U.S. at 819.

### 1. The Assumption of Jurisdiction by Either Court over Any Res or Property

There is no res involved in this dispute. This factor is thus irrelevant to the abstention inquiry. See Arkwright-Boston Mfrs. Mut. Ins. Co. v. City of New York, 762 F.2d 205, 210 (2d Cir. 1985); see also Ackoff-Ortega v. Windswept Pac. Entm't Co., 98 F. Supp. 2d 530, 536 (S.D.N.Y. 2000).

### 2. Desirability of Avoiding Piecemeal Litigation

The Supreme Court has stated that "the most important factor in our decision to approve the dismissal [in Colorado River] was the 'clear federal policy . . . [of] avoidance of piecemeal adjudication.'" Moses H. Cone Mem'l Hosp. v. Mercury Constr. Corp., 460 U.S. 1, 16, 74 L. Ed. 2d 765, 103 S. Ct. 927 (1983) (quoting Colorado River, 424 U.S. at 819); see also Arkwright-Boston Mfrs., 762 F.2d at 211 ("The danger of piecemeal litigation is the paramount consideration . . . ."); American Alliance Ins. Co. v. Eagle Ins. Co., 961 F. Supp. 652, 656 (S.D.N.Y. 1997) (same). However, the "mere potential for conflict in the results of the adjudications, does not, without more, warrant staying [the] exercise of federal jurisdiction." Colorado River, 424 U.S. at 815; see also GBA Contracting Corp. v. Fidelity and Deposit Co. of Md., 2001 U.S. Dist. LEXIS 32, No. 00 Civ. 1333, 2001 WL 11060, at *2 (S.D.N.Y. Jan. 4, 2001).

Radioactive has filed a Cross-Complaint in the California Action that is identical to the Complaint in this action. See Gibson Decl. at 3; see also Conditional Cross-Complaint of Radioactive J.V., Ex. E to Gibson Decl. Although not a determinative factor, the existence of duplicative litigation weighs in favor of abstention. See Telesco v. Telesco Fuel and Masons' Materials, Inc., 765 F.2d 356, 362 (2d Cir. 1985) (affirming abstention in part because "the federal and state actions are essentially the same"); see also Arkwright-Boston, 762 F.2d at 211 ("Maintaining virtually identical suits in two forums . . . would waste judicial resources and invite duplicative effort."); Tarka v. Greenfield Stein & Senior, LLP, 2000 U.S. Dist. LEXIS 11203, No. 00 Civ. 1262, 2000 WL 1121557, at *5 (S.D.N.Y. Aug. 8, 2000) (same); Inn Chu Trading Co. v. Sara Lee Corp., 810 F. Supp. 501, 508 (S.D.N.Y. 1992) (abstaining where the issue in the federal case was "at the core of the state action" and recognizing that the overriding concerns expressed in the abstention cases are "the avoidance of piecemeal or purely duplicative litigation and the concomitant waste of judicial resources").

The California court has already refused to dismiss the action between Manson and Radioactive, finding that UMG controlled all the contracts in question and that dismissal would lead to piecemeal litigation. See California Order; California Tr. at 4-6, 10, 22, 25. That court also determined that piecemeal litigation in New York and California would make settlement of the case far more difficult. See California Order; California Tr. at 25.

Radioactive implicitly argues that Manson and Garbage are distinct. See Plaintiff's Memorandum of Points and Authorities in Opposition to Shirley Manson's Motion to Stay or Dismiss This Action ("Pl. Opp.") at 15, 16 n.11. Neither has an interest in the litigation of the other, and there is no need for all of the claims to be adjudicated together. See id. Garbage can record without Manson, and Manson can record without Garbage. This is disingenuous. Manson is the public image of Garbage. Notably, Radioactive's President himself wrote that "Garbage has become Shirley Manson." 4/15/97 Radioactive Memo from Gary Kurfirst, Ex. 17 to Marmaro Decl., at 345. To the record-buying world Garbage and Manson are one and the same, and all of the contracts in dispute necessarily concern all of Garbage's members, Manson included.

Both the New York federal action and the California Action concern the eventual relationship between Garbage and UMG. A number of the contracts concerning Garbage's relationship with UMG — the Almo-Garbage Agreement, the Manson Inducement Letter, and the Almo-Radioactive Agreement — contain California forum selection clauses, making it impossible to fully litigate Garbage's status in New York. Separate litigation of the different contracts increases the likelihood that this dispute will drag on and decreases the likelihood of settlement. This factor weighs heavily in favor of abstention.

3. Order in Which the Actions Were Filed

The California Action was filed on January 29, 2001. The New York federal action was filed on March 7, 2001. However, "priority should not be measured exclusively by which complaint was filed first, but rather in terms of how much progress has been made on the two actions." Moses H. Cone Mem'l Hosp., 460 U.S. at 21. Radioactive argues that the federal action has progressed further because Radioactive has already provided discovery in compliance with Federal Rule of Civil Procedure 26(a) and because it has already made a non-jurisdictional motion, namely the motion for partial summary judgment addressed above. See Pl. Opp. at 14-15. This argument is somewhat misleading. Discovery in the California Action has proceeded more slowly, at least in part, because of Radioactive's unilateral refusal to comply with Manson and Garbage's discovery requests. See Defendant Shirley Manson's Reply Memorandum of Points and Authorities in Support of Her Motion to Dismiss or, in the Alternative, to Stay this Action ("Def. Rep. Mem.") at 6; Plaintiffs' Reply to Radioactive Records, J.V.'s Separate Statement of Items in Dispute Regarding Plaintiffs' Motion to Compel Responses to First Set of Requests for Admission ("Motion to Compel"), Ex. A to 5/30/01 Declaration of Christina Harvell Brown, counsel for defendant, in Support of Defendant Shirley Manson's Reply Memorandum P 2. Radioactive also asserts that depositions taken by Garbage in California should not be considered because Garbage is not a proper party to Radioactive's dispute with Manson. See Def. Rep. Mem.; Motion to Compel.

Arguably, both actions have progressed at an even pace. Nonetheless, because the burden is on the moving party to demonstrate exceptional circumstances, this factor weighs against abstention. See McConnell v. Costigan, 2000 U.S. Dist. LEXIS 16592, *20, No. 00 Civ. 4598, 2000 WL 1716273, at *7 (S.D.N.Y. Nov. 16, 2000) ("Because neither case is significantly advanced, the factor weighs against abstention.").

4. Inconvenience of the Federal Forum

Manson argues that it is inconvenient to litigate the case on both coasts, especially as Garbage is currently in Wisconsin recording its third album. See Def. Mem. at 16. Radioactive asserts that the convenience of the federal forum is demonstrated by the express New York forum selection clause in the Manson-Radioactive Agreement. See Pl. Opp. at 15.

The Manson-Radioactive Agreement is in dispute in both the federal and state actions. There will undoubtedly be considerable overlap in discovery. Witnesses and parties will be forced to travel back and forth between California and New York. Furthermore, discovery and testimony concerning the Manson-Radioactive Agreement is likely to cover many of the same issues, documents, and witnesses as will be involved in Garbage's larger dispute with UMG. Because all parties, including Radioactive, Manson and Garbage, are already litigating the issues underlying this dispute in California, the New York forum is clearly inconvenient for all involved. This factor weighs in favor of abstention.

### 5. Which Law Provides the Rule of Decision

All the claims here are state law claims. "The absence of any significant federal interests in this action provides additional grounds for abstention." Cadle Co. v. Bankers Fed. Sav. FSB, 929 F. Supp. 636, 639 (E.D.N.Y. 1996); see also Loral Fairchild Corp. v. Matsushita Elec. Indus. Co., 840 F. Supp. 211, 217 (E.D.N.Y. 1994) ("When state law will apply to the bulk of the claims this factor will weigh in favor of a federal court abstaining."). However, as discussed above, New York rather than California law governs disputes concerning the Manson-Radioactive Agreement. This does not necessarily make abstention inappropriate. "Simply because this court sits in New York does not mean that it can apply New York state law any better than the California court. Federal courts are obliged to give comity to state courts and not to assume expertise where none may lie." Loral Fairchild Corp., 840 F. Supp. at 217 (citing Carnegie-Mellon University v. Cohill, 484 U.S. 343, 350, 98 L. Ed. 2d 720, 108 S. Ct. 614 (1988)). This factor therefore weighs slightly in favor of abstaining.

### 6. Can the State Court Adequately Protect Plaintiff's Rights?

All of Radioactive's claims against Manson in this action have also been asserted in Radioactive's Cross-Complaint in the California Action. There is no reason to believe that the California court cannot protect Radioactive's rights. See Wiggin & Co. v. Ampton Invs., Inc., 66 F. Supp. 2d 549, 553 (S.D.N.Y. 1999) ("Wiggin's rights are adequately protected in the California Action, where it can assert (as counterclaims) the same claims raised here."). This factor weighs in favor of abstention.

### 7. Balancing the Factors

In the current action the first factor is irrelevant, the second, fourth, fifth and sixth factors weigh in favor of abstention and only the third factor weighs slightly against it. The Second Circuit has held the "no single factor is necessarily decisive, and the weight to be given to any one factor may vary greatly from case to case, depending on the particular setting of the case." Village of Westfield v. Welch's, 170 F.3d 116, 121 (2d Cir. 1999) (quotation marks and citations omitted). However, in balancing the factors, there is a strong presumption against surrendering jurisdiction. See Colorado River, 424 U.S. at 813.

"The Court ruled, in Colorado River, that a district court may abstain from exercising its authority when a state forum has concurrent jurisdiction, and when wise judicial administration, giving regard to conservation of judicial resources and comprehensive disposition of litigation, counsels such abstention." Arkwright-Boston, 762 F.2d at 211 (quotation marks, citation, and alteration omitted). The essential question involved in both this dispute and the California Action is the future relationship of Garbage and UMG. This Court's exercise of jurisdiction will lead to duplicative efforts, piecemeal litigation, and the possibility of inconsistent determinations. Worse, the multiple actions in different courts decrease the chances of both settlement and efficient resolution of the underlying dispute between Garbage and UMG. Allowing this action to proceed will only waste judicial resources. Accordingly, defendant's motion to dismiss this action pursuant to the Colorado River abstention doctrine is granted.

## IV. CONCLUSION

For the reasons set forth above, both plaintiff's motion for partial summary judgment and defendant's motion to dismiss are granted. The Clerk of the Court is directed to close this case.

SO ORDERED:

_____

In *Radioactive, J.V. v. Manson*, 153 F. Supp. 2d 462 (S.D.N.Y. 2001), the question is, what state is designated as controlling, if there needs to be interpretation of the contract?

In the following case, *Vanguard Recording Soc. v. Kweskin*, 276 F. Supp. 563 (S.D.N.Y. 1967), defendant recording society entered into a recording contract with the musician's band, as well as the musician himself (Jim Kweskin of Jug Band Fame). Both contracts were for a one-year period, with two options for a one-year extension. It's a question of interpreting the recording contract so as to determine the length of the contract; plaintiff seeks a preliminary injunction.

Vanguard Recording Soc. v. Kweskin
United States District Court for the Southern District of New York
October 26, 1967
No. 67 Civ. 3133
276 F. Supp. 563

## MEMORANDUM

BONSAL, District Judge.

Plaintiff, Vanguard Recording Society, Inc. (Vanguard), instituted this action in Supreme Court, New York County, based on a contract between it and the defendant Jim Kweskin (Kweskin) dated April 17, 1963. Thereafter, on August 17, 1967, defendants Warner Bros. Records, Inc. (Warner Bros.) and Kweskin removed the action to this court on the ground of diversity of citizenship.

Vanguard moves pursuant to Rule 65, F.R.Civ.P., for a preliminary injunction enjoining:

a) defendants Kweskin and Warner Bros. from performing any agreements between them for the recording and sale of phonograph records embodying the performances of Kweskin;

b) defendant Warner Bros. from entering agreements with third persons for the production or distribution of phonograph records embodying the performances of Kweskin, from advertising or using the name and likeness of Kweskin with regard to phonograph records, and from interfering with the exclusive recording agreement that Vanguard claims exists between it and Kweskin;

c) defendant Warner Bros., its licensees and agents from manufacturing, selling or distributing any phonograph records embodying the performances of Kweskin, and ordering Warner Bros. to destroy any master tape recordings or other material embodying the performances of Kweskin.

Plaintiff's motion for a preliminary injunction is denied.

Kweskin is the leader of a musical group called "Jim Kweskin and The Jug Band," or "Jim Kweskin Jug Band" (hereinafter referred to as the Jug Band). The Jug Band entered into a recording contract with Vanguard dated April 1, 1963 (the Jug Band contract), that provided for an initial term until April 30, 1964 and provided for two options, each permitting Vanguard to extend the contract for one year by giving the Jug Band written notice at least 30 days prior to the expiration of the existing term of the contract. Thereafter, Kweskin entered into the recording contract with Vanguard dated April 17, 1963 (the solo contract), that also provided for an initial term until April 30, 1964 and for two options on the same terms as those in the Jug Band contract. In other respects, the provisions in the Jug Band contract are the same as those in the solo contract. Both contracts provide in part as follows:

"1 - We [Vanguard] hereby agree to employ your personal services as a recording artist for the purpose of making phonograph records and you [the Jug Band and Kweskin respectively] hereby agree to record solely and exclusively for us according to the terms and provisions of this agreement.

"2 - * * * A minimum of sixteen 45 or 78 rpm record sides shall be recorded during the initial term of this agreement, and additional recordings shall be made at our election. The musical compositions to be recorded shall be mutually agreed upon between you and us, and each recording shall be subject to our approval as satisfactory for manufacture and sale. We shall have the right to call upon you to repeat any work until a satisfactory master recording has been made.

"6 - During the term of this agreement you will not perform for the purpose of making phonograph records for any person other than us, * * * and you acknowledge that your services are unique and extraordinary."

"11 - If, by reason of illness, injury, accident or refusal to work, you fail to perform for us in accordance with the provisions of paragraph 2 of this agreement, * * * without limiting our rights in any such event, we shall have the option without liability to suspend operation of paragraph 2 of this agreement for the duration of any such contingency by giving you written notice thereof; and, at our election, a period of time equal to the duration of such suspension shall be added to the end of the then current period of the term hereof, and then such period and the term of this agreement shall be accordingly extended."

On February 23, 1967, Warner Bros. entered into a recording contract with the Jug Band (the Warner Bros. contract), and since that date, an LP album with recordings of the Jug Band has been made and 11,000 to 12,000 of the albums have been distributed at a cost of some $21,000. According to the affidavit of its Vice-President, Warner Bros. is a financially solvent corporation with cash on hand in excess of $10 million and a gross annual business of some $24 million.

Vanguard contends that, for the reasons hereinafter stated, the solo contract, which had an initial term of one year running until April 30, 1964, is still in effect, and that it is entitled to a preliminary injunction. (Vanguard also claims that the Jug Band contract is still in effect, but in its motion it is relying only on the solo contract.) At oral argument, all parties agreed that determination of the motion for a preliminary injunction did not require an evidentiary hearing.

It is Vanguard's position that Kweskin refused to perform from March 3, 1964 to April 21, 1965 (a period of 1 year, 1 month and 18 days), justifying Vanguard in suspending the solo contract under paragraph 11 and in adding this period to the then current term of the contract, thereby extending it until April

21, 1966. Since the suspension continued after the expiration of the original term of the contract, viz., April 30, 1964, Vanguard argues that for purposes of paragraph 11, the original term did not end on April 30, 1964, but ended when Vanguard lifted the suspension on April 21, 1965, and that it was entitled to add the period of suspension to the new date, April 21, 1965. Vanguard then renewed the solo contract until April 21, 1967 under the first option and until April 21, 1968 under the second option. On January 12, 1967 Vanguard again suspended the solo contract under paragraph 11 and claims that the contract is now in its second year with more than a year remaining before it expires. Vanguard contends that Kweskin ratified its interpretation of the contract by performing under the solo contract on July 11, 19 and 20, 1966 and on August 18 and 22, 1966.

Kweskin, on the other hand, denies that his performances make Vanguard's interpretation of the contract binding on him, and contends that even if the solo contract was still in effect in July and August 1966, two letters from Vanguard to him dated July 27, 1966 and August 22, 1966 released him from any obligations he had thereunder. Vanguard denies that these letters constituted a release, claiming that they were an offer that Vanguard withdrew by letter to Kweskin and the Jug Band dated November 29, 1966.

Vanguard's motion for a preliminary injunction must be denied since the affidavits, exhibits and pleadings before the court evidence issues of fact which can only be resolved at trial. See Willheim v. Investors Diversified Services, Inc., 303 F.2d 276 (2d Cir. 1962); G. P. Putnam's Sons v. Lancer Books, Inc., 239 F. Supp. 782, 787 (S.D.N.Y. 1965); Paramount Pictures Corp. v. Holden, 166 F. Supp. 684 (S.D.Calif. 1958). These issues of fact include, but are not limited to, the following:

1) If, as appears from the papers before the court, the Warner Bros. contract is with the Jug Band and not with Kweskin individually, does the solo contract give Vanguard the right to enjoin performances by the Jug Band? The solo contract appears to relate only to performances by Kweskin as an individual and not to performances by him as a member of the Jug Band.

2) Did Kweskin refuse to perform under the solo contract?

3) If Kweskin did refuse to perform, which he denies, did such refusal end by June 12, 1964 as Kweskin contends or did it continue until April 21, 1965 as Vanguard contends?

4) Did Kweskin ratify Vanguard's interpretation of the solo contract by performing for Vanguard on July 11, 19 and 20, 1966 and on August 18 and 22, 1966?

5) If the solo contract was in effect in July and August 1966, did Vanguard, by reason of the letters from Vanguard to Kweskin dated July 27, 1966 and August 22, 1966, release Kweskin from his obligations?

6) Assuming that Kweskin is still bound by the solo contract, are his services so unique and extraordinary as to warrant the issuance of an injunction? See Madison Square Garden Corp. v. Carnera, 52 F.2d 47 (2d Cir. 1931); Machen v. Johansson, 174 F. Supp. 522, 529 n. 8 (S.D.N.Y.1959); Harry Rogers Theatrical Enterprises, Inc. v. Comstock, 225 App.Div. 34, 232 N.Y.S. 1 (1st Dept. 1928).

Vanguard has not shown that it is reasonably certain to prevail at trial or that it will suffer irreparable injury outweighing the harm that a preliminary injunction is likely to cause to Kweskin and other members of the Jug Band. See, e.g., Symington Wayne Corp. v. Dresser Industries, Inc., 383 F.2d 840 (2d Cir. 1967); Rosemont Enterprises, Inc. v. Random House, Inc., 366 F.2d 303 (2d Cir. 1966), cert. denied, 385 U.S. 1009, 87 S. Ct. 714, 17 L. Ed. 2d 546 (1967).

There is serious doubt that Vanguard is correct in interpreting paragraph 11 of the solo contract so as to give it the right to extend the contract until April 21, 1966. Under paragraph 11 Vanguard could add a period of time equal to the duration of any suspension to the end of the then current term of the contract. Since the initial term was to expire on April 30, 1964, the period of suspension could only extend the contract until sometime in June 1965 rather than until April 21, 1966. Vanguard so interpreted paragraph 11 in the Jug Band contract (letter of July 8, 1966 from Vanguard to Kweskin and the Jug Band), and this appears more reasonable than the construction here urged. If the suspension extended the solo contract only until June 1965, then on April 21, 1965 the contract would have approximately two months more to run and Vanguard would receive the same period of performance as it would have received had there been no suspension. On the other hand, if the suspension extended the contract until April 21, 1966, then Vanguard would receive a period of performance that was 10 months longer than the period of performance it would have otherwise received.

If Vanguard was entitled to extend the solo contract only until June 1965, then Vanguard did not validly exercise the first and second options to renew and the contract would not presently be in effect.

According to Vanguard's interpretation of the solo contract, it is entitled to turn a one-year contract with two one-year renewal options into a contract that will run for more than five years. If Vanguard's interpretation of the contract is correct, it would appear that the contract was harsh and unreasonable and on equitable grounds the court would decline to issue a preliminary injunction. See Machen v. Johanssen, supra, at 530-31; see also Welcome Wagon, Inc. v. Morris, 224 F.2d 693 (4th Cir. 1955).

Vanguard has not shown that it is reasonably certain to prove at trial that Kweskin ratified its interpretation of the contract (see Hopwood Plays, Inc. v. Kemper, 263 N.Y. 380, 189 N.E. 461 (1934); Mohawk National Bank v. Chalifaux, 33 Misc.2d 987, 227 N.Y.S.2d 526 (Schenectady Co. Ct. 1962)) or that the letters of July and August 1966 did not release Kweskin.

Even if Vanguard had made a stronger showing of probable success at trial, Vanguard's motion would be denied in the exercise of the court's discretion because Vanguard has not shown that if a preliminary injunction is denied it will suffer irreparable injury outweighing the harm that a preliminary injunction is likely to cause to the defendants and other members of the Jug Band. See, e.g., Symington Wayne Corp. v. Dresser Industries, Inc., supra; Paramount Pictures Corp. v. Holden, supra. It appears that Warner Bros. will be able to respond in full to any damages Vanguard proves at trial it is entitled to recover. On the other hand, a preliminary injunction is likely to restrain performances by the other members of the Jug Band as well as Kweskin since they and Kweskin perform as a group. Moreover, it appears that Warner Bros. has already begun the distribution of its album with the recordings of the Jug Band, has entered into contracts for the distribution of the album, and has incurred substantial advertising expenses.

The foregoing constitutes the court's findings of fact and conclusions of law. Rule 52(a), F.R.Civ.P.

Vanguard's motion for a preliminary injunction is denied.

It is so ordered.

_____

The court denied plaintiff's request for the remedy of a preliminary injunction to restrain the musician from selling records. The court denied the preliminary injunction on the grounds that plaintiff did not show that it was reasonably certain to prevail at trial, or that it would have suffered such irreparable harm that would outweigh the harm a preliminary injunction would likely cause to the musician, the band, and the company.

In the following case, *Fred Ahlert Music Co. v. Warner/Chappell Music, Inc.*, 155 F.3d 17 (2d Cir. 1998), the court looks into the assignment of royalties for derivative works; here, the musical composition, "Bye Bye Blackbird."

Fred Ahlert Music Corp. v. Warner/Chappell Music, Inc.
United States Court of Appeals for the Second Circuit
January 8, 1998, Argued; July 14, 1998, Decided
Docket No. 97-7705
155 F.3d 17

WALKER, Circuit Judge:

This appeal requires us to consider the scope of the "Derivative Works Exception" of the Copyright Act of 1976, 17 U.S.C. § 304(c)(6)(A). The Copyright Act of 1976 ("the 1976 Act") expanded the rights of authors and their heirs by automatically extending the life of their copyrights by 19 years, for a total of 75 years, see 17 U.S.C. §§ 304(a)-(b), and by allowing authors (or, if the authors are deceased, their statutory heirs) to terminate, for the period of the extended copyrights, any domestic copyright interests in their work that they may have granted to others, see 17 U.S.C. §§ 304 (c)(1)-(3). The purpose of the termination provision is to protect the interests of authors, who may have bargained away their rights without a full appreciation of the value of their work, as well as the interests of authors' surviving spouses and children. See Woods v. Bourne Co., 60 F.3d 978, 982 (2d Cir. 1995); Larry Spier, Inc. v. Bourne Co., 953 F.2d 774, 778-80 (2d Cir. 1992). Thus, the 1976 Act creates a completely new property right in the copyright for 19 years, and allows the author and his or her heirs to exploit it. See id. at 779; H.R. Rep. No. 94-1476, reprinted in 1976 U.S.C.C.A.N. 5659, 5756 (1976).

However, an author's termination rights are not unlimited. The 1976 Act's Derivative Works Exception permits a grantee or licensee who prepares a derivative work before termination to continue to utilize the derivative work during the extended renewal term "under the terms of the grant." 17 U.S.C. § 304(c)(6)(A). A derivative work is "a work based upon one or more preexisting works, such as a . . . sound recording . . . . A work consisting of editorial revisions, annotations, elaborations, or other modifications which, as a whole, represent an original work of authorship, is a 'derivative work.'" Id. at § 101. The Exception seeks to protect public access to the derivative work as well as the rights of persons who have invested in creating the derivative work. See Woods, 60 F.3d at 986; Donald A. Hughes, Jr., Jurisprudential Vertigo: The Supreme Court's View of "Rear Window" is for the Birds, 60 Miss. L.J. 239, 251-52 (1990).

In this action, both the appellee, Fred Ahlert Music Corp. ("Ahlert"), and the appellant, Warner/Chappell Music, Inc. ("Warner"), claim the right to license the use of a 1969 Joe Cocker recording, a derivative work based on the copyrighted musical composition "Bye Bye Blackbird" (the "Song"), in the soundtrack and soundtrack album of the motion picture "Sleepless in Seattle." Warner's predecessor in interest authorized preparation of the Cocker derivative pursuant to a grant from the Song's co-authors, Mort Dixon and Ray Henderson.

The statutory heirs of Mort Dixon terminated, pursuant to the 1976 Act, the rights held by Warner in the Song that were attributable to Dixon; the termination was to be effective in 1982. Warner claims a continued right to royalties, however, on the basis that the inclusion of the Cocker derivative on the movie soundtrack and soundtrack album is a post-termination utilization of a derivative work within the meaning of the Derivative Works Exception. Ahlert, successor-in-interest to Dixon's heirs, argues that Warner has no rights pertaining to the use of the Cocker derivative on the "Sleepless in Seattle" soundtrack or on the soundtrack album because those uses were not authorized "under the terms of the grant," and thus do not fall within the Exception. We agree with Ahlert, and affirm.

### BACKGROUND

"Bye Bye Blackbird" was written by Mort Dixon and Ray Henderson, who registered their copyright in the Song on May 3, 1926. Under the Copyright Act of 1909, Pub. L. 60-349, 35 Stat. 1075 (1909) (previously codified at 17 U.S.C. §§ 1-216) (repealed 1976), the copyright in a musical composition was effective for 28 years and renewable for an additional 28 years by the author. See Mills Music, Inc. v. Snyder, 469 U.S. 153, 157, 83 L. Ed. 2d 556, 105 S. Ct. 638 (1985). On May 6, 1953, the copyright was effectively renewed in the names of both authors; it was to have expired on December 31, 1982. Prior to renewal, each author assigned his interest in the copyright to Remick Music Corporation ("Remick"), the predecessor in interest to Warner. On March 23, 1956, Dixon died.

On or about May 2, 1969, Warner granted a non-exclusive mechanical license to A&M Records ("A&M"). This license authorized A&M to record and manufacture a phonorecording of the Song performed by recording artist Joe Cocker. The agreement "covered only the particular recording mentioned herein of said musical composition." That recording was identified in the agreement as "RECORD NO. SP 4182" by "RECORDING ARTIST Joe Cocker." Pursuant to this license, A&M produced a version of the Song performed by Joe Cocker (the "Cocker derivative").

In 1976, Congress enacted a sweeping revision of the Copyright laws. See Pub. L. No. 94-553, 90 Stat. 2541 (1976) (codified at 17 U.S.C. §§ 101-810); see also Mills Music, 469 U.S. at 159-62. Among these changes, the new 17 U.S.C. § 304(b) automatically extended the renewal term of the copyright for an additional 19 years, through December 31, 2001 (the "extended renewal term"), for a total copyright term of 75 years. The 1976 Act also allowed the authors of copyrighted material (or if deceased, their statutory heirs) to terminate any grant of a transfer or license in a copyrighted work for the duration of the extended renewal term where the grant was executed before 1978. 17 U.S.C. § 304(c). On January 3, 1978, pursuant to the 1976 Act, Dixon's statutory heirs Yvonne Dixon Cresci and Estelle Barbara Kalish served formal notice terminating Dixon's grant to Remick, effective May 3, 1982. Thus, Warner's domestic rights in the Song reverted to Dixon's heirs. See 17 U.S.C. § 304(c)(6). On February 24, 1986, Dixon's heirs signed an agreement transferring their interest in the Song to the plaintiff, music publisher Ahlert.

In 1992, Tri-Star Pictures, Inc. ("TriStar") sought permission from Ahlert to include the Song on the soundtrack of the motion picture "Sleepless in Seattle." Ahlert provided TriStar with a quote for use of the Song in the United States. Because Warner retained the foreign rights to the copyright after termination, Ahlert directed TriStar to seek a quote from Warner for foreign use of the Song. In May 1993, Warner issued a synchronization and performance license to TriStar specifying one background vocal usage of the Song (an edited version of the Cocker derivative) and five background instrumental uses (recorded specifically for the film) on the "Sleepless in Seattle" soundtrack. In June, 1993, Ahlert issued a synchronization and performance license to TriStar authorizing identical uses of the Song. Ahlert's license granted domestic rights to TriStar; Warner's license granted foreign rights. Ahlert claims that it awarded TriStar a synchronization license at a reduced rate in anticipation of the royalties Ahlert expected to receive as a result of the eventual release of a soundtrack album.

Subsequently, in July 1993, Ahlert, through its agent The Harry Fox Agency, Inc. ("Fox"), issued a mechanical license to TriStar's affiliate, Sony Music Entertainment, Inc. ("Sony"), for use of the Song, as embodied by the Cocker derivative, on the "Sleepless in Seattle" soundtrack album. On August 20, 1993, Warner wrote a letter to Fox (which also represented Warner) asserting that "Warner Bros. Inc. retains all rights derived from uses of [the Cocker derivative], including mechanical royalties earned from uses of [the Song] on the ["Sleepless in Seattle"] soundtrack album." As a result of this letter, and despite Ahlert's protests, Fox canceled Ahlert's license to Sony, and instead issued a mechanical license to Sony on Warner's behalf. Since that time, Sony has paid royalties to Fox from sales of the "Sleepless in Seattle" soundtrack album, and in turn Fox has remitted these royalties to Warner.

On February 8, 1996, Ahlert brought this action in the United States District Court for the Southern District of New York (Harold Baer, Jr., District Judge). The complaint requested that the district court "declare and adjudge the following:"

A. The use of the Song in phonorecords made from the soundtrack of the motion picture SLEEPLESS IN SEATTLE is not a use of the Song within the Derivative Works Exception . . . .

B. AHLERT, not WARNER, is entitled to license the use of the Song in the making and distributing of all phonorecords . . . which reproduce the [Cocker derivative], and to receive all mechanical royalties attributable to the Dixon Share payable therefor, except phonorecords made and distributed by A&M Records, Inc. and identified as "Record No. SP 4182," the subject of the 1969 WARNER mechanical license to A&M Records.

C. WARNER shall account for, and pay to AHLERT, a sum equal to the amount of all mechanical royalties paid to WARNER for use of the Dixon Share in the Soundtrack Album, together with prejudgment interest . . . .

D. AHLERT shall be granted such other and further relief as the court may deem to be just and proper.

Warner counterclaimed, seeking, inter alia, an accounting of all royalties that Ahlert received from granting TriStar the June, 1993, synchronization and performance license for the domestic right to use the Cocker derivative on the "Sleepless in Seattle" soundtrack.

Both parties moved for summary judgment. On April 14, 1997, the district court issued an order granting Ahlert's motion, denying Warner's motion, and dismissing Warner's counterclaims. See Fred Ahlert Music Corp. v. Warner/Chappell Music, Inc., 958 F. Supp. 170 (S.D.N.Y. 1997). The district court declared (1) that inclusion of the Song in the "Sleepless in Seattle" soundtrack and soundtrack album was not within the Exception, and (2) that Ahlert "is entitled to license . . . the United States use of the" Song, as embodied by the Cocker derivative, during the extended renewal term, and "to receive 50% of all mechanical royalties . . . payable for the use of the Song . . . excluding phonorecords made and distributed by A&M Records and identified as 'Record No. SP 4182.'" Pursuant to this declaration, the district court ordered Warner (1) to pay Ahlert $ 118,781.06, constituting 50% of the mechanical royalties paid to Warner by Sony, and (2) to account for and pay to Ahlert 50% of all other mechanical royalties paid to Warner during the extended renewal term, except from the sale of "phonorecords made and distributed by A&M Records and identified as 'Record No. SP 4182.'" The district court further awarded prejudgment interest to Ahlert. Warner appeals, challenging the district court's conclusion that the mechanical license it issued to Sony is not covered by the Derivative Works Exception, and arguing that the scope of the district court's judgment was overbroad.

### DISCUSSION
### I. Standard of Review

We review de novo the district court's award of summary judgment, drawing all inferences and resolving all ambiguities in favor of the party opposing the motion. See *Ryan v. Grae & Rybicki, P.C.*, 135 F.3d 867, 869 (2d Cir. 1998).

## II. Derivative Works Exception

As noted above, the Copyright Act of 1976 had a major effect on the rights of the parties to this dispute. Section 304(b) automatically extended the copyright renewal term for 19 years. Section 304(c) gave Dixon's heirs (to whose interests Ahlert has succeeded) the right to exploit this extended renewal term by allowing them to terminate Dixon's grant to Remick (Warner's predecessor in interest). Upon termination, all rights possessed by Remick and Warner reverted to Dixon's heirs, including the right to license uses of the Song and receive any consequent royalties. But there is one notable caveat—the Derivative Works Exception:

A derivative work prepared under authority of the grant before its termination may continue to be utilized under the terms of the grant after its termination, but this privilege does not extend to the preparation after the termination of other derivative works based upon the copyrighted work covered by the terminated grant.

17 U.S.C. § 304(c)(6)(A).

The Derivative Works Exception reflects Congress's judgment that the owner of a derivative work should be allowed to continue to use the derivative work after termination, "both to encourage investment by derivative work proprietors and to assure that the public retains access to the derivative work." Note, *The Errant Evolution of Termination of Transfer Rights and the Derivative Works Exception*, 48 Ohio St. L.J. 897, 912 (1987). Without the Exception, the creator of a derivative work (and, indeed, the public at large) could be held hostage to the potentially exorbitant demands of the owner of the copyright in the underlying work.

The parties to the present case do not dispute that the Cocker derivative is a "derivative work prepared under authority of the grant before its termination." Rather, they dispute whether the inclusion of the Cocker derivative on the soundtrack and soundtrack album constitutes "utilization under the terms of the grant." The district court found that it was not, and therefore concluded that Ahlert was entitled to receive the contested royalties. Warner appeals from this determination. In order to resolve this question, we must determine what is meant by the phrase "the terms of the grant."

The Supreme Court interpreted the meaning of "the terms of the grant" in *Mills Music, Inc. v. Snyder*, 469 U.S. 153, 83 L. Ed. 2d 556, 105 S. Ct. 638 (1985). That case involved a controversy between a music publisher and the heirs of Ted Snyder, a co-author of the copyrighted musical composition "Who's Sorry Now." The original copyright was registered in 1923 by a publishing company partially owned by Snyder. When that company went bankrupt, the bankruptcy trustee assigned the copyright to music publisher Mills Music. In 1940, Mills Music and Snyder entered into an agreement whereby Snyder assigned his interest in all renewals of the copyright to Mills Music. In exchange, Mills Music agreed to pay certain royalties to Snyder, including 50 percent of all net royalties received for mechanical reproductions of "Who's Sorry Now."

In 1951, Mills Music registered the renewed copyright. It then issued over 400 licenses to record companies authorizing various recordings of "Who's Sorry Now." These record companies paid royalties to Mills Music, which in turn remitted 50 percent of those royalties to Snyder. On January 3, 1978, Snyder's heirs served notice of termination on Mills Music effective January 3, 1980, pursuant to the 1976 Act's termination provision. Mills Music claimed that after termination, Snyder's heirs were entitled to only 50 percent of the royalties from pre-termination derivative recordings of "Who's Sorry Now," as was agreed to in the original 1940 grant from Snyder to Mills Music. The heirs claimed that they were entitled to the full 100 percent of these royalties.

Resolution of the dispute turned on whether the "terms of the grant" preserved by the Exception included only the approximately 400 licenses from Mills Music to the record companies, or whether it also included the terms of the original 1940 grant from Snyder to Mills Music entitling the latter to 50% of the mechanical royalties. The Supreme Court first examined the text of the Derivative Works Exception. For convenience, we set forth this text a second time.

A derivative work prepared under authority of the grant before its termination may continue to be utilized under the terms of the grant after its termination, but this privilege does not extend to the preparation after the termination of other derivative works based upon the copyrighted work covered by the terminated grant. 17 U.S.C. § 304(c)(6)(A) (emphasis added). Because the word "grant" appears three times in the Exception, the Court assumed that Congress intended to give the word the same meaning throughout. Mills Music, 469 U.S. at 164-65. Logically, the third reference to "the terminated grant" had to refer to Snyder's 1940 grant to Mills Music. See id. at 164. The Court next considered the first reference to the word "grant," in the phrase "derivative works prepared under authority of the grant." Because "the 1940 grant . . . expressly gave Mills the authority to license others to make derivative works," and because "each of the 400-odd sound recordings" at issue was authorized by Mills Music while it was owner of the copyright, the Court concluded that "whether the phrase . . . is read to encompass both the original grant to Mills and the subsequent licenses that Mills issued, or only the original grant, . . . the word 'grant' must refer to the 1940 grant from Snyder to Mills." Id. at 165.

Finally, the Court interpreted the phrase "under the terms of the grant." In order to give the word "grant" a consistent meaning throughout § 304(c)(6)(A), the Court reasoned that this language necessarily encompassed the original 1940 grant from Snyder to Mills Music. However, "the terms of the grant" for a particular derivative work also had to include the subsequent license between Mills Music and the record company that prepared the derivative work. See id. at 165-66. Thus, the Court concluded that "the phrase 'under the terms of the grant' as applied to any particular licensee would necessarily encompass both the 1940 grant and the individual license executed pursuant thereto." Id. at 166-67 (quoting § 304(c)(6)(A)). In other words, the "terms of the grant" include the "entire set of documents that created and defined each licensee's right to prepare and distribute [the] derivative work[]," id. at 167, both the individual license requiring the licensee to pay royalties to Mills Music, and the 1940 grant from Snyder to Mills Music entitling the latter to keep 50 percent of those royalties and requiring it to remit the remaining 50 percent to Snyder's heirs. Indeed, unless the preserved "terms of the grant" included the original grant from Snyder to Mills Music, the Court noted that "there would be neither a contractual nor a statutory basis for paying any part of the derivative-works royalties to the Snyders." Id. Therefore, the Court ruled that Mills Music was entitled to keep 50 percent of the disputed royalties. See also Woods v. Bourne Co., 60 F.3d 978, 987 (2d Cir. 1995) (interpreting Mills Music "to preserve during the post- termination period the panoply of contractual obligations that governed pre-termination uses of derivative works by derivative work owners or their licensees."

The Supreme Court in Mills Music did not specifically address the question before us: whether the author or the publisher has the authority to license new uses of a pre-termination derivative work after termination. When the Mills Music case was in the district court, Judge Weinfeld determined that after termination, the publisher retained the authority to license "new [uses] of old derivative works that it first licensed prior to termination of the [1940 grant] with royalties to be shared as [they were] before termination" (assuming of course that those new uses were not themselves new derivative works). Harry Fox Agency, Inc. v. Mills Music, Inc., 543 F. Supp. 844, 868 (S.D.N.Y. 1982), rev'd, 720 F.2d 733 (2d Cir. 1983), rev'd, Mills Music v. Snyder, 469 U.S. 153, 83 L. Ed. 2d 556, 105 S. Ct. 638 (1985). The district court reasoned that it would be illogical to impose a limitation on Mills Music's rights on the basis of licenses which Mills Music itself had issued and which were never a part of the original grant from Snyder to Mills Music. Id. Neither the Second Circuit Court of Appeals, which reversed the district court's judgment, nor the Supreme Court, which in turn reversed the Second Circuit, touched on the question of post-termination licensing of pre-termination derivative works.

We are not persuaded by the district court's reasoning in Harry Fox Agency. In effect, Judge Weinfeld's holding would enforce the terms of the original grant from the author to the music publisher but ignore the terms of the subsequent grant from the music publisher to the record company, at least when it came to authorizing post-termination uses of pre-termination derivative works. But, as the Supreme Court in Mills Music makes clear, the "entire set of documents that created and defined each licensee's right to prepare and distribute [the] derivative work[]" must be enforced. 469 U.S. at 167 (emphasis added). As one commentator has noted, "if the entire pre-termination transaction is what is being preserved, then the limitations on the record companies are preserved as well, and any attempt to change them after termination is . . . outside of 'the terms of the grant.'" Howard B. Abrams, Who's Sorry Now? Termination Rights and the Derivative Works Exception , 62 U. Det. L. Rev. 182, 235 (1985) (quoting 17 U.S.C. § 304(c)(6)(A)); see also Howard B. Abrams, The Law of Copyright § 12.05[F][5][d][iv], at 12-50 (1998) (district court decision in Harry Fox Agency "seems to be in fundamental conflict with" the Supreme Court's Mills Music decision); id. at 12-58 ("If a particular post-termination exploitation of the derivative work cannot be undertaken within the terms of the pre-termination grant, then it is the post-termination copyright owner who must authorize and be entitled to compensation for the particular post-termination exploitation of the copyright."). But see 3 Melville B. Nimmer & David Nimmer, Nimmer on Copyright § 11.02[B], at 11-18.10 (1997) (concluding that new uses of a pre-termination derivative work "would not be the subject of termination because the post-termination licenses would simply constitute the further utilization of the previously prepared derivative work").

To determine, then, whether inclusion of the Cocker derivative on the "Sleepless in Seattle" soundtrack and soundtrack album is "under the terms of the grant," we must examine the scope of both the original grant from Dixon to Warner's predecessor in interest, and the subsequent grant from Warner to A&M authorizing production of the Cocker derivative. Although the original grant would presumably authorize this new use, plainly Warner's license to A&M does not. As the district court found, that license is a narrow one granting A&M the right to use "Bye Bye Blackbird" for the limited purpose of recording the Cocker derivative and releasing it as "Record No. SP 4182." This grant does not authorize any additional releases of the Cocker derivative, much less its inclusion on a movie soundtrack. Just as Warner continues to benefit from the terms of the second grant, pursuant to which it receives royalties from sales of the Cocker derivative on A&M Record No. SP 4182, it is bound by those terms of the second grant which limit its exploitation of the Song to sales of that phonorecord. Cf. Mills Music, 469 U.S. at 167 n.35 (criticizing dissent for "reading the 'terms of the grant' to include only those terms defining the amount of the royalty payments . . . . The statute itself . . . refers to 'the terms of the grant' — not to some of the terms of the grant.").

This result is consistent with the purposes of the Derivative Works Exception, which seeks to protect the rights of persons who have invested in creating the derivative work as well as to protect public access to derivative works. See Woods, 60 F.3d at 986; Hughes, Jurisprudential Vertigo, 60 Miss. L.J. at 251-52; Note, Errant Evolution, 48 Ohio St. L.J. at 912. Neither interest would be furthered if Warner, rather than Ahlert, had the power to authorize new uses of the Cocker derivative. First, Warner's investment in the Cocker derivative is already protected because it may continue to receive its share of royalties from the sale of the A&M phonorecord. Second, ruling for Warner would not increase public access to the Cocker derivative. Any new use of the Cocker derivative would have to be specifically licensed, and there is no reason to believe Warner would authorize new uses more frequently than would Ahlert. Cf. Woods, 60 F.3d at 986 ("The goal of keeping derivative works in public circulation does not require that publishers rather than authors receive royalties for their use."). And of course, a ruling for Ahlert is more consistent with the general thrust of § 304, which is designed to protect the interests of authors and their heirs and to maximize their ability to exploit the value of their Songs during the extended renewal term. See Note, Errant Evolution, 48 Ohio St. L.J. at 912.

In sum, when Dixon's heirs terminated Warner's domestic copyright interest in the Song pursuant to 17 U.S.C. § 304(c), the right to authorize new uses of the Song as embodied by the Cocker derivative reverted to the heirs, because that right is not within the "terms of the grant" preserved by the Derivative Works Exception. The district court properly entered judgment in favor of Ahlert.

### III. Scope of the District Court's Judgment

Finally, Warner argues that the district court's judgment was too broad because it encompassed relief neither sought by Ahlert in the complaint nor litigated at trial. The district court ordered Warner to account for and pay to [Ahlert] a sum equal to the amount of 50% of all other mechanical royalties paid to defendant for United States use of the Song in phonorecords first licensed and distributed during the extended renewal copyright term, . . . excluding phonorecords made and distributed by A&M Records and identified as "Record No. SP 4182."

Warner claims that any award to Ahlert should have been limited to "the amount of all mechanical royalties paid to WARNER for use of the Dixon Share in the Soundtrack Album, together with prejudgment interest," as was requested in the complaint. We disagree.

In its prayer for relief, Ahlert asked the district court to "grant[] such other and further relief as the court may deem to be just and proper," invoking the district court's power, pursuant to 28 U.S.C. § 2202, to provide any "further necessary or proper relief based on a declaratory judgment or decree . . .

against any adverse party whose rights have been determined by such judgment." A district court may grant further relief, including monetary damages, whether or not it "had been demanded, or even proved, in the original action for declaratory relief." Edward B. Marks Music Corp. v. Charles K. Harris Music Publ'g, 255 F.2d 518, 522 (2d Cir. 1958); accord Insurance Servs. of Beaufort, Inc. v. Aetna Cas. and Sur. Co., 966 F.2d 847, 851-52 (4th Cir. 1992); Horn & Hardart Co. v. National Rail Passenger Corp., 269 U.S. App. D.C. 53, 843 F.2d 546, 548-49 (D.C. Cir. 1988); see also Beacon Constr. Co. v. Matco Elec. Co., 521 F.2d 392, 399-400 (2d Cir. 1975) ("further relief" under § 2202 includes damages); Alexander & Alexander, Inc. v. Van Impe, 787 F.2d 163, 166 (3d Cir. 1986); Security Ins. Co. v. White, 236 F.2d 215, 220 (10th Cir. 1956).

The district court declared that Ahlert, rather than Warner, has the authority to license new uses of the Song, as embodied by the Cocker derivative, for the duration of the extended renewal term. The relief awarded by the district court followed directly from that declaration: because Ahlert is entitled to receive royalties from post-termination licenses, the judgment awarding those royalties to Ahlert was "proper relief based on a declaratory judgment." 28 U.S.C. § 2202. Although Warner argues that "recovery of some of the royalties the Court has awarded . . . may independently be barred by the statute of limitations, laches, or other defenses," Appellant's Brief at 35, it nowhere indicates which royalties might be so barred, or what "other defenses" might bar relief. Furthermore, the record reveals no objection to the scope of relief by Warner in the district court. We will not vacate an award, otherwise proper under § 2202, on the basis of unpreserved claims of theoretical error.

## CONCLUSION

The judgment of the district court is affirmed.

---

This is a case about the assignment of royalties from a copyrighted song pursuant to the Copyright Act of 1976, 17 U.S.C. Section 101-810. There were two assignees. The court held that the authors' heirs terminated appellant, Warner/Chappell Music's domestic copyright in the song. Warner/Chappell's original license to A&M only authorized Joe Cocker's original recording and did not approve of any other use thereof. The right to reissue new uses of the song reverts to the heirs and is not excepted by the derivative works exception (17 U.S.C. Section 304 (c)(6)A)): The right to authorize new uses of the song reverted to the heirs who then assigned their right, to appellee, Fred Ahlert Music Group. But, Ahler was entitled to royalties under the mechanical license it issued to Sony for the right to use the song on a soundtrack album.

The Copyright Act of 1976 creates a new property right in the copyright for 19 years which allows the author or the heirs to exploit it as they will. Key to the Act is the Derivative Works Exception, which allows grantee (or licensee) who prepares a derivative work before termination of the life of the copyright, to continue to use the derivative work during the extended renewal term "under the terms of the grants" (17 U.S.C. Section 304 (c)6(A)).

Everyone wants to claim the right to license the distinctive 1969 Joe Cocker derivative work based on copyrighted "Bye Bye Blackbird," which was used in "Sleepless in Seattle." Who gets the royalties? The Fred Ahlert Music Group is the successor-in-interest to the author's heirs. The Court held that Warner/Chappell has no rights to the use of Cocker's derivative on either the "Sleepless in Seattle" soundtrack or soundtrack album since those uses were not authorized "under the terms of the grant" and do not fall within the Derivative Works Exception.

Granz v. Harris
United States Court of Appeals for the Second Circuit
May 15, 1952, Argued; August 20, 1952, Decided
No. 240, Docket 22324
198 F.2d 585

This is an appeal by the plaintiff from a judgment dismissing his complaint on the merits after trial to the court without a jury. The complaint sought rescission of a contract of sale of master phonographic recordings of portions of a jazz concert presented by the plaintiff, damages for breach of the contract, an accounting of profits, a permanent injunction, and attorney's fees in the amount of $ 3,000. Federal jurisdiction rests on diversity of citizenship. The district judge rendered an opinion, reported in 98 F.Supp. 906, and made detailed findings of fact and conclusions of law in conformity with his opinion. Only two of the findings of fact are attacked by the appellant. They will be discussed hereinafter.

Norman Granz is a well-known promoter and producer of jazz concerts under the designation 'Jazz At The Philharmonic.' One such concert he caused to be recorded in its entirety on a sixteen-inch master disc from which he re-recorded on six twelve-inch master discs that part of the concert constituting the rendition of two musical compositions entitled 'How High the Moon' and 'Lady Be Good.' These master discs, three for each composition, revolved at 78 revolutions per minute, and were usable in manufacturing commercial phonograph records of the same size and playable at the same speed as the master discs. Granz sold the master discs to the defendant pursuant to a contract dated August 15, 1945. The contract required that in the sale of phonograph records manufactured from the purchased masters the defendant should use the credit-line 'Presented by Norman Granz' and explanatory notes which Granz had prepared. Some time in 1948 the defendant re-recorded the musical content of the purchased masters on ten-inch 78 rpm masters from which he manufactured phonograph records of the same size and speed. Such records he sold both in an album and separately. Concededly, at first the album cover did not conform to the contract in that, although it bore the designation 'Jazz At The Philharmonic' it did not contain the credit-line or the explanatory notes, but the court found that the cover was later corrected upon the plaintiff's demand. He found also that there was no deletion of music in the ten-inch 78 rpm records. In 1950 the defendant re-recorded the entire contents of the purchased masters on a ten-inch 33 1/3 rpm master and from this manufactured records of the same size and speed for retail sale.

The questions presented by the appeal are whether any right of the plaintiff was violated by the defendant: (1) by manufacturing and selling ten-inch 33 1/3 rpm records; or (2) by manufacturing and selling ten-inch 78 rpm records; or (3) by selling records singly instead of as part of an album containing both 'How High the Moon' and 'Lady Be Good.'

On the authority of RCA Mfg. Co. v. Whiteman, 2 Cir., 114 F.2d 86, certiorari denied 311 U.S. 712, 61 S.Ct 393, 85 L.Ed. 463, and a finding that the contract was one of sale rather than license, the district court answered the first question in the negative 98 F.Supp. 906, 910. We agree with this conclusion and see no need to add to his opinion.

He also gave a negative answer to the third question, 98 F.Supp. 910-911. We adopt this reasoning and conclusion on this point also.

Determination of the second question turns upon findings of fact. Obviously a ten-inch record revolving at 78 revolutions a minute has a shorter playing time and a smaller content than a twelve-inch recording at the same speed. Findings 25 and 26 state that all that was deleted in the smaller record was audience reaction consisting of whistles, cheers and screams; that there was no deletion of music, and the plaintiff's contribution to the original musical production was not changed or affected in any way; and 'Accordingly, when the defendant, at the plaintiff's insistence, corrected the album covers of the ten-inch 78 rpm records to conform to the agreement, he was not, as claimed, attributing to the plaintiff the work of some one else.' The court based his finding that there was no deletion of music on his own listening to the records (exhibits 4 and 14 played in the court room) and on the testimony of Mr. Hammond, a musical expert called by the plaintiff. A perusal of this expert's testimony discloses statements patently at odds with the judge's findings. Nor can we understand, after ourselves listening to the records, the judge's finding that nothing but audience reaction was omitted from the ten-inch records. Fully eight minutes of music appear to us to have been omitted, including saxophone, guitar, piano and trumpet solos. In our opinion the trial judge's finding that there was no substantial musical deletions is erroneous.

We are therefore faced with the question whether the manufacture and sale by the defendant of the abbreviated ten-inch records violated any right of the plaintiff. Disregarding for the moment the terms of the contract, we think that the purchaser of the master discs could lawfully use them to produce the abbreviated record and could lawfully sell the same provided he did not describe it as a recording of music presented by the plaintiff. If he did so describe it, he would commit the tort of unfair competition. But the contract required the defendant to use the legend 'Presented by Norman Granz,' that is, to attribute to him the musical content of the records offered for sale. This contractual duty carries by implication, without the necessity of an express prohibition, the duty not to sell records which make the required legend a false representation. In our opinion, therefore, sale of the ten-inch abbreviated records was a breach of the contract. No specific damages were shown to have resulted. As such damages are difficult to prove and the harm to the plaintiff's reputation as an expert in the presentation of jazz concerts is irreparable, injunctive relief is appropriate. Hence we think the plaintiff was entitled to an injunction against having the abbreviated ten-inch records attributed to him unless he waived his right. As already noted the district court found that the album cover of the shortened record was corrected 'at the plaintiff's insistence,' and consequently the defendant was not 'attributing to the plaintiff the work of some one else.' The only evidence we can discover to support the theory of waiver is the following bit of testimony by the defendant who was called as a witness by the plaintiff:

'As soon as I have received the letter from his (Granz's) attorney, probably about a couple of weeks later or month later, I called in my attorney and he said, What is Norman Grantz's complaint, and he said he wanted to see his attorney, and he said he did not like the arrangement, and that was the question discussed, change the cover.'

What this testimony means is far from clear. Even if Granz's attorney requested that the cover be corrected immediately and without waiting for the case to come to trial, we are not satisfied that this would necessarily operate as a waiver of Granz's right to an injunction, if sale of the abbreviated records under the legend 'Presented by Norman Granz' constituted a breach of contract or the tort of unfair competition, as we have found it did. Whether he intended to waive all claims or whether that result would follow regardless of his intention depends upon what was said and done in the negotiations regarding correction of the cover. We think the case must be remanded for additional evidence on this point and a finding as to what, if anything, Granz did consent.

Dismissal of the complaint is affirmed with respect to sales of the ten-inch 33 1/3 rpm records and with respect to selling records singly. With respect to the sale of ten-inch 78 rpm records and the claim of attorney's fees the cause is remanded for further proceedings in conformity with the opinion. One-half costs of appeal are awarded the appellant.

The dismissal of the complaint was affirmed with respect to the sales of 10" 33 1/3 rpm records and also with respect to the sale of single records. But, with respect to the sale of 10" 78 rpm records and the claim of attorney fees, the cause is remanded so as to develop additional evidence on this point. However, plaintiff was entitled to an injunction as to those records that did not contain the entire composition. Defendant's contractual duty implied a duty not to sell records which attributed a false representation. The sale of these falsely represented records would constitute a breach of contract and thus the granting of an injunction. In short, substantial cutting of the original work (still under the less-than-accurate title, "Presented by Norman Glanz,") constitutes misrepresentation, and, therefore, plaintiff Glanz is entitled to an injunction from having falsely represented records attributed to him.

## Exclusive Recording Agreement

THIS AGREEMENT ("Agreement") is made and entered into as of the _____ day of August, 2015 ("Effective Date"), by and between Joshua Doe Records, LLC, ( herein referenced as "Company" and/or "Joshua Doe Records, LLC"), a Texas corporation having its principal place of business at 8888 Sunflower Drive, Houston, Texas, 77777, and John Doe (herein referenced as "Artist" and/or "John Doe"), an individual, located at 3399 Tulip Road, Houston, Texas 77777.

In consideration of the mutual promises contained herein, it is hereby agreed as follows:

1. (a) Company, hereby engages Artist to provide original masters or record for Company, masters embodying the performances of Artist, and Artist hereby accepts such engagement and agrees to provide original masters or record masters embodying the performances of Artist exclusively for Company, during the term hereof and all extensions and renewals.

   (b) The rights herein granted to Company, and the obligations of Artist shall be for the world ("Territory").

   (c) Artist is authorized, empowered and able to enter into and fully perform its obligations under this agreement. Neither this agreement nor the fulfillment hereof by any party infringes upon the rights of any Person.

2. The term of this Agreement shall be for a period of two (2) years commencing on the date hereof ("Initial Period"). Artist hereby grants to Company, one (1) consecutive separate options to extend the term for further periods of one (1) year each ("Option Periods"), each upon the same terms and conditions applicable to the Initial Period, except as otherwise hereinafter set forth. The Initial Period and every Option Period for which Company, has exercised its option are hereinafter sometimes referred to together as the "Term". Each option shall be automatically exercised, unless written notice to the contrary is sent to Artist at least thirty (30) days prior to the date that the Term would otherwise expire.

3.  During the initial period, Artist shall provide original master or record masters the equivalent in playing time of one CD, not less than forty-five (45) minutes. Said masters are herein and hereby owned by Company, pursuant to all of the terms and conditions of this Agreement, particularly Paragraph 20 hereof and said masters shall be deemed recorded and delivered hereunder during the Initial term. Company, has the option to require an additional master in the equivalent in playing time of one CD during the Initial Period and each subsequent period.

4.  (a) During the Term, Artist shall not perform for the purpose of making records, for anyone other than Company, for distribution in the Territory and Artist shall not authorize the use of Artist's name, likeness, or other identification for the purpose of distributing, selling, advertising or exploiting records, cd's, audio digital recordings for anyone other than Company, in the Territory. Artist shall take reasonable measures to prevent the manufacture, distribution and sale at any time by any Person other than Company, to use Artist's name (including professional name or sobriquet), Likeness (including picture, portrait, or caricature) or biography in connection with the manufacture and/or exploitation of Masters or Phonograph Records.

    (b) Artist shall not perform any selection recorded hereunder for the purpose of making records for anyone other than Company, for distribution in the Territory (I) for a period of ten (10) years after the initial date of release of the respective record containing such selection or (ii) for a period of two (2) years after the expiration or other termination of this Agreement, whichever is later ("Re-recording Restriction").

    (c) Should Artist make any sound recording during the Term for motion pictures, television, electrical transcriptions or any other medium or should Artist after the Term perform for any such purpose any selection recorded hereunder to which the Recording Restriction then applies, Artist will do so only pursuant to a written agreement prohibiting the use of such recordings directly or indirectly, for record purposes in the Territory. Artist shall furnish Company, a copy of the provisions of any such contract relating to the foregoing. Such contract, if any, may be negotiated by Company, on behalf of Artist; or Company, must be a party to all such contracts.

5. All original masters provided or masters recorded by Artist during the Term from the inception of the recording thereof and all reproductions derived therefrom, together with the performances embodied thereon, shall be the property of Company, for the world free form any claims whatsoever by Artist or any person deriving any rights or interest from Artist. Without limiting the generality of the foregoing, Company, and its designee(s) shall have the exclusive and unlimited right to all the results and proceeds of Artist's recording services rendered during the Term, including, but not limited to the exclusive, unlimited and perpetual rights throughout the world:

(a) To manufacture, advertise, sell, lease, license, distribute or otherwise use or dispose of, in any or all fields of use by any method now or hereafter known, records embodying the masters recorded by Artist during the term, all upon such terms and conditions as Company, may elect, or at its discretion, to refrain therefrom;

(b) To use and publish and to permit others to use and publish Artist's name (including any professional name heretofore, or hereafter adopted by Artist), photographs, likeness, and biographical material concerning Artist for advertising and trade purposes in connection with all masters recorded by Artist and all Pictures produced during the Term.

(c) To obtain copyrights and renewals thereof in sound recordings and the musical compositions embodied thereon recorded by Artist during the Term in Company's name as owner and employer-for-hire of such sound recordings;

(d) To release records derived from masters recorded by Artist during the Term under any name, trademark or label which Company, or its subsidiaries, affiliates or licensees may from time to time elect. Artist agrees that the initial United States release during the Term hereof embodying masters recorded by Artist hereunder shall be in Company's sole discretion.

(e) To perform such records publicly and to permit public performances thereof by means of radio broadcast, television or any other method now or hereafter known.

(f) Without limitation we, and/or our subsidiaries, affiliates and licensees shall have the right to make records or other reproductions of the performances embodied in such recordings by any method now or hereafter known, and to see and deal in the same under any trademark or trade names or labels designated by us, or we may at our election refrain therefrom.

6.  (a) Artist acknowledges that the sale of records is speculative and agrees that the judgment of Company, with regard to any matter affecting the sale, distribution or exploitation of such records shall be binding and conclusive upon Artist. Except as otherwise specifically set forth in subparagraph 6(b) hereof, nothing contained in this Agreement shall obligate Company, to make sell, license, or distribute records manufactured from masters delivered hereunder.

(b) Provided that Artist is not in breach of this Agreement, and if Company, is in receipt of completed, fully edited and mixed technically satisfactory masters sufficient to comprise each newly recorded required CD hereunder embodying Artist's studio performances of material not previously recorded by Artist ready for Company's, manufacture of records therefrom, together with all materials therefore, Company, agrees to commercially release each CD recorded and delivered hereunder within one hundred and eighty (180) days following completion or delivery of Artist's providing the original master or recording masters for Company,.

(c) It is understood and agreed that if Company, shall have failed to so release any such CD, Artist shall have the right to notify Company, in writing of Company's such failure and of Artist's desire that the Term of this Agreement be terminated if Company, does not, within sixty (60) days after Company, receives such notice from Artist commercially release the applicable CD in the U. S. Unless Company, can show where such release was prevented due to unavoidable conditions including but not limited to; any labor controversy or adjustment thereof or to any other cause not entirely within Company's control or which Company, cannot by reasonable diligence have avoided, Company, is materially hampered in the recording, manufacture, distribution or sale of records, or Company's normal business operations become commercially impractical. Such suspension shall be upon written notice to you and shall last for the duration of any such contingency.

At Company's election, a period equal to the duration of such suspension shall be added at the end of the then current period for the term hereof, and such period and the term hereof shall be accordingly extended. It is specifically understood and agreed that Company, shall have no liability whatsoever to Artist and Artist's only remedy shall be to terminate the Term of this Agreement by written notice to Company, within fifteen (15) days following the expiration of such extended periods. Failure to provide such notice within the specified time constitutes waiver of the Artist's option to terminate.

7.  For your services rendered, and for the rights herein, Company, may make a non-returnable advance payment to you, within fourteen (14) days after the services are rendered at each recording session, and each such payment shall constitute an advance and be charged against your royalties, if and when earned, under this or any other agreement between Artist and Company,. Within fourteen (14) days after the services are rendered at each recording session Company, may pay for the services of the Company, musicians, vocalists, arrangers and copyists, and such payments and other recording costs shall be charged against your royalties, if and when earned, under this or any other agreement between Artist and Company,.

8.  (a) (i) Except as otherwise provided in subparagraph 8 (a)(ii) hereof, Company, is not responsible for and shall not pay any recording costs, pressing and promotional costs, subject to Company, approval if applicable before royalties are calculated, incurred in the production and release of all masters subject to this Agreement. All such costs paid by Company, shall be deducted from any and all monies becoming payable to Artist under this or any other agreement between the parties hereto.

    (ii) Notwithstanding the provisions of subparagraph 9 (a) hereof, in the event that Company, elects to require Artist to record and deliver the Additional Masters, or if Company, wishes to remix any of the master delivery in connections with the first LP, all costs so paid by Company, shall be advances against and recoupable by Company, out of all royalties payable to Artist pursuant to this or any other agreement between the parties hereto.

(b) Company, shall be solely responsible for and shall pay all monies becoming payable to Artist and all other parties rendered services or otherwise in respect of sales of the recording derived from masters subject to this Agreement.

9.  (a) Each master recorded and delivered hereunder shall be produced by a producer selected by Company, (unless produced prior to signing with Company,). Company, shall be solely responsible for and shall pay all monies becoming payable to all producers hired by Company,. All such sums so paid by Company, shall be deducted from any and all monies otherwise payable to Artist under this or any other agreement between the parties hereto.

10. Conditions upon Artist'S full and faithful performance of all the material terms hereof, Company, shall pay Artist the following royalties in respect of records subject to this Agreement:

    (a) Company, shall credit Artist's Royalty Account pursuant to and in accordance with the following royalty schedule for records manufactured and sold in the United States:

| Recording Periods | Minimum Sides | Royalty Rates |
|---|---|---|
| Initial Period (First Year) | _____ | _____ |
| Initial Period (Second Year) | _____ | _____ |
| 1$^{st}$ Option Period (1 year) | _____ | _____ |

*Royalty Rate- Percentage times ninety (90% percent of net records sold and for which Company, has been paid times the retail price retained by Company, of records manufactured in the United States. This rate shall also apply to 7" or 12" Singles or their equivalent. (In the event Company's distributor pays on the basis of eighty-five (85%) or ninety (90%) percent of retail, then Company, shall pay on the same basis as distributor).

(b)(I) With respect to retail sales outside the United States of all records derived from masters recorded and delivered during the Term, the royalty rate shall be one half of the U.S. Rate, or the U.S. rate prorated down the percentage which Company's royalty rate is reduced, the amount will be determined by whichever is the lesser amount.

(ii) The royalty rate herinafter set forth in subparagraph 10(b)(I) shall be hereinafter referred to as the "Basic Foreign Rate."

(iii) Notwithstanding to the contrary anything contained herein, with respect to records sold in Brazil, Greece, Portugal, India, Kenya, Zambia, Zimbabwe, Nigeria and any other territory in which governmental or other authorities place limits on the royalty rates permissible for remittance to the United States, in respect of records sold in such territory (ies), the rate shall equal the lesser of (A) the Basic Foreign Rate or (B) the effective royalty rate permitted by such governmental or other authority for remittances to the United States less a royalty equivalent to two (2%) percent of the retail list price and such monies as Company, or its licensees shall be required to pay to all applicable union funds in respect of said sales.

(iv) Royalties in respect of sales of records outside the United States shall be computed in the same national currency as Company, is accounted to by is licensees and shall be paid to Artist at the same rate of exchange as Company, is paid. It is understood that such royalties will not be due and payable until payment thereof is received by or credited to Company, in the United States according to governmental regulations. Royalties therefore shall not be credited to Artist's account during the continuance of such inability of Company, to receive payment, or (ii) if the royalties not credited to Artist's account exceed the amount, if any, by which Artist's account is in a debit position, then Company, will, after Artist's request and at Artist's expense, and if Company, is able to do so, deposit such excess royalties to Artist crediting the applicable foreign currency in a foreign depository. Deposit as aforesaid shall fulfill Company's obligations under this Agreement as to record sales to which such royalty payments are applicable.

(c) With respect of records sold (I) through any direct mail or mail order distribution, method, including, without limitation, record club distribution, (ii) by distribution through retail outlets in conjunction with special advertisements on radio or television or (iii) by any combination of the methods set forth above, the royalty payable in connection therewith shall be one half (1/2) of Company's net earned royalty receipts in respect of reported sales through such channels after Company, shall have first deducted all third party payments for which Company, is responsible. No royalties shall be payable with respect to records given away as "bonus" or "free" records as a result of joining a record club or plan or of purchasing a required number of records with respect to records received by members of any such club operation either in an introductory offer in connection with joining such club or upon recommending that another join such club operation.

(d)(I) With respect to mid-priced CDs, the royalty rate shall be two-thirds (2/3) of the Basic U.S. LP rate of Basic Foreign Rate, as the case may be provided that during the Term, Company, shall not release in the United States any such mid-priced CD comprised solely of masters delivered hereunder prior to nine (9) months following Company's initial United States release of such CD as a full-priced record, unless Artist shall consent in writing.

(ii) With respect to budget, CDs, the royalty rate shall be one-half (1/2) of the Basic U.S. LP Rate or Basic Foreign Rate, as the case may be, provided that during the Term Company, shall not release in the United States any such budget CD comprised solely of masters delivered hereunder prior to eighteen (18) months following Company's initial United States release of such CD as full priced record, unless Artist shall consent thereto.

(e) With respect to EP's, the royalty rate shall be three-fourths (3/4) of the Basic U.S. LP Rate or Basic Foreign Rate, as the case may be.

(f) Notwithstanding anything to the contrary contained in this Agreement, in the event that Company, (or its licensee(s)) shall in any country(ies) of the Territory adopt a policy applicable to the majority of CDs in Company's (or its licensee(s)); then current catalogue pursuant to which the retail list price of an CD is reduced subsequent to its initial release, then the royalty rates otherwise payable to Artist under this Agreement shall be reduced in proportion that such reduced retail list price retained by Company, of such CD as initially released in the applicable country.

(g) With respect to "compact disc" LPs, the royalty rate shall be the Basic U.S. LP Rate retained by Company, or Basic Foreign Rate, as the case may be.

(h) In the event that Company, shall sell or license third parties to sell "records" via telephone, satellite, cable or other direct transmission to the consumer over wire or through the air, Artist shall be paid royalties with respect thereto at the Basic U.S. Singles Rate as retained by Company,, Basic U.S. LP Rate as retained by royalties payable in connection with such sales, the retail list price as retained by Company, if such "records" shall be deemed to be the then current retail list price of tape copies of such records and in the case of records which have no tape equivalent, the corresponding price of the disc (but not in the United States, eighty-five (85%) percent of the then current retail list price retained by Company, of such tape copies or corresponding disc), and the packaging deduction for such sales shall be made in accordance with subparagraph 10(s)(iii) of this Agreement.

(i) The royalty rate payable for records sold to the United States government, its subdivisions, departments and agencies, and to educational institutions and libraries shall be one-half (1/2) of the otherwise applicable basic U.S. rate and shall be based upon the retail list price as retained by Company, (Post Exchange list price where applicable of such records).

(j) There shall be no royalty rate paid for records sold as "premiums." It is understood that Company, shall not use Artist's name or likeness in connection with any such premium record as an endorsement of any product or service.

(k) The royalty rate payable for records sold in the form of pre-recorded tape (whether reel-to-reel or cartridge) or any other form (other than disc), shall be the applicable royalty rate otherwise payable, provided that if the retail list price of any record sold in pre-recorded tape form or any form (other than disc) shall be less than the retail list price of the corresponding record in disc form, the royalty rate otherwise payable reduced in the proportion that the retail list price of the applicable record in pre-recorded tape form (or such for other than disc) bears to the retail list price of such record (in disc form).

(l) Company, shall have the right to license the masters to third parties for record use and/or all other types of use on a flat-fee basis. Company, shall credit Artist's royalty account with twenty-five (25%) percent of the net amount received by Company, under each such license after Company, shall have first deducted all third party payments for which Company, is responsible.

(m) As to records not consisting entirely of masters recorded and delivered hereunder, the royalty rate otherwise payable to Artist hereunder with respect to sales of any such record shall be prorated by multiplying such royalty rate by a fraction, the numerator of which is the total number of masters embodied thereon.

(n) As to masters embodying performances of Artist together with the performances of any other Artist(s), the royalty rate otherwise payable hereunder with respect to sales of any record derived from any such master of the recording cost and/or advances otherwise payable by Company, hereunder with respect to any such master shall be prorated by multiplying such royalty rate less any recording costs and/or advances by a fraction the numerator of which is one and the denominator of which is the total number of Artists whose performances are embodied on such master.

(o) Company, shall have the right to include or to license others to include any one or more of the masters in promotional records on which such masters and other recordings are included, which promotional records are designed for sale at a substantially lower price than the regular price of Company's LPs. No royalties shall be payable on sales of such promotional records.

(p) No royalties shall be payable in respect of: (I) records given away or furnished on a "no-charge basis to "one-stops", rack jobbers, distributors or dealers, whether or not affiliated with Company,, provided that such records do not exceed 300 non-royalty bearing Singles out of every 1,000 Singles distributed and non-royalty bearing LPs out of every 1,000 LPs distributed, and provided further that Company, shall have the right to exceed the aforesaid limitations for short term special promotions or marketing campaigns. The number of records distributed on a no-charge basis shall not, for any such short term promotion or campaign exceed an additional ten (10%) percent of the total number of records distributed. Company, shall use reasonable efforts to notify Artist of any such short term special promotion or campaign, but Company's failure to do so shall not be a breach of this Agreement or in any manner affect Company's right to distribute records on a non-royalty basis as aforesaid; and heretofore (ii) records given away or sold at or below stated wholesale prices for promotional purposes to disc jockey, record reviewers, radio and television stations and networks, motion picture companies, music publishers, Company's employees, Artist or other customary recipients of promotional records or for use on transportation facilities, (iii) records sold as scrap, salvage, overstock or "cut-outs", (iv) records sold below cost. No royalties shall be payable on any sales by Company's licensees until payment has been received by or credited to Company, in the United States. This paragraph shall be governed by the agreement between Company, and its distributor. In the event that distributor adopts a different policy as to the contents of this paragraph, then said distributors' policy shall prevail as between Company, and Artist in calculating all royalties payable first.

(q) As to records sold at a discount to "one-stops", rack jobbers, distributors or dealers, whether or not affiliated with Company,, in lieu of the records given away or furnished on a "no-charge" basis as provided in subparagraph 10(p)(I) above, the applicable royalty rate otherwise payable hereunder with respect to such records shall be reduced in the proportion that said discount wholesale price bears to the usual stated wholesale price, provided that said reduction in the applicable royalty rate does not exceed that percentage limitation set forth in subparagraph 10(q)(I) above.

(r) The royalty rate provided for in this Paragraph 10 shall be applied against the retail list price as retained by Company, (less Company's container deductions, excise taxes, duties and other applicable taxes) for ninety (90%) of records sold which are paid for and not returned. The term for "retail list price" as retained by Company, as used in this Agreement shall mean (I) for records sold in the United States, the manufacturer's suggested retail price in the United States less any amounts contracted out by Company, and (ii) for records sold outside the United States, the manufacturer's suggested retail price in the country of manufacture or sale, as Company, is paid. In those countries where a manufacturer's suggested retail price is not utilized or permitted, the generally accepted retail price shall be utilized.

Notwithstanding the foregoing (A) the retail list price for a "Disco-Single" shall be deemed to be the retail list price for a Single, except for Disco-Singles sold in the United States the retail list price therefore shall be deemed to be the lesser of one hundred fifty (150%) percent of the retail list price of a Single or the actual retail list price of such Disco-Single and (B) with respect to "compact discs" or other audio-file records in any configuration manufactured, distributed and sold by Company's normal retail channels in the United States a royalty equal at the same penny rate as Company, is paid on cassette tapes. In computing sales, Company, shall have the right to deduct all returns made at any time and for any reason. In the event Company, is paid on the basis of 100% of the retail list price then Artist will be paid on the same basis.

(s) Company's, container deductions shall be a sum equal to (I) ten (10%) percent of the retail list price for records in disc form (other than "compact discs" records), (ii) twelve and one-half (12 ½%) of retail list price for records in disc form in "double-fold" jackets or covers or in jackets which contain an insert or any other special elements, and (iii) twenty (20%) percent of the retail list price of pre-recorded tape, thereof for reel-to-reel tapes, cartridges, cassettes and any other types of recordings other than discs; and twenty-five per cent (25%) for compact discs. In the event that the deduction for packaging charged by Company's, distributor is different than the amounts herein, then the amount deducted by Company's, distributor shall prevail.

(t) The royalty rate pursuant to this paragraph 10 will apply to the first 1,000,000 units of sales of each album consisting of Master Recordings made during the first Option period. The royalty rate will be 50% rather than 30.0% on the next 500,000 units sold. The royalty rate on sales of the next 1,000,000 units sold will be 50%. The royalty that OP 2 shall begin at is the initial royalty rate and it shall be credited the same point increases upon reaching the above mentioned levels of sales.

11. Statements as to royalties payable hereunder shall be sent by Company, to Artist within thirty (30) days after the expiration of each semiannual period for the preceding semiannual period ending June 1 and December 1. Concurrently with the rendition of each

statement, Company, shall pay Artist all royalties shown to be due by such statement, after deducting all recording costs paid by Company,, all payments made on behalf of Artist and all advances made to Artist prior to the rendition of the statement. No statements need be rendered by Company, for any such quarterly period after the expiration of the Term hereof. All payments shall be made to the order of Artist and shall be sent to Artist at Artist's address first above written. Company, shall be entitled to maintain a single account with respect to all recordings subject to this or any other agreement between the parties hereto. Company, may maintain reserves and reserves the right not to, however, in the event that Company, does agree regarding such reserves: (I) with respect to LPs in disc form, each base reserve as initially established shall not exceed twenty-five (25%) percent of records shipped during the applicable accounting period and shall, at the end of two (2) years from the date established, be reduced to twenty 20% percent; (ii) with respect to LPs in tape form, each base reserve as initially established shall not exceed twenty-five (25%) percent of tapes shipped during the applicable accounting period and shall at the end of two (2) years from the date established, be reduced to twenty (20%) percent; and (iii) with respect to Singles, each base reserve as initially established shall not exceed thirty-five (35%) percent of records shipped during the applicable accounting period and shall, at the end of two (2) years from the date established, be reduced to twenty (20%) percent. Company, shall fully liquidate each base reserve within five (5) years from the date that such base reserve was established. At such time as reserve is liquidated, it shall be deemed to be a sale in the period in which it was liquidated. Artist shall be deemed to have consented to all accountings rendered by Company, hereunder and said accountings shall be binding upon Artist and not subject to any objection by Artist for any reason unless specific objection, in writing, stating the basis thereof, is given to Company, within one (1) year after the date rendered, and after such written objection, unless, suit is instituted within one (1) year after the date upon which Company, notifies Artist that it denies the validity of the objection.

12. Artist shall have the right at Artist's sole cost and expense to appoint a Certified Public Accountant who is not then currently engaged in an outstanding audit of Company's books and records as same pertain to sales of records subject hereto as to which royalties are payable hereunder, provided that any such examination shall be

for a reasonable duration, shall take place at Company's offices or the office of Legal Counsel for Company,, during normal business hours on reasonable prior written notice and shall not occur more than once in any calendar year.

13. (a)  All notices to Artist may be served upon a principal or officer of Artist personally, by prepaid telegram, or by depositing the same, postage prepaid, Certified Mail Return Receipt Requested (CMRRR) in any mailbox, chute, or other receptacle authorized by the United States Postal Service for mail, addressed to Artist at Artist's address first above written.

(b) All notices to Company, shall be in writing and shall be sent postage prepaid by registered or certified mail, return receipt requested, and addressed to Company's address first above written.

14.  (a)  All musical compositions or material recorded pursuant to this Agreement which are written or composed, in whole or in part by Artist or any producer of the masters subject hereto, or which are owned or controlled, directly or indirectly, in whole or in part, by Artist and/or Artist and or any Producer of the masters subject hereto (herein called "Controlled Compositions") shall be and are hereby licensed to Company, for the United States at a royalty per selection equal to seventy-five (75%) percent of the minimum statutory per selection rate (without regard to playing time) effective on the earlier of (I) the date such masters are required to be delivered hereunder or (ii) the date such masters are delivered to Company, hereunder. The aforesaid seventy-five (75%) percent per selection rate shall hereinafter sometimes be referred to as the "Per Selection Rate." Notwithstanding the foregoing, the maximum aggregate mechanical royalty rate which Company, shall be required to pay in respect of any Single, Disco-single or LP hereunder, regardless of the total number of all compositions contained therein, shall not exceed two (2) times, and ten (10) times the Per Selection Rate, respectively and in respect of any EP hereunder, regardless of the total number of all compositions contained thereon, shall not exceed the per Selection rate times the total number of masters contained therein. In this connection, it is specifically understood that in the event that any single, Disco-Single, EP or LP contains other compositions in addition to the Controlled Compositions and the aggregate mechanical royalty rate provided in this Paragraph 14, the aggregate rate for the Controlled Compositions contained thereon shall be reduced by the aforesaid excess over said applicable rate. Additionally, Company, shall have the right with respect to any Single, Disco-Single, EP or LP, the

aggregate mechanical royalty rate for which exceeds the applicable rate provided in this Paragraph 14 to deduct such excess payable thereon from any and all monies payable to Artist pursuant to this or any other agreement between the parties hereto. All mechanical royalties payable hereunder shall be paid on the basis of net records sold hereunder for which royalties are payable to Artist pursuant to this Agreement. Notwithstanding anything to the contrary contained herein, mechanical royalties payable in respect to Controlled Compositions for sales of records for any use other than as describe in subparagraphs 10 (a), (e), (g), and (k) hereof shall be seventy-five (75%) percent of the otherwise applicable Per Selection Rate. Controlled Compositions with rearranged versions of any musical compositions in the public domain, when furnished by Artist for recording hereunder, shall be free of administration of copyright in any Controlled Compositions with rearranged versions of any musical compositions in the public domain, when furnished by Artist for recording hereunder, shall be free of administration of copyright in any Controlled Composition shall be made subject to the provisions hereof any inconsistencies between the terms of this Agreement and mechanical licenses issued to and accepted by Company, shall be determined by the terms of the Agreement. If any Single, Disco-Single, EP or LP contains other compositions in addition to the Controlled Compositions, Artist will obtain for Company's benefit mechanical licenses covering such composition on the same terms and conditions applicable to Controlled Compositions pursuant to this Paragraph 14.

(b)      In respect of all Controlled Compositions performed in Pictures, Company, is hereby granted an irrevocable perpetual worldwide license to record and reproduce such compositions in such Pictures and to distribute and perform such Pictures including, but not limited to, all Video shows thereof, and to authorize to others to do so. Company, will not be required to make any payment in connection with those uses, and that licenses shall apply whether or not Company, received any payment in connection with those Pictures. Simultaneously with Artist's submission to Company, of the information required pursuant to subparagraph 21 (c) (I) hereof, Artist shall furnish Company, with a written acknowledgment from the person(s) or entity(ies) controlling the copyright in each non Controlled Compositions to be embodied on any Picture confirming the terms upon which said person(s) or entity(ies) to forthwith issue to Company, (and its designees), may require. Royalties in connection with licenses for the use of non-Controlled Compositions pertaining to Pictures and Video shows are included in the royalties set forth in subparagraph 21 (d) hereof, as described in subparagraph 21 (d) (ii). If the copyright in any Controlled

Composition is owned or controlled by anyone else, Artist will cause that person, firm or corporation to grant Company, the same rights described in this Paragraph 14, on the same terms.

15.    (a)    In the event that the Artist for any reason fails to timely fulfill any of its production and delivery commitments to Company, hereunder in accordance with all the terms and conditions of this Agreement, then, in addition to any other rights or remedies which Company, may have, Company, shall have the right, upon written notice to Artist at any time prior to the expiration of then current Period. (I) to terminate the Agreement without further obligation to Artist as to unrecorded or undelivered masters, (ii) to reduce the minimum number of masters required to be recorded and delivered during the then current Period to the number which have been timely recorded and delivered during such period, or (iii) such default plus one hundred and fifty (150) days with the time for the exercise by Company, of its options to extend the term and the dates of commencement of subsequent Option Periods deemed extended accordingly.  It is specifically understood that Company, may exercise any or all of its rights pursuant to subparagraphs 15 (a) (I), (ii) and (iii) hereof at any time(s) prior to the date the Term would otherwise expire.   Company's obligations hereunder shall be suspended for the duration of any such default.  The provisions of this subparagraph shall not result in an extension of the Term for a period in excess of enforcement of personal services agreements.

(b)    (i) Upon reasonable notice from Company,, Artist shall be available for and shall assist Company, with all forms of promotion such as but not limited to in store, radio and trade interviews.  The parties acknowledge that this provision is a material provision of this agreement. Company, as a remedy can estimate damages to profit as a result of lack of promotion and withhold such damage from royalties due to Artist.

(ii)    Artist may tour in conjunction with promotion of recordings subject to this Agreement, but all tour schedules must be submitted to and approved by Company,.   Approval will not be unreasonably withheld.

(c)    Company, reserves the right, at their election, to suspend the operation of this Agreement for the duration of any of the following contingencies, if for by reason of any such contingency, it is materially hampered in their performance of the obligations under this Agreement or its normal business operations are delayed or become agencies or officers, and any order, regulation, ruling or action of any labor union or association of Artists, musicians, companies or employees affecting Company's control. Any such suspension due to a labor controversy which involves only Company, shall be limited to a period of six (6) months.

(d)      If Artist's voice should be materially or permanently impaired, then in addition to any other rights or remedies which Company, may have, Company, shall have the right, upon written notice to Artist, to terminate this Agreement and shall thereby be relieved of any liability in connection with undelivered masters.

16.      Artist expressly acknowledges that Artist's services hereunder are of a special, unique and intellectual character which gives them peculiar value, and that by any breach in the term, condition or covenant hereof, Company, will be caused immediate irreparable injury. Artist expressly agrees that Company, shall be entitled to seek injunctive and other equitable relief, as permitted by law, to prevent a breach or threatened breach of this Agreement, or any portion thereof, by Artist which relief shall be in addition to any other rights or remedies, for damages which are otherwise available to Company,.

17.      (a)      Artist warrants and represents that neither Artist is under any disability, restriction or prohibition, whether contractual or otherwise, with respect to Artist's right to execute this Agreement or Artist's right to perform its terms and conditions. Without limiting the foregoing, Artist specifically warrants and represents that no prior obligations, contracts or agreements of any kind undertaken or entered into by Artist, will interfere in any manner with the complete performance of this Agreement by Company,, Artist, or with Artist's right to record any and all selections hereunder. Artist warrants and represents that there are not in existence any prior unreleased masters embodying Artist's performance.

(b)      Artist warrants and represent that no materials, or any use thereof, will violate any law or infringe upon or violate the rights of any third party. "Material(s)", as used in this subparagraph 17 (b) shall include (i) all musical compositions and other material contained on masters subject thereto, with masters recorded hereunder, (ii) each name used by Artist, in connection with masters recorded hereunder, and (iii) all other material, ideas, other intellectual properties, or elements furnished or selected by Artist and contained in or used in connection with any masters recorded hereunder or the packaging, sale distribution, advertising, publicizing, or other exploitation thereof.

(c)      Artist agrees to and does hereby indemnify, save and hold Company, harmless from any and all loss and damage (including court costs and reasonable attorney's fees) arising out of, connected with or as a result of any inconsistency with, failure or breach or threatened breach by Artist of any warranty, representation, agreement, undertaking or covenant contained in this Agreement including without limitation, any claim by any third party in connection with the foregoing.  In addition to any other rights or remedies Company, may have by reason of any such inconsistency , failure, breach, threatened breach or claim, Artist shall reimburse Company,, on demand, for any payment made by Company, at any time after the date hereof with respect to any loss, damage, or liability resulting therefrom and in addition thereto Company, shall have the right to deduct from any and all monies otherwise payable to Artist under this or any other agreement between the parties hereto a sum(s) equal to such loss, and reasonable attorney's fee.  Company, shall give Artist notice of any third party claim to which the foregoing indemnity applies and Artist shall have the right to participate in the defenses of any such claim through counsel of Artist's own choice and at Artist's expense.  Pending the determination of any such claim, Company, may withhold payment of all monies under this or any other agreement between the parties hereof in any amount consistent with such claim.

18.      Wherever in this agreement Artist's approval or consent is required, such approval or consent shall not be unreasonably withheld. Company, may require Artist to formally give or withhold such approval or consent by giving Artist written notice requesting same and by furnishing Artist with the information or materials in respect of which such approval or consent is sought.  Artist shall give Company, written notice of approval or disapproval within five (5) days after such notice.  Artist shall not hinder nor delay the scheduled release of any record hereunder.  In the event of disapproval or no consent, the reasons therefore shall be stated.  Failure to give such notice to Company, as aforesaid  shall be deemed to be consent or approval.

19.      (a)      During the Term, Company, and Artist warrants and represents the Company, and Artist shall become and remain a member in good standing of any labor unions with which the Company, may at any time have agreements lawfully requiring such union membership, including, but not limited to, the American Federation of Musicians and the American Federation of Television and Radio Artists.  All masters subject hereto shall be produced in accordance with the rules and regulations of all unions having jurisdiction.

(b)     Notwithstanding any provision in this contract to the contrary, it is specifically understood and agreed by all parties hereto:

(i)     They are bound by all the terms and provisions of the AFTRA CODE OF FAIR PRACTICE for Phonograph recordings.

(ii)     That should there be any inconsistency between this contract and said CODE OF FAIR PRACTICE, the said CODE OF FAIR PRACTICE shall prevail, but nothing in this provision shall affect terms, compensation or conditions provided in this contract which are more favorable to members of AFTRA that the terms, compensation, and conditions provided for in said CODE OF FAIR PRACTICE.

(iii)     If the terms of this contract is of longer duration than the term of said Code, then from and after the expiration date of the Code (a) the provisions of this contract shall be deemed modified to conform to any agreement or modifications negotiated or agreed to in a renewal or extension of the code; and (b) while no code is in effect the existence of this contract shall not prevent the Artist from engaging in any strike or work stoppage without penalty by way of damage or otherwise to you for AFTRA. In the event Artist engages in such strike or stoppage Company, may suspend this contract for the duration of the strike or stoppage and may have the option of extending the term of this contract for a period of time equal to the length of such strike or stoppage which option must be exercised by written notice give to you within thirty (30) days after the end of the strike or stoppage. Artist represents that he/she is or will become a member of the American Federation of Televisions and Radio Artists in good standing.

20.     (a)     Artist hereby sells, transfers and assigns to Company, irrevocably all rights, title and interests in and to the master embodying Artist's performances the titles of which are listed on Schedule "A" annexed hereto and made a part hereof, from the inception of recordings thereof (hereinafter in this Paragraph 20 referred to as the "Master"), including without limitation, the Company's (or its designee's) name as employer-for-hire such copyrights and all renewals and extensions thereof, perpetually and throughout the Territory.

(b)     Artist will facilitate the Masters to Company, at its offices in Houston, Texas not later than simultaneously with the execution of this Agreement, unless said masters are already in the possession of Company,.

(c)     The Masters will be deemed to have been recorded under this Agreement during the initial Period of the Term of this Agreement.

(d)     Artist hereby warrants and represents:

(i)     No records have been manufactured from the Masters by Artist or any other person, firm or corporation for distribution in the Territory, and neither Artist nor any other person, firm or corporation has or shall have the right to distribute, market and/or sell any records embodying the Masters in Territory, and none of the musical compositions performed in the Masters have been performed by Artist for the making of any other master recordings, other than those records already pressed.

(ii)     Artist has not, nor has any other person, would or assigned to any other party or otherwise disposed of any right, power, and authority to do so, and was not bound by an agreement which would restrict such person from rendering such services or granting such rights.

(iii)     (1)     Each person who rendered any service in connection with, or who otherwise contributed in any way to the making of the Masters, or who granted to Artist any of the rights referred to in this Agreement, had the full right, power, and authority to do so, and was not bound by any agreement which would restrict such person from rendering such services or granting such rights.

(2)     All recording costs and expenses with respect to the making of the Masters have been paid in full.

(3)     All necessary licenses for the recording of the compositions performed in the Masters have been obtained from the copyright owners, and all monies payable under such license or otherwise by reason of such recording have been paid. The foregoing does not apply to any monies payable to such copyright owners in connection with the manufacture of sale of records derived from the Masters.

(4)     All the Masters were made in accordance with the rules and regulations of the American Federation of Musicians ("AFM"), the American Federation of Television and Radio Artists ("AFTRA") and all other unions having jurisdiction.

(iv)     Company, shall have the sole and exclusive right to manufacture, advertise, distribute, sell and otherwise exploit and deal throughout the Territory in the Masters and records and other reproductions derived therefrom, free from any liability or obligation to make any payments therefore, except as expressly provided in this Agreement.

(v)     Artist will execute, and acknowledge and deliver to Company, such further instruments and documents, and will otherwise cooperate with Company, as Company, shall request at any time, for the purpose of establishing or evidencing the rights granted Company, herein, or otherwise to implement the intent of this Paragraph 20 Company, shall give Artist five day notice to sign such documentation and in the event that after said five days the documentation is not signed then Company, may sign the documents in the name of and on behalf of Artist.

(e)     It is understood and agreed that provisions of this Paragraph 20 are of the essence of this agreement.

21.     (a)     In addition to Artist's recording commitments as set forth in Paragraph 3 of this Agreement, Artist shall comply with requests, if any, made by Company, in connection with the production of Pictures. In this connection, Artist shall appear on dates and at places requested by Company, for the filming, taping or other fixation of audio-visual recordings. Artist shall perform services with respect thereto as Company, deems desirable in a timely and first-class manner. Artist acknowledges that the production of Pictures, involved matters of judgment with the respect to art and taste, which judgment shall be exercised by Company, and Company's decisions with respect thereto shall be final. Company, will endeavor to consult with Artist as to the Production of pictures.

(b)(1) Each Picture produced during the Term of this Agreement shall be owned by Company, (including the worldwide copyrights therein and thereto and all extensions and renewals thereof) to the same extent as Company's rights in master recordings made under this Agreement.

(ii)     Company, will have the unlimited right to manufacture Video shows of the Picture to rent, sell, distribute, transfer, sublicense or otherwise deal in such Video shows under any trademarks, trade names and labels; to exploit the Picture by any means now or hereafter known or developed; or refrain Artist from any such exploitation, throughout the world.

(c)(I) Company, agrees to advance all costs actually incurred in the production of Pictures made by Company,. Company, shall submit to Artist for Artist's reasonable approval; in writing, the following information: (I) the musical compositions and other material to be embodied thereon; (ii) the general concept therefore and (iii) the producer, director, and any other key personnel therefor. Following Company's receipt of Artist's approval of said information, within Three (3) days of delivery to Artist, if written approval is not received within the specified time limits Company, shall commence production of the Picture. (iv) All sums paid by Company, in connection with each Picture shall be an advance against and recoupable by Company, out of all royalties becoming payable to Artist pursuant to this or any other agreement between the parties hereto.

(ii)       Each of the following sums, if any, paid by Company, in connection with each Picture shall be an advance against and recoupable by Company, out of all royalties becoming payable to Artist pursuant to this or any other agreement between the parties hereto.

(A)       All expenses incurred by Company, in connection with the preparation and production of the Picture and the conversion of the Picture to Video Masters that are made to serve as prototypes for the duplication of the Video shows of the Picture.

(B)       All of Company's direct out-of-pocket costs (such as for rights, Artists [including Artist], other personnel, facilities, materials, services, and the use of equipment) in connection with all steps in the production of the Picture and the process leading to and including the production of such Video Masters (including, but not limited to, packaging costs and the costs of making and delivering duplicate copies of such Video Master); and

(C)       If in connection therewith Company, furnishes any of its own facilities, materials, services for equipment for which Company, has a standard rate, the amount of such standard rate or if there is not standard rate, the market value for the services or thing furnished.

(iii)       All sums that Company, in its sole discretion deems necessary or advisable to pay in connection with the production of Pictures and the exploitation of Company's, rights therein in order to clear rights or to make any contractual payments that are due or may become due on the part of Company, to Artist, Artist and any other person, firm or corporation by virtue of the exploitation of Company's rights therein, in order to avoid, satisfy or make unnecessary any claims or demands by any person, firm or corporation claiming the right to payment therefor, including, but not limited to, any payment of an actual or alleged copyright owner, patent owner, union-related trust fund, pension plan or other entity, and any payment for an actual or alleged re-run fee, residual, royalty, license fee or otherwise shall constitute advances against and recoupable out of all royalties becoming payable to you pursuant to this or any other agreement between the parties hereof. No payment pursuant to this subparagraph 21 (c) (iii) shall constitute a waiver of any of the Artist's express of implied warranties and representations.

(d)(I) Conditioned upon Artist full and faithful performance of all of the terms and conditions of this Agreement, Company, shall pay Artist royalties equal to twenty-five (25%) percent of Company's Video Net Receipts with respect to Company's exploitation of Pictures subject to this Agreement. Monies earned and received by Company, from any licensee (rather than monies earned and received by the licensee) in respect of exploitation of Pictures shall be included in the computation of Video Net Receipts.

(ii) The royalties provided in subparagraph 21 (d)(I) include any royalty obligations Company, may have to any other person, firm or corporation who supplied services or rights used in connection with Pictures, including, without limitation, producers, directors, extras, and music publishers, and any such royalties shall be deducted from the royalties otherwise payable to Artist.

(iii) With respect to audiovisual material embodying Pictures made hereunder together with other audiovisual material, royalties payable to Artist shall be computed by multiplying the royalties otherwise applicable by a fraction, the numerator of which is the amount of playing time in such audiovisual material of Pictures made hereunder and the denominator of which is the total number of Artists whose performances are embodied on such Pictures.

(e) Company, shall have the right to use and allow others to use each Picture for advertising and promotional purposes with no payment to Artist. As used herein, "advertising and promotional purposes" shall mean all uses for which Company, received no monetary consideration from licensees in excess of reasonable amount as legal fees, administrative costs or similar type payments and as reimbursement for transaction cost incurred by Company, in connection with such uses, such as tape, duplication costs, shipping, handling and insurance costs.

(f)(i) During the Term of this Agreement, no person, firm or corporation other than Company, will be authorized to make, sell, broadcast or otherwise exploit audio-visual materials unless: (A) Artist first notifies Company, of all of the material terms and conditions of the proposed agreement pursuant to which the audio-visual materials are to be made, sold, broadcast or otherwise exploited, including, but not limited to, the titles of the compositions covered by the proposed agreement, the format to be used, the manner of exploitation proposed, and the identities of all proposed parties to the agreement, and that the agreement be made exclusively with the Company,. Royalties to be paid subject to such agreement will be paid according to subparagraph 21 (f) (ii) hereof.

(ii) If Company, does not accept an offer made to it pursuant to this subparagraph 21(f), such non-acceptance shall not be considered a waiver of any of Company's rights pursuant to this Agreement. Such rights include, without limitation, the right to prevent authorizing any use of masters owned by or exclusively licensed to Company, unless Company, so agrees. Artist shall not act in contravention of such rights.

(g) In all other respects (e.g. the times for accountings to be rendered, and warranties and representations made by Artist) Pictures and Video Masters shall be governed by the same terms and conditions as are applicable to masters subject to this Agreement.

22. Intentionally deleted.

23. Company, shall prepare the artwork for the album covers used in connection with the releases hereunder in the United States, during the Term of this Agreement, of each newly-recorded LP required to be recorded and delivered hereunder (hereafter, the "Artwork"), upon prior written notice to Company, and only upon all of the following conditions:

(a) Before preparation and incurring of any expenses in connection with the album Artwork, Artist may discuss completely with a representative of Company's, art department, the proposed artwork to be produced by Company,, all of which shall be subject to the decision of Company's art department. Company, will endeavor to consult with Artist as to the album Artwork.

(b)     Company, will deliver all such Artwork prepared by Company, to Artist for Artist's reasonable approval, prior to the printing of said album cover.  If such approval is withheld the printing can proceed 5 days after Artist has viewed the final product.

24.     All sums paid by Company, in connection with independent promotion, shall be an advance against and recoupable to Company, out of all royalties becoming payable to Artist pursuant to this or any other agreement between the parties.

25.     For the purposes of this Agreement, the following definitions shall apply:

(a)     "Master", "Master Recording" or "Recording" means any recording of sound, whether or not coupled with a visual image, by any method and on any substance or material, whether now or hereafter known, which is intended for use in the recording, production and/or manufacture of Photograph Records.

(b)     "LP" or "CD"- A twelve (12") inch 33 1/3 rpm double-sided long-playing record of not less than 45 minutes of playing time.  A compact disc of not less than 45 minutes of playing time.  Multiple sets which consist of more than (1) LP intended to be released, packaged and sold together for a single overall practice, shall be deemed to be the equivalent of the one (1) LP for the purposes of this Agreement, but shall not be recorded or delivered hereunder without Company's prior written consent.

(c)     "Records", "phonograph records", recordings' and "sound recordings" — All forms of recording and reproduction by which sound may be recorded now know or which may hereafter become known, manufactured or sold primarily for home use, juke box use, or use on or in means of transportation, including, without limiting the foregoing, magnetic recording tape, film, electronic video recordings, disc of any speed size, and any other medium or device for the production of artistic performance manufactured or sold primarily for home use, juke box use or use on or in means of transportation, whether with (I) sound alone or (ii) sound synchronized with visual images.

(d)     "Delivery", "deliver" or "delivered". The actual receipt by Company, of completed, fully mixed, leadered and edited masters comprising each LP, commercially satisfactory to Company, and ready for

Company's manufacture of records, together with all materials, consents, approvals, licenses and permissions.

(e)  "Recording costs" — Wages, fees, advances and payments of any nature to or in respect of all musicians, vocalists, conductors, arrangers, orchestrators, engineers, producers, copyists, etc.: payments to a trustee or fund based on wages to the extent required by any agreement between and any labor organization or trustee, all studio, tape, editing, mixing, remixing, mastering, and engineering costs, all costs of travel, per diems, rehearsal halls, non-studio facilities and equipment, and all other costs and expenses incurred in producing the master recordings hereunder which are then customarily recognized as recording costs in the recording industry.

(h)  "Mid-priced LP" - , an LP which bears a suggested retail list price in the applicable country of the Territory of at least sixty-seven (67%) percent but not more than eighty (80%) percent of the suggested retail list price of the majority of Company's licensees as applicable, then-current newly-released LPS.

(i)  "Budget LP" — an LP which bears a suggested retail list price in the applicable country of the Territory or less than sixty-seven (67%) percent of the suggested retail list price of the majority of Company's or Company's, retail list price of the majority of Company's, or Company's licensee's as applicable then-current newly-released LPs.

(j)  "Picture" — motion Pictures or other audiovisual works that have a soundtrack substantially featuring performances of Artist.

(k)  "Video shows" — Videocassette, Videodiscs or any other devices or any other devices, now or hereafter known or developed, that enable the Picture to be perceived visually, with or without sound, when used in combination with or as part of a piece of electronic, mechanical, or other apparatus.

(l)  "Videodisc" — a disc-type video show that enables the Picture to be perceived visually, with or without sound, through a television-type playback system or device.

(m)  "Videocassette" — a Video show other than Videodisc (e.g., a Video show in the form of prerecorded tape).

(n)      "Video Masters"- master Video shows.

(o)      "Video Receipts" – monies earned and received by Company, from exploitation of Pictures less a twenty (20%) percent gross distribution fee, and less any out-of-pocket expenses copyright, union and other third party payments, taxes and adjustments borne by Company, in connection with such exploitations and collection and receipt by Company, OF such movies.

(p)      "Any other agreement between the parties hereto" any agreements between Company, on the one part, and Artist (or any other entity furnishing Artist's recordings or services) or Artist, on the other part, pertaining to Artist's recording services or recordings.

26.      Company, may assign its rights under this agreement in whole or in part to any subsidiary, affiliated or controlling corporation, to any person owning or acquiring, a substantial, portion of the stock or assets of Company,, or to any partnership or other venture in which Company, may participate.  Company, may also assign its rights to any of its licensees if advisable in Company's sole discretion to implement the license granted. Artist may not assign its rights under this agreement.

27.      This Agreement sets both the entire agreement between the parties with respect to the subject matter hereof.  No modification, amendment, waiver, termination or discharge of this Agreement shall be binding upon Company, unless confirmed by a written instrument signed by an officer of the Company,.  A waiver by Company, of any term or condition of this Agreement in any instance does not affect our rights thereafter to enforce such provision nor does it constitute any default. All of Company's, rights, options and remedies in this Agreement shall be cumulative and none of them shall be in limitation of any remedy, option or right available to Company,.  Should any provision of this Agreement be adjudicated by a court of competent jurisdiction as void, invalid or inoperative, such decision shall not affect any other provision hereof, and the remainder of this Agreement will be effective, as though such void, invalid or inoperative provision has not been contained herein.  It is agreed that all accountings and payments required herein, and all grants made herein, shall survive and continue beyond the expiration or earlier termination of this Agreement. No breach of this Agreement by Company, shall be deemed material unless within thirty (30) days after Artist learns of such breach, Artist serves written notice thereof on Company, specifying the nature thereof and Company, fails to cure such breach, if any, within ninety (90) days (except

sixty (60) days if such alleged breach is the payment of monies hereunder) after receipt of such notice. The remedy for such breach shall be specific performance only unless hampered by conditions listed heretofore in section 6(c).

28.    This Agreement shall be deeded to have been made in the state of Texas and its validity, construction, performance and breach shall be governed by the laws of the State of Texas applicable to agreements made and to be wholly performed therein. Artist agrees to submit itself to the jurisdiction of the Federal or State courts located in Houston in any action which may rise out of this agreement and said courts shall have executive jurisdiction over all disputes between Company, AND Artist pertaining to this Agreement and all matters related thereto. In this regard, any process in any action or proceeding commenced in the courts of the State of Texas arising out of any claim, dispute or disagreement under this Agreement may, among other methods, be served upon Artist by delivering or mailing the same, via registered or certified mail, addressed to Artist at the address provided herein for notices to Artist: any such delivery or mail service shall be deemed to have the same force and affect as personal service within the State of Texas. Nothing contained herein shall constitute a waiver of any other remedies available to Company,. Nothing contained in this Paragraph 28 shall preclude Company, from joining Artist in an action brought by a third party against Company, in any jurisdiction, although Company's, failure to join Artist in any such action in one instance shall not constitute a waiver of any of Company's, rights with respect thereto, or with respect to any subsequent action brought by a third party against Company,.

29.    Artist hereby grants to Company, and its licensees the exclusive right, throughout the world, to use and authorize the use of Artist's name, portraits, pictures, licenses, and biographical material, either alone or in conjunction with other elements, in connection with the sale, lease, licensing or other disposition of merchandising rights. For the rights granted by Artist to Company, in this paragraph, Company, shall pay Artist a royalty of twenty-five (25%) percent of Company's, net royalty receipts derived from the exploitation of such rights, after deducting all costs and third party payments relating thereto, and such royalty shall be accounted to Artist in the manner otherwise provided herein. Relative to any and all activities conducted and contemplated by this paragraph, Company, agrees to regularly and reasonably inform Artist in writing of progress to submit to Artist, within thirty (30) days of execution, copies of all contracts entered into by Company, relative to those activities provided for in this paragraph.

30.     This Agreement shall not become effective until executed by all parties.

31.     <u>Grant of Rights</u>

(a)     Assignment of Copyrights.  Artist hereby sells, transfers, and assigns to Company, its successors and assigns, an undivided fifty (50%) of the publishing interest in the Compositions, including without limitation, the copyrights therein and any and all renewals and/or extensions thereof throughout the world (the "Territory"), and all claims and causes of actions related to the Compositions accruing at any time and all other rights of whatsoever nature in the Composition, including without limitation, the titles, words and music for the Compositions and every arrangement, adaptation and version thereof.  Artist will execute and deliver to Company, such instruments of transfer and other documents regarding the rights of Company, in the Compositions subject to this agreement as Company, may reasonably request to carry out the purposes of this agreement, and Company, may sign such documents in your name or the name of any Controlled Songwriter and make appropriate disposition of them.

31.2    <u>Administration</u>.  Company, and its Licensees will have the sole, exclusive and perpetual right, throughout the Territory to:

(a)     License and cause others to license the exploitation of the Compositions, including, without limitation, the right to license broadcast and other public performances and the right to license the manufacture distribution and sale of Phonograph Records embodying any one or more Compositions.

(b)     Administer and grant rights in the Composition and the copyrights therein.

(c)     Print, publish and sell printed edition of the Compositions.

(d)     Collect all monies payable during the term and Retention Period, with respect to the Compositions, in addition to all monies due prior to the date hereof, and all performance royalties payable to you with respect to the compositions by the American Society of Composers, Authors and Publishers (ASCAP), Broadcast Music, Inc. (BMI), or any other applicable performing rights society (hereinafter collectively the "Societies"), but excluding any songwriter share of public performance income. If a Society in any territory does not license any particular public performance of a Composition it is understood Company, may license that use directly and all income received by Company, in connection with such licenses shall be deemed Gross Income and subject to accounting hereunder.

(e)     Make arrangements, or otherwise adapt or change any one or more Composition in any manner.

(f)     Otherwise administer the Composition and the copyrights therein and to act as the publisher thereof and exercise all such rights as fully as if the copyrights were registered in Company's name alone and Company, alone were the sole and exclusive owner thereof and of the Compositions.

31.3    Power of Attorney.    Artist hereby irrevocably authorizes, empowers and appoints Company, Artist's true and lawful attorney, for the term of the copyrights (including songwriter copyrights) in the respective Compositions and any renewals or extensions thereof, to secure any renewal period for Company's benefit, to initiate and compromise any claim or action with respect to the Compositions including any claim or action against infringers of Company, or Artist's rights in the Compositions and to execute in Artist name, and the name of any Controlled Songwriter, any and all documents and/or instruments necessary or desirable to accomplish the foregoing and/or to evidence Company's, ownership of the copyrights during such period and/or to effectuate Company's, rights hereunder. The power granted herein is coupled with an interest and irrevocable right. Company, will cause the copyrights in the Composition to be registered or re-registered jointly in the name of Company, and Artist and such additional parties as appropriate.

31.4    Name and Likeness.    Company, and any License of Company, each shall have the right and may grant to others the right to reproduce, print, or disseminate any likeness in the exploitation of musical compositions and the marketing of other merchandise of any kind. During the term of this agreement neither you nor any Controlled Songwriter shall authorize any Party other than Company, to use the name or likeness of controlled Songwriter (or any professional, group, or other assumed or fictitious name used by Controlled Songwriters) in connection with the exploitation of musical compositions.

32.    Group Provisions

(a)    Your obligations under this Agreement are joint and several. All references to the "you" include both members of the group inclusively and each member individually, unless otherwise specified. A breach of any term or provision or a disaffirmance or attempted disaffirmance of this Agreement for a reason by any one of the individuals comprising your members shall, at Company's, election, be deemed a breach by all members comprising the group.

(b)    Additional individuals may become members of your group only with Company's prior written consent. Company, shall have the right to designate such new members. You shall cause any individual so approved by Company, to be bound by all terms and provisions of this Agreement, and you shall upon our request, cause such individual to execute and deliver such documents as Company, may deem necessary or expedient to evidence such individual's agreement to be bound.

(c)(i) If any of your members ("leaving member") ceases, refuses, neglects, or fails to perform as a member of the group for any reason whatsoever, you will notify Company, thereof promptly. The leaving member will be replaced by a new member, if Company, so agrees in writing. The new member will be deemed substituted as a party to this Agreement in the place of the leaving member and you will cause the new member to execute and deliver to Company, such instruments as Company, in its judgment, may require to accomplish that substitution. Thereafter, you will have no further obligation to furnish the services of the leaving member for performances under this Agreement, including, without limitation, a subparagraphs (b) (c) and (d) of this paragraph. You will not permit any musician to perform in place of the leaving member in making Master Recordings under this Agreement unless that musician has executed and delivered to Company, the substitution instruments referred to above.

(ii)    Company, will have the right to terminate the Term of this Agreement with respect to the remaining members of the Artist by notice given to you at any time before the expiration of ninety (90) days after Company, 's receipt of your notice provided in (a) above. In the event of such termination, all of the members of the Artist will be deemed leaving members as of the date of such termination notice, and paragraph (c) will apply to all of them; collectively or individually as Company, elects.

(iii)     Company, shall have the option to engage the exclusive services of each leaving member as a recording Artist ("Leaving Member Option").  The leaving Member Option may be exercised by Company, by notice to the leaving member at any time before the receipt of your notice under section (a) above, as the case may be.  If Company, exercises that Option, the leaving member(s) concerned will be deemed to have executed Company's, standard form of term recording agreement for the services of an individual recording Artist or an approved budget basis without recording fund provision and containing the following provisions:

(1)     The term will commence on the date of Company's execution of such Leaving Member Option and may be extended by Paragraph 1 of this Agreement, for the same number of additional Contract Periods as the number of Option Contract Periods, if any, remaining pursuant to Paragraph 1 at the time of Company's exercise of the Leaving Member Option (but at least two (2) such additional periods in any event);

(2)     The Minimum Recording Commitment for each Contract Period such Term will be Master Recording sufficient to comprise two (2) 12" singles or its equivalent, with overall options equivalent to that granted to Company, in Paragraph 3 of this Agreement.

(3)     The royalty percentage rates in respect of records and video-records embodying performances recorded during that term will be the same as provided herein, and

(4)     In your royalty account under this Agreement is an unrecouped position at the date of Company's exercise of the Leaving Member Option, a pro-rata part of the amount of that unrecouped balance, determined by computing the percentage of the original group being retained by Company, will constitute an Advance recoupable from those royalties.

(d)     No leaving member shall have the right thereafter to use any professional name or service mark utilized by any other of your members at any time during the Term of this Agreement, or any service mark similar thereto.  Furthermore such leaving member shall not have the right to promote herself/himself, or allow herself/himself to be promoted as, "formerly of (the Mark)" or by any similar label.

33. **Non Disparagement**

Artist agrees that at no time hereafter will it or any of its officers, employees, agents or representatives make, disclosure or cause to be disclosed any negative, adverse or disparaging statement or information concerning Joshua Doe Records LLC, or its business affairs, or concerning any officer, director, agent, representative or employee of Joshua Doe Records LLC.

34. **Release**

Artist, on their own behalf, and on behalf of their employers, employees, affiliates, attorneys, agents, successors, assigns and parent companies hereby release, discharge and agree to hold harmless Joshua Doe Records, LLC, and each of their respective affiliates, and all of their respective officers, employees, directors, agents, attorneys and assigns from any and all claims whatsoever arising from your professional appearances, participations and performances, whatsoever or for any fees or damages whatsoever, resulting from your professional appearances, participations and performances, which you now have or hereinafter may have, in accordance with the terms of this Agreement.

35. **Limited Liability**

In the event of any dispute with Joshua Doe Records, LLC, in connection with Artist's professional appearances or performances, Artist warrants and represents that Artist will seek remedies against Joshua Doe Records, LLC only, and Artist will not bring or commence any action whatsoever against any officer, director, agent, representative, or member of Joshua Doe Records, LLC, in an individual capacity. If any court or arbitrator of competent jurisdiction shall agree to hear a dispute action brought by Artist against any officer, director, agent, representative or member of Joshua Doe Records, LLC, in an individual capacity, then the aforementioned officer, director, agent, representative or member of Joshua Doe Records, LLC, against whom such an action has been commenced may use this paragraph as a full and complete defense to any such action, and Artist shall be liable for any costs and attorneys' fees incurred by the officer, director, agent, representative or member defending such action.

YOU UNDERSTAND THAT THIS IS AN IMPORTANT LEGAL DOCUMENT PURSUANT TO WHICH YOU GRANT TO Company, CERTAIN EXCLUSIVE SERVICES FOR ALL OF THE WORLD FOR A PERIOD IN EXCESS OF TEN (10) YEARS. YOU HEREBY REPRESENT AND WARRANT THAT YOU HAVE BEEN ADVISED OF YOUR RIGHT TO RETAIN INDEPENDENT LEGAL COUNSEL IN CONNECTION WITH THE NEGOTIATION AND EXECUTION OF THIS AGREEMENT AND THAT YOU HAVE EITHER RETAINED AND HAVE BEEN REPRESENTED BY SUCH LEGAL COUNSEL, OR HAVE KNOWINGLY AND VOLUNTARILY WAIVED YOUR RIGHT TO SUCH LEGAL COUNSEL AND DESIRE TO ENTER INTO THIS AGREEMENT WITHOUT THE BENEFIT OF LEGAL REPRESENTATION.

IN WITNESS WHEREOF, the parties hereto have executed this Agreement on the day and year first above written.

**This Agreement is non-binding until executed by all Parties**

**Joshua Doe Records, LLC**

BY: _____

Joshua Doe, Authorized Agent for
Joshua Doe Records, LLC

**Artist**

_____

John Doe p/k/a "John Doe"

Questions and Discussion

1. The use or threat thereof of an injunction is a key piece in settling contractual difficulties. In professional league sports, the athlete agrees in the standard player's contract to allow injunction relief to enforce the contract. But, you can't enter equity with unclean hands. And, in the music business, most hands are dirty—whether some hands are dirtier than others is probably a moot point. Another defense to a recording contract is that it is unconscionable—that is, it shocks the conscience. Forcing a 17-year-old rapper to a 10-year contract, with an automatic 10-year renewal, and saying take it or leave it, might be sufficiently one-sided and mean-spirited to allow the artist to void the contract under the doctrine of unconscionability.

2. More on Cal. Civ. Code Section 3423, "When injunction may not be granted." An employee can be enjoined by his employer from performing extraordinary service to others during an option period (*Warner Bros. Pictures, Inc., v. Bridle*, 192 P.2d 949 (Cal. 1948)).

Code Section 3423 limits the availability of injunctive relief from the breach of a contract for personal service in writing where the minimum compensation is not less than $6,000 per year; however, when read in conjunction with Cal. Civ. Code Section 3391, subd. 2, it demands a minimum standard of fairness as a condition for equitable enforcement of an exclusivity clause in a personal service contract (*Motown Record Corp. v. Brockert*, 207 Cal. Rptr. 574 (Cal. App. 1984)).

3. *Lamothe v. Atl. Recording Corp.*, 847 F.2d 1403 (9th Cir. 1988), concerns the question of credit by the authors of two songs who sued for omission of their names from an album cover and sheet music of their co-written songs. The court held that the plaintiffs had a legitimate interest in protecting their work from the false designation of being the creation of another. Therefore, the two songwriters were deprived of recognition and profits from the release of their songs. Credit is Money! Discuss.

4. There are many clauses in a recording contract. *Radioactive, J.V.* emphasizes the importance of the choice of law clause that designates which state's law is controlling if a question of interpretation arises. In that case, the forum state's laws were applicable because of the state's relationship to the recording contract, since that agreement specifically designated the law of New York to be the forum state for rules of decision if disputes occured.

5. In the Exclusive Recording Agreement, note in Clause 35, in capital letters, the agreement indicates THAT THIS IS AN IMPORTANT LEGAL DOCUMENT. It also mentions THAT YOU HAVE BEEN ADVISED OF YOUR RIGHT TO RETAIN INDEPENDENT LEGAL COUNSEL. Is that enough? In some cases, should a guardian ad litem be appointed, regardless of the age?

# Chapter 6
# Accountability Under Recording Contracts

Accountability for record contracts or production contracts or distribution contracts begins with the contract itself. Do not buy into a bad deal. Payment is an integral part of the artist-record company agreement. Make sure that the recording company accomplishes what they have promised. Draft each contract with accountability in mind for every promise and every method of payment. Be careful with studio costs and advances. Learn to understand the nuances of the royalty statement.

Hire an accountant who is experience in the entertainment industry. There are formats for calculating domestic and international royalties. There are payment schedules for mechanical royalties and single-song royalties that must be honored; breach of these schedules or any other material promise could taint the entire agreement so that it would be voidable. You have a right to review the royalty process. You have a right to challenge the royalty statement. The agreements incorporate audits; and there should be time limitations on these audits.

In a chapter entitled, "Show Me the Money!: Financial Accounting," Eric Beall in *Making Music Make Money* admonishes that one must be careful when it comes to attempts by the record company (or publisher) to recoup expenses. "[A]ny recoupable expenses will need to be identified specifically on the writer's accounting statement. . . " (Eric Beall, Making Music Make Money 81 (Boston, 2014)).

In your recording contract, there should be sections entitled "Royalty Accountings," "Foreign Sales," "Licenses for Musical Compositions," and "Warranties; Representations; Restrictions; Indemnities." There should also be a definition of "Advance." There are numerous horror stories where the advances devoured the royalties even when the song was a hit! Accounting and auditing is the key to accountability. In boxing, there are separate contracts between the boxer-manager, boxer-promoter, boxer-trainer, boxer-lawyer, and boxer-cutman. After advances are paid out, there literally might be nothing left for the boxer. Eighty percent of all professional athletes are broke after six years.

Another sign of perhaps failed accountability is the frequency of bankruptcy proceedings for members of the music businsess. In re Taylor, 913 F. 2d 102 (3d Cir. 1990) (which follows) dissects the bankruptcy proceedings of James Taylor (the other one), the lead singer of Kool and the Gang. Taylor seeks "the bankruptcy court's approval of his decision to reject certain executory contracts, including a music-publishing agreement dated November 13, 1985, between the debtor, and the appellant, Delightful Music, Ltd." (at 104). The "Bankruptcy Code permits a debtor-in-possession to reject an executor contract for personal services, with the court's approval . . ."(at 108).

In re Taylor
United States Court of Appeals for the Third Circuit
June 25, 1990, Argued; September 4, 1990, Filed
No. 89-5700
913 F.2d 102

## OPINION OF THE COURT

FULLAM, District Judge.

James Taylor, as debtor-in-possession in this Chapter 11 bankruptcy proceeding, sought the bankruptcy court's approval of his decision to reject certain executory contracts, including a music-publishing agreement dated November 13, 1985, between the debtor and the appellant, Delightful Music, Ltd. The latter objected, moved to dismiss the bankruptcy petition, and requested the court to abstain from ruling on the rejection request.

The Bankruptcy Court granted permission to reject the executory contract, and refused to dismiss the bankruptcy petition or abstain. The district court upheld these rulings, In re Taylor, 103 Bankr. 511 (D.N.J. 1989), and Delightful now appeals.

Under 28 U.S.C. § 158(d), this court has jurisdiction to review "final" orders. In the bankruptcy context, finality is accorded a somewhat flexible, pragmatic definition, see, In re Comer, 716 F.2d 168, 171 (3d Cir. 1983). The order approving rejection of appellant's contracts fully and finally resolved a discrete set of issues, leaving no related issues for later determination; we conclude that that order is final and appealable for purposes of § 158(d) and 28 U.S.C. § 1291. See generally, Century Glove v. First Amer. Bank of N.Y., 860 F.2d 94, 97-99 (3d Cir. 1988). The order refusing to dismiss the bankruptcy petition is likewise appealable, In the Matter of Christian, 804 F.2d 46 (3rd Cir. 1986).

This appeal presents an issue which has not previously been addressed in any reported appellate decision, namely, whether executory contracts for the personal services of the debtor may be rejected under § 365 of the Bankruptcy Code. Appellant argues that personal-service contracts are not, and cannot become, part of the estate being dealt with in the bankruptcy court, and therefore cannot be rejected or otherwise affected in a Chapter 11 proceeding. Alternatively, appellant argues that rejection should not have been permitted in this case because it was not sought in good faith and would not benefit the estate. A final argument is that the bankruptcy petition should have been dismissed because the debtor was not insolvent at the time the petition was filed, and lacked a genuine reorganization purpose, and because the petition was not filed in good faith.

## I. Factual Background

James Taylor is a well-known professional musician and entertainer. From 1979 until mid-February 1988, he served as the lead singer and principal songwriter in a group known as "Kool and the Gang" ("The Group").

The services of The Group were furnished pursuant to various contracts arranged through "furnishing companies" - corporate entities in which various members of The Group held ownership interests. Thus, Quintet Associates, Ltd. was a corporation formed by the members of The Group to handle its recording contracts. Fresh Start Music, Inc. handled The Group's musical publishing business. A third corporation, variously known as Road Gang Enterprises, Inc. and/or Road Gang Associates, Ltd., arranged The Group's concerts and tours.

Until 1985, Quintet contracted to provide The Group's exclusive recording services to DeLite Recorded Sound Corp., and the individual members of The Group were required to furnish their recording services to Quintet so that Quintet could fulfill its contractual obligations to DeLite. In 1985, DeLite assigned its rights to Polygram Records, Inc., which entered into a new agreement with Quintet. Mr. Taylor and the other individual members of The Group executed "inducement letters" assenting to these arrangements. Concomitantly, Quintet entered into a music-publishing agreement with the appellant, Delightful Music, Ltd., which was a corporate affiliate of DeLite. This arrangement, too, was sanctioned by "inducement letters" executed by Mr. Taylor and other members of The Group.

In November 1986, similar arrangements were concluded between Fresh Start and Polygram for the services of Group members as songwriters; by this agreement, Polygram was required to pay royalties for songs written by Group members but not recorded by The Group.

In consequence of these contractual arrangements, appellant obtained the exclusive worldwide copyrights in all of the musical compositions of The Group, and of Mr. Taylor as a principal writer for The Group. Appellant was obliged to secure and protect copyrights, make master recordings and other audio-visual reproductions of The Group's compositions, print, publish and sell sheet music of The Group's compositions, market these products and issue licenses, and collect performance fees. And Mr. Taylor was contractually obligated to compose and perform, as a principal member of The Group, musical compositions sufficient to produce at least eight record albums (subject to various options). In the event Mr. Taylor should terminate his membership in The Group, he would remain personally liable to fulfill his remaining obligations as a solo artist — i.e., to compose and perform enough musical compositions to produce the required minimum number of albums — under a "leaving member clause" in the pertinent agreements.

Upon completion of a February 1988 tour of The Group, Mr. Taylor left The Group to pursue a solo career. The bankruptcy petition was filed on May 23, 1988. At that time, only one album had been released.

Beginning at least as early as 1985, The Group and its various related corporate entities experienced financial difficulties, apparently due in large part to life-styles involving unduly lavish expenditures, in excess of the substantial income generated by their performances. They borrowed money, from banks, their agent, and their pension funds, and these advances were secured by assignments of future revenues under the recording agreements, as well as by the personal guarantees of The Group members, including Mr. Taylor.

When the bankruptcy petition was filed, Mr. Taylor was in the following unenviable position: he was owed substantial amounts by Group entities, but with virtually no prospect of payment; he was contractually obliged to write and perform enough musical compositions to provide at least seven additional albums, but any revenues these efforts might generate would be retained by The Group's creditors; and he had personally guaranteed the obligations of The Group and its related entities in amounts greatly in excess of the remaining equity in his home, which was his only significant asset.

## II. Dismissal of the Bankruptcy Petition

If the bankruptcy court and district court erred in refusing to dismiss the bankruptcy proceeding in its entirety, the issue of contract-rejection would be moot. We therefore first address the dismissal question.

In affirming the bankruptcy court's refusal to dismiss the petition, the district court found that the "debtor's current financial condition justifies the filing of a voluntary petition in bankruptcy". Taylor, 103 Bankr. at 521. The court noted that the bankruptcy petition lists liabilities totaling $ 4,518,701.50 ($ 2,530,730 secured, $ 1,987,969.50 unsecured), and assets totaling only $ 734,215. The court further concluded that appellant had not established that the petition was filed in bad faith. We review the factual component of these findings under the clearly erroneous standard, and the legal component de novo.

Appellant contends that, if the personal liabilities of the debtor had not been improperly confused with the debts of the various Group entities, and if the debtor's personal liabilities had been properly evaluated to reflect their contingent nature, the debtor's financial picture would not be nearly bleak enough to warrant filing for bankruptcy; in addition, appellant argues, inter alia, that many of the listed liabilities are not enforceable against the debtor for various reasons: that the debtor was merely an accommodation-maker, whose liability was extinguished by the acts of the other parties; and that the debtor's obligations had been canceled by virtue of novations or settlement agreements. We reject these arguments.

Even if debtor's contingent liabilities (approximately $ 1.2 million in amount) were disregarded, his debts would greatly exceed his assets. Moreover, appellant's argument rests upon an unduly optimistic view as to the remoteness of the contingency. The district court expressly found that the debtor was not a mere accommodation party — he was, after all, personally guaranteeing repayment of loans to Group entities (owned by The Group members) for the direct benefit of the members of The Group, himself included. Whether a novation occurred as to certain of these guaranty transactions depends upon the intent of the parties. This is a factual question, and the findings set forth in the record are not clearly erroneous.

In short, we conclude that the order appealed from, to the extent appellant's motion to dismiss the bankruptcy proceeding was denied, must be affirmed.

### III. Rejection of Executory Contracts for Personal Services

As set forth in § 1107, a debtor-in-possession in a Chapter 11 proceeding has the same powers with respect to executory contracts as a trustee. And 11 U.S.C. § 365 provides as follows:

"(a) Except as provided [in subsection (c) of this section], the trustee, subject to the court's approval, may assume or reject any executory contract or unexpired lease of the debtor.

" . . .

"(c) The trustee may not assume or assign any executory contract or unexpired lease of the debtor . . . if —

"(1)(A) applicable law excuses a party, other than the Debtor, to such contract or lease from accepting performance from or rendering performance to an entity other than the debtor or the debtor in possession . . . and

"(B) such party does not consent to such assumption or assignment."

It is clear that contracts for personal services fall within (c)(1)(A), since "applicable law" excuses the parties from accepting performance from, or rendering performance to, non-signatories.

Thus, § 365(a) permits a trustee to assume or reject any executory contract, but § 365(c) adds the limitation that a trustee may not assume or assign an executory contract for personal services unless the parties consent.

On its face, the statute places no restrictions on a trustee's right to reject a personal services contract. This is not in the least surprising, since, as we read the statute, it implicitly provides that any executory contract which is not assumed — either in the course of the proceedings, or in the reorganization plan approved by the court — is automatically rejected. See 11 U.S.C. § 365(g)(1).

Appellant argues that this straightforward reading of the plain language of § 365 is inappropriate, because it does not take into account other provisions of the Bankruptcy Code, most notably § 541(a)(6) which, in defining "property of the estate," makes clear that the proceeds of the debtor's post-petition personal services are excluded from the estate. Since an executory contract for the debtor's personal services is not part of the estate, the argument continues, such a contract is not within the "jurisdiction" of the trustee, and the trustee simply has no power to deal with such a contract. This line of argument rests upon some fundamental misconceptions.

To the extent that money is due the debtor for pre-petition services under a personal services contract, the debtor's claim for those sums is undoubtedly an asset of the estate which passes to the trustee/debtor-in-possession. And this is so regardless of whether the trustee later affirms or rejects the contract. Stated otherwise, the issue of affirmance or rejection relates only to those aspects of the contract which remained unfulfilled as of the date the petition was filed. It serves no useful purpose to speak generally about whether "the contract" becomes part of "the estate". The real question is the status of the reciprocal rights and obligations of the contracting parties arising after the petition was filed. As to these, the "assume or reject" dichotomy means simply that if the trustee wishes to obtain for the estate the future benefits of the executory portion of the contract, the trustee must also assume the burdens of that contract, as an expense of bankruptcy administration (i.e., having priority over all pre-bankruptcy claims of creditors).

It is simply a non sequitur to suggest that a trustee may not reject an executory contract because it is not property of the estate. It is the trustee's decision (whether to assume or reject) that determines whether the benefits of an executory contract will or will not become property of the estate. And that decision is obviously within the power ("jurisdiction") of the trustee.

Personal services contracts differ from other executory contracts only in that the consent of the parties is required before the trustee has authority to assume them — a qualification which reflects the peculiar nature of such contracts and the widespread distaste for involuntary servitude. On the other hand, H the trustee's authority to reject extends to all executory contracts — including personal-services contracts.

When an executory contract is not assumed (is rejected), 11 U.S.C. § 365(g) provides:

"(g) . . . The rejection of an executory contract . . . constitutes a breach of such contract . . .

"(1) if such contract or lease has not been assumed under this section or under a plan confirmed under Chapter 9, 11 or 13 of this title, immediately before the date of the filing of the petition . . . .

Appellant has a claim against the debtor's estate for whatever damages the rejection/breach has occasioned. This claim, like the claims of other creditors, will have to be dealt with in the reorganization plan.

The parties' research has uncovered only two reported decisions directly pertinent to this appeal. In In re Noonan, 17 Bankr. 793 (Bky. S.D.N.Y. 1982), the court permitted the trustee to reject an executory personal-services contract in a Chapter 11 proceeding which had been voluntarily converted to a Chapter 7. In In re Carrere, 64 Bankr. 156 (Bky. C.D.Cal. 1986), the court ruled that a debtor in possession or trustee has no "standing" to reject a personal services executory contract (since the "trustee has no interest in the contract, he has no standing to act at all under § 365", 64 Bankr. at 159). In Carrere, a TV actress contractually committed to perform in a daytime serial program was offered a more lucrative role on another program, and the court found that the sole purpose in filing for bankruptcy was to enable her to reject her existing contract and accept the new offer, in order to improve her financial position — a purpose not compatible with the true aim of the bankruptcy law. It seems probable that the principal basis for the court's decision was its conclusion that the bankruptcy proceeding itself might well have been dismissed. At any rate, for the reasons already discussed, we reject the notion that a trustee lacks power to deal with personal-service contracts.

The remaining issue is whether this particular executory contract was properly rejected. Since we are dealing with a personal-services contract which could not be assumed without the parties' consent, and which would therefore, sooner or later, be deemed rejected in the absence of such consent, the debtor-in-possession was confronted with an extremely limited choice: he could reject the contract, or he could defer decision pending formulation of a plan of reorganization — in case the parties might change their minds and consent to assumption of the contract in the plan itself. In these circumstances, the traditional "business judgment" test of benefit to the estate, see, Sharon Steel Corp. v. National Fuel Gas Distrib. Corp., 872 F.2d 36, 39-40 (3d Cir. 1989) has only limited application. We have no hesitation in concluding that no useful purpose would have been served by delaying the rejection decision. Indeed, the task of formulating a successful reorganization plan is undoubtedly aided by promptly clarifying the potential availability of some or all of the revenues from the debtor's post-petition creative efforts.

## IV. Conclusion

The district court properly decided that the Bankruptcy Code permits a debtor-in-possession to reject an executory contract for personal services, with court approval; that rejection of appellant's contract was appropriate; and that the bankruptcy proceeding should not be dismissed. We affirm those rulings. To the extent the appeal challenges the refusal to abstain, the appeal is dismissed.

Willie Nelson Music Co. v. Commissioner
United States Tax Court
December 12, 1985, Filed
Docket Nos. 1174-85, 1193-85
1985 U.S. Tax Ct. LEXIS 9

OPINION

These cases are before the Court on petitioners' motions to seal filed in each case on May 16, 1985. They were called for hearing at Washington, D.C. on June 5, 1985, at which time counsel for the parties appeared and presented argument. At the conclusion of the hearing, the Court took the motions under advisement.

Respondent, in his notice of deficiency issued on October 15, 1984 to Willie Nelson Music Company, petitioner in docket number 1174-85, determined the following deficiencies and additions to tax:

Additions to tax, I.R.C. 1954

Personal Income Holding

| Year | Tax | Company Tax | Total | Sec. 6651(a) | Sec. 6653(b) | Sec. 6654 |
|------|------|------|------|------|------|------|
| 1972 | $ 1,288 | $ 3,198 | $ 4,486 | $ 1,122 | 0 | $ 130 |
| 1973 | 5,333 | 13,234 | 18,567 | 4,642 | 0 | 537 |
| 1974 | 7,610 | 15,250 | 22,860 | 5,715 | 0 | 661 |
| 1975 | 6,387 | 17,443 | 23,830 | 0 | $ 11,915 | 0 |
| 1976 | 16,589 | 32,268 | 48,857 | 0 | 24,429 | 0 |
| 1977 | 20,145 | 34,964 | 55,109 | 0 | 27,555 | 0 |
| 1978 | 58,396 | 63,972 | 122,368 | 0 | 61,184 | 0 |
|  |  |  |  |  |  |  |
|  | $ 115,748 | 180,329 | 296,077 | 11,479 | 125,083 | 1,328 |

Willie Nelson Music Co., a Tennessee corporation, had its principal office in Danbury, Connecticut, on the date its petition was filed.

Respondent, in his notice of deficiency issued on October 15, 1984, to petitioners Willie H. Nelson and Connie Nelson, petitioners in docket number 1193-85, determined the following deficiencies and additions to tax:

Additions to tax, I.R.C. 1954

| Years | Income tax | Sec. 6653(b) | Sec. 6653(a) |
|-------|-----------|--------------|--------------|
| 1975 | $ 259,775 | $ 141,995 | 0 |
| 1976 | 405,180 | 283,312 | 0 |
| 1977 | 384,389 | 305,290 | 0 |
| 1978 | 465,408 | 0 | $ 23,270.40 |
| | | | |
| | 1,514,752 | 730,597 | 23,270.40 |

Petitioners in docket number 1193-85 were residents of Austin, Texas, at the time they filed their petition.

On January 15, 1985, petitions in both dockets were filed. On March 15, 1985, respondent filed a motion to extend the time within which to answer. Respondent's motion was granted on March 20, 1985 extending his answer due dates to May 20, 1985. On May 16, 1985, petitioners filed identical motions to seal pursuant to Rule 103(a). On May 24, 1985, respondent filed his memorandum of law in opposition to motions to seal. Petitioners filed a reply to respondent's memorandum of law on June 3, 1985.

In their motions to seal, petitioners seek a protective order sealing the entire record of both cases (including but not limited to all pleadings, depositions, exhibits, papers, and filings) to be opened only by order of the Court and directing that the parties and their counsel in these cases be prohibited from disclosing to the media or public the contents of the sealed records. At the hearing, petitioners' counsel modified his motions in requesting that the records be sealed only up to the time of trial.

In support of their motions, petitioners argue that Willie H. and Connie Nelson as nationally known personalities are subject to "intense and continual" scrutiny by the media. The Willie Nelson Music Co. (hereinafter referred to as the company) is wholly owned and controlled by Willie H. and Connie Nelson, and, as a result, the company is also subject to "intense and continual" scrutiny by the media. Petitioners contend that the media coverage has attached undue credibility to respondent's allegations and has resulted in wide publicity and sensationalization. Thus, petitioners assert that they have been seriously and irreparably damaged by the public's impressions. Petitioners maintain that the damage is caused in part by newspaper headlines which indicate that petitioners are subject to criminal prosecution, thus causing petitioners undue embarrassment and considerable emotional distress. Additionally, petitioners urge that, as a result of the publicity, they have been financially injured in that now they are unable to negotiate large up front payments in long-term endorsement contracts.

Respondent opposes petitioners' motions and argues that common law, statutory law, and the Constitution require that the motions be denied.

Our research has failed to disclose any reported Tax Court case where the fraud additions to tax have been determined and the record was sealed, nor has any such case been advanced by the parties. Since Rule 103(a) is derived from Rule 26(c), Federal Rules of Civil Procedure, we have looked to decisions interpreting Rule 26(c), Fed. R. Civ. P., for guidance in our decision herein.

Rule 103(a) provides, in relevant part:

RULE 103. PROTECTIVE ORDERS

(a) Authorized Orders: Upon motion by a party or any other affected person, and for good cause shown, the Court may make any order which justice requires to protect a party or other person from annoyance, embarrassment, oppression, or undue burden or expense, including but not limited to one or more of the following:

\* \* \* \*

(6) That a deposition or other written materials, after being sealed, be opened only by order of the Court.

(7) That a trade secret or other information not be disclosed or be disclosed only in a designated way.

(8) That the parties simultaneously file specified documents or information enclosed in sealed envelopes to be opened as directed by the Court.

[Emphasis added.]

As a general rule, common law, statutory law, and the U.S. Constitution support the proposition that official records of all courts, including this Court, shall be open and available to the public for inspection and copying. Nixon v. Warner Communications, Inc., 435 U.S. 589, 597 (1978) (where a transcript of some 22 hours of tape recordings was furnished to reporters, but, release of Watergate tapes used as evidence in criminal trial to copy, broadcast, and sell denied); In re Coord. Pretrial Proc. in Pet. Prod. Antitrust, 101 F.R.D. 34, 38 (C.D.Cal. 1984) ("umbrella" protective order partially lifted and only that material which contained trade secrets or was actually commercially sensitive was to remain subject to protection); In re , 45 C.C.P.A. 701, 248 F.2d 956, 959 (1957), and cases cited therein (where the court directed its clerk to provide copies of decision of Patent Office Board of Appeals as set forth in the transcript of record filed in patent appeal); section 7461. However, the right to inspect and copy judicial records is not absolute. Nixon v. Warner Communications, Inc., supra at 598-599; Brown & Williamson Tobacco Corp. v. F.T.C., 710 F.2d 1165, 1179 (6th Cir. 1983).

It is beyond question, and petitioners agree, that this Court has broad discretionary power to control and seal, if necessary, records and files in its possession, and the standard for review thereof is for abuse of discretion. Belo Broadcasting Corp. v. Clark, 654 F.2d 423, 430-434 (5th Cir. 1981); Nixon v. Warner Communications, Inc., supra at 598; Crystal Grower's Corp. v. Dobbins, 616 F.2d 458, 461 (10th Cir. 1980) (documents claimed to be privileged under the attorney-client privilege and work product immunity doctrine remain under seal); secs. 7458 and 7461; Rule 103(a). In the instant cases, to determine whether the sealing of these records in any manner is appropriate, in exercising our discretion, we must weigh the interests of the public, which are presumptively paramount against those advanced by the parties. Nixon v. Warner Communications, Inc., supra at 602; Crystal Grower's Corp. v. Dobbins, supra at 461; Coe v. U.S. Dist. Court for Dist. of Colorado, 676 F.2d 411, 414 (10th Cir. 1982); [13] In re Agent Orange Product Liability Litigation, 98 F.R.D. 539, 545 (E.D.N.Y. 1983) (only materials filed in connection with specific summary judgment motions unsealed).

In these cases, members of the public have an interest in free access to the facts and in understanding disputes that are presented to this forum for resolution. They also have an interest in assuring that courts are fairly run and judges are honest. Coe v. U.S. Dist. Court for Dist. of Colorado, supra at 414; Crystal Grower's Corp. v. Dobbins, supra at 461. Nevertheless, the presumptive right to access may be rebutted by a showing that there are countervailing interests sufficient to outweigh the public interest in access.

For example, where a motion to seal encompasses documents governed by the attorney work-product privilege or the contents of communications subject to the attorney-client privilege, the public interest in protecting those privileges would take precedence over the interest to inspect and copy court records. In re Agent Orange Product Liability Litigation, supra at 545, and cases cited therein; Crystal Grower's Corp. v. Dobbins, supra at 462. If disclosure of documents would amount to use of the court process for gratification of private spite or public scandal, then the public's interest in its right of access diminishes. Nixon v. Warner Communications, Inc., supra at 598, and cases cited therein. Additionally, the constitutional right to privacy in avoiding disclosure of personal matters may outweigh the public's right of access. Tavoulareas v. Washington Post Co., 724 F.2d 1010, 1017-1021 (D.C. Cir. 1984), and cases there cited (where it was held that a corporation had a constitutionally protected privacy interest in avoiding public disclosure of sensitive commercial information not used at trial of a libel action); Plante v. Gonzalez, 575 F.2d 1119, 1132-1137 (5th Cir. 1978), cert. denied 439 U.S. 1129 (1979); cf. Coe v. U.S. Dist. Court for Dist. of Colorado, supra.

Public interests are weighed against those advanced by the party seeking the protective order, and, in its discretion, a court may seal the record or portions thereof where justice so requires and the party seeking such relief demonstrates good cause. American Telephone & Telegraph Co. v. Grady, 594 F.2d 594, 596 (7th Cir. 1979); Rule 103(a). However, a party may not rely on mere conclusory statements or his attorney's unsupported self-serving hearsay statements to establish good cause. In re Coord. Pretrial Proc. in Pet. Prod. Antitrust, supra at 44; Sacks v. Frank H. Lee Co., 18 F.R.D. 500, 501 (S.D.N.Y. 1955). In Sacks, the court stated that the affidavit of plaintiff's attorney was "an utterly insufficient showing that the testimony sought will betray any secrets."

A party must come forth with appropriate testimony and factual data to support claims of harm that would occur as a consequence of disclosure. Wyatt v. Kaplan, 686 F.2d 276, 283 (5th Cir. 1982); United States v. United Fruit Co. 410 F.2d 553 n. 11 (5th Cir. 1969) (protective order prohibiting disclosure of divestiture plans upheld where affidavit was supported with numerous examples of harm that would occur upon disclosure). In Apco Oil Corp. v. Certified Transportation, Inc., 46 F.R.D. 428, 432 (W.D. Mo. 1969), the court said, "It is not necessary to add that the burden of proof will rest upon plaintiff at such a hearing and that the determination of whether good cause does or does not exist must be based upon appropriate testimony and other factual data, not the unsupported contentions and conclusions of counsel." (Emphasis supplied.)

Historically, good cause has been demonstrated and records sealed where patents, trade secrets, or confidential information are involved. However, a showing that the information would harm a party's reputation is generally not sufficient to overcome the strong common law presumption in favor of access to court records. "Indeed, common sense tells us that the greater the motivation a corporation has to shield its operations the greater the public's need to know." Brown & Williamson Tobacco Corp. v. F.T.C., supra at 1179-1180.

In Application of Sarkar, 575 F.2d 870 (C.C.P.A. 1978), a patent application proceeding, the court granted Sarkar's motion to seal the record. The court found that the seal was justified by Sarkar's showing that the application contained material constituting a trade secret. Thus, to encourage patent applicants to pursue their rights to patents and provide the public with early disclosure of inventions, the court determined that legitimate trade secrets must be protected. Application of Sarkar, supra at 872.

Courts also acknowledge that confidential business information (e.g., pricing information, customer lists, sales volume) requires protection. The rationale in granting protective orders where documents contain this type of information is that if these facts were disclosed, the moving party would suffer great competitive disadvantage and irreparable harm. Essex Wire Corp. v. Eastern Electric Sales Co., 48 F.R.D. 308, 310 (E.D. Pa. 1969) (subject matter of protective arrangement between one defendant and foreign supplier, the release of which would cause great competitive disadvantage, protected); Doe v. A Corp., 709 F.2d 1043 (5th Cir. 1983) (house counsel, after resignation, barred by his ethical obligations as a lawyer from prosecuting litigation as class representative of other employees; case records sealed); Chesa Intern., Ltd. v. Fashion Associates, Inc., 425 F. Supp. 234 (S.D.N.Y. 1977) (protective order issued to protect defendant's competitive position); Covey Oil Co. v. Continental Oil Co., 340 F.2d 993 (10th Cir. 1965) (non-party witnesses required to comply with subpoena duces tecum requesting trade secrets relating to price, cost, and volume of sales of gasoline; however, use thereof for business or competitive purposes proscribed); Ames Co. v. Bostitch, Inc., 235 F. Supp. 856 (S.D.N.Y. 1964) (limited protective order issued). In all these cases access to the protected documents was granted, but the extent to which the parties could use them was limited by the courts. Hence, from these cases it is clear that the paramount concern is to accord the parties access to all relevant and necessary information so that they can adequately prepare their cases without permitting improper or unfair use of the materials produced. See, e.g., Boeing Airplane Co. v. Coggeshall, 280 F.2d 654 (D.C. Cir. 1960), which involved three appeals from orders by the District Court on motions relating to a petition to enforce a subpoena duces tecum issued by the Tax Court. Boeing wanted the documents for its own use and the Tax Court's use in a proceeding before the Tax Court under section 108 of the Renegotiation Act of 1951. There the court found that enforcement of the subpoena was warranted, but said the District Court could properly examine in camera individual papers for stated purposes, e.g., privilege, trade secrets.

Courts have not only accorded business entities' "confidential" information protection but have also issued protective orders to protect an individual's confidentiality and right to privacy. Sendi v. Prudential-Bache Securities, 100 F.R.D. 21 (D.D.C. 1983); In re Smith, 656 F.2d 1101 (5th Cir. 1981); In re Caswell, 18 R.I. 835, 29 A. 259 (1893) (where the court in holding that no one has a right to examine or obtain copies of public records from mere curiosity, or for the purpose of creating public scandal, refused to turn over judicial records respecting a divorce). However, these cases bear no resemblance to the instant cases.

In Sendi v. Prudential-Bache Securities, supra, the court issued a protective order in which the moving parties' tax returns were filed under seal, and any contents thereof, reflected in the pleadings or memoranda, were also sealed. The court recognized the special privacy and confidentiality interests accorded tax returns and balanced these interests against the need for discovery. See section 6103, respecting confidentiality of returns and return information. Here, petitioners have no special privacy or confidentiality interest that is protected by statute. In fact, as public figures they may have given up many privacy rights.

The court in In re Smith, supra, ordered petitioner Smith's name to be permanently obliterated from records or pleas of guilty and sealed all pleadings, records, documents, and orders to protect Smith's reputation. The Smith case arose out of an investigation, by the U.S. attorney's office in Dallas, Texas, of bribery allegations concerning the Army and Air Force Exchange Service (AAFES). Mr. Smith was the head of AAFES. The investigation resulted in more than 25 convictions (none of which involved Smith) involving AAFES employees, Government contractors, and military sales representatives. Two of the Government contractors waived indictment and entered guilty pleas in United States of America v. Churchill Sales Co., Criminal No. CR 3-80-165 (N.D. Tex., Aug. 1, 1980); and United States of America v. Martin Taylor Co., Criminal No. 3-80-198 (N.D. Tex., Sept. 4, 1980). At the Churchill Sales and Martin Taylor plea hearings, despite the fact no evidence or testimony existed to support her statement, the assistant U.S. attorney read in open court, and filed in the above criminal cases, factual resumes which named Smith as a recipient of payments. After each of the plea hearings in the District Court, the media covering the AAFES bribery scandal reported that Mr. Smith had been paid bribe moneys by various businesses dealing with AAFES.

Following several months of adverse publicity, Smith filed motions in both the above-mentioned criminal cases asking the District Courts to either strike any mention of his name from the resumes and records or to seal the record. These motions were denied. Shortly after these rulings, Mr. Smith notified the personnel division of his intention to retire. Upon retirement, Smith was to receive his normal retirement pay commensurate with his employment grade plus an additional retirement annuity because of his participation in the executive management program (EMP). Approval for his retirement was soon acknowledged. Smith's attorney then filed a petition in the Circuit Court of Appeals for the Fifth Circuit seeking a writ of mandamus to compel the District Court to grant the relief requested in the motions. On the same day the writ of mandamus was filed, the Commander of AAFES issued notice to Smith that he was being suspended from the EMP. The only reasons given for the suspension were that Smith had been accused of wrongdoing in the two factual resumes previously discussed. After several months of AAFES administrative actions, amended and additional motions, and several orders entered by the administrative panel of the Circuit Court, the status of Smith remained essentially as it was on the day he retired, he had been retired with his regular retirement but his EMP benefits were being held in abeyance pending further AAFES proceedings. Thus, Smith showed that he suffered actual financial injury. The Court of Appeals granted the petition for writ of mandamus and noted at page 1107 —

The presumption of innocence, to which every criminal defendant is entitled, was forgotten by the Assistant United States Attorney in drafting and reading aloud in open court the factual resumes which implicated [Smith] in criminal conduct without affording him a forum for vindication.

Accordingly, we find the inclusion of Mr. Smith's name in the factual resumes were [sic] a violation of his liberty and property rights guaranteed by the Constitution and hold that [Smith's] motions to strike and seal should have been granted in the proceedings below.

In re Smith, supra, is distinguishable from the instant cases in that it arose out of a criminal case in which Smith was not a party and therefore was not able to testify on his behalf or given an opportunity to rebut the charges. In fact, Smith was not indicted on any bribery charge and the accusations made by the assistant U.S. attorney were totally unwarranted and without support. What is of significance here is that Smith demonstrated he suffered actual financial injury subsequent to the denial of his motions and that he had been subject to adverse publicity. Petitioners have totally failed to make such a showing.

Furthermore, petitioners have not demonstrated any harm (financial or otherwise) that they have suffered or will suffer if their motions are denied; their contentions are wholly unsupported by the record. Petitioners are correct when they argue that Rule 103(a) permits this Court, in its discretion, to seal its records including pleadings to protect a party from embarrassment or harassment. Nevertheless, merely asserting annoyance and embarrassment is wholly insufficient to demonstrate good cause.

We have carefully studied the thirty-seven newspaper articles submitted on petitioners' behalf at the hearing. All of them were published in Texas newspapers in February 1985: twelve of the articles were published on February 6, twenty-two on February 7, two on February 8 and one on February 9. None of them, in our opinion, even remotely suggest that petitioners are subject to criminal prosecution, albeit thirty-one of the articles report that Willie Nelson has been accused of civil tax fraud. Twenty-six articles report that petitioners' counsel, who is one of petitioners' counsel in these cases, was contacted and his replies were to the effect that it is believed the IRS position is grossly exaggerated, petitioner is certainly not guilty of any fraud, we expect to prevail in the litigation, or since the matter is in the courts we will let it be resolved there. On the whole, we think the articles gave a factual report on petitioners' tax situation and, in fact, emphasized petitioners' claims that all of the deficiencies and additions to tax are in controversy and that no part of any underpayment is due to fraud.

Petitioners further claim that the publications they submitted have caused the public to question Willie Nelson's availability for performances in light of "potential criminal prosecution." Petitioners did not show one instance where this happened. In fact, since the filing of the petitions, Willie Nelson has performed at the Merriweather Post Pavillion in Maryland; appeared in Plains, Georgia, to help former President and Mrs. Carter celebrate Plains' 100th

Birthday; performed at his annual July 4 picnic in Austin, Texas; and performed 5 nights at New York City's Radio City Music Hall. On May 6, 1985, Willie Nelson won the Academy of Country Music's single record of the year award for "To All The Girls I Loved Before," which he sang with Julio Iglesias. If anything, in our view, Willie Nelson's popularity and desirability as a performer has remained intact, if not, increased.

We think a few final observations are in order. Attached to each petition is a full copy of the statutory notice of deficiency, which lists all of respondent's determinations. The petitions on file contest all of those determinations and in the appropriate portions thereof "facts" are alleged. Respondent, in his yet to be filed answers, must set forth facts to sustain his determinations under section 6653(b), the burden of proof for which is placed upon him. Sec. 7454(a) and Rules 36(b) and 142(b). Thereafter, petitioners may file replies controverting respondent's answers wherein they shall set forth "a clear and concise statement of every ground, together with the facts in support thereof, on which the petitioner relies affirmatively or in avoidance of any matter in the answer on which the Commissioner has the burden of proof." See Rule 37(b). Moreover, trials before this Court "shall be conducted in accordance with such rules of practice and procedure * * * as the Tax Court may prescribe and in accordance with the rules of evidence applicable in trials without a jury in the U.S. District Court of the District of Columbia." See sec. 7453 and Rule 143(a).

On these records, after exhaustive analysis and research, we find and hold that petitioners have demonstrated no probative evidence of good cause sufficient to outweigh the public interests. The possibility that petitioners' status as nationally known entertainers may cause these cases to gain some notoriety is not a compelling enough reason to seal these records up to the time of trial. See U.S. v. Hooker Chemicals & Plastics Corp., 90 F.R.D. 421, 426 (W.D.N.Y. 1981). Since good cause has not been demonstrated, petitioners' motions will be denied.

To reflect the foregoing,

Appropriate orders will be issued.

The I.R.S. refused to seal Willie Nelson's tax proceedings. The court can seal records up to the time of the trial to prevent annoyance, embarrassment, and opposition. But, here, the Court avers that the requisite good cause was not shown, and therefore, their motions to seal are denied.

In re Carrere
United States Bankruptcy Court for the Central District of California
July 16, 1986, Filed
No. LA 86-03670-GM
64 B.R. 156

## MEMORANDUM OF OPINION RE MOTION TO REJECT EXECUTORY CONTRACT
### GERALDINE MUND, United States Bankruptcy Judge
### STATEMENT OF FACTS

In August, 1985, Tia Carrere ("Carrere") entered into a personal services contract with American Broadcasting Company ("ABC") whereby she agreed to perform in the television series "General Hospital" from that time until August, 1988 ("ABC Contract"). Under the terms of the contract, Carrere was guaranteed employment on the average of 1 1/2 performances per week. She was to be paid between $600 and $700 for each 60-minute program in which she performed.

While the contract with ABC was still in effect, Carrere agreed to make an appearance on the show "A Team." Under the terms of her agreement with Steven J. Cannell Productions ("A Team Contract"), if she became a regular on A Team, she would make considerably more money over the life of the contract than if she remained on General Hospital.

Although a state court suit was filed by ABC against Carrere for breach of contract due to her agreement with A Team, it appears that no actual breach of the ABC contract will take place until the option in the A Team Contract has been exercised.

On March 4, 1986, Carrere filed her voluntary petition under Chapter 11. The next day she filed a Notice of Rejection of Executory Contract, seeking to reject the ABC Contract. A motion to reject the ABC Contract was filed by the debtor and the matter was set for hearing.

In her declaration in support of the motion to reject, Carrere makes it clear that her primary motivation in seeking the protection of this Court was to reject the contract with ABC so as to enter into the more lucrative contract with A Team. In fact, she claims she did not enter into the contract with A Team until she had obtained advice that the bankruptcy would allow her to reject the contract with ABC. In her schedules she claims unsecured debt only. Her stated liabilities are $76,575 and her assets are $13,191. The amount of debts is disputed by ABC.

ABC vigorously opposed the rejection of its contract and has sought extensive discovery concerning Carrere's liabilities and motivations in filing this bankruptcy. ABC also brought a motion to dismiss the Chapter 11 proceeding on the grounds that it was filed in bad faith.

## ANALYSIS

The key issue to be determined by this Court is whether a debtor, who is a performer under a personal services contract, is entitled to reject the contract by virtue of the provisions of 11 U.S.C. § 365. If so, what criteria must be applied?

A Personal Services Contract is not Property of the Estate in Chapters 7 or 11

The concept of § 365 is that the trustee, in administering the estate, may assume (and even assign) contracts which are advantageous to the estate and may reject contracts which are not lucrative or beneficial to the estate. 2 Collier on Bankruptcy (15th Ed.) para. 365.01. It is not the trustee's duty to benefit the debtor's future finances, but he is to maintain the property of the estate for the benefit of the creditors.

The threshhold issue to be determined is whether the ABC contract is "property of the estate." If it is not, the trustee has no standing to assume or reject it.

When the Bankruptcy Code became operable in 1979, it radically expanded the concept of property of the estate. Under the Bankruptcy Act of 1898, § 70 identified specific items which would become property of the estate. The Bankruptcy Code begins with the concept that everything is property of the estate unless it is specifically excluded or unless the debtor thereafter exempts it.

11 U.S.C. § 541(a)(6) states that property of the estate does not include "earnings from services performed by an individual debtor after the commencement of the case." This is limited to cases under Chapter 7 or 11, as post-petition earnings of the debtor become property of the estate in Chapter 13 cases (11 U.S.C. § 1306). The post-petition earnings from personal services contracts are thus excluded from the Chapter 7 or Chapter 11 estate. Does this exclude the contract itself?

Although no specific legislative history is set forth describing the language of 11 U.S.C. § 541(a)(6), it appears clear that by removing from the estate post-petition earnings from personal services contracts, Congress was intending to retain the concept of § 70(a)(5). The language of § 541(a)(6), which excludes post-petition proceeds from property of the estate, is an enactment of case law which specified that where an executory contract between the debtor and another is based upon the personal service or skill of the debtor, the Trustee does not take title to the debtor's rights in the contract. Ford, Bacon & Davis, Inc. v. M. A. Holahan, 311 F.2d 901 (5th Cir. 1962). (See discussion in 4A Collier on Bankruptcy, (14th Ed.) § 70(a)(5), paragraph 70.22).

Under the Code, it has been held that a contract for personal services is excluded from the estate pursuant to both § 541(a)(6) and § 365(c). In re Bofill, 25 Bankr. 550 (Bankr. S.D.N.Y. 1982). The foremost recent opinion on this matter is In re Noonan, 17 Bankr. 793 (Bankr. S.D.N.Y. 1982), which is cited by both sides in support of their respective positions. While Noonan is usually cited for the proposition that a debtor may not be forced to assume a personal services contract, it also deals with the personal services contract as property of the estate.

In Noonan the debtor was also a performer. He had entered into a personal services contract with a recording company, which wished to exercise its option and require him to record new albums. Noonan, a debtor-in-possession, sought to reject the contract. When the recording company vigorously opposed Noonan's motion, Noonan converted to Chapter 7, knowing that the trustee could not assume the contract, nor could he force the debtor to perform. Therefore the contract would be automatically rejected.

The recording company moved to reconvert to Chapter 11 and to be allowed to confirm a creditor's plan requiring Noonan to assume the contract and perform under it. The Court denied the motion. Among the grounds for denial was the holding that a personal services contract is not property of the estate. Noonan at 797-8.

The Noonan case did not deal with the issue of rejection of a personal services contract, for the debtor's motion to reject was never heard. But the case clearly held that a personal services contract is not property of the estate. The Court finds this line of reasoning to be persuasive.

Since the trustee has no interest in the contract, he has no standing to act at all under § 365. Therefore, he cannot assume or reject the contract.

The Rights of a Debtor-in-Possession are No Greater Than Those of a Trustee

An argument might be made that the debtor-in-possession, by virtue of the fact that she is also the individual who can perform the contract, has greater rights than the trustee and therefore can assume or reject the contract. The Court does not agree with this.

Upon the filing of a Chapter 11, Ms. Carrere created a new entity called a debtor-in-possession. That debtor-in-possession is not identical to the debtor herself. She is granted the rights and duties of a trustee (11 U.S.C. § 323). Therefore while the debtor (Tia Carrere) may have duties under the ABC contract and may wish to reject those duties, the debtor-in-possession (who represents the estate of Tia Carrere) has no rights or duties whatsoever in the contract and therefore is a stranger to it.

In her role as debtor-in-possession, she has no interest in the proceeds of the personal services contract, nor in the contract itself. The contract never comes under the jurisdiction of the Bankruptcy Court. The Court has no interest, the estate has no interest, and even if the debtor-in-possession were allowed by consent of all parties to assume the contract under 11 U.S.C. § 365, the assumption would not create an asset of the estate, for the proceeds would not be an asset of the estate, nor would the contract be assignable. Therefore, no rights of assumption are vested in the debtor-in-possession.

The only one who has rights or duties under the contract is the debtor herself. But the statutory scheme of Section 365(d)(1) does not allow the debtor to reject an executory contract. It only allows the trustee to do so.

Therefore this Court finds that § 365 concerning assumption or rejection of a contract does not apply to a personal services contract in a bankruptcy case under Chapter 7 or 11, whether or not a trustee has been appointed.

It Would be Inequitable to Allow the Contract to be Rejected

Beyond the legal arguments described above, the Court is concerned about the good faith issue of allowing a debtor to file for the primary purpose of rejecting a personal services contract. A personal services contract is unique and money damages will often not make the employer whole. In weighing the rights of the employer to require performance against the rights of the performer to refuse to perform, California courts have allowed the employer to seek an injunction against the performer so that she could not breach the negative promises not to compete. Warner Bros. Pictures v. Brodel, 31 Cal.2d 766, 192 P.2d 949 (1948). It is this very remedy that Carrere seeks to avoid.

The Bankruptcy Court is a court of equity, as well as a court of law. It would be inequitable to allow a greedy debtor to seek the equitable protection of this Court when her major motivation is to cut off the equitable remedies of her employer.

For that reason this Court finds that there is not "cause" to reject this contract, if the major motivation of the debtor in filing the case was to be able to perform under the more lucrative A Team contract. It is clear that for Carrere this is the major motivation, even if it is not the sole motivation. Therefore, rejection is denied for lack of cause.

Rejection Would Not Relieve the Debtor of a Possible Negative Injunction

There is yet another issue that arises and impacts on the ultimate outcome of such cases: if rejection were permitted, what would be its effect on the creditor's right to seek a negative injunction against the debtor?

Rejection of an executory contract constitutes a breach, which is deemed to have occurred immediately before the date of the filing of the petition (11 U.S.C. § 365(g)(1)). The claim for monetary damages thus becomes a claim in the estate (11 U.S.C. § 502(g)).

But a rejection under the Bankruptcy Code only affects the monetary rights of the creditor. It does not disturb equitable, non-monetary rights that the creditor may have against the debtor because of the breach of contract.

This issue was raised in In re Mercury Homes Development Co., 4 Bankr. Ct. Dec. (CRR) 837 (Bankr. N.D.Ca. 1978). The debtor/vendor of a condominium rejected the land sale contract. The buyer requested specific performance; the trustee argued that the only remedy left to the buyer was his unsecured claim for monetary damages. The court rejected the trustee's argument and held that the buyer was entitled to enforce the equitable remedies given to it by state law.

While the Mercury Homes case does not differentiate between the equitable rights that the aggrieved party has against the debtor and those that he has against the trustee, the Court finds no reason in this situation to make any such distinction. California law has given ABC an equitable remedy: to seek a negative injunction against Carrere and thereby prevent her from performing elsewhere. Rejection of the ABC contract would not interfere with ABC's rights to seek that equitable remedy. Rejection would merely categorize any claim for monetary damages as a pre-petition debt. Therefore, whether this Court were to allow rejection or not, Carrere cannot use the Bankruptcy Code to protect her from whatever non-monetary remedies are enforceable under state law.

On both the legal and equitable grounds set forth above, Carrere's Motion to Reject this contract is denied.

---

In *MCA Records, Inc. v. Newton-John*, 90 Cal. App. 3d 18 (1970), famous Australian singer Olivia Newton-John appeals from a temporary injunction which bars her from recording with anyone but plaintiff "or until April 1, 1982 . . ." The court modified by deleting "or until April 1, 1982" if that date should occur during the pendency of this action. The court held that this phrase was misleading and inappropriate for a preliminary injunction. In *Foxx v. Williams*, 244 Cal. App. 2d 223 (1966), famous blue comedian and star of Sanford and Son, Redd Fox, sued record company for a declaration of rights and an accounting. The record company counter-sued to recover monies paid by mistake. It also sought an injunction to prohibit breaches of contract. The injunction failed, but the court affirmed the trial court's determination that the payments to Redd Foxx should be refunded.

Foxx v. Williams
Court of Appeal of California, Second Appellate District, Division Four
August 15, 1966
Civ. No. 28545
244 Cal. App. 2d 223

Plaintiff Redd Foxx, an entertainer in nightclubs and on phonograph records, brought this action against Walter D. Williams, Jr., Dootone Record Manufacturing, Inc., and others, for a declaration of rights, accounting, and other relief under a written contract called "Artist Recording Royalty Agreement." Dootone cross-complained against Foxx to recover moneys paid by mistake, for damages, and for an injunction to prohibit breaches of the contract. After a court trial, judgment was entered declaring the rights of the parties, awarding a money judgment in favor of cross-complainant for overpayments, and enjoining Foxx. We have here Foxx' appeal from the judgment.

In the latter part of 1955, while Foxx was performing at the Club Oasis in Los Angeles, defendant Williams suggested that he be allowed to record Foxx' comedy routine there and find out if phonograph records made therefrom would be salable. Foxx had been a performer for many years but had never made a successful phonograph record. His one previous attempt had sold about 40 copies. Williams was established in the record manufacturing and distributing business, being the president and sole stockholder of defendant Dootone Record Manufacturing, Inc.

The market tests were encouraging, and on January 6, 1956, Foxx and Dootone entered into a written agreement, which will be referred to as the first contract. It stated "we [Dootone] hereby employ you [Foxx] for the purpose of making phonograph records," and provided for a royalty to Foxx of 2 percent of the distributor price. As a minimum, four sides were to be recorded, and additional recordings were to be made at Dootone's election. The term of the contract was one year from the date of execution, with the option in Dootone to renew for an additional two years.

The option in the first contract was not exercised. On January 28, 1957, the parties executed another writing similar in form to the first, but calling for a royalty of 3 percent of the distributor price. This contract also expired at the end of one year, the option not having been exercised.

On April 4, 1958, the parties entered into the third contract, this time for a term of five years, with the option to extend for two years more. This contract provided that "a minimum of 12 78 RPM record sides, or the equivalent thereof shall be recorded, and additional recordings shall be made at our [Dootone's] election." The royalty was 3 percent of the list price (as distinguished from 3 percent of the distributor price provided for in the second contract). The distributor price is approximately one-half of the list price.

To place in context the problems of interpretation which are involved here, the authorship of those writings should be mentioned. The first and second contracts were on a mimeographed form, with the royalty rate and minimum number of record sides typed in. Williams testified that he obtained this form from another manufacturer and changed only the name of the company. Williams further testified:

"Q. Now, with respect to Contract 3, who made that one?

"A. I did, after research and inquiry in the industry.

"Q. Did you consult an attorney?

"A. No.

"Q. Used somebody else's form again?

"A. No, I consulted a number of contracts that were in use at the time and consolidated the items that I thought —

"Q. Took what you thought would be the best from each one?

"A. Yes, that is right."

Between April 4, 1958, and April 6, 1961, Foxx recorded for Dootone under the third contract 16 longplaying records, 26 extended play records and 5 single records. This was many times over the minimum specified in the agreement. It has been stipulated that Dootone has given the notice required to extend the stated term of this contract for its sixth and seventh years.

Commencing in 1956, Dootone submitted to Foxx semi-annual statements purporting to show the number of copies sold of each record and the royalty due. Each statement was accompanied by a check for the balance due as shown by the statement. Foxx made no effort to verify the accuracy of any of these statements except that on one occasion in 1957 an accountant employed by him for tax purposes examined some of Dootone's books.

In early 1961, on a trip east, Foxx talked to some distributors who told him how well his records were selling and who, as he testified, "just sort of aroused my curiosity as to whether I was getting a fair shake and that's how I got started in the thing." Foxx consulted an attorney, and this action was filed April 6, 1961.

At the trial, which was conducted in September 1963, Foxx conceded that Dootone had correctly reported the number of records sold. Foxx' principal contentions then were (1) that after April 4, 1958, all royalties, including those on records made under the 1956 and 1957 contracts, should be computed at 3 percent of the list price, which was approximately double the distributor price, and (2) that the charges which Dootone had made against the royalties for studio costs were improper. The trial court held against plaintiff on both of these points.

With respect to the cross-complaint the trial court found that there had been a mistake in computing royalties, and that Dootone was entitled to recover the amount of its overpayments for the period of two years immediately preceding the filing of the cross-complaint. It also found that Foxx had entered into an agreement with another manufacturer to make recordings as soon as he was legally free to do so, and concluded that, unless restrained, Foxx would make records for a manufacturer other than Dootone. The findings of fact also contain this statement:

"That Cross Complainant has suffered damage and injury by reason of Cross Defendant's refusal to make or produce recordings since April 6, 1961, but that such damages are exceedingly difficult to compute and that it would be more equitable and to the best interests of both parties to extend the term of the contract of April 4, 1958, by a term equal to that period during which Cross Defendant has refused to perform rather than to impose damages for such failure. That the total period during which Cross Defendant has refused to perform is two years, five months and ten days. That the contract of April 4, 1958, provided, inter alia, that should Plaintiff Redd Foxx fail to make recordings at times designated by Defendant Dootone Record Manufacturing, Inc. the then current recording year might be extended for such period of time as shall elapse until the Plaintiff Redd Foxx renders the required services."

The judgment, which was entered October 9, 1963, includes an injunction in the following language:

"It Is Further Considered, Ordered And Adjudged that Plaintiff and Cross Defendant Redd Foxx be, and he is hereby restrained and enjoined during the term of the contract of April 4, 1958, as extended to and including September 14, 1967, from making sound recordings for any other person, firm or corporation, or from making, distributing, selling or authorizing any other person, firm or corporation, to make, distribute or sell any phonograph records, or from recording for himself or any other person, firm or corporation any sound recordings or from using his name, likeness or any other identification in connection with any sound recordings except those made and produced by Defendant Dootone Record Manufacturing, Inc. That such injunction shall remain in full force and effect only so long as royalties earned by Plaintiff under the contract of April 4, 1958, equal or exceed the sum of $ 3,000 for any royalty period beginning with the royalties due on December 31, 1963, and that if on that date or thereafter royalties fall below the sum of $ 3,000 for any six-month royalty period as that term is defined in said contract then such injunction shall be dissolved and shall be of no further force or effect but the dissolution of said injunction, in the event it occurs, shall be without prejudice to any other remedies available to Defendant Dootone Record Manufacturing, Inc. as provided by operation of law or under the terms of the contract of April 4, 1958."

After Foxx had perfected his appeal in this court he filed a petition for writ of supersedeas on August 13, 1965, to stay the enforcement of that injunction. On August 20, 1965, this court made its order staying the enforcement of the injunction until further order of this court.

### The Royalty Rate on the First Two Contracts

The first point argued by Foxx on this appeal is that, after the third contract had been executed on April 4, 1958, Dootone was thereafter obligated to pay a royalty of 3 percent of the list price on all records, including those which had been made under the 1956 and 1957 contracts. The language of the three agreements on this subject is unambiguous, and Foxx' theory is clearly incorrect. The first two contracts call for a royalty computed upon the distributor price. The third contract provides for "a royalty of 3% of the list price in the country of manufacture, of 90% of all records sold embodying performances hereunder on both sides thereof, . . ." It is conceded that the period for Foxx' performance under the first two contracts had expired before the third was executed. There are no circumstances shown which would justify interpreting the third contract as changing the royalty terms for records theretofore made under the first two agreements.

Foxx' brief refers to the testimony which he gave, without objection, that around April 4, 1958, he had a discussion in which Williams told him that he would get "three percent of everything," including records made before that time. According to Foxx, Williams did not say 3 percent of what. It was "Just three percent." Williams was asked if he remembered such a conversation and he answered "No."

Even assuming that Foxx' testimony should be accepted as undenied, it shows no more than that a party made an oral promise which was at variance with the written agreement. Under the circumstances such a statement has no legal effect. The 1958 contract appears to have been adopted as the final and complete expression of the agreement of the parties — an "integration," as that term is used in the Restatement of Contracts section 228.

"The parol evidence rule, as is now universally recognized, is not a rule of evidence but is one of substantive law. It does not exclude evidence for any of the reasons ordinarily requiring exclusion, based on the probative value of such evidence or the policy of its admission. The rule as applied to contracts is simply that as a matter of substantive law, a certain act, the act of embodying the complete terms of an agreement in a writing (the 'integration'), becomes the contract of the parties. The point then is, not how the agreement is to be proved, because as a matter of law the writing is the agreement. Extrinsic evidence is excluded because it cannot serve to prove what the agreement was, this being determined as a matter of law to be the writing itself. The rule comes into operation when there is a single and final memorial of the understanding of the parties. When that takes place, prior and contemporaneous negotiations, oral or written, are excluded; or, as it is sometimes said, the written memorial supersedes these prior or contemporaneous negotiations. (See Civ. Code, § 1625; Code Civ. Proc., § 1856; . . .” (Estate of Gaines, 15 Cal.2d 255, 264-265 [100 P.2d 1055].)

The 1958 contract is in some respects ambiguous and uncertain, but this much is clearly established by the writing: that the royalty specified therein applies to records “embodying performances hereunder,” and not to recordings made under the earlier contracts.

Foxx complains of a number of rulings made by the trial court sustaining objections during his testimony. So far as can be determined from the transcript, what was excluded was Foxx’ attempt to testify to oral statements of Williams which were in conflict with the royalty clause of the 1958 contract. Such statements were properly excluded under the rule referred to above. The trial court advised counsel that evidence would be received for the purpose of interpretation, but counsel failed to show the trial court and has not suggested here any way in which the excluded answers would assist the court in interpreting the writing, as distinguished from proving a conflicting oral promise.

The Overpayments

Williams testified that all of the royalty statements until 1961 had been made up by a bookkeeper who had computed the royalties under the 1956 and 1957 contracts on the basis of retail list rather than distributor's price; that he, Williams, did not discover this until he made an investigation sometime after this action had been filed; and that he would not have approved the payments if he had known. The trial court accepted this testimony as true, and its finding on this factual issue is conclusive here. (People v. Hills, 30 Cal.2d 694, 700 [185 P.2d 11].) The finding of fact supports the judgment for refund of the overpayments.

The law applicable to such overpayments is set forth in American Oil Service v. Hope Oil Co., 194 Cal.App.2d 581, 587 [15 Cal.Rptr. 209]: “Whether the payments were made voluntarily or through mistake depended upon the intentions of plaintiff in making them. These were to be judged in light of the facts that were known to plaintiff. Means of knowledge were not the equivalent of knowledge. We would suppose that most mistakes of fact occur through failure to resort to means of knowledge.”

This rule of law was restated and applied in the second appeal of that case. (American Oil Service v. Hope Oil Co., 233 Cal.App.2d 822, 830 [44 Cal.Rptr. 60].)

## Studio Costs

The only studio costs which Foxx contended were unnecessary were the expenditures for food and liquor served to the studio audiences. The reasonableness of these charges is established by the testimony of Williams, and the trial court's finding on this factual matter is not reviewable on appeal. There remains the question of law whether any studio costs were deductible from the royalties under the contracts.

Williams conceded in his testimony that he charged against Foxx' royalties "studio costs," which he said, include "all costs pertaining to making the sound production." When a recording was made in a studio (as distinguished from a nightclub where a paying audience was present) the practice was to invite a group of persons to attend and provide background laughter for Foxx' performance. Williams purchased food and drink for these guests to put them in the proper mood for their participation. This expense was included in the "studio costs" charged against the artist's royalties. The royalty statements contained no itemization of "studio costs." All charges which Dootone claimed against royalties were lumped in a single item called "advances and charges" at the bottom of each royalty statement.

The 1956 and 1957 contracts said nothing about charging the artist for studio expense. Those agreements simply declare that "we hereby employ you for the purpose of making phonograph records" and "We will pay you in respect of recordings made hereunder, a royalty" at the specified rate. Foxx should not have been charged any studio costs for recordings made under those two contracts.

The third agreement is altogether different in form. It includes the following language:

"1. The Artist(s) hereby sells, assigns, transfers and delivers to the Company, its successors and assigns, certain creative sound productions, recordings or masters for the purpose of making phonograph records.

"....

"4. For the services of the musicians hereunder, and for your services as a vocalist, we will make a non-returnable payment within fourteen days after the services are rendered, at the rate of union scale of musicians and per side to you as vocalist. Such payments shall be charged against your royalties when earned. We will render an accounting to you within forty-five (45) days after June 30th and after December 31st of each year during which records made hereunder are sold.

"....

"9. Company will advance compensation and/or other costs of recording (including without limitation thereto, so-called 'studio costs' and where applicable, costs of acquiring the rights to reproduce from sound-tracks or other devices on which Artist's vocal performances are embodied and the rights to sell phonograph records made therefrom), for arrangements, copying, orchestrations, any amounts payable to the sound or recording technicians and personnel, conductor, musicians, and/or other accompanying artists, e.g., choral accompanists, together with all amounts Company is required to pay by reason of any regulation of or agreement with any agency, union or guild, in connection with the recording of the performances for each recording session. Artist agrees to supply such instrumentations, orchestrations and arrangements as Artist may have for the selections to be recorded without any additional payment to Artist, but if the Company's use thereof occasions any additional obligation to the arranger or orchestrator or other person, Company pay same and charge same as an advance against Artist's royalties."

The words of sale contained in paragraph 1 indicate an intention to treat the artist, for accounting purposes at least, as the producer of the sound recording who then sells the master record to Dootone.

Paragraphs 4 and 9 obligate Dootone to advance the necessary studio costs and other production expenses, to be recouped out of royalties. The first sentence of paragraph 9, which covers studio costs generally, does not specifically call for repayment, but the word "advance," in its context, supplies that meaning. Reading paragraphs 4 and 9 together with the language of paragraph 1 which obligates the artist to sell "sound productions, recordings or masters," we can only conclude that the intention was to charge the cost of production against the artist, and to collect it as an offset against royalties. Thus the studio costs incurred in recording after April 4, 1958, were proper charges.

Foxx offered no evidence as to what studio charges, if any, were made against him under the 1956 and 1957 contracts. Only three royalty statements were offered in evidence, only one of which was for a period prior to 1958. Each statement shows a lump sum identified only as "advances and charges" which is deducted from royalties earned. These sums are not explained or itemized. There was testimony that from time to time Dootone advanced cash to Foxx for his personal use, and thus there is no basis for inferring that any part of the amounts called "advances and charges" was for recording expenses.

During the trial Williams produced in court a number of checks which had been written by Dootone for costs of recording sessions which had been charged to Foxx. The checks were not offered in evidence. The attorney for Foxx stated that the total was $ 2,179.32 and that "Those cover the period from '58 to '61." Since the contract of April 4, 1958, authorizes the deduction of studio costs, and since there is no showing that any amount was deducted for recordings made prior to that date, Foxx is not entitled to any recovery.

The Injunction

Civil Code section 3423 provides in part:
"An injunction can not be granted:
". . . .
"Fifth — To prevent the breach of a contract, other than a contract in writing for the rendition or furnishing of personal services from one to another where the minimum compensation for such service is at the rate of not less than six thousand dollars per annum and where the promised service is of a special, unique, unusual, extraordinary or intellectual character, which gives it peculiar value the loss of which can not be reasonably or adequately compensated in damages in an action at law, the performance of which would not be specifically enforced; . . ."
Similar language appears in Code of Civil Procedure section 526.

It is a familiar rule that a contract to render personal services cannot be specifically enforced. (Civ. Code, § 3390; Lyon v. Goss, 19 Cal.2d 659, 674 [123 P.2d 11]; Poultry Producers etc. Inc. v. Barlow, 189 Cal. 278, 288 [208 P. 93]; see 5A Corbin on Contracts, § 1204, p. 398.) It follows that the breach of such a contract may not be enjoined except in cases falling within the exception provided for in the quoted statute. The 1958 contract recites that the artist's performances "are of a special, unique, unusual, extraordinary and intellectual character which gives them a peculiar value," and at pretrial the parties agreed that such characterization was correct. There remains the question whether this is a contract "where the minimum compensation for such service is at the rate of not less than six thousand dollars per annum."

At the trial the parties stipulated to the amounts which Foxx had received as royalties each year from 1956 through 1962, but these figures were not broken down to show what portion was paid for recordings made under the 1958 contract. The royalty statement for the six months ending June 30, 1963, which was the accounting period immediately preceding the trial, showed total royalties for the period as $ 2,682.27, less advances and charges of $ 156.

We do not place our decision upon the absence of proof of the amount of royalties earned under the 1958 contract. In our opinion this royalty contract does not meet the requirements of the injunction statute even though it should ultimately appear that the royalties earned, over any given period, should exceed the rate of $ 6,000 per year.

An injunction which forbids an artist to accept new employment may be a harsh and powerful remedy. The monetary limitation in the statute is intended to serve as a counterweight in balancing the equities. The Legislature has concluded that an artist who is not entitled to receive a minimum of $ 6,000 per year by performing his contract should not be subjected to this kind of economic coercion. Under the statutory scheme, an artist who is enjoined from accepting new employment will at least have the alternative of earning $ 6,000 or more per year by performing his old contract.

The trial court's solution to the problem was to grant the injunction for only so long as the royalties for each half year equaled $ 3,000. This means that the artist is enjoined for 7 1/2 months at a time (6 months plus the 45 days thereafter which the contract allows for the preparation of the royalty statement) without any assurance of earning anything. This is not what the statute calls for.

The portion of the judgment which enjoins Foxx must be deleted.

The elimination of the injunction does not require a remand of the case to the trial court for consideration of a new remedy for the breach of contract. Although the trial court made a finding that Dootone had suffered damage, there was no evidence to support it. Under the circumstances the most that Dootone would be entitled to for Foxx' breach would be nominal damages. A judgment should not be reversed simply to permit such a recovery. (Chaparkas v. Webb, 178 Cal.App.2d 257, 262 [2 Cal.Rptr. 879].)

### Extension of the Contract

Based upon the stipulated fact that Foxx had "failed and refused to make any recordings . . . from and after April 6, 1961," the trial court computed the period of his refusal, to the date the trial ended, as two years, five months and ten days, and added it to the term of the 1958 contract. The judgment declares that the contract of April 4, 1958, is in effect to and including September 14, 1967.

This portion of the judgment is erroneous for two independent reasons, which will be discussed separately.

The first is that there is nothing in the 1958 contract or elsewhere in the evidence which would justify extending the term during which Foxx is required to record for Dootone and abstain from recording for anyone else. Paragraph 12 of the agreement provides that "during the term" the artist will not record for anyone other than Dootone, but this negative covenant contains no language calling for an extension of the term or of the period of exclusivity.

The duty of Foxx to make recordings during the term of the 1958 contract is set forth in the following language:

"These creative sound productions, recordings or masters, are to be made during the term of this contract and a minimum of 12 78 RPM record sides, or the equivalent thereof, shall be recorded, and additional recordings shall be made at our [Dootone's] election."

It is undisputed that recordings exceeding the minimum had been made prior to the commencement of the action, and there is no evidence of any "election" by Dootone to make recordings other than those which were made.

The trial court's remarks indicate it relied upon paragraph 15 of the 1958 contract which reads as follows:

"15. Should Artist, for any reason whatever, be unavailable for the making of recordings at the times designated by the Company as herein provided, or fail to make recordings at such times, the then current 'recording year' hereof may be extended by the Company for such period of time as shall elapse until Artist renders the required services for the Company. The Company shall have at least thirty (30) days' notice before the Company is required to arrange for the making by Artist of the recordings for which Artist was unavailable or which Artist failed to make as aforesaid."

Preliminarily it is noted that the words "the then current 'recording year'" are not defined in the contract, nor are they used elsewhere, except in paragraph 17, the force majeure clause, which will be discussed later. This incongruity of language is explained by Williams' testimony that he consulted a number of contracts used by others and "consolidated the items" that he thought were the best in each. To make paragraph 15 applicable it is necessary to interpret "the then current 'recording year'" to mean the term of the contract.

The form of paragraph 15 suggests that it was lifted from a contract in which the artist was obligated to make a determinable number of recordings within a "recording year," but at times designated by the company. The paragraph provides that if the artist fails to make recordings "at such times," the "recording year" may be extended "for such period of time as shall elapse until Artist renders the required services. . . ."

Such extension is not necessarily for a period equal to the time during which the artist was in default. Rather it is for the period which shall elapse until the artist "renders the required services." The distinction is a substantial one.

It is obvious, from the nature of the business, that the parties did not contemplate that Foxx would be engaged continuously in making records for the entire seven-year term of the contract. The evidence shows that each recording session was about three hours in length, and Foxx testified that he needed eight to ten days to prepare his material for each recording session. The parties must have recognized that they had time to produce a great many more recordings than the market could absorb. The actual number which could be made and sold profitably was not a matter that could be determined when the contract was written. Hence the parties left it to Dootone to call for more recordings as its business judgment dictated. Foxx' obligation under the contract was not to render a given number of days, weeks or years of service, but to make as many records during the seven-year period as Dootone elected to finance, produce and market.

The language of paragraph 15 may be contrasted with the force majeure clause, which is paragraph 17. The latter provides that in the event of fire, strikes, et cetera, the company may suspend its obligations and "A number of days equal to the total of all such days of suspension shall be added to the then current 'recording year.'"

The extension under paragraph 17, unlike paragraph 15, is for a period measured by the period of nonperformance.

Since an extension under paragraph 15 is only for the period which shall elapse "until Artist renders the required services," it is necessary to inquire what are the required services. Since Foxx had made more than the minimum, he was not obligated to make any more unless Dootone so elected, of which there is no evidence. Foxx' refusal to perform after April 6, 1961, constituted an anticipatory breach of the contract, which justified Dootone's suing him immediately on the contract. (Gold Min. & Water Co. v. Swinerton, 23 Cal.2d 19, 29 [142 P.2d 22].) But without proof that Dootone had elected to make any more recordings, the extension provided for in paragraph 15 was not applicable at all.

### The Seven-Year Statute

The second reason why the court should not have extended the contract is found in Labor Code section 2855 which reads:

"A contract to render personal service, other than a contract of apprenticeship as provided in Chapter 4 of this division, may not be enforced against the employee beyond seven years from the commencement of service under it. Any contract, otherwise valid, to perform or render service of a special, unique, unusual, extraordinary, or intellectual character, which gives it peculiar value and the loss of which can not be reasonably or adequately compensated in damages in an action at law, may nevertheless be enforced against the person contracting to render such service, for a term not to exceed seven years from the commencement of service under it. If the employee voluntarily continues his service under it beyond that time, the contract may be referred to as affording a presumptive measure of the compensation."

Dootone contends that Foxx was engaged in an independent calling, and points out that section 2855 uses the word "employee," thereby excluding independent contractors from its coverage. In support of the argument that Foxx was not an employee, Dootone relies upon the cases arising under the Workmen's Compensation Act and cases applying the doctrine of respondeat superior to impose liability upon a master for the torts of his servant. Counsel also produced, in opposing the issuance of a writ of supersedeas, affidavits showing that, for accounting purposes, Dootone always treated Foxx as an independent contractor; that there never was any withholding of income tax, social security tax or state disability assessment which the law requires with respect to employees.

We do not think such considerations are determinative of the applicability of section 2855. The definitions of "employee" and "independent contractor" in the Workmen's Compensation Law (Lab. Code, §§ 3350- 3353) are said to be the meanings "used in this division," i.e., division 4 of the Labor Code, not division 3 wherein section 2855 is found. The public policy which underlies the doctrine of respondeat superior is altogether distinct from the legislative policy which is expressed in section 2855. (See De Haviland v. Warner Bros., Inc., 67 Cal.App.2d 225 [153 P.2d 983], for explanation of the history and purpose of § 2855.)

Section 2855 is a part of Labor Code division 3, which is headed "Employment Relations." This division includes the following definition:

"§ 2750. The contract of employment is a contract by which one, who is called the employer, engages another, who is called the employee, to do something for the benefit of the employer or a third person."

Division 3 also contains, in chapter 3 thereof, headed "Master and Servant," this definition:

"§ 3000. A servant is one who is employed to render personal service to his employer, other than in the pursuit of an independent calling, and who in such service remains entirely under the control and direction of the employer, who is called his master."

It appears from a reading of these definitions that, at least in division 3 of the Labor Code, the Legislature has given a broader meaning to the word "employer" than to "master," and, inferentially, that "employee" is broader than "servant."

In determining whether or not the contract before the court is "a contract to render personal service," we consider what the artist was required to do in the performance of the agreement. An examination of the contract in the light of the surrounding circumstances leads us to the conclusion that Foxx' performance was rendition of personal service, and that he was an employee, as that term is used in division 3 of the Labor Code.

The first two contracts between Dootone and Foxx were by their express terms contracts to render personal services as an employee. The opening sentence of each was as follows:

"This contract for your personal services as a vocalist between Dootone Records as the employer, and you as the vocalist, and we hereby employ you for the purpose of making phonograph records."

The manner in which services were performed remained the same throughout the entire period from 1955 to the commencement of the action in 1961. Foxx prepared his own material at home, using his own library of joke books and his own experience as a comedian, making up new jokes and adapting old ones. Williams suggested some material but Foxx says he used very little of it. Recording sessions were held either in a recording studio or at a nightclub where Foxx was performing. Foxx brought with him the material which he had written and which his wife had copied on the typewriter. Foxx then put his script on a music stand in front of a microphone and performed.

Williams testified, without contradiction, that he made all of the arrangements for these recording sessions. This means Dootone selected the place of recording, selected and operated (or arranged for) the recording equipment, determined whether other persons should be present for background, selected and invited all of the other persons who were to participate, and paid the cost of all of this. Foxx' performance was recorded on tape. Williams edited the tape, selecting the best material which would give a recording of the desired length. From this, Dootone produced the records. The following testimony by Foxx (which is uncontradicted) is illuminating:

"Q. Did you ever know before the album was actually produced what was going to be on the album?

"A. I never knew, I just recorded the material. Mr. Williams, he finished the product.

"Q. Did you ever have any discussions with him about that subject?

"A. Yes, we discussed it quite a bit, to no avail, because I would ask him sometimes to edit it. He said he was the producer, you do what you do and I'll take care of my end."

As indicated above in the discussion of "studio costs," the language of the 1958 contract is susceptible to the interpretation that Foxx was to produce the recordings and sell them to Dootone. But the surrounding circumstances, and particularly the manner in which the parties were performing, both before and after April 4, 1958, indicate that those provisions were for accounting purposes only, and did not change the employer-employee relationship which had existed since January 1956.

A case relied upon by Dootone provides an excellent contrast with the facts here, and thereby illustrates the point. Ketcham v. Hall Syndicate, Inc., 37 Misc.2d 693 [236 N.Y.S.2d 206], affd. 19 App.Div.2d 611 [242 N.Y.S.2d 182], was an action brought by the creator of a cartoon strip for a declaration of rights under a 10-year contract whereby he had agreed to deliver his cartoon panels to the New York office of a news syndicate. Plaintiff there contended that the contract could not be enforced against him after seven years, because of California Labor Code section 2855. The court gave judgment against plaintiff, holding that section 2855 did not apply, both because plaintiff was not an employee, and because the law of New York, not California, governed.

Although the statement of facts in the Ketcham case is brief, it seems clear that plaintiff there created an artistic product, reduced to tangible form, and then sold it to defendant, together with the privilege of reproducing it commercially. In the case at bench Foxx served as a writer and a performer. His performance, combined with the managerial, artistic and technical skills of

Dootone's employees, resulted in an intangible product, recorded sound, which Dootone used in the production of salable merchandise.

Ketcham, by himself, produced an article which he shipped across the country to the Hall Syndicate. Foxx, by himself, produced nothing. His skill and artistry were essential ingredients, but no recording would have resulted without the application of the capital, management and technical work supplied by Dootone. There is no evidence that Foxx was qualified by training or experience to assume the responsibility for making a recording, or that anyone expected him to do so. Except for Foxx' complaints about not being consulted on editing, and not being allowed to invite his friends to the recording sessions, there is no evidence that anyone ever contemplated that he would do more than come in with a script, as instructed, and render services as a performer.

We are mindful that this contract did not call for full-time employment, and that the greater part of Foxx' time was devoted to his other calling as a nightclub entertainer. Although this fact may to some extent dilute the policy considerations discussed in the De Haviland opinion (67 Cal.App.2d at p. 235), the statute makes no distinction between full-time and part-time employment.

Although Foxx' contract did not require his continuous performance, the relationship of the parties, as shown by the evidence, compels the conclusion that this is a "contract to render personal service" which is subject to the seven-year limitation.

## Reuse of Material

Foxx contends on this appeal that the trial court erred in failing to declare unenforceable paragraph 12 (f) of the 1958 contract. By this provision Foxx agreed in substance that for five years after the expiration of the contract he would not make any phonograph records embodying any composition which he had recorded under the agreement. Foxx argues that this provision is unreasonable and should be annulled on that ground.

The record on appeal shows that this contention was never made in the trial court. The second amended complaint, upon which the case went to trial, contains no mention of paragraph 12 (f) and no request for a declaration of rights on this subject. The joint pretrial statement and the pretrial order are likewise silent. Neither party offered any evidence of circumstances which would assist the court in determining whether this clause is reasonable or unreasonable. It does not appear that the subject was presented to the trial court in any way. Appellant is not entitled to raise the issue for the first time on appeal. ( Everly Enterprises, Inc. v. Altman, 54 Cal.2d 761, 765 [8 Cal.Rptr. 455, 356 P.2d 199].) The application of this rule is especially compelling here since evidence might have been offered to show the purpose and effect of the clause to prove its reasonableness, if the issue had been raised.

## The Accounting

At the time this appeal was argued and submitted Foxx made a "motion for order for accounting by respondent and in the alternative for an order of reference to the superior court." In support of the motion Foxx declared that, on June 30, 1961 (after the commencement of this action), Dootone gave him a statement showing overpayments amounting to $ 18,236.64 under the 1956 and 1957 contracts, and that for each accounting period thereafter Dootone has made deductions from his royalties based upon this claimed offset. Foxx further declares that, although the trial court awarded Dootone recovery of only $ 8,128.52 for overpayments under the 1956 and 1957 contracts, Dootone has now withheld an amount in excess of that sum and claims the right to withhold more. In response, Williams has filed a declaration in which he asserts that Dootone was entitled to offset interest and costs and other items.

The motion itself is an attempt to litigate in this court matters which should properly be raised in the superior court, either on a motion to declare the judgment satisfied, or on remand of this action or in a new action. Hence we deny the motion by an order filed concurrently herewith. But the issue adverted to serves to illustrate a defect in the judgment which must be considered.

In this action, in which the plaintiff and the cross-complainant each has been found to have a valid claim against the other, the judgment fails to state the dollar balance due from one to the other as of any given date. The trial court made findings that Dootone has "properly accounted to Plaintiff for all records sold and properly charged Plaintiff with expenses as permitted under the contracts." The judgment contains declarations construing the contracts and provides that Dootone "is hereby ordered to pay to Plaintiff" royalties computed at the rates specified in the court's findings. The judgment also provides that Dootone "have and recover from Cross Defendant Redd Foxx the sum of $ 4,708.59 as overpayments made on the contract of January 6, 1956; and the sum of $ 3,419.93 as overpayments made on the contract of January 28, 1957, from and after July 12, 1959 to December 31, 1960."

Apparently the finding that Dootone had "properly accounted" was intended to mean only that Dootone's reports of sales and expenses were correct, not that Dootone had paid Foxx all of his royalties. Instead of determining and stating in dollars the amount of the royalties earned and unpaid to date, the trial court gave what was in terms a mandatory injunction to Dootone to pay royalties at specified rates. A proper decision in the trial court would have required a computation of the royalties earned and unpaid as of the end of the most recent accounting period, an offset of the overpayments, and the determination of a balance, for which judgment could have been entered in favor of one party or the other.

The reason no such decision was given in this case is that counsel failed to introduce evidence from which the balance could be computed. The error was invited, but we cannot ignore the defect in the judgment, for to do so would only compound the difficulty. The issue will not be at rest until a court determines what the actual amounts are. Since the action must be remanded to the trial court for this purpose, the account may as well be brought down to date.

The judgment is reversed and the action remanded to the superior court with directions to determine the balance then due as between plaintiff and Dootone, under the three contracts, using, so far as applicable, the findings of fact heretofore made, and to enter a judgment consistent with this opinion.

---

Redd Foxx's attempt to seek an accounting of payments from his record company resulted in the court ordering him to re-pay the record company for money paid to him by mistake. In *Campbell v. Accuff-Rose Music, Inc.*, 510 U.S. 569 (1994), rap group 2 Live Crew was sued for their parody of Roy Orbison's "Oh, Pretty Woman" by their song, "Pretty Woman." Acuff-Rose Music could not prove market harm. The U.S. Supreme Court stated that the court of appeals erred in concluding that the commercial nature of the parody had rendered it presumptively unfair. The parody was held to be fair use, and, thus, did not constitute copyright infringement.

Campbell v. Acuff-Rose Music, Inc.
Supreme Court of the United States
November 9, 1993, Argued; March 7, 1994, Decided
No. 92-1292
510 U.S. 569

JUSTICE SOUTER delivered the opinion of the Court.

We are called upon to decide whether 2 Live Crew's commercial parody of Roy Orbison's song, "Oh, Pretty Woman," may be a fair use within the meaning of the Copyright Act of 1976, 17 U.S.C. § 107 (1988 ed. and Supp. IV). Although the District Court granted summary judgment for 2 Live Crew, the Court of Appeals reversed, holding the defense of fair use barred by the song's commercial character and excessive borrowing. Because we hold that a parody's commercial character is only one element to be weighed in a fair use enquiry, and that insufficient consideration was given to the nature of parody in weighing the degree of copying, we reverse and remand.

I.

In 1964, Roy Orbison and William Dees wrote a rock ballad called "Oh, Pretty Woman" and assigned their rights in it to respondent Acuff-Rose Music, Inc. See Appendix A, infra, at 594. Acuff-Rose registered the song for copyright protection.

Petitioners Luther R. Campbell, Christopher Wongwon, Mark Ross, and David Hobbs are collectively known as 2 Live Crew, a popular rap music group. In 1989, Campbell wrote a song entitled "Pretty Woman," which he later described in an affidavit as intended, "through comical lyrics, to satirize the original work . . . ." App. to Pet. for Cert. 80a. On July 5, 1989, 2 Live Crew's manager informed Acuff-Rose that 2 Live Crew had written a parody of "Oh, Pretty Woman," that they would afford all credit for ownership and authorship of the original song to Acuff-Rose, Dees, and Orbison, and that they were willing to pay a fee for the use they wished to make of it. Enclosed with the letter were a copy of the lyrics and a recording of 2 Live Crew's song. See Appendix B, infra, at 595. Acuff-Rose's agent refused permission, stating that "I am aware of the success enjoyed by 'The 2 Live Crews', but I must inform you that we cannot permit the use of a parody of 'Oh, Pretty Woman.'" App. to Pet. for Cert. 85a. Nonetheless, in June or July 1989, 2 Live Crew released records, cassette tapes, and compact discs of "Pretty Woman" in a collection of songs entitled "As Clean

As They Wanna Be." The albums and compact discs identify the authors of "Pretty Woman" as Orbison and Dees and its publisher as Acuff-Rose.

Almost a year later, after nearly a quarter of a million copies of the recording had been sold, Acuff-Rose sued 2 Live Crew and its record company, Luke Skyywalker Records, for copyright infringement. The District Court granted summary judgment for 2 Live Crew, reasoning that the commercial purpose of 2 Live Crew's song was no bar to fair use; that 2 Live Crew's version was a parody, which "quickly degenerates into a play on words, substituting predictable lyrics with shocking ones" to show "how bland and banal the Orbison song" is; that 2 Live Crew had taken no more than was necessary to "conjure up" the original in order to parody it; and that it was "extremely unlikely that 2 Live Crew's song could adversely affect the market for the original." 754 F. Supp. 1150, 1154-1155, 1157-1158 (MD Tenn. 1991). The District Court weighed these factors and held that 2 Live Crew's song made fair use of Orbison's original. Id., at 1158-1159.

The Court of Appeals for the Sixth Circuit reversed and remanded. 972 F.2d 1429, 1439 (1992). Although it assumed for the purpose of its opinion that 2 Live Crew's song was a parody of the Orbison original, the Court of Appeals thought the District Court had put too little emphasis on the fact that "every commercial use . . . is presumptively . . . unfair," Sony Corp. of America v. Universal City Studios, Inc., 464 U.S. 417, 451, 78 L. Ed. 2d 574, 104 S. Ct. 774 (1984), and it held that "the admittedly commercial nature" of the parody "requires the conclusion" that the first of four factors relevant under the statute weighs against a finding of fair use. 972 F.2d at 1435, 1437. Next, the Court of Appeals determined that, by "taking the heart of the original and making it the heart of a new work," 2 Live Crew had, qualitatively, taken too much. Id., at 1438. Finally, after noting that the effect on the potential market for the original (and the market for derivative works) is "undoubtedly the single most important element of fair use," Harper & Row, Publishers, Inc. v. Nation Enterprises, 471 U.S. 539, 566, 85 L. Ed. 2d 588, 105 S. Ct. 2218 (1985), the Court of Appeals faulted the District Court for "refusing to indulge the presumption" that "harm for purposes of the fair use analysis has been established by the presumption attaching to commercial uses." 972 F.2d at 1438-1439. In sum, the court concluded that its "blatantly commercial purpose . . . prevents this parody from being a fair use." Id., at 1439.

We granted certiorari, 507 U.S. 1003 (1993), to determine whether 2 Live Crew's commercial parody could be a fair use.

## II.

It is uncontested here that 2 Live Crew's song would be an infringement of Acuff-Rose's rights in "Oh, Pretty Woman," under the Copyright Act of 1976, 17

U.S.C. § 106 (1988 ed. and Supp. IV), but for a finding of fair use through parody. From the infancy of copyright protection, some opportunity for fair use of copyrighted materials has been thought necessary to fulfill copyright's very purpose, "to promote the Progress of Science and useful Arts . . . ." U.S. Const., Art. I, § 8, cl. 8. For as Justice Story explained, "in truth, in literature, in science and in art, there are, and can be, few, if any, things, which in an abstract sense, are strictly new and original throughout. Every book in literature, science and art, borrows, and must necessarily borrow, and use much which was well known and used before." Emerson v. Davies, 8 F. Cas. 615, 619 (No. 4,436) (CCD Mass. 1845). Similarly, Lord Ellenborough expressed the inherent tension in the need simultaneously to protect copyrighted material and to allow others to build upon it when he wrote, "while I shall think myself bound to secure every man in the enjoyment of his copy-right, one must not put manacles upon science." Carey v. Kearsley, 4 Esp. 168, 170, 170 Eng. Rep. 679, 681 (K. B. 1803). In copyright cases brought under the Statute of Anne of 1710, English courts held that in some instances "fair abridgements" would not infringe an author's rights, see W. Patry, The Fair Use Privilege in Copyright Law 6-17 (1985) (hereinafter Patry); Leval, Toward a Fair Use Standard, 103 Harv. L. Rev. 1105 (1990) (hereinafter Leval), and although the First Congress enacted our initial copyright statute, Act of May 31, 1790, 1 Stat. 124, without any explicit reference to "fair use," as it later came to be known, the doctrine was recognized by the American courts nonetheless.

In Folsom v. Marsh, 9 F. Cas. 342 (No. 4,901) (CCD Mass. 1841), Justice Story distilled the essence of law and methodology from the earlier cases: "look to the nature and objects of the selections made, the quantity and value of the materials used, and the degree in which the use may prejudice the sale, or diminish the profits, or supersede the objects, of the original work." Id., at 348. Thus expressed, fair use remained exclusively judge-made doctrine until the passage of the 1976 Copyright Act, in which Justice Story's summary is discernible:

"§ 107. Limitations on exclusive rights: Fair use

"Notwithstanding the provisions of sections 106 and 106A, the fair use of a copyrighted work, including such use by reproduction in copies or phonorecords or by any other means specified by that section, for purposes such as criticism, comment, news reporting, teaching (including multiple copies for classroom use), scholarship, or research, is not an infringement of copyright. In determining whether the use made of a work in any particular case is a fair use the factors to be considered shall include —

"(1) the purpose and character of the use, including whether such use is of a commercial nature or is for nonprofit educational purposes;

"(2) the nature of the copyrighted work;

"(3) the amount and substantiality of the portion used in relation to the copyrighted work as a whole; and

"(4) the effect of the use upon the potential market for or value of the copyrighted work.

"The fact that a work is unpublished shall not itself bar a finding of fair use if such finding is made upon consideration of all the above factors." 17 U.S.C. § 107 (1988 ed. and Supp. IV).

Congress meant § 107 "to restate the present judicial doctrine of fair use, not to change, narrow, or enlarge it in any way" and intended that courts continue the common-law tradition of fair use adjudication. H. R. Rep. No. 94-1476, p. 66 (1976) (hereinafter House Report); S. Rep. No. 94-473, p. 62 (1975) (hereinafter Senate Report). The fair use doctrine thus "permits [and requires] courts to avoid rigid application of the copyright statute when, on occasion, it would stifle the very creativity which that law is designed to foster." Stewart v. Abend, 495 U.S. 207, 236, 109 L. Ed. 2d 184, 110 S. Ct. 1750 (1990) (internal quotation marks and citation omitted).

The task is not to be simplified with bright-line rules, for the statute, like the doctrine it recognizes, calls for case-by-case analysis. Harper & Row, 471 U.S. at 560; Sony, 464 U.S. at 448, and n.31; House Report, pp. 65-66; Senate Report, p. 62. The text employs the terms "including" and "such as" in the preamble paragraph to indicate the "illustrative and not limitative" function of the examples given, § 101; see Harper & Row, supra, at 561, which thus provide only general guidance about the sorts of copying that courts and Congress most commonly had found to be fair uses. Nor may the four statutory factors be treated in isolation, one from another. All are to be explored, and the results weighed together, in light of the purposes of copyright. See Leval 1110-1111; Patry & Perlmutter, Fair Use Misconstrued: Profit, Presumptions, and Parody, 11 Cardozo Arts & Ent. L. J. 667, 685-687 (1993) (hereinafter Patry & Perlmutter).

The first factor in a fair use enquiry is "the purpose and character of the use, including whether such use is of a commercial nature or is for nonprofit educational purposes." § 107(1). This factor draws on Justice Story's formulation, "the nature and objects of the selections made." Folsom v. Marsh, supra, at 348. The enquiry here may be guided by the examples given in the preamble to § 107, looking to whether the use is for criticism, or comment, or news reporting, and the like, see § 107. The central purpose of this investigation is to see, in Justice Story's words, whether the new work merely "supersede[s] the objects" of the original creation, Folsom v. Marsh, supra, at 348; accord, Harper & Row, supra, at 562 ("supplanting" the original), or instead adds something new, with a further purpose or different character, altering the first with new expression, meaning, or message; it asks, in other words, whether and to what extent the new work is "transformative." Leval 1111. Although such transformative use is not absolutely necessary for a finding of fair use, Sony, supra, at 455, n. 40, the goal of copyright, to promote science and the arts, is generally furthered by the creation of transformative works. Such works thus lie at the heart of the fair use doctrine's guarantee of breathing space within the confines of copyright, see, e. g., Sony, supra, at 478-480 (BLACKMUN, J., dissenting), and the more transformative the new work, the less will be the significance of other factors, like commercialism, that may weigh against a finding of fair use.

This Court has only once before even considered whether parody may be fair use, and that time issued no opinion because of the Court's equal division. Benny v. Loew's Inc., 239 F.2d 532 (CA9 1956), aff'd sub nom. Columbia Broadcasting System, Inc. v. Loew's Inc., 356 U.S. 43, 2 L. Ed. 2d 583, 78 S. Ct. 667 (1958). Suffice it to say now that parody has an obvious claim to transformative value, as Acuff-Rose itself does not deny. Like less ostensibly humorous forms of criticism, it can provide social benefit, by shedding light on an earlier work, and, in the process, creating a new one. We thus line up with the courts that have held that parody, like other comment or criticism, may claim fair use under § 107. See, e. g., Fisher v. Dees, 794 F.2d 432 (CA9 1986) ("When Sonny Sniffs Glue," a parody of "When Sunny Gets Blue," is fair use); Elsmere Music, Inc. v. National Broadcasting Co., 482 F. Supp. 741 (SDNY), aff'd, 623 F.2d 252 (CA2 1980) ("I Love Sodom," a "Saturday Night Live" television parody of "I Love New York," is fair use); see also House Report, p. 65; Senate Report, p. 61 ("Use in a parody of some of the content of the work parodied" may be fair use).

The germ of parody lies in the definition of the Greek parodeia, quoted in Judge Nelson's Court of Appeals dissent, as "a song sung alongside another." 972 F.2d at 1440, quoting 7 Encyclopedia Britannica 768 (15th ed. 1975). Modern dictionaries accordingly describe a parody as a "literary or artistic work that imitates the characteristic style of an author or a work for comic effect or ridicule," or as a "composition in prose or verse in which the characteristic turns of thought and phrase in an author or class of authors are imitated in such a way as to make them appear ridiculous." For the purposes of copyright law, the nub of the definitions, and the heart of any parodist's claim to quote from existing material, is the use of some elements of a prior author's composition to create a new one that, at least in part, comments on that author's works. See, e. g., Fisher v. Dees, supra, at 437; MCA, Inc. v. Wilson, 677 F.2d 180, 185 (CA2 1981). If, on the contrary, the commentary has no critical bearing on the substance or style of the original composition, which the alleged infringer merely uses to get attention or to avoid the drudgery in working up something fresh, the claim to fairness in borrowing from another's work diminishes accordingly (if it does not vanish), and other factors, like the extent of its commerciality, loom larger. Parody needs to mimic an original to make its point, and so has some claim to use the creation of its victim's (or collective victims') imagination, whereas satire can stand on its own two feet and so requires justification for the very act of borrowing. See ibid.; Bisceglia, Parody and Copyright Protection: Turning the Balancing Act Into a Juggling Act, in ASCAP, Copyright Law Symposium, No. 34, p. 25 (1987).

The fact that parody can claim legitimacy for some appropriation does not, of course, tell either parodist or judge much about where to draw the line. Like a book review quoting the copyrighted material criticized, parody may or may not be fair use, and petitioners' suggestion that any parodic use is presumptively fair has no more justification in law or fact than the equally hopeful claim that any use for news reporting should be presumed fair, see Harper & Row, 471 U.S. at 561. The Act has no hint of an evidentiary preference for parodists over their victims, and no workable presumption for parody could take account of the fact that parody often shades into satire when society is lampooned through its creative artifacts, or that a work may contain both parodic and nonparodic elements. Accordingly, parody, like any other use, has to work its way through the relevant factors, and be judged case by case, in light of the ends of the copyright law.

Here, the District Court held, and the Court of Appeals assumed, that 2 Live Crew's "Pretty Woman" contains parody, commenting on and criticizing the original work, whatever it may have to say about society at large. As the District Court remarked, the words of 2 Live Crew's song copy the original's first line, but then "quickly degenerate into a play on words, substituting predictable lyrics with shocking ones . . . [that] derisively demonstrate how bland and banal the Orbison song seems to them." 754 F. Supp. at 1155 (footnote omitted). Judge Nelson, dissenting below, came to the same conclusion, that the 2 Live Crew song "was clearly intended to ridicule the white-bread original" and "reminds us that sexual congress with nameless streetwalkers is not necessarily the stuff of romance and is not necessarily without its consequences. The singers (there are several) have the same thing on their minds as did the lonely man with the nasal voice, but here there is no hint of wine and roses." 972 F.2d at 1442. Although the majority below had difficulty discerning any criticism of the original in 2 Live Crew's song, it assumed for purposes of its opinion that there was some. Id., at 1435-1436, and n.8.

We have less difficulty in finding that critical element in 2 Live Crew's song than the Court of Appeals did, although having found it we will not take the further step of evaluating its quality. The threshold question when fair use is raised in defense of parody is whether a parodic character may reasonably be perceived. Whether, going beyond that, parody is in good taste or bad does not and should not matter to fair use. As Justice Holmes explained, "it would be a dangerous undertaking for persons trained only to the law to constitute themselves final judges of the worth of [a work], outside of the narrowest and most obvious limits. At the one extreme some works of genius would be sure to miss appreciation. Their very novelty would make them repulsive until the public had learned the new language in which their author spoke." Bleistein v. Donaldson Lithographing Co., 188 U.S. 239, 251, 47 L. Ed. 460, 23 S. Ct. 298 (1903) (circus posters have copyright protection); cf. Yankee Publishing Inc. v. News America Publishing, Inc., 809 F. Supp. 267, 280 (SDNY 1992) (Leval, J.) ("First Amendment protections do not apply only to those who speak clearly, whose jokes are funny, and whose parodies succeed") (trademark case).

While we might not assign a high rank to the parodic element here, we think it fair to say that 2 Live Crew's song reasonably could be perceived as commenting on the original or criticizing it, to some degree. 2 Live Crew juxtaposes the romantic musings of a man whose fantasy comes true, with degrading taunts, a bawdy demand for sex, and a sigh of relief from paternal responsibility. The later words can be taken as a comment on the naivete of the original of an earlier day, as a rejection of its sentiment that ignores the ugliness of street life and the debasement that it signifies. It is this joinder of reference and ridicule that marks off the author's choice of parody from the other types of comment and criticism that traditionally have had a claim to fair use protection as transformative works.

The Court of Appeals, however, immediately cut short the enquiry into 2 Live Crew's fair use claim by confining its treatment of the first factor essentially to one relevant fact, the commercial nature of the use. The court then inflated the significance of this fact by applying a presumption ostensibly culled from Sony, that "every commercial use of copyrighted material is presumptively . . . unfair . . . ." Sony, 464 U.S. at 451. In giving virtually dispositive weight to the commercial nature of the parody, the Court of Appeals erred.

The language of the statute makes clear that the commercial or nonprofit educational purpose of a work is only one element of the first factor enquiry into its purpose and character. Section 107(1) uses the term "including" to begin the dependent clause referring to commercial use, and the main clause speaks of a broader investigation into "purpose and character." As we explained in Harper & Row, Congress resisted attempts to narrow the ambit of this traditional enquiry by adopting categories of presumptively fair use, and it urged courts to preserve the breadth of their traditionally ample view of the universe of relevant evidence. 471 U.S. at 561; House Report, p. 66. Accordingly, the mere fact that a use is educational and not for profit does not insulate it from a finding of infringement, any more than the commercial character of a use bars a finding of fairness. If, indeed, commerciality carried presumptive force against a finding of fairness, the presumption would swallow nearly all of the illustrative uses listed in the preamble paragraph of § 107, including news reporting, comment, criticism, teaching, scholarship, and research, since these activities "are generally conducted for profit in this country." Harper & Row, supra, at 592 (Brennan, J., dissenting). Congress could not have intended such a rule, which certainly is not inferable from the common-law cases, arising as they did from the world of letters in which Samuel Johnson could pronounce that "no man but a blockhead ever wrote, except for money." 3 Boswell's Life of Johnson 19 (G. Hill ed. 1934).

Sony itself called for no hard evidentiary presumption. There, we emphasized the need for a "sensitive balancing of interests," 464 U.S. at 455, n.40, noted that Congress had "eschewed a rigid, bright-line approach to fair use," id., at 449, n.31, and stated that the commercial or nonprofit educational character of a work is "not conclusive," id., at 448-449, but rather a fact to be "weighed along with other[s] in fair use decisions," id., at 449, n.32 (quoting House Report, p. 66). The Court of Appeals's elevation of one sentence from Sony to a per se rule thus runs as much counter to Sony itself as to the long common-law tradition of fair use adjudication. Rather, as we explained in Harper & Row, Sony stands for the proposition that the "fact that a publication was commercial as opposed to nonprofit is a separate factor that tends to weigh against a finding of fair use." 471 U.S. at 562. But that is all, and the fact that even the force of that tendency will vary with the context is a further reason against elevating commerciality to hard presumptive significance. The use, for example, of a copyrighted work to advertise a product, even in a parody, will be entitled to less indulgence under the first factor of the fair use enquiry than the sale of a parody for its own sake, let alone one performed a single time by students in school. See generally Patry & Perlmutter 679-680; Fisher v. Dees, 794 F.2d at 437; Maxtone-Graham v. Burtchaell, 803 F.2d 1253, 1262 (CA2 1986); Sega Enterprises Ltd. v. Accolade, Inc., 977 F.2d 1510, 1522 (CA9 1992).

B

The second statutory factor, "the nature of the copyrighted work," § 107(2), draws on Justice Story's expression, the "value of the materials used." Folsom v. Marsh, 9 F. Cas. at 348. This factor calls for recognition that some works are closer to the core of intended copyright protection than others, with the consequence that fair use is more difficult to establish when the former works are copied. See, e.g., Stewart v. Abend, 495 U.S. at 237-238 (contrasting fictional short story with factual works); Harper & Row, 471 U.S. at 563-564 (contrasting soon-to-be-published memoir with published speech); Sony, 464 U.S. at 455, n.40 (contrasting motion pictures with news broadcasts); Feist, 499 U.S. at 348-351 (contrasting creative works with bare factual compilations); 3 M. Nimmer & D. Nimmer, Nimmer on Copyright § 13.05[A][2] (1993) (hereinafter Nimmer); Leval 1116. We agree with both the District Court and the Court of Appeals that the Orbison original's creative expression for public dissemination falls within the core of the copyright's protective purposes. 754 F. Supp. at 1155-1156; 972 F.2d at 1437. This fact, however, is not much help in this case, or ever likely to help much in separating the fair use sheep from the infringing goats in a parody case, since parodies almost invariably copy publicly known, expressive works.

C

The third factor asks whether "the amount and substantiality of the portion used in relation to the copyrighted work as a whole," § 107(3) (or, in Justice Story's words, "the quantity and value of the materials used," Folsom v. Marsh, supra, at 348) are reasonable in relation to the purpose of the copying. Here, attention turns to the persuasiveness of a parodist's justification for the particular copying done, and the enquiry will harken back to the first of the statutory factors, for, as in prior cases, we recognize that the extent of permissible copying varies with the purpose and character of the use. See Sony, supra, at 449-450 (reproduction of entire work "does not have its ordinary effect of militating against a finding of fair use "as to home videotaping of television programs); Harper & Row, supra, at 564 ("Even substantial quotations might qualify as fair use in a review of a published work or a news account of a speech" but not in a scoop of a soon-to-be-published memoir). The facts bearing on this factor will also tend to address the fourth, by revealing the degree to which the parody may serve as a market substitute for the original or potentially licensed derivatives. See Leval 1123.

The District Court considered the song's parodic purpose in finding that 2 Live Crew had not helped themselves overmuch. 754 F. Supp. at 1156-1157. The Court of Appeals disagreed, stating that "while it may not be inappropriate to find that no more was taken than necessary, the copying was qualitatively substantial. . . . We conclude that taking the heart of the original and making it the heart of a new work was to purloin a substantial portion of the essence of the original." 972 F.2d at 1438.

The Court of Appeals is of course correct that this factor calls for thought not only about the quantity of the materials used, but about their quality and importance, too. In Harper & Row, for example, the Nation had taken only some 300 words out of President Ford's memoirs, but we signaled the significance of the quotations in finding them to amount to "the heart of the book," the part most likely to be news-worthy and important in licensing serialization. 471 U.S. at 564-566, 568 (internal quotation marks omitted). We also agree with the Court of Appeals that whether "a substantial portion of the infringing work was copied verbatim" from the copyrighted work is a relevant question, see id., at 565, for it may reveal a dearth of transformative character or purpose under the first factor, or a greater likelihood of market harm under the fourth; a work composed primarily of an original, particularly its heart, with little added or changed, is more likely to be a merely superseding use, fulfilling demand for the original.

Where we part company with the court below is in applying these guides to parody, and in particular to parody in the song before us. Parody presents a difficult case. Parody's humor, or in any event its comment, necessarily springs from recognizable allusion to its object through distorted imitation. Its art lies in the tension between a known original and its parodic twin. When parody takes aim at a particular original work, the parody must be able to "conjure up" at least enough of that original to make the object of its critical wit recognizable. See, e.g., Elsmere Music, 623 F.2d at 253, n.1; Fisher v. Dees, 794 F.2d at 438-439. What makes for this recognition is quotation of the original's most distinctive or memorable features, which the parodist can be sure the audience will know. Once enough has been taken to assure identification, how much more is reasonable will depend, say, on the extent to which the song's overriding purpose and character is to parody the original or, in contrast, the likelihood that the parody may serve as a market substitute for the original. But using some characteristic features cannot be avoided.

We think the Court of Appeals was insufficiently appreciative of parody's need for the recognizable sight or sound when it ruled 2 Live Crew's use unreasonable as a matter of law. It is true, of course, that 2 Live Crew copied the characteristic opening bass riff (or musical phrase) of the original, and true that the words of the first line copy the Orbison lyrics. But if quotation of the opening riff and the first line may be said to go to the "heart" of the original, the heart is also what most readily conjures up the song for parody, and it is the heart at which parody takes aim. Copying does not become excessive in relation to parodic purpose merely because the portion taken was the original's heart. If 2 Live Crew had copied a significantly less memorable part of the original, it is difficult to see how its parodic character would have come through. See Fisher v. Dees, supra, at 439.

This is not, of course, to say that anyone who calls himself a parodist can skim the cream and get away scot free. In parody, as in news reporting, see Harper & Row, supra, context is everything, and the question of fairness asks what else the parodist did besides go to the heart of the original. It is significant that 2 Live Crew not only copied the first line of the original, but thereafter departed markedly from the Orbison lyrics for its own ends. 2 Live Crew not only copied the bass riff and repeated it, but also produced otherwise distinctive sounds, interposing "scraper" noise, overlaying the music with solos in different keys, and altering the drum beat. See 754 F. Supp. at 1155. This is not a case, then, where "a substantial portion" of the parody itself is composed of a "verbatim" copying of the original. It is not, that is, a case where the parody is so insubstantial, as compared to the copying, that the third factor must be resolved as a matter of law against the parodists.

Suffice it to say here that, as to the lyrics, we think the Court of Appeals correctly suggested that "no more was taken than necessary," 972 F.2d at 1438, but just for that reason, we fail to see how the copying can be excessive in relation to its parodic purpose, even if the portion taken is the original's "heart."

As to the music, we express no opinion whether repetition of the bass riff is excessive copying, and we remand to permit evaluation of the amount taken, in light of the song's parodic purpose and character, its transformative elements, and considerations of the potential for market substitution sketched more fully below.

The fourth fair use factor is "the effect of the use upon the potential market for or value of the copyrighted work." § 107(4). It requires courts to consider not only the extent of market harm caused by the particular actions of the alleged infringer, but also "whether unrestricted and widespread conduct of the sort engaged in by the defendant . . . would result in a substantially adverse impact on the potential market" for the original. Nimmer § 13.05[A][4], p. 13-102.61 (footnote omitted); accord, Harper & Row, 471 U.S. at 569; Senate Report, p. 65; Folsom v. Marsh, 9 F. Cas. at 349. The enquiry "must take account not only of harm to the original but also of harm to the market for derivative works." Harper & Row, supra, at 568.

Since fair use is an affirmative defense, its proponent would have difficulty carrying the burden of demonstrating fair use without favorable evidence about relevant markets. In moving for summary judgment, 2 Live Crew left themselves at just such a disadvantage when they failed to address the effect on the market for rap derivatives, and confined themselves to uncontroverted submissions that there was no likely effect on the market for the original. They did not, however, thereby subject themselves to the evidentiary presumption applied by the Court of Appeals. In assessing the likelihood of significant market harm, the Court of Appeals quoted from language in Sony that "'if the intended use is for commercial gain, that likelihood may be presumed. But if it is for a noncommercial purpose, the likelihood must be demonstrated.'" 972 F.2d at 1438, quoting Sony, 464 U.S. at 451. The court reasoned that because "the use of the copyrighted work is wholly commercial, . . . we presume that a likelihood of future harm to Acuff-Rose exists." 972 F.2d at 1438. In so doing, the court resolved the fourth factor against 2 Live Crew, just as it had the first, by applying a presumption about the effect of commercial use, a presumption which as applied here we hold to be error.

No "presumption" or inference of market harm that might find support in Sony is applicable to a case involving something beyond mere duplication for commercial purposes. Sony's discussion of a presumption contrasts a context of verbatim copying of the original in its entirety for commercial purposes, with the noncommercial context of Sony itself (home copying of television programming). In the former circumstances, what Sony said simply makes common sense: when a commercial use amounts to mere duplication of the entirety of an original, it clearly "supersede[s] the objects," Folsom v. Marsh, supra, at 348, of the original and serves as a market replacement for it, making it likely that cognizable market harm to the original will occur. Sony, supra, at

451. But when, on the contrary, the second use is transformative, market substitution is at least less certain, and market harm may not be so readily inferred. Indeed, as to parody pure and simple, it is more likely that the new work will not affect the market for the original in a way cognizable under this factor, that is, by acting as a substitute for it ("superseding [its] objects"). See Leval 1125; Patry & Perlmutter 692, 697-698. This is so because the parody and the original usually serve different market functions. Bisceglia, ASCAP, Copyright Law Symposium, No. 34, at 23.

We do not, of course, suggest that a parody may not harm the market at all, but when a lethal parody, like a scathing theater review, kills demand for the original, it does not produce a harm cognizable under the Copyright Act. Because "parody may quite legitimately aim at garroting the original, destroying it commercially as well as artistically," B. Kaplan, An Unhurried View of Copyright 69 (1967), the role of the courts is to distinguish between "biting criticism [that merely] suppresses demand [and] copyright infringement[, which] usurps it. " Fisher v. Dees, 794 F.2d at 438.

This distinction between potentially remediable displacement and unremediable disparagement is reflected in the rule that there is no protectible derivative market for criticism. The market for potential derivative uses includes only those that creators of original works would in general develop or license others to develop. Yet the unlikelihood that creators of imaginative works will license critical reviews or lampoons of their own productions removes such uses from the very notion of a potential licensing market. "People ask . . . for criticism, but they only want praise." S. Maugham, Of Human Bondage 241 (Penguin ed. 1992). Thus, to the extent that the opinion below may be read to have considered harm to the market for parodies of "Oh, Pretty Woman," see 972 F.2d at 1439, the court erred. Accord, Fisher v. Dees, supra, at 437; Leval 1125; Patry & Perlmutter 688-691.

In explaining why the law recognizes no derivative market for critical works, including parody, we have, of course, been speaking of the later work as if it had nothing but a critical aspect (i.e., "parody pure and simple," supra, at 591). But the later work may have a more complex character, with effects not only in the arena of criticism but also in protectible markets for derivative works, too. In that sort of case, the law looks beyond the criticism to the other elements of the work, as it does here. 2 Live Crew's song comprises not only parody but also rap music, and the derivative market for rap music is a proper focus of enquiry, see Harper & Row, supra, at 568; Nimmer § 13.05B. Evidence of substantial harm to it would weigh against a finding of fair use, because the licensing of derivatives is an important economic incentive to the creation of originals. See 17 U.S.C. § 106(2) (copyright owner has rights to derivative works). Of course, the only harm to derivatives that need concern us, as discussed above, is the harm of market substitution. The fact that a parody may impair the market for derivative uses by the very effectiveness of its critical commentary is no more relevant under copyright than the like threat to the original market.

Although 2 Live Crew submitted uncontroverted affidavits on the question of market harm to the original, neither they, nor Acuff-Rose, introduced evidence or affidavits addressing the likely effect of 2 Live Crew's parodic rap song on the market for a nonparody, rap version of "Oh, Pretty Woman." And while Acuff-Rose would have us find evidence of a rap market in the very facts that 2 Live Crew recorded a rap parody of "Oh, Pretty Woman" and another rap group sought a license to record a rap derivative, there was no evidence that a potential rap market was harmed in any way by 2 Live Crew's parody, rap version. The fact that 2 Live Crew's parody sold as part of a collection of rap songs says very little about the parody's effect on a market for a rap version of the original, either of the music alone or of the music with its lyrics. The District Court essentially passed on this issue, observing that Acuff-Rose is free to record "whatever version of the original it desires," 754 F. Supp. at 1158; the Court of Appeals went the other way by erroneous presumption. Contrary to each treatment, it is impossible to deal with the fourth factor except by recognizing that a silent record on an important factor bearing on fair use disentitled the proponent of the defense, 2 Live Crew, to summary judgment. The evidentiary hole will doubtless be plugged on remand.

### III.

It was error for the Court of Appeals to conclude that the commercial nature of 2 Live Crew's parody of "Oh, Pretty Woman" rendered it presumptively unfair. No such evidentiary presumption is available to address either the first factor, the character and purpose of the use, or the fourth, market harm, in determining whether a transformative use, such as parody, is a fair one. The court also erred in holding that 2 Live Crew had necessarily copied excessively from the Orbison original, considering the parodic purpose of the use. We therefore reverse the judgment of the Court of Appeals and remand the case for further proceedings consistent with this opinion.

It is so ordered.

---

The decision of the U.S. Supreme Court in *Campbell v. Acuff-Ross Music*, 510 U.S. 569 (1994), allowed rappers to parody other compositions, even though the parody was for commercial purposes.

In the following case, *Papa's-June Music, Inc. v. McLean*, 924 F. Supp. 1154 (S.D.N.Y. 1996), the court held that an oral agreement was insufficient to transfer copyright ownership to defendant. Furthermore, the court dismissed plaintiff's fraud claim for failure to allege a fraud claim distinct from its breach of contract claim; however, the court granted plaintiff's permission to amend its complaint with respects to all of his claims except the fraud claim.

Papa's-June Music, Inc. v. McLean
United States District Court for the Southern District of New York
April 11, 1996, Dated; April 12, 1996, FILED
95 Civ. 5396 (MGC)
921 F. Supp. 1154

MEMORANDUM OPINION AND ORDER
CEDARBAUM, J.

This diversity action involves a dispute over control of the copyright in twelve songs on a record album entitled "She." Papa's-June Music, Inc., a Delaware corporation of which the performer Harry Connick, Jr. is the chief executive officer and principal shareholder, alleges that it had an oral contract providing for a seventy/thirty percent division of royalties and copyright ownership with Ramsey McLean, author of the lyrics. The alleged oral agreement also gave Papa's-June the exclusive right to exploit the songs. The complaint asserts claims for breach of contract, unjust enrichment, restitution, tortious interference with contract relations, declaratory judgment and fraud. McLean has moved to dismiss the claims other than fraud on the ground that section 204 of the Copyright Act, 17 U.S.C. § 204 (1988), bars enforcement of an oral agreement transferring rights of copyright ownership. McLean has also moved to dismiss the fraud claim on the ground that under New York law an allegation that a party to an agreement never intended to comply with the terms of the agreement does not state a claim for fraud. For the reasons that follow, the motion to dismiss is granted, and Papa's-June is granted leave to amend the complaint with respect to the claims other than fraud.

### Allegations of the First Amended Complaint

This dispute concerns twelve songs on an album called "She" that was publicly released in 1994. The complaint alleges that ownership of the copyright and division of royalties for these songs are governed by an agreement between the parties originally made in 1990.

In late 1989, Connick began to prepare an album entitled "We Are in Love." (First Am. Compl. P 9.) McLean sent him a folder of "poems." (Id.) Connick rewrote some of the words, composed the music, and recorded the songs between March and April 1990. (Id. P 10.) Five of the "jointly written" songs were ultimately selected for the "We Are in Love" album, which was released on June 4, 1990. (Id. PP 10, 13.) In April 1990, the parties entered into a Co-Publishing Agreement, under the terms of which Papa's-June and McLean own seventy and thirty percent, respectively, of the copyrights in the five "jointly written songs" on the "We Are in Love" album. (Id. P 11.) Royalties are divided according to the same percentages. (Id.) Papa's-June has the exclusive right to license and publicly perform the songs. (Id.) The "jointly written songs" on the "We Are in Love Album" are also subject to the controlled composition clause in Connick's contract with his record company, Sony. (Id.) That clause sets the royalty rate paid by Sony at seventy-five percent of the statutory rate applicable to compulsory licenses under the Copyright Act. (Id. P 3.)

In early 1991, McLean sent Connick a folder of "poems" for the "Blue Light, Red Light" album. (Id. P 14.) Connick rewrote some of the words, composed the music, and recorded the songs in June and July 1991. (Id.) Some of the "jointly written" songs were included on the "Blue Light, Red Light" album, which was released on September 3, 1991. (Id.) On January 12, 1992, McLean signed an amendment to the Co-Publishing Agreement, which stated that the "jointly written compositions" on the "Blue Light, Red Light" album would be governed by the terms of the original Co-Publishing Agreement. (Id. P 15.)

When Connick began planning the "She" album, McLean sent him a folder of "poems." (Id. P 16.) Connick rewrote some of the words, composed the music, and recorded the songs. (Id.) On May 24, 1994, the master disk was delivered to Sony for manufacture and distribution. (Id. P 17.) The "She" album was publicly released on July 12, 1994. (Id. P 19.) According to the complaint, Papa's-June believed that McLean had delivered the "poems" for the "She" album with the understanding that the songs based on these "poems" would be governed by the terms of the Co-Publishing Agreement. (Id. P 21.) On June 8, 1994, McLean notified Papa's-June that he wanted a different arrangement for the "jointly written songs" on the "She" album. (Id. P 18.) On July 15, 1994, Papa's-June sent McLean an amendment to the Co-Publishing Agreement that would have extended its terms to the songs on the "She" album. (Id. P 20.) McLean refused to sign the amendment. (Id.)

In early 1995, Papa's-June sent McLean two checks for his share of the royalties from the songs on the "She" album. (Id. P 22.) Unbeknownst to Papa's-June, McLean also received two royalty checks from Sony. (Id.) McLean cashed all four checks. (Id.) McLean refused to refund to Papa's-June the royalty amount in excess of his thirty percent share under the Co-Publishing Agreement, approximately $ 60,000. (Id.) McLean has represented to various performance rights organizations around the world that he owns fifty percent of the copyright in the songs on the "She" album, is entitled to fifty percent of the royalties, and has an equal right to license the songs. (Id. P 24.)

## Discussion

On a motion to dismiss the complaint pursuant to Fed. R. Civ. P. 12(b)(6), the factual allegations of the complaint are accepted as true, Leatherman v. Tarrant County Narcotics Intelligence & Coordination Unit, 507 U.S. 163, 113 S. Ct. 1160, 1161, 122 L. Ed. 2d 517, 522 (1993), and all reasonable inferences are drawn in favor of the plaintiff, Bolt Elec., Inc. v. City of New York, 53 F.3d 465, 469 (2d Cir. 1995). A motion to dismiss should be granted only if it appears beyond doubt that the plaintiff can prove no set of facts that would entitle it to relief. Id.

### I. Claims Other Than Fraud

The complaint alleges that the songs on the "She" album were "jointly written" by Connick and McLean. (Id. PP 1, 18.) McLean argues that since he is a joint author of the songs on the "She" album, he is entitled to an undivided one-half interest in the joint works. Section 204 of the Copyright Act requires a signed writing to effect a transfer of copyright ownership. McLean argues that since there has been no such writing with regard to the songs on the "She" album, he retains all his rights as a joint author of those songs, including the right to license them. Papa's-June argues that even though the complaint alleges that the songs on the "She" album are "jointly written," they are derivative works based on McLean's "poems," and that no writing is required for what is effectively a non-exclusive license agreement between Papa's-June and McLean for the use of McLean's poems. Alternatively, Papa's-June argues that even if the songs on the "She" album are joint works, no writing is required because the writing requirement of the Copyright Act does not apply to transfers between joint authors. Papa's-June also contends that there are writings that satisfy the requirements of the Copyright Act.

The Copyright Act defines a "joint work" as a work prepared by two or more authors with the intention that their contributions be merged into inseparable or interdependent parts of a unitary whole. 17 U.S.C. § 101 (1988 & Supp. 1993). The parts of a work are "interdependent" when they have some meaning standing alone but achieve their primary significance because of their combined effect, as in the case of the words and music of a song. See Childress v. Taylor, 945 F.2d 500, 505 (2d Cir. 1991); H.R. Rep. No. 1476, 94th Cong., 2d Sess. 120 (1976), reprinted in 1976 U.S.C.C.A.N. 5659, 5736 (citing words and music of a song as example of interdependent parts of a joint work); S. Rep. No. 473, 94th Cong., 1st Sess. 103-04 (1975) (same). The requisite intent to create a joint work exists when the putative joint authors intend to regard themselves as joint authors. Childress, 945 F.2d at 507-08. It is not enough that they intend to merge their contributions into one unitary work. Id. at 507.

The complaint alleges that McLean sent Connick "poems" and that Connick rewrote some of the words to make them singable. (First Am. Compl. P 16.) From this, Papa's-June argues that McLean did not intend that his "poems" would be used as lyrics when he created them, and could not have intended that he and Connick would be joint authors of the songs on the "She" album. However, the complaint also alleges that the songs on the "She" album were "jointly written" by Connick and McLean. (First Am. Compl. PP 1, 18.) Indeed, the complaint alleges that McLean and Connick had "jointly written" songs for Connick's previous albums as well. (Id. PP 10-12, 14-15.) Papa's-June's after-the-fact argument that McLean only contributed "poems" is inconsistent with the allegations of the complaint taken as a whole.

A "transfer of copyright ownership" is defined by the Copyright Act as "an assignment, . . ., or any other conveyance, . . . of a copyright or of any of the exclusive rights comprised in a copyright." 17 U.S.C. § 101. The Copyright Act presumes that the authors of a joint work are each entitled to an equal undivided interest in the copyright. See 17 U.S.C. § 201(a) (1988); Childress, 945 F.2d at 508. Each joint author also has an independent right to use or license the joint work. See Community for Creative Non-Violence v. Reid, 270 U.S. App. D.C. 26, 846 F.2d 1485, 1498 (D.C. Cir. 1988), aff'd, 490 U.S. 730, 104 L. Ed. 2d 811, 109 S. Ct. 2166 (1989); cf. 17 U.S.C. § 106 (1988 & Supp. 1993) (copyright owner has the exclusive right to authorize reproductions, performances, displays, derivative works and distribution of copies of the copyrighted work). An agreement that alters these presumptions effects a "transfer of copyright ownership" between the joint authors. Under the terms of the Co-Publishing Agreement, instead of each joint author owning an equal undivided interest in the copyrights in the songs on the "She" album, Papa's-June owns seventy percent of the copyrights and McLean owns thirty percent. Instead of each author having an independent right to license or publicly perform the joint works, the Co-Publishing Agreement gives these rights exclusively to Papa's-June. Therefore, the complaint alleges a "transfer of copyright ownership" between McLean and Papa's-June.

Section 204(a) of the Copyright Act provides that a "transfer of copyright ownership, . . ., is not valid unless an instrument of conveyance, or a note or memorandum of the transfer, is in writing and signed by the owner of the rights conveyed or such owner's duly authorized agent." 17 U.S.C. § 204(a). Papa's-June argues that section 204(a) does not apply to transfers between the authors of a joint work. The starting point for interpretation of a statute is always its language. Community for Creative Non-Violence, 490 U.S. at 739, 104 L. Ed. 2d at 824. The only explicit exemption in section 204 is for transfers of copyright that occur by operation of law. Section 204 does not contain language exempting copyright transfers between joint authors. The Copyright Act treats the authors of a joint work as co-owners of the copyright. 17 U.S.C. § 201(a).

Papa's-June has not presented any authority that transfers of copyright ownership between co-owners who are not joint authors are exempt from the requirements of section 204(a). And there is nothing in the language of the Copyright Act which suggests that transfers between co-owners who are joint authors should be treated differently.

Papa's-June argues that section 204(a) was designed to protect authors from unscrupulous third parties, not from their joint authors. In support of this position, it cites Eden Toys, Inc. v. Florelee Undergarment Co., 697 F.2d 27 (2d Cir. 1982). Papa's-June reads Eden Toys too narrowly. The issue there was whether Eden Toys had standing to sue based on an exclusive license that was initially embodied in an oral agreement but was later formalized in a written agreement. Id. at 36. In holding that the later writing could satisfy the requirements of the Copyright Act, the Second Circuit also noted that the purpose of section 204(a) was "to protect copyright holders from persons mistakenly or fraudulently claiming oral licenses." Id.; see also Effects Associates, Inc. v. Cohen, 908 F.2d 555, 557 (9th Cir. 1990) (section 204 ensures that creator will not inadvertently give away his copyright and forces party who wants to use copyright to negotiate with the creator to determine precisely what rights are being transferred and at what price), cert. denied, 498 U.S. 1103, 112 L. Ed. 2d 1086, 111 S. Ct. 1003 (1991). Although Eden Toys addressed a transfer of copyright ownership between parties that were not joint authors, the reasoning is just as applicable to transfers between joint authors. An author can mistakenly or fraudulently claim an oral transfer of copyright ownership from his joint author. If joint authors are forced to put their agreement into writing, there is less opportunity for fraud or mistake. Moreover, if an agreement to alter the statutory presumptions of equal ownership and equal right to license and perform the joint work is put into writing, the joint authors will have less need to resort to the courts to resolve disputes about the terms of their mutual understanding. See Effects Associates, 908 F.2d at 557. I therefore hold that the writing requirement of section 204(a) is applicable to transfers between joint authors.

Section 204(a) does not mandate a particular form of transfer document. As Judge Kozinski has noted, a writing memorializing the assignment of copyright interests "doesn't have to be the Magna Carta; a one-line pro forma statement will do." Id. However, the terms of any writing purporting to transfer copyright interests, even a one-line pro forma statement, must be clear. See Playboy Enterprises, Inc. v. Dumas, 831 F. Supp. 295, 308 (S.D.N.Y. 1993), aff'd in part and rev'd in part on other grounds, 53 F.3d 549 (2d Cir. 1995). While it is not required that the writing explicitly mention "copyright" or "exclusive rights," see Schiller & Schmidt, Inc. v. Nordisco Corp., 969 F.2d 410, 413 (7th Cir. 1992), the better practice is that it should, 1 William F. Patry, Copyright Law and Practice at 390; cf. Playboy Enterprises, 53 F.3d at 564 (writing that did not expressly mention copyright failed to meet requirements of section 204(a)). And, of course, the owner of the copyright interests being conveyed must sign the document. 17 U.S.C. § 204(a).

The complaint alleges that in early 1995 McLean cashed two royalty checks from Papa's-June for the jointly written songs on the "She" album. (First Am. Compl. P 22.) Papa's-June has supplemented the allegations of the complaint with an affidavit which states that royalty statements attached to the checks indicated that McLean's share of the royalties for the songs on the "She" album was thirty percent. (Wilkins Aff. P 13, Exh. 1 & 2.) Papa's-June argues that by endorsing the checks McLean agreed that the terms of the Co-Publishing Agreement would govern the jointly written songs on the "She" album.

Papa's-June cites Dean v. Burrows, 732 F. Supp. 816 (E.D. Tenn. 1989) for the proposition that endorsed checks satisfy the writing required by section 204(a). In Dean, a critical issue was the date on which the creator of a mold design for a ceramic animal figurine had transferred his copyright interests. Both the creator and the purchaser testified that the transfer occurred in March 1984 and that the creator had prepared a written transfer agreement in March 1984. Id. at 823. However, the agreement was not dated and was not signed or notarized until well over a year later, on November 8, 1985, a delay the court attributed to the purchaser's lack of legal advice on the technicalities of copyright law. Id. at 818-19, 823. The court held that a check dated March 10, 1984, with the notation that it was payment for "mold designs and molds," endorsed by the creator, negotiated, posted and cancelled in March 1984, complied with the requirements of section 204(a). Id. at 823.

The decision in Dean was influenced by two factors, neither of which are present here. First, there was substantial uncontroverted evidence of an agreement to transfer copyright ownership when the check was endorsed by the creator. Both parties to the transfer testified that such an agreement existed. They also testified that the transferor had prepared contemporaneously with the transfer and negotiation of the check an unsigned writing which memorialized the terms of the agreement. By contrast, when Papa's-June sent McLean the royalty checks in early 1995, it had known since June 8, 1994 that McLean wanted a different arrangement for the jointly written songs on the "She" album. (First Am. Compl. P 18.) Furthermore, in July 1994 McLean rejected Papa's-June's proposed amendment to the Co-Publishing Agreement and reasserted his demand for a new arrangement. (Id. P 20.) In sum, the complaint alleges that there was sharp disagreement between Papa's-June and McLean at the time McLean endorsed the royalty checks. The unsigned agreement in Dean was prepared by the transferor, not the transferee. In this case, the royalty statements, which McLean never signed, were prepared by the transferee, Papa's-June, and not by McLean, the transferor.

Second, there was writing on the check in Dean which indicated, however inarticulately, that copyright ownership was being transferred. In this case, neither the royalty checks nor the attached royalty statements mention a transfer of copyright ownership. There is a notation at the bottom of the second page of the royalty statements — "@ 30%" — underneath the totals for the songs from the "She" album. Papa's-June argues that this notation on the attached royalty statements put McLean on notice that by endorsing the royalty checks he was agreeing to all the terms of the Co-Publishing Agreement, an eleven-page document (not including schedules) that covers among other things ownership, licensing and performance rights. In light of the disagreement between Papa's-June and McLean at the time McLean endorsed the checks, the notations on the royalty statements indicate nothing more than the fact that the royalty checks are for an amount equal to thirty percent of the total royalties for the jointly written songs on the "She" album. Cf. 1 Patry, supra, at 392 (transfer agreements should be construed in favor of copyright transferor because section 204(a) reflects the policy judgment that copyright owners should retain all rights unless specifically transferred).

Papa's-June's claims for breach of contract, quasi-contract, restitution, declaratory judgment and tortious interference with contractual relations are all premised on the allegation that the terms of the Co-Publishing Agreement govern the jointly written songs on the "She" album. Because the complaint does not allege a signed writing as required by section 204(a), there was no transfer of copyright ownership between Papa's-June and McLean, and the jointly written songs on the "She" album are not governed by the terms of the Co-Publishing Agreement. Papa's-June and McLean each have an equal undivided interest in the copyright in these songs and an independent right to license and perform them. Therefore, McLean's motion to dismiss the non-fraud claims for failure to state a claim is granted.

Papa's-June also argues that the alleged agreement with McLean affects only the division of royalties, not McLean's copyright interests in the jointly written songs on the "She" album. This argument is not consistent with the allegations of the complaint. The complaint alleges that the songs on the "She" album are governed by all the terms of the Co-Publishing Agreement, including the provisions regarding ownership of the copyright and the right to perform and license the songs. (First Am. Compl. PP 3, 26, 43-44.) However, an agreement concerning royalties does not constitute a "transfer of copyright ownership" within the meaning of 17 U.S.C. § 101. To the extent that Papa's-June has a good-faith basis upon which to allege that there was an agreement concerning the collection and distribution of royalties for the songs on the "She" album, it may so amend the complaint within the next thirty days.

## II. Fraud Claim

The complaint alleges that when McLean submitted his lyrics to Connick, McLean never intended that the jointly written songs on the "She" album would be governed by the terms of the Co-Publishing Agreement. (First Am. Compl. P 55.) McLean, however, knew that Connick and Papa's-June believed that the songs on the "She" album would be governed by the terms of the Co-Publishing Agreement. (Id. P 58.) According to the complaint, by not disclosing his secret intention to seek a different arrangement for the songs on the "She" album, McLean fraudulently induced Connick to use his lyrics. (Id. P 60.) The issue is whether McLean can be held separately accountable on a claim of fraud for failure to disclose his intention not to perform in accordance with the Co-Publishing Agreement.

In Sabo v. Delman, 3 N.Y.2d 155, 160, 164 N.Y.S.2d 714, 716, 143 N.E.2d 906 (1957), the New York Court of Appeals held that a promise made with the undisclosed intention of not performing constitutes a misrepresentation of a material fact upon which an action for rescission may be predicated. See also Channel Master Corp. v. Aluminium Ltd. Sales, Inc., 4 N.Y.2d 403, 408, 176 N.Y.S.2d 259, 263, 151 N.E.2d 833 (1958) (one who fraudulently misrepresents himself as intending to perform an agreement is liable regardless of whether the agreement is enforceable). It is important to note that the allegedly fraudulent representations at issue in Sabo were not contained in the contracts between the parties. They were alleged to be express representations made to induce contracts for assignment of patents. 3 N.Y.2d at 158-59, 164 N.Y.S.2d at 715-16.

Most courts that have subsequently considered the issue have held that a contract claim cannot be converted into a fraud claim by the addition of an allegation that the promisor intended not to perform when he made the promise. E.g., Caniglia v. Chicago Tribune-New York News Syndicate, Inc., 204 A.D.2d 233, 234, 612 N.Y.S.2d 146, 147 (App. Div. 1st Dep't 1994); Guterman v. RGA Accessories, Inc., 196 A.D.2d 785, 786, 602 N.Y.S.2d 116, 117 (App. Div. 1st Dep't 1993); Gordon v. Dino De Laurentiis Corp., 141 A.D.2d 435, 436, 529 N.Y.S.2d 777, 779 (App. Div. 1st Dep't 1988); Comtomark, Inc. v. Satellite Communications Network, Inc., 116 A.D.2d 499, 500, 497 N.Y.S.2d 371, 372 (App. Div. 1st Dep't 1986); Spellman v. Columbia Manicure Mfg. Co., 111 A.D.2d 320, 323, 489 N.Y.S.2d 304, 307 (App. Div. 2d Dep't 1985); L. Fatato, Inc. v. Decrescente Distrib. Co., 86 A.D.2d 600, 601, 446 N.Y.S.2d 120, 121-22 (App. Div. 2d Dep't 1982); Chase v. United Hospital, 60 A.D.2d 558, 559, 400 N.Y.S.2d 343, 344 (App. Div. 1st Dep't 1977); Wegman v. Dairylea Coop., Inc. 50 A.D.2d 108, 113, 376 N.Y.S.2d 728, 734-35 (App. Div. 4th Dep't 1975); Miller v. Volk & Huxley, Inc., 44 A.D.2d 810, 810, 355 N.Y.S.2d 605, 606-07 (App. Div. 1st Dep't 1974); PI, Inc. v. Quality Prods., Inc., 907 F. Supp. 752, 761 (S.D.N.Y. 1995); Sudul v. Computer Outsourcing Servs., 868 F. Supp. 59, 62 (S.D.N.Y. 1994); Best

Western Int'l, Inc. v. CSI Int'l Corp., 1994 U.S. Dist. LEXIS 11815, *12, 1994 WL 465905, at *4 (S.D.N.Y. Aug. 23, 1994); cf. New York University v. Continental Ins. Co., 87 N.Y.2d 308, 1995 N.Y. LEXIS 4752, *11, 1995 WL 761955, at *3 (N.Y. Dec. 27, 1995) (general allegations that defendant entered into a contract while lacking the intent to perform it are insufficient to support claim for fraud). Contra Bibeau v. Ward, 193 A.D.2d 875, 877, 596 N.Y.S.2d 948, 950 (App. Div. 3rd Dep't 1993); Stewart v. Jackson & Nash, 976 F.2d 86, 89 (2d Cir. 1992); Bower v. Weisman, 650 F. Supp. 1415, 1423 (S.D.N.Y. 1986).

To maintain a claim for fraud, a plaintiff must allege: (1) a legal duty separate and apart from the contractual duty to perform, see Van Neil v. Berger, 632 N.Y.S.2d 48, 48 (App. Div. 4th Dep't 1995); Strasser v. Prudential Sec., Inc., 630 N.Y.S.2d 80, 82 (App. Div. 1st Dep't 1995); Locascio v. Aquavella, 185 A.D.2d 689, 690, 586 N.Y.S.2d 78, 79 (App. Div. 4th Dep't 1992); Mastropieri v. Solmar Constr. Co., 159 A.D.2d 698, 700, 553 N.Y.S.2d 187, 189 (App. Div. 2d Dep't 1990); Tesoro Petroleum Corp. v. Holborn Oil Co., 108 A.D.2d 607, 607, 484 N.Y.S.2d 834, 835 (App. Div. 1st Dep't 1985); Sudul, 868 F. Supp. at 63; Best Western Int'l, Inc., 1994 U.S. Dist. LEXIS 11815, *15, 1994 WL 465905, at *4-5; G.D. Searle & Co. v. Medicore Communications, Inc., 843 F. Supp. 895, 909 (S.D.N.Y. 1994); (2) a fraudulent representation collateral or extraneous to the contract, see Deerfield Communications Corp. v. Chesebrough-Ponds, Inc., 68 N.Y.2d 954, 956, 510 N.Y.S.2d 88, 89, 502 N.E.2d 1003 (1986); Sforza v. Health Ins. Plan of Greater New York, Inc., 210 A.D.2d 214, 214-15, 619 N.Y.S.2d 734, 736 (App. Div. 2d Dep't 1994); McKernin v. Fanny Farmer Candy Shops, Inc., 176 A.D.2d 233, 234, 574 N.Y.S.2d 58, 59 (App. Div. 2d Dep't 1991); Wallace v. Crisman, 173 A.D.2d 322, 322, 573 N.Y.S.2d 654, 654 (App. Div. 1st Dep't 1991); Metropolitan Transp. Auth. v. Triumph Advertising Prods., Inc., 116 A.D.2d 526, 527, 497 N.Y.S.2d 673, 675 (App. Div. 1st Dep't 1986); PI, Inc., 907 F. Supp. at 761; Sudul, 868 F. Supp. at 63; or (3) special damages proximately caused by the fraudulent representation that are not recoverable under the contract measure of damages, see Deerfield Communications, 68 N.Y.2d at 956, 510 N.Y.S.2d at 89-90; Wallace, 173 A.D.2d at 322, 573 N.Y.S.2d at 654; Tuck Indus. v. Reichhold Chems., Inc., 151 A.D.2d 565, 566, 542 N.Y.S.2d 701, 702 (App. Div. 2d Dep't 1989); Metropolitan Transp. Auth., 116 A.D.2d at 527-28, 497 N.Y.S.2d at 675; Tesoro, 108 A.D.2d at 607, 484 N.Y.S.2d at 835; Lehman v. Dow Jones & Co., 783 F.2d 285, 296 (2d Cir. 1986); Sudul, 868 F. Supp. at 63; Best Western Int'l, Inc., 1994 U.S. Dist. LEXIS 11815, *15, 1994 WL 465905, at *5; Landgarten v. Noise Cancellation Technologies, 1993 U.S. Dist. LEXIS 11088, 1993 WL 312999 at *3 (S.D.N.Y. Aug. 11, 1993).

The recent decision of the New York Court of Appeals in Graubard Mollen Dannett & Horowitz v. Moskovitz, 86 N.Y.2d 112, 629 N.Y.S.2d 1009, 653 N.E.2d 1179 (1995), does not change the law in this area. Graubard was a suit by a law firm against a former partner who, it was alleged, breached his fiduciary duty and his retirement contract when he persuaded a major client to leave the firm with him. The firm also asserted a claim for fraud based on oral promises made by the former partner at the time the retirement agreement was presented to the partnership for its approval, promises which the former partner never intended to honor. Although the Court of Appeals concluded that the law firm had stated a viable fraud claim, it also held that apart from the contract, the former partner owed his firm a fiduciary duty not to solicit clients of the firm prior to his resignation. Id. at 119, 629 N.Y.S.2d at 1013. Moreover, the oral representations that were the basis of the fraud claim were collateral to the provisions of the retirement agreement. Id. at 116, 629 N.Y.S.2d at 1011. Thus, Graubard is consistent with the lower court decisions cited above.

The complaint does not allege a fraud claim that is sufficiently distinct from the breach of contract claim. It merely appends allegations about McLean's state of mind to the claim for breach of contract. There is no allegation that McLean owed Connick or Papa's-June a duty separate and apart from the alleged obligations under the Co-Publishing Agreement. Papa's-June does not allege that McLean's fraudulent representations were collateral to the Co-Publishing Agreement. Nor does Papa's-June seek special damages attributable to the fraud that are not recoverable under the contract claim. Because the only fraud alleged arises out of the same facts that serve as the basis for the breach of contract claim, Papa's-June's fraud claim fails to state a claim for fraud on which relief can be granted. Locascio, 185 A.D.2d at 690, 586 N.Y.S.2d at 79. The fact that Papa's-June's non-fraud claims are barred by the writing requirements of the Copyright Act does not change this conclusion. See Gutterman, 196 A.D.2d at 785-86, 602 N.Y.S.2d at 117 (dismissing fraud claim where breach of contract claim is barred by Statute of Frauds); McKernin, 176 A.D.2d at 234, 574 N.Y.S.2d at 59-60 (same); Chase, 60 A.D.2d at 559, 400 N.Y.S.2d at 344 (same). Therefore, McLean's motion to dismiss the fraud claim pursuant to Fed. R. Civ. P. 12(b)(6) is granted.

## Conclusion

For the foregoing reasons, McLean's motion to dismiss the complaint in its entirety is granted. Papa's-June is granted leave to file an amended complaint within thirty days alleging claims other than fraud to the extent that it has a good-faith basis upon which to allege that there was an enforceable agreement concerning the collection and distribution of royalties for the jointly written songs on the "She" album.

SO ORDERED.

———————

Papa's-June Music, Inc. was allowed 30-days to amend its complaint (except for the fraud claim), to the extent that it had a good-faith basis upon which to allege that there was an enforceable agreement concerning the collection and distribution of royalties for the jointly written songs on the "She" album.

In the following case, *Marcy Playground, Inc. v. Capitol Records*, 6 F. Supp. 2d 277 (S.D.N.Y 1998), plaintiff producers moved for a preliminary injunction seeking to enjoin the continued distribution of an album and single recording, alleging that the records were released without the designation of proper credit for plaintiffs' contributions as producers.

Marcy Playground, Inc. v. Capitol Records
United States District Court for the Southern District of New York
July 13, 1998, Decided; July 14, 1998, Filed
98 Civ. 2853 (LAK)
6 F. Supp. 2d 277

MEMORANDUM OPINION
LEWIS A. KAPLAN, District Judge.

Plaintiffs here seek to enjoin the continued distribution of the hit album entitled Marcy Playground and the "single" entitled Sex and Candy on the theory that these recordings have been released without crediting the plaintiffs for their alleged contributions as producers and therefore violate the Lanham Act and plaintiffs' contractual rights. The Court concludes that plaintiffs have failed to show the necessary threat of immediate and irreparable injury both because they delayed too long in seeking interlocutory relief and because the alleged irreparable injury is speculative. In any case, plaintiffs have not shown a strong likelihood of success on the merits because the facts critical to determination of the action are sharply disputed and have failed to demonstrate that the balance of hardships tips decidedly in their favor. Accordingly, the motion for a preliminary injunction is denied.

## Facts
## Background

Plaintiff Jared Kotler and defendant John Wozniak meet as high school classmates and budding musicians in the mid-1980's. Both aspired to careers in the music business. Their paths diverged, but they resumed contact in or about 1993 or 1994. Although the details of Kotler's right to have done so are hotly disputed, Kotler obtained a "demo" recording which included, perhaps among other things, certain of Wozniak's compositions, and submitted it to EMI-America, then a significant record company. While this did not result in a deal, Don Rubin of EMI expressed interest in considering additional material, although the parties disagree as to whether the additional material in which he was interested consisted only of Wozniak's music or of the joint efforts of Wozniak and Kotler.

In 1995, Wozniak moved to New York. He and Kotler began playing together on an almost daily basis, Wozniak on guitar and Kotler on drums. According to Kotler, they agreed that the pair would perform and record together as a two-member musical group known as "Marcy Playground," that

Kotler would be the producer of the project, and that Jeff White, Kotler's cousin and the financier of their efforts, would be the executive producer. Wozniak, on the other hand, contends that he coined and began using the name "Marcy Playground" years before, although he does not directly dispute the other aspects of Kotler's account of this phase of their endeavors.

Whatever the precise arrangements among Kotler, White and Wozniak, the group, assisted by studio musicians, participated in a significant recording session in the spring of 1995 at Sabella Recording Studios in Roslyn, New York. The session was financed by White. The group recorded 13 to 15 compositions by Wozniak, with Wozniak on guitar and Kotler on drums, although the parties are at loggerheads concerning who "produced" the recording.

### The EMI Deal and the Formation of Marcy Playground, Inc.

The product of the Sabella Recording session was another "demo" which was submitted to EMI. This led to a live audition on May 31, 1995 at which EMI executives expressed an intention to sign a record deal with Marcy Playground, which of course then included Kotler as its drummer. Wozniak, to be sure, contends that he was the "key artist" whose presence was the real attraction to EMI.

Although success appears to have been on the horizon, Wozniak contends that it had become increasingly clear to him by mid-1995 that Marcy Playground was being harmed because Kotler's skills as a drummer were not at a professional level. Although it is unclear whether there a connection with Wozniak's claimed dissatisfaction with Kotler's drumming, he and Kotler recruited Dylan Keefe, a bass guitarist, and Keefe began playing with them over the summer of 1995.

At about this time, White suggested that the group retain a music industry lawyer in connection with the EMI recording deal, and the trio — White, Kotler and Wozniak-retained Fred Davis for that purpose. Marcy Playground, Inc. ("MPI"), the corporate plaintiff was formed, with Kotler and Wozniak each allegedly owning 45 percent of the shares and White the balance, to exploit the products of the group — although Wozniak claims that he was neither consulted nor advised concerning the implications of this step and asserts that Davis had a conflict of interest in representing all three in this connection.

On October 27, 1995, MPI entered into a recording contract, signed on its behalf by Wozniak, with EMI pursuant to which it granted EMI the exclusive recording artist services of Wozniak and Kotler performing as Marcy Playground. The contract was accompanied by a so-called Inducement Letter in which MPI represented and agreed that it possessed the exclusive right to the services of Wozniak and Kotler as recording artists and that it was the sole owner of their product to date including what the parties have referred to as the Original

Marcy Playground Recordings. The Original Marcy Playground Recordings were intended as the source of the first two albums of the three album EMI deal.

### The Emergence of the Dispute

On the heels of the signing of the EMI deal, Wozniak and Kotler fell out. Keefe began to accompany the group's live performances, allegedly over Kotler's objection. According to Wozniak, EMI executives and other music industry professionals expressed concern that Kotler's allegedly poor drum performances were hurting the group. Wozniak and Keefe persuaded Kotler to play second guitar behind Wozniak and to permit Wozniak's friend, Dan Rieser, to play the drums. Tension was in the air.

By the spring of 1996, EMI had not released the first album contemplated by the recording agreement, which came to be known as Marcy Playground. It was at about this point, Kotler claims, that a senior EMI executive threatened to withhold release of ,the album unless Kotler agreed to stop performing as a member of Marcy Playground. In any case, it is undisputed that Kotler stopped performing with Marcy Playground at about this point.

Wozniak contends that the absence of any final agreement among himself, Kotler and White at the time of Kotler's departure from the group threatened to delay or prevent release of the first album and that EMI executives assisted in settlement discussions among the combatants. Kotler requested, among other things, that he be credited on the album as co-producer and that a Kotler/White production company logo be included on the outer packaging, both to further their alleged ambitions as record producers. Wozniak, allegedly "in an effort to defuse a volatile, painful situation and because [he] believed a settlement was close," agreed. The album was released in February 1997 with the credits Kotler had requested. The anticipated settlement among White, Kotler and Wozniak thereupon failed to materialize.

Marcy Playground was not an immediate success, achieving only insignificant sales in the first weeks following its release. In the meantime, EMI ceased record operations in April-May 1997. Some time later, its affiliate, defendant Capitol Records, Inc. ("Capitol") assumed the MPI recording agreement and decided to reissue Marcy Playground. According to Kotler, Wozniak, his agent and Capitol insisted that he and White agree to the previously rejected settlement proposal as a condition for giving Kotler and the Kotler/White entity (Mighty Slim Productions) the same credit on the reissued album as on the original. Wozniak and his agent rejoin that they decided to eliminate the producer credits previously given to Kotler, White and their company because those credits never reflected the reality of what had occurred and were given only as a gratuitous gesture in anticipation of a settlement that never was consummated. Capitol, for its part, says that it was aware of conflicting claims as to who had produced what, that it had no way to determine the truth, and that it therefore acted in conformity to the alleged custom of the industry by accepting the information provided by the band's manager, who at that point of course was Wozniak's creature.

Marcy Playground was reissued on September 25, 1997 and has become a substantial success. Approximately 1.5 million copies have been sold, and the album remains number 54 on the relevant Billboard magazine chart. An undetermined number remains in Capitol's inventory.

It should be noted also that Capitol on March 12, 1998 released the first "single" from Marcy Playground, which is entitled Sex and Candy and actually includes three songs only one of which is also on Marcy Playground. Sex and Candy, however, was deleted from Capitol's catalog on April 4, 1998, and there are no plans for any additional printings.

### Post-Reissue Settlement Discussions and this Litigation

There were sporadic efforts to resolve the dispute between Wozniak and Kotler from the time of Marcy Playground's initial release in March 1997 through its reissuance in late September 1997 punctuated by the expected exchange of "pleasantries" when Kotler learned that the credits would be revised for the reissued album. By the time of the reissuance, the parties had set forth their positions and retreated in silence to their respective corners. As indicated above, however, the reissued album rapidly achieved great success. On November 20, 1997, plaintiff's counsel contacted Capitol and raised the issue of settlement once again. This appears to have resulted in a reopening of talks on December 1, 1997.

The parties understandably have lavished a great deal of attention on their respective accounts of the discussions that ensued in the December 1997 to March 1998 period. Both are mindful of the adverse impact of unexplained or unjustified delay on a movant's prospects for preliminary injunctive relief. The defendants seek to portray the communications between the parties during this period as only remotely connected to settlement and, in any case, characterized by long and unexplained delays on the plaintiffs' part so as to charge plaintiffs with undue delay in making this motion. The plaintiffs, on the other hand, claim that negotiations "were continuous, bilateral, progressive and fruitful" and seek to tax the defendants with responsibility for any delays that did occur.

Resolution of this dispute appears quite likely impossible absent a substantial evidentiary hearing. Even on plaintiffs' version, however, "the parties' settlement negotiations . . . came to abrupt, unexpected and rather shocking closure in mid-March . . ." Hence, plaintiffs waited approximately five weeks before filing this action on April 22, 1998 and almost three months after the cessation of talks before seeking a preliminary injunction.

## Discussion

The Court is met at the outset with a dispute as to the applicable standard for issuance of a preliminary injunction in this case. Defendants argue that the injunction plaintiffs seek — which would restrain inter alia any further distribution or sale of Marcy Playground or Sex and Candy — effectively would force a product recall and alter that status quo and therefore must be considered against the standard applicable to mandatory preliminary injunctions. In their reply papers, plaintiffs disavow any request for a product recall, indicating that they would be quite content with a restraint on any further sale or distribution at Capitol's level. Plaintiffs' concession thus eliminates one of the props supporting defendants' argument that the injunction sought is mandatory in character, but ignores the fact that they seek to alter the status quo.

An injunction that is prohibitory to one person often will seem mandatory to another, and the distinction does not necessarily determine which standard applies to the application. As the plaintiffs are not entitled to relief even under the most relaxed standard, however, there is no need to explore this interesting issue.

Under the usual standard, the movant, in order to obtain a preliminary injunction, must demonstrate "(a) irreparable harm and (b) either the likelihood of success on the merits or (c) sufficiently serious questions going to the merits to make them a fair ground for litigation and a balance of hardship tipping decidedly toward the party requesting preliminary relief." A clear showing of threatened irreparable harm, as the foregoing suggests, is indispensable. Accordingly, examination of plaintiffs' claim of irreparable injury is the proper starting point for analysis.

### Irreparable Injury

Insofar as is relevant to the present motion, the complaint in this case alleges that the defendants' distribution of Marcy Playground and Sex and Candy without the proper credits to Kotler, White and their production entity violates Section 43(a) of the Lanham Act because it falsely suggests that Wozniak was the sole producer and that the plaintiffs were not involved in the production. The claim is one of reverse palming off— essentially, the removal of the name or mark of the source of the product and its sale under the wrongdoer's name or mark. Plaintiffs claim that they are threatened with irreparable injury because they are being deprived of credit for their role in bringing these recordings into existence, a deprivation that allegedly is particularly harmful because Kotler and White are seeking to establish themselves in the music industry.

Irreparable injury ordinarily is presumed in copyright, trademark and trade dress infringement cases. As the theory underlying the presumption rests on the difficulty of remedying confusion in the market place by an award of damages, the Court assumes that the presumption applies in a case like this one. But it is equally well established that "any such presumption of irreparable harm is inoperative if the plaintiff has delayed either in bringing suit or in moving for preliminary injunctive relief."

In this case, Marcy Playground was re-released, without giving the credits that plaintiffs regard as their due, on September 25, 1997. Plaintiffs brought this action on or about April 22, 1998, more than six months later. They did not seek a preliminary injunction until mid-June 1998, almost nine months later. Even if the Court were to accept plaintiffs' account of the discussions between the parties in the period September 1997 through March 1998 and to assume (as seems likely) that the diligent pursuit of settlement negotiations is a legally sufficient excuse for delay, it would remain undisputed that the discussion broke down entirely in mid-March. Thus, on the view of the evidence most favorable to plaintiffs, there was an unexplained delay of about five weeks in bringing suit and of three months in seeking a preliminary injunction.

Not every delay in seeking interlocutory relief defeats the presumption of irreparable injury in cases such as this. The cases reflect that "delay attributable to good faith investigation or a failure to realize the severity of the infringement does not." But here there is no excuse whatever for the delay from mid-March until mid-June. This delay is more than sufficient basis for concluding that any presumption of irreparable injury has been vitiated. Moreover, while the Court need not rely on the interval from September through March, the fact that plaintiffs did not seek relief during that period despite the alleged pendency of settlement discussions further undercuts their claim of irreparable injury.

The conclusion that the presumption has fallen away is not necessarily dispositive, as the Court of Appeals has not yet held that unexcused delay alone necessarily defeats a preliminary injunction motion, particularly in the face of District Court findings of irreparable injury based upon evidence before it. But the Court need not determine this unresolved question, as the evidence before it would not support a finding of irreparable injury in the absence of the presumption. Indeed, it would sap the lifeunder from the presumption even if breath remained in it.

To begin with, there is precious little basis for supposing that there is any real confusion in the market place. We are dealing, after all, with production credits on printed materials accompanying recorded popular music. There is no reason to suppose that a single recording has been sold or not sold, or that a single consumer cares, whether Kotler is listed as co-producer or White as executive producer. The music is sold for other reasons entirely.

Second, there is no convincing basis for concluding that the careers of Kotler and/or White will be affected in any material way by whether they are credited on these materials. While the Court assumes that those in the music business who might consider dealing with Kotler or White as record producers would consider their prior production experience as relevant, the question whether their names are listed on the reissued recordings as the result of an interlocutory court order pending the resolution of a dispute as to whether they in fact performed those functions seems of little consequence. The important facts are that Kotler and White claim to have performed those functions, Wozniak denies it, and the matter is in litigation. Those facts would not be altered by a preliminary injunction. The only evidence to the contrary are the conclusory and unsubstantiated assertions of irreparable injury by Kotler and White, the persuasiveness of which is significantly undercut by their relative inexperience in the music business and their manifest self interest. Indeed, if the liner credits were as important as they now claim, they would have sought a preliminary injunction months ago.

Third, the movant for a preliminary injunction must show not only that irreparable injury is possible, but that it is likely. Plaintiffs' showing certainly does not rise to that level. The most that can be said is that they have advanced a speculative theory.

Finally, it is evident that any injury the sale of the reissued album might cause already has occurred in virtually all material respects. While the parties have been somewhat imprecise as to the exact numbers of copies in distribution, at least one million copies actually have been sold and somewhere between 300,000 and 500,000 appear to be in the hands of retailers and, by virtue of plaintiffs' concession, would be unaffected by any preliminary injunction. Thus, the allegedly incorrect album liner has been distributed very extensively whereas the parties agree that any injunction would affect only a comparatively small number of albums remaining in Capitol's inventory. Hence, a preliminary injunction here would be very much like locking the barn door after the horse is gone.

For all these reasons, the Court finds that plaintiffs have failed to demonstrate any material threat of irreparable injury. Indeed, the circumstances suggest something else entirely — that plaintiffs are seeking to use the threat of disruption of marketing of a highly successful recording as leverage in seeking an advantageous settlement.

### Balance of Hardships

Even if plaintiffs had demonstrated a threat of irreparable injury, they would not be entitled to a preliminary injunction absent proof that the balance of hardships tips decidedly in their favor, as the Court is not prepared to say on this record that they have established a likelihood of success. Plaintiffs have not produced such evidence.

In the event that a preliminary injunction were wrongly denied, the injury to plaintiffs is the risk that their nascent reputations as record producers might be injured by the lack of credits on the album liners. On the other hand, the erroneous issuance of a preliminary injunction would interrupt the marketing of a hit recording that is generating very substantial revenues, revenues in which the plaintiffs are likely to share in the event they prevail in this case. While it is relatively certain that such an interruption would have a significant and negative impact on the revenue stream, there would be no reliable means of estimating that effect. In consequence, the balance here is straightforward. On the one hand, an erroneous denial of an injunction risks a speculative adverse impact on the plaintiff. An erroneous grant, on the other hand, seems quite likely to result in significant but unmeasurable economic injury to the defendants and, in all likelihood, to the plaintiffs as well. In these circumstances, plaintiffs have not carried their burden.

## Conclusion

For the foregoing reasons, plaintiffs' motion for a preliminary injunction is denied. The foregoing constitute the Court's findings of fact and conclusions of law, supplementing those contained in its oral opinion in open court.

SO ORDERED.

Bell v. Streetwise Records, Ltd.
United States District Court for the District of Massachusetts
June 11, 1986
Civil Action No. 83-4086-Z
640 F. Supp. 575

ZOBEL, D.J.
MEMORANDUM OF DECISION ZOBEL, D.J.

Plaintiffs Bell, Bivins, Brown, DeVoe and Tresvant, members of a singing group, are known to teenagers across the nation and around the world by the name "New Edition." Together with their present recording company, MCA Records, Inc. ("MCA"), they seek to establish their exclusive right to appear, perform and record under that mark. Defendants and counter-claimants (hereinafter "defendants"), Boston International Music, Inc. ("BIM"), and Streetwise Records, Ltd. ("Streetwise") produced, recorded and marketed the first New Edition long-playing album, "Candy Girl," as well as the singles from that album. Defendants claim that they employed the five individual plaintiffs to serve as a public front for a "concept" which they developed, and to promote musical recordings embodying that "concept." Because the mark New Edition allegedly identifies those recordings, and not the group members, defendants assert that they are its rightful owners. Each side has asked that this court enjoin the other from using the mark.

The amended complaint charges defendants with violations of § 43(a) of the Lanham Act, 15 U.S.C.A. § 1125(a)(West 1982), of the Massachusetts antidilution statute, Mass. Gen. Laws ch. 110B, § 12 (West Supp. 1986), of the Massachusetts nonstatutory law of unfair competition, and of Mass. Gen. Laws ch. 93A, § 11 (West 1984), which prohibits unfair or deceptive acts or practices. Defendants' counterclaims mirror the claims of plaintiffs.

This court first addressed the parties' cross-motions for preliminary injunctive relief in December 1983. Both motions were denied: defendants', because they had failed to make the requisite showing for preliminary relief, and plaintiffs', because their 1983 disaffirmance of their recording contracts with defendant Streetwise barred them from seeking the aid of a court of equity. The Court of Appeals for the First Circuit vacated this court's decision. Noting that it did "not view the 'unclean hands' doctrine as sufficient to justify continuation of public confusion," Bell v. Streetwise Records, Ltd., 761 F.2d 67, 76 (1st Cir. 1985)(Breyer and Coffin, JJ., concurring), and that both parties should be given the opportunity to amplify the record, it remanded the case for an exclusive award of rights to the mark.

A week-long evidentiary hearing was held in December 1985. A few months earlier, after learning that plaintiffs intended to release new records under the New Edition mark, defendants requested an "interim" injunction which this court denied. In affirming, the Court of Appeals clarified its earlier opinion, stating, "the district court should take a fresh look at the ownership issue in light of all the evidence." It further noted that "the prior ruling of the concurring judges in this case was not intended to designate Streetwise as the 'presumptive owner' of the name NEW EDITION." Bell v. Streetwise Records, Ltd., 787 F.2d 578 (1st Cir. 1986) (per curiam). Having examined all the evidence before me through the "new 'legal lens'" prescribed by the Court of Appeals, id. at 2 (quoting Bell, supra, 761 F.2d at 76), I conclude that plaintiffs are entitled to a preliminary injunction. Because they cannot sustain their ownership claim and have thus failed to show a likelihood of success on the merits, defendants' motion is denied.

## FINDINGS OF FACT AND RULINGS OF LAW
### Background

The five plaintiffs, calling themselves New Edition, form one of the hottest song-and-dance acts on the entertainment scene today. They have released four albums, numerous singles and several videos. They have performed throughout this country, filling major concert halls. They have toured Britain and Germany, and have plans for an upcoming trip to Japan. They have appeared on television shows, at charity events, and — the crowning sign of success — they have even been featured in a COKE commercial.

The group got its start in 1981 when four of the five current members performed in a talent show at Roscoe's Lounge, in Boston. They were each about thirteen years old at the time and they called themselves New Edition. Travis Gresham, who knew Bell and Tresvant from the marching band he directed, saw the show and thought they had potential. Within a week or two he became their manager and Brook Payne, who had collaborated with Bell, Bivins and Brown on an earlier endeavor, became their choreographer.

Gresham booked a series of performances for the group. Their sixth engagement, on November 15, 1981, was the "Hollywood Talent Night" at the Strand Theatre, where the group performed a medley of songs made famous by the Jackson Five. First prize and plaintiffs' goal for the night was a recording contract with Maurice Starr, president of defendant BIM, who originated and organized the event. New Edition came in second but Starr, who had an agenda of his own, decided to work with them anyway.

Maurice Starr, who partly from his "Hollywood Talent Nights" had become something of a local celebrity, had been in the music business for a long time. Starr — originally Larry Johnson — performed with his five brothers in a rock band in the early seventies. Modelled after the Jackson Five, whom they sought to emulate, Starr and his brothers called themselves the Johnson Six. They achieved moderate success but broke up in the mid-seventies when they became too mature for the image.

It was around this time that Starr began developing the "concept," which, in its final form, he dubbed "black bubble gum music of the eighties." The concept is essentially the Jackson Five updated by the addition of modern elements like synthesizers (electronic instrumentation) and rap (speaking parts). As early as 1972 Starr began to search for the right kids to act out his concept. In November 1981, when he first encountered Bell, Bivins, Brown and Tresvant, he was still looking.

Although he decided to work with them, Starr believed plaintiffs were short on talent. They had no training to speak of; none could read or write music. Nevertheless, he used the four boys to create a demonstration tape of a song he had composed earlier, entitled Candy Girl. Starr played all the instruments, sang background vocals and did the arranging and mixing. He had to teach the thirteen-year-old group members everything, and while it is disputed whether lead singer Ralph Tresvant had to record his part bar-by-bar or note-by-note, it is clear Starr ran the show in the sound studio.

The tape was completed in the winter of 1982, and Starr expended considerable effort attempting to sell it to a recording company. He finally connected with Streetwise in the following fall. In the meantime, under the supervision of Gresham and Payne, plaintiffs continued to rehearse their dance routines and to perform locally. Starr played little if any role in these activities.

During this period Starr and the group members had three disagreements, all stemming from Starr's desire to make the group more like the Jackson Five. First, Starr insisted they acquire a fifth member. The boys resisted, but Starr prevailed. Plaintiffs selected Ronnie DeVoe, a nephew of Brook Payne, whom Starr approved. Second, he wanted the group to grow "afros." They refused. Third, and perhaps most significant, he wanted the newly expanded group to change its name to the MaJic Five [sic]; the upper case "J," not surprisingly, to evoke "Jackson." Plaintiffs were adamantly opposed and remained New Edition.

In November and December of 1982, Streetwise entered into separate recording contracts with each of the five plaintiffs, who were at the time approximately age fourteen. Each contract granted to Streetwise the exclusive right to use the name. Each, except Tresvant's, confirmed that the name "The New Edition" was wholly owned by BIM.

Streetwise released the "Candy Girl" single in February 1983. The long-playing album — containing ten songs selected, produced, and for the most part written by Starr — came out the following June. Streetwise launched an unusually extensive and elaborate promotional campaign, placing advertisements in print and on radio, and producing three videos. After the single was released, plaintiffs — high school students at the time — performed every weekend night, in Massachusetts and beyond. At first they "lip-synched" to a recorded track; later they sang to a live band. For a period of time Starr accompanied them on these tours, announcing the group, playing instruments (four simultaneously, he testified), and performing background vocals. The records and the group were smash hits.

Sometime in the summer of 1983 plaintiffs began to perform without Starr. In August, they fired Gresham and Payne. That same month they performed in Britain and Germany. In September they acquired new management and in November they disaffirmed their contracts with Streetwise. After defendants revealed plans to issue New Edition records featuring five different young singers, and after they sought federal registration of the New Edition mark, plaintiffs commenced this lawsuit.

One postscript completes the evidentiary picture before the court. In January of 1984, Jheryl Busby, a senior vice president at MCA, was dragged by his fourteen-year-old son to see a performance of New Edition. None too impressed, he left to meet a friend at a nearby hotel. Young girls had swarmed the place. When he asked his friend what was going on he was told, "that group, New Edition, is staying here and those little girls have been looking for them all night." Busby signed the group.

### Discussion

A party seeking preliminary injunctive relief must satisfy four requirements: (1) that there is a likelihood of success on the merits; (2) that absent relief it will suffer irreparable harm; (3) that the harm it will suffer if an injunction is not granted outweighs the harm defendant will suffer if restrained; and (4) that injunctive relief is consistent with the public interest. Planned Parenthood League of Massachusetts v. Bellotti, 641 F.2d 1006 (1st Cir. 1981); Kingsmen v. K-Tel International Ltd., 557 F. Supp. 178, 181 (S.D.N.Y. 1983).

Although neither side concedes any of these prerequisites, the primary focus was on the first — the likelihood of success on the merits.

In order to prevail on the merits, plaintiffs or defendants must establish that the mark is valid and protectable, that they own the mark, and that use of the mark by the opposing party is likely to confuse the public. See, e.g., Estate of Presley v. Russen, 513 F. Supp. 1339, 1362 (D.N.J. 1981).

Both sides concede that New Edition is a distinctive mark, protectable under state and federal law; it is accordingly unnecessary to pass on that issue. They also concede, and the opinion of the Court of Appeals assumes, that use of the mark by both plaintiffs and defendants will lead to public confusion. Thus this court must decide the sole remaining issue: who owns the mark.

## I.

It is settled law that ownership of a mark is established by priority of appropriation. Blanchard Importing & Distributing Co. v. Charles Gilman, 353 F.2d 400, 401 (1st Cir. 1965), cert. denied, 383 U.S. 968, 16 L. Ed. 2d 308, 86 S. Ct. 1273 (1966). Priority is established not by conception but by bona fide usage. The claimant "must demonstrate that his use of the mark has been deliberate and continuous, not sporadic, casual or transitory." La Societe Anonyme des Parfums LeGalion v. Jean Patou, Inc., 495 F.2d 1265, 1272 (2d Cir. 1974)(citing 3 Callmann, Unfair Competition, Trademarks & Monopolies § 76.2(d) (1969)). While it is not required that a product be an instant success the moment it hits the market, its usage must be consistent with a "present plan of commercial exploitation." Id. at 1273. Finally, while the Lanham Act is invoked only through use in interstate commerce, common law rights can be acquired through interstate or intrastate usage. Noah's Inc. v. Nark, Inc., 560 F. Supp. 1253, 1258 (E.D. Mo. 1983), aff'd, 728 F.2d 410 (8th Cir. 1984)(citing Weiner King, Inc. v. Weiner King Corp., 201 U.S.P.Q. 894, 908 (TTAB 1979)).

With these principles in mind, I make the following findings of fact. First, on the basis of testimony by Mr. Busby and by defendants' expert, Thomas Silverman, I find that there is only one relevant market at issue here: the entertainment market. Second, I find that as of the release of "Candy Girl" in February 1983 — the first use in commerce — plaintiffs, calling themselves New Edition, had publicly performed in the local entertainment market on at least twenty occasions. Those performances (for which they frequently received compensation; albeit in nominal amounts), the promotional efforts by Travis Gresham on their behalf, their regular rehearsals with Gresham and Payne, their attempt to win a recording contract, and their hard work with Maurice Starr to further their career, all evidence a "present plan of commercial exploitation."

I accordingly conclude that plaintiffs have acquired legal rights to the mark New Edition through their prior use in intrastate commerce. Even if defendants' use had been the first in interstate commerce, they used the name simultaneously in Massachusetts, where plaintiffs had already appropriated it. And while it is well recognized that a junior user may occasionally acquire superior rights to a mark it used in good faith and in a different market, see 2 J. McCarthy, Trademarks and Unfair Competition, § 26:3 at 289-92 (2d ed. 1984), and cases cited therein, that was obviously not the case here. On this basis alone, plaintiffs own the mark.

## II.

Even assuming there was no prior appropriation by the plaintiffs, however, they nonetheless own the mark under the controlling standard of law.

Defendants correctly state that in the case of joint endeavors, where prior ownership by one of several claimants cannot be established, the legal task is to determine which party "controls or determines the nature and quality of the goods which have been marketed under the mark in question." See In re Polar Music International AB, 714 F.2d 1567 (Fed. Cir. 1983). The difficulty in performing that task in this case, however, is in deciding what the "goods" are. The parties have given the court little guidance in how to go about making that determination. Rather, each side baldly asserts the result that leads most logically to a decision in its favor. Defendants claim the goods are the recordings; plaintiffs claim they are the entertainment services of Bell, Bivins, Brown, DeVoe and Tresvant.

The role of "public association" in determining ownership has been much disputed in this case. Defendants have argued, and the Court of Appeals has confirmed, that the "finding that the public associate[s] the name NEW EDITION with the plaintiffs [does not compel] the conclusion that the name belong[s] to the plaintiffs." Bell, supra, 761 F.2d at 76. See, e.g., Wallpaper Mfgrs. Ltd. v. Crown Wallcovering Corp., 680 F.2d 755, 762 (C.C.P.A. 1982) ("Trademark rights are neither acquired or lost on the basis of comparative popularity. . . .") But defendants are wrong when they say that public association plays no part in determining ownership. It is crucial in establishing just what the mark has come to identify, i.e., what the "goods" are. 1 J. McCarthy, Trademarks and Unfair Competition, § 16:14 at 755-57 (2d ed. 1984).

In order to determine ownership in a case of this kind, a court must first identify that quality or characteristic for which the group is known by the public. It then may proceed to the second step of the ownership inquiry, namely, who controls that quality or characteristic. 1 J. McCarthy, supra, § 16:14 at 757. See also General Business Services, Inc. v. Rouse, 208 U.S.P.Q. 893, 900 (E.D. Penn. 1980); Five Platters, Inc. v. Purdie, 419 F. Supp. 372 (D. Md. 1976).

As a preliminary matter, I find that the norm in the music industry is that an artist or group generally owns its own name. This case does not fit into one of the clearer exceptions to this rule. The name New Edition has not been assigned, transferred, or sold. See, e.g., Kingsmen v. K-Tel International Ltd., supra; Marshak v. Green, 505 F. Supp. 1054 (S.D.N.Y. 1981); Rare Earth, Inc. v. Hoorelbeke, 401 F. Supp. 26 (S.D.N.Y. 1975). Nor is New Edition a "concept group," whose name belongs to the person or entity that conceived both concept and name. Compare O & L Associates v. Del Conte, No. 83-7939, slip op. (S.D.N.Y. Dec. 3, 1984).

With respect to defendants, although Maurice Starr's contribution to the "Candy Girl" records was substantial, I find that all the functions he performed were consistent with the duties of a producer. He was credited and compensated separately for each role. Similarly, while Streetwise's promotional work was unusually extensive, and though it proceeded at considerable risk, marketing — or "educating your label," as one witness put it — is a normal function of a recording company.

With respect to the plaintiffs themselves, as noted elsewhere in this opinion, they existed and performed as New Edition long before defendants released "Candy Girl." They had already used songs of the Jackson Five. Their membership has been essentially constant; they were not, as defendants contend, replaceable actors in a play written by Maurice Starr. (Compare Rick v. Buchansky, supra, where the four-person "Vito and the Salutations" had had twenty-two different members, including ten different "Vitos," to its one manager, Rick — who was found to own the name.) They were individual persons that the public came to know as such. While defendants would have us believe this is only the result of their successful promoting, I find that it was personality, not marketing, that led to the public's intimacy with plaintiffs. The "magic" that sold New Edition, and which "New Edition" has come to signify, is these five young men.

Based on the totality of the evidence, I conclude that the quality which the mark New Edition identified was first and foremost the five plaintiffs with their distinctive personalities and style as performers. The "goods" therefore are the entertainment services they provide. They and no one else controlled the quality of those services. They own the mark.

## CONCLUSION

I accordingly conclude that plaintiffs have demonstrated a likelihood of success on the merits, and that defendants have failed to do so. I am also persuaded by the testimony of Jheryl Busby, that failure to enjoin defendants would irreparably injure plaintiffs by weakening the mark — far in excess of the minor injury this injunction will cause defendants. Finally, as the Court of Appeals has made plain, the public interest will best be served by an exclusive award of the name.

For all these reasons, plaintiffs' motion requesting a preliminary injunction is allowed. Defendants' motion is denied. Plaintiffs shall prepare and the parties shall attempt to agree on a form of injunction. If they are unable to agree, plaintiffs shall file their proposal and defendants their objections no later than June 25, 1986.

---

In *Bell v. Streetwise Records, Inc.*, 640 F. Supp. 575 (D. Mass. 1986), the five members of New Edition were granted a preliminary injunction to establish their exclusive right to appear, perform, and record under that mark.

## PRODUCTION AND DISTRIBUTION AGREEMENT

This Production and Distribution Agreement (the **"Agreement"**) is made and entered into on January, 2015 (the **"Effective Date"**), between John Doe Records, LLC **("Company"**), a music recording and distribution company organized under the laws of the State of California and Joshua Doe **("Artist"**), collectively, with Company, the **"Parties"**), and:

WHEREAS, Company is engaged in the business of producing, duplicating, packaging, marketing, and distributing, sound recordings and songs, far wholesale and retail sales; and

WHEREAS, Artist is currently engaged in a new project (the **"New Project"**) of writing and recording of scores and lyrics (the "New Project Songs"), for the subsequent marketing, distribution, and sale, by Company; and

WHEREAS, Company shall produce, duplicate, package, market, distribute, and sell, physical and digital media containing the New Project Songs, as written and recorded by Artist as its New Project;

NOW THEREFORE, in consideration of the mutual promises and benefits accruing to each of the Parties hereunder, the Parties agree to the following.

1.    COMPANY'S OBLIGATIONS

    A.    <u>Production and Distribution of Initial New Project CDs</u>

        **1.**    Company shall reproduce, from the master recording received from the Artist (the **"Master Recording"**), the New Project Songs on a master compact disc (the **"Master CD"**) and, thereafter, shall have the Master CD duplicated in an initial pressing of **1,000** compact discs (the **"Initial New Project CDs"**).

        2.    Company shall provide graphic design, album art, and promotional materials, for the Initial New Project CDs; and shall package the Initial New Project CDs for distribution and sale, with UPC markings. Thereafter, Company shall market, distribute, and sell, the Initial New Project CDs.

        3.    Company shall be responsible for the arrangement of, and the payment of the costs and expenses of, the reproduction, duplication, marketing, distribution, and sale, of the Initial New Project CDs, as contemplated and **set** forth in this Agreement.

        4.    Company shall collect all proceeds from its distribution and sale of the Initial New Project CDs, and shall account to Artist for, on a semi-annual basis, all collected proceeds and its associated costs and expenses, as further provided in this Agreement.

        5.    Company shall use its best efforts to market, distribute, and sell, the Initial New Project CDs, through such channels and means as it, in good faith, shall determine to be effective and appropriate, including the use of website, mail-order, electronic, digital, and other, means of marketing, distribution and sales.

6.      Company, upon receipt from the Artist, shall handle the Master Recording with all due care and shall return the Master Recording to the Artist as soon as is practicable following Company's production use thereof, and, in no event, later than 30 days thereafter.

B.      Production and Distribution of Subsequent New Project CDs

1.      Company, upon consultation with the Artist and the agreement of the Parties, and following the distribution and sale of the Initial New Project CDs, shall use its best efforts to produce and duplicate from the Master CD, additional compact discs (the **"Subsequent New Project CDs"**) and shall use its best efforts to market, distribute, and sell, the Subsequent New Project CDs.

2.      Company, as further provided in this Agreement, shall be responsible for the arrangement of, and payment of the costs and expenses of, the reproduction, duplication, marketing, distribution, and sale, of the Subsequent New Project CDs, as contemplated and set forth in this Agreement.

3.      Company shall account to Artist for, on a semi-annual basis, all collected proceeds and its associated costs and expenses, as further provided in the Agreement.

**4.**      The Initial New Project CDs and the Subsequent New Project CDs are referred to herein, collectively, as the **"New Project CDs."**

C.      Production and Distribution of Initial New Project Vinyl

**1.**      Company shall reproduce, from the master recording received from the Artist (the **"Master Recording"**), the New Project Songs on an LP vinyl album {the **"Master Vinyl"**) and, thereafter, shall have the Master Recording duplicated in an initial pressing of 500 vinyl records (the **"Initial** New **Project Vinyl"**).

2.      Company shall provide graphic design, album art, and promotional materials, for the Initial New Project Vinyl; and shall package the Initial New Project Vinyl for distribution and sale, with UPC markings. Thereafter, Company shall market, distribute, and sell, the Initial New Project Vinyl.

3.      Company shall be responsible for the arrangement of, and the payment of the costs and expenses of, the reproduction, duplication, marketing, distribution, and sale, of the Initial New Project Vinyl, as contemplated and set forth in this Agreement.

4.      Company shall collect all proceeds from its distribution and sale of the Initial New Project Vinyl, and shall account to Artist for, on a semi-annual basis, all collected proceeds and its associated costs and expenses, as further provided in this Agreement.

5.      Company shall use its best efforts to market, distribute, and sell, the Initial New Project Vinyl, through such channels and means as it, in good faith, shall determine to be effective and appropriate, including the use of

website, mail-order, electronic, digital, and other, means of marketing, distribution and sales.

      6.      Company, upon receipt from the Artist, shall handle the Master Recording with all due care and shall return the Master Recording to the Artist as soon as is practicable following Company's production use thereof, and, in no event, later than 30 days thereafter.

      <u>D.</u>      <u>Production and Distribution of Subsequent New Project Vinyl</u>

      I.      Company, upon consultation with the Artist and the agreement of the Parties, and following the distribution and sale of the Initial New Project Vinyl, shall use its best efforts to produce and duplicate from the Master Recording, additional vinyl (the "Subsequent New Project Vinyl") and shall use its best efforts to market, distribute, and sell, the Subsequent New Project Vinyl.

      2.      Company, as further provided in this Agreement, shall be responsible for the arrangement of, and payment of the costs and expenses of, the reproduction, duplication, marketing, distribution, and sale, of the Subsequent New Project Vinyl, as contemplated and set forth in this Agreement.

      3.      Company shall account to Artist for, on a semi-annual basis, all collected proceeds and its associated costs and expenses, as further provided in the Agreement.

      4.      The Initial New Project Vinyl and the Subsequent New Project Vinyl are referred to herein, collectively, as the "New Project Vinyl."

2.      ARTIST'S OBLIGATIONS

      A.      Artist shall cooperate with Company, regarding promotional appearances, information and photographic sessions, and other promotional activities, related to the marketing, distribution, and sale, of the New Project, as requested by Company, which shall be reasonable in scope and necessary to the marketing, distribution, and sale, of the New Project.

      B.      Artist shall choose the recording studio and studio musicians, and shall provide the scores, lyrics, and instruments required for the recording of the New Project. Additionally, the Artist, as further provided in this Agreement, shall pay all costs and expenses related to the recording of the New Project Songs and production of the Master Recording.

      C.      Artist shall use no materials in the New Project which could cause the Artist or Company to incur any royalty payment to, or infringement of any copyright belonging to, any person or entity not a party hereto.

3.      FINANCIAL AND ACCOUNTING MATTERS

      A.      <u>Costs and Expenses</u>

      1.      The Artist shall be responsible for, and shall pay, all costs and expenses relating to the recording of the New Project Songs and the production of the Master Recording.

      2.      Company shall be responsible for, and shall pay, all

costs and expenses relating to the production and reproduction of the Master Recording (CD and Vinyl) and the production, duplication, marketing, distribution, and sales, of the New Project CDs and New Project Vinyl (the "New Project Costs"). The New Project Costs shall consist of the following:

- Cases and compact discs for the New Project CDs;
- Associated printing of art included with the New Project CDs;
- Album and album sleeve for the New Project Vinyl;
- Associated printing of art included with the New Project Vinyl;
- Printed marketing and promotional materials for the New Project
- Mailing and delivery costs relating to the distribution and sale of the New Project;

3.      Unless otherwise agreed by the Parties, the New Project Costs shall not include any portion of the general overhead, fixed costs, or other internal costs of Company.

B.      Recoupment of New Project Costs

Company shall be entitled to its recoupment of the New Project Costs, determined on a semi-annual basis, prior to any distribution of sales proceeds to the Parties, hereunder.

Therefore, the distributions of the sales proceeds made to the Parties, hereunder, shall be net of the New Project Costs (the "Net Proceeds") incurred by Company.

C.      Distribution of Net Proceeds

1.      Distributions of Net Proceeds to the Parties shall be accounted for, and made, within 30 days of each 6 month cycle. Company will deliver to Artist, with each semiannual distribution of Net Proceeds, a semi-annual accounting of the sales, the sales proceeds, and New Project Costs, related to the marketing, distribution, and sales, of the New Project during the previous period.

2.      Each of the Parties shall be entitled to a semi-annual distribution, equal in amount to 50% of the Net Proceeds.

4.      DISTRIBUTION RIGHTS

Artist hereby grants to Company, during the term of this Agreement, the exclusive license to market, distribute, and sell, the digital and physical formats of New Project Songs, worldwide.

5.      RIGHTS REGARDING NEW PROJECT SONGS

A.      The Artist also hereby grants to Company, during the term of this Agreement, the non-exclusive right to use and exploit any or all of the New Project Songs, as contained on the Master Recording, in any motion pictures, television productions, or other audio-visual medium, provided that

Company shall consult with Artist and the Parties shall agree thereto, prior to such use or exploitation of New Project Songs.

B.      Unless otherwise agreed, the Parties shall, each, be entitled to 50% of the proceeds and revenues flowing from, and produced by, the use and exploitation of the New Project Songs (the "Use Proceeds"), and, within 30 days of each 6 month period Company shall remit 50% of such Use Proceeds to Artist, together with a semi-annual accounting of its receipt of such Use Proceeds.

C.      The use or exploitation of the New Project Songs, by Company or any other party, in any motion pictures, television productions, or other audio-visual medium, whether nationally or internationally, shall terminate on or before the termination of this Agreement, unless otherwise agreed by the Parties, prior to such use or exploitation.

6.      OTHER RIGHTS

A.      Artist, notwithstanding anything to the contrary contained in this Agreement, shall retain all copyrights, ownership of the Master Recording, mechanical royalties, rights of publicity, and publishing rights, with respect to the New Project Songs, the Master Recording, New Project CDs, and New Project Vinyl.

B.      Company, upon production of the New Project CDs, shall provide 100 of the New Project CDs and 50 of the New Project Vinyl to the Artist at no cost. Thereafter Company shall provide to Artists additional New Project CDs and New Project Vinyl, equal in amount to the amount of the New Project CDs and New Project Vinyl sold by Artist during the preceding 6 month period, but, in no event, inure than the New Project CDs and New Project Vinyl remaining in the inventory of Company.

C.      Artist may purchase additional CDs from Company for $5 per unit. Artist may purchase additional Vinyl from Company for $8 per unit.

7. TERM AND TERMINATION OF AGREEMENT

A.      This Agreement, unless renewed by the Parties, shall continue seven years from the Effective Date, provided that New Project CDs and New Project Vinyl sold prior to the date of termination of this Agreement may be shipped to buyers and sale proceeds received, prior to the date of termination. A final accounting of New Project Costs and proceeds received, together with a final distribution of the Net Proceeds and the Use Proceeds to the Parties, shall be made by Company within 60 days of the date of termination of this Agreement.

B.      The Parties agree that, in the event of a breach of, or non-compliance under, this Agreement, by either Party, the compliant Party, upon ten (10) days written notice to the noncompliant Party, may terminate this Agreement, if such non-compliant Party fails to cure such breach or non-compliance, within said ten day notice period.

C.      Further, if the breach or event of non-compliance constitutes, results from, or results in, the failure to remit the Net Proceeds or the Use Proceeds, as required under this Agreement, to the proper Party, an amount equal to 22%, per annum, of such =emitted proceeds, calculated from the date such remittance was due and payable, shall be paid by the non-compliant Party, as liquidated damages hereunder, for such breach or event of noncompliance.

8.      MISCELLANEOUS

A.      This Agreement constitutes the sole and entire Agreement between the Parties, and no modification of this Agreement shall be binding on the Parties, unless set forth in writing and signed by each of the Parties.

B.      This Agreement is entered into, in contemplation of, and shall be governed by, the laws of the State of California, including those laws that govern the choice of law relating to this Agreement.

C.      This Agreement may be executed in counter parts, and each such executed counter-part shall constitute this Agreement.

D.      This Agreement may not be assigned or transferred by either of the Parties, unless such assignment is agreed to, in writing, by each of the Parties.

WHEREUPON, the Parties hereto have set their hands and executed this Agreement, as of the above-referenced Effective Date.

**Joshua Doe ("Artist")**                                    **John Doe Records**
**("Company")**

_____                    _____

Questions and Discussion

1. *In re Taylor*, 913 F.2d 102, gives a good synopsis of the dilemma a musician might face: "When the bankruptcy petition was filed, Mr. Taylor was in the following unviable position: he was owed substantial amounts by Group entities, but with virtually no prospect of payment; he was contractually obligated to write and perform enough musical compositions to provide at least seven additional albums, but any revenues these efforts might generate would be retained by the Group's creditors; and he had personally guaranteed the obligations of The Group and its related entities in amounts greatly in excess of the remaining equity in his home, which was his only significant asset" (at 105) Catch-22? Unconscionable? Would better contract drafting help? "Several albums" is excessive.

2. *In re Carrere*, 64 B.R. 1566 (1986), is different than *In re Taylor* because the court held that Carrere's bankruptcy filing was fraudulent and a means to reject a contract of employment with "General Hospital" so she could accept a more lucrative agreement to perform in the "A-Team." She was not able to reject the General Hospital Contract. "Carrere cannot use the Bankruptcy Code to protect her from whatever non-monetary remedies are enforceable under state law" (at 160). Yes, she should have looked into other remedies. But, perhaps she could have explained her financial difficulties in a more sympathetic manner. What do you think? Maybe it was timing? She filed her voluntary petition under Chapter 11, and the next day she filed a Notice of Rejection of Executory Contract, seeking to void the ABC contract for employment as an actor with General Hospital. Perhaps she was given bad legal advice. Legal malpractice, anyone?

3. Poor Redd Foxx. In Foxx v. Williams, 244 Cal. App. 2d 223 (1966), the great "Sanford & Son" comedian sought an accounting for his live comedy albums. Although they did not grant defendant record company's request for an injunction to prohibit breaches of contract, they did force Redd to refund the payments that were allegedly paid to him by mistake. The contract in question was called "Artist Recording Royalty Agreement." There were many successful albums. Defendant claims that a mistake in computing royalties resulted in an overpayment of royalties. Does this happen often? I think not. There is always the discussion of "studio costs." And, here, defendant paid for the food and liquor, Catch-22? If the books were cooked, who is in the best position to police them? Is the record company a fiduciary or an adversary?

4. Spend some time looking at the "Production and Distribution Agreement." What clauses would you amend if you were the lawyer for the record company? What clauses would you amend if you were the lawyer for the artist?

# Chapter 7
# Record Distribution Agreements

In the old days, there were many record distributors available; now, there are few. I'm not saying that this is why CDs are sold from the trunks of late-model cars, but it does make one ponder. "Distribution agreements are those agreements between two record companies where one company (the distributor) agrees to distribute the recorded product of another company (the distributed) on the distributed company's own label" (Richard Schulenberg, Legal Aspects of the Music Industry 775 (1999)). The distributor's job is to do the selling. The contract itself will spell out the distributor's obligations and the obligations of the distributed label. The agreement also will include representation and warranties, distribution fees, free goods, reserves, inventory, termination, and manufacturing (see Schulenberg, Chapter 14, "Distribution Agreements," Legal Aspects of the Music Industry 375-401)).

In the following case of *Platinum Record Co. v. Lucasfilm, Ltd.*, 566 F. Supp. 226 (D.N.J. 1983), defendant gave plaintiff's predecessor-in-interest the "master recording" rights to form popular songs for use on the *American Graffiti* motion picture soundtrack in January 1973. In 1980, the film was released for sale and rental to the public on videocassettes and video discs. "The last distribution of the picture forms the basis of plaintiff's action before this court" (at 227).

Platinum Record Co. v. Lucasfilm, Ltd.
United States District Court for the District of New Jersey
June 15, 1983
Civ. A. No. 82-1018
566 F. Supp. 226

CLARKSON S. FISHER, Chief Judge.

Plaintiff, Platinum Record Company, Inc., has brought suit against defendants Universal City Studios, Inc. and MCA, Inc. for breach of contract, misappropriation, unjust enrichment, and tortious interference with business opportunities. Defendants have moved for summary judgment on the merits. For the reasons outlined herein, the motion is granted.

In January 1973 Lucasfilm, Ltd. entered into an agreement (Agreement) with Chess Janus Records, plaintiff's predecessor-in-interest. Under this Agreement Chess Janus gave Lucasfilm the right to use the "master recordings" or "matrixes" of four popular songs for use on the soundtrack of the motion picture American Graffiti. The conditions for the use of the recordings were set out in paragraph 2 of the Agreement:

(f) Subject to our performance of the terms and conditions herein contained, you agree that we have the right to record, dub and synchronize the above mentioned master recordings, or portions thereof, into and with out motion picture and trailers therefor, and to exhibit, distribute, exploit, market and perform said motion picture, its air, screen and television trailers, perpetually throughout the world by any means or methods now or hereafter known.

Lucasfilm produced American Graffiti under a contract with Universal, and the film was released by a Universal subsidiary for national theatrical exhibition in August 1973. American Graffiti proved to be a major commercial success in its theatrical release and has subsequently been shown on cable television and on network and local television. In 1980 MCA Distributing Corp., a Universal affiliate, released the film for sale and rental to the public on video cassettes and video discs. This last distribution of the picture forms the basis of plaintiff's action before this court.

Plaintiff contends that its predecessor's Agreement with Lucasfilm, Ltd. (to whose rights defendants have suceeded) did not include the right to distribute American Graffiti on video discs and video cassettes. It asserts that the Agreement does not "speak for itself" in providing defendants with these rights. In any event, plaintiff believes it necessary to look beyond the actual terms of the Agreement to determine the parties' intent at the time of contracting.

Plaintiff argues that the contracting parties' state of mind (as to whether or not video discs and video cassettes were to be included under the Agreement) remains to be determined, and that this presents a material issue of fact which precludes summary judgment at this point.

Paragraph 2 of the Agreement specifically gives defendants the right "to exhibit, exploit, market and perform [American Graffiti] perpetually throughout the world by any means or methods now or hereafter known" (emphasis added). This language is extremely broad and completely unambiguous, and precludes any need in the Agreement for an exhaustive list of specific potential uses of the film. As a previous motion-picture-related case cited by plaintiff itself has held, "if the words are broad enough to cover the new use, it seems fairer that the burden of framing and negotiating an exception should fall on the grantor." Bartsch v. Metro-Goldwyn-Mayer, Inc., 391 F.2d 150, 155 (2d Cir.1968). Similarly, in the recent case of Rooney v. Columbia Pictures Industries, 538 F. Supp. 211 (S.D.N.Y. 1982), a district court found that "where . . . a party has acquired a contractual right which may fairly be read as extending to media developed thereafter," the other party may not escape that part of the agreement by showing that the specific nature of the new development was not foreseen at the time. Id. at 229. It is obvious that the contract in question may "fairly be read" as including newly developed media, and the absence of any specific mention in the Agreement of videotapes and video cassettes is thus insignificant.

Plaintiff places great emphasis on its argument that the showing of American Graffiti on video discs and video cassettes is not an exhibition of the film as covered by the Agreement. It presents no clear-cut definition, however, which would set out exactly what does or does not qualify as exhibition of a motion picture. Plaintiff apparently does not feel that the term encompasses only theatrical showings, as it has registered no objections in the past to the repeated showing of American Graffiti on cable and over-the-air television. I am persuaded by the rationale adopted by the Rooney court when it found that whether the exhibition apparatus is a home videocassette player or a television station's broadcast transmitter, the films are 'exhibited' as images on home television screens." Rooney v. Columbia Pictures Industries, 538 F. Supp. at 228. A motion picture is exhibited when it is presented for viewing by an audience on a theater or television screen; the video cassette and video disc operate as a means of exhibition, not as something of an altogether different nature from exhibition.

Finally, plaintiff insists that, even if the terms of the Agreement clearly give defendants rights to the music in question for home video presentation, we should look behind the written contract to determine whether the parties actually intended it to encompass this area. It has already been established that it is immaterial whether plaintiff anticipated all potential future developments in the manner of exhibiting motion pictures. There was no mistake as to the terms of the contract, as plaintiff alleges. Thus, there are no material facts remaining to be determined in this case.

Defendants' motion for summary judgment is granted. An order accompanies this opinion. No costs.

Buffalo Broad. Co. v. ASCAP
United States Court of Appeals for the Second Circuit
November 1, 1983, Argued; January 18, 1984, Finally Submitted;
September 18, 1984, Decided
Nos. 83-7058, 83-7060, 83-7062 — August Term, 1983
744 F.2d 917

NEWMAN, Circuit Judge.

Once again we consider the lawfulness under section 1 of the Sherman Antitrust Act of the blanket license offered by the American Society of Composers, Authors and Publishers (ASCAP) and Broadcast Music, Inc. (BMI). The license permits the licensee to perform publicly any musical composition in the repertory of the licensor. In this litigation the blanket license is challenged by a class of licensees comprising all owners of "local" television stations in the United States, i.e., stations not owned by any of the three major television networks, ABC, CBS, and NBC. After a bench trial in the District Court for the Southern District of New York (Lee P. Gagliardi, Judge), the blanket license was held to be an unreasonable restraint of trade. Buffalo Broadcasting Co. v. ASCAP, 546 F. Supp. 274 (S.D.N.Y. 1982). ASCAP and BMI were enjoined from licensing to local television stations non-dramatic music performing rights for any "syndicated" program. For reasons that follow, we conclude that the evidence was insufficient as a matter of law to show that the blanket license is an unlawful restraint of trade in the legal and factual context in which it currently exists. We therefore reverse the judgment of the District Court.

## Background
### I. The Parties

The five named plaintiffs own and operate one or more local television stations. They represent a class of all owners of local television stations in the United States who obtain music performing rights pursuant to license agreements with ASCAP and/or BMI. The class does not include the three major television networks, ABC, CBS, and NBC, each of which owns five television stations. The class includes approximately 450 owners who, because of multiple holdings, own approximately 750 local television stations. Only one owner has opted out of the class. The class includes some relatively small corporations that own a single station with relatively modest revenue and some major corporations with significant television revenue and profits, such as Metromedia, Inc., which owns seven stations including those in the major markets of New York City (WNEW-TV) and Los Angeles (WTTV). Since 1949 most stations have been represented in negotiations with ASCAP and BMI by the All-Industry Television Station Music License Committee ("the All-Industry Committee").

Defendant ASCAP is an unincorporated membership association of composers, authors, and publishers of music, formed in 1914. It has approximately 21,000 writer and 8,000 publisher members. It holds non-exclusive licenses for the non-dramatic performing rights to more than three million musical compositions. BMI is a non-profit corporation organized in 1939 by radio broadcasters. It has approximately 38,000 writer and 22,000 publisher affiliates. Its repertory, for which it holds non-exclusive licenses for non-dramatic performing rights, includes more than one million compositions. The eleven individual defendants represent two classes of defendants that include all persons from whom ASCAP and BMI have obtained the non-exclusive right to license non-dramatic music performing rights to others.

## II. Music, Rights, and Licenses

The subject matter of this litigation is music transmitted by television stations to their viewer-listeners. Television music is classified as either theme, background, or feature. Theme music is played at the start or conclusion of a program and serves to enhance the identification of the program. Background music accompanies portions of the program to heighten interest, underscore the mood, change the pace, or otherwise contribute to the overall effect of the program. Feature music is a principal focus of audience attention, such as a popular song sung on a variety show.

More particularly, we are concerned with the licensing of non-dramatic performing rights to copyrighted music, that is, the right to "perform" the music publicly by transmitting it, whether live or on film or tape, to television audiences. This performance right is created by the Copyright Act as one of the exclusive rights enjoyed by the copyright owner. 17 U.S.C. § 106(4) (1982). Also pertinent to this litigation is the so-called synchronization right, or "synch" right, that is, the right to reproduce the music onto the soundtrack of a film or a videotape in synchronization with the action. The "synch" right is a form of the reproduction right also created by statute as one of the exclusive rights enjoyed by the copyright owner. Id. § 106 (1). The Act specifically accords the copyright owner the right to authorize others to use the various rights recognized by the Act, including the performing right and the reproduction right, id. § 106, and to convey these rights separately, id. § 201(d)(2). The Act recognizes that conveyance of the various rights protected by copyright may be accomplished by either an exclusive or a non-exclusive license. Id. § 101.

Music performed by local television stations is selected in one of three ways. It may be selected by the station itself, or by the producer of a program that is sold to the station, or by a performer spontaneously. The stations select music for the relatively small portion of the program day devoted to locally produced programs. The vast majority of music aired by television stations is selected by the producers of programs supplied to the stations. In some instances these producers are the major television networks, but this litigation is not concerned with performing rights to music on programs supplied to the local stations by the major networks because the networks have blanket licenses from ASCAP and BMI and convey performing rights to local stations when they supply network programs. Apart from network-produced programs, the producers of programs for local stations are "syndicators" supplying the stations with "syndicated" programs. Most syndicated programs are feature length movies or one-hour or half-hour films or videotapes produced especially for television viewing by motion picture studios, their television production affiliates, or independent television program producers. However, the definition of "syndicated program" that was stipulated to by the parties also includes live, non-network television programs offered for sale or license to local stations. These syndicated programs are the central focus of this litigation. The third category of selected music, songs chosen spontaneously by a performer, accounts for a very small percentage of the music aired by the stations. These spontaneous selections of music can occur on programs produced either locally or by the networks or by syndicators.

Syndicators wishing to include music in their programs may either select pre-existing music (sometimes called "outside" music) or hire a composer to compose original music (sometimes called "inside" music). Most music on syndicated programs, up to 90% by plaintiffs' estimate, is inside music commissioned through the use of composer-for-hire agreements between the producer and either the composer alone or the composer and a corporation entitled to contract for a loan of the composer's services. Composer-for-hire agreements are normally standard form contracts. The salary paid to the composer, sometimes called "up front money," varies considerably from a few hundred dollars to several thousand dollars. The producer for whom a "work made for hire" was composed is considered by the Act to be the author and (unless the producer and composer have otherwise agreed) owns "all of the rights comprised in the copyright." Id. § 201(b). However, composer-for-hire agreements for syndicated television programs typically provide that the producer assigns to the composer and to a music publishing company the performing right to the music composed pursuant to the agreement.

When the producer wishes to use outside music in a film or videotape program, it must obtain from the copyright proprietor the "synch" right in order to record the music on the soundtrack of the film or tape. "Synch" rights vary in price, usually within a range of $150 to $500. When the producer wishes to use inside music, as is normally the case, it need not obtain the "synch" right because it already owns this right by virtue of the "work made for hire" provision of the Act.

Whether the producer decides to use outside or inside music, it need not acquire the television performing right since neither the making of the program nor the selling of the program to a television station is a "performance" of the music that would require a performing right. The producer is therefore free either to sell the program without the performing right and leave it to the station to obtain that right, or to obtain the performing right from the copyright proprietor, usually the composer and a publishing company, and convey that music performing right to the station along with the performing rights to all other copyrighted components of the program. If the producer obtains the music performing right from the copyright proprietor and conveys it to the station, the transaction is known as "source licensing" or "clearance at the source." If the station obtains the music performing right directly from the copyright proprietor, the transaction is known as "direct licensing."

The typical arrangement whereby local television stations acquire music performing rights in syndicated and all other programs is neither source licensing nor direct licensing. Instead, the stations obtain from ASCAP and BMI a blanket license permitting television performance of all of the music in the repertories of these organizations. The license is conveyed for a fee normally set as a percentage of the station's revenue. That fee, after deduction of administrative expenses, is distributed to the copyright proprietors on a basis that roughly reflects the extent of use of the music and the size of the audience for which the station "performed" the music. The royalty distribution is normally divided equally between the composer and the music publishing company.

In addition to offering stations a blanket license, ASCAP and BMI also offer a modified form of the blanket license known as a "program" or "per program" license. The program license conveys to the station the music performing rights to all of the music in the ASCAP or BMI repertory for use on the particular program for which the license is issued. The fee for a program license is a percent of the revenue derived by the station from the particular program, i.e., the advertising dollars paid to sponsor the program.

The blanket license contains a "carve-out" provision exempting from the base on which the license fee is computed the revenue derived by the station from any program presented by motion picture or transcript for which music performing rights have been licensed at the source by the licensor, i.e., ASCAP or BMI. The program license contains a more generous version of this provision, extending the exemption to music performing rights licensed at the source either by ASCAP/BMI or by the composer and publisher. Thus, for film and videotaped syndicated programs, a station can either obtain a blanket license for all of its music performing rights and reduce its fee for those programs licensed at the source by ASCAP/BMI, or obtain program licenses for each of its programs that use copyrighted music and avoid the fee for those programs licensed at the source by either ASCAP/BMI or by the composers and publishers.

### III. Prior Litigation

The merits of the current lawsuit cannot properly be assessed without consideration of the extensive history of litigation concerning the licensing of music performing rights. In 1941 an antitrust suit brought by the United States against ASCAP and BMI was settled by entry of consent decrees, imposing some limitations on the operations of ASCAP and BMI. Those decrees, however, permitted ASCAP and BMI to obtain exclusive licenses for music performing rights from their members and affiliates. The exclusive nature of these licenses prevented those requiring performing rights from negotiating directly with composers for rights to individual compositions. That limitation precipitated suit by operators of movie theaters, who successfully challenged the blanket license they were obliged to take from ASCAP in order to exhibit films with music from the ASCAP repertory. Alden-Rochelle, Inc. v. ASCAP, 80 F. Supp. 888 (S.D.N.Y. 1948). See also M. Witmark & Sons v. Jensen, 80 F. Supp. 843 (D. Minn. 1948), appeal dismissed, 177 F.2d 515 (8th Cir. 1949).

The restraining nature of the ASCAP blanket license, as applied to movie theater operators, prompted the Government to reopen the 1941 ASCAP consent decree and secure in 1950 a significant amendment. The amended decree, known as the "Amended Final Judgment," prohibits ASCAP from acquiring exclusive music performing rights, limiting it solely to non-exclusive rights. ASCAP is also prohibited from limiting, restricting, or interfering with the right of any member to issue to any user a non-exclusive license for music performing rights.

The Amended Final Judgment requires ASCAP to grant a blanket license to anyone requesting it. The decree also requires ASCAP to offer to any television or radio broadcaster a program license. ASCAP is also required "to use its best efforts to avoid any discrimination among the respective fees fixed for the various types of licenses which would deprive the licensees or prospective licensees of a genuine choice from among such various types of licenses." Amended Final Judgment, para. VIII, 546 F. Supp. at 278 n.6. Finally, in the event license applicants believe they are being overcharged, the decree permits any applicant for a blanket or program license to apply to the District Court for the determination of a "reasonable" fee, and in such a proceeding, "the burden of proof shall be on ASCAP to establish the reasonableness of the fee requested by it." Id. para. IX(A), 546 F. Supp. at 278-79 n.6.

In 1951 local television stations instituted suit pursuant to the Amended Final Judgment to determine reasonable license fees and terms. United States v. ASCAP (Application of Voice of Alabama, Inc.), 11 F.R.D. 511. (S.D.N.Y. 1951). In 1954 the parties reached agreement to set the per program license rate at 9% of the revenue of programs using ASCAP music and to reduce the blanket license rate to 2.05% of total station revenue, less certain deductions. In light of this agreement the Voice of Alabama proceeding was discontinued.

In 1961 local television stations requested from ASCAP a modified blanket license that excluded syndicated programs. When ASCAP refused, the stations sued in the consent decree court to require ASCAP to issue such a license. The District Court declined to require such a license, United States v. ASCAP (Application of Shenandoah Valley Broadcasting, Inc.), 208 F. Supp. 896 (S.D.N.Y. 1962), aff'd, 331 F.2d 117 (2d Cir.), cert. denied, 377 U.S. 997, 12 L. Ed. 2d 1048, 84 S. Ct. 1917 (1964). In affirming, this Court observed that if the blanket license was serving to restrain trade unreasonably in violation of the antitrust laws, the stations' remedy was to urge the Department of Justice to seek modification of the consent decree or to initiate a private suit. 331 F.2d at 124.

Rather than press an antitrust challenge, the stations initiated another round of fee determination pursuant to the consent decree. That litigation, known as the Shenandoah proceeding, was settled upon the parties' agreement that the form of blanket and program licenses then in use "may be entered into lawfully by each party to this proceeding" and that the rate for the blanket license was reduced to 2% of 1964-65 revenue plus 1% of incremental revenue above that base. United States v. ASCAP (Application of Shenandoah Valley Broadcasting, Inc.), Civ. No. 13-95 (S.D.N.Y. July 28, 1969) (final order). The All-Industry Committee reported to the stations that this rate reduction would save them approximately $53 million through 1977, an estimate that was exceeded because of the rapid growth of station revenue.

Thereafter, while the local television stations took blanket licenses from ASCAP and BMI, the legality of the license was challenged by a network licensee, CBS. Its suit, filed in 1969, was dismissed by Judge Lasker after an eight-week trial. CBS, Inc. v. ASCAP, 400 F. Supp. 737 (S.D.N.Y. 1975). Judge Lasker ruled that the evidence failed to show that the blanket license restrained CBS from obtaining music performing rights to individual compositions if it chose to seek and pay for them. On appeal, this Court reversed, ruling that the blanket license was an unlawful price-fixing device, a per se violation of section 1. CBS, Inc. v. ASCAP, 562 F.2d 130 (2d Cir. 1977). That decision was reversed by the Supreme Court, which ruled that the blanket license was not a per se violation of section 1. BMI, Inc. v. CBS, Inc., 441 U.S. 1, 99 S. Ct. 1551, 60 L. Ed. 2d 1 (1979). Upon remand from the Supreme Court, we affirmed Judge Lasker's decision, agreeing that the blanket license had not been proven to be a restraint of trade. CBS, Inc.

v. ASCAP, 620 F.2d 930 (2d Cir. 1980) ("CBS-remand"), cert. denied, 450 U.S. 970, 101 S. Ct. 1491, 67 L. Ed. 2d 621 (1981).

Perhaps encouraged by our 1977 ruling in favor of CBS, the local stations began this litigation in 1978. A four-week bench trial occurred in 1981 before Judge Gagliardi, resulting in the decision now on appeal. That decision holds that the blanket licensing of music performing rights to local television stations unreasonably restrains trade in violation of section 1 and enjoins ASCAP and BMI from granting to local television stations music performing rights in any syndicated programs. With respect to syndicated programs, the injunction thus bars ASCAP and BMI from offering either blanket or program licenses and also prohibits them from conveying performing rights with respect to such programs on any basis at all.

## Discussion
## A. Estoppel

As a threshold issue, ASCAP contends that the local stations are estopped from challenging the lawfulness of the blanket license as applied to them by reason of the position they took in settlement of the Shenandoah rate determination proceeding. Specifically, ASCAP relies on the fact that the stations settling that litigation represented to the District Court that the ASCAP blanket license "may be entered into lawfully" and that ASCAP in effect bargained for that representation by giving up at least $53 million in license fees. There is undeniable force to the contention that those who secured benefits exchanged in part for a representation to the District Court that the blanket license is lawful ought not to be heard to assert the contrary. See Chance v. Board of Examiners, 561 F.2d 1079, 1092 (2d Cir. 1977). But the argument is not necessarily a winning one for three reasons: It was not asserted in the trial court, it rests on a consent decree that applied to a term of years ending in 1977, and its force in the antitrust context is not free from doubt. Cf. Bernstein v. Universal Pictures, Inc., 517 F.2d 976, 981-82 (2d Cir. 1975) (plaintiff who has previously asserted contrary legal position still deserving of antitrust relief).

We are persuaded to move past the estoppel argument, without determining its validity, and consider the merits of the lawsuit. In the first place, the argument is a matter of considerable dispute, and, if not forfeited by failure to raise it in the trial court, the argument comes to us on a record that inadequately develops the facts as to whom the estoppel binds and whom it benefits. Second, even if the estoppel argument bars the claims of those local television stations for whom the All-Industry Committee spoke when negotiating the Shenandoah settlement, it is not at all clear that it would bar the claims of the approximately 200 stations that have come into existence since the 1969 settlement. Finally, there is uncertainty whether the estoppel would inure to the benefit of ASCAP's co-defendant, BMI, which was not a party to the Shenandoah proceeding. Without resolving our doubts on these points, we proceed to consider the merits of the dispute.

### B. Is There a Restraint?

We think the initial and, as it turns out, dispositive issue on the merits is whether the blanket licensing of performing rights to the local television stations has been proven to be a restraint of trade. See CBS-remand, supra, 620 F.2d at 934-35. Arguably the answer is a fortiori after the Supreme Court's decision and our decision on remand in the CBS litigation. The Supreme Court noted that "the necessity for and advantages of a blanket license for [television and radio networks] may be far less obvious than is the case when the potential users are individual television or radio stations . . . ." 441 U.S. at 21. And on remand we upheld the blanket license against the claim of a network. However, for several reasons, it does not follow that the local stations lose simply because the CBS network lost. First, the Supreme Court's observation concerned the relative pro-competitive effects of the blanket license for a network compared to local stations. Even though the pro-competitive effects may be greater when the licensees are local stations, those pro-competitive effects do not necessarily outweigh the anti-competitive effects. Second, the Supreme Court's comparative statement does not determine the threshold issue of whether the blanket licensing of performing rights to local television stations is a restraint at all. The fact that CBS did not prove that blanket licensing of networks restrained competition does not necessarily mean that blanket licensing of local stations may not be shown to be a restraint. Finally, in CBS-remand we reviewed a District Judge's ruling that no restraint had been proved; here, we review a ruling that the local stations proved the existence of a restraint.

In reaching his conclusions as to the existence of a restraint, Judge Gagliardi endeavored to apply the mode of analysis we had used in CBS-remand. We there noted that trade is restrained, sometimes unreasonably, when rights to use individual copyrights or patents may be obtained only by payment for a pool of such rights, but that the opportunity to acquire a pool of rights does not restrain trade if an alternative opportunity to acquire individual rights is realistically available. 620 F.2d at 935-36. We recognized, as CBS had urged, that a plaintiff will not be held to have an alternative "available" simply because some imaginable possibility exists. We agreed that CBS's "alternative" of hiring composers to fill its need for music was not the sort of realistic alternative that prevented the blanket license from being a restraint. "An antitrust plaintiff is not obliged to pursue any imaginable alternative, regardless of cost or efficiency, before it can complain that a practice has restrained competition." Id.

at 936. What we examined in CBS-remand, as Judge Lasker had done in the District Court, was whether the plaintiff had proved that it lacked a realistic opportunity to obtain performance rights from individual copyright holders.

We continue to believe that this is the appropriate inquiry, especially in light of the Supreme Court's recent decision concerning the NCAA's attempt to regulate the televising of college football games. NCAA v. Board of Regents of the University of Oklahoma, 468 U.S. 85, 104 S. Ct. 2948, 82 L. Ed. 2d 70 (1984). Two aspects of that ruling are especially pertinent. First, the Court was there concerned, as we are here, with an agreement whereby a pool of rights was conveyed. In determining that the agreement constituted a restraint, the Court stated, "Since as a practical matter all member institutions need NCAA approval, members have no real choice but to adhere to the NCAA's television controls." Id. at 2963 (emphasis added) (footnote omitted). Thus, the restraining effect of the challenged agreement arose not by virtue of its terms alone, but because as a "practical" matter no "real" alternative existed whereby individual negotiations could occur between member schools and television broadcasters. Second, the Court had occasion to characterize the blanket license for music performing rights that it had sustained against a per se challenge in CBS and stated that under the blanket license "each individual remained free to sell his own music without restraint." Id. at 2968 (emphasis added). NCCA thus reinforces our view that the first issue is whether the local television stations have proven that they lack, as a "practical" matter, a "real" alternative to the blanket license for obtaining music performing rights.

In reaching the conclusion that plaintiffs had proven the lack of realistically available alternatives to the blanket license, Judge Gagliardi gave separate consideration to three possibilities: the program license, direct licensing, and source licensing. We consider each in turn.

Program License. Judge Gagliardi based his conclusion that a program license is not realistically available to the plaintiffs essentially on two circumstances: the cost of a program license and the reporting requirements that such a license imposes on a licensee. "The court therefore concludes that the per program license is too costly and burdensome to be a realistic alternative to the blanket license." 546 F. Supp. at 289 (footnote omitted). Without rejecting any subsidiary factual finding concerning the availability of a program license, we reject the legal conclusion that it is not a realistic alternative to the blanket license.

The only fact found in support of the conclusion that the program license is "too costly" is that the rates for such licenses are seven times higher than the rates for blanket licenses. Id. The program license rate is 9%; the blanket license rate is between 1% and 2%. This difference in rates does not support the District Court's conclusion for several reasons. First, the rates are charged against different bases. The blanket license rate is applied to a station's total revenue;

the program license rate is applied only to revenue from a particular program. Since the base for the blanket license fee includes revenue from network programs, for which the networks have already acquired performing rights by virtue of their blanket licenses, as well as some local programs that use no music it is inevitable that the rate for a local station's blanket license will be less than the rate for a program license taken solely to permit use of music on a particular program.

Second, the degree of difference between the two rates is largely attributable to the stations themselves. In negotiating a revision of license rates in the Shenandoah proceeding in 1969, the All-Industry Committee elected not to press for reduction of the program license rate and instead concentrated on securing a reduction of the blanket license rate, believing, as it informed the broadcasters it represented, that "the critical matter at this time was to get the best possible blanket license." Having preferred to win a lower price for only the blanket license, the stations are in no position to point to the widened differential between rates to show that program licenses are not realistically available.

Third, the only valid test of whether the program license is "too costly" to be a realistic alternative is whether the price for such a license, in an objective sense, is higher than the value of the rights obtained. But plaintiffs presented no evidence that the price of the program license is "higher" in terms of value received. Instead, they rely, as did the District Court, on a comparison between the program license rate and the blanket license rate. That comparison, defendants contend, leads to the anomalous result that the more the blanket license is a bargain, the more it is likely to be a restraint. The anomaly is more apparent than real. Within reasonable price ranges, the program license is not an unrealistic alternative to the blanket license simply because the rate for the latter is less. The differential in rates may reflect the inherent difference in the bundle of rights being conveyed. Even if the blanket license is objectively the "better buy" for most users, the program license would be a realistic alternative so long as it was fairly priced for those who might find it preferable for reasons other than price. But if the program license were available only at a price beyond any objectively reasonable range, the "bargain" nature of the blanket license would not immunize it from characterization as a restraint. Sellers of alternatives may not set absurdly high prices at which they have no real intention of making sales and then point to the cheaper price of the package under attack to argue that it is not a restraint but the object of customer preference.

Thus, while the relative cheapness of the blanket rate does not necessarily mean that it is not a restraint, the absence of evidence that the program license has been artificially priced higher than is reasonable for value received bars any conclusion that the program license is "too costly" to be a realistic alternative.

The fact that very few stations have elected to take program licenses is not evidence that they are priced beyond an objectively reasonable price range. It may simply reflect, as defendants believe, that the blanket license has virtues of convenience that make it a legitimate object of customer preference.

Fourth, even if there were evidence that showed the program license rate to be too "high," that price is always subject to downward revision by Judge Conner, who currently supervises the administration of the Amended Final Judgment. Two aspects of that judgment are especially pertinent to any claim that the price of the program license is too "high." In a proceeding to redetermine rates, the burden is on ASCAP to prove the reasonableness of the rates charged, and the judgment expressly requires ASCAP "to use its best efforts to avoid any discrimination among the respective fees fixed for the various types of licenses which would deprive the licensees or prospective licensees of a genuine choice from among such various types of licenses," Amended Final Judgment P VIII, 546 F. Supp. at 278 n.6 (emphasis added). The availability of a judicially enforceable requirement of a "reasonable" fee precludes any claim that the program license rate is too high, especially in the context of television stations regularly represented by a vigorous committee with the demonstrated resources, skill, and willingness to invoke the rate-adjustment process.

In addition to cost, Judge Gagliardi considered the program license not realistically available because of the burdens of required record-keeping that accompany its use. This conclusion is similarly flawed by the lack of evidence that the record-keeping requirements have been unnecessarily imposed. Since the program license permits only selective use of copyrighted music, it is inevitable that some reporting requirements would be reasonable to assure proper use. The District Court made no finding that any aspect of the record-keeping is objectively unnecessary, and plaintiffs offered no evidence to this effect. As with price, the apparent benefit of the blanket license in sparing the user record-keeping may simply reflect inherent differences in the two products. In any event, the program license has been shown only to require more record-keeping than the blanket license; it has not been shown to require burdens objectively unreasonable, such as would support a conclusion that the program license is not realistically available. Finally, though we do not decide the point, it would appear that any aspect of the record-keeping requirement that prevents the stations from having a "genuine choice" between the program and the blanket license would be subject to revision under the Amended Final Judgment.

The lack of evidence that the program license is not realistically available has a two-fold significance in determining whether the blanket license has been shown to be a restraint. First, the program license itself remains as an alternative to the blanket license for the local stations to acquire performing rights to the music on all of their syndicated programs. That consequence is not necessarily determinative since the program license is in reality a limited form of the blanket license and, like the blanket license, is subject to the objection that its use by stations would continue the present practice whereby no price competition occurs among individual songs with respect to licensing of performing rights. However, the availability of the program license has a second and more significant consequence: The program license provides local stations with a fall-back position in the event that they forgo the blanket license and then encounter difficulty in obtaining performing rights to music on some syndicated programs either by direct licensing or by source licensing. Whether those alternatives were proven to be unavailable as realistic alternatives is our next inquiry.

Direct Licensing. The District Court concluded that direct licensing is not a realistic alternative to the blanket license without any evidence that any local station ever offered any composer a sum of money in exchange for the performing rights to his music. That evidentiary gap exists despite the 21-year interval between entry of the Amended Final Judgment and the trial of this case, during which the local stations had ample opportunity to determine whether performing rights could be directly licensed.

The District Court declined to attach any significance to the absence of purchase offers from stations directly to copyright proprietors for two related reasons. Judge Gagliardi concluded, first, that direct licensing could not occur without the intervention of some agency to broker the numerous transactions that would be involved and, second, that the television stations lack the market power to induce anyone to come forward and perform that brokering function. 546 F. Supp. at 290. We have no quarrel with the first proposition. Some intermediary would seem essential to negotiate performing rights licenses between thousands of copyright proprietors and hundreds of local stations, in the same manner that the Harry Fox Agency for years has brokered licenses for "synch" rights between copyright proprietors and program producers.

However, we see no evidentiary support for the District Court's second proposition — that no one would undertake the brokering function for direct licensing of performing rights. Judge Gagliardi was led to this conclusion, not on the basis of any evidence of an expressed reluctance on anyone's part to broker direct licensing, but because of his view of the difference between the market power of CBS and that of the local television stations. In CBS Judge Lasker had found, 400 F. Supp. at 779, and we had emphasized, 620 F.2d at 938, that if CBS were to seek direct licensing, "copyright proprietors would wait at CBS' door." In this case, Judge Gagliardi found that "local television stations acting individually and severally would possess no such awesome power over copyright owners." 546 F. Supp. at 290. From this finding he concluded, "Since no lines would form at the doors of local television stations, no centralized machinery would arise to facilitate direct licensing." Id.

This reasoning escalates a characterization of the evidence in CBS into a minimum requirement for future cases. The plaintiffs in this case do not discharge their burden of proving that local stations cannot realistically obtain direct licenses by showing that they have less market power than CBS, "'the giant of the world in the use of music rights,'" CBS v. ASCAP, supra, 400 F. Supp. at 771 (quoting testimony of a former CBS vice-president). The issue is whether the local stations have been shown to lack power sufficient to give them a realistic opportunity to secure direct licenses. To conclude that they do not simply because no one of them is as powerful as CBS disregards the functioning of a market. Sellers are induced to sell by a perception of aggregate demand, existing or capable of stimulation. The automobile manufacturers who recently decided to bring back the convertible car did not await a fleet order from the nation's largest user of automobiles; they responded to the actual and anticipated consumer preferences of individual car buyers, whose individual market power is surely no greater than that of the least successful television station. Thus, it avails plaintiffs nothing to cite the testimony of Salvatore Chiantia, president of the National Music Publishers Association, that as a publisher he would not line up at the door of KID-TV in Idaho Falls to license performing rights. Brief for Appellees at 52. What is pertinent is Chiantia's point that while it would be difficult for him to have a staff that would wait at the doors of 700 television stations, "if [direct licensing] was the way I was going to get my music performed, I would have to devise a system which would make it possible for me to license." The plaintiffs have not presented evidence to show that a brokering mechanism would not handle direct licensing transactions if the stations offered to pay royalties directly to copyright proprietors.

The alleged infeasibility of direct licensing is further undermined by the acknowledged ability of the stations to secure direct licensing of music needed for thier locally produced programming. Judge Gagliardi observed, "Since local television stations deal directly with the composers or copyright owners of the music contained in locally-produced programs, stations would not encounter difficulties in finding and obtaining music licenses from those composers and copyright owners." 546 F. Supp. at 289 n.37. Nevertheless, he concluded that, because local stations would be paying double for such direct licenses so long as they held a blanket license, "direct licensing would not be a realistically available alternative unless the blanket license were discarded entirely." Id. at 289-90 n.37. But if the stations can realistically obtain direct licenses for local programming by offering reasonable amounts of money, they can avoid double payment by forgoing the blanket license. Their response is that they dare not do so because they will then be unable to secure performing rights to music on syndicated programs, which constitute the bulk of their program day. But, as we have previously noted, the availability of the program license enables them to forgo the blanket license and still obtain music rights for any program for which direct licensing proves infeasible. Alternatively, they can pursue source licensing, to which we now turn.

Source Licensing. As Judge Gagliardi noted, the "current availability and comparative efficiency of source licensing have been the focus of this lawsuit." Id. at 291. The availability of source licensing is significant to the inquiry as to whether the blanket license is a restraint because so much of the stations' programming consists of syndicated programs for which the producer could, if so inclined, convey music performing rights. Most of these syndicated programs use composer-for-hire music. As to such music, the producer starts out with the rights of the copyright, including the performing right, by operation of law, 17 U.S.C. § 201(b), unless the hiring agreement otherwise provides. Thus it becomes important to determine whether the stations can obtain from the producer the music performing right, along with all of the other rights in a syndicated program that are conveyed to the stations when the program is licensed. As to "inside" music, source licensing would mean that the producer would either retain the performing right and convey it to the stations, instead of following the current practice of assigning it to the composer and a publishing company, or reacquire the performing right from the composer and publisher for conveyance to the stations. As to "outside" music, source licensing would mean that the producer would have to acquire from the copyright proprietor the performing right, in addition to the "synch" right now acquired.

Plaintiffs sought to prove that source licensing was not a realistic alternative by presenting two types of evidence: "offers" from stations and analysis of the market. Prior to bringing this lawsuit, the stations had not sought to obtain performing rights via source licensing. Perhaps prompted by the evidentiary gap emphasized in our decision in CBS-remand or by the taunting of defendants in this litigation, plaintiffs began in mid-1980, a year and one-half after the suit was filed, to create a paper record designed to show the unavailability of source licensing.

Various techniques were used. Initially, some stations simply inserted into the standard form of licensing agreement for syndicated programs a new clause specifying that the producer has obtained music performing rights and that the station need not do so. No offer of additional compensation for the purchase of the additional rights was made. Not surprisingly most producers declined to agree to the proposed clause. A vice-president of MCA Television Limited ("MCA"), one of the major syndicators, replied to KAKE-TV, "It is surprising to me that the station would attach a Rider of such magnitude without previously discussing it with us. . . . You are apparently asking us to undertake the clearance of the music performance rights in [the "Rockford Files" TV series] without offering any additional payment. . . . We are unable to accept the amendment. . . . This does not mean, of course, that a different approach is unacceptable. It does, however, mean that a change of this magnitude should be discussed well in advance so that our respective concerns can be addressed."

Another approach, evidenced by King Broadcasting Co.'s letter to MCA, attached a music performing rights rider to the standard syndication licensing agreement and added, "If [sic] an additional fee is in order, we would certainly consider favorably any such reasonable fee." Another approach, adopted by Chronicle Broadcasting Co. in letters to various syndicators, was a request for source clearance of music performing rights with the comment, "Chronicle recognizes that this contemplated change . . . may [sic] in some instances require an adjustment in the basic program license fees." Metromedia, Inc., owner of several stations, went further and asked Twentieth Century-Fox Television ("Fox"), "Since you are the 'seller', what is the price you would affix to the altered product [the syndication license including music performing rights]?" In reply Fox made the entirely valid point that since syndication licensing without music performing rights had been the industry practice for years, it was Metromedia's "responsibility to advise us in what manner you would like" to change the current arrangements. Notably absent from all of the correspondence tendered by the plaintiffs is the customary indicator of a buyer's seriousness in attempting to make a purchase — an offer of a sum of money.

Judge Gagliardi properly declined to give any probative weight to the plaintiffs' transparent effort to assemble in the midst of litigation evidence that they had seriously tried to obtain source licensing. He found "plaintiffs' source licensing foray so darkened by the shadow of the approaching trial that its results may not be relied upon to support either side." 546 F. Supp. at 292. Nevertheless the District Court concluded that source licensing was not a realistic alternative because the syndicators "have no impetus to depart from their standard practices and request and pay for television performing rights merely in order to pass them along to local stations." Id. This conclusion does not follow from some of the Court's factual findings and rests on a view of the syndication market that is contradicted by other findings.

The District Court viewed the syndication market as one in which the balance of power rests with the syndicators and the stations have no power to "compel" a reluctant syndicator to change to source licensing. Id. Yet the Court found that there are eight major syndicators, id. at 280 & n.13, and that they distribute only 52% of all syndicated programs, id. at 281, hardly typical of a non-competitive market. Moreover, the Court characterized production of syndicated programs as a "risky business," id. at 282, a finding fully supported by the evidence. It may be that the syndicator of a highly successful program has the upper hand in negotiating for the syndication of that program and would not engage in source licensing for music in that program simply to please any one station, but it does not follow that the market for the wide range of syndicated programs would be unresponsive to aggregate demand from stations willing to pay a reasonable price for source licensing of music performing rights.

The District Court recognized that, even under its view of a syndication market weighted in favor of the syndicators, source licensing could be said to be unavailable only if stations would not offer "premium prices." Id. at 292. There is no subsidiary finding as to what prices the Court thought stations would have to offer to obtain source licensing. That is not surprising in view of the failure of the plaintiffs to present evidence to show either what such prices might be or that they would be "premium" in the sense of significantly exceeding an objectively reasonable value of the rights obtained. Nor is the alleged unwillingness of the producers to undertake source licensing established by the fact that some producers own music publishing companies that receive royalties as their distributive share of the fees stations pay for the blanket license. The undisputed evidence shows that these fees are far too small to persuade syndicators to refuse to undertake source licensing in the face of reasonable offers. BMI, for example, typically distributes to a publisher between 50 cents and 85 cents for theme and background music in a half-hour episode of a syndicated program shown on a single station; by contrast, the syndication licensing fee can exceed $ 60,000 for a single episode of a popular series shown in a major television market. Though some of the major producers that own music publishing companies have received more than $1 million in annual television distributions of music royalties, those royalties are a small fraction of their syndication revenue.

Defendants vigorously assert that whatever reluctance producers may have to undertake source licensing reflects their view of the efficiency of the blanket license. They contend that the blanket license may not properly be found to be a restraint simply because producers of syndicated programs regard it as efficient. We need not determine whether defendants have correctly analyzed the motivation of those syndicators who have expressed reluctance to undertake source licensing. Our task, in determining whether plaintiffs have presented evidence sufficient to support a conclusion that the blanket license is a restraint of trade, is not to psychoanalyze the sellers but to search the record for evidence that the blanket license is functioning to restrain willing buyers and sellers from negotiating for the licensing of performing rights to individual compositions at reasonable prices. Plaintiffs have simply failed to produce such evidence.

Instead they suggest that source licensing is not a realistic alternative because the agreements producers have made with composers and publishers are a "contractual labyrinth," Brief for Appellants at 53 n.73, and because the composers have precluded price competition among songs by "splitting" performing rights from "synch" rights, id. at 2. But plaintiffs have made no legal challenge to the "composer-for-hire" contracts by which "inside" music is customarily obtained for syndicated programs, with provisions for producers to assign performing rights to composers and publishers. And composers have not "split" performing rights from "synch" rights; they have separately licensed distinct rights that were created by Congress. Moreover, the composers' grant of a performing rights license to ASCAP/BMI is on a non-exclusive basis. That circumstance significantly distinguishes this case from Alden-Rochelle, where ASCAP's acquisition of exclusive licenses for performing rights was held to restrain unlawfully the ability of motion picture exhibitors to obtain music performing rights directly from ASCAP's members.

The Claimed Lack of Necessity. Plaintiffs earnestly advance the argument that the blanket license, as applied to syndicated programming, should be declared unlawful for the basic reason that it is unnecessary. In their view, the blanket license is suspect because, where it is used, no price competition occurs among songs when those who need performing rights decide which songs to perform. The resulting absence of price competition, plaintiffs urge, is justifiable only in some contexts such as night clubs, live and locally produced programming of television stations, and radio stations, which make more spontaneous choices of music than do television stations.

There are two fundamental flaws in this argument. First, it has not been shown on this record that the blanket license, even as applied to syndicated television programs, is not necessary. If all the plaintiffs mean is that a judicial ban on blanket licensing for syndicated television programs would not halt performance of copyrighted music on such programs and that some arrangement for the purchase of performing rights would replace the blanket license, we can readily agree. Most likely source licensing would become prevalent, just as it did in the context of motion pictures in the aftermath of Alden-Rochelle. But a licensing system may be "necessary" in the practical sense that it is far superior to other alternatives in efficiency and thereby achieves substantial saving of resources to the likely benefit of ultimate consumers, who usually end up paying whenever efficient practices are replaced with inefficient ones.

Moreover, the evidence does not establish that barring the blanket license as to syndicated programs would add any significant price competition among songs that the blanket license allegedly prevents. When syndicators today decide what music to select for their programs, they do so in the vast majority of instances, by deciding which composer to hire to compose new music for their programs. As to that "inside" music, which plaintiffs estimate accounts for 90% of music on syndicated programs, there is ample price competition: Prices paid as "up front" money in order to hire composers vary significantly. Even when syndicators consider use of pre-existing music (for which copyright protection has not expired), there is some price competition affecting the choice of that "outside" music because prices for "synch" rights vary. With this degree of price competition for music on syndicated programs already in place, it is entirely a matter of speculation whether replacement of the blanket license with source licensing would add any significant increment to price competition at the point where the syndicators decide which music to use. And since music is such a small portion of the total cost of a syndicated program to the television stations, and would still be even if performing rights were acquired at the source and included in the total price to the station, it is also a matter of speculation whether any significant increase in price competition for music would occur when television stations decide which syndicated programs to purchase in a world of source licensing. Viewed in the context of what is known about the way music is now obtained by syndicators and the entirely speculative nature of what benefits might occur if blanket licensing were prohibited, the evidence does not show that the blanket license is unnecessary to achieve its present efficiencies.

The second flaw in the argument is more fundamental. Even if the evidence showed that most of the efficiencies of the blanket license could be achieved under source licensing, it would not follow that the blanket license thereby becomes unlawful. The blanket license is not even amenable to scrutiny under section 1 unless it is a restraint of trade. The fact that it may be in some sense "unnecessary" does not make it a restraint. This is simply a recognition of the basic proposition that the antitrust laws do not permit courts to ban all practices that some economists consider undesirable. Since the blanket license restrains no one from bargaining over the purchase and sale of music performance rights, it is not a restraint unless it were proven that there are no realistically available alternatives. As we have discussed, the plaintiffs did not present evidence to establish the absence of realistic alternatives. It is therefore irrelevant whether, as plaintiffs contend, the blanket license is not as useful or "necessary" in the context of syndicated programming on local television stations as it is in other contexts. Not having been proven to be a restraint, it cannot be a violation of section 1.

The blanket license has been challenged in a variety of contexts. It has been upheld for use by nightclubs and bars, BMI v. Moor-Law, Inc., 527 F. Supp. 758 (D. Del. 1981), aff'd mem., 691 F.2d 490 (3d Cir. 1982), by radio stations, K-91, Inc. v. Gershwin Publishing Corp., 372 F.2d 1 (9th Cir. 1967), cert. denied, 389 U.S. 1045, 19 L. Ed. 2d 838, 88 S. Ct. 761, 156 U.S.P.Q. (BNA) 720 (1968), and by a television network, CBS-remand, supra. Without doubting that the context in which the blanket license is challenged can have a significant bearing on the outcome, we hold that the local television stations have not presented evidence in this case permitting a conclusion that the blanket license is a restraint of trade in violation of section 1.

The judgment of the District Court is therefore reversed.

———————

American Society of Composers, Authors, and Publishers (ASCAP) and Broadcast Music, Inc. (BMI) successfully appeal from lower court decision in favor of plaintiffs who were owners of local television stations in a class action antitrust lawsuit. Plaintiffs contend that the "preferred" method of licensing music performance rights through "blanket" licensing, which allows TV stations blanket rights to use all pieces of music held by ASCAP and BMI, is an impermissible restraint of trade since this licensing structure restrains plaintiffs from seeking performance rights for individual compositions. The court disagrees, since the TV stations still have the option of "program licensing"; even though it is rarely used, it is still a viable option, hence blanket licensing is not an unlawful restraint of trade.

Glovaroma, Inc. v. Maljack Prods., Inc.
United States District Court for the Northern District of Illinois, Eastern
Division
September 23, 1999, Decided; September 28, 1999, Docketed
96 C 3985
71 F. Supp. 2d 846

MEMORANDUM OPINION AND ORDER

Plaintiffs Glovaroma, Inc. ("Glovaroma"), the Zappa Family Trust (the "Trust"), and Gail Zappa allege that Maljack Productions, Inc. ("MPI") violated the Copyright Act, 17 U.S.C. §§ 101-1332, and the Trademark Act, 15 U.S.C. §§ 1051-1127. Plaintiffs also have a claim for an accounting. Both parties now move the court for summary judgment pursuant to Rule 56 of the Federal Rules of Civil Procedure. For the reasons set forth below, the court denies plaintiffs' motion for summary judgment but grants defendant's motion for summary judgment in part and denies it in part.

**Background**

The late Frank Zappa was a legendary rock-and-roll music icon who created many musical works using both audio and video mediums. Since Frank Zappa's death, his widow Gail Zappa has controlled the rights to her deceased husband's creative works through Glovaroma and the Trust. Glovaroma creates and produces videotapes of Frank Zappa's creative works under the registered trademark "Honker Home Video." Gail Zappa owns the right to use Frank Zappa's name, voice, photograph, and likeness as a successor-in-interest. Defendant MPI, an Illinois corporation, is in the business of licensing and distributing video products.

In December 1987, Gail Zappa and MPI reached an oral agreement that gave MPI the right to produce and distribute five Frank Zappa videos under the Honker Home Video trademark label. The videos that are part of this dispute are "Baby Snakes," "Uncle Meat," "Video From Hell," "The True Story of Frank Zappa's 200 Motels," and "The Amazing Mr. Bickford" (the "Videos"). Pursuant to this agreement, MPI a license to manufacture, rent, sublease, advertise, and market copies of these Videos in the United States. In 1987, MPI began distributing four of the Videos. Early in 1990, MPI began distributing the fifth video.

At Gail Zappa's request, an accounting firm reviewed MPI's financial records and determined that MPI was under-reporting sales of the Videos and miscalculating royalty payments. In May 1994, Gail Zappa demanded that MPI return all videos, advertising, and promotional materials belonging to Glovaroma; destroy all Zappa video inventory in MPI's possession; and provide an affidavit to that effect. MPI neither provided an affidavit nor remitted payment. Furthermore, MPI continued to sell-off its existing inventory. (Def.'s 12(M) P 18.) MPI did not, however, duplicate any more Videos or video sleeves. (Def.'s 12(M) P 18.)

The copyright registration certificates for the Videos identify Frank Zappa as the author of the new matter. His personal efforts, which were not as "work made for hire," include editing, new lyrics and music, writing, producing, and directing. (Gerber Decl. Exs. O, Q, S, U, W.) The certificates identify part of the new matter as "work made for hire." (Def.'s 12(M) P 4.) MPI contends that no written "work made for hire" agreements exist for the Videos.

The registration certificates for the video sleeves accompanying the videos "Baby Snakes," "Uncle Meat," "Video From Hell," and "The True Story of Frank Zappa's 200 Motels" (the "Four Sleeves") identify Honker Home Video as the author and describe the work as "work made for hire." (Def.'s 12(M) PP 6-7.) Frank Zappa created the Four Sleeves with help from Greg Gorman, Cal Schenkel, and perhaps others. (G. Zappa Dep. 149-55.) Frank Zappa's personal efforts included graphic design and art direction. (Id.)

Glovaroma does business as Honker Home Video. (Def.'s 12(M) P 8.) Glovaroma had no employees who designed the Four Sleeves. (Def.'s 12(M) P 9.) Furthermore, MPI claims that no written "work made for hire" agreements exist for the Four Sleeves. (Def.'s 12(M) PP 5, 10.)

The copyright registration certificate for "The Amazing Mr. Bickford" video sleeve (the "Bickford sleeve") identifies Cal Schenkel as the author. (Def.'s 12(M) P 11.) The registration certificate further states that Schenkel transferred copyright ownership of the Bickford sleeve to Frank Zappa "by agreement." (Def.'s 12(M) P 12.) MPI claims, however, that no written agreement regarding the transfer of copyright ownership exists between Schenkel and Frank Zappa. (Def.'s 12(M) P 13.) In 1993, Frank and Gail Zappa reached a written assignment agreement and transferred their ownership of all tangible and intangible property to the Zappa Family Trust. (Plaintiffs.' Resp. Ex. D.)

With respect to the trademark infringement claim, MPI contends that it never signed an agreement that inured its use of the Honker Video label to Glovaroma's benefit. (Def.'s 12(M) P 22.) Therefore, MPI claims that it is the owner of the Honker Home Video label because it initiated the use of the trademark in commerce. (Def.'s 12(M) P 20.) Moreover, MPI only used the Honker Home Video label after May 1994 to sell its existing inventory. (Def.'s 12(M) P 23.) Finally, MPI contends that Gail Zappa's objection to the royalty report in April 1989 demonstrates her earliest knowledge of the alleged under-reporting. (Def.'s 12(M) P 24.)

## Analysis

Both parties move the court to enter summary judgment on their behalf under Rule 56 of the Federal Rules of Civil Procedure. The court will render summary judgment only if the factual record shows "that there is no genuine issue as to any material fact and the moving party is entitled to a judgment as a matter of law." Bratton v. Roadway Package Sys., Inc., 77 F.3d 168, 173 (7th Cir. 1996) (quoting Fed. R. Civ. P. 56(c)). The court will not render summary judgment if "a reasonable jury could return a verdict for the nonmoving party." Sullivan v. Cox, 78 F.3d 322, 325 (7th Cir. 1996) (citing Anderson v. Liberty Lobby, Inc., 477 U.S. 242, 248, 91 L. Ed. 2d 202, 106 S. Ct. 2505 (1986)). In ruling on a motion for summary judgment, the court views the facts in the light most favorable to the nonmoving party. See Bratton, 77 F.3d at 171 (citation omitted); Sullivan, 78 F.3d at 325 (citation omitted).

On a motion for summary judgment, the moving party "bears the initial burden of showing that no genuine issue of material fact exists." Hudson Ins. Co. v. City of Chicago Heights, 48 F.3d 234, 237 (7th Cir. 1995) (citing Celotex Corp. v. Catrett, 477 U.S. 317, 323, 91 L. Ed. 2d 265, 106 S. Ct. 2548 (1986)). Then the burden shifts to the nonmoving party, which "must set forth specific facts showing that there is a genuine issue for trial." Fed. R. Civ. P. 56(e); accord NLFC, Inc. v. Devcom Mid-America, Inc., 45 F.3d 231, 234 (7th Cir. 1995) (citations omitted).

These burdens are reflected in Rule 12 of the Local General Rules for the Northern District of Illinois. See Waldridge v. American Hoechst Corp., 24 F.3d 918, 921-22 (7th Cir. 1994). Under Rule 12(M)(3), the moving party must submit a statement of material facts in the form of short numbered paragraphs supported by specific references to the factual record. Under Rule 12(N)(3), the nonmoving party must submit a response to each such paragraph, including (in the case of disagreement) specific references to the factual record. If the nonmoving party fails to disagree with a fact in the moving party's 12(M) statement, the court will deem that fact admitted. See Local Rule 12(N)(3). Similarly, if the nonmoving party disagrees with a fact in the moving party's statement but fails to support its disagreement with a specific reference to the factual record, the court may deem that fact admitted as well. See Fed. R. Civ. P. 56(e); Flaherty v. Gas Research Institute, 31 F.3d 451, 453 (7th Cir. 1994) (citations omitted). The Seventh Circuit Court of Appeals has "repeatedly upheld the strict enforcement of these rules." Waldridge, 24 F.3d at 922; see also, e.g., Knoblauch v. DEF Express Corporation., 86 F.3d 684, 690 (7th Cir. 1996).

## I. Copyright Infringement
### A. The Video Sleeves

To establish copyright infringement, plaintiffs' must prove that they own the copyrights and that defendant copied the "constituent elements of the work that are original." See Feist Publications, Inc. v. Rural Tel Serv. Co., 499 U.S. 340, 361, 113 L. Ed. 2d 358, 111 S. Ct. 1282 (1991). Generally, plaintiffs can prove ownership by a copyright registration. See 17 U.S.C. § 401(c). Under the Copyright Act (the "Act"), copyright ownership "vests initially in the author or authors of the work." 17 U.S.C. § 201(a). "As a general rule, the author is the party who actually creates the work, that is, the person who translates an idea into a fixed, tangible expression entitled to copyright protection." Community for Creative Non-Violence v. Reid, 490 U.S. 730, 737, 104 L. Ed. 2d 811, 109 S. Ct. 2166 (1989). The Copyright Act, however, creates an exception for "works made for hire." 17 U.S.C. § 201(b).

In a "work made for hire," the "author" and initial owner of the copyright is not the creator of the work but the employer or the party that commissioned the work. Section 201(b) provides:

In the case of work made for hire, the employer or other person for whom the work was prepared is considered the author for purposes of this title, and, unless the parties have expressly agreed otherwise in a written instrument signed by them, owns all the rights comprised in the copyright.

Id. Section 101 defines a "work made for hire" as:

(1) a work prepared by an employee within the scope of his or her employment; or

(2) a work specially ordered or commissioned for use as a contribution to a collective work, as part of a motion picture or other audiovisual work, as a translation, as a supplementary work, as a compilation, as an instructional text, as a test, as answer material for a test, or as an atlas, if the parties expressly agree in a written instrument signed by them that work shall be considered a work made for hire.

17 U.S.C. § 101.

The two parts of this test are mutually exclusive. Specifically, the first paragraph of section 101 applies to works created by employees, and the second applies to works created by independent contractors. See Community for Creative Non-Violence, 490 U.S. at 742-43. The CCNV Court held that "employee" and "employer" in section 101 (a) narrowly describes the traditional agency view of the employer-employee relationship. MPI has challenged Glovaroma's valid ownership of the video sleeves for "Baby Snakes," "Uncle Meat," "Video From Hell," and "The True Story of Frank Zappa's 200 Motels," (the "Four Sleeves"). The copyright registration identifies the author of these video sleeves as Honker Home Video and states that the sleeves were "works made for hire." (Gerber Decl. Exs. R, T, V, X.) Glovaroma is doing business as Honker Home Video. (Def.'s 12(M) P 8.) Therefore, Glovaroma must present evidence that it either (1) hired employees who created the video sleeves or (2) commissioned an independent contractor, pursuant to a written agreement, to create the video sleeves.

MPI contends that Glovaroma had no employees who designed video sleeves. (Def.'s 12(M) P 9). In their response, plaintiffs contend that this statement is a misinterpretation of Gail Zappa's testimony. Gail Zappa testified that Frank Zappa created video sleeves in association with Glovaroma, but she did not know whether this was done in an employment relationship. (Plaintiffs.' 12(N) P 9.)

Under Local Rule 12(N)(3), a party opposing summary judgment must serve and file "a response to each numbered paragraph in the moving party's statement, including, in the case of any disagreement, specific references to the affidavits, parts of the record, and other supporting materials relied upon." If the nonmoving party fails to comply with this requirement, the court will deem that fact admitted.

Glovaroma, through its failure to provide any affidavits or deposition testimony that would create a genuine factual issue whether Frank Zappa and Glovaroma were in an employment relationship, has failed to meet its burden under Local Rule 12(N)(3). Gail Zappa's uncertainty regarding the relationship between the two parties is an insufficient denial under the requirements of Local Rule 12(N). Thus, for purposes of this motion, the court assumes that Glovaroma had no employees who designed the sleeves.

Consequently, Glovaroma could only have obtained ownership of the Four Sleeves if it commissioned an independent contractor. A work created by an independent contractor can constitute a "work made for hire" only if it fits one of the nine narrowly drawn categories of works, and then only by compliance with the writing requirement. See Community for Creative Non-Violence, 490 U.S. at 748; see also 17 U.S.C. § 101. One of these categories is a "supplemental work."

Section 101 describes a supplementary work as:

a work prepared for publication as a secondary adjunct to a work by another author for the purpose of introducing, concluding, illustrating, explaining, revising, commenting upon, or assisting in the use of the other work, such as forewords, afterwords, pictorial illustrations, maps, charts, tables, editorial notes, musical arrangements, answer material for tests, bibliographies, appendixes, and indexes, and an "instructional text" in a literary, pictorial, or graphic work prepared for publication and with the purpose of use in systematic instructional activities.

17 U.S.C. § 101 (emphasis added). The copyright registrations describe these Four Sleeves as artwork or cover photographs. (Gerber Decl. Exs. R, T, V, X.) Clearly, the Four Sleeves are supplementary works.

Glovaroma must also produce, however, a written agreement between Frank Zappa and Glovaroma that expressly states that Frank Zappa's work on the Four Sleeves was considered "work made for hire." In Schiller & Schmidt, Inc., v. Nordisco Corp., 969 F.2d 410, 412 (7th Cir. 1992), Judge Posner stated that the requirement of a written statement for specially commissioned works not only serves to protect people against false claims of oral agreements but also ensures the goal of defining ownership rights in intellectual property so that such property will be readily marketable. Furthermore, the written execution must occur before the creation of the work. See id.

MPI contends that no written "work made for hire" agreements exist between Glovaroma and Frank Zappa for the four video sleeves. (Def.'s 12(M) P 10.) In response, Glovaroma states that "Gail Zappa is not necessarily the person with the most knowledge of the subject, and Defendant has not shown for purposes of summary judgment that the agreements do not exist." (Def.'s 12(M) P 10.)

While MPI bears the initial responsibility of informing the court of the basis for its motion and identifying those portions of the deposition that it believes demonstrate the absence of a genuine issue of material fact, MPI does not have to prove affirmatively the nonexistence of a written "work made for hire" agreement. See Celotex, 477 U.S. at 323; see also Fed. R. Civ. P. 56. Therefore, Gail Zappa's deposition testimony satisfies MPI's initial burden that no written "work made for hire" agreements existed between Glovaroma and Frank Zappa. (G. Zappa Dep. p. 155.)

Specifically, Gail Zappa was uncertain of whether a "work made for hire" agreement or copyright assignment existed and, moreover, which video or video sleeve it covered. Because of this uncertainty, Glovaroma must provide evidence from a party with actual knowledge of an agreement or assignment to create a genuine issue of material fact. Glovaroma's 12(N) response fails to meet this burden. Therefore, for the purposes of this summary judgment motion, Glovaroma is not the author of, and is not entitled to enforce, the copyright for the Four Sleeves.

Because no written "work made for hire" agreements exist for the Four Sleeves, the creator of the works is the rightful owner of the video sleeves. See Schiller & Schmidt, 969 F.2d at 413 ("The creator of the property is the owner, unless he is an employee creating the property within the scope of his employment or the parties have agreed in a writing signed by both that the person who commissioned the creation of the property is the owner."). The issue then becomes who created the Four Sleeves?

Per Gail Zappa's uncontroverted testimony, Frank Zappa created the Four Sleeves with help from Greg Gorman, Cal Schenkel, and perhaps others. (G. Zappa Dep. 149-55.) According to section 101 of the Copyright Act, "a work prepared by two or more authors with the intention that their contributions be merged into inseparable or interdependent parts of a unitary whole" is a "joint work." A contributor is not considered an "author," and does not gain a co-owner copyright interest, unless her contribution, standing alone, is copyrightable. See Erickson v. Trinity Theatre, Inc., 13 F.3d 1061, 1070 (7th Cir. 1994). From Gail Zappa's uncontroverted testimony, Frank Zappa was a graphic artist, a designer, and the art director for the Four Sleeves. Therefore, his efforts were more than de minimis and he is the creator, or one of the creators, for each of the Four Sleeves.

In a joint work, each of the authors is an owner of the work as a tenant in common. See Picture Music, Inc. v. Bourne, Inc., 314 F. Supp. 640, 646 (S.D.N.Y. 1970), aff'd, 457 F.2d 1213 (2d Cir. 1972). Absent an agreement to the contrary, each author has an undivided interest in the work. Furthermore, the joint owner cannot assign the work or grant an exclusive license without the written consent of the other co-owners. See 17 U.S.C. § 204(a). A co-owner can, however, transfer his undivided interest in the work. Therefore, whether Frank Zappa was the sole creator or a co-owner of the Four Sleeves, he could transfer his copyright interest.

Consequently, the issue becomes whether Frank Zappa transferred his ownership interest in the Four Sleeves to the Zappa Family Trust (the "Trust"). Under the Copyright Act, "[a] transfer of copyright ownership other than by operation of law is not valid unless an instrument of conveyance, or a note or memorandum of the transfer, is in writing and signed by the owner of the rights conveyed or such owner's duly authorized agent." 17 U.S.C. § 204(A).

In April 1993, Frank and Gail Zappa transferred their individual rights to all tangible and intangible property to the Trust. The written transfer of ownership includes "any copyrights and all renewals and extensions thereof, [and] any trademarks and service marks, applications and registrations therefor." (Plaintiffs.' Resp. Ex. D.) The plain meaning of this conveyance satisfies the section 204(a) writing requirement. Therefore, the Trust is, at a minimum, a co-owner in the Four Sleeves and is, therefore, entitled to bring a copyright infringement action.

### B. The "The Amazing Mr. Bickford" video sleeve

As noted above, transfer of copyright ownership requires a signed agreement between the parties. See 17 U.S.C. § 204(a). The copyright certificate for "The Amazing Mr. Bickford" sleeve (the "Bickford sleeve") identifies Cal Schenkel as the author. (Gerber Decl. Ex. P.) Moreover, the certificate states that Schenkel transferred copyright ownership to Frank Zappa "by agreement." MPI contends that no written agreement exists to transfer the Bickford sleeve copyright from Schenkel to Frank Zappa. (Def.'s 12(M) P 13.) Plaintiffs respond that MPI has not shown that no written agreement exists and that "the only evidence in the matter to date is the deposition of Gail Zappa, who simply does not know whether the agreements exist."

Defendant does not have to prove affirmatively the nonexistence of purported evidence to satisfy summary judgment requirements; the court has already ruled that plaintiffs' argument is deficient for purposes of summary judgment. Consequently, the Trust can only obtain ownership of the Bickford sleeve if the court finds that the mere filing of a certificate of registration containing the "assignment" language is prima facie evidence of the Trust's copyright ownership.

The Copyright Act provides:

In any judicial proceedings the certificate of registration made before or within five years after first publication of the work shall constitute prima facie evidence of the validity of the copyright and of the facts stated in the certificate. The evidentiary weight to be accorded the certificate of the registration made thereafter shall be within the discretion of the court.

17 U.S.C. § 410(c) (emphasis added). The registration certificate for the Bickford sleeve satisfies this five-year requirement. The work was first published on May 15, 1989, and Frank Zappa registered the copyright on December 6, 1993. (Gerber Decl. Ex. P.) The certificate names Frank Zappa as the copyright owner by assignment from Schenkel.

Therefore, plaintiffs have created a rebuttable presumption that Frank Zappa was the owner of the Bickford sleeve copyright on or before December 6, 1993. Although defendant has questioned whether any assignment from Schenkel to Zappa in fact exists, defendant has not introduced any factual evidence to counter the registration certificate. Consequently, for purposes of this motion for summary judgment, Frank Zappa owned the Bickford sleeve copyright and properly transferred it to the Trust under the April 9, 1993 agreement. (Plaintiffs. Resp. Ex. D (stating that the transfer of copyrights from Frank Zappa to the Trust includes those "hereafter acquired"); see also Gerber Decl. Ex. N (recording the transfer of the Bickford sleeve from Frank Zappa to the Trust).)

C. The Five Videos

MPI also challenges Plaintiffs ownership of the "Baby Snakes," "Uncle Meat," "Video From Hell," "The True Story of Frank Zappa's 200 Motels," and "The Amazing Mr. Bickford" videos (the "Videos"). As noted above, a work created by an independent contractor can constitute a "work made for hire" only if it fits one of the nine narrowly drawn categories of works in Section 101, and then only by compliance with the writing requirement. See Community for Creative Non-Violence, 490 U.S. at 748. One of the categories is "audiovisual work"; the Videos fit into this category.

With respect to whether the writing requirement of Section 101 is satisfied, the copyright registration certificate for each video recites that it consists of preexisting matter and new matter. (Gerber Decl. Exs. O, Q, S, U, W.) The certificates also state that Frank Zappa is the author of the new matter and identifies the new matter as "work made for hire." MPI contends that no written "work made for hire" agreements exists for any of the five videos. Plaintiffs respond that MPI has not shown that no written agreement exists and that "the only evidence in the matter to date is the deposition of Gail Zappa, who simply does not know whether the agreements exist." As the court ruled above, plaintiffs' response does not create a genuine issue of material fact. Therefore, the Videos are not "works made for hire," and their creator is the copyright owner. See Schiller & Schmidt, 969 F.2d at 413.

Frank Zappa was, at a minimum, a joint author of the new matter in these Videos. The registration certificates state that part of Frank Zappa's contribution to the Videos was not a "work made for hire." His personal efforts included editing, new lyrics and music, writing, producing, and directing. Three of the five certificates were registered within five years of the first publication of the work. Therefore, per section 410(c), the certificates are prima facie evidence of the validity of the copyrights and the facts stated on the certificates. The other two certificates, for "Video from Hell" and "Uncle Meat," were registered within seven years of first publication. Because defendant has adduced no facts to contravene Frank Zappa's contributions to these two videos, the court, in its 410(c) discretion, accepts the certificates as prima facie evidence of the facts stated thereon. Consequently, for purposes of this motion for summary judgment, the court finds that Frank Zappa owned, or jointly owned, the copyrights for the Videos and properly transferred them, or his interest in them, to the Trust under the April 9, 1993 agreement. Therefore, the Trust has the right to bring a copyright infringement action for the Videos.

### D. Infringement

Having established that the Trust is entitled to sue for infringement of the sleeve and the video copyrights, the next issue is whether MPI infringed the copyrights by "selling-off" its existing inventory after Gail Zappa revoked their oral agreement. Under 17 U.S.C. § 106(3), the copyright owner has the exclusive right "to distribute copies . . . of the copyrighted work to the public by sale or other transfer of ownership or by rental, lease or lending." Moreover, the copyright owner has the authority to transfer its exclusive rights, subject to a writing requirement. Section 204(a) provides that an exclusive license "is not valid unless an instrument of conveyance or note or memorandum of the transfer, is in writing and signed by the owner of the rights conveyed." This provision protects copyright holders from persons who mistakenly or fraudulently claim oral licenses. Furthermore, this provision allows licensees to defend themselves against copyright infringement actions.

Plaintiffs contend that their licensing agreement with MPI is not enforceable because no written agreement exists that grants defendant an exclusive right to copy and distribute their works. MPI argues that because plaintiffs permitted MPI to manufacture the videos and video sleeves, MPI was entitled to sell-off its existing inventory after Gail Zappa rescinded the oral license.

A copyright holder can grant an implied nonexclusive license through conduct or an oral agreement. See I.A.E., Inc. v. Shaver, 74 F.3d 768, 775 (7th Cir. 1996). A nonexclusive license does not transfer copyright ownership to the licensee but does grant the licensee the right to use the copyrighted work. See id.

A nonexclusive license is, therefore, an exception to the writing requirement of section 204. In fact, consent given in the form of mere permission or lack of objection is also equivalent to a nonexclusive license and is not required to be in writing. Although a person holding a nonexclusive license has no standing to sue for copyright infringement, the existence of a license, exclusive or nonexclusive, creates an affirmative defense to a claim of copyright infringement.

Id. (citations omitted).

The I.A.E. court suggests several objective factors to use when evaluating whether an implied license exists: the copyright registration certificate language, any written agreements between the parties, deposition testimony, and "the delivery of the copyrighted material without warning that its further use would constitute copyright infringement. " See id. at 776. In I.A.E., the registration certificates stated that the copyrighted designs were to be used for a particular purpose. See id. No such restrictions exist on the Videos or sleeve certificates; therefore, defendant was not under notice that it exceeding the purpose of the copyrights when it duplicated and distributed the videos.

Furthermore, both parties agree that MPI had a license to manufacture and distribute plaintiffs' works until around May 9, 1994. (Second Am. Compl. PP 11-14; Def.'s 12(M) P 15.) Furthermore, on January 15, 1991, Gail Zappa wrote defendant, "isn't it time to redo our 'deal'." (Def.'s 12(M) Ex. L.) Although this memorandum lacks the term "transfer" or "copyright," the minimum requirement is merely "a mutual intent to transfer the copyright interests." M. & D. Nimmer, Nimmer on Copyrights § 10.03[A][2], p. 10-37 (1997). Therefore, the court finds that a nonexclusive license existed until on or about May 9, 1994.

Both parties acknowledge that defendant did not duplicate the videos or the sleeves after plaintiffs canceled the license. (Def.'s 12(M) P 17.) Moreover, they agree that after this date defendant sold its remaining inventory. (Id. P 18.) The issue before the court is whether these final sales constitute a copyright infringement. The record is not clear about what agreements the parties had before May 9, 1994. For example, the court does not know whether their agreement contained a termination date or not. Furthermore, the court does not know if the parties had an agreement about how to wrap up business after the termination. Therefore, the extent of the infringement, if any, is a matter to be left to the jury. Accordingly, the court denies both parties' motions for summary judgment on the copyright infringement claim.

## II. The Trademark Infringement Claim

Plaintiffs allege in Count V that defendant continued to use the trademark "Honker Home Video" after plaintiffs requested the defendant to cease distribution of the Zappa videos under the Honker label. According to the Trademark Act, any person who shall, without consent of the registrant, use in commerce any reproduction, counterfeit, copy, or colorable imitation of a registered mark in connection with the sale, offering for sale, distribution, or advertising of any goods . . . [where] such use is likely to cause confusion . . . shall be liable in a civil action to the registrant.

15 U.S.C. § 1114(1). Plaintiffs' alleged ownership of the trademark is based on their registration of the label in February 1988. (Plaintiffs.' 12(M) P 4.)

A trademark is infringed when an unauthorized party creates consumer confusion by using a similar mark on similar goods. However, "trademark law generally does not reach the sale of genuine goods bearing a true mark even though such sale was without the owner's consent." Weil Ceramics & Glass, Inc. v. Dash, 878 F.2d 659, 671 (3d Cir. 1989). Furthermore, no claim for infringement is generally found where plaintiff authorized the defendant to use the mark. See Genin, Trudeau & Co. v. Integra Dev. Int'l, 845 F. Supp. 611 (N.D. Ill. 1994). Thus, where defendant continued to sell product bearing plaintiff's trademark even after plaintiff canceled their agreement, defendant was not found liable for trademark infringement. See Advanced Sports Concepts, Inc. v. Baden Sports Inc., 1993 U.S. Dist. LEXIS 20311, 29 U.S.P.Q.2D (BNA) 1227, 1229-30 (S.D. Ohio 1993). And, where defendant's products bearing the mark were genuine and qualitatively equivalent to those produced by plaintiff, no infringement was found because "there is no likelihood of confusion or loss of good will." Genin, 845 F. Supp. at 615-16.

Plaintiffs argue that they own the Honker Home Video Mark because they registered it on February 2, 1988. (Plaintiffs.' Resp. Ex. C.) Defendant responds that it owns the mark because it initiated use of the mark. (Ali Decl. P 6.) Despite which party owns the Honker Home Video mark, "there is no likelihood of confusion" from MPI's continued use of the mark after plaintiffs canceled the license. Plaintiffs have not met their burden of satisfying the prima facie case for infringement; they adduced no evidence showing any consumer confusion over the Honker mark after May 9, 1994. The inventory that defendant sold after the license lapsed was identical to the inventory produced and sold before May 9, 1994. The videos sold with the mark after May 9 were genuine; consumers are not going to be confused by seeing the mark on a Zappa video sold after May 9. The mark was not diminished by having the rest of defendants inventory sold after May 9. Therefore, the court finds that defendant did not create any consumer confusion by continuing to sell its Honker Home Video inventory after May 9, 1994. Consequently, the court does not have to determine who, in fact, owns the Honker mark. The court grants defendant's motion for summary judgment and dismisses plaintiffs' claim for trademark infringement.

### III. Plaintiffs' Claim for Accounting

MPI argues that the court should grant it summary judgment on plaintiffs' accounting claim. Specifically, MPI claims that the court lacks equity jurisdiction over the claim, that there is no federal jurisdiction over the claim as it seeks no monetary relief, and that the applicable statute of limitations has time-barred the claim.

The existence of an account, or the fact that an accounting is necessary, does not confer equitable jurisdiction. See Webster v. Hall, 388 Ill. 401, 58 N.E.2d 575 (Ill. 1944). An accounting claim is improper without a specific, recognized factual predicate. Plaintiffs allege that the factual predicate in the instant case is that the accounts involved are "complex." MPI contends that this issue is not complex and points to plaintiffs' expert testimony that only three issues exist. Moreover, the expert's audit report fully explains the issues in four pages. Consequently, MPI argues that the accounting is not so complex that a jury could not understand it. Plaintiffs admit to the statements regarding their expert's testimony and fail to even discuss the issue in their Response and Cross-Motion for Summary Judgment.

Plaintiffs failed to address this issue. Moreover, even looking in a light most favorable to plaintiffs, the fact that plaintiffs' expert identified only three issues and fully discussed those issues demonstrates that the factual predicate, upon which plaintiffs base the accounting claim, is baseless.

The accounting claim must also fail as it is beyond the applicable statute of limitations. Specifically, Illinois applies a five-year limitation to an accounting claim. See Kedzierski v. Kedzierski, 899 F.2d 681, 682 (7th Cir. 1990). Gail Zappa first became aware of the accounting claim on April 1989 when she first protested MPI's first royalty report. Again, Plaintiffs' counsel does not even address this issue in its Response and Cross-Motion for Summary Judgment. As a result, the court grants MPI's motion for summary judgment and dismisses plaintiffs' accounting claim.

### Conclusion

The court grants in part and denies in part MPI's motion for summary judgment. Specifically, the court grants MPI's motion for summary judgment on the trademark infringement and accounting claims. The court denies MPI's motion for summary judgment on the copyright infringement claim. Plaintiffs' motion for summary judgment is denied. The parties should discuss settlement before the next court date.

---

*Glovaroma* involves the Zappa Family Trust lawsuit against a distributor of video products for infringement under the copyright Act, 17 U.S.C. Section 101-1332, and the Trademark Act, 15 U.S.C. Section 1051. Plaintiffs are a family trust for the late rock-and-roll icon/genius, Frank Zappa ("Help I'm a Rock"). Plaintiff's spouse had made a verbal agreement with defendant to produce and distribute five videos created by the deceased musician. Plaintiffs sued defendant after an accounting firm determined that defendant under-reported sales and miscalculated royalties. The court grants defendant's motion for summary judgment on trademark infringement and accounting, but denies defendant's motion for summary judgment on the copyright infringement claim.

### DISTRIBUTION AGREEMENT

This Agreement made this 21st, day of November 2015, by and between John Doe Music Group, whose principal place of business is 1234 Smith Street, Houston, Texas 77777 (hereinafter called Record Company) and Joshua Doe, Inc., f/s/o Joshua Doe, whose principal place of business is located at 5555 Azalea Lane, Houston, Texas 77777 (hereinafter Artist).

Whereas, Record Company desires to distribute Master recording of Joshua Doe (hereinafter Artist); and

Whereas, the Artist has unique skills and expertise in the administration of production of sound recordings. Now, therefore, in consideration of the respective promises herein, the parties agree as follows:

1.  Artist shall provide the arranging, producing, engineering, and musicianship, for the recording of 10-12 songs with a combined length of approximately 70 minutes. Record company and Artist shall mutually approve all material to be recorded, including the number of compositions to be recorded.

2.  Artist shall supply all talent, including, singers and musicians. Selection of dates of recording, studio or facilities where recording, mixing, remixing, and other recording tasks are to take place are the responsibility of the Artist. Record Company's representative shall have the right to be present at all and any recording sessions. Record Company will have final approval on recording production.

3.  All artwork for project shall be delivered to Record Company no later than November 30th, 2015.

4.  Artist warrants that copyright infringement in no way is involved in said recording project on works provided by Artist.

5.  Artist further warrants that all songs written from this project will be the sole responsibility of the Artist. The Artist will maintain and controlled all Publishing from said project.

6.  The Master Recordings herein described from the inception of recording thereof, all artwork and photographs involved, and all performances embodied therein, shall be sole property of Joshua Doe, Inc., after Exploitation Period. John Doe Music Group shall have the exclusive right to copyright such Master Recordings in its name as the owner thereof and to secure any and all renewals and extensions of such copyright under our distribution agreement. The Exploitation Period as to Accepted Project shall commence upon the release date of February 2016 and shall continue thereafter until a date which is two (2) years.

7.  For the Master herein Record Company shall pay to Artist Fifty Percent (50%) of ($2.75) sales John Doe Music Group collects from Distribution Company for each compact disc (CD) master exploitation, from record one, and Fifty Percent (50%) of any and all revenue received, for each Single Song electronic, digital, or any format now know, or hereafter developed, for single song content transfer or Download. Any money paid to artist or on artist behalf shall be non-recoupable to Artist. Artist will be responsible for paying producers, writers, publishers and any and

all royalties that are due to persons that are associated with this project.

8.     John Doe Music Group will be responsible for the cost of promotion, manufacturing, radio, retail and any cost associated with the sale of the project at record company sole discretion and shall not be recoupable against the Artist royalties.

9.     Artist will have a 20% reserve against returns to be held for a period of one year. Or in accordance to John Doe Music Group distribution deal.

10.     Company will compute royalties payable to you hereafter as of June 30$^{th}$ and December 31$^{st}$ for each preceding six month period during which records as to which royalties are payable hereunder sold, and will render a statement and pay such royalties prior to each succeeding October 15$^{th}$ and April 15$^{th}$ respectively. All royalty statements provided to Artist shall include a copy of all royalty computation statements and compensation paperwork provided to Record Company by Distributor reflecting the number of records sold.

11.     At any time within the twelve (12) months after a royalty statement is provided hereunder you shall have the right to give said Record Company written notice of your intention to examine said books and records with respect to such statement. Such examination shall be commenced within thirty (30) days after the date of such notice, at your sole cost and expense, by a certified public accountant or attorney designated by you. Audit shall be conducted during company business hours.

12.     In all trade advertisements, paid advertising, liner notes, labels, CD's, cassettes, cassette singles, single sleeves and album covers exactly as follows: Joshua Doe, Inc. f/s/o Joshua Doe.

13.     This agreement is entered into in the State of Texas and shall be governed by the laws and practices of the State of Texas. In the event of any action, suit, or proceeding arising from or based upon this contract brought by either party hereto against the other, the prevailing party shall be entitled to recover from the other its attorneys' fees in connection therewith in addition to the costs of such action, suit, or proceeding.

14.     This agreement sets forth the entire covenant between the parties with respect to the subject matter hereof. In witness whereof, the parties have here onto set their hands the day and year as first written above.

_____        _____

President                         Joshua Doe, Inc.
John Doe Music Group         f/s/o Joshua Doe
1234 Smith Street              5555 Azalea Lane
Houston, Texas 77777        Houston, Texas 77777

Questions and Discussion

1. In *Glovaroma, Inc. v. Maljack Prods.*, 71 F. Supp. 2d 846 (1999), the judge suggested that the parties should discuss settlement before the next date. What does that mean? The judge denied the accounting claim, stating that the "existence of an account, or the fact that an accounting is necessary does not confer equitable jurisdiction." An accounting claim is improper without a specific, recognized factual predicate. Plaintiffs allege that the factual predicate in the instant case is that the accounts involved are complex" (at 857, footnote omitted). Is this another example of poor legal preparation?

2. In *Platinum Record Co. v. Lucasfilm, Ltd.*, 566 F. Supp. 226 (1983), the court looks at "after-developed media" and its effect on a preexisting contract. Film Company gave plaintiff's predecessor-in-interest the "master recordings" of four popular songs for use on the soundtrack of the motion picture "American Graffiti." Defendant distributed the movie on videocassettes and video discs. Defendant's motion for summary judgment is granted on the grounds that the wording in the relevant contract was extremely broad and unambiguous in permitting defendants to distribute the movie on videocassettes and video discs. Another outcome would come about—a case of the tail wagging the dog. Isn't there any way to change the language in the original contract that would favor plaintiff record company more?

3. In *Buffalo Broadcasting Co. v. ASCAP*, 744 F.2d 917 (1984) the court found for ASCAP and BMI, asserting that their "blanket" licensing for the licensing of music to local television stations was not a violation of the antitrust laws. Remember, in "Dumb and Dumber," when Jim Carrey was ecstatic to find out that he had a "one-in-a-million" chance with Lauren Holly? Is that the case here? The local stations have an option, namely, "program" licensing; but, even the court agrees that because of cost and availability, "blanket" licensing is the only real option. What do you think?

4. Look at the enclosed Distribution Agreement. How would you change or ameliorate or strengthen it, if you were hired by distributor? Or, if you were hired by the artist?

# Chapter 8
# Songwriters and Producers, Performing Rights Societies, and Copyright Enforcement

The performing rights societies act as the policeman and cashier for payment to the artists of their royalty income. They work on the copyright laws of the various countries. They ensure copyright enforcement. The three most prevalent are: ASCAP (American Society of Composers, Authors, and Publishers); BMI (Broadcast Music, Inc.), and SESAC (Society of European Stage Authors & Composers).

A working description of ASCAP and BMI can be found in *Buffalo Broad. Co. v. ASCAP*, 744 F.2d 917, 920 (2d Cir. 1984):

> Defendant ASCAP is an unincorporated membership association of composers, authors, and publishers of music, formed in 1914. It has approximately 21,000 writers and 8,000 publisher members. It holds non-exclusive licenses for the non-dramatic performing rights to more than three million musical compositions. BMI is a non-profit corporation organized in 1939 by radio broadcasters. It has approximately 38,000 writers and 22,000 publisher affiliates. Its repertory, for which it holds non-exclusive licenses for non-dramatic performing rights, includes more than one million compositions.

"SESAC and SESAC Latina (a branch of SESAC devoted exclusively to Spanish-language music) use a computerized system for the identification and tracking of musical compositions . . ." (Schulenberg, Legal Aspects of the Music Industry 369).

Frank Music Corp. v. MGM, Inc.
United States Court of Appeals for the Ninth Circuit
January 9, 1985; September 23, 1985, Decided
Nos. 83-6426, 83-6460
772 F.2d 505

FLETCHER, Circuit Judge:

This copyright infringement suit arises out of defendants' use of five songs from plaintiffs' dramatico-musical play Kismet in a musical revue staged at defendant MGM Grand Hotel in 1974-76. After a bench trial, the district court found infringement and awarded the plaintiffs $22,000 as a share of defendants' profits. Plaintiffs appeal and defendants cross-appeal. We affirm in part, reverse in part, and remand.

## I. FACTS

The original version of Kismet was a dramatic play, written by Edward Knoblock in 1911. Knoblock copyrighted the play as an unpublished work in that year and again as a published work in 1912. Knoblock's copyright expired in 1967, and the dramatic play Kismet entered the public domain.

In 1952, plaintiff Edwin Lester acquired the right to produce a musical stage production of the dramatic play Kismet. Lester hired plaintiffs Luther Davis and Charles Lederer to write the libretto and plaintiffs Robert Wright and George Forrest to write the music and lyrics for the musical adaptation. In 1953 and 1954, Lederer and Davis copyrighted their dramatico-musical play Kismet, and in 1953, Wright and Forrest assigned to plaintiff Frank Music Corporation the right to copyright all portions of the musical score written for Kismet. Frank Music subsequently obtained copyrights for the entire musical score and for each of the songs in the score.

In 1954, Lederer, Wright, and Forrest entered into a license agreement with Loew's, Inc., a predecessor of Metro-Goldwyn-Mayer, Inc., ("MGM, Inc.") granting to it the right to produce a musical motion picture based on plaintiffs' play. MGM released its motion picture version of Kismet, starring Howard Keel and Ann Blyth, in 1955.

The story presented in the MGM film and in plaintiffs' dramatico-musical play is essentially the same as that told in Knoblock's dramatic play. It is the tale of a day in the life of a poetic beggar named Hajj and his daughter, Marsinah. The story is set in ancient Baghdad, with major scenes in the streets of Baghdad, the Wazir's palace, an enchanted garden, and the Wazir's harem.

On April 26, 1974, defendant MGM Grand Hotel premiered a musical revue entitled Hallelujah Hollywood in the hotel's Ziegfield Theatre. The show was staged, produced, and directed by defendant Donn Arden. It featured ten acts of singing, dancing, and variety performances. Of the ten acts, four were labeled as "tributes" to MGM motion pictures of the past, and one was a tribute to the "Ziegfield Follies." The remaining acts were variety numbers, which included performances by a live tiger, a juggler, and the magicians, Siegfried and Roy.

The Ziegfield Theatre, where Hallelujah Hollywood was performed, is a lavish showplace. Its special features, including huge elevators used to raise or lower portions of the stage and ceiling lifts capable of lowering performers down into the audience during the shows, reportedly provide impressive special effects.

Act IV of Hallelujah Hollywood, the subject of this lawsuit, was entitled "Kismet," and was billed as a tribute to the MGM movie of that name. Comprised of four scenes, it was approximately eleven and one-half minutes in length. It was set in ancient Baghdad, as was plaintiffs' play, and the characters were called by the same or similar names to those used in plaintiffs' play. Five songs were taken in whole or in part from plaintiffs' play. No dialogue was spoken during the act, and, in all, it contained approximately six minutes of music taken directly from plaintiffs' play.

The total running time of Hallelujah Hollywood was approximately 100 minutes, except on Saturday nights when two acts were deleted, shortening the show to 75 minutes. The show was performed three times on Saturday evenings, twice on the other evenings of the week.

On November 1, 1974, plaintiffs informed MGM Grand that they considered Hallelujah Hollywood to infringe their rights in Kismet. MGM Grand responded that it believed its use of plaintiffs' music was covered by its blanket license agreement with the American Society of Composers, Authors and Publishers ("ASCAP"). In 1965, plaintiffs had granted to ASCAP the right to license certain rights in the musical score of their play Kismet.

Plaintiffs filed this action, alleging copyright infringement, unfair competition, and breach of contract. MGM Grand continued to present Hallelujah Hollywood, including Act IV "Kismet," until July 16, 1976, when the hotel substituted new music in Act IV. In all, the "Kismet" sequence was used in approximately 1700 performances of the show.

## II. DISCUSSION
### A. Scope of the ASCAP License

Paragraph one of the ASCAP license gives MGM Grand the right to perform publicly "non-dramatic renditions of the separate musical compositions" in the ASCAP repertory. Paragraph three excludes from the license "dramatico-musical works, or songs [accompanied by] visual representation of the work from which the music is taken. . . ." The district court addressed both of these clauses and concluded that Act IV of Hallelujah Hollywood was nondramatic but contained visual representations of plaintiffs' play. The court therefore held that Act IV exceeded the scope of the ASCAP license. We review de novo the district court's interpretation of the agreement because the court interpreted the agreement from the face of the document and as a matter of law. In re Financial Securities Litigation, 729 F.2d 628, 631-32 (9th Cir. 1984). We apply the clearly erroneous standard to its findings as to the sufficiency of the visual representations.

We agree with the result reached by the district court, but not with its approach. We agree that Act IV "Kismet" was accompanied by "visual representation" of plaintiffs' play. Accordingly, defendants' use was excluded from the ASCAP license by the express terms of paragraph three. We conclude, however, that there is no reason to consider, as the district court did, whether Act IV was "non-dramatic."

The district court found the following "visual representations": plaintiffs' songs were performed in Hallelujah Hollywood by singers identified as characters from plaintiffs' Kismet, dressed in costumes designed to recreate Kismet, and the performance made use of locale, settings, scenery, props, and dance style music of the type used in plaintiffs' work.

The defendants do not challenge the finding that their production contained these visual representations. They argue, instead, that the district court failed to give sufficient consideration to whether the visual representations in Act IV were "of the work from which the music is taken," i.e., plaintiffs' Kismet. Defendants suggest that this distinction is important because plaintiffs' Kismet is a derivative work. They argue that many of the visual representations, (e.g., street scenes in ancient Baghdad, swarming bazaars, and an oriental palace), could be said to be derived from Edward Knoblock's 1911 dramatic version of Kismet rather than from plaintiffs' Kismet. Since Knoblock's play is in the public domain, defendants contend these visual representations are not protectable by plaintiffs' copyright. Defendants further argue that other elements of the "visual representations," such as choreography style and character names, also are not protectable by copyright.

We find defendants' arguments unpersuasive for two reasons. First, their suggestion that they might have derived portions of Act IV from Knoblock's 1911 play is directly contradicted in the record. Arden created Act IV as a tribute to the MGM musical Kismet, which was derived from plaintiffs' play. While preparing Act IV, he obtained the Broadway score of plaintiffs' play and screened the MGM motion picture. The record does not show that any of Act IV was based on Knoblock's 1911 dramatic version of Kismet.

More important, defendants' argument is unpersuasive because it is simply irrelevant. The question we face is not whether the "visual representations" are copyrightable, but whether the use of a copyrighted work exceeds the scope of an ASCAP license because visual representations accompanied the songs. The license agreement does not refer to "copyrightable" visual representations. The district court was not clearly erroneous in finding that Act IV "Kismet" was accompanied by sufficient visual representations derived from plaintiffs' play to place the songs' use beyond the scope of the ASCAP license.

The district court properly concluded that defendants infringed plaintiffs' copyrights in Kismet.

### B. Recovery for Infringement

The Copyright Act of 1909 provided three forms of recovery to a plaintiff whose copyright had been infringed: actual damages, infringer's profits, or statutory "in lieu" damages. The Act provided for recovery of "such damages as the copyright proprietor may have suffered due to the infringement, as well as all the profits which the infringer shall have made from such an infringement. . . ." 17 U.S.C. § 101(b) (1970). The Act further provided that a court could award "in lieu of actual damages and profits, such damages as to the court shall appear to be just" within certain prescribed minima and maxima. Id.

A court making an award for copyright infringement must, if possible, determine both the plaintiff's actual damages and the defendant's profits derived from the infringement. Sid & Marty Krofft Television Productions, Inc. v. McDonald's Corp., 562 F.2d 1157, 1172 (9th Cir. 1977) (Krofft I). In this circuit, we have construed section 101(b) of the 1909 Act as allowing recovery of the greater of the plaintiff's damage or the defendant's profits. Krofft I, 562 F.2d at 1176; Universal Pictures Co. v. Harold Lloyd Corp., 162 F.2d 354, 376 (9th Cir. 1947).

### 1. Actual Damages

"Actual damages" are the extent to which the market value of a copyrighted work has been injured or destroyed by an infringement. 3 M. Nimmer, Nimmer on Copyright § 14.02, at 14-6 (1985). In this circuit, we have stated the test of market value as "what a willing buyer would have been reasonably required to pay to a willing seller for plaintiffs' work." Krofft I, 562 F.2d at 1174.

The district court declined to award actual damages. The court stated that it was "unconvinced that the market value of plaintiffs' work was in any way diminished as a result of defendant's infringement." We are obliged to sustain this finding unless we conclude it is clearly erroneous. Fed. R. Civ. P. 52(a); see County of Ventura v. Blackburn, 362 F.2d 515, 521 (9th Cir. 1966); Shapiro, Bernstein & Co. v. 4636 S. Vermont Ave., Inc., 367 F.2d 236, 241 (9th Cir. 1966).

Plaintiffs contend the district court's finding is clearly erroneous in light of the evidence they presented concerning the royalties Kismet could have earned in a full Las Vegas production. Plaintiffs did offer evidence of the royalties Kismet had earned in productions around the country. They also introduced opinion testimony, elicited from plaintiff Lester and from Kismet's leasing agent, that a full production of Kismet could have been licensed in Las Vegas for $7,500 per week. And they introduced other opinion testimony to the effect that Hallelujah Hollywood had destroyed the Las Vegas market for a production of plaintiffs' Kismet.

In a copyright action, a trial court is entitled to reject a proffered measure of damages if it is too speculative. See Peter Pan Fabrics, Inc. v. Jobela Fabrics, Inc., 329 F.2d 194, 196-97 (2d Cir. 1964). Although uncertainty as to the amount of damages will not preclude recovery, uncertainty as to the fact of damages may. Universal Pictures Co. v. Harold Lloyd Corp., 162 F.2d at 369; see also 3 M. Nimmer, supra, § 14.02, at 14-8 to -9. It was the fact of damages that concerned the district court. The court found that plaintiffs "failed to establish any damages attributable to the infringement." (emphasis in original). This finding is not clearly erroneous.

Plaintiffs offered no disinterested testimony showing that Hallelujah Hollywood precluded plaintiffs from presenting Kismet at some other hotel in Las Vegas. It is not implausible to conclude, as the court below apparently did, that a production presenting six minutes of music from Kismet, without telling any of the story of the play, would not significantly impair the prospects for presenting a full production of that play. Based on the record presented, the district court was not clearly erroneous in finding that plaintiffs' theory of damages was uncertain and speculative.

### 2. Infringer's Profits

As an alternative to actual damages, a prevailing plaintiff in an infringement action is entitled to recover the infringer's profits to the extent they are attributable to the infringement. 17 U.S.C. § 101(b); Krofft, 562 F.2d at 1172. In establishing the infringer's profits, the plaintiff is required to prove only the defendant's sales; the burden then shifts to the defendant to prove the elements of costs to be deducted from sales in arriving at profit. 17 U.S.C. § 101(b). Any doubt as to the computation of costs or profits is to be resolved in favor of the plaintiff. Shapiro, Bernstein & Co. v. Remington Records, Inc., 265 F.2d 263 (2d Cir. 1959). If the infringing defendant does not meet its burden of proving costs, the gross figure stands as the defendant's profits. Russell v. Price, 612 F.2d 1123, 1130-31 (9th Cir. 1979), cert. denied, 446 U.S. 952, 100 S. Ct. 2919, 64 L. Ed. 2d 809 (1980).

The district court, following this approach, found that the gross revenue MGM Grand earned from the presentation of Hallelujah Hollywood during the relevant time period was $24,191,690. From that figure, the court deducted direct costs of $18,060,084 and indirect costs (overhead) of $3,641,960, thus arriving at a net profit of $2,489,646.

Plaintiffs' challenge these computations on a number of grounds. Several of the objections plaintiffs raise require only brief discussion; we dispose of these in the margin. But three of their objections are more serious, and deserve closer scrutiny. Plaintiffs claim the district court erred in allowing deductions for overhead expenses for two reasons: because the infringement was "conscious and deliberate," and because defendants failed to show that each item of claimed overhead assisted in the production of the infringement. Plaintiffs also contend the court erred in not including in gross profits some portion of MGM's earnings on its hotel and gaming operations.

A portion of an infringer's overhead properly may be deducted from gross revenues to arrive at profits, at least where the infringement was not willful, conscious, or deliberate. Kamar International, Inc. v. Russ Berrie & Co., 752 F.2d 1326, 1331 (9th Cir. 1984); Sammons v. Colonial Press, Inc., 126 F.2d 341, 351 (1st Cir. 1942); 3 M. Nimmer, supra, § 14.03[B], at 14-16.1. Plaintiffs argue that the infringement here was conscious and deliberate, but the district court found to the contrary. The court's finding is not clearly erroneous. Defendants believed their use of Kismet was protected under MGM Grand's ASCAP license. Although their contention ultimately proved to be wrong, it was not implausible. Defendants reasonably could have believed that their production was not infringing plaintiffs' copyrights, and, therefore, the district court was not clearly erroneous in finding that their conduct was not willful. See Kamar International, Inc. v. Russ Berrie & Co., 752 F.2d at 1331.

We find more merit in plaintiffs' second challenge to the deduction of overhead costs. They argue that defendants failed to show that each item of claimed overhead assisted in the production of the infringement. The evidence defendants introduced at trial segregated overhead expenses into general categories, such as general and administrative costs, sales and advertising, and engineering and maintenance. Defendants then allocated a portion of these costs to the production of Hallelujah Hollywood based on a ratio of the revenues from that production as compared to MGM Grand's total revenues. The district court adopted this approach.

We do not disagree with the district court's acceptance of the defendants' method of allocation, based on gross revenues. Because a theoretically perfect allocation is impossible, we require only a "reasonably acceptable formula." Sammons v. Colonial Press, Inc., 126 F.2d at 349; see Kamar International, Inc. v. Russ Berrie & Co., 752 F.2d at 1333. We find, as did the district court, that defendants' method of allocation is reasonably acceptable.

We disagree with the district court, however, to the extent it concluded the defendants adequately showed that the claimed overhead expenses actually contributed to the production of Hallelujah Hollywood. Recently, in Kamar International, we stated that a deduction for overhead should be allowed "only when the infringer can demonstrate that [the overhead expense] was of actual assistance in the production, distribution or sale of the infringing product." 752 F.2d at 1332 (citation omitted); accord Sheldon v. Metro-Goldwyn-Mayer Pictures Inc., 106 F.2d 45, 54, 42 U.S.P.Q. (BNA) 540 (2d Cir. 1939) (Sheldon I), aff'd, 309 U.S. 390, 84 L. Ed. 825, 60 S. Ct. 681 (1940). We do not take this to mean that an infringer must prove his overhead expenses and their relationship to the infringing production in minute detail. See Sheldon I, 106 F.2d at 52; Sterns-Roger Manufacturing Co. v. Ruth, 87 F.2d 35, 41-42 (10th Cir. 1936). Nonetheless, the defendant bears the burden of explaining, at least in general terms, how claimed overhead actually contributed to the production of the infringing work. See Kamar International, Inc. v. Russ Berrie & Co., 752 F.2d at 1333; Taylor v. Meirick, 712 F.2d 1112, 1121-22 (7th Cir. 1983) ("It is too much to ask a plaintiff who has proved infringement also to do the defendant's cost accounting.").

We do not doubt that some of defendants' claimed overhead contributed to the production of Hallelujah Hollywood. The difficulty we have, however, is that defendants offered no evidence of what costs were included in general categories such as "general and administrative expenses," nor did they offer any evidence concerning how these costs contributed to the production of Hallelujah Hollywood. The defendants contend their burden was met when they introduced evidence of their total overhead costs allocated on a reasonable basis. The district court apparently agreed with this approach. That is not the law of this circuit. Under Kamar International, a defendant additionally must show that the categories of overhead actually contributed to sales of the infringing work. 752 F.2d at 1332. We can find no such showing in the record before us. Therefore, we conclude the district court's finding that "defendants have established that these items of general expense [the general categories of claimed overhead] contributed to the production of 'Hallelujah Hollywood'" was clearly erroneous.

Plaintiffs next challenge the district court's failure to consider MGM Grand's earnings on hotel and gaming operations in arriving at the amount of profits attributable to the infringement. The district court received evidence concerning MGM Grand's total net profit during the relevant time period, totaling approximately $395,000,000, but its memorandum decision does not mention these indirect profits and computes recovery based solely on the revenues and profits earned on the production of Hallelujah Hollywood (approximately $24,000,000 and $2,500,000 respectively). We surmise from this that the district court determined plaintiffs were not entitled to recover indirect profits, but we have no hint as to the district court's reasons.

Whether a copyright proprietor may recover "indirect profits" is one of first impression in this circuit. We conclude that under the 1909 Act indirect profits may be recovered.

The 1909 Act provided that a copyright proprietor is entitled to "all the profits which the infringer shall have made from such infringement. . . ." 17 U.S.C. § 101(b). The language of the statute is broad enough to permit recovery of indirect as well as direct profits. See 3 M. Nimmer, supra, § 14.03[A], at 14-15; cf. Nucor Corp. v. Tennessee Forging Steel Service, Inc., 513 F.2d 151, 153 (8th Cir. 1975) (common law copyright infringement action; issue of whether infringing use of copyrighted architectural plans resulted in lower manufacturing costs to defendants was properly put to jury). At the same time, a court may deny recovery of a defendant's profits if they are only remotely or speculatively attributable to the infringement. See 3 M. Nimmer, supra, § 14.03[A]; see, e.g., Roy Export Co. v. Columbia Broadcasting System, Inc., 503 F. Supp. 1137, 1156-57 (S.D.N.Y. 1980) (profits from an infringing unsponsored television broadcast could not be ascertained since benefit received by CBS "consists of unmeasurable good-will with affiliates and increased stature and prestige vis-a-vis competitors."), aff'd, 672 F.2d 1095 (2d Cir.), cert. denied, 459 U.S. 826, 74 L. Ed. 2d 63, 103 S. Ct. 60 (1982).

The allowance of indirect profits was considered in Sid & Marty Krofft Television Productions, Inc. v. McDonald's Corp., 1983 Copyright L. Rep. (CCH) P25,572 at 18,381 (C.D. Cal. 1983) (Krofft II), on remand from 562 F.2d 1157 (9th Cir. 1977), a case involving facts analogous to those presented here. The plaintiffs, creators of the "H.R. Pufnstuf" children's television program, alleged that they were entitled to a portion of the profits McDonald's earned on its food sales as damages for the "McDonaldland" television commercials that infringed plaintiffs' copyright. The district court rejected as speculative the plaintiffs' formula for computing profits attributable to the infringement. However, the court's analysis and award of in lieu damages indicate that it considered indirect profits recoverable. The court stated, in awarding $1,044,000 in statutory damages, that "because a significant portion of defendants' profits made from the infringement are not ascertainable, a higher award of [statutory] in lieu damages is warranted." Id. at 18,384; see also Cream Records Inc. v. Jos. Schlitz Brewing Co., 754 F.2d 826, 828-29 (9th Cir. 1985) (discussed supra note 7) (awarding profits from the sale of malt liquor for Schlitz's infringing use of plaintiff's song in television commercial).

Like the television commercials in Krofft II, Hallelujah Hollywood had promotional value. Defendants maintain that they endeavor to earn profits on all their operations and that Hallelujah Hollywood was a profit center. However, that fact does not detract from the promotional purposes of the show — to draw people to the hotel and the gaming tables. MGM's 1976 annual report states that "the hotel and gaming operations of the MGM Grand — Las Vegas continue to be materially enhanced by the popularity of the hotel's entertainment[, including] 'Hallelujah Hollywood', the spectacularly successful production revue. . . ." Given the promotional nature of Hallelujah Hollywood, we conclude indirect profits from the hotel and gaming operations, as well as direct profits from the show itself, are recoverable if ascertainable.

### 3. Apportionment of Profits

How to apportion profits between the infringers and the plaintiffs is a complex issue in this case. Apportionment of direct profits from the production as well as indirect profits from the hotel and casino operations are involved here, although the district court addressed only the former at the first trial.

When an infringer's profits are attributable to factors in addition to use of plaintiff's work, an apportionment of profits is proper. Sheldon v. Metro-Goldwyn Pictures, Inc., 309 U.S. 390, 405-06, 84 L. Ed. 825, 60 S. Ct. 681 (1939) (Sheldon II); Universal Pictures Co. v. Harold Lloyd Corp., 162 F.2d at 377. The burden of proving apportionment, (i.e., the contribution to profits of elements other than the infringed property), is the defendant's. Lottie Joplin Thomas Trust v. Crown Publishers, Inc., 592 F.2d 651, 657 (2d Cir. 1978). We will not reverse a district court's findings regarding apportionment unless they are clearly erroneous. See Shapiro, Bernstein & Co. v. 4636 S. Vermont Ave., Inc., 367 F.2d at 241-42.

After finding that the net profit earned by Hallelujah Hollywood was approximately $2,500,000, the district court offered the following explanation of apportionment:

While no precise mathematical formula can be applied, the court concludes in light of the evidence presented at trial and the entire record in this case, a fair approximation of the profits of Act IV attributable to the infringement is $22,000.

The district court was correct that mathematical exactness is not required. However, a reasonable and just apportionment of profits is required. Sheldon II, 309 U.S. at 408; Universal Pictures Co. v. Harold Lloyd Corp., 162 F.2d at 377.

Arriving at a proper method of apportionment and determining a specific amount to award is largely a factual exercise. Defendants understandably argue that the facts support the district court's award. They claim that the infringing material, six minutes of music in Act IV, was an unimportant part of the whole show, that the unique features of the Ziegfield Theater contributed more to the show's success than any other factor. This is proved, they argue, by the fact that when the music from Kismet was removed from Hallelujah Hollywood in 1976, the show suffered no decline in attendance and the hotel received no complaints.

Other evidence contradicts defendants' position. For instance, defendant Donn Arden testified that Kismet was "a very important part of the show" and "[he] hated to see it go." Moreover, while other acts were deleted from the shortened Saturday night versions of the show, Act IV "Kismet" never was.

We reject defendants' contention that the relative unimportance of the Kismet music was proved by its omission and the show's continued success thereafter. Hallelujah Hollywood was a revue, comprised of many different entertainment elements. Each element contributed significantly to the show's success, but no one element was the sole or overriding reason for that success. Just because one element could be omitted and the show goes on does not prove that the element was not important in the first instance and did not contribute to establishing the show's initial popularity.

The difficulty in this case is that the district court has not provided us with any reasoned explanation of or formula for its apportionment. We know only the district court's bottom line: that the plaintiffs are entitled to $22,000. Given the nature of the infringement, the character of the infringed property, the success of defendants' show, and the magnitude of the defendants' profits, the amount seems to be grossly inadequate. It amounts to less than one percent of MGM Grand's profits from the show, or roughly $13 for each of the 1700 infringing performances.

On remand, the district court should reconsider its apportionment of profits, and should fully explain on the record its reasons and the resulting method of apportionment it uses. Apportionment of indirect profits may be a part of the calculus. If the court finds that a reasonable, nonspeculative formula cannot be derived, or that the amount of profits a reasonable formula yields is insufficient to serve the purposes underlying the statute, then the court should award statutory damages. See infra Part II.B.5.

4. Liability of Joint Infringers

The district court granted judgment of $22,000 "against defendants" in the plural. Yet if the district court intended that each of the defendants be jointly and severally liable for the $22,000 award, this was error.

When a copyright is infringed, all infringers are jointly and severally liable for plaintiffs' actual damages, but each defendant is severally liable for his or its own illegal profit; one defendant is not liable for the profit made by another. MCA, Inc. v. Wilson, 677 F.2d 180, 186 (2d Cir. 1981); 3 M. Nimmer, supra, § 12.04[C][3], at 12-50; see Cream Records, Inc. v. Jos. Schlitz Brewing Co., 754 F.2d at 829.

The rule of several liability for profits applies, at least, where defendants do not act as partners, or "practically partners." Compare Belford, Clarke & Co. v. Scribner, 144 U.S. 488, 507-508, 36 L. Ed. 514, 12 S. Ct. 734 (1892) (printer held jointly liable for publisher's profits on infringing book since they were "practically partners."), with Sammons v. Colonial Press, Inc., 126 F.2d at 346-47 (court refused to hold printer jointly liable for publisher's profits since printer was paid a fixed price for work, payable whether or not infringing books made profit). Defendants assert that Arden and MGM Grand are jointly liable since they "worked closely together" in producing the infringing work. This is a fact question for the district court to consider on remand. The court should consider whether Arden was an employee or an independent contractor rather than a partner. Relevant to this determination, among others, are such factors as whether Arden received a fixed salary or a percentage of profits and whether he bore any of the risk of loss on the production.

Arden may be liable for profits he earned in connection with the production of Hallelujah Hollywood, but amounts paid to him as salary are not to be considered as profits. See MCA, Inc. v. Wilson, 677 F.2d at 186. But if Arden did earn profits from the production, such as royalties, he is liable for a proportionate amount of these. Concomitantly, defendant MGM Grand would be entitled to deduct any such royalties as costs in arriving at its own profits. See Smith v. Little, Brown & Co., 396 F.2d 150, 151-52 (2d Cir. 1968); see Cream Records, Inc. v. Jos. Schlitz Brewing Co., 754 F.2d at 829 (interpreting the 1976 Act).

The court must also determine whether MGM, Inc., MGM Grand's parent corporation, should be held liable for the infringement. A parent corporation cannot be held liable for the infringing actions of its subsidiary unless there is a substantial and continuing connection between the two with respect to the infringing acts. 3 M. Nimmer, supra, § 12.04[A], at 12-44 to -45.

If the district court finds a "substantial and continuing connection" between MGM Grand and MGM, Inc., then MGM, Inc., may also be liable for its profits. But to the extent any such profits are merely passed on from its subsidiary, MGM Grand, the plaintiffs should be given only one recovery, to be satisfied by either MGM, Inc. or MGM Grand.

5. Statutory "In Lieu" Damages

Statutory damages are intended as a substitute for profits or actual damage. When injury is proved but neither the infringer's profits nor the copyright holder's actual damages can be ascertained, an award of statutory "in lieu" damages is mandatory. Russell v. Price, 612 F.2d at 1131-32; Pye v. Mitchell, 574 F.2d 476, 481 (9th Cir. 1978); Sid & Marty Krofft Television Productions, Inc. v. McDonald's Corp., 562 F.2d 1157, 1178-79 (9th Cir. 1977)

(Krofft I). But if either profits or actual damages or both can be ascertained, the trial court has discretion to award statutory damages. Krofft I, 562 F.2d at 1178. Such an award must be in excess of the amount that would have been awarded as profits or actual damages. Id. We review a district court's award or refusal to award statutory damages for abuse of discretion. Russell v. Price, 612 F.2d at 1132.

A determination as to whether to award statutory damages must abide the district court's reconsideration of whether to award damages based on profits. On remand, the district court should keep in mind the purposes underlying the remedy provisions of the Copyright Act, i.e., to provide adequate compensation to the copyright holder and to discourage wrongful conduct and deter infringements. See F.W. Woolworth Co. v. Contemporary Arts, Inc., 344 U.S. 228, 233, 97 L. Ed. 276, 73 S. Ct. 222 (1952); Kamar International, Inc. v. Russ Berrie & Co., 752 F.2d at 1332; Russell v. Price, 612 F.2d at 1131. Thus, in determining whether to exercise its discretion to award statutory damages, the district court must consider whether the amount of profits that have been proved accomplish the purposes of the statute. If not, it should exercise its discretion to award statutory "in lieu" damages that do effectuate the statutory purposes.

The $22,000 awarded by the district court obviously is too little to discourage wrongful conduct or to deter infringement.

### 6. Attorneys' Fees

The plaintiffs requested that the district court award attorneys' fees under 17 U.S.C. § 116 (1970). The court omitted mention of plaintiffs' request in its memorandum decision, although during the course of the proceedings, it had noted that the issue was before it. On remand, the district court can address this issue.

### C. Plaintiffs' Other Claims

In addition to claims for copyright infringement, plaintiffs pleaded claims for unfair competition and breach of contract. The district court rejected both of these ancillary claims. We affirm.

### 1. Unfair Competition

To prevail on a claim of unfair competition, a plaintiff must demonstrate a likelihood of confusion. Walt Disney Productions v. The Air Pirates, 581 F.2d 751, 760 (9th Cir. 1978), cert. denied, 439 U.S. 1132, 99 S. Ct. 1054, 59 L. Ed. 2d 94 (1979); Alpha Industries, Inc. v. Alpha Steel Tube & Shapes, Inc., 616 F.2d 440,

443 (9th Cir. 1980). Any findings of fact underlying a determination as to likelihood of confusion are subject to the clearly erroneous test, but determination of whether, based on those facts, a likelihood of confusion exists is a legal conclusion. Alpha Industries, 616 F.2d at 443-44; J. B. Williams Co., Inc. v. Le Conte Cosmetics, Inc., 523 F.2d 187, 190 (9th Cir. 1975), cert. denied, 424 U.S. 913, 47 L. Ed. 2d 317, 96 S. Ct. 1110, 188 U.S.P.Q. (BNA) 720 (1976).

Plaintiffs attempted to prove unfair competition by showing that the title "Kismet" had acquired secondary meaning referring to their play. The only evidence offered by plaintiffs on this issue was the testimony of plaintiff Edwin Lester who claimed that the original 1911 Kismet was a "dead issue." Defendants introduced evidence that the 1911 Kismet and a silent movie produced from that play in 1912 had been very popular and widely acclaimed. The trial court's finding that the title "Kismet" had not acquired secondary meaning referring to plaintiff's play, is not clearly erroneous. Moreover, since Act IV "Kismet" was only an 11-minute segment of a 100-minute revue, we agree that audiences were not likely to confuse the two versions.

### 2. Breach of Contract

Finally, plaintiffs urge that the district court denied them due process in dismissing their breach of contract claim against MGM, Inc. The court indicated at the outset of the trial that it would not exercise pendent jurisdiction and would not receive evidence on the contract claim or the unfair competition claim. But at the end of the trial, the court permitted post-trial briefs, specifying that they should include issues relating to plaintiffs' pendent claims. The court stated it would take additional evidence on those claims if necessary. Since plaintiffs apparently did not offer any additional evidence, the district court did not err in dismissing the contract claim based on the evidence before it. Accordingly, plaintiffs' due process challenge has no merit.

### III. CONCLUSION

We affirm the district court's finding that defendants' use of plaintiffs' Kismet exceeded the scope of the ASCAP license. We also affirm the district court's finding that plaintiffs failed to prove actual damages. We vacate the award of defendants' profits derived from the infringement and remand to the district court for further proceedings consistent with this opinion.

AFFIRMED in part, REVERSED in part, and REMANDED with directions.

---

In *Frank Music Corp. v. MGM*, 772 F.2d 505, the court found that the hotel casino infringed the copyright holder's copyright of the musical Kismet, and awarded the holder $22,000 as a share of the hotel's casino profits. The case was remanded to ascertain proper apportionment of infringer's profits.

Joplin Enterprises v. Allen
United States District Court for the Western District of Washington, Seattle
Division
June 2, 1992, Decided; June 2, 1992, Filed and Entered
NO. C91-1035C
795 F. Supp. 349

## REVISED OPINION AND ORDER
### I. Introduction

This matter is before the court on (1) defendants' motion for partial judgment on the pleadings under Fed. R. Civ. P. 12(c), (2) defendants' motion for a declaratory judgment under Fed. R. Civ. P. 57, and (3) plaintiffs' motion for judgment on the pleadings under Fed. R. Civ. P. 12(c).

### II. Background

Janis is a two-act play about Janis Joplin, a renowned rock and blues singer who, sadly, died young in 1970. Act I fictionally portrays Ms. Joplin's experiences over the course of a day previous to an evening's concert performance. Its forty-six page script focuses on visions of artistic inspiration and their colloquies with Ms. Joplin. Act I contains only one song. Defendants concede, for the purposes of their motions, that Act II simulates an evening's concert performance by Mr. Joplin.

Plaintiffs believe that the play violates both copyright law and Janis Joplin's right of publicity. They demanded that Janis close, and, when the production did not cease, they filed this lawsuit. Janis ended its production run shortly thereafter.

### III. Discussion
Defendants' Motions

Defendants move for a judgment on the pleadings pursuant to Fed. R. Civ. P. 12(c), dismissing plaintiffs' second cause of action, infringement of the right of publicity. They also move, pursuant to Fed. R. Civ. P. 57, for a declaratory judgment that Janis is not subject to any state law protecting proprietary interests in the names and likenesses of public figures.

In ruling upon defendants' motions, the curt must first determine which law applies to the issues presented therein. Washington's choice of law rule apply here. Klaxon Co. v. Stentor Electric Manufacturing Co., 313 U.S. 487, 85 L. Ed. 1477 , 61 S. Ct. 1020 , 49 U.S.P.Q. (BNA) 515 (1941).

The right of publicity is a "property right." Acme Circus Operating Co., Inc. v. Kuperstock, 711 F.2d 1538, 1541, 221 U.S.P.Q. (BNA) 420 (11th Cir. 1983). Accord Rogers v. Grimaldi, 875 F.2d 994, 10 U.S.P.Q.2D (BNA) 1825 (2nd Cir. 1989); Cal. Civ. Code § 990(b) (West Supp. 1992) ("the rights recognized under this section are property rights"). Janis Joplin was domiciled in California and her right of publicity descended to her devisees in California. Thus, under Washington's choice of law rules, Washington looks to the law of California to determine whether the allegedly infringed property right exists at all in this case. James A.R. Nafziger, Conflict of Laws: a Northwest Perspective 187 (1985); See also In re Grady's Estate, 79 Wash. 2d 41, 483 P.2d 114 (1971). If a right of publicity exists in California, Washington then applies the law of the state having the most significant relationship to this conflict to determine whether that right has been tortiously infringed. Bush v. O'Connor, 58 Wash. App. 138, 143, 791 P.2d 915 (1990).

California Civ. Code Section 990 delineates California's statutory right of publicity for deceased personalities. It applies by its language and by legal authority only to the exclusively commercial use of Ms. Joplin's persona in merchandise, advertising or endorsements. Cf. Leidholdt v. L.F.P. Inc., 860 F.2d 890, 895 (9th Cir. 1988) (applying this proposition to living celebrities' rights of publicity under similar California and New York statutes), cert. denied, 489 U.S. 1080, 103 L. Ed. 2d 837 , 109 S. Ct. 1532 (1989). Indeed, by its plain language the statute specifically excepts from its purview "a play, book . . . [or] musical composition . . . ." (emphasis added). Cal. Civ. Code § 990(n)(1). Although a common law right of publicity also exists in California, that right of publicity is not descendible and did not pass to plaintiffs. Guglielmi v. Spelling-Goldberg Prod., 25 Cal. 3d 860, 160 Cal. Rptr. 352, 455, 603 P.2d 454, 205 U.S.P.Q. (BNA) 1116 (1979).

As a matter of law, Acts I and II of Janis must be viewed together in the context of plaintiffs' right of publicity claims. Plaintiffs have attempted to pursue their claims against Act II of Janis as if Act I did not exist or could be analyzed separately. Yet they admit that "as written and produced [Janis ] occurs in two acts." They also admit that Act I is "a protected form of expression." Plaintiffs' Memorandum in Opposition at 14. In fact, plaintiffs do not argue, nor can they, that if Janis is analyzed as a whole it is not a play subject to the provisions of Cal. Civ. Code § 990.

California Civ. Code § 990 clearly contemplates examining the use of a deceased personality's name, voice, etc., in terms of the total context in which it appears. Where a use is for the purpose of advertising goods or services, it is prohibited. Identical use in the context of a play is protected. To analyze Act II of Janis out of context would destroy the statutory exemption.

Moreover, even cases not decided under California law, which are cited by plaintiff in support of its right of publicity claim, stand for the proposition that a theatrical production must be examined in its entirety. For example, both *Estate of Presley v. Russen*, 513 F. Supp. 1339, 211 U.S.P.Q. (BNA) 415 (D.N.J. 1981), and *Apple Corps v. Leber*, 12 Media L. Rep. 2280, 229 U.S.P.Q. (BNA) 1015 (Cal. Super. Ct. 1986), indicate that the right of publicity claim must be applied to Janis as a whole.

Allowing plaintiffs to assert a right of publicity only in a severable Act II would legitimate right of publicity claims based, for example, on a photograph in the back of a stage set, a comedian's imitation of a famous figure, or a celebrity's likeness on the cover of a biography. The right of publicity cannot rationally reach so far. Therefore, Act II of Janis occurs in the context of Act I and constitutes only a portion of the entire play. Under California law, plaintiffs cannot state a legally cognizable right of publicity claim in this case.

The court notes that if Washington law applied to the issue of whether plaintiffs' right of publicity claim is colorable at law, its holding would be the same. Neither Washington's legislature nor its courts have addressed the right of publicity issue. Therefore plaintiffs have neither a right of publicity nor a remedy for tortious interference with that right under Washington law. This court is not willing to extrapolate, from Washington's recognition of a right to privacy, a descendible right of publicity applicable to this case or a remedy for interference with such a right under Washington law, especially given the fact that the Washington State Constitution places an even higher value upon the principle of free speech than the Federal Constitution. See, e.g., *Bering v. Share*, 106 Wash. 2d 212, 721 P.2d 918 (1986) (Article 1 Section 5 of the Washington State Constitution provides greater protections to the rights of free speech than afforded under the First Amendment); *O'Day v. King County*, 109 Wash. 2d 796, 749 P.2d 142 (1988) (Washington's overbreadth analysis less tolerant than federal overbreath analysis); cf. *Rogers v. Grimaldi*, 875 F.2d 994, 10 U.S.P.Q.2D (BNA) 1825 (2d Cir. 1989) (determining that if Oregon recognized the right of publicity, the right would be limited to control of commercial advertisements for the sale of goods and services, in part because the free speech clause of Oregon's Constitution provides broader free speech rights than the First Amendment).

"In considering a rule 12(c) motion, the court must accept as true all of the well-pleaded facts in the complaint and may not dismiss the action unless the court is convinced that the plaintiff can prove no set of facts in support of his claim which would entitle him to relief." *Bloor v. Carro, et al.*, 754 F.2d 57 (9th Cir. 1985) (internal quotations and citations omitted). As the court has indicated, no issues of material fact can exist in this case which could alter a judgment against plaintiffs on the right of publicity issue.

Finally, this court declines defendants' invitation to depart from the usual rule that it should avoid direct constitutional adjudication whenever possible. County Court of Ulster County v. Allen, 442 U.S. 140, 60 L. Ed. 2d 777 , 99 S. Ct. 2213 (1979) courts have a strong duty to avoid constitutional issues that need not be resolved in adjudicating a case). The court notes, however, the clear direction in which constitutional law points. In a case different from this one only in that it involved a book and not a play, a New York court held that "the protection of the right of free expression is so important that we should not extend any right of publicity, if such exists, to give rise to a cause of action against publication of a . . . work about a deceased person." Frosch v. Grosset & Dunlap, Inc., 75 A.D.2d 768, 427 N.Y.S.2d 828, 829 (App. Div. 1980). This court agrees with the reasoning of the Frosh opinion.

Defendants' Motion for Partial Judgment on the Pleadings is GRANTED. Plaintiffs' second cause of action, infringement of the right of publicity, is DISMISSED. Defendants' Motion for Declaratory Judgment is DENIED.

Plaintiffs' Motion

Plaintiffs move for judgment on the pleadings pursuant to Fed. R. Civ. P. 12(c), requesting that the court dismiss defendants' antitrust counterclaims. Because defendants do not allege per se violations of either § 1 or § 2 of the Sherman Act, their claims must be evaluated under the rule of reason. Cascade Cabinet Co. v. Western Cabinet & Millwork, 710 F.2d 1366, 1370 9th Cir. 1983). Market definition is "essential" to claims under § 1 and § 2 in which the rule of reason is applied. Gough v. Rossmoor Corp., 585 F.2d 381, 389 (9th Cir. 1978).

The relevant product market includes "the pool of goods or services that enjoy reasonable interchangeability of use and cross-elasticity of demand." Id. (quoting Oltz v. St. Peter Community Hosp., 861 F.2d 1440, 1446 (9th Cir. 1988). The two factors to focus upon are (1) reasonable interchangeability of the products, and (2) the purchaser's willingness to substitute one commodity for another. United States v. E.I. duPont de Nemours & Co., 351 U.S. 377, 393-404, 100 L. Ed. 1264 , 76 S. Ct. 994 (1956).

A substantial body of case law indicates that the market proposed by defendants is too narrow to support a cause of action. For example, in cases involving relatively narrow markets, courts have held that the relevant market is not so limited as to include just one product. Theater Party Associates, Inc. v. Shubert Organization, Inc., 1988-2 Trade Cases (CCH) P 68,251 (S.D.N.Y. 1988) (proposed market for Phantom of the Opera rejected). See also Belfiore v. New York Times Co., 826 F.2d 177, 180 (2d Cir. 1987) (proposed market for The New York Times rejected); Seidenstein v. National Medical Enterprises, Inc., 769 F.2d 1100, 1106 (5th Cir. 1985); Shaw v. Rolex Watch, U.S.A., Inc., 673 F. Supp. 674 (S.D.N.Y. 1987) (proposed market for Rolex watches rejected); Disenos Artisticos

E Industriales, S.A. v. Work, 676 F. Supp. 1254, 6 U.S.P.Q.2D (BNA) 1161 (E.D.N.Y. 1987) (proposed market for Lladro figurines rejected). In these cases, courts have granted motions to dismiss, thus preventing the matter from going to the jury.

In Theatre Party Assoc., the court rejected a proposed market consisting of tickets for Phantom of the Opera, noting that "plaintiff had failed to explain why other forms of entertainment, namely other Broadway shows, the opera, ballet or even sporting events are not adequate substitute products." Theatre Party Assoc., at 154-55. Similarly, here, defendants cannot rationally explain why their market does not include live performances of dramatic plays or concerts, other depictions of the lives of female rock and blues vocalists, or movies and plays about historically significant musicians of the sixties. Therefore, Plaintiffs' Motion to Dismiss Defendants' Antitrust Counterclaims is GRANTED. Defendants' counterclaims under the Sherman Act are DISMISSED, for failure to plead a relevant market in which plaintiffs have, or could have, monopoly power.

---

Plaintiff Corporations, representing the estate of the much grieved Janis Joplin, sued defendant performers and production company for copyright infringement and right of publicity when defendants produced a two-act play entitled *Janis*. Defendants answered with antitrust and right-of-publicity counterclaims. The claims were dismissed, however, the case was set for trial on the copyright infringement claim.

In the following case, *Estate of Presley v. Russen*, 513 F. Supp. 1339 (D. N. J. 1981), the court grants a preliminary injunction against the "Big El" show.

Estate of Elvis Presley v. Russen
United States District Court for the District of New Jersey
April 16, 1981
Civ. A. No. 80-0951
513 F. Supp. 1339

ON MOTION FOR A PRELIMINARY INJUNCTION, FINDINGS OF FACT AND CONCLUSIONS OF LAW

During his lifetime, Elvis Presley established himself as one of the legends in the entertainment business. On August 16, 1977, Elvis Presley died, but his legend and worldwide popularity have survived. As Presley's popularity has subsisted and even grown, so has the capacity for generating financial rewards and legal disputes. Although the present case is another in this line, it presents questions not previously addressed. As a general proposition, this case is concerned with the rights and limitations of one who promotes and presents a theatrical production designed to imitate or simulate a stage performance of Elvis Presley.

This action is currently before the court on a motion by plaintiff, the Estate of Elvis Presley, for a preliminary injunction pursuant to Rule 65 of the Federal Rules of Civil Procedure. It seeks a preliminary injunction restraining defendant, Rob Russen, d/b/a THE BIG EL SHOW (hereafter Russen), or anyone acting or purporting to act in his or its behalf or in collaboration with it from using the name and service mark THE BIG EL SHOW and design, the image or likeness or persona of Elvis Presley or any equivalent, the names Elvis, Elvis Presley, Elvis in Concert, The King, and TCB or any equivalent or similar names on any goods, in any promotional materials, in any advertising or in connection with the offering or rendering of any musical services.

Plaintiff instituted suit on April 9, 1980 for federal law unfair competition (false designation of origin under § 43(a) of the Lanham Trademark Act, 15 U.S.C. § 1125(a), common law unfair competition, common law trademark infringement, and infringement, of the right of publicity. This court has jurisdiction by virtue of 15 U.S.C. § 1121, 28 U.S.C. § 1332, and 28 U.S.C. § 1338. Venue is properly laid in the District of New Jersey by 28 U.S.C. § 1391. Plaintiff seeks a permanent injunction, an impounding and delivery to plaintiff of promotional and advertising materials, letterheads, business cards and other materials, an accounting of defendant's profits, and an award of treble damages and of reasonable attorneys' fees. Defendant answered the allegations contained in the complaint and also filed a counterclaim alleging that the plaintiff's actions were in violation of the anti-trust laws of the United States.

On October 2, 1980, the court conducted a hearing on the preliminary injunction motion, which is being submitted upon the proof taken at the hearing, pleadings, depositions, affidavits, exhibits, and written briefs. This opinion incorporates the court's findings of fact and conclusions of law as authorized by Rule 52(a) of the Federal Rules of Civil Procedure.

Every Finding of Fact that may be a Conclusion of Law is adopted as such; and every Conclusion of Law that may be a Finding of Fact is adopted as such.

## FINDINGS OF FACT

Plaintiff

1. Plaintiff is the Estate of Elvis Presley (hereafter the Estate) located in Memphis, Tennessee, created by the Will of Elvis Presley and is, under the laws of the State of Tennessee, a legal entity with the power to sue and be sued. (Tennessee Code Annotated § 35-618; Exhibit P 26).

2. The Estate came into being upon the death of Elvis Presley on August 16, 1977. (Parker, Affidavit).

3. During his career, Elvis Presley established himself as one of the premier musical talents and entertainers in the United States, Europe and other areas of the world. He was the major force behind the American Rock and Roll movement, and his influence and popularity has continued to this day. During Presley's legendary career, his talents were showcased in many ways. He performed in concert, setting attendance records and selling out houses in Las Vegas and other cities in which his tour appeared. He starred in numerous motion pictures including one entitled Viva Las Vegas, which is also the name of the movie's title song which Presley sang. He made records which sold over one million copies and appeared on television programs and in television specials made from his tour programs. (Jarvis Testimony, Tr. pp. 42-63).

4. The Elvis Presley tours were billed as "Elvis in Concert," and his nightclub performances were billed as the Elvis Presley Show, while Elvis Presley shows in Las Vegas were billed simply as "Elvis." Most of Elvis Presley's record albums used the name ELVIS on the cover as part of the title. One of his albums was entitled ELVIS IN CONCERT. (Hanks, Affidavit; Jarvis Testimony, Tr. pp. 45, 49, 63; Exhibits, P 10, 12, 16).

5. Elvis Presley adopted the initials TCB along with a lightning bolt design to identify entertainment services provided by him. This insignia appeared on letterheads, jackets for personnel associated with the show, a ring worn by Presley while performing, and tails of Presley's airplanes. Also, Presley's band was identified as the TCB band. (Jarvis Testimony, Tr. pp. 45-46, 53-57; Exhibits, P 17A, 17B).

6. Elvis Presley's nickname was "THE KING." (Jarvis Testimony, Tr. p. 57).

7. Although Elvis Presley exhibited a range of talents and degrees of change in his personality and physical make-up during his professional career, he, in association with his personal manager, Thomas A. (Col.) Parker, developed a certain, characteristic performing style, particularly as to his live stage shows. His voice, delivery, mannerisms (such as his hips and legs gyrations), appearance and dress (especially a certain type of jumpsuit and a ring), and actions accompanying a performance (such as handing out scarves to the audience), all contributed to this Elvis Presley style of performance. (Jarvis Testimony, Tr. pp. 45-53; Exhibits P 10, 12, 16).

8. One particular image or picture of Presley became closely associated with and identifiable of the entertainment provided by Elvis Presley. This image (hereafter referred to as the "Elvis pose") consisted of a picture or representation of Elvis Presley dressed in one of his characteristic jumpsuits with a microphone in his hand and apparently singing. (Exhibits P 10, 12, 16).

9. Elvis Presley exploited his name, likeness, and various images during his lifetime through records, photographs, posters, merchandise, movies, and personal appearances. (Exhibits P 1, 12, 13, 16, 20, 21, 27; Jarvis Testimony, Tr. pp. 44-64).

10. As a result of Presley's own talent, as well as of the various promotional efforts undertaken on his behalf, the popularity of Elvis Presley and his entertainment services, as identified by certain trademark and service marks, reached worldwide proportions. Elvis Presley productions achieved a reputation for a certain level of quality and performance. Goodwill attached to Presley's performances and the merchandise bearing his name and picture.

11. From nearly the beginning of his life as an entertainer, Elvis Presley was represented in his career by Thomas A. (Col.) Parker. (Exhibit P 25; Parker Affidavit).

12. On March 26, 1956, Elvis Presley having reached age 21 entered into an agreement with Col. Parker, amending an agreement entered into in 1955 between Col. Parker and Elvis Presley and his parents, making Parker Elvis Presley's "sole and exclusive Advisor, Personal Representative and Manager in any and all fields of public and private entertainment." (Exhibit P 25).

13. Throughout Presley's professional career, Parker continued to supervise and authorize the commercialization of Presley's name, image, picture, and/or likeness. He granted different entities the right to use Elvis' name, image, picture or likeness on such merchandise as posters, statues, and buttons, for a limited time in return for a percentage on the sales of the articles involved. (Parker Affidavit). On July 26, 1956, Col. Parker, with Presley's approval, entered into an agreement with Special Projects, Inc. granting to it for a term of one (1) year a commercial license for the use of the name, photograph and likeness of Elvis Presley "in connection with the sale, marketing and exploitation of consumer items." (Exhibit P 27).

14. The working relationship between Presley and Parker begun in 1955 appears to have continued throughout Presley's career. Although there are some gaps in the documents showing this relationship during the next 22 years, the evidence presented sufficiently supports their continuing association. (Parker Affidavit; Davis Affidavit).

15. In particular, on January 22, 1976, Elvis Presley entered into an agreement (Exhibit P 1) with Col. Parker, d/b/a All Star Shows, whereby he authorized Parker to set up tours, promotion, merchandising sales and any other medium involving the artistry of Elvis Presley and to generally act as his agent for merchandising projects, personal appearances, motion picture performances, and "any other projects involving the personal services, name, photo or any likeness of the Artist," Elvis Presley. The agreement also sets forth the responsibilities of Presley and Parker with respect to the shows. "Presley is responsible for the presentation of the stage performance" and Col. Parker handles the "advertising and promotion of the show." Thus, Presley did not authorize any rights associated directly with the performances, and how they were to be conducted.

This agreement which recognizes Presley's existing contracts did not preclude Elvis Presley from arranging any activities, including merchandising or performing, on his own behalf. The terms of the agreement appear to negate any implication of an "assignment," which would necessarily preclude Elvis Presley himself from entering into agreements pertaining to the use of his name, likeness and image. The agreement, which was limited to a seven (7) year period, gave Parker supervision of merchandising projects and a power of attorney-in-fact for specified purposes, but did not assign or sell the rights of Elvis Presley to his name, likeness or image.

16. In 1974, Boxcar Enterprises, Inc. was incorporated. Col. Parker and Elvis Presley were two of the original subscribers to the stock in the corporation. According to the charter of the corporation, it was formed for the purpose of, inter alia, publishing music, managing entertainers, producing records, producing motion pictures, producing entertainment, selling merchandise and otherwise generally engaging in the broad range of activities corporations may undertake. Col. Parker, Elvis Presley, and Tom Diskin, the President of Boxcar, did subscribe to shares in the corporation, for which shares Elvis Presley gave a consideration of three thousand dollars ($ 3,000.00). (Hanks Affidavit and Exhibits; Diskin Affidavit).

17. Col. Parker is the majority shareholder in and Chairman of the Board of Boxcar Enterprises, Inc. and he, under the terms of his agreement with Elvis Presley, licensed or sublicensed Boxcar Enterprises, Inc. to act on behalf of Elvis Presley to create and promote merchandise and articles using the name, likeness and image of Elvis Presley. (Exhibits P 5; Diskin Affidavit; Parker Affidavit).

18. There have been no licenses or assignments by Elvis Presley to Boxcar Enterprises, Inc. There have been only letters setting in writing the agreed division of the royalties and income from the sale of merchandise by Boxcar Enterprises, Inc. (Diskin Affidavit; Exhibit P 5. See Parker Affidavit).

19. The right to the commercial use of the name, likeness and image which Boxcar Enterprises has is derived from the license or sublicense granted to Boxcar by Col. Parker. Col. Parker's rights derive from the January 22, 1976 contract (Exhibit P 1) he entered into with Elvis Presley which will terminate in 1983. It is understood that the Parker-Boxcar agreement terminates at the same time. (Exhibit P 6; Diskin Affidavit. See Parker Affidavit).

20. In a letter dated August 23, 1977, one week after Elvis Presley's death, Vernon Presley, Elvis' father and the executor of Elvis' estate, asked Col. Parker to "carry on according to the same terms and conditions" of the agreement between Elvis Presley and Col. Parker dated January 22, 1976. (Exhibit P 3). In June 1979, after Vernon Presley's death, the Estate of Presley, through its representatives again reaffirmed the agreement between Col. Parker and Elvis Presley. (Exhibit P 4). The Estate's continued desire to have Col. Parker market the name, likeness and image of Elvis and, thus, obtain income for the estate is based on the Estate's position that Parker "could probably make the most of the opportunity that was there plus maintain the quality that he and Elvis had maintained throughout the period of their relationship." (Hanks Testimony Tr. pp. 22-26).

21. Boxcar Enterprises, Inc. and the Estate agreed by letter dated August 24, 1977, to Boxcar's continued payment to the Estate of royalties from the sale of merchandise. (Exhibit P 2).

22. Two days after Elvis Presley's death, on August 18, 1977, Boxcar Enterprises, Inc. granted an exclusive license to Factors Etc., Inc. (Factors) to use the name, likeness, characters, symbols, designs and visual representations of Elvis Presley, termed the "Feature," on merchandise throughout the world for a period of eighteen (18) months, renewable for four (4) one-year periods thereafter. The license specifically reserved to the licensor the right, title and interest to the Feature and specifically stated that the rights granted were not an assignment but only a license. The license sets forth quality control provisions for standards for the merchandise and specifically states that the rights licensed shall revert to the licensor upon the termination of the license. (Exhibit P 6; Turner Testimony, Tr. pp. 67-68).

23. As an inducement for Factors Etc., Inc. to enter into the license agreement with Boxcar Enterprises, Inc., Vernon Presley as Executor of the Estate, executed the agreement on a separate page, confirming "the truth of the representations and warranties of Boxcar contained in the agreement." (Exhibit P 6).

24. In the license between Boxcar and Factors, Boxcar sets forth that it "has exclusive ownership of all rights to the use of the Feature," that it is "the sole owner of the entire right, title and interest in the Feature when used in connection with ... merchandise," and that it has the "full right, authority and power to enter into this Agreement." (Exhibit P 6). Because of Boxcar's arrangement with Col. Parker, his control of Boxcar and his exclusive representation contract of Elvis Presley for seven years (or until 1983) (Exhibit P 1; Hanks Affidavit, Minutes of First Meeting of Incorporation), these representations, considering the time period of the license to Factors, though not completely accurate, were true as far as necessary for Factor's protection to operate under the license. No one else had the license rights for merchandise but Col. Parker/Boxcar. Given the time frame of the execution of the agreement (two days after Elvis Presley's death) and knowing of the agreement (Exhibit P 1) between Elvis Presley and Col. Parker, Vernon Presley's signature as "an inducement" cannot be considered an assignment of rights or a confirmation of an assignment, but rather an affirmation of Col. Parker's/Boxcar's exclusive license rights for a period of years. The continued understanding of the parties confirms that there has been no assignment of rights by Elvis Presley or his Estate but merely the licensing of the right to exploit commercially Elvis Presley's name, likeness and image for merchandise for a limited period of time. (Turner Testimony, Tr. p. 67; see Diskin Affidavit).

25. Elvis Presley's popularity did not cease upon his death. His records and tapes are still sold in considerable dollar and unit amounts and Elvis Presley movies are still shown in theaters and on television. Elvis Presley merchandise is still in demand and sold. Also, many people travel to Memphis, Tennessee to visit Presley's gravesite and to see Graceland Mansion, his former home. The extent of Presley's continued popularity and the value and goodwill associated with him and his performances on, for example, records, film and tape, is evidenced by the over seven (7) million dollars in royalty and licensing payments which Presley's estate received in the first two years of its existence. (Hanks Affidavit; Hanks Testimony, Tr. p. 19; Parker Affidavit. See Davis Affidavit).

26. The agreements, including the Boxcar-Factors contract, relative to the commercial use of Elvis Presley's name, likeness and image are terminable. Upon their termination the existing rights to the name, likeness and image of Elvis Presley revert ultimately to the Estate. (Turner Testimony, Tr. p. 67; Diskin Affidavit).

27. Further, the Estate, during the existence of the agreements, that is, prior to their termination, has an interest in protecting the licensed rights not only for their value upon their reversion to it, but also to protect its continued royalties, which it receives from the licensees' sales of records, movies, merchandise and television performances of Elvis Presley. The Estate's licensees advertise and promote the marks identifying Presley's entertainment services

and licensed merchandise to maintain their commercial value and goodwill. (Exhibit P 2; Hanks Testimony, Tr. pp. 18-20, 76-77).

28. The Estate has entered into a license agreement for the use of the logo TCB and the lightning bolt design to identify a band composed of the members of Elvis Presley's back-up band. The Estate receives royalties. (Exhibit P 23; Jarvis Testimony, Tr. p. 55; Hanks Testimony, Tr. pp. 76-77).

29. The Estate, with the agreement of Col. Parker, has entered into a movie contract with Warner Bros. Studio for a movie about Elvis Presley. (Exhibit P 22; Hanks Testimony, Tr. p. 76).

30. The Estate and its licensees, and sub-licensees and during his lifetime, Elvis Presley and his representatives and those with whom he had contracts or licenses have taken actions to protect the rights of the Estate and of the licensees. (Parker, Affidavit; Davis Affidavit; Hanks Testimony, Tr. pp. 82-83). For example, the Estate has filed an opposition against the registration by defendant Russen of a trademark (Hanks Testimony, Tr. pp. 82-83) and Factors Etc., Inc. has instituted law suits. (See Factors Etc., Inc. v. Pro Arts, Inc., 444 F. Supp. 288 (S.D.N.Y.1977) (preliminary injunction), aff'd, 579 F.2d 215 (2nd Cir. 1978), cert. denied, 440 U.S. 908, 99 S. Ct. 1215, 59 L. Ed. 2d 455 (1979); 496 F. Supp. 1090 (S.D.N.Y.1980) (permanent injunction); Factors Etc., Inc. v. Creative Card Co., 444 F. Supp. 279 (S.D.N.Y.1977); Memphis Development Foundation v. Factors Etc., Inc., 441 F. Supp. 1323 (W.D.Tenn.), rev'd, 616 F.2d 956 (6th Cir. 1980).)

Defendant

31. Defendant, Rob Russen d/b/a THE BIG EL SHOW (hereafter Russen) is the producer of THE BIG EL SHOW.

32. THE BIG EL SHOW is a stage production patterned after an actual Elvis Presley stage show, albeit on a lesser scale, and featuring an individual who impersonates the late Elvis Presley by performing in the style of Presley. The performer wears the same style and design of clothing and jewelry as did Presley, hands out to the audience scarves as did Presley, sings songs made popular by Presley, wears his hair in the same style as Presley, and imitates the singing voice, distinctive poses, and body movements made famous by Presley. (Exhibit P 11, 12, 14, 15; Exhibit D to Defendant's Answer; Jarvis Testimony, Tr. pp. 45-53; Russen Deposition, pp. 27-28, 54-55, 59).

33. Russen charges customers to view performances of THE BIG EL SHOW or alternatively charges fees to those in whose rooms or auditoriums THE BIG EL SHOW is performed who in turn charge customers to view THE BIG EL SHOW. (Exhibit D to Defendant's Answer).

34. THE BIG EL SHOW production runs for approximately ninety minutes. The show opens with the theme from the movie "2001 A Space Odyssey" which Elvis Presley also used to open his stage shows. (Exhibit D to Defendant's Answer; Jarvis Testimony, Tr. p. 62). The production centers on Larry Seth, "Big

EI," doing his Elvis Presley impersonation and features musicians called the TCB Band. The TCB Band was also the name of Elvis Presley's band; however THE BIG EL SHOW TCB Band does not consist of musicians from Presley's band. (Jarvis Testimony, Tr. pp. 53-57; Exhibits P 11, 14, 15, 17A-C, 23; Russen Deposition, pp. 53-54).

35. From the inception of THE BIG EL SHOW, the star was Larry Seth. Seth, who is under a long-term contract with THE BIG EL SHOW, recently "retired" from the show; but he may return. (Russen Affidavit; see Russen Deposition, p. 171). THE BIG EL SHOW has continued its performances by using replacements for Seth. (Russen Deposition, pp. 91-92).

36. THE BIG EL SHOW was first presented in 1975 (Russen Affidavit; Russen Deposition, p. 22; Exhibit D to Defendant's Answer) and has been performed in the United States and Canada. For example, performances have been given in cities and towns in Connecticut, Maryland, New Jersey, Pennsylvania, and Nevada (one engagement at a Hotel-Casino in Las Vegas). (Russen Deposition, pp. 28-33, 37, 91; Exhibits P 14, 19, 17C; Exhibit D to Defendant's Answer). In addition, Larry Seth as the star of THE BIG EL SHOW has appeared on television talk shows in Philadelphia and Las Vegas, and on the David Suskind Show, a nationally syndicated program. (Exhibit P 17C; Russen Deposition, pp. 55-56, 167).

37. Russen has advertised the production as THE BIG EL SHOW and displayed a photograph of the star, Larry Seth, or an artist's rendering of Seth dressed and posed as if in performance. The advertisements make such statements as "Reflections on a Legend … A Tribute to Elvis Presley," "Looks and Sounds LIKE THE KING," "12 piece Las Vegas show band." (Russen Deposition, p. 176; Exhibits P 14, 15).

38. Although the various pictures and artist's rendering associated with THE BIG EL SHOW are photographs of Larry Seth, or based on such photographs (Russen Affidavit; Exhibit P 28), a reasonable viewer upon seeing the pictures alone would likely believe the individual portrayed to be Elvis Presley. Even with a side-to-side comparison of photographs of Larry Seth as Big El and of certain photographs of Elvis Presley, it is difficult, although not impossible, to discern any difference.

39. On October 18, 1978, Russen applied to the United States Patent and Trademark Office to register the name THE BIG EL SHOW and the design feature, of that name, i. e., an artist's rendition of Larry Seth as Big El, as a service mark. (Exhibit P 28). Plaintiff did prepare and timely file its Notice of Opposition in the United States Patent and Trademark Office to contest the defendant's right to register the mark. (Exhibit F to Plaintiff's Memorandum in Support of the Motion for Preliminary Injunction). The proceeding before the Trademark Trial and Appeal Board has been stayed by the Board pending the results in the suit before this court.

40. Russen has produced or had produced for him records of THE BIG EL SHOW (including two albums and three 45 RPMs). (Russen Deposition, pp. 72-74; see Exhibits P 11, 13, 18). Only a limited number of these records were pressed, and they were made for sales and promotional purposes. (Russen Deposition, pp. 73-74). One record album, entitled "Viva Las Vegas" (Exhibit P 11), has on the cover of the jacket only the title and an artist's sketch which upon reasonable observation appears to be of Elvis Presley. It is only on the back of the jacket in a short blurb and in the credits that the name BIG EL SHOW appears. It is also indicated that the show stars Larry Seth as Big El and features the TCB Band. The other album (Exhibit P 13) is entitled BIG EL SHOW "In Concert" and also features an artist's drawing, ostensibly of Big El, but which looks like Elvis Presley, with microphone in hand, singing. Only one of the 45s has been presented to this court. THE BIG EL SHOW insignia (Exhibit P 28) appears on both sides. The artists are designated as Larry Seth and TCB Orchestra, on Side I, and Larry Seth and PCB (sic) Orchestra on Side II.

41. In addition to selling records at performances of THE BIG EL SHOW, Russen sold Big El pendants and a button with the picture of Larry Seth as Big El. (Russen Deposition, pp. 77-78).

42. Russen began to produce THE BIG EL SHOW and to use his certain identifying marks, such as THE BIG EL SHOW logo, after Presley had become famous as one of the premier performers in the world and had used and established certain marks as strongly identifying his services and the merchandise licensed or sub-licensed by him.

43. Russen has never had any authorization from, license or contractual relation with Elvis Presley or with the Estate of Elvis Presley in connection with the production of THE BIG EL SHOW. (Parker Affidavit; Hanks Affidavit; Hanks Testimony, Tr. pp. 79-80).

## DISCUSSION and CONCLUSIONS OF LAW
### I. Standing

The issue of standing requires us to determine "whether the plaintiff has "alleged such a personal stake in the outcome of the controversy' as to warrant his invocation of federal court jurisdiction and to justify exercise of the court's remedial powers on his behalf." Warth v. Seldin, 422 U.S. 490, 498-99, 95 S. Ct. 2197, 2205, 45 L. Ed. 2d 343 (1975) (emphasis in original). Plaintiff has shown that it has an economic interest in the protection of the rights it asserts, for it receives royalty or percentage payments from those who sell merchandise using the name, likeness and image of Elvis Presley. Further, it receives payments from record sales, has entered into motion picture contracts and has licensed the TCB logo. (Cf. Factors Etc., Inc. v. Pro Arts, Inc., 579 F.2d 215, 222 (2nd Cir. 1978) ("... income interest, continually produced from Boxcar's exclusive right of commercial exploitation should inure to Presley's estate at death like any other intangible property right.")).

Perhaps an even more compelling reason for granting standing than the Estate's income from the current licensing agreements, is the Estate's protection of and future ability to generate income from those property rights, such as the use of trademarks or service marks, associated with Elvis Presley's entertainment services which became owned by Presley's estate after his death. See generally Trademarks and Tradenames, 74 Am.Jur.2d, § 25 (1974). It has been shown that those parties who have entered into agreements with Elvis Presley, or with his Estate, to make use of the name, likeness and image of Presley have been licensees. None of the agreements between Elvis Presley and others, including his manager and agent, Thomas A. (Col.) Parker, indicate that Presley assigned his right, title and interest to those property rights connected with his name, likeness and/or image. While the terms, "assignment," "exclusive license," and "license" are frequently used by courts and practitioners interchangeably, the differences are significant. An assignment passes legal and equitable title to the property while a license is mere permission to use. Assignment is the transfer of the whole of the interest in the right while in a license the owner retains the legal ownership of the property. Vandenburgh, Trademark Law and Procedure, 2d Ed. § 7.31; Gilson, Trademark Protection and Practice § 6.01.

An assignment presupposes the transfer of the entire interest in a trademark, while a license involves the transfer of something less than the entire interest, and does not affect the licensor's title. The assignee becomes the new owner while the licensee is a mere user. If the grant of an exclusive use of a trademark is limited as to duration or area, it will not confer title thereto upon the licensee or upon the party who purchases the trademarked article for resale. The licensee acquires only the right to a limited use of the trademark, for the title to the reversionary interest in that use remains with the owner.... The licensor is merely estopped from challenging the licensee's use of the mark under the agreement. In principle, an assignment is permanent and perpetual, while a license is temporary, provisional or conditional. (emphasis added).

Callmann, The Law of Unfair Competition, Trademarks and Monopolies (hereafter "Callmann"), § 78.2 (3d ed. 1969). Thus, even if Presley had licensed certain property rights such as service marks, the ownership of these rights and standing to protect them, remained with Presley, and, after his death became part of the assets of his estate. If, as is alleged by the plaintiff, the defendant's use of certain logos or advertising is likely to have a negative impact on these intangible property rights or on the goodwill associated with Presley or his Estate, then a sufficient reason for granting standing exists. As it has been noted with respect to trademark infringement, "standing to sue exists in anyone who "is or is likely to be damaged' by the defendant's use of the disputed mark, and the parties need not be direct competitors. Fleischmann Distilling Corp. v. Maier Brewing Co., 314 F.2d 149, 151 (9th Cir. 1963), cert. den., 374 U.S. 830, 83 S. Ct. 1870, 10 L. Ed. 2d 1053." National Lampoon, Inc. v. American Broadcasting Cos., Inc., 376 F. Supp. 733, 746 (S.D.N.Y.), affirmed, 497 F.2d 1343 (2nd Cir. 1974). In addition, we are convinced that "the (plaintiff's) personal stake in the outcome (is) compelling enough to assure aggressive and conscientious advocacy and that the issues" … (are not) … "so nebulous as to create the danger of judicial inquiry beyond customary bounds." Schiaffo v. Helstoski, 492 F.2d 413 (3rd Cir. 1974).

## II. Laches and Acquiescence

Russen, having asserted the defenses of laches, and acquiescence in his Answer, argues that a preliminary injunction should not be granted. Although it has been noted that "there are cases in which preliminary injunctive relief has been held barred by laches … (citations omitted)," Selchow & Righter Co. v. Book-of-the Month Club, Inc., 192 U.S.P.Q. 530, 532 (S.D.N.Y.1976) (action for trademark and copyright infringement, unfair competition and trademark dilution); see Saratoga Vichy Spring Co., Inc. v. Lehman, 625 F.2d 1037, 1041 (2nd Cir. 1980) (federal trademark, unfair competition, false designation of origin); Le Sportsac, Inc. v. Dockside Research, Inc., 478 F. Supp. 602, 609 (S.D.N.Y.1979), "the laches defense is reserved for those rare cases where a protracted acquiescence by plaintiff induces a defendant to undertake substantial activities in reliance on the acquiescence." McNeil Laboratories, Inc. v. American Home Products Corp., 416 F. Supp. 804, 809 (D.N.J.1976). See, e.g., Jenn-Air Corp. v. Penn Ventilator Co., 464 F.2d 48 (3rd Cir. 1972); John Wright, Inc. v. Casper Corp., 419 F. Supp. 292 (E.D.Pa.1976); Callmann, § 87.3(b). In any event "laches generally is not a bar to injunctive relief against unfair competition." Great Atlantic & Pacific Tea Co. v. A & P Trucking Corp., 51 N.J.Super. 412, 423, 144 A.2d 172 (App.Div.), modified and remanded, 29 N.J. 455, 149 A.2d 595 (1959). The equitable defense of acquiescence " "(a)s distinguished from laches, constitutes a ground for denial of relief only upon a finding of conduct on the plaintiff's part that amounted to an assurance to the defendant, express or implied, that the plaintiff would not assert his trademark rights against the defendant.' (citations omitted)" Carl Zeiss Stiftung v. VEB Carl Zeiss Jena, 433 F.2d 686, 704 (2nd Cir. 1970).

In deciding whether the defendant has made a sufficiently strong showing of laches or acquiescence, we must examine the particular circumstances of the case. Id. at 703-04. See Playboy Enterprises, Inc. v. Chuckleberry Publishing, Inc., 486 F. Supp. 414, 434-35 (S.D.N.Y.1980). Our review of the available evidentiary sources indicates certain unsettled facts; however, we cannot conclude that the defendant has met his burden of proving, for the purposes of this preliminary injunction motion, laches or acquiescence.

In the first place, the defendant has not made a sufficient showing of implicit or explicit consent or inexcusable delay by the plaintiff. Although there is evidence that THE BIG EL SHOW, with Larry Seth starring, has been performed since 1975 (Findings of Fact # 35, # 36, supra ), Russen's application to register the mark THE BIG EL SHOW and DESIGN states that the first use of the mark was in June of 1978.

Of more importance, there is a significant question as to the "knowledge and acquiescence" of the Estate or its representatives or of Elvis Presley or his representatives. Russen stated that Presley and his manager, Col. Parker, were aware of the existence of THE BIG EL SHOW, that he, Russen, had spoken via telephone with Col. Parker, in June of 1977, and that Col. Parker had indicated that neither he nor Presley had any objection to THE BIG EL SHOW being performed or using the name THE BIG EL SHOW. (Russen Affidavit).

This purported acceptance by Parker is apparently contradicted by Parker's statement that "at no time was defendant granted any rights by me, Boxcar Enterprises or anyone on behalf of Elvis Presley, to use Elvis' name, image, picture or likeness in any theatrical or entertainment endeavor." (Parker Affidavit). In addition, Joseph Hanks, a co-executor of the Estate of Elvis Presley, indicated that the Estate's files contained no references to Russen or THE BIG EL SHOW and that neither he nor any of the co-executors authorized or approved any uses by the defendant of Elvis Presley's name or image. (Hanks Affidavit; Hanks Testimony, Tr. p. 79). Finally, as noted above, the Estate of Elvis Presley and its licensee, Factors Etc., Inc., have taken steps, in addition to the present suit, to protect the rights of the Estate. The Estate did file a timely Notice of Opposition to Russen's application to register THE BIG EL SHOW and DESIGN as a service mark (Exhibit P 28; Exhibit F to Plaintiff's Memorandum in Support of the Motion for Preliminary Injunction), and Factors has instituted different legal actions.

Russen has also failed to show adequately that he was prejudiced by the delay. Although we assume Russen may have made some expenditures to produce and promote THE BIG EL SHOW and a limited number of records, Russen has failed to establish that his activities constituted the necessary prejudice. See Alfred Dunhill of London, Inc. v. Kasser Distillers Prods. Corp., 350 F. Supp. 1341, 1364-68 (E.D.Pa.1972), aff'd without opinion, 480 F.2d 917 (3rd Cir. 1973); Tisch Hotels, Inc. v. Americana Inn, Inc., 350 F.2d 609, 615 (7th Cir. 1965). See also Jenn-Air Corp., supra.

Since we have concluded that Russen has not made a sufficient showing of laches or acquiescence by Presley or his representatives or by the Estate of Presley to bar a preliminary injunction, we must now decide if a preliminary injunction should issue.

### III. Preliminary Injunction Standards

To prevail on a motion for a preliminary injunction, the moving party must show that it has a reasonable likelihood of eventual success in the litigation, that it will be irreparably injured pendente lite if relief is not granted, that a balance of equities favor the plaintiff, and that the public interest considerations support the preliminary injunction's issuance. SK&F, Co. v. Premo Pharmaceutical Laboratories, Inc., 625 F.2d 1055 (3rd Cir. 1980). See Tefal, S.A. v. Products International Co., 186 U.S.P.Q. 545, 547-48 (D.N.J.1975), aff'd, 529 F.2d 495, 497 (3rd Cir. 1976); Fotomat Corp. v. Photo Drive-Thru, Inc., 425 F. Supp. 693, 701 (D.N.J.1977); McNeil Laboratories, supra. These elements will be evaluated in light of the various causes of action asserted by the plaintiff. We shall first examine the likelihood of plaintiff's success on each claim.

### A. Likelihood of Success on the Merits

1. Right of Publicity

The plaintiff has asserted that the defendant's production, THE BIG EL SHOW, infringes on the right of publicity which plaintiff inherited from Elvis Presley.

The right of publicity is a concept which has evolved from the common law of privacy and its tort "of the appropriation, for the defendant's benefit or advantages, of the plaintiff's name or likeness." The term "right of publicity" has since come to signify the right of an individual, especially a public figure or a celebrity, to control the commercial value and exploitation of his name and picture or likeness and to prevent others from unfairly appropriating this value for their commercial benefit. The idea generally underlying an action for a right of privacy is that the individual has a right personal to him to be let alone and, thus, to prevent others from invading his privacy, injuring his feelings, or assaulting his peace of mind. In contrast, underlying the right of publicity concept is a desire to benefit from the commercial exploitation of one's name and likeness.

In the present case, we are faced with the following issues: a. Does a right of publicity and the concomitant cause of action for its infringement exist at common law in New Jersey; if so, does this right descend to the estate at the death of the individual? Assuming the existence and inheritability of a right of publicity, does the presentation of THE BIG EL SHOW infringe upon the plaintiff's right of publicity?

a. Right of Publicity in New Jersey

Although the courts in New Jersey have not used the term "right of publicity," they have recognized and supported an individual's right to prevent the unauthorized, commercial appropriation of his name or likeness. In the early and widely cited case of Edison v. Edison Polyform Mfg. Co., 73 N.J.Eq. 136, 67 A. 392 (1907), Thomas Edison sought to enjoin a company which sold medicinal preparations from using the name Edison as part of its corporate title or in connection with its business and from using his name, picture, or endorsement on the label of defendant's product or as part of the defendant's advertising. In granting the requested relief, the court concluded that:

If a man's name be his own property, as no less an authority than the United States Supreme Court says it is ... it is difficult to understand why the peculiar cast of one's features is not also one's property, and why its pecuniary value, if it has one, does not belong to its owner rather than to the person seeking to make an unauthorized use of it.

Id. at 141. This idea that an individual has a property right in his name and likeness was reemphasized in Ettore v. Philco Television Broadcasting Corporation, 229 F.2d 481, 491-92 (3rd Cir.), cert. denied, 351 U.S. 926, 76 S. Ct. 783, 100 L. Ed. 1456 (1956) (interpreting New Jersey law) and Canessa v. Kislak, 97 N.J.Super. 327, 235 A.2d 62 (Law Div.1967). Cf. Palmer v. Schonhorn, 96 N.J.Super. 72, 232 A.2d 458 (Ch.1967). (The court did not characterize the right as property. However, the court held:

that although the publication of biographical data of a well-known figure does not per se constitute an invasion of privacy, the use of that same data (as well as the name) for the purpose of capitalizing upon the name by using it in connection with a commercial project other than the dissemination of news or articles or biographies does.

Id. at 79, 232 A.2d 458.) Judge Lynch in his thoughtful opinion in Canessa initially found that "in the concept of "right of privacy' there is implicit the right of property, at least in the instance of an appropriation by defendant of another's likeness." 97 N.J.Super. at 339, 235 A.2d 62. After a comprehensive examination of a number of cases occurring prior to Canessa, Judge Lynch decided that:

Entirely apart, however, from the metaphysical niceties, the reality of a case such as we have here is, in the court's opinion, simply this: plaintiffs' names and likenesses belong to them. As such they are property. They are things of value. Defendant has made them so, for it has taken them for its own commercial benefit.

New Jersey has always enjoined the use of plaintiff's likeness and name on the specific basis that it was a protected property right. It is as much a property right after its wrongful use by defendant as it might be before such use.

We therefore hold that, insofar as plaintiffs' claim is based on the appropriation of their likeness and name for defendant's commercial benefit, it is an action for invasion of their "property" rights and not one for "injury to the person."

97 N.J.Super. at 351-52, 235 A.2d 62.

In following the approach taken by pre-1968 cases evaluating New Jersey law, we conclude that, today, a New Jersey court would allow a cause of action for infringement of a right of publicity. In addition, this right, having been characterized by New Jersey courts as a property right, rather than as a right personal to and attached to the individual, is capable of being disassociated from the individual and transferred by him for commercial purposes. We thus determine that during his life Elvis Presley owned a property right in his name and likeness which he could license or assign for his commercial benefit.

In deciding whether this right of publicity survived Presley's death, we are persuaded by the approach of other courts which have found the right of publicity to be a property right. These courts have concluded that the right, having been exercised during the individual's life and thus having attained a concrete form, should descend at the death of the individual "like any other intangible property right." Factors Etc., Inc. v. Creative Card Co., 444 F. Supp. 279, 284 (S.D.N.Y.1977). As Chief Justice Bird of the California Supreme Court has explained:

...granting protection after death provides an increased incentive for the investment of resources in one's profession, which may augment the value of one's right of publicity. If the right is descendible, the individual is able to transfer the benefits of his labor to his immediate successors and is assured that control over the exercise of the right can be vested in a suitable beneficiary. "There is no reason why, upon a celebrity's death, advertisers should receive a windfall in the form of freedom to use with impunity the name or likeness of the deceased celebrity who may have worked his or her entire life to attain celebrity status. The financial benefits of that labor should go to the celebrity's heirs...." (citations omitted).

Lugosi, 25 Cal.3d at 846, 160 Cal.Rptr. at 344, 603 P.2d at 446 (Bird, C. J., dissenting). Following the line of reasoning in the above cases, we hold that Elvis Presley's right of publicity survived his death and became part of Presley's estate.

b. Theatrical Imitations and The Right of Publicity

Having found that New Jersey supports a common law right of publicity, we turn our attention to a resolution of whether this right of publicity provides protection against the defendant's promotion and presentation of THE BIG EL SHOW. In deciding this issue, the circumstances and nature of defendant's activity, as well as the scope of the right of publicity, are to be considered. In a recent law journal article, the authors conducted an extensive and thorough analysis of the cases and theories bearing on media portrayals, i. e., the portrayal of a real person by a news or entertainment media production. Felcher & Rubin, Privacy, Publicity, and the Portrayal of Real People by the Media, (hereinafter "Portrayal") 88 Yale L.J. 1577, 1596 (1979). They concluded that "(t)he primary social policy that determines the legal protection afforded to media portrayals is based on the First Amendment guarantee of free speech and press." Id. at 1596. Thus, the purpose of the portrayal in question must be examined to determine if it predominantly serves a social function valued by the protection of free speech. If the portrayal mainly serves the purpose of contributing information, which is not false or defamatory, to the public debate of political or social issues or of providing the free expression of creative talent which contributes to society's cultural enrichment, then the portrayal generally will be immune from liability. If, however, the portrayal functions primarily as a means of commercial exploitation, then such immunity will not be granted. See generally Portrayal, supra, at 1596-99.

The idea that the scope of the right of publicity should be measured or balanced against societal interests in free expression has been recognized and discussed in the case law and by other legal commentators. In general, in determining whether a plaintiff's right of publicity can be invoked to prevent a defendant's activity, the courts have divided along the lines set out above. In cases finding the expression to be protected, the defendant's activity has consisted of the dissemination of such information as "thoughts, ideas, newsworthy events, ... matters of public interest," Rosemont Enterprises, Inc. v. Random House, Inc., 58 Misc.2d 1, 6, 294 N.Y.S.2d 122, 129 (Sup.Ct.1968), aff'd mem., 32 App.Div.2d 892, 301 N.Y.S.2d 948 (1969) (biography of Howard Hughes) and fictionalizations. The importance of protecting fictionalizations and related efforts as against rights of publicity was explained by Chief Justice Bird of the California Supreme Court:

Contemporary events, symbols and people are regularly used in fictional works. Fiction writers may be able to more persuasively, more accurately express themselves by weaving into the tale persons or events familiar to their readers. The choice is theirs. No author should be forced into creating mythological worlds or characters wholly divorced from reality. The right of publicity derived from public prominence does not confer a shield to ward off caricature, parody and satire. Rather, prominence invites creative comment.

Guglielmi, 25 Cal.3d at 869, 160 Cal.Rptr. at 358, 603 P.2d at 460 (Bird, C. J., concurring).

On the other hand, most of those cases finding that the right of publicity, or its equivalence, prevails have involved the use of a famous name or likeness predominantly in connection with the sale of consumer merchandise or "solely "for purposes of trade e.g., merely to attract attention.' (without being artistic, informational or newsworthy) Grant v. Esquire, Inc., 367 F. Supp. 876, 881 (S.D.N.Y.1973) (unauthorized use of photo of Cary Grant in fashion article)." Ali v. Playgirl, Inc., 447 F. Supp. 723, 727, 728-29 (S.D.N.Y.1978) (unauthorized drawing of nude man, recognizable as Muhammed Ali, seated in corner of boxing ring). In these cases, it seems clear that the name or likeness of the public figure is being used predominantly for commercial exploitation, and thus is subject to the right of publicity. As the court in Palmer v. Schonhorn, supra, noted, "While one who is a public figure or is presently newsworthy may be the proper subject of news or informative presentation, the privilege does not extend to commercialization of his personality through a form of treatment distinct from the dissemination of news or information." Id. 96 N.J.Super. at 78, 232 A.2d 458 quoting Gautier v. Pro-Football, Inc., 304 N.Y. 354, 359, 107 N.E.2d 485 (1952) (emphasis added by Palmer court).

In the present case, the defendant's expressive activity, THE BIG EL SHOW production, does not fall clearly on either side. Based on the current state of the record, the production can be described as a live theatrical presentation or concert designed to imitate a performance of the late Elvis Presley. The show stars an individual who closely resembles Presley and who imitates the appearance, dress, and characteristic performing style of Elvis Presley. The defendant has made no showing, nor attempted to show, that the production is intended to or acts as a parody, burlesque, satire, or criticism of Elvis Presley. As a matter of fact, the show is billed as "A TRIBUTE TO ELVIS PRESLEY." In essence, we confront the question of whether the use of the likeness of a famous deceased entertainer in a performance mainly designed to imitate that famous entertainer's own past stage performances is to be considered primarily as a commercial appropriation by the imitator or show's producer of the famous entertainer's likeness or as a valuable contribution of information or culture. After careful consideration of the activity, we have decided that although THE BIG EL SHOW contains an informational and entertainment element, the show serves primarily to commercially exploit the likeness of Elvis Presley without contributing anything of substantial value to society. In making this decision , the court recognizes that certain factors distinguish this situation from the pure commercial use of a picture of Elvis Presley to advertise a product. In the first place, the defendant uses Presley's likeness in an entertainment form and, as a general proposition, "entertainment ... enjoys First Amendment protection." Zacchini v. Scripps-Howard Broadcasting Co., 433 U.S. 562, 578, 97 S. Ct. 2849, 2859, 53 L. Ed. 2d 965 (1977). See, e.g., Southeastern Promotions, Ltd. v. Conrad, 420 U.S. 546, 557-58, 95 S. Ct. 1239, 1246, 43 L. Ed. 2d 448 (1975) (the musical play "Hair"); Joseph Burstyn, Inc. v. Wilson, 343 U.S. 495, 501, 72 S. Ct. 777, 780, 96 L. Ed. 1098 (1952) (the motion picture "The Miracle"); Goldstein v. Town of Nantucket, 477 F. Supp. 606, 608 (D.Mass.1979) (public performance of

Nantucket's traditional folk music). However, entertainment that is merely a copy or imitation, even if skillfully and accurately carried out, does not really have its own creative component and does not have a significant value as pure entertainment. As one authority has emphasized:

The public interest in entertainment will support the sporadic, occasional and good-faith imitation of a famous person to achieve humor, to effect criticism or to season a particular episode, but it does not give a privilege to appropriate another's valuable attributes on a continuing basis as one's own without the consent of the other.

Netterville, "Copyright and Tort Aspects of Parody, Mimicry and Humorous Commentary," 35 S.Cal.L.Rev. 225, 254 (1962).

In the second place, the production does provide information in that it illustrates a performance of a legendary figure in the entertainment industry. Because of Presley's immense contribution to rock "n roll, examples of him performing can be considered of public interest. However, in comparison to a biographical film or play of Elvis Presley or a production tracing the role of Elvis Presley in the development of rock "n roll, the information about Presley which THE BIG EL SHOW provides is of limited value.

This recognition that defendant's production has some value does not diminish our conclusion that the primary purpose of defendant's activity is to appropriate the commercial value of the likeness of Elvis Presley. Our decision receives support from two recent cases. In Price v. Worldvision Enterprises, Inc., 455 F. Supp. 252 (S.D.N.Y.1978), aff'd without opinion, 603 F.2d 214 (2nd Cir. 1979), the court found that the protection of the right of publicity could be invoked by the widows and beneficiaries, respectively, of Oliver Hardy and Stanley Laurel to enjoin the production or distribution of a television series entitled "Stan "n Ollie," wherein two actors would portray the comedians Laurel and Hardy. Although the facts bearing on the content of the program are not entirely clear, it appears that the show was to be based on old Laurel and Hardy routines which the comedy team performed during the careers and was not a biographical portrayal of the lives of the two men. In this regard, the court can be deemed to have decided that an inherited "right of publicity" can be invoked to protect against the unauthorized use of the name or likeness of a famous entertainer, who is deceased, in connection with an imitation, for commercial benefit, of a performance of that famous entertainer.

In Zacchini v. Scripps-Howard Broadcasting Co., 433 U.S. 562, 97 S. Ct. 2849, 53 L. Ed. 2d 965 (1977) the Supreme Court addressed a situation which implicated both a performer's right of publicity and the First Amendment. The Court held that the First Amendment did not prevent a state from deciding that a television news show's unauthorized broadcast of a film showing plaintiff's "entire act," a fifteen second human cannonball performance, infringed plaintiff's right of publicity.

In reaching its conclusion, the Court reasoned that "(t)he broadcast of (the) film of petitioner's entire act poses a substantial threat to the economic value of that performance," id. at 576, 97 S. Ct. at 2857-2858; that

the broadcast of petitioner's entire performance, unlike the unauthorized use of another's name for purposes of trade or the incidental use of a name or picture by the press, goes to the heart of petitioner's ability to earn a living as an entertainer. Thus, in this case, Ohio has recognized what may be the strongest case for a "right of publicity" involving, not the appropriation of an entertainer's reputation to enhance the attractiveness of a commercial product, but the appropriation of the very activity by which the entertainer acquired his reputation in the first place.

Id. at 576, 97 S. Ct. at 2857-2858; and that the "protection (of the right of publicity) provides an economic incentive for the performer to produce a performance of interest to the public." Id.

In the present case, although the defendant has not shown a film of an Elvis Presley performance, he has engaged in a similar form of behavior by presenting a live performance starring an imitator of Elvis Presley. To some degree, the defendant has appropriated the "very activity (live stage show) by which (Presley initially) acquired his reputation ..." id. at 576, 97 S. Ct. at 2857-2858, and from which the value in his name and likeness developed. The death of Presley diminishes the impact of certain of the court's reasons, especially the one providing for an economic incentive to produce future performances. However, through receiving royalties, the heirs of Presley are the beneficiaries of the "right of the individual to reap the reward of his endeavors." Id. at 573, 97 S. Ct. at 2856. Under the state's right of publicity, they are entitled to protect the commercial value of the name or likeness of Elvis Presley from activities such as defendant's which may diminish this value.

We thus find that the plaintiff has demonstrated a likelihood of success on the merits of its right of publicity claim with respect to the defendant's live stage production. In addition, we find this likelihood of success as to the defendant's unauthorized use of Elvis Presley's likeness on the cover or label of any records or on any pendants which are sold or distributed by the defendant.

2. Common Law Trademark or Service Mark Infringement

Since the plaintiff does not assert any Federal or State of New Jersey trademark or service mark registrations, any trademark or service mark infringement claims are governed by the common law, which provided the basis for and essentially parallels the protection provided by the Federal or State statutory schemes. See Dallas Cowboys Cheerleaders v. Pussycat Cinema, 604 F.2d 200, 203 n.3 (2nd Cir. 1979); Scott Paper Co. v. Scott's Liquid Gold, Inc., 589 F.2d 1225, 1228 (3rd Cir. 1978); House of Westmore v. Denney, 151 F.2d 261,

265 (3rd Cir. 1945); Caesars World, Inc. v. Caesar's Palace, 490 F. Supp. 818, 823 (D.N.J.1980); D. C. Comics, Inc. v. Powers, 465 F. Supp. 843, 846 (S.D.N.Y.1978), aff'd on reargument, 482 F. Supp. 494 (S.D.N.Y.1979). In order to prevail on a statutory or common law trademark or service mark infringement claim, the plaintiff must establish that the names or symbols are valid, legally protectible trademarks or service marks; that they are owned by the plaintiff; and that the defendant's subsequent use of the same or similar marks to identify goods or services is infringing, i. e., is likely to create confusion as to the origin of the goods or services. See, e.g., Scott Paper Co., supra; Perfectform Corp. v. Perfect Brassiere Co., Inc., 256 F.2d 736 (3rd Cir. 1958); Caesars World, Inc., supra; Fotomat Corp., supra; Time Mechanisms, Inc., supra. Actions for trademark (or service mark) infringement serve both to protect the "right of the public to be free of confusion and the synonymous right of a trademark (or service mark) owner to control his product's (or service's) reputation." James Burrough, Ltd. v. Sign of Beefeater, Inc., 540 F.2d 266, 274 (7th Cir. 1976), rev'd on retrial, 572 F.2d 574 (7th Cir. 1978).

Plaintiff asserts that Elvis Presley, during his lifetime, created and owned valid trademarks or, more specifically, service marks for musical entertainment services in the names of ELVIS, ELVIS PRESLEY, and THE KING, the phrase ELVIS (or ELVIS PRESLEY) IN CONCERT, the logo composed of the letters TCB and lightning bolt design, and the likeness of Elvis Presley, and that these marks were all legally protectible. After Presley's death the rights in these marks were acquired by the plaintiff, which is entrusted with the preservation and management of the property and rights of the decedent, Elvis Presley, for the benefit of Presley's heirs. The plaintiff points out that, in the fulfillment of its obligations, it has entered into a number of agreements licensing the use of the marks in various ways, including records, movies, merchandise and television performances of Presley, and that the licensees have continued to promote these trademarks and service marks. Thus, the plaintiff claims that since the service marks or trademarks are property rights and have continued to be used to identify the musical entertainment services of Presley, these marks have been inherited by and continue to exist in the plaintiff estate. Finally, the plaintiff argues that the defendant's uses of the name THE BIG EL SHOW, the logo composed of THE BIG EL SHOW name and the likeness ostensibly of Larry Seth as he appears in THE BIG EL SHOW, the term THE KING, the initials TCB with or without a lightning bolt, and all likenesses of Elvis Presley (whether or not they are really of Larry Seth as he appears or appeared in THE BIG EL SHOW) to identify his production, constitute infringements of plaintiff's marks.

Each of plaintiff's points will be evaluated in seriatim in the context of the requirements for an infringement claim.

a. Validity of Marks

A service mark is defined as "a word, name, symbol, device or any combination thereof adopted and used in the sale or advertising of services to identify the service of the entity and distinguish them from the services of others." Caesars World, Inc., 490 F. Supp. at 822; 15 U.S.C. § 1127; N.J.S.A. 56:3-13.1(B). See generally 3 Callmann, "common law rights are acquired in a service mark by adopting and using the mark in connection with services rendered. (citations omitted)." Caesars World, Inc., 490 F. Supp. at 822. Since the plaintiff is principally claiming, at the present time, that its marks identify Elvis Presley entertainment services, we will focus on the validity of the names and symbols as service marks. However, it should be noted that these marks also might be trademarks which identify goods, id., or particular products licensed by the marks' owner. See Dallas Cowboys Cheerleaders v. Pussycat Cinema, 467 F. Supp. 366, 373 (S.D.N.Y.), affirmed, 604 F.2d 200 (2nd Cir. 1979).

(1). Names

The plaintiff claims that the names ELVIS, ELVIS IN CONCERT, ELVIS PRESLEY, and THE KING are valid and protectible service marks. Our review of the record indicates that the first three names have not been used only to identify a particular individual, Elvis Presley. Rather they have been used in advertising, such as for performances, concerts, and on records, to identify a service. They have appeared in close association with a clear reference (i. e., IN CONCERT OR SHOW) to entertainment services of Presley. Thus, they have attained service mark status. See Five Platters, Inc., supra (the name "The Platters" functions as a service mark to identify the services of a singing and entertainment group); In re Carson, supra (the name JOHNNY CARSON functions as a service mark to identify entertainment services rendered by John W. Carson).

With respect to the name THE KING, the plaintiff has not established this name as a valid service mark. The record reveals that Elvis Presley's nickname was The King. However, plaintiff has not presented sufficient evidence as to how the name was used to identify services, see Hirsch v. S. C. Johnson & Son, Inc., 90 Wis.2d 379, 280 N.W.2d 129, 138-39 (1979), and thus to function as a service mark. Of course, the plaintiff is not precluded from establishing the term THE KING as a valid service mark by presenting appropriate evidence at trial.

(2). Logo

The plaintiff has presented sufficient evidence, for the purposes of a preliminary injunction, of connection with Presley entertainment services or business, to establish the logo composed of the initials TCB with or without the lightning bolt design as a service mark. For example, the logo was used on Presley's letterhead and on business cards, see, e.g., Re Reichold Chemicals, Inc., 167 U.S.P.Q. 376 (TMT & App. Bd. 1970); Re Pierce, 164 U.S.P.Q. 369 (TMT

& App. Bd. 1970); 1 McCarthy, Trademarks and Unfair Competition, § 16:11, and it appeared on the tails of Presley's airplanes. See generally Boston Professional Hockey Ass'n, supra; Fotomat Corp., supra.

(3). Likeness and Image

The plaintiff asserts that the likeness and image of Elvis Presley serves as a service mark; however, the available evidence does not support such a broad position. Rather, the record only supports a conclusion that a picture or illustration of Elvis Presley dressed in one of his characteristic jumpsuits and holding a microphone in a singing pose is likely to be found to function as a service mark. This particular image (hereinafter referred to as the "Elvis Pose") has appeared in promotional and advertising material for concerts and on record albums. Thus, even though the "Elvis Pose" identifies the individual performer, we find it also has been used in the advertising and sale of Elvis Presley entertainment services to identify those services. See generally Dallas Cowboys Cheerleaders, Inc. v. Pussycat Cinema, 467 F. Supp. 366 (S.D.N.Y.), affirmed, 604 F.2d 200 (2nd Cir. 1979). The court recognizes that the "Elvis Pose" has appeared in somewhat different forms; for example, the color of the outfit or the direction of the face has been altered. We do not find such changes to be determinative. Rather, we find the following idea persuasive reasoning for treating the "Elvis Pose" as a service mark:

"It is settled that a person may change the display of a mark at any time because whatever rights he may possess in the mark reside in the term itself rather than in any particular form or arrangement thereof.... The only requirement in these instances is that the mark be modified in such a fashion as to retain its trademark impact and symbolize a single and continuing commercial impression. That is, a change which does not alter its distinctive characteristics represents a continuity of trademark rights. Thus, where the distinctive character of the mark is not changed, the mark is, in effect, the same and the rights obtained by virtue of the earlier use of the prior form inure to the later form. (citations omitted)"

Ilco Corporation v. Ideal Security Hardware Corporation, 527 F.2d 1221, 1224 (C.C.P.A.1976).

b. Protectibility

The requirements for a valid trademark or service mark to be considered protectible under the common law or the Lanham Act, depend on the characteristics of the marks themselves. Inherently distinctive trademarks or service marks, such as fanciful or arbitrary or non-descriptive, but suggestive, words and symbols, gain protected status upon their first adoption and use; while, non-inherently distinctive marks only achieve protection if the mark is shown to have secondary meaning. See McCarthy, supra, §§ 15:1, 16:2; Scott

Paper Co. v. Scott's Liquid Gold, Inc., 439 F. Supp. 1022, 1034 (D.Del.1977), rev'd, 589 F.2d 1225 (3rd Cir. 1978). A trademark or service mark attains secondary meaning if the consuming public has come to recognize the mark not only as an identification of the goods or services but as a symbol indicating that the goods or services emanate from a single source, even though the identity of that source may in fact be unknown. Id.

Of the five names or symbols found to be valid service marks, the three containing the personal names (surname or first name) of Elvis Presley, will be considered as non-inherently distinctive terms. The evidence sufficiently shows that these marks have been used for a long period of time through various promotions and uses, such as in advertising and on records (as well as in connection with certain licensed products), and have acquired a secondary meaning associated with Elvis Presley entertainment services as distinct from other entertainment services. See Scott Paper Co., 589 F.2d at 1228; Wyatt Earp Enterprises, Inc. v. Sackman, Inc., 157 F. Supp. 621 (S.D.N.Y.1958) (name as televised by plaintiff in television show identified with merchandise upon which name licensed to appear). Cf. Five Platters, Inc., supra (the name, "The Platters" developed secondary meaning connected with singing and entertainment services by widespread circulation of records, public performances, and other promotional efforts).

The mark composed of the TCB and lightning bolt logo can be characterized as inherently distinctive since it is unique and arbitrary. See Q-Tips, Inc., supra; Standard Brands, Inc. v. Smidler, 151 F.2d 34 (2nd Cir. 1945); Caesars World, Inc., 490 F. Supp. at 822-23. In the alternative, we also find that there is sufficient evidence of use of the mark in association with Elvis Presley entertainment services to show that the mark has acquired a secondary meaning of identifying the source of Presley entertainment services. Thus, the logo is protectible.

Finally, we find that there is sufficient evidence in the record for us to conclude that the particular "Elvis Pose" service mark, although perhaps a descriptive mark in that it illustrates the service, has acquired secondary meaning through its use in advertising and promoting of the entertainment services of Elvis Presley (as well as in identifying licensed products). See generally Dallas Cowboys Cheerleaders, Inc. v. Pussycat Cinema, 604 F.2d 200 (2nd Cir. 1979); Volkswagenwerk Akg. v. Rickard, 175 U.S.P.Q. 563 (C.D.Tex.), affirmed, 492 F.2d 474 (5th Cir. 1972). Volkswagenwerk Akg. v. Rose'Vear Enterprises, Inc., 199 U.S.P.Q. 744 (TMT & App.Bd.1978), affirmed, 592 F.2d 1180 (C.C.P.A.1979).

### c. Ownership

Trademarks and service marks are in the nature of property rights. See Hanover Milling Co. v. Metcalf, 240 U.S. 403, 36 S. Ct. 357, 60 L. Ed. 713 (1915). They "can be alienated like any piece of property," McCarthy, supra, § 2:6; however, "unlike patents and copyrights, (they) have no existence independent of the article, service or business in connection with which the mark is used. Id. at § 2:7. See United Drug Co. v. Theodore Rectanus Co., 248 U.S. 90, 39 S. Ct. 48, 63 L. Ed. 141 (1918). We find that after Presley's death, the rights to use the service marks and trademarks identifying the entertainment services of Elvis Presley and the merchandise licensed by him passed to Presley's legal representative as a part of the assets of his estate. See generally Trademarks and Tradenames, 74 Am.Jur.2d 325 (1974); Dilworth v. Hake, 64 S.W.2d 829, 830 (Tex.Civ.App.1933) (right to use trade name descended as part of estate to executrix.) See also Ward-Chandler Bldg. Co. v. Caldwell, 8 Cal.App.2d 375, 47 P.2d 758 (1935). Plaintiff through the trustee and executor of the estate, is entrusted with the preservation and management of the property and rights of the decedent for the benefit of the decedent's heirs. Restatement of Trusts 2d § 174 et seq. (1957). Thus, as long as these marks continue to be used to identify Elvis Presley entertainment services, which are still available in such forms as records, video tapes, movies, and television performances, the marks will continue to exist and will not be considered abandoned. See generally McCarthy, supra, § 17:3; La Societe Anonyme des Parfums Le Galion v. Jean Patou, Inc., 495 F.2d 1265, 1271 (2nd Cir. 1974) ("The user who first appropriates the mark obtains an enforceable right to exclude others from using it as long as the initial appropriation and use are accompanied by an intention to continue exploiting the mark commercially.")

Although the record does not provide extensive evidence of the plaintiff's use of the five service marks (or trademarks), we conclude that the evidence is sufficient, for the preliminary injunction motion, to find that plaintiff still owns and properly uses the marks. For example, the plaintiff has licensed the use of the TCB logo to identify Presley's former back up band. The fact that the band previously performed with Presley is significant since there is a connection to Presley's entertainment services. The plaintiff also continues to receive royalties from licensing agreements wherein the licensees advertise and promote the service marks or trademarks to identify Elvis Presley records, movies, merchandise and television performances. In this regard, it should be re-emphasized that the "Elvis Pose" identified earlier is the only specific image of Elvis Presley for which there is sufficient evidence in the record to qualify as a service mark or trademark.

d. Likelihood of Confusion

The plaintiff claims that the defendant's uses in connection with THE BIG EL SHOW production of: the initials TCB with and without a lightning bolt, any artist's renderings or pictures, purportedly of Larry Seth as he appears in THE BIG EL SHOW, which resemble Elvis Presley, the name THE BIG EL SHOW, and the logo composed of the name THE BIG EL SHOW and the artist's rendering, and the term THE KING, constitute infringements of plaintiff's service marks. Because we find that the term THE KING, unlike the other items, has not been used by the defendant as a mark to identify his entertainment service, we will not consider this term in the infringement claim.

The test for infringement of common law service marks or trademarks, which is the same as for statutorily registered marks, see House of Westmore, 151 F.2d at 265, is whether the defendant has made a subsequent unauthorized use of marks, which are the same or similar to those marks used by the plaintiff, in the sale or advertising of his goods or services to identify those goods or services; and the defendant's use creates a likelihood of confusion or deception as to the source of those goods or services. See James Burrough Ltd. v. Sign of Beefeater, Inc., 540 F.2d 266, 275 (7th Cir. 1976); Tefal, S.A. v. Products International Co., 186 U.S.P.Q. 545, 548 (D.N.J.1975), affirmed, 529 F.2d 495 (3rd Cir. 1976); DeCosta v. Columbia Broadcasting System, Inc., 520 F.2d 499, 513-15 (1st Cir.), cert. denied, 423 U.S. 1073, 96 S. Ct. 856, 47 L. Ed. 2d 83 (1975); Perfectform Corporation, 256 F.2d at 741; Caesars World, Inc., 490 F. Supp. at 823; Fotomat Corp., 425 F. Supp. at 703; Time Mechanisms, Inc., 422 F. Supp. at 914; Great Atlantic & Pacific Tea Co. v. A & P Trucking Corp., 29 N.J. 455, 149 A.2d 595 (1959); N.J.S.A. 56:3-13.11. See generally 3 Callmann, supra, § 80. The facts that Elvis Presley has died and, it is undisputed that almost no one would expect to see Elvis Presley performing live in THE BIG EL SHOW does not preclude a finding of infringement. The likelihood of confusion test refers to source, and, thus, may be satisfied if the plaintiff proves that consumers viewing the defendant's marks are likely to believe that plaintiff sponsored THE BIG EL SHOW production or licensed defendant to use the marks in connection with the show or was in some other way associated or affiliated with the production. See Dallas Cowboys Cheerleaders, Inc. v. Pussycat Cinema, 604 F.2d 200, 205 (2nd Cir. 1979); James Burrough Ltd. v. Sign of Beefeater, Inc., 540 F.2d at 274.

The determination of likelihood of confusion necessitates our weighing various factors including, but not necessarily limited to, the strength of the plaintiff's mark, the degree of similarity between the marks, the intent of the defendant in adopting the allegedly infringing mark, the similarity of products or services involved, trade channels, manners of marketing and predominant purchasers, and the evidence of actual confusion. Q-Tips, Inc., 206 F.2d at 147-48; Caesars World, Inc., 490 F. Supp. at 823-24; Fotomat Corp., 425 F. Supp. at

703; McNeil Laboratories, Inc. v. American Home Products Corporation, 416 F. Supp. 804, 806 (D.N.J.1976). By applying these factors in light of our earlier findings of fact and discussions about plaintiff's marks, we have reached certain conclusions based on general comparisons applicable to all of the marks and on specific comparisons of each mark.

(1). Strength of Plaintiff's Marks

The strength or weakness of plaintiff's marks is an important consideration. In general, "strong marks are given ... protection over a wide range of related products (or services) and variations on appearance of the mark (, while) weak marks are given a narrow range of protection both as to products (or services) and as to visual variations." 1 McCarthy, supra, § 11:24. See Family Circle, Inc. v. Family Circle Associates, Inc., 332 F.2d 534 (3rd Cir. 1964). "The term "strength' as applied to trademarks refers to the distinctiveness of the mark, or more precisely, its tendency to identify the goods sold under the mark as emanating from a particular, although possibly anonymous, source. (citations omitted)." McGregor-Doniger, Inc. v. Drizzle, Inc., 599 F.2d 1126, 1131 (2nd Cir. 1979). In view of our earlier discussion concerning the protectibility of plaintiff's marks, it is not necessary to conduct an extensive inquiry. For the purposes of this motion we find that plaintiff's service marks (ELVIS, ELVIS PRESLEY, ELVIS IN CONCERT, TCB with the lightning bolt and, to a lesser degree, without the lightning bolt, and the "Elvis Pose") have acquired great distinctiveness, in the eyes of the public and strongly identify Elvis Presley entertainment services and the source, although not necessarily known by name, of those services. See generally 1 McCarthy, supra, §§ 3:1-3, 11:1-24. However, we do consider the TCB logo to be somewhat weaker than the others since it has received less public exposure.

(2). Similarity of the Marks

It is well-recognized that the greater the similarity between plaintiff's and defendant's marks, the greater the likelihood of confusion. See generally 2 McCarthy, supra, §§ 23:3-23:16; Exxon Corp. v. Texas Motor Exchange of Houston, 628 F.2d 500, 505 (5th Cir. 1980). An evaluation of similarity generally entails a comparison with respect to similarity of appearance, pronunciation, and meaning. See Caesars World, Inc., 490 F. Supp. at 824; 2 McCarthy, supra, § 23:4; Restatement of Torts, § 729(a) (1938). In the present case, appearance is the most dominant element, and similarity of appearance is determined "on the basis of the total effect of the designation, rather than on a comparison of individual features." Restatement of Torts § 729, comment b (1938). Using these general guidelines, we reach the following conclusions.

The defendant's first mark can be considered the initials TCB. The defendant's logo of TCB with the lightning bolt, and, to a slightly lesser degree, without the lightning bolt, is essentially identical to plaintiff's corresponding mark.

The second of the defendant's marks can be characterized as any of the artist's renderings or pictures, which are purportedly of the performer Larry Seth as he appears in THE BIG EL SHOW, standing alone without being part of THE BIG EL SHOW logo. (See, e.g., Exhibit P. 11). We find that such pictures are highly similar to the image of Elvis Presley portrayed in the "Elvis Pose." The use of an artist's rendering or sketch rather than a photograph does not diminish the resemblance.

The third mark, the name THE BIG EL SHOW, which is the name of defendant's production, is not as similar to one of the plaintiff's marks as the first two are. The plaintiff's marks ELVIS and ELVIS IN CONCERT provide the closest bases for comparison. Using the factors of appearance and pronunciation, we find that there is some similarity between plaintiff's marks and defendant's mark but the extent of similarity is less than for the first two marks. The resemblance results because the EL in THE BIG EL SHOW is the first two letters of ELVIS, and it sounds similar, and the defendant's EL appears in the same type of blocked, capital letters as does plaintiff's ELVIS.

The fourth mark in question, and perhaps the most important, is the defendant's logo composed of the words THE BIG EL SHOW and the artist's rendering (Exhibit P. 28). Considering the total effect conveyed by this mark, we find there is a high degree of similarity with plaintiff's "Elvis Pose" and a slightly lower degree of similarity with the names ELVIS and ELVIS IN CONCERT. (See discussion, supra ). The connection in defendant's logo of the name THE BIG EL SHOW with the picture that looks like Elvis Presley results in the letters EL being more suggestive in meaning of the marks ELVIS and ELVIS PRESLEY.

(3). Defendant's Intent

Although the intent of the defendant in adopting a mark is only one of the factors, see Q-Tips, Inc., supra, if a plaintiff can demonstrate that a defendant adopted a mark with the intent of obtaining unfair commercial advantage from the reputation of the plaintiff, then "that fact alone "may be sufficient to justify the inference that there is confusing similarity.' Restatement of Torts § 729, comment f (1938)." Amstar Corp. v. Domino's Pizza, Inc., 615 F.2d 252 (5th Cir. 1980). See John Wright, Inc. v. Casper Corp., 419 F. Supp. 292, 320 (E.D.Pa.1976). See also Perfectform Corporation, 256 F.2d at 741-42.

Because of the nature of the defendant's service, the defendant's intent as specifically related to his marks is interwoven with his intent as to the origin and presentation of the production. We have no doubt that a reason for Russen's starting his show was to capitalize on the popularity of Elvis Presley. It is also quite apparent that the show, the service in question, was designed to simulate or imitate a performance by Elvis Presley. The available evidence bearing on the defendant's reasons for adopting his marks must be considered in light of the nature of the production. It is possible that producer Russen adopted his marks in order to tell the public something about the production and to promote the show. On the other hand, such marks could have been designed mainly to deceive the public and to trade on the good will associated with plaintiff's marks.

Because the record contains a relative paucity of information bearing on defendant's intent, it is difficult to draw many strong conclusions. Based on our review, we make the following observations as to intent. Russen was well aware of Presley's TCB mark and adopted the same mark because of its connection to the Elvis Presley organization. See Caesars World, Inc., 490 F. Supp. at 825 (defendant's claim of innocent adoption negated by evidence of defendant's prior awareness of plaintiff's mark). He stated that he got the idea to use TCB as the name of his band because it is the name of Elvis Presley's fan clubs and serves as Presley's motto. We find that the use of TCB in connection with defendant's production was totally unnecessary and was done only to benefit from the good will which attached to Presley and his performances and organization.

As to the name THE BIG EL SHOW and the artist's rendering or picture of the performer Larry Seth as he appears in the show, we are unable to conclude that the defendant adopted these marks mainly to "bask in the reflected popularity" generated by plaintiff's marks. See Q-Tips, Inc., 206 F.2d at 147 (3rd Cir.), cert. denied, 346 U.S. 867, 74 S. Ct. 106, 98 L. Ed. 377 (1953). The defendant indicated that the name, THE BIG EL SHOW, was thought up by Larry Seth, the star of the production, and agreed to by the defendant Russen. The defendant also indicated that the artist's rendering or pictures were all of Larry Seth as the BIG EL. The plaintiff has not offered any other evidence, beyond the marks themselves, to prove improper motive. We conclude that there is insufficient evidence that the defendant adopted the name or used the pictures predominantly for the purpose of misleading or deceiving the public rather than for suggesting the nature of THE BIG EL SHOW production.

(4). Similarity of Services

As a rule, "the greater the similarity between the products and services (provided by the defendant and plaintiff), the greater the likelihood of confusion." Exxon Corp. v. Texas Motor Exchange of Houston, 628 F.2d 500, 505 (5th Cir. 1980). See generally Restatement of Torts § 731(e), comment d (1938). In the present case, the services of the plaintiff and of the defendant cannot be considered identical, but they are very similar. In general terms, each party's services can be described as musical entertainment provided by one singer or performer with instrumental or vocal background provided by others. There is some difference in the forms of presentation, since plaintiff's entertainment is provided mainly in the forms of records, film, video tape, and audio tape, while defendant's entertainment mainly appears as live, stage productions. The defendant, however, has also produced records, albeit in limited numbers, of THE BIG EL SHOW. In addition, both parties have engaged in forms of licensing or sub-licensing their marks to appear on such merchandise as photographs, pendants, and buttons.

A more specific reason for finding strong similarity is that both parties' entertainment services involve Elvis Presley. The plaintiff provides actual performances of Presley, while the defendant provides an imitation of an Elvis Presley performance. The fact that the plaintiff does not provide live stage performances of Presley, admittedly an impossibility due to Presley's current state, makes identical services virtually impossible and does lessen the similarity somewhat. In any event, direct competition or identity of services or products is not required to prove likelihood of confusion. Great Atlantic & Pacific Tea Co., supra.

See Scarves by Vera, Inc. v. Todo Imports Ltd., supra, (544 F.2d 1167 (2d Cir. 1976)) (women's scarves and apparel with women's cosmetics and fragrances); James Burrough Ltd. v. Sign of the Beefeater, Inc., supra (liquor with restaurant selling liquor); Union Carbide Corp. v. Ever-Ready, Inc., supra (531 F.2d 366 (7th Cir. 1976)) (batteries and lamps with lightbulbs and lamps); Alfred Dunhill of London, Inc. v. Kasser Distillers Products Corp., 350 F. Supp. 1341 (E.D.Pa.1972), aff'd without opinion, 480 F.2d 917 (3rd Cir. 1973) (pipe tobacco and bar accessories with scotch whiskey).

Scott Paper Co., 589 F.2d at 1230.

(5). Similarity of Channels of Trade, Manners of Marketing, and Predominant Purchasers

Similarities of channels of trade, manners of marketing, and predominant purchasers of plaintiff's and defendant's services, as well as licensed goods, increase the possibilities of confusion. See, e.g., Exxon Corp. v. Texas Motor Exchange of Houston, 628 F.2d at 505; DeCosta supra; Schmid Laboratories v. Youngs Drug Products, 482 F. Supp. 14, 19-20 (D.N.J.1979); Fotomat Corp., supra ; Restatement of Torts §§ 729(c), 731(c), (d), comment d (1938). The evidence in the record bearing on these factors is sketchy. By drawing some reasonable inferences from the available information and speculating on certain points, we have concluded that there is some similarity between the trade channels and marketing campaigns and that there is more similarity between the purchasers of the two services.

The enterprises of Presley, and more recently of plaintiff, have been national, including the New Jersey, Pennsylvania region, and international in scope and distribution. Since Presley's death, his performances as embodied in records and tapes have continued to be sold in major retail outlets. In addition, plaintiff's licensees and sublicensees have conducted marketing campaigns in order to sell a variety of merchandise. Plaintiff has also indicated that a movie about Presley has been filmed and will be released; however, the evidence does not reveal how much of the actual Presley performances will be included in the movie or when and where the movie will be exhibited. Plaintiff has not provided any other evidence that it is currently presenting any entertainment services in theaters or nightclubs. Plaintiff, however has introduced a license agreement allowing Presley's former band to use the TCB logo on a record and in association with personal appearances.

The defendant's show has had a much smaller and more localized market. Although THE BIG EL SHOW has appeared in different American towns and cities, including Las Vegas, it basically has been localized in the Northeast generally and the New Jersey-Pennsylvania region specifically. The performances usually have been presented in smaller nightclubs, although there was an engagement at a Las Vegas hotel, and the show has been advertised on a local basis.

One particularly important aspect of the defendant's advertising is the emphasis placed on the disputed marks in the records, ads, and promotional materials themselves. The picture or artist's rendering, which we have already found to have an extremely close resemblance to plaintiff's mark, is highlighted along with the name THE BIG EL SHOW, except on one of the album covers which only has a sketch of the performer. The name and the written material, such as "A TRIBUTE TO ELVIS PRESLEY," does suggest the production is a type of simulation or imitation intended to honor Presley, but does not reveal the name of the star or any information as to the producer or sponsor of the show. In essence, there is nothing to negate the reasonable impression that the artist's rendering or picture is of Elvis Presley.

The marketing of limited quantities of THE BIG EL SHOW records and merchandise also appears to be on a highly localized and small scale basis. Most of the records were given away for promotional purposes. Those records which have been sold were distributed in a few stores in the New Jersey-Pennsylvania region; while the merchandise was sold mainly at THE BIG EL SHOW performances. Interestingly, Elvis Presley merchandise was also sold at THE BIG EL SHOW performances, and the evidence shows this to be the only side-by-side sale outlet of plaintiff's and defendant's products. In addition, another similarity exists in that both parties utilized a TCB logo with a lightning bolt on their stationery.

Based on the sketchy information in the record, we conclude that there is only some similarity between the marketing campaigns and the trade channels. See DeCosta, supra.

The similarity between the predominant purchasers is greater than that between the marketing campaigns and trade channels. Because defendant's enterprise, THE BIG EL SHOW, is a stylized imitation of an Elvis Presley performance, it seems likely that it would appeal to many of the same members of the public who are interested in and patronize plaintiff's entertainment services. These purchasers could be called members of the Elvis Presley consuming public. Of course, there are also significant areas of difference between the "customers." For example, since the defendant's production usually has been presented in nightclubs, the customers may attend mainly for the nightclub aspect and not the production; while plaintiff's services, because of their current forms of presentation, would appeal more to home entertainment consumers (but the release of the movie could extend the appeal of plaintiff's services to members of the public who patronize nightclubs and theaters.)

(6). Actual Confusion

Plaintiff has not presented any evidence of actual confusion by members of the consuming public. Plaintiff has not shown, for example by survey evidence, that people seeing THE BIG EL SHOW or advertisements for it thought the production was associated with the plaintiff or with Elvis Presley entertainment services. Although a showing of actual confusion could be significant, such evidence is not necessary to a finding of likelihood of confusion, see, e.g., Amstar Corp., supra; Caesars World, Inc., 490 F. Supp. at 825; Fotomat Corp., 425 F. Supp. at 703. See generally 2 McCarthy § 23:2, particularly where the party seeks only preliminary equitable relief. See, e.g., D. C. Comics, Inc., supra.

(7). Likelihood of Confusion Conclusion

In determining the existence of a likelihood of confusion, we must look through "the eyes of "ordinary purchasers, buying with ordinary caution,' McLean v. Fleming, 96 U.S. 245, 251, 24 L. Ed. 828 (1878), including people whose purchasers are motivated by appearance and general impressions, Dresser Industries, Inc. v. Heraeus Engelhard Vacuum, Inc., 395 F.2d 457, 462 (3rd Cir. 1968), cert. denied, 393 U.S. 934, 89 S. Ct. 293, 21 L. Ed. 2d 270 (1968)." Fotomat Corp., 425 F. Supp. at 703. An analysis of likelihood of confusion can be a complex process because of the variety of factors to be considered and because of the subjective and conjectural nature inherent in the process. In formulating our final conclusions we have used the perspective of the "ordinary purchaser" as our guide in balancing the extent and strength of the similarities against those of the dissimilarities. Based both on our evaluations of defendant's marks in light of the multiple factors and on our general sense impressions we have reached the following conclusions. The defendant's uses of both the initials TCB with or without the lightning bolt and of any artist's rendering or picture which resembles the "Elvis Pose," alone or as part of THE BIG EL SHOW logo, as service marks or trademarks to identify the defendant's production, records, or merchandise create a likelihood of confusion as to source or sponsorship. Although our analysis of the various factors provides ample support for our conclusion, we are especially persuaded by the strength of plaintiff's marks in the entertainment industry and the virtual equivalence of these two marks of the defendant with the corresponding marks of the plaintiff.

In making our decision, it is not necessary to conclude that the public be led to believe that defendant's show is composed of actual Elvis Presley performances or is produced by the plaintiff. It is not even necessary that the public know who the plaintiff is. What is required and what we find is that the ordinary purchaser generally familiar with plaintiff's marks is likely to believe that defendant's show is somehow related to, associated with, or sponsored by the same people or entity that provides the actual Elvis Presley entertainment services identified by its own marks. It is not at all unreasonable for the public to believe that this entity, which is the plaintiff, the Estate of Elvis Presley, has decided to license or sponsor a form of entertainment closely related to its other entertainment services. The public, realizing that an actual Elvis Presley live stage show is now impossible, might assume that the plaintiff's only alternative in order to enter this specific area of the entertainment field was to produce or sponsor an imitation of a real Elvis Presley performance, perhaps by using members of the actual Presley performing troupe or production staff or by supplying costumes or other official Presley items. It is also highly possible that consumers seeing the defendant's TCB logo or the advertisements highlighting the likeness of Elvis Presley might believe that the show is a multimedia presentation and incorporates films or recordings of actual Elvis Presley performances.

Our decisions with respect to the name THE BIG EL SHOW alone and in association with any pictures or artist's renderings resembling the "Elvis Pose" are closer. After careful consideration of the various factors, we have concluded that the use of the name THE BIG EL SHOW by itself does not create a likelihood of confusion, but its use as part of the logo or in connection with misleading pictures does create such confusion.

By attaching the artist's rendering to the name THE BIG EL SHOW to form the logo, the defendant has gone beyond allowable bounds. The likelihood of confusion associated with the artist's rendering is not sufficiently diminished by the use of the name with it. The picture, which certainly appears to be of Elvis Presley, provides the major triggering mechanism for the appeal to the public. The purchasing public seeing the picture and the name is likely to have a very similar reaction to the logo, believing the picture to be of Elvis, as it would if the picture were presented alone. The addition of the name may help to confirm that the production is an imitation of an actual Presley performance, but it really does not dispel any confusion as to plaintiff's association with or sponsorship of the production.

Thus, based on the current state of the record, we have found a likelihood of confusion with respect to the defendant's marks of TCB with or without the lightning bolt, any artist's renderings or pictures which resemble the "Elvis Pose," and the logo. The plaintiff has established the likelihood of its ultimate success on the merits of its infringement claims as to these marks. The plaintiff has not established the same likelihood as to the defendant's use of THE BIG EL SHOW, alone, as the name or mark for its production.

### 3. Common Law Unfair Competition

Plaintiff has alleged that the defendant's use of the names THE BIG EL SHOW, THE BIG EL SHOW IN CONCERT, THE KING, TCB (with or without the lightning bolt), the pictures resembling Elvis Presley and the presentation of the production imitating an Elvis Presley performance itself constitute common law unfair competition. Plaintiff claims that defendant's show, in combination with his advertising and promotion, should give rise to legal restraints because the defendant has "by unfair means usurped(ed) the goodwill and distinctive attributes of the business so constructed by (plaintiff)." House of Westmore, Inc. v. Denney, 151 F.2d 261, 265 (3rd Cir. 1945).

The claim of common law unfair competition, which is governed in this case by New Jersey law, covers a broader spectrum of behavior than trademark or service mark infringement. "In fact the common law of trademarks is but a part of the broader law of unfair competition." Hanover Star Milling Co. v. Metcalf, 240 U.S. 403, 413, 36 S. Ct. 357, 360, 60 L. Ed. 713 (1916). Unfair competition "may be distinguished from infringement in that it does not involve the violation of the exclusive right to use a word, mark or symbol, but rather involves any violation of a right arising from the operation of an established business." House of Westmore v. Denney, 151 F.2d at 265. The focus in trademark litigation is on whether an alleged symbol or name functions to identify and distinguish one's goods or services and whether the usage by another of the same or similar mark is likely to confuse customers. Under unfair competition, the focus, generally, is on the buyer's likely confusion between two products or services based on an examination of everything that is likely to have an impact upon the purchaser. 1 McCarthy, Trademarks and Unfair Competition § 2:2 (1973). Many types of behavior are capable of constituting unfair competition. As one New Jersey court has noted:

... equity broadly concerns itself with the suppression of injurious deception and fraud whatever the means by which they are wrongfully accomplished. It must be realized that injunctive relief is not confined to the protection of those having trademarks and trade-names. It reaches beyond to encompass all cases in which it is evident that fraud and deception are practiced by one in disparaging or capturing the trade of a competitor. The ingenuity of the unfair competitor thus eludes classification but not always the restraint of a court of equity.

American Shops, Inc. v. American Fashion Shops of Journal Square, Inc., 13 N.J.Super. 416, 421, 80 A.2d 575 (App.Div.1951).

One common form of unfair competition is closely linked to an action for trademark infringement and involves the use of the same or similar name, or symbols of a competitor or non-competitor. As in trademark infringement, the test is the likelihood of confusion or deception among actual or prospective customers of the plaintiff. Where the necessary and probable tendency of the defendant's simulation or resemblance of plaintiff's trade name is to mislead the public into believing that the defendant's business is that of or connected with plaintiff's, then neither actual confusion nor actual fraudulent intent need be shown, for the court is then concerned with the consequences of defendant's act and not the motive for them. (Citations omitted).

Great Atlantic & Pacific Tea Co. v. A & P Trucking Co., 51 N.J.Super. 412, 420, 144 A.2d 172 (App.Div.1958), modified and remanded, 29 N.J. 455, 459, 149 A.2d 595 (1959). See Perfectform Corporation v. Perfect Brassiere Co., 256 F.2d 736, 741-42 (3rd Cir. 1958); Caesars World, Inc. v. Caesar's Palace, 490 F. Supp. 818, 828 (D.N.J.1980); Fotomat Corp. v. Photo Drive-Thru, Inc., 425 F. Supp. 693, 708-09 (D.N.J.1977). In addition, as with the trend in trademark infringement, injunctive relief will be granted "upon proof of likelihood of confusion as to source or sponsorship despite the diverse nature of the products or services involved. (citations omitted)." Great Atlantic & Pacific Tea Co. v. A & P Trucking Corp., 29 N.J. at 455, 149 A.2d 595.

In light of our earlier discussion, in the service mark infringement context, of the likelihood of confusion as to the names and symbols used by the defendant, it is unnecessary for an extended analysis here. It is generally acknowledged that the same facts supporting a suit for trademark or service mark infringement will support a suit for unfair competition. See, e.g., Amstar Corp. v. Domino's Pizza, Inc., 615 F.2d 252, 265 (5th Cir. 1980); New West Corp. v. NYM Company of California, Inc., 595 F.2d 1194, 1201 (9th Cir. 1979); James Burrough Ltd. v. Sign of the Beefeater, Inc., 540 F.2d 266, 274 n.16 (7th Cir. 1976); Time Mechanisms, Inc. v. Qonaar Corp., 422 F. Supp. 905, 915 (D.N.J.1976); American Shops, Inc. v. American Fashion Shops of Journal Square, Inc., 13 N.J.Super. at 421, 80 A.2d 575. Thus, our earlier decisions regarding likelihood of confusion and probable success on the merits also hold for the unfair competition claims. Because there are fewer restrictions for a showing of unfair competition and more leeway in the exercise of our equitable powers, we conclude that our findings of likelihood of confusion are even stronger. As Judge Gerry has explained, "it is possible to be guilty of unfair competition even when trademark infringement is not present, if use of a similar but noninfringing mark or device is combined with unfair practices in a manner which is likely to deceive purchasers regarding the origin of goods (or services) under all the circumstances. (citations omitted)." Fotomat Corp. v. Photo Drive-Thru, Inc., 425 F. Supp. at 709. Therefore, even assuming the names ELVIS, ELVIS PRESLEY, and ELVIS IN CONCERT, the TCB logo, and the "Elvis Pose" have not functioned as service marks, the current uses by the defendant of THE BIG EL SHOW logo (words and Presley likeness), the pictures resembling Presley, and the initials TCB in his advertising and business and promotional materials are still likely to deceive the public as to the origin or sponsorship of the show itself.

As to the defendant's uses of the name THE BIG EL SHOW, without any accompanying photographs or artist's renderings, and the term THE KING, we still do not find a likelihood of confusion or deception. The plaintiff has not made a sufficient showing of unfair practices or other circumstances to convince us that the defendant's proper use of these two items constitutes unfair competition.

In addition to its claims against the defendant's use of certain names or symbols in its business, advertising, or promotional materials, the plaintiff argues that the defendant's production, itself, constitutes unfair competition. The plaintiff asserts that the packaging together of the image, dress, and style of Elvis Presley into an hour and one-half production designed to simulate an actual Elvis Presley production results in unfair competition since the audience viewing the performance is necessarily deceived into believing it is dealing with a service of the Estate of Elvis Presley. Plaintiff mainly relies on a type of unfair competition known as "unreasonable" or unprivileged imitation. As the Third Circuit recently noted in S K & F, Co. v. Premo Pharmaceutical Lab., 625 F.2d 1055 (3rd Cir. 1980), the New Jersey cases define this tort "in roughly the same manner as did the First Restatement of Torts." Id. at 1062. Sections 711(c) and 741 provide the guidelines. The Restatement of Torts § 711(c) (1938) indicates that:

(one) who

(c) markets goods with an unprivileged imitation of the physical appearance of another's goods is liable to the other for the relief appropriate under [the ensuing Restatement rules with regard to calculation of damages].

The definition is set forth in § 741 of the Restatement as follows:

One who markets goods, the physical appearance of which is a copy or imitation of the physical appearance of the goods of which another is the initial distributor, markets them with an unprivileged imitation, under the rule stated in § 711, if his goods are of the same class as those of the other and are sold in a market in which the other's interest is protected, and

(b) the copied or imitated feature has acquired generally in the market a special significance identifying the other's goods and

(i) the copy or imitation is likely to cause prospective purchasers to regard his goods as those of the other, and

(ii) the copied or imitated feature is nonfunctional, or, if it is functional, he does not take reasonable steps to inform prospective purchasers that the goods which he markets are not those of the other.

See, e.g., French Amer. Reeds. Mfg. Co. v. Park Plastics Co., 20 N.J.Super. 325, 332-34, 90 A.2d 50 (App.Div.1952). See also Squeezit Corp. v. Plastic Dispensers, Inc., 31 N.J.Super. 217, 106 A.2d 322 (App.Div.1952). The plaintiff specifically points to United Cigar Stores Co. v. United Confectioners, 92 N.J.Eq.

449, 113 A. 226 (Ch.1921) to support its position. In that case, which involved similar store fronts, the court concluded that

defendants' stores have been "dressed" in such striking simulation and imitation of the appearance of complainants' store as to deceive a very large part, if not practically all, the interested public who did not know otherwise, into thinking that defendants' stores were a part of or compartments in complainants' establishment, and, at least as to a substantial part of the public, to mislead them into patronizing defendants' stores in the mistaken belief that it was complainants' store which they were in fact patronizing as they intended to do.

Id. at 450, 113 A. 226.

Upon reviewing the record we find that the plaintiff has not presented sufficient evidence, such as eyewitness accounts, films, or video tapes, to show that the defendant's entire production is such a duplication of plaintiff's services that members of the public likely would be deceived into believing the production originated with the plaintiff. Even assuming the defendant's production is shown to have a striking resemblance to an Elvis Presley concert, as embodied in a form such as film or video tape, this resemblance by itself, and without other evidence tending to show a deception of the public as to the origin of the production, probably would not constitute unfair competition in the same manner as a striking resemblance to a distinctive trade or business dress would. Unlike an outside appearance of a store, the presentation of the defendant's production, itself, which occurs in a theater or club, cannot act to mislead customers into attending a performance of the defendant's show in the mistaken belief that it is associated with the plaintiff. Rather, the defendant's advertising and promotional materials for the show function to induce and attract potential customers in a manner similar to a building design or a package for a product. See, e.g., Fotomat Corp., 425 F. Supp. at 709-10; Time Mechanisms, Inc., 422 F. Supp. at 915. See also Squeezit Corp., 31 N.J.Super. at 223-24, 106 A.2d 322.

In any event, even assuming the similarity in shows should be considered, we are convinced that the doctrine of unfair competition was not designed to attach strict liability to a good faith and non-confusing imitation of an entertainment service, such as a concert by a famous performer like Presley, particularly where the original performer is no longer living. As noted in Chaplin v. Amador, 93 Cal.App. 358, 362, 269 P. 544, 546 (1928), a case involving an unfair competition claim and an imitation of a performer:

The case of plaintiff does not depend on his right to the exclusive use of the role, garb and mannerisms, etc.; it is based upon fraud and deception. The right of action in such a case arises from the fraudulent purpose and conduct of appellant and injury caused to the plaintiff thereby, and the deception to the public.

Id. at 362, 269 P. at 546. (Emphasis in original). See also Lone Ranger v. Cox, 124 F.2d 650 (4th Cir. 1942). Cf. West v. Lind, 186 Cal.App.2d 563, 9 Cal.Rptr. 288 (Cal.App.1960).

In deciding whether the defendant's activities constitute unfair competition, we must go beyond the question of whether THE BIG EL SHOW production is similar to an actual Elvis Presley performance as recorded on film, video tape, records, etc. Rather, our analysis must focus on the totality of the factors bearing on whether the defendant by his activities in the marketplace has attempted to deceive or confuse the public into believing THE BIG EL SHOW is connected with the actual Elvis Presley performances or sponsored by the same people, Elvis Presley's estate or its licensees, who have been presenting actual Elvis Presley entertainment services. See, e.g., DeCosta v. Columbia Broadcasting System, Inc., 520 F.2d 499, 513-15 (1st Cir.), cert. denied, 423 U.S. 1073, 96 S. Ct. 856, 47 L. Ed. 2d 83 (1975); Lone Ranger v. Cox, supra; Ideal Toy Corp. v. Kenner Products, Etc., 443 F. Supp. 291, 307-09 (S.D.N.Y.1977); Wyatt Earp Enterprises v. Sackman, Inc., 157 F. Supp. 621 (S.D.N.Y.1958). After considering these circumstances in light of our earlier findings as to likelihood of confusion, we conclude that the plaintiff has adequately demonstrated a likelihood of success on the merits as to part of its unfair competition claim. The plaintiff has made a sufficient showing of the deceptive impact of the defendant's advertising and promotional materials and other communication to the public but has not made such a showing with respect to the nature or composition of the defendant's show, itself.

### 4. Section 43(a) of the Lanham Act

The plaintiff argues that the defendant has violated § 43(a) of the Lanham Act, 15 U.S.C. § 1125(a), by his use of the name THE BIG EL SHOW, the initials TCB, the phrase THE BIG EL SHOW IN CONCERT, the picture or artist's rendering which looks like Elvis Presley, and the logo composed of the name and artist's rendering. The plaintiff also claims that the defendant has violated § 43(a) by his complete adoption of the performance style, accouterment and songs made famous by Presley, and by his advertising of "A Tribute to Elvis Presley."

Section 43(a) of the Lanham Act ("Act"), 15 U.S.C. § 1125(a), created a "distinct federal statutory tort," Franklin Mint, Inc. v. Franklin Mint, Ltd., 331 F. Supp. 827, 831 (E.D.Pa.1971), "designed to afford broad protection against various forms of unfair competition and false advertising," John Wright, Inc. v. Casper Corp., 419 F. Supp. 292, 324-25 (E.D.Pa.1976), aff'd in part, rev'd and remanded in part sub. nom. Donsco, Inc. v. Casper Corp., 587 F.2d 602 (3rd Cir. 1978), including deceptive and misleading advertising. See Nature's Bounty, Inc. v. SuperX Drugs Corp., 490 F. Supp. 50, 54 (E.D.N.Y.1980). The Third Circuit recently has noted that § 43(a) ... proscribes not only acts that would technically qualify as trademark infringement, but also unfair competitive practices involving actual or potential deception. L'Aiglon Apparel, Inc. v. Lana Lobell, Inc., 214 F.2d 649, 650-51 (3d Cir. 1954); see Ives Labs., Inc. v. Darby Drug Co., 601 F.2d (631) at 641-42 ((2d Cir. 1979)) (§ 43(a) creates federal statutory torts of unfair competition beyond simple trademark infringement); Quabaug Rubber Co. v. Fabiano Shoe Co., 567 F.2d 154, 160 (1st Cir. 1977) (s 43(a) standing to sue extends beyond trademark owner to other injured parties); Alfred Dunhill Ltd. v. Interstate Cigar Co., 499 F.2d 232, 236 (2d Cir. 1974) (s 43(a) extends rights to parties injured by false advertising).

S K & F, Co. v. Premo Pharmaceutical Laboratories, Inc., 625 F.2d 1055, 1065 (3rd Cir. 1980).

Although § 43(a) may proscribe competitive torts not covered by trademark infringement law or common law unfair competition, S K & F, Co., 625 F.2d at 1065, as a general rule, the same facts which would support an action for trademark (or service mark) infringement or common law unfair competition (facts indicating a likelihood of confusion as to source or sponsorship of goods or services) would support an action for unfair competitive practices under § 43(a). See, e.g., New West Corp. v. NYM Co. of Cal., Inc., 595 F.2d 1194, 1201 (9th Cir. 1979); Boston Professional Hockey Association, Inc. v. Dallas Cap & Emblem Manufacturing, Inc., 510 F.2d 1004, 1010 (5th Cir.), cert. denied, 423 U.S. 868, 96 S. Ct. 132, 46 L. Ed. 2d 98 (1975); National Lampoon, Inc. v. American Broadcasting Co., Inc., 376 F. Supp. 733, 746 (S.D.N.Y.), aff'd, 497 F.2d 1343 (2nd Cir. 1974); Frederick Warne & Co., Inc. v. Book Sales, Inc., 481 F. Supp. 1191, 1195 (S.D.N.Y.1979); John Wright, Inc., 419 F. Supp. at 325. See also, S K & F, Co., 625 F.2d at 1065. Because we have already addressed the strength or secondary meaning and the concomitant likelihood of confusion as to each of the names or symbols, as well as to the production itself, we do not find it necessary to conduct a similar examination here. Those conclusions as to likelihood of success on the merits are sufficient to suggest that a similar result is likely for the § 43(a) claims.

As noted, one of the purposes of § 43(a), as distinguished from the common law of unfair competition, is to protect "consumers as well as commercial interests from the effects of false advertising." 2 McCarthy, Trademarks and Unfair Competition, supra, § 27:2 at 246. In view of the qualifications attached to our unfair competition decision, we will address some comments to the permissible scope of the defendant's advertising for the stage production. In this regard, we have found three lines of cases addressing unfair competition and § 43(a) claims to be especially informative. The cases are those where a violation occurs when a record is advertised so as to represent falsely the true nature or extent, if any, of the participation of a performer, see, e.g., RCA Records v. Kory Records, Inc., 197 U.S.P.Q. 908 (E.D.N.Y.1978); CBS, Inc. v. Springboard International Records, 429 F. Supp. 563 (S.D.N.Y.1976); CBS, Inc. v.

Gusto Records, Inc., 403 F. Supp. 447 (M.D.Tenn.1974); Decca Records v. Musicor Records, 314 F. Supp. 145, 166 U.S.P.Q. 57 (S.D.N.Y.1970); Shaw v. Time-Life Records, 38 N.Y.2d 201, 379 N.Y.S.2d 390, 341 N.E.2d 817 (1975), where a violation occurs where deceptive title or advertising is used in connection with a movie or stage production, see, e.g., Dallas Cowboys Cheerleaders, Inc. v. Pussycat Çinema, Ltd., 467 F. Supp. 366 (S.D.N.Y.), aff'd, 604 F.2d 200 (2nd Cir. 1979); Robert Stigwood Group, Ltd. v. Sperber, 457 F.2d 50 (2nd Cir. 1972); Warner Bros., Inc. v. Film Ventures International, 403 F. Supp. 522 (C.D.Cal.1975), and where a violation does not occur where a competitor makes a copy of an unprotected product (or service) of the plaintiff's, and truthfully advertises it as a copy by using the name or trademark of the plaintiff, without his consent, to identify the originator or the product copied. See, e.g., Saxony Products, Inc. v. Guerlain, Inc., 513 F.2d 716 (9th Cir. 1975), aff'd in part, rev'd in part on different grounds, 594 F.2d 230 (9th Cir. 1979); Smith v. Chanel, Inc., 402 F.2d 562 (9th Cir. 1968); Societe Comptoir de L'Industrie Cotonniere Etablissements Boussac v. Alexander's Dept. Stores, Inc., 299 F.2d 33 (2nd Cir. 1962). These cases emphasize the significance of and techniques for preventing and alleviating deceptive and misleading advertising, while stressing the need for providing the public with truthful information about the products or services and their sources or sponsorship.

Assuming arguendo defendant's presentation of a stage show imitating an actual Elvis Presley performance were permissible, defendant would be allowed to use a name and advertising material which suggests something about the production's content. However, the success of the production or service should depend on the quality of the production, itself, and not on the ability of the defendant to deceive the public and to benefit unfairly from the goodwill attached to plaintiff's entertainment services of actual Elvis Presley performances. The defendant would have to make clear in all communications (including, but not limited to, advertising and promotional materials, theater programs or playbills, and record covers) to the consuming public that his production is not affiliated with, sponsored by, or in any other way connected with the same people who provide actual Elvis Presley entertainment services. In this respect, the defendant's current advertisements and promotional materials (see Exhibits P. 14, 15, 19), as well as the album covers (see Exhibits P. 11, 13) and labels on the 45 RPM records (see Exhibit P. 18), are not adequate. They highlight those items, THE BIG EL SHOW logo and pictures or artist's renderings which appear to be of Elvis Presley, which we already have concluded are likely to cause confusion. The use by the defendant only of phrases such as "REFLECTIONS ON A LEGEND … A TRIBUTE TO ELVIS PRESLEY," "Looks and Sounds like The KING," and "LIVE ON STAGE" does not diminish the confusion engendered by the use of the logo or artist's renderings to identify the production. In order to reduce this confusion, the defendant's representations and communications to the consuming public should incorporate in some manner the following ideas: that the production, or recording of the production, is a stage show, called THE BIG EL SHOW, which stars Larry Seth (or whoever is currently starring); that THE BIG EL SHOW is an attempted imitation of a performance or stage show of the late Elvis Presley; who the producer of THE BIG EL SHOW and of the record is; that neither THE BIG EL SHOW nor any recording is authorized or sponsored or licensed by the Estate of Elvis Presley; and that no one involved in the production of actual Elvis Presley performances or films or records is involved in THE BIG EL SHOW or the records of the show. In addition, in order to properly apprise potential customers that the star of THE BIG EL SHOW actually looks like Elvis Presley, the defendant should be able to use properly identified and legally obtained photographs of Elvis Presley to compare with photographs of the star of THE BIG EL SHOW.

### B. Irreparable Injury

Having found that the plaintiff is likely to succeed on the merits as to certain claims, we must next examine the second requirement for a plaintiff seeking a preliminary injunction. The plaintiff must demonstrate that irreparable injury will result if an injunction is not granted pendente lite.

### 1. Right of Publicity

Although the plaintiff has shown a likelihood of success on the merits of its right of publicity claim, the plaintiff has not made a sufficient showing that irreparable injury will result if the defendant's production is not preliminarily enjoined. In making this decision, we note that we are treating a right of publicity claim different than a service mark infringement or unfair competition claim. Because the doctrine of the right of publicity emphasizes the protection of the commercial value of the celebrity's name or likeness, the plaintiff must demonstrate sufficiently that the defendant's use of the name and likeness of the celebrity has or is likely to result in an identifiable economic loss. In contrast, in the context of the service mark infringement, unfair competition, and § 43(a) of the Lanham Act claims, we found that irreparable injury could result even in the absence of economic harm per se. One reason for this difference in approach stems from the public deception which is part of the latter three causes of action, but not part of the right of publicity claim. As a result of such public deception or confusion as to source, the plaintiff is being harmed. The plaintiff is being unfairly compelled to place the control of the good will attached to its entertainment services in the hands of the defendant.

In addition, and perhaps even more importantly, the close relationship in this case between the right of publicity and the societal considerations of free expression supports the position that the plaintiff in seeking relief for an infringement of its rights of publicity should demonstrate an identifiable economic harm. As we noted earlier, the defendant's activity when viewed simply as a skilled, good faith imitation of an Elvis Presley performance, i. e., without the elements leading to a likelihood of confusion, is, in some measure, consistent with the goals of freedom of expression. Thus, before the harsh step of barring defendant's activity is undertaken, the plaintiff should have to make a showing of immediate, irreparable harm to the commercial value of the right of publicity and should not be able to rely on an intangible potentiality.

In light of these comments, we find that the plaintiff has not made a sufficient showing that the presentation of this particular production, THE BIG EL SHOW, has resulted in any loss of commercial benefits to the plaintiff or will result in an irreparable commercial harm in the near future. The plaintiff has not adequately demonstrated that the existence of defendant's activity has led to or is likely to lead to a diminished ability of the plaintiff to profit from the use of Elvis Presley's name or likeness. For example, there is insufficient evidence that plaintiff's (or its licensees') ability to enter into agreements licensing the use of Presley's name or likeness in connection with consumer products is seriously jeopardized by defendant's activity. As a matter of fact, it is even possible that defendant's production has stimulated the public's interest in buying Elvis Presley merchandise or in seeing films or hearing records embodying actual Elvis Presley performances. See Zacchini, supra, 433 U.S. at 575 n.12, 97 S. Ct. at 2857 n.12 (conjecturing that the broadcast of the film showing plaintiff's act might stimulate the public interest in seeing the act live). Thus, the defendant's show will not be preliminarily enjoined.

The considerations preventing the issuance of a preliminary injunction as to the show do not sufficiently apply to the sale of pendants or records even though the sales are limited. Since the plaintiff, through its licensing programs, also engages in the sale of such items, this situation is similar to that in Factors Etc., Inc. v. Pro Arts, Inc., 579 F.2d 215 (2nd Cir. 1978), cert. denied, 440 U.S. 908, 99 S. Ct. 1215, 59 L. Ed. 2d 455 (1979) and Factors Etc., Inc. v. Creative Card Co., 444 F. Supp. 279 (S.D.N.Y.1977), where irreparable harm was found. We find that irreparable injury would result from the continued sale and distribution of pendants displaying Elvis Presley's likeness or of records whose covers or labels display pictures or artist's renderings which are or appear to be of Elvis Presley.

2. Service Mark Infringement, Common Law Unfair Competition, and § 43(a) of the Lanham Act

As a general proposition, in the contexts of service mark (or trademark) infringement and unfair competition, including § 43(a) of the Lanham Act, the plaintiff who demonstrates a likelihood of confusion as to source, and thus, likelihood of success on the merits, will have formed a strong basis for showing irreparable injury. See, e.g., Playboy Enterprises, Inc. v. Chuckleberry Publishing, Inc., 486 F. Supp. 414, 429 (S.D.N.Y.1980); Russ Berrie & Co., Inc. v. Jerry Elsner Co., Inc., 482 F. Supp. 980, 990 (S.D.N.Y.1980); Louis Rich, Inc. v. Horace W. Longacre, Inc., 423 F. Supp. 1327 (E.D.Pa.1976); United Cigar Stores Co. of America v. United Confectioners, 92 N.J.Eq. 449, 450, 113 A. 226 (E. & A. 1921). This results because:

A plaintiff who has demonstrated service mark infringement and unfair competition faces the probability of lost trade and appropriation of its good will. The damages in such a case are by their very nature irreparable and not susceptible of adequate measurement. Tefal, S.A. v. Products International Co., 186 U.S.P.Q. 545, 548 (D.N.J.1975), aff'd, 529 F.2d 495, 497 (3d Cir. 1976). Plaintiff's lack of ability to control the nature and quality of services provided under an infringing service mark, even if defendant matches the high quality of plaintiff's services, constitutes irreparable injury. Ambassador East, Inc. v. Orsatti, Inc., 257 F.2d 79, 82 (3d Cir. 1958); Chips " N Twigs, Inc. v. Chip-Chip, Ltd., 414 F. Supp. 1003 (E.D.Pa.1976).

Fotomat Corp. v. Photo Drive-Thru, Inc., 425 F. Supp. 693 at 696, 711 (D.N.J.1977). See also McNeil Laboratories v. American Home Products Corp., 416 F. Supp. 804, 809 (D.N.J.1976); Franklin Mint, Inc. v. Franklin Mint, Ltd., 331 F. Supp. 827, 830 (E.D.Pa.1971). A similar position prevails even in connection with non-competing goods or services. As Judge Learned Hand explained in his classic statement on the subject.

(A) merchant may have a sufficient economic interest in the use of his mark outside the field of his own exploitation to justify interposition by a court. His mark is his authentic seal; by it he vouches for the goods which bear it; it carries his name for good or ill. If another uses it, he borrows the owner's reputation, whose quality no longer lies within his own control. This is an injury, even though the borrower does not tarnish it, or divert any sales by its use; for a reputation, like a face, is the symbol of its possessor and creator, and another can use it only as a mask.

Yale Electric Corp. v. Robertson, 26 F.2d 972, 974 (2nd Cir. 1928). See James Burrough, Ltd. v. Sign of Beefeater, Inc., 540 F.2d 266, 275-76 (7th Cir. 1976); Professional Golfers Association of America v. Bankers Life & Casualty Co., 514 F.2d 665, 669-70 (5th Cir. 1975); Great Atlantic & Pacific Tea Co. v. A & P Trucking Corp., 29 N.J. 455, 458-60, 149 A.2d 595 (1959).

In the present case, the plaintiff's service marks are widely known and represent high quality entertainment services and substantial good will. The plaintiff has a significant stake in continuing to ensure that the services or products identified by these marks maintain these standards. If the defendant were allowed to continue to use those names or symbols (THE BIG EL SHOW logo, the initials TCB with or without a lightning bolt, and pictures or artist's renderings which closely resemble Elvis Presley) previously found to engender confusion as to source, the plaintiff would be harmed seriously by the deprivation of its ability to control the nature and quality of a service which the public believes it provides. We find that "(t)his deprivation ... constitutes irreparable injury." Franklin Mint, Inc., 331 F. Supp. at 830. In addition, the plaintiff has a right to be protected from the probable damage to its good will if the purchasing public believes that the plaintiff has sponsored or helped produce THE BIG EL SHOW and is dissatisfied with the show. Such a loss of intangible value cannot be accurately measured and compensated in damages.

### C. The Balance of Equities

Recognizing our earlier conclusions as to likelihood of success on the merits and irreparable injury, we find that the hardships to the defendant in complying with a preliminary injunction would not outweigh the harm to the plaintiff resulting from a failure to grant a preliminary injunction. Since the preliminary injunction would not prevent the defendant from using the name THE BIG EL SHOW or from presenting the production itself, the harm to the defendant should not be significant. This conclusion actually is supported by the defendant's own arguments as to the equities. The defendant claims only two equitable considerations: that THE BIG EL SHOW is his and his family's major source of income and that THE BIG EL SHOW has generated its own good will with the public. Although we feel the defendant has not made an adequate showing of both of these claims, it is not necessary to consider this in our decision. Since our preliminary injunction would not stop the production or the use of the name THE BIG EL SHOW, the defendant's main concerns are alleviated. The defendant has not indicated that changing the advertising and promotional material and the logo or discontinuing the use of TCB will cause any real financial damage or have any other adverse impact. The effect of an injunction on defendant's sales of records also would not have any significant financial impact because of the limited number of records and extent of distribution. Finally, any loss in trade to the defendant should be due only to the fact that the defendant will no longer be using confusion to trade on the good will and reputation of the plaintiff. Any expenses incurred by the defendant in complying with the preliminary injunction could be easily calculated and adequately compensated by an award of monetary damages if the defendant ultimately prevails. See Louis Rich, Inc. v. Horace W. Longacre, Inc., 423 F. Supp. 1327, 1340 (E.D.Pa.1976). We conclude that the relative hardship to the defendant is outweighed by the potential harm to the plaintiff if the defendant is not preliminarily enjoined from those actions likely to cause confusion.

### D. Public Interest

The public interest requirement in cases of unfair competition or service mark (or trademark) infringement generally favors preliminary injunctions where the moving party has demonstrated a likelihood of success because "the public is ... interested in fair competitive practices and clearly opposed to being deceived in the marketplace." McNeil Laboratories, Inc. v. American Home Products Corporation, 416 F. Supp. 804, 809 (D.N.J.1976). See S K & F, Co. v. Premo Pharmaceutical Laboratories, Inc., 625 F.2d 1055, 1067 (3rd Cir. 1980). A potential attendee at THE BIG EL SHOW or a potential buyer of a BIG EL SHOW record is entitled to know that the production has no connection with plaintiff or with the actual Elvis Presley performances. We conclude that the public interest favors our granting preliminary relief.

## IV. Conclusion

In accordance with the reasons set forth herein, a preliminary injunction will be entered as reflected in the attached order.

ORDER

This matter having been brought before the court on the 29th day of October, 1980; and

The court having considered the testimony, briefs, proposed findings of fact and conclusions of law, exhibits, affidavits, depositions and oral argument; and

For the reasons stated in the court's opinion filed this day,

It is on this 16th day of April, 1980 ORDERED that the defendant Rob Russen, d/b/a THE BIG EL SHOW, his agents, servants, employees and attorneys and all persons in active concert and participation with him or acting on his behalf are restrained and enjoined, pending final determination of this action, from the following:

1. Using the initials TCB (whether in capital letters or lower case letters) alone or in combination with a lightning bolt design, in connection with any advertising, promotional materials, or business material, including letterheads and business cards, or on any covers or labels of records, or on any merchandise, or to refer to any band or orchestra, or in any manner whatsoever to refer to a concert or musical event or entertainment service not conducted or sponsored or licensed by plaintiff or under its authority;

2. Using any pictures, sketches, artist's renderings (or any other such forms) of Elvis Presley or which appear to be of or resemble the "Elvis Pose" as

described or which are likely to lead persons into the mistaken belief that it is of Elvis Presley, in any advertising, promotional materials, or business materials or in any other notices or communications to identify an entertainment service or business, or on any record cover or label, or on any product, in any manner tending to deceive the purchasing public into the belief that the services or products provided by the defendant are sponsored or licensed by, or in any other way connected with the plaintiff;

3. Using any future advertisements or promotional materials, including but not limited to posters, newspaper advertisements, playbills, brochures, photograph albums, for the defendant's production of THE BIG EL SHOW which are not consistent with the general guidelines set forth in the opinion this date;

4. Using THE BIG EL SHOW logo or mark (Exhibit P 28), which is composed of the name THE BIG EL SHOW and the artist's sketch which closely resembles the "Elvis Pose," in connection with any advertising, promotional materials, or business material, including letterheads and business cards, or on any covers or labels of records, or on any merchandise, or to refer to any band or orchestra, or in any manner whatsoever to refer to a concert or musical event or entertainment service not conducted or sponsored or licensed by plaintiff or under its authority;

5. Further distribution or sale of any copies of records (33 RPMs, LPs, or 45 [1383] RPMs, singles), including those designated as Exhibits P 14, 15, 19, which album covers or labels display an actual picture or artist's sketch of Elvis Presley or a picture, artist's rendering, or sketch closely resembling and appearing to be of Elvis Presley; and shall neither transfer nor remove from the jurisdiction any such records;

6. Further distribution or sale of any pendants or merchandise displaying an actual picture or sketch of Elvis Presley or a picture, artist's rendering, or sketch closely resembling and appearing to be of Elvis Presley; and shall neither transfer nor remove from the jurisdiction any such pendants or merchandise;

7. Committing any other acts calculated or likely to lead persons to the mistaken belief that any event or service produced, provided, or presented by defendant emanates from plaintiff or is sponsored, approved, licensed, or supervised by plaintiff, or is in any other way connected with plaintiff; and

8. Infringing on any of plaintiff's service marks set forth in the opinion this date.

It is FURTHER ORDERED that the restraints herein contained shall become effective upon the plaintiff's giving security in the amount of Twenty-five Thousand Dollars ($ 25,000.00), in accordance with the provisions of Rule 65(c) of the Federal Rules of Civil Procedure, for the payment of such costs and damages as the defendant may incur or suffer if the defendant is found to have been improperly enjoined, such bond to be approved as to form and substance by the court; and

It is FURTHER ORDERED that the premium of said bond shall be an item of taxable cost.

Questions and Discussion

1. Richard Schulenberg explains ASCAP as follows: "ASCAP collects for public performances of its members' music by monitoring 'public performances for profit.' The revenue collected for licenses (radio and television broadcasters, theaters, concert halls, bars, hotels, etc.) is allocated to the works of members based upon the method of performance" (Schulenberg, Legal Aspects of the Music Industry 366). Is this method still feasible in our global E-universe?

2. BMI is a performance rights society and deals only with the licensing and administration of public performance for profit. It collects license fees from the users of the music and then allocates the revenue to its member publishers and composers" (Schulenberg at 368). Again, is this method still feasible in our global E-universe?

3. Neighboring rights are "[c]ertain rights which are not explicitly covered by American copyright law and consequently are not recognized in the United States either by law or by custom, do exist in other countries, either thorough conventions, national laws, or both" (Schulenberg at 369). Neighboring rights may include related rights in photographs, portraits, Kramer's coffee table book on coffee tables, etc. If that's the case, what is the best way to handle a world tour of your recently signed NGB ("New Girl Band")?

4. We have included various documents from ASCAP, BMI, and SESAC. Take a look. Can you see any situation where your artist might join all three organizations? Think about it.

# Chapter 9
# Promotion of Recording Artists

A part of the record contract, and other music industry contracts, is the requirement to promote the recording artist. The record company must use good faith and best efforts. But, what does that mean? The absolute dearth of *any* promotion could be viewed as a material breach and thus would make the contract voidable on the part of the artist. If there are no sales, then there is no money for anyone; there are, of course, a nearly endless list of mediums in which you can promote your artist. Try to be cost effective. Contemplate billboards, even those that are rented by the day. Use a variety of methods— don't put all your apples in one basket. Radio can be very effective, especially if your artist fits into a particular genre, which just happens to be the same genre du jour of that particular radio station. Think about websites, social media, I-Phones, etc. Maybe connect with a charity—it's good karma, and good business. Remember to stick to your budget.

In the following case, *Motown Record Corporation v. Brockert*, 160 Cal. App. 3d 123 (1984), famous singer Teena Marie, erstwhile duet partner with Rick James, is faced with Motown's motion for injunctive relief against breach of exclusivity provision of personal service contract. The California Court of Appeals reversed the trial court's order granting a preliminary injunction barring Tina Marie from performing her singing and songwriting talents for anyone else than Motown Record Corp.

Motown Record Corp. v. Brockert
Court of Appeal of California, Second Appellate District, Division Seven
September 17, 1984
Civ. No. 69060
160 Cal. App. 3d 123

This appeal arises from a contract dispute between Motown Record Corporation (Motown) and Jobete Music Company, Inc. (Jobete) and singer, songwriter Tina Marie Brockert, known professionally as Teena Marie. (See also Motown Record Corp. v. Superior Court (1984) 155 Cal.App.3d 482 [202 Cal.Rptr. 227].)

Teena Marie appeals from a preliminary injunction restraining her from performing her singing and songwriting talents for anyone other than Motown and Jobete until their contracts expire. At the heart of this appeal is an issue which has received considerable attention in law reviews but has never been addressed by the appellate courts. The issue is whether a clause in a personal services contract giving the employer the option to pay the employee a minimum of $ 6,000 a year satisfies the statutory minimum compensation requirement for an injunction restraining breach of the contract. (See, e.g., Note, Statutory Minimum Compensation and the Granting of Injunctive Relief to Enforce Personal Services Contracts in the Entertainment Industries: The Need for Legislative Reform (1979) 52 So.Cal.L.Rev. 489, (hereafter Statutory Minimum Compensation); Tannenbaum, Enforcement of Personal Service Contracts in the Entertainment Industry (1954) 42 Cal.L.Rev. 18 (hereafter Tannenbaum); Light, The California Injunction Statute and the Music Industry: What Price Injunctive Relief? (1982) 7 Colum. J. Art & L. 141, (hereafter Light); Schlesinger, Six Thousand Dollars Per Year (Dec. 1968) Bev. Hills Bar J. 25 (hereafter Schlesinger).)

We have concluded this option clause does not satisfy the statutory requirement of minimum compensation.

Facts and Proceedings Below

In 1976, Teena Marie entered into contracts as a recording artist and songwriter with Motown and Jobete respectively. At the time she signed these contracts she was an unknown in the music business. Her experience consisted of singing with local bands at weddings, parties, and shopping centers and roles in school musicals. She had written some songs but none had been recorded or released commercially.

The Motown and Jobete contracts were admitted into evidence at the hearing on the preliminary injunction. Each contract was for an initial period of one year and granted the companies six options to renew the agreements for one-year periods on the same terms applicable to the initial period. Teena Marie and the companies were in the sixth and last option period when their dispute arose. Each contract contained an exclusivity clause providing that during the term of the contract, including any renewals, Teena Marie may not perform like services for another employer. The contracts further provided each company with the option, exercisable at any time, to pay Teena Marie "compensation at the rate of not less than $ 6,000 per annum."

Between 1979 and 1980 Teena Marie recorded four albums for Motown. All were successful. Indeed her fourth and last album, "It Must Be Magic," achieved gold record status, selling more than 400,000 copies. During this time she also wrote songs for Jobete.

In May 1982, Teena Marie informed Motown and Jobete she would no longer perform under the contracts and gave a written notice of recision. In August 1982, Motown and Jobete sued Teena Marie for breach of contract and injunctive and declaratory relief, among other things. The following month, more than six years after she began performing under the contracts, Motown and Jobete exercised their options to pay Teena Marie at the rate of $ 6,000 per year. In November 1982, Teena Marie informed Motown and Jobete she had signed a recording contract with another company and intended to commence performing for that company later in the month.

Upon learning of her intention to perform for another company, Motown and Jobete sought a preliminary injunction under the exclusivity clauses of their contracts to prevent Teena Marie from performing services for another employer until her contracts with them expired in 1983.

The trial court granted a preliminary injunction in essence restraining Teena Marie from performing as a singer or songwriter for anyone other than Motown and Jobete until April 9, 1983, the purported expiration date of her contracts. This appeal followed.

Discussion

Before turning to the major issue in this case, we address the preliminary questions whether this appeal is moot and whether, to be enforceable by injunction, the contract must guarantee the performer a minimum of $ 6,000 per year. We then explain why we believe the option clause does not satisfy the minimum compensation requirement of Civil Code section 3423.

## I. The Appeal is Not Moot.

All the operative clauses of the injunction are modified by the words "until and including April 9, 1983." This suggests Teena Marie may do any of the enjoined acts after April 9, subject to Motown's and Jobete's remedies at law. However, the companies have not conceded this point although they have had the opportunity to do so in the trial court and in this court. While urging this appeal is moot, the companies' brief carefully skirts the issue of whether Teena Marie is still prohibited under the preliminary injunction from recording or otherwise using songs produced or conceived on or before April 9, 1983.

A further controversy remains with respect to the order granting the preliminary injunction. Pursuant to the injunction and Code of Civil Procedure section 529, the companies were required to file an undertaking in the sum of $ 50,000 "for the purpose of indemnifying [Teena Marie] for such damage as [she] may sustain by reason of" the preliminary injunction. If it should be determined on this appeal that the companies were not entitled to the injunction, Teena Marie may be entitled to recover upon this undertaking. ( Rees v. Gardner (1960) 185 Cal.App.2d 630, 633 [8 Cal.Rptr. 505].)

An additional reason for proceeding to the merits of this appeal lies in the fact it involves an issue of continuing public interest which is likely to recur yet evade appellate scrutiny. (See Liberty Mut. Ins. Co. v. Fales (1973) 8 Cal.3d 712, 715 [106 Cal.Rptr. 21, 505 P.2d 213], and cf. Lemat Corp. v. Barry (1969) 275 Cal.App.2d 671, 673, fn. 2 [80 Cal.Rptr. 240].)

As we noted above, the major question in this appeal, whether the $ 6,000 option clause satisfies the statutory requirement of minimum compensation, has never been addressed by an appellate court in the 65-year history of Civil Code section 3423, subdivision Fifth. Nevertheless it is a question the resolution of which will affect a large segment of California business; not only the entertainment and sports industries but virtually any enterprise where the employee's service is of "a special, unique, unusual, extraordinary or intellectual character." (Ibid.) The resolution of this question will have ramifications on the cost of services and competition in those businesses which will ultimately impact California consumers. Furthermore, as one commentator has noted, use of the $ 6,000 option clause has worked in favor of the employer in negotiating contract disputes with employees. (Statutory Minimum Compensation, supra, at pp. 491-492.) If this advantage is not justified under the statute, we should act to clarify the meaning of the statute.

Because personal services contracts are typically of short duration, especially in the entertainment field (Statutory Minimum Compensation, supra, at pp. 499-500, Light, supra, at p. 170, fn. 40), it is likely appellate review of injunctions prohibiting breach of the exclusivity clause may continue to be thwarted by the expiration of the contract term.

Under all the circumstances, we conclude this appeal is not moot.

## II. History of the Minimum Compensation Requirement in the California Legislature and Courts.

A brief history of the minimum compensation requirement of section 3423, subdivision Fifth, is an important aid to understanding the issues underlying the option clause.

It has long been a principle of equity that a contract to perform personal services cannot be specifically enforced. (Poultry Producers etc. v. Barlow (1922) 189 Cal. 278, 288 [208 P. 93]; Note, Equity — Negative Covenants in Contracts for Personal Service (1937) 10 So.Cal.L.Rev. 347-348.) In the mid-19th Century an exception to this rule was born in England that where the employee both covenants to perform for the employer and not to perform elsewhere, equity will enjoin a breach of the negative covenant not to perform elsewhere although it cannot specifically enforce the affirmative covenant to perform for the employer. (Lumley v. Wagner (1852) 42 Eng. Rep. 687.) The infant doctrine was not warmly embraced even in the country of its birth. (Whitwood Chem. Co. v. Hardman (1891) 2 Ch. 416; 5A Corbin on contracts (1964) § 1208, p. 415.) And, while it has gradually gained acceptance in the United States, it has been questioned by some eminent legal scholars. (See, e.g., comments of Justice Holmes quoted in Note, Lumley v. Wagner Denied (1894) 8 Harv. L.Rev. 172 and 11 Williston on Contracts (3d ed. 1968) § 1447, pp. 1018-1019.)

When the California Civil Code was adopted in 1872 it did not include a Lumley exception to the rule prohibiting specific performance of personal services contracts. Section 3423, as originally enacted, provided, "An injunction cannot be granted: . . . 5. To prevent the breach of a contract, the performance of which would not be specifically enforced." ( Farnum v. Clarke (1906) 148 Cal. 610, 615 [84 P. 166].) After discussing the Lumley line of cases and another line of cases holding to the contrary, the court in Anderson v. Neal Institutes Co. (1918) 37 Cal.App. 174, 178 [173 P. 779] observed: "Subdivision 5 of section 3423 is free from ambiguity or uncertainty. It clearly declares as the law in this state the rule laid down in one of two opposing lines of authority . . . that the court will not interfere by injunction to prevent the violation of an agreement of which, from the nature of the subject, there could be no decree of specific performance."

A year after Anderson v. Neal Institutes Co. was decided, the California Legislature amended section 3423 to allow a limited version of Lumley. (Stats. 1919, ch. 226, § 1, p. 328.) As originally introduced, the legislation would have prohibited an injunction "[to] prevent the breach of a contract, other than a contract in writing for the rendition or furnishing of personal services from one to another, the performance of which would not be specifically enforced." The original bill was amended to add the stipulation "where the minimum compensation for such service is at the rate of not less than six thousand dollars per annum." (Italics added.) It was amended again to require that the promised service be of a unique character the loss of which cannot be adequately compensated in damages. (J. of the Sen., Forty-Third Sess. (1919) pp. 534, 1255, 1349.)

In the 65 years since the current version of section 3423, subdivision Fifth, was adopted only two cases have interpreted the $ 6,000 minimum compensation requirement: Foxx v. Williams (1966) 244 Cal.App.2d 223 [52 Cal.Rptr. 896] and MCA Records Inc. v. Newton-John (1979) 90 Cal.App.3d 18 [153 Cal.Rptr. 153].

Comedian Redd Foxx brought an action for an accounting, declaratory and other relief against the recording company which was distributing his albums. The company cross-complained for injunctive relief to prevent Foxx from breaching the exclusivity clause of his contract. The trial court granted the injunction restraining Foxx "'from making sound recordings for any other person . . . so long as royalties earned by [Foxx] under the contract . . . equal or exceed the sum of $ 3000 [for each six-month royalty period].'" (Id., at p. 230.) On appeal the appellate court found the royalty payments were entirely contingent upon sales of Foxx' albums and, therefore, did not guarantee Foxx would receive any money while the injunction was in effect. (Id., at p. 236.)

"[This] royalty contract does not meet the requirements of the injunction statute even though it should ultimately appear that the royalties earned, over any given period, should exceed the rate of $ 6,000 per year . . . . [para. ] The Legislature has concluded that an artist who is not entitled to receive a minimum of $ 6,000 per year by performing his contract should not be subjected to this kind of economic coercion." (Ibid.)

Thirteen years later the minimum compensation requirement was again an issue in a suit for injunctive relief. (MCA Records Inc. v. Newton-John, supra, 90 Cal.App.3d 18.) Unlike Foxx, who at the time of his suit was a struggling nightclub comic, Olivia Newton-John was an international star when her case came before the court. The agreement at issue provided for her to record and deliver to MCA two albums a year for two years and, at MCA's option, additional albums in three periods of one year each. In return, MCA agreed to pay royalties and a nonreturnable advance of $ 250,000 for each album recorded in the initial two-year period and $ 100,000 for each album recorded in the option years. Newton-John was required to pay her recording costs out of her advances. (90 Cal.App.3d at p. 21.) In opposing injunctive relief to enforce the exclusivity clause of this contract, Newton-John argued requiring her to bear the costs of production reduced the $ 100,000 payments in the option years below the $ 6,000 minimum required for an injunction. The appellate court interpreted section 3423, subdivision Fifth, as providing that "A party to a personal service contract may not be enjoined from rendering personal services to others unless, under the terms of the contract, she is guaranteed minimum annual compensation of $ 6,000." (d., at p. 22.) The court upheld the injunction on the basis of the trial court's finding of fact that after deducting recording costs Newton-John would still net at least $ 6,000 a year and she controlled whether that sum was received. All Newton-John had to do was make the promised record each year and keep her production costs below $ 94,000. The record company had to pay her the non-refundable $ 100,000 advance no matter whether the record succeeded in the marketplace. (Ibid.) Foxx was distinguished on the ground the comedian's contract "did not guarantee him annual compensation of $ 6,000." (Ibid.)

In response to Foxx and MCA many California record companies adopted the practice of including a clause in their contracts giving the company the right at any time during the contract to agree to pay the artist a minimum compensation of $ 6,000 a year. (Schlesinger, supra, at p. 29; Statutory Minimum Compensation, supra, at p. 508.) The clause in Teena Marie's contract is typical of such provisions. (See, Schlesinger, supra., at p. 29.) In this manner the company hedges its bets on the success of its artists. If the artist is not selling, the company does not exercise its option. If the artist catches on with the public and begins to make a substantial sum of money for the company, the company plays its "option" card to keep the artist from jumping to another label.

As the case at bar indicates, the company may wait until the last possible moment to exercise its option. Motown and Jobete filed suit against Teena Marie in August 1982 but waited until September 1982 to exercise the option clauses. The request for a preliminary injunction was filed two months later. Thus, the companies purchased an insurance policy worth a considerable sum for a minimal premium just prior to the time they could be fairly certain a loss would occur. If the option clause meets the statutory requirement of minimum compensation, the company can buy its insurance policy on the courthouse steps on its way to seek an injunction. Indeed, Schlesinger suggests the company may be able to buy its insurance policy after the "accident" has occurred; that is, after the artist has already signed and recorded with another company. (Schlesinger, supra, at p. 30.)

### III. A Party to a Personal Services Contract May Not Be Enjoined From Rendering Personal Services to Others Unless, Under the Terms of the Contract, the Performer is Guaranteed Minimum Annual Compensation of $ 6,000.

Foxx v. Williams, supra, 244 Cal.App.3d 223, and MCA Records Inc. v. Newton-John, supra, 90 Cal.App.3d 18, appear unambiguous on this point. Nevertheless, the erroneous interpretations of Civil Code section 3423 by the trial court and the companies indicate the point bears repeating.

The record in the proceedings below indicates the trial judge erroneously believed for purposes of injunctive relief it did not matter what compensation was provided by the contract as long as the performer actually received at least $ 6,000 per year. The court, in Foxx, addressed this precise issue and held that unless the contract itself provides for compensation of at least $ 6,000 a year the "contract does not meet the requirements of the injunction statute even though it should ultimately appear that the royalties earned, over any given period, should exceed the rate of $ 6,000 per year." (244 Cal.App.2d at p. 236; and see MCA, supra, 90 Cal.App.3d at p. 22.)

The companies argue by exercising their option to pay Teena Marie $ 6,000 a year a new contract came into existence which did guarantee her the statutory sum and it was this new contract guaranteeing $ 6,000 a year — not the old contract giving them an option to pay $ 6,000 a year — that they were seeking to enforce by injunction. In support of this argument the companies cite cases describing an option contract as a kind of contract within a contract: the initial contract — an irrevocable and continuing offer to perform an act — and the final contract — the underlying promises to which the option relates. (See, e.g. Dawson v. Goff (1954) 43 Cal.2d 310, 316-317 [273 P.2d 1], Caras v. Parker (1957) 149 Cal.App.2d 621, 627 [309 P.2d 104].) We reject this interpretation of the contracts in this case.

The contracts between the companies and Teena Marie are not option contracts with respect to the exclusivity clause. In the contracts, Teena Marie does not give the companies the option to enjoy her services exclusively on condition they pay her $ 6,000 a year. Rather, the promise to perform exclusively for the companies is one of the terms to which Teena Marie agrees from the outset of the contracts. In addition, the authorities cited, Dawson and Caras, do not hold when an option is exercised a new contract is created. Indeed, the case relied on in both opinions, Warner Bros. Pictures Inc. v. Brodel (1948) 31 Cal.2d 766, 772 [192 P.2d 949, 3 A.L.R.2d 691], indicates just the opposite. The issue in Warner Bros. was whether a contract to perform services was made at the time an option contract for those services was given. The court held the contract to perform the services was made when the option contract was made. (Id., at pp. 771-773.)

Alternatively, the companies argue the letters they sent Teena Marie advising her they had elected to "revise" her contract and guarantee her no less than $ 6,000 per year constituted new contracts modifying the former ones. (See Civ. Code, § 1698, subd. (a).) The California Supreme Court has interpreted the language of section 1698 literally, holding that an executory written modification must meet the requirements of a valid contract. (See, Timbie, Modification of Written Contracts in California (1972) 23 Hast. L.J. 1549, 1553.) Specifically, the court has held the modification must be supported by new consideration. (Main St. etc. v. L. A. Trac. Co. (1900) 129 Cal. 301, 305 [61 P.

937].) Accordingly, an executory agreement to pay more for the same performance is unenforceable. (Fairlane Estates v. Carrico Constr. Co. (1964) 228 Cal.App.2d 65, 71 [39 Cal.Rptr. 35].) In this case, Teena Marie was required by the original contracts to perform exclusively for the companies. Consequently there was no consideration for the purported modification of the contracts. Were we to interpret defendants' letters as attempts to create new contracts, the new contracts would be unenforceable by Teena Marie and, thus, would not guarantee her compensation at the rate of $ 6,000 a year.

Even if exercising the option clauses created "new" contracts, we question whether the provisions of the contracts regarding compensation meet the requirement of section 3423. In order to obtain an injunction to prevent the breach of a personal services contract the compensation for services under that contract must be at the rate of not less than six thousand dollars. The fact the performer was being paid at least $ 6,000 under some other contract with the same employer would not satisfy the statute. For example, if the performer had two personal services contracts with the same employer, one to record songs and the other to write songs, the fact the performer was guaranteed $ 6,000 a year under the recording contract would not support injunctive relief to prevent breach of the songwriting contract. Nor would a $ 6,000 guarantee under the songwriting contract support injunctive relief to enforce the record making contract.

The contracts in the case at bench appear to attempt such a set off of compensation. The recording contract with Motown provides, "Any amounts paid under [the $ 6,000 compensation clause] may be credited against monies thereafter payable to you pursuant to this or any other agreement between [Motown] and you, or between [Motown's] associated, affiliated, or subsidiary corporations and you." The songwriting contract with Jobete contains virtually identical language. There is no dispute Motown and Jobete are associated or affiliated corporations. If Teena Marie received $ 6,000 in 1982 from Jobete for songwriting, she would be guaranteed nothing from Motown for recording. Moreover, there is evidence suggesting Teena Marie performed other services for Motown and possibly Jobete as a producer, technician and the like. Presumably she received compensation for these efforts unrelated to her singing, songwriting and recording work. If she was already receiving $ 6,000 a year as a sound technician, for example, then she would be guaranteed nothing under the contracts before us.

Accordingly, these cagily drafted option clauses might not guarantee a cent in additional compensation for Teena Marie's songwriting and recording services or, at best, she would be guaranteed a single $ 6,000 a year payment for her services under both contracts.

Still, because we hold a contract giving the employer the discretion to pay the performer $ 6,000 a year if and when it chooses does not meet the requirements of section 3423, we need not decide whether the provisions for setting off compensation in the contracts before us would, independently, require refusal of injunctive relief.

Thus, we turn to the question left unanswered by Foxx and MCA: does an option guarantee $ 6,000 a year at some time in the future satisfy the statutory requirement of "a contract in writing . . . where the minimum compensation . . . is at a rate of not less than six thousand dollars per annum . . . ."

One of Teena Marie's songs is entitled "Don't Turn Your Back On Me." Here, it could be said, we answer her plea.

### IV. A Clause in a Personal Services Contract Giving the Employer the Option to Pay the Employee at Least $ 6,000 a Year Does Not Satisfy the Minimum Compensation Requirement for Injunctive Relief.

(A) From the statutory language it appears the Legislature was referring to contracts which guarantee the performer a minimum of $ 6,000 per year from the outset.

The availability of injunctive relief from breach of contract is limited by section 3423, subdivision Fifth, to "a contract in writing for the rendition . . . of personal services . . . where the minimum compensation for such service is at the rate of not less than six thousand dollars per annum." (Italics added.) The most reasonable, common sense reading of this language is that "minimum compensation for such service" refers back to the "contract in writing for . . . personal services." To be subject to specific enforcement, the contract must have as one of its terms a compensation provision providing for payment at the minimum rate of $ 6,000 per year. In other words, agreeing to payment of the minimum compensation is not a condition precedent to the granting of injunctive relief; it is a threshold requirement for admission of the contract into the class of contracts subject to injunctive relief under the statute.

This reading of the statute is implicit in the Foxx and MCA decisions. In Foxx the court found the contract did not meet the minimum compensation requirement of section 3423 even though the potential for earning $ 6,000 a year or more existed under the contract. (244 Cal.App.2d at pp. 231, 236.) Similarly, under the option clause, the artist has merely the potential of earning $ 6,000 a year; there is no guarantee this compensation will ever be paid. Distinguishing Foxx, the court in MCA observed, "Unlike [Olivia Newton-John], who is guaranteed minimum annual compensation of $ 200,000 in the form of nonreturnable advances in addition to any royalties she may receive, Foxx' sole compensation was in the form of royalties contingent upon prospective sales which could amount to nothing." (90 Cal.App.3d at pp. 22-23.) We believe the option clause is analogous to the contingent payment rejected in Foxx. It is nothing more than a new arrangement of an old song.

(B) The option clause would defeat the legislative intent to limit injunctive relief to contracts where not only the services are special or unique but the performer herself is a person of distinction in her field at the time of entering the contract.

The language of section 3423 and the Fifth subdivision in particular is clearly language of limitation. (Poultry Producers etc. v. Barlow, supra, 189 Cal. at p. 288; Lemat Corp v. Barry, supra, 275 Cal.App.2d 671, 678.) It will be remembered subdivision 5 as originally drafted would have excepted from the prohibition against injunctive relief any personal services contract. (See Discussion, ante, at p. 130.) The bill was amended to add the stipulation the contract must provide for minimum compensation at the rate of $ 6,000 per year.

While the legislative history does not explicitly state the intent of the minimum compensation amendment it is reasonable to believe Senator Lyon, who introduced the bill, and Senator Chamberlin who proposed the minimum compensation amendment, both members of the Judiciary Committee, were familiar with Lumley v. Wagner, Anderson v. Neal Institutes Co. as well as other leading cases on the subject and that the amendment was intended to incorporate the policies reflected in those decisions.

We begin our review with Lumley itself, Johanna Wagner was not an unknown member of a chorus line at the time her case arose. She was one of Europe's best known opera singers, niece of Richard Wagner and "cantatrice of the Court of His Majesty the King of Prussia." (Light, supra, at p. 144; 23 Encyclopedia Britannica (1942) at p. 278; Lumley v. Wagner, supra, 42 Eng. Rep. at p. 687.) Her contract with Lumley called for her to perform at Her Majesty's Theatre in London twice a week for three months at the rate of 100 pounds per week; (id., at p. 688) a significant sum considering the wage of a unionized bricklayer in London at the same time was less than two pounds per week. (23 Encyclopedia Britannica, supra, at p. 270.)

It was not uncommon for courts of that time to distinguish Lumley v. Wagner on the ground that there the services of an exceptional artist and a considerable sum were involved. Among the best known of these cases are Whitwood Chem. Co. v. Hardman, supra, 2 Ch. 416, Arthur v. Oakes (7th Cir. 1894) 63 F. 310 and Dockstader v. Reed (1907) 121 App.Div. 846 [106 N.Y.S. 795]. Thus, at the time section 3423 was amended there was a discernible trend toward enforcing negative covenants against the "prima donnas" but not the "spear carriers." (See Carter v. Ferguson (1890) 58 Hun. 569 [12 N.Y.S. 580, 581]; and see generally, 11 Williston on Contracts, supra, § 1450, pp. 1042-1043; 5A Corbin on Contracts, supra, § 1209, p. 417; 4 Pomeroy, Equity Jurisprudence (5th ed. 1941) § 1343, p. 943.)

Aside from the Lumley line of cases there is an even older judicial tradition which helps to explain why the California Legislature sought to limit injunctive relief to performers of star quality. A fundamental reason why courts will not order specific performance of personal services contracts is because such an order would impose on the courts a difficult job of enforcement and of passing judgment upon the quality of performance. (See 11 Williston on Contracts, supra, § 1423, pp. 782-783; 5A Corbin on Contracts, supra, § 1204, p. 400; Poultry Producers etc. v. Barlow, supra, 189 Cal. 278, 288-289; Light, supra, at p. 143.) As Corbin observes in his treatise, "An artist does not work well under compulsion, and the court might find it difficult to pass judgment upon the performance rendered." (5A Corbin, supra, § 1204, p. 400.)

As the court in Lumley candidly admitted, it had no power to compel Madame Wagner to sing at Lumley's theatre but the injunction prohibiting her from performing elsewhere might well accomplish the same result. (42 Eng. Rep. at p. 693.) Thus there is a danger an artist prohibited from performing elsewhere may feel compelled to perform under the contract and, under the stress of the situation, turn in an unsatisfactory performance. This would lead to further litigation between the parties on the adequacy of the artist's performance; the very thing the courts traditionally sought to avoid. (See, e.g., Bethlehem Engineering Export Co. v. Christie (2d Cir. 1939) 105 F.2d 933, 935 [125 A.L.R. 1441] (Hand, J.).) There is less likelihood of this conundrum arising if the performer is of great renown. Such a performer may well choose not to perform rather than risk her reputation by delivering a sub-par performance. (See Clark, supra, at pp. 690, fn. 11.)

In 1919 the sum of $ 6,000 a year was more than five times the average national wage of $ 1,142. (Historical Statistics of the United States (1976) at p. 164, Table: Average Annual Earnings of Employees: 1900 to 1970.) This is equivalent to setting the minimum compensation figure at $ 100,000 today. (Based on the 1982 median income level of $ 20,171. See Statistical Abstract of the United States (1984) at p. 459, Table 754.) By selecting such a large sum, the Legislature indicated an intent injunctive relief not be available against a performer, however capable, who had not yet achieved distinction. The fact the bill was further amended to provide the services must be special is a further indication the Legislature intended the statute to apply only to persons who had attained "star quality" no matter how special their services might be.

Without doubt the passage of time has diluted the effect of this legislative intent but the option clauses before us would totally wash it away. It would allow a record company to bind the entire student body of "Rydell High" to personal services contracts (and pay them nothing) on the off-chance one of them turns out to be Olivia Newton-John.

It is no answer to say that by the time Motown and Jobete sought injunctive relief to enforce the exclusivity clauses Teena Marie had become a star. Motown and Jobete did not contract with a star. By their own admission they contracted with a "virtual unknown." Nothing in section 3423 prevents the companies from seeking damages from Teena Marie for breach of the exclusivity clause. That section merely says for reasons of public policy the exclusivity clause of a contract can only be enforced by injunction when the contract is with a performer of requisite distinction as measured by the compensation the employer is willing to pay. Moreover, as we explain below, allowing the companies, once they judge the artist to have achieved star quality, to enforce the exclusivity clause by injunction would violate the concept of fundamental fairness which is also embodied in section 3423.

The option clause violates the concept of fundamental fairness embodied in Civil Code section 3423.

We agree with the court in Foxx, supra that the $ 6,000 minimum compensation requirement was intended to balance the equities between employer and performer. (244 Cal.App.2d at p. 236.) This is quite clear when section 3423 is read in connection with Civil Code section 3391, subdivision 2, which provides specific performance cannot be enforced against a party as to whom the contract is not "just and reasonable." Taken together those sections demand a minimum standard of fairness as a condition on equitable enforcement of an exclusivity clause in a personal services contract. (See Light, supra, at p. 153.)

"As one grows more experienced and skillful there should be a reasonable opportunity to move upward and to employ his abilities to the best advantage and for the highest obtainable compensation." (De Haviland v. Warner Bros. Pictures (1944) 67 Cal.App.2d 225 [153 P.2d 983], 235.) "[Any] agreement that limits a person's ability to follow his vocation must be strictly construed . . . ." ( Lemat Corp. v. Barry, supra, 275 Cal.App.2d at pp. 678-679.) Therefore, "[an] injunction which forbids an artist to accept new employment may be a harsh and powerful remedy. The monetary limitation in the statute is intended to serve as a counterweight in balancing the equities. The Legislature has concluded that an artist who is not entitled to receive a minimum of $ 6,000 per year by performing his contract should not be subjected to this kind of economic coercion." (Foxx, supra, 244 Cal.App.2d at p. 236.)

If we were to hold the option clause satisfies section 3423, we would nullify the $ 6,000 compensation requirement as a counterweight on the employer. Whereas the $ 6,000 compensation requirement was intended to balance the equities, the $ 6,000 option clause is intended to allow record companies to avoid payment of minimum compensation while retaining the power of economic coercion over the artist. (Statutory Minimum Compensation, supra, at p. 508; Light, supra, at p. 165; Schlesinger, supra, at p. 29.) This is accomplished in two ways. First, the option clause gives the company the coercive power of a credible threat of injunctive relief without it having to guarantee or pay the artist anything. The threat of a prohibitory injunction may be just as effective as the injunction itself in discouraging the artist from seeking more lucrative employment. (Statutory Minimum Compensation, supra at p. 519.) Second, in practice, the company will exercise its option to pay minimum compensation only when it is certain the artist intends to breach the exclusivity clause by performing for another and, even then, only when exercising the option is necessary to enable the company to assert in court the contract does indeed provide for the statutory minimum compensation. (Light, supra, at p. 165.) Of course, by then, the company's agreement to pay the artist a minimum of $ 6,000 a year is meaningless. If the artist was not already earning far in excess of that amount from royalties, the artist's worth to the company would not justify the expense of litigating the case. The record company is in fact merely "electing" to pay that which it would have to pay anyway as a result of royalties from sales. (Schlesinger, supra, at p. 29.)

Based on the foregoing we conclude the option clauses in the Motown and Jobete contracts do not support equitable relief in the form of an injunction restraining Teena Marie from performing for other employers.

The order granting a preliminary injunction is reversed.

———————

In *Brockert*, the court revisits *Lumley v. Wagner*, 42 E.R. 687 (1852), but stays away from their results, probably because there is a difference between the "prima donnas" (Johanna Wagner) and the "spear carriers" (Teena Marie— no offense, she has a beautiful voice) (*Brockert* at 160 Cal. App. 3d 123,127 (footnotes omitted)).

In the following case, *Kenford Co. v. County of Erie*, 67 N.Y.2d 257 (NY 1986), the court looks at an action for breach of contract where the court disallows as damages the loss of prospective profits for plaintiff's contemplated 20-year operation of a domed stadium that was to be constructed by defendant Erie County.

Kenford Co. v. County of Erie
Court of Appeals of New York
March 18, 1986, Argued; May 6, 1986, Decided
No Number in Original
67 N.Y.2d 257

OPINION OF THE COURT

The issue in this appeal is whether a plaintiff, in an action for breach of contract, may recover loss of prospective profits for its contemplated 20-year operation of a domed stadium which was to be constructed by defendant County of Erie (County).

On August 8, 1969, pursuant to a duly adopted resolution of its legislature, the County of Erie entered into a contract with Kenford Company, Inc. (Kenford) and Dome Stadium, Inc. (DSI) for the construction and operation of a domed stadium facility near the City of Buffalo. The contract provided that construction of the facility by the County would commence within 12 months of the contract date and that a mutually acceptable 40-year lease between the County and DSI for the operation of said facility would be negotiated by the parties and agreed upon within three months of the receipt by the County of preliminary plans, drawings and cost estimates. It was further provided that in the event a mutually acceptable lease could not be agreed upon within the three-month period, a separate management contract between the County and DSI, as appended to the basic agreement, would be executed by the parties, providing for the operation of the stadium facility by DSI for a period of 20 years from the completion of the stadium and its availability for use.

Although strenuous and extensive negotiations followed, the parties never agreed upon the terms of a lease, nor did construction of a domed facility begin within the one-year period or at any time thereafter. A breach of the contract thus occurred and this action was commenced in June 1971 by Kenford and DSI.

Prolonged and extensive pretrial and preliminary proceedings transpired throughout the next 10 years, culminating with the entry of an order which affirmed the grant of summary judgment against the County on the issue of liability and directed a trial limited to the issue of damages ( Kenford Co. v County of Erie, 88 AD2d 758, lv dismissed 58 NY2d 689). The ensuing trial ended some nine months later with a multimillion dollar jury verdict in plaintiffs' favor. An appeal to the Appellate Division resulted in a modification of the judgment. That court reversed portions of the judgment awarding damages for loss of profits and for certain out-of-pocket expenses incurred, and directed a new trial upon other issues ( Kenford Co. v County of Erie, 108 AD2d 132). On appeal to this court, we are concerned only with that portion [261] of the verdict which awarded DSI money damages for loss of prospective profits during the 20-year period of the proposed management contract, as appended to the basic contract. That portion of the verdict was set aside by the Appellate Division and the cause of action dismissed. The court concluded that the use of expert opinion to present statistical projections of future business operations involved the use of too many variables to provide a rational basis upon which lost profits could be calculated and, therefore, such projections were insufficient as a matter of law to support an award of lost profits. We agree with this ultimate conclusion, but upon different grounds.

Loss of future profits as damages for breach of contract have been permitted in New York under long-established and precise rules of law. First, it must be demonstrated with certainty that such damages have been caused by the breach and, second, the alleged loss must be capable of proof with reasonable certainty. In other words, the damages may not be merely speculative, possible or imaginary, but must be reasonably certain and directly traceable to the breach, not remote or the result of other intervening causes ( Wakeman v Wheeler & Wilson Mfg. Co., 101 NY 205). In addition, there must be a showing that the particular damages were fairly within the contemplation of the parties to the contract at the time it was made (Witherbee v Meyer, 155 NY 446). If it is a new business seeking to recover for loss of future profits, a stricter standard is imposed for the obvious reason that there does not exist a reasonable basis of experience upon which to estimate lost profits with the requisite degree of reasonable certainty (Cramer v Grand Rapids Show Case Co., 223 NY 63; 25 CJS, Damages, § 42 [b]).

These rules must be applied to the proof presented by DSI in this case. We note the procedure for computing damages selected by DSI was in accord with contemporary economic theory and was presented through the testimony of recognized experts. Such a procedure has been accepted in this State and many other jurisdictions (see, De Long v County of Erie, 60 NY2d 296). DSI's economic analysis employed historical data, obtained from the operation of other domed stadiums and related facilities throughout the country, which was then applied to the results of a comprehensive study of the marketing prospects for the proposed facility in the Buffalo area. The quantity of proof is massive and, unquestionably, represents business and industry's most advanced and sophisticated method for predicting the probable results of contemplated projects. Indeed, it is difficult to conclude what additional relevant proof could have been submitted by DSI in support of its attempt to establish, with reasonable certainty, loss of prospective profits. Nevertheless, DSI's proof is insufficient to meet the required standard.

The reason for this conclusion is twofold. Initially, the proof does not satisfy the requirement that liability for loss of profits over a 20-year period was in the contemplation of the parties at the time of the execution of the basic contract or at the time of its breach (see, Chapman v Fargo, 223 NY 32; 36 NY Jur 2d, Damages, §§ 39, 40, at 66-70). Indeed, the provisions in the contract providing remedy for a default do not suggest or provide for such a heavy responsibility on the part of the County. In the absence of any provision for such an eventuality, the commonsense rule to apply is to consider what the parties would have concluded had they considered the subject. The evidence here fails to demonstrate that liability for loss of profits over the length of the contract would have been in the contemplation of the parties at the relevant times.

Next, we note that despite the massive quantity of expert proof submitted by DSI, the ultimate conclusions are still projections, and as employed in the present day commercial world, subject to adjustment and modification. We of course recognize that any projection cannot be absolute, nor is there any such requirement, but it is axiomatic that the degree of certainty is dependent upon known or unknown factors which form the basis of the ultimate conclusion. Here, the foundations upon which the economic model was created undermine the certainty of the projections. DSI assumed that the facility was completed, available for use and successfully operated by it for 20 years, providing professional sporting events and other forms of entertainment, as well as hosting meetings, conventions and related commercial gatherings. At the time of the breach, there was only one other facility in this country to use as a basis of comparison, the Astrodome in Houston. Quite simply, the multitude of assumptions required to establish projections of profitability over the life of this contract require speculation and conjecture, making it beyond the capability of even the most sophisticated procedures to satisfy the legal requirements of proof with reasonable certainty.

The economic facts of life, the whim of the general public and the fickle nature of popular support for professional athletic endeavors must be given great weight in attempting to ascertain damages 20 years in the future. New York has long recognized the inherent uncertainties of predicting profits in the entertainment field in general (see, Broadway Photoplay Co. v World Film Corp., 225 NY 104) and, in this case, we are dealing, in large part, with a new facility furnishing entertainment for the public. It is our view that the record in this case demonstrates the efficacy of the principles set forth by this court in Cramer v Grand Rapids Show Case Co. (223 NY 63, supra), principles to which we continue to adhere. In so doing, we specifically reject the "rational basis" test enunciated in Perma Research & Dev. Co. v Singer Co. (542 F2d 111, cert denied 429 U.S. 987) and adopted by the Appellate Division.

Accordingly, that portion of the order of the Appellate Division being appealed from should be affirmed.

Contemporary Mission, Inc. v. Famous Music Corp.
United States Court of Appeals for the Second Circuit
November 22, 1976, Argued; May 18, 1977, Decided
Docket No. 76-7403, No. 575 - September Term, 1976
557 F.2d 918

MESKILL, Circuit Judge:

This is an appeal by Famous Music Corporation ("Famous") from a verdict rendered against it in favor of Contemporary Mission, Inc. ("Contemporary"), in the United States District Court for the Southern District of New York, after a jury trial before Judge Richard Owen. Contemporary cross-appeals from a ruling which excluded testimony concerning its prospective damages. The dispute between the parties relates to Famous' alleged breach of two contracts.

## I. The Facts.

Contemporary is a nonprofit charitable corporation organized under the laws of the State of Missouri with its principal place of business in Connecticut. It is composed of a small group of Roman Catholic priests who write, produce and publish musical compositions and recordings. In 1972 the group owned all of the rights to a rock opera entitled VIRGIN, which was composed by Father John T. O'Reilly, a vice-president and member of the group. Contemporary first became involved with Famous in 1972 as a result of O'Reilly's efforts to market VIRGIN.

Famous is a Delaware corporation with its headquarters in the Gulf + Western Building in New York City. It is a wholly-owned subsidiary of the Gulf + Western Corporation, and, until July 31, 1974, it was engaged in the business of producing musical recordings for distribution throughout the United States. Famous' president, Tony Martell, is generally regarded in the recording industry as the individual primarily responsible for the successful distribution of the well-known rock operas TOMMY and JESUS CHRIST SUPER.

The relationship between Famous and Contemporary was considerably more harmonious in 1972 than it is today. At that time, Martell thought he had found, in VIRGIN, another TOMMY or JESUS CHRIST SUPER*, and he was anxious to acquire rights to it. O'Reilly, who was encouraged by Martell's expertise and enthusiasm, had high hopes for the success of his composition. On August 16, 1972, they executed the so-called "VIRGIN Recording Agreement" ("VIRGIN agreement") on behalf of their respective organizations.

The terms of the VIRGIN agreement were relatively simple. Famous agreed to pay a royalty to Contemporary in return for the master tape recording of VIRGIN and the exclusive right to manufacture and sell records made from the master. The agreement also created certain "Additional Obligations of Famous" which included, inter alia: the obligation to select and appoint, within the first year of the agreement, at least one person to personally oversee the nationwide promotion of the sale of records, to maintain contact with Contemporary and to submit weekly reports to Contemporary; the obligation to spend, within the first year of the agreement, no less than $50,000 on the promotion of records; and the obligation to release, within the first two years of the agreement, at least four separate single records from VIRGIN. The agreement also contained a non-assignability clause which is set out in the margin.

On May 8, 1973, the parties entered into a distribution contract which dealt with musical compositions other than VIRGIN. This, the so-called "Crunch agreement," granted to Famous the exclusive right to distribute Contemporary's records in the United States. Famous agreed to institute a new record label named "Crunch," and a number of records were to be released under it annually. Contemporary agreed to deliver ten long-playing records and fifteen single records during the first year of the contract. Famous undertook to use its "reasonable efforts" to promote and distribute the records. Paragraph 15 of the Crunch agreement stated that a breach by either party would not be deemed material unless the non-breaching party first gave written notice to the defaulting party and the defaulting party failed to cure the breach within thirty days. The notice was to specify the nature of the alleged material breach. The contract prohibited assignment by Contemporary, but it contained no provision relating to Famous' right to assign.

Although neither VIRGIN nor its progeny was ever as successful as the parties had originally hoped, the business relationship continued on an amicable basis until July 31, 1974. On that date, Famous' record division was sold to ABC Records, Inc. (ABC). When O'Reilly complained to Martell that Famous was breaking its promises, he was told that he would have to look to ABC for performance. O'Reilly met with one of ABC's lawyers and was told that ABC was not going to have any relationship with Contemporary. On August 21, 1974, Contemporary sent a letter to Famous pursuant to paragraph 15 of the Crunch agreement notifying Famous that it had "materially breached Paragraph 12, among others, of [the Crunch] Agreement in that [it had] attempted to make a contract or other agreement with ABC-Dunhill Record Corporation (ABC Records) creating an obligation or responsibility in behalf of or in the name of the Contemporary Mission." This lawsuit followed.

## II. The Jury Verdict.

Contemporary brought this action against several defendants and asserted several causes of action. By the time the case was submitted to the jury the only remaining defendant was Famous and the only remaining claims were that (1) Famous had failed to adequately promote the VIRGIN and Crunch recordings prior to the sale to ABC, (2) Famous breached both the VIRGIN and Crunch agreements when it sold the record division to ABC, and (3) Famous breached an oral agreement to reimburse Contemporary for its promotional expenses. The latter claim has no relevance to this appeal.

The district judge submitted the case to the jury in two parts: the first portion as to liability and the second concerning damages. The court's questions and the jury's answers as to liability and damages are set forth below:

Liability Questions

1. Has plaintiff established by a fair preponderance of the credible evidence that Famous breached the Virgin agreement by failing to adequately promote Virgin in its various aspects as it had agreed?

Yes.

2. If you find a failure to adequately promote, did that cause plaintiff any damage?

Yes.

3. Did the assignment of the Virgin contract by Famous to ABC cause any damage to plaintiff?

Yes.

4. Did plaintiff establish by a fair preponderance of the credible evidence that Famous failed to use "its reasonable efforts consistent with the exercise of sound business judgment" to promote the records marketed under the Crunch label?

No.

5. Did plaintiff establish by a fair preponderance of the credible evidence that there was a refusal by ABC to perform the Crunch contract and promote plaintiff's music after the assignment?

Yes.

6. If your answer is "yes" to either 4 or 5 above, did such a breach or breaches of the Crunch agreement cause plaintiff any damage?

Yes.

7. Did Tony Martell, on behalf of Famous, in talking to any member of plaintiff, make any agreement to reimburse plaintiff for the expense of its members promoting their music around the country?

Yes.

Damage Questions

1. To what damages is plaintiff entitled under the Virgin agreement?

$68,773.

2. To what damages is plaintiff entitled under the Crunch agreement? $104,751.

3. To what unallocated damages as between the Virgin and Crunch and oral agreements is plaintiff entitled - if any? $21,000.

4. To what damages, if any, is plaintiff entitled under the oral agreement? $16,500.

III. Discussion.

On this appeal, Famous attacks the verdict on several grounds. Their first contention is that the evidence was insufficient to support the jury's response to liability question number 1. Their second contention is that the jury's response to liability question number 4 precludes a recovery for non-performance of the Crunch agreement. Their third contention is that Contemporary failed to comply with the notice provision of the Crunch agreement. Their final contention is that Contemporary is estopped from suing for a breach of the Crunch agreement. We find none of these arguments persuasive.

A. The VIRGIN Agreement.

Judge Owen charged the jury as a matter of law that Famous breached the VIRGIN agreement by assigning it to ABC without getting from ABC a written agreement to be bound by the terms of the VIRGIN agreement. A reading of paragraph 29 of the agreement reveals that that charge was entirely correct, and Famous does not challenge it on this appeal. Famous vigorously contends, however, that the jury's conclusion, that it had failed to adequately promote VIRGIN prior to the sale to ABC, is at war with the undisputed facts and cannot be permitted to stand. O'Connor v. Pennsylvania R.R. Co., 308 F.2d 911, 915 & n.5 (2d Cir. 1962). In particular they argue that they spent the required $50,000 and appointed the required overseer for the project. The flaw in this argument is that its focus is too narrow. The obligations to which it refers are but two of many created by the VIRGIN agreement. Under the doctrine of Wood v. Lucy, Lady - Duff Gordon, 222 N.Y. 88, 118 N.E. 214 (1917), Famous had an obligation to use its reasonable efforts to promote VIRGIN on a nationwide basis. That obligation could not be satisfied merely by technical compliance with the spending and appointment requirements of paragraph 14 of the agreement. Even assuming that Famous complied fully with those requirements, there was evidence from which the jury could find that Famous failed to adequately promote VIRGIN. The question is a close one, particularly in light of Martell's obvious commitment to the success of VIRGIN and in light of the efforts that were in fact exerted and the lack of any serious dispute between the parties prior to the sale to ABC. However, there was evidence that Famous prematurely terminated the promotion of the first single record, "Got To Know," shortly after its release, and that Famous limited its promotion of the second record, "Kyrie," to a single city, rather than promoting it nationwide. Moreover, there was evidence that, prior to the sale to ABC, Famous underwent a budget reduction and cut back its promotional staff. From this, the jury could infer that the promotional effort was reduced to a level that was less than adequate. On the whole, therefore, we are not persuaded that the jury's verdict should be disturbed.

B. The Crunch Agreement.

There is no dispute that the sale of Famous' record division to ABC constituted an assignment of the Crunch agreement to ABC. The assignment of a bilateral contract includes both an assignment of rights and a delegation of duties. See 3 Williston on Contracts § 418 (3d ed. 1960). The distinctions between the two are important.

Perhaps more frequently than is the case with other terms of art, lawyers seem prone to use the word "assignment" inartfully, frequently intending to encompass within the term the distinct [concept] of delegation. . . . An assignment involves the transfer of rights. A delegation involves the appointment of another to perform one's duties.

J. Calamari & J. Perillo, Contracts § 254 (1970) (footnote omitted). Famous' arguments with respect to the Crunch agreement ignore this basic distinction, and the result is a distortion of several fundamental principles of contract law.

It is true, of course, as a general rule, that when rights are assigned, the assignor's interest in the rights assigned comes to an end. When duties are delegated, however, the delegant's obligation does not end.

One who owes money or is bound to any performance whatever, cannot by any act of his own, or by any act in agreement with any other person, except his creditor, divest himself of the duty and substitute the duty of another. "No one can assign his liabilities under a contract without the consent of the party to whom he is liable."

This is sufficiently obvious when attention is called to it, for otherwise obligors would find an easy practical way of escaping their obligations. . . .

3 Williston on Contracts § 411 (3d ed. 1960) (footnote omitted). This is not to say that one may not delegate his obligations. In fact, most obligations can be delegated - as long as performance by the delegate will not vary materially from performance by the delegant. The act of delegation, however, does not relieve the delegant of the ultimate responsibility to see that the obligation is performed. If the delegate fails to perform, the delegant remains liable.

Davidson v. Madison Corp., 257 N.Y. 120, 125, 177 N.E. 393, 394 (1931); Devlin v. Mayor, 63 N.Y. 8, 16 (1875).

Judge Owen correctly charged the jury that "after the assignment of the contract by Famous to ABC, Famous remained liable for any obligation that was not fulfilled by ABC." This was a correct statement of the law, and Famous' assault upon it, while valiant, is without merit.

Our conclusion also disposes of Famous' evidentiary argument. The argument is that since Famous is being held liable for a breach by ABC, and since the only proof of a breach by ABC was proof of ABC's repudiation, and since the evidence of repudiation was hearsay, there was no admissible proof of a breach by ABC, and, therefore, Famous cannot be held liable. This argument fails because it was unnecessary for Contemporary to prove that ABC breached, or repudiated, any obligation. All Contemporary was required to do was to prove that no one performed Famous' obligation to promote after the sale to ABC. This it clearly did. Performance by ABC would have been an affirmative defense for Famous, but in order to prevail it was not necessary for Contemporary to disprove an affirmative defense that was neither pled nor proved by Famous. Because Contemporary's proof of ABC's refusal to perform was unnecessary to make out its cause of action, we need decide whether that proof was admissible.

Famous also maintains that, even if there were a breach, Contemporary is barred from asserting it, because it failed to adequately comply with the notice requirement contained in the Crunch agreement. We find this argument unpersuasive. The letter sent by Contemporary to Famous shortly after the sale to ABC gave Famous adequate notice that Contemporary considered the contract to have been materially breached as a result of the sale, which had led to the "illegal seizure of our property from the marketplace," an obvious reference to evidence that the Crunch (and VIRGIN) record inventory had been removed from retail stores and shipped to ABC without notice to Contemporary, with probable harm to promotion and sales. Indeed, Famous' president, Martell, had advised O'Reilly of this fact before the latter's visit to ABC in early August 1974. While it is true that the letter directs Famous' attention to "Paragraph 12, among others," and that a breach of paragraph 12 was not the basis for Contemporary's ultimate recovery, under the circumstances, it would be hypertechnical to upset the verdict on the ground that the notice was insufficient. We decline to construe the notice provision as if it were a common law pleading requirement under which every slip would be fatal. The purpose of the written notice requirement was to permit Famous within 30 days to cure any material breach. Contemporary's August 19, 1974, telegram, construed in the light of the earlier Martell-O'Reilly conversation with respect to the removal of the record inventory from retail stores was sufficient to place Famous under a duty to communicate immediately with ABC and to insure that the contract was being performed according to its terms. Had it done so, it would have found (as had O'Reilly a few days earlier) that ABC was not fulfilling Famous' obligations under the contract but was taking the position that it would not have anything to do with Contemporary. The problem for Famous, of course, was that, having sold its entire record division to ABC, it had stripped itself of its ability to cure the breach.

Famous' final contention is that Contemporary is estopped from suing for a breach of the Crunch agreement. According to Famous, because Contemporary has always claimed that the assignment was void ab initio, it is estopped to claim that Famous is vicariously liable for a breach by ABC, because if the assignment was void, ABC had no obligation which could have been breached. This argument is without merit because it is premised upon the mistaken notion that Famous is being held liable for a breach by ABC. Such is not the case. The basis for the recovery is not a breach by ABC, it is a breach by Famous after the sale to ABC.

### IV. The Cross-Appeal.

During the trial, Contemporary sought to introduce a statistical analysis, together with expert testimony, in order to prove how successful the most successful of its single recordings, "Fear No Evil," would have become if the VIRGIN agreement had not been breached as a result of the sale to ABC. Based upon its projection of the success of that recording, Contemporary hoped to prove what revenues that success would have produced. Judge Owen excluded this evidence on the ground that it was speculative. Freund v. Washington Square Press, Inc., 34 N.Y.2d 379, 314 N.E.2d 419, 357 N.Y.S.2d 857 (1974).

There can be no dispute that Contemporary "is entitled to the reasonable damage flowing from the breach of" the VIRGIN agreement by Famous, and that "the measure of the damage is the amount necessary to put [Contemporary] in [the] exact position as [it] would have been if the contract had not been breached." Perma Research & Dev. v. Singer Co., 542 F.2d 111, 116 (2d Cir.), cert. denied, 429 U.S. 987, 50 L. Ed. 2d 598, 97 S. Ct. 507 (1976). Nor can there be any dispute as to the New York rules concerning the measure of proof required to prove the existence of damage and the measure of proof necessary to enable the jury to fix its amount. It is clear that the existence of damage must be certain - a requirement that operates with particular severity in cases involving artistic creations such as books, Freund v. Washington Square Press, Inc., supra, movies, Broadway Photoplay Co. v. World Film Corp., 225 N.Y. 104, 121 N.E. 756 (1919), plays, Bernstein v. Meech, 130 N.Y. 354, 29 N.E. 255 (1891), and, by analogy, records. What all of these have in common is their dependence upon taste or fancy for success. When the existence of damage is uncertain or speculative, the plaintiff is limited to the recovery of nominal damages. On the other hand, if the plaintiff has given valuable consideration for the promise of performance which would have given him a chance to make a profit, the defendant should not be allowed to deprive him of that performance without compensation unless the difficulty of determining its value is extreme. Especially is this true where there is no chance of loss.

11 Williston on Contracts § 1346, at 242 (3d ed. 1968). Thus, under the long-standing New York rule, when the existence of damage is certain, and the only uncertainty is as to its amount, the plaintiff will not be denied a recovery of substantial damages. See Lee v. Joseph E. Seagram & Sons, Inc., 552 F.2d 447, 456 (2d Cir. 1977); W. L. Hailey & Co. v. County of Niagara, 388 F.2d 746, 753 (2d Cir. 1967) (collecting New York cases). Moreover, the burden of uncertainty as to the amount of damage is upon the wrongdoer, Perma Research & Dev. v. Singer, supra, 542 F.2d at 116, and the test for admissibility of evidence concerning prospective damages is whether the evidence has any tendency to show their probable amount. Duane Jones Co. v. Burke, 306 N.Y. 172, 192, 117 N.E.2d 237, 247-48 (1954). The plaintiff need only show a "stable foundation for a reasonable estimate of royalties he would have earned had defendant not breached." Freund v. Washington Square Press, Inc., supra, 34 N.Y.2d at 383, 314 N.E.2d at 421, 357 N.Y.S.2d at 861. "Such an estimate necessarily requires some improvisation, and the party who has caused the loss may not insist on theoretical perfection." Entis v. Atlantic Wire & Cable Corp., 335 F.2d 759, 763 (2d Cir. 1964). "The law will make the best appraisal that it can, summoning to its service whatever aids it can command." Sinclair Rfg. Co. v. Jenkins Co., 289 U.S. 689, 697, 77 L. Ed. 1449, 53 S. Ct. 736 (1933).

We are confident that under the principles enunciated above the exclusion of the evidence proffered by Contemporary was error. This is not a case in which the plaintiff sought to prove hypothetical profits from the sale of a hypothetical record at a hypothetical price in a hypothetical market. At the time of the sale to ABC, the record was real, the price was fixed, the market was buying and the record's success, while modest, was increasing. Even after the promotional efforts ended, and the record was withdrawn from the marketplace, it was carried, as a result of its own momentum, to an additional 10,000 sales and to a rise from approximately number 80 on the "Hot Soul's Singles" chart of Billboard magazine to number 61. It cannot be gainsaid that if someone had continued to promote it, and if it had not been withdrawn from the market, it would have sold more records than it actually did. Thus, it is certain that Contemporary suffered some damage in the form of lost royalties. The same is not true, however, of the existence of damage in the form of lost opportunities for concert tours, theatrical tours or similar benefits. While it is certain that some sales were lost as a result of the failure to promote, we cannot believe that under Freund the New York courts would accept what Famous' counsel aptly described at trial as Contemporary's "domino theory" of prospective damages. The theory is that if "Fear No Evil" had become a "hit," its success would have stimulated additional sales of the full two-record VIRGIN album and would have generated sufficient popular acceptance to enable Contemporary to obtain bookings for a nationwide concert tour. We hold that these additional benefits are too dependent upon taste or fancy to be considered anything other than speculative and uncertain, and, therefore, proof of damage in the form of such lost benefits was properly excluded by Judge Owen. Freund v. Washington Square Press, Inc., supra; see Devlin v. Mayor, supra, 63 N.Y. at 25-26.

We next turn to the question of whether the evidence as to the amount of lost royalties was relevant under the standards set out above. Because "Fear No Evil" ultimately reached number 61 on the record charts, Contemporary offered a statistical analysis of every song that had reached number 61 during 1974. This analysis showed that 76 percent of the 324 songs that had reached number 61 ultimately reached the top 40; 65 percent reached the top 30; 51 percent reached the top 20; 34 percent reached the top 10; 21 percent reached the top 5; and 10 percent reached number 1. If the trial judge had admitted this evidence, Contemporary was prepared to offer the testimony of an expert witness who could have converted these measures of success into projected sales figures. The sales figures could be converted into lost royalties in accordance with the terms of the VIRGIN agreement.

Famous vigorously maintains, and Judge Owen agreed, that the data was incomplete because it failed to account for such factors as the speed with which the various records rose upward (the most successful records generally rise quickly - passing number 61 in their third or fourth week - "Fear No Evil" had risen relatively slowly - number 61 in ten weeks); the reputations of the various artists performing the recordings (Contemporary had no prior hit records and was relatively unknown); and the size and ability of the company promoting the recordings. We agree that a more accurate prediction of the success of "Fear No Evil" would be likely to result if the statistical analysis accounted for these and other factors. The omission of these factors from Contemporary's study affects only the weight of the evidence, however, and not its admissibility. Evidence need not be conclusive in order to be relevant. North American Philips Co. v. Church, 375 F.2d 93, 97 (2d Cir. 1967). Standing alone, the study tended to prove that it was more likely than not that "Fear No Evil" would be among the 51 percent of recordings that reached the top 20. If Famous wished to offer proof that would tend to cast doubt on the accuracy of that prediction, it would be free to do so. In this way, all of the evidence tending to show the probable amount of Contemporary's damages would be placed before the jury. While it is true that the jury would be required to speculate to some degree with respect to whether "Fear No Evil" would be within any particular percentage, such is the nature of estimation. If the amount of damage were certain, no estimation would be required. But the uncertainty exists, and since it is a product of the defendant's wrongful conduct, he will not be heard to complain of the lack of precision. Entis v. Atlantic Wire & Cable Corp., supra, 335 F.2d at 763.

Because Freund does not bar proof of lost royalties and because the proffered evidence was relevant on that issue, Fed. R. Evid. 401, Judge Owen was required to admit it, Fed. R. Evid. 402, unless he found that "its probative value [was] substantially outweighed by the danger of unfair prejudice, confusion of the issues, or misleading the jury." Fed. R. Evid. 403. It may be, for example, that "in the frame within which [they were sought to be] used . . . the [statistics], though relevant, became an item of prejudicial overweight." Marx & Co. v. Diners' Club, Inc., 550 F.2d 505, 511 & n.19 (2d Cir. 1977). Similarly, it may be that if Contemporary was unprepared to offer an analysis of factors other than the bare statistics, those statistics, standing alone, would be misleading and would therefore not provide a "stable foundation for a reasonable estimate of royalties" that would have been earned if Famous had not breached. Freund v. Washington Square Press, Inc., supra, 34 N.Y.2d at 383, 314 N.E.2d at 421, 357 N.Y.S.2d at 861. Because Judge Owen did not reach these issues, and because we believe it would be inappropriate for this Court to engage in Rule 403 balancing in the first instance, the case must be remanded to the district court for the purpose of making a Rule 403 determination. The resolution of that issue will, in turn, determine whether Contemporary should be given the new trial on the issue of damages which it seeks on its cross-appeal.

The judgment of the district court is affirmed in all respects except as to its ruling with regard to lost royalties, and the case is remanded to the district court for further proceedings in accordance with this opinion.

———————

*Contemporary Mission* again looks into whether alleged damages for lost royalties are too speculative to be determined with any certainty. This was an assigned contract, but defendant is still under a duty to ensure that the contract is performed according to its terms. The court held that additional benefits such as lost opportunities for concert tours, theatrical tours, or similar benefits are too dependent upon fickle public tastes to be anything other than speculative. As the N.Y. Court of Appeals stated in *Kenford* (at 67 N.Y. 2d 257, 263), "New York has long recognized the inherent uncertainties of predicting profits in the entertainment field. . . "

The following case of *Peterson v. Lightfoot*, 47 Cal. App. 646 (1920), concerns a request for an accounting in a dissolving partnership.

Peterson v. Lightfoot
Court of Appeal of California, First Appellate District, Division Two
May 21, 1920, Decided
Civ. No. 3373
47 Cal. App. 646

BRITTAIN, J. The defendant appeals from a judgment in a suit for partnership accounting. The judgment provided that the assets of the partnership be sold by a commissioner, and upon the return of the commissioner and the equal division of the assets between the parties, a final judgment be entered dissolving the partnership or declaring it dissolved.

The respondent contends that the judgment is a non-appealable interlocutory order. The findings and conclusions of law finally determined the rights of the parties, leaving only the transmutation of the assets into cash and their equal division to be done. The appellant claims that the court was in error in determining that the assets ordered to be sold belonged to the partnership and he claims ownership of them himself. If his contentions in this regard should be sustained by the appellate court after the sale of his property, he would be without remedy or find himself compelled to resort to a doubtful remedy against the purchaser at the commissioner's sale. For all practical purposes of disposing of the issues tried the judgment was final. "The question, as affecting the right of appeal, is not what the form of the order may be, but what is its legal effect." ( Estate of West, 162 Cal. 352, [122 P. 953]; Byrne v. Hoag, 126 Cal. 283, [58 P. 688]; People v. Bank of Mendocino County, 133 Cal. 107, [65 P. 124]; Clark v. Dunnam, 46 Cal. 204.)

There was no written agreement by which the partnership was formed. From the oral testimony of the partners and others, the trial court found that the claim of the appellant that the partnership was one of profits only was not sustained. There was evidence to support this finding and it is controlling on this appeal. The appellant states that there is but one question to be determined, and that is whether the name "Redlands Auto Service" was a part of the assets of the partnership.

From the findings it appears that in May, 1914, the defendant purchased an automobile on which he caused to be painted the name in question. For about three weeks he operated the machine for hire under that name to designate the business in which he was engaged. In June he associated with himself, his brother, who owned another automobile, which was thereafter similarly used. The partnership business was operated under the firm name of "Redlands Auto Service." Shortly after, during the same month, the plaintiff became a member of the partnership, he contributing $ 640 to the common fund, that being the value of each of the machines then used in the business. In April, 1915, the defendant's brother sold his interest to the partnership, then composed of the parties to this suit. Thereafter the business was carried on under the same name it had been carried on from the time the first partnership was formed. In December, 1914, while the partnership was composed of the three men, the defendant caused the name "Redlands Auto Service" to be registered in the office of the Secretary of State in his own name. This was done without the knowledge of the plaintiff, who was not informed of the fact until after the dissolution of the partnership in July, 1918. During all the intervening time the business of the partnership was carried on under that name. It was further found, and the finding is supported by the evidence and by reasonable inferences therefrom, that at the time of the formation of the partnership the name had no value, but by the joint efforts of the partners in conducting the business from June, 1914, to July, 1918, when the partnership was dissolved, "the goodwill of the partnership business, including the right, title, and interest of said partnership in said firm name, became, and at the time of the dissolution of said partnership was, and now is, of the value of $ 800."

The appellant's contentions that the adoption and use of a trade name immediately fixes its status as personal property, and that a single act of use with the intent to continue that use confers a right in the original user may be conceded without affecting the propriety of the judgment. The suit for partnership accounting is one addressed to the equitable jurisdiction of the court. (Andrade v. Superior Court, 75 Cal. 459-463, [17 P. 531].)

Under the facts found, even though the name was originally owned by the appellant, the court, in adjusting the respective interests of the parties, properly considered all the circumstances. The name, which had been used for three weeks, was of no value. The respondent went into the business carried on by the appellant at the request of the latter as a partner. It was agreed that the appellant's automobile, which had value, should be used in the business, but the ownership retained. It was also agreed that the money invested in the business by the respondent should be used for the purchase of a machine. Before the termination of the partnership each of the partners had in use in the business two automobiles owned by them separately. On dissolution each retained his own tangible property. The name which was worthless when the partnership was formed was an asset and apparently the only asset of the business at that time. It was made valuable by the joint efforts of the two partners. If it had been some other kind of tangible personal property so worthless as not to have been the subject of agreement, but a part of the business establishment when the partnership was formed, and had had bestowed upon it the work of both partners for a period of three years, in use constantly as partnership property and without claim by the original owner, until at the time of the dissolution it came to have a substantial value produced solely by their joint work, it would be manifestly inequitable that it should be given to one only of the two who had produced the value.

It is said in the appellant's brief that the recordation of the name added nothing to his common-law rights. Neither could the secret recordation of the name by the appellant cause any diminution of the rights of his partner. The relationship was confidential and the recordation by one of the partners of the name under which the partnership had been doing business for six months, in contemplation of law, was in the interest of the partnership.

From an examination of the entire record it does not appear that incidental matters touched upon in the briefs require notice here.

The judgment is affirmed.

---

*Boogie Kings v. Guillory*, 188 So. 2d 445 (La. App. 1966), looks into the very typical situation of a former band member (maybe even a "key" member) who challenges a trial court order in favor of appellee band association in an action brought by the band association to enjoin the former band member from using the trade name, "Boogie Kings."

In the following case, *Marshak v. Green*, 505 F. Supp. 1054 (S.D.N.Y. 1981), similar to *Boogie Kings*, we look at the name of the estimable group, The Drifters.

Marshak v. Green, 505 F. Supp. 1054
United States District Court for the Southern District of New York
January 26, 1981
79 Civ. 3458
505 F. Supp. 1054

The defendant Doc Green, together with Charles Thomas and Elsbeary Hobbs (not named as defendants), filed on December 17, 1976 in the United States Patent and Trademark Office a service-mark application in the name of "The Drifters," a partnership composed of all three. The Drifters, as the aforesaid applicants, assigned to plaintiff Larry Marshak all their right, title and interest in the pending application. The registration was issued by the Patent Office on January 3, 1978 and covers the mark "THE DRIFTERS" used for "ENTERTAINMENT SERVICES NAMELY A SINGING GROUP." Marshak has been the manager of The Drifters musical group which included defendant Green since 1971.

In July 1979, Marshak commenced this action against Doc Green and David Rick, the manager of a singing group formed shortly before and using the name The Drifters. Plaintiff charges that such use by the defendants constituted an infringement of the registered service mark, unfair competition, and dilution of the mark. He seeks injunctive relief against defendants' continued use of the mark to represent their services and in the promotion thereof, as well as damages and an accounting of defendants' profits. Defendants, in addition to contending that the assignment of the registration application on which plaintiff bases his ownership is invalid and that plaintiff does not have a right to the exclusive use of the mark, seek cancellation of the registration. Further, they counterclaim for an accounting of monies allegedly owed defendant Green by plaintiff from the time Green performed for plaintiff as a Drifter.

After a thorough review of the trial testimony, including the transcript of the hearing on a preliminary injunction, exhibits and an evaluation of the credibility of witnesses, the Court finds that the plaintiff has sustained his burden of proof as to his respective claims and is entitled to relief; likewise, the defendants have failed to meet their burden on the counterclaims, which are dismissed.

Events Prior to 1970

A group known as "The Drifters" originally achieved prominence in the late 1950s and early 1960s. Green, Hobbs and Thomas were part of The Drifters when the group was most successful at the end of the 1950s and early 1960s and they recorded popular hit songs such as "There Goes My Baby" and "Save The Last Dance For Me." During this period they were under the management of George Treadwell. In addition to Thomas, Hobbs and Green, who were publicly recognized as part of The Drifters, there were others who at times played with the group. Although the membership of the group was not constant, the evidence establishes that Thomas, Hobbs and Green recorded on all or most of The Drifters' hit records, and their pictures appeared on the covers of several albums that have been continuously available to the public since then. The Drifters continued to record hit songs through 1966; by that time Thomas, Hobbs and Green, as well as others who had participated in the hit songs, had for various reasons stopped singing actively with the group.

The Period Subsequent to 1970

Thomas, Hobbs and Green resumed performing together under the name of The Drifters in 1969 and have been managed by plaintiff Marshak since 1971. During the 1970s, Thomas, Hobbs and Green now and then performed along with one or two others and continued to be recognized by the public as "The Drifters." Under the plaintiff's direction, they made records, tapes, appeared on television and performed live concerts throughout the country (including one at the White House).

There is no evidence that during this decade any other group was so identified by the public as The Drifters, or that any other group had an unrestricted right to the name, although defendants sought to prove that plaintiff's group was not the exclusive user of the name "The Drifters." Thus, they suggested that Faye Treadwell, George Treadwell's widow, has continued to manage a group of Drifters since his death, and that this group had at least as great a right as plaintiff to "The Drifters" name. But the evidence was insufficient to support this claim. The evidence establishes that following a 1971 infringement suit brought by Mrs. Treadwell against Marshak in New York State Supreme Court, she had agreed to restrict her group's performances to Europe. Further, defendants asserted that Bill Pinckney, a former member of the group, currently performs under "The Drifters" name. Again, defendants offered no direct evidence substantiating this position; to the contrary, the proof establishes that Marshak has an agreement with Pinckney licensing Pinckney to use "The Drifters" name only in the South.

Typical of defendants' efforts in support of their position that plaintiff's use of "The Drifters" is not exclusive is the testimony of James Hudson, a rock manager and producer. He testified that, throughout the 1970s, he booked plaintiff's group and understood The Drifters to include Thomas, Hobbs, Green and another. Although he heard of others using the name, he was not personally familiar with them nor did he know if they had any right to the name. This vague and inconclusive testimony fails to support defendants' claim that plaintiff's group did not have exclusive use of the service mark prior to applying to register it in 1976.

In 1976, after reading that another singing group, The Platters, had, because of their service-mark registration, been successful in preventing others from using its name, plaintiff urged Thomas, Hobbs and Green to apply to register "The Drifters" to protect their right to the exclusive use of the name. Marshak agreed that, if they assigned their rights under the application to him, he would continue as their manager and be vigilant in stopping others from using "The Drifters" name. The three considered plaintiff's offer out of his presence and for their mutual benefit signed both the application and the assignment of their own free will and with the understanding that the purpose was to protect their right to the name. As already noted, the service mark was finally registered on January 3, 1978. Since then, Marshak has been active in policing the mark and instituted several lawsuits based on alleged infringement.

Thomas, Hobbs and Green continued to perform together under plaintiff's management until June 1979, when Green, claiming dissatisfaction with the group's financial arrangements, broke away and formed another group, managed by defendant Rick, also using the name "The Drifters." Green's group, which performs in the same style as plaintiff's, has appeared in many of the same locations as plaintiff's and solicited trade through many of the same agents and clubs.

The essence of plaintiff's infringement and unfair-competition claims, under both federal and New York law, "is that the use of the infringing term creates the likelihood of consumer confusion; the facts supporting both are also substantially the same. The essential inquiry is whether an appreciable number of ordinarily prudent prospective (customers) are likely to be confused or misled." Several factors are considered, including the strength of the prior user's mark, the degree of similarity, and the defendants' good faith in adopting the mark.

Plaintiff has clearly shown a likelihood of confusion. Defendants' group has performed in the same areas and in the same style as plaintiff's; they use the same name; they are in direct competition. Green himself testified that the public, in buying tickets to a concert, was likely to be confused as to which group was performing. Further, producer Hudson, called as a witness by defendants, testified that, whenever he booked defendants' group, he could not guarantee that plaintiff's group would not appear in the same area.

Defendants in their own promotional material make no attempt to distinguish between the groups. In one such example, a flyer, defendants describe Green as an original member of The Drifters and as having appeared with the group in concerts, on television, and on records, none of which refers to defendants' group. The flyer lists eleven hit recordings, including "There Goes My Baby" and "Save The Last Dance For Me," all of which were recorded well before 1979, when Green's group was formed. Finally, it designates defendant Rick as the person to contact to book the group. Defendants in promoting their own group were thus trading on the name and goodwill of plaintiff's group.

Moreover, defendant Rick evinced an express intention to capitalize on plaintiff's goodwill. Having been sought out by Green for help in forming a new group after Green left plaintiff's group, Rick chose the name The Drifters precisely because "the only thing that draws is a name that is well known or halfway known or whatever," and that The Drifters is such a name. In short, defendants intended to capitalize on plaintiff's right to the use of "The Drifters." They deliberately used the name aware they had no right thereto, with consequent confusion of the public.

Plaintiff has affirmatively established that "The Drifters" is a valuable name that has been well known both within the industry and to the consuming public over a long period of time. Indeed, Rick clearly acknowledged that in selecting the name for his own group. He further noted that, in his capacity as an agent before he formed his own Drifters group with Green, when he wanted to book The Drifters, he would contact Marshak.

From the time Thomas, Hobbs and Green resumed performing together in 1969 until Green left the group in 1979, these men were recognized by the public as The Drifters, and they were a unit when they applied to register their mark in December 1976 and assigned all their rights in the application for the mark to plaintiff Marshak.

The registration for the service mark "The Drifters," issued on the application of defendant Green and Thomas and Hobbs, his co-partners, is prima facie evidence of the validity of the mark. Thus, in challenging its validity, defendants Green and Rick not only have the burden of coming forward with evidence, but also they "must put something more into the scales than the registrant." Defendants have simply not met this burden on any of their defenses.

With respect to their defense of nonexclusive use, they have produced no competent, direct evidence to support their claims that other groups used and had a right to "The Drifters" name. No member of such a group testified, nor were any indicia of their existence, like recordings or billboards, produced.

Further, defendants' attack on the service-mark application itself is unavailing. They contend that the application contains false allegations as to exclusive use, continuous use, and first use. Putting aside for the moment the issue whether they are estopped from challenging statements Green made under oath and from which he benefitted for several years until he left plaintiff's group, defendants have not met their burden of proof. First, they have utterly failed to present adequate proof that plaintiff's group's use was not exclusive. Further, Drifters' records have been continuously available, and defendants have not demonstrated any intention by plaintiff's assignors to abandon the name. Finally, any irregularity in the alleged date of first use 1959 was insignificant and not prejudicial.

There are additional considerations in rejecting defendants' attack on the application. Although, in general, neither opposition to registration nor a petition for cancellation under 15 U.S.C., section 1064, is a prerequisite to a cancellation counterclaim in an infringement action, failure to act at the administrative level by one in a position to do so may make such a counterclaim "smack of tactical afterthoughts." Here, Green swore to and signed the application seeking the benefits of the registration and the assignment of the application to Marshak; Rick knew all along of plaintiff's group and the great value of its name, though he denied specific knowledge of the registration until shortly before the suit was commenced; and Green continued to perform with plaintiff's group after the application was filed and, indeed, for over a year after the registration was final.

Defendants' failure to meet their burden on this issue is wholly apart from any considerations of estoppel to attack the application which Green signed and from which, for a time, he reaped benefits. Courts adhere to traditional common-law contract principles even in trademark cases as long as holding a party to his obligations is not inconsistent with the public policy of preventing confusion and deception as to the origin of goods or services. Where a party, as here, applies for the benefits of service-mark registration and then receives such benefits over a period of time, he is estopped from challenging the validity of the mark under these traditional principles.

Defendants' contention that the assignment of the application to plaintiff was invalid is without merit. Marshak's promise to provide greater protection for the name was adequate consideration for the promise, and the instrument itself recites that consideration was furnished. Further, defendants' claim that no goodwill was transferred by this assignment is without merit. Not only did the instrument itself provide for the transfer of goodwill, but also the use of the mark that is, the singing in The Drifters style by Thomas, Hobbs and Green remained unchanged in the public eye. The essence of what Marshak acquired was "the right to inform the public that (he) is in possession of the special experience and skill symbolized by the name of the original concern, and of the sole authority to market its [services]." Here, the goodwill was clearly transferred.

The record thus indicates that plaintiff's mark is valid and strong, that defendants use the same name in the same manner as does plaintiff, and in the same geographic area. Plaintiff has demonstrated that defendants' use of "The Drifters" infringes on his mark, is likely to confuse the consuming public and, further, constitutes unfair competition. Moreover, the infringement was intentional. "That [defendants] persuaded [themselves they] had a legal right to pursue the course [they] did diminishes neither the fact of [their] violation of [Marshak's] rights, nor the force of its impact upon the consumer. That a course is stubbornly pursued does not render it innocent. The very persistence in the infringing conduct over the prompt protest of [Marshak] not only emphasizes its wilfulness, but continues the wrong, entitling [Marshak] to judicial redress."

Marshak is thus entitled to a decree as sought by him enjoining defendants from continuing to perform under the name "The Drifters" or any variant thereof. The decree shall include a prohibition against use of the mark "The Drifters" on any billboard or other promotional material and a requirement that defendants surrender to plaintiff any promotional materials bearing the name "The Drifters."

The defendants' conduct was deliberate and intended to pirate potential customers from the plaintiff by their unjustified use of "The Drifters." Their conduct was calculated to appropriate the goodwill attaching to plaintiff's right to "The Drifters." As a result, the defendants were unjustly enriched, and this alone entitles plaintiff to an accounting. An accounting is further justified to deter others in similar positions from infringing valid marks.

Plaintiff has met his burden and shown gross receipts for concerts actually performed by defendants' group in the amount of $ 31,450. Although defendants failed to put in any evidence on elements of cost or deduction, as required by the statute, this Court in equity must seek a realistic figure for defendants' profits. Marshak himself testified that the deductible expenses for a group, even before paying performers, were considerable, including commissions, gas and tolls, amortization of vehicle, uniform rentals and general office expenses. However, no precise figures were supplied. In the circumstances, the Court will afford the defendants an opportunity to submit evidence with respect thereto. A hearing is set for Tuesday, February 3, 1981, at 2:15 p.m., courtroom 1506, at which time the evidence will be limited to deductible expenses from gross income.

Plaintiff also seeks to recover attorneys' fees under an amendment to section 35 of the Lanham Act allowing such fees "in exceptional cases." Despite defendants' intentional infringement of plaintiff's mark, the Court, exercising its discretion, finds that the circumstances do not warrant an award of attorneys' fees in this case. Plaintiff is entitled to taxation of statutory costs.

Defendant Green has failed entirely in presenting evidence in support of his counterclaim for damages and an accounting of monies allegedly owed him by Marshak arising out of Green's performances with plaintiff's group through 1979. Although Green expressed dissatisfaction with the amounts received for various performances, in part because he believed that others were earning more money, he conceded that he had no financial records, relied on what others knew or speculated on for his information, and did not know the amount of expenses deducted from gross receipts. In the circumstances, and considering that Green continued to perform with plaintiff throughout the 1970s without filing suit, Green's counterclaims must be dismissed.

Submit decree in accordance with the foregoing.

The foregoing shall constitute the Court's Findings of Fact and Conclusions of Law.

Giammarese v. Delfino
United States District Court for the Northern District of Illinois Eastern
Division
September 29, 1977
No. 75 C 1051
1977 U.S. Dist. LEXIS 13720

McGarr, District Judge.

This is an action by three members of a musical group known as "The Buckinghams" in which it is alleged that the trade name "The Buckinghams" has been appropriated and used, and a confusingly similar trade name ("The Nu-Buckinghams") has been used by another group of musicians playing songs of the same genre as those the plaintiffs' group had played, all to the plaintiffs' damage and in contravention of both state and federal trademark and unfair competition laws. Although various members of the second group are named as defendants, none of these persons have been served, and the only defendants before this court are Mr. Micolis, a former member of the original group, who is alleged to have promoted the second group and licensed its use of the subject trade name, Mr. Gab Garland, alleged to be a producer for the second group, and the Norby Walters Association, alleged to be managers for the second group. Plaintiffs' second amended complaint seeks relief in the form of a preliminary and a final injunction, damages, an accounting for profits, and cancellation of defendant Miccolis' registration of the subject trade name with the U.S. Patent and Trademark Office.

A hearing was held in this court on the issue of whether or not a preliminary injunction should issue in this matter and, on January 21, 1976, an order was entered enjoining defendants from

directly or through agents using the name 'Buckinghams', or 'Nu-Buckinghams', or from acting in any way intended to lead the public into believing that they, or any musical group which they participate in, sponsor, license, book or manage are the original Buckinghams, or a group sponsored or approved by the original Buckinghams.

Among the findings of fact and conclusions of law made by the court at that time were the following: "that in 1965 there was an original group known as the Buckinghams, who were a viable and recognizable organization," and that plaintiffs and defendant Miccolis were members of that organization; that Mr. Miccolis left the group in September, 1966; that when he left, Mr. Miccolis "took with him no rights to the name" ("The Buckinghams"); that a certain recording made while Miccolis was still a member of the group became a "hit" in January, 1967; that the group became inactive in 1971; that, even though the original Buckinghams are no longer performing together, there had been no showing that plaintiffs had abandoned the name and that, indeed, plaintiffs have demonstrated their continued interest in the name by protests to defendant Miccolis over his claim to the name, registration of the name with the State of Illinois, and the release of an album, "Made in Chicago", in 1975. Specifically, this court found that "the album reinforces the continuity of the name in the public mind and the persons and organizations involved with it, and these are the original Buckinghams." This court also found that the promotion of the second group is "calculated to deceive the public into believing that the currently performing group is the original Buckinghams, the same group, that is responsible for the original 'hit' records that the public is familiar with."

Defendants appealed this court's order granting plaintiffs' prayer for preliminary injunction, and the Court of Appeals for the Seventh Circuit, in an opinion dated January 4, 1977, affirmed. The Court of Appeals specifically approved this court's finding that defendant Miccolis, upon separating himself from the original group, possessed no ownership interest in the name "The Buckinghams", and that, therefore, any purported licensing by him of use of the name was of no effect. Finding that the original group constituted a partnership and that ownership of the good will and of the name to which it was attached resided in the partnership as partnership property, and not as property of the individual partners, the Court of Appeals held that defendant Miccolis was "clearly not possessed of a sufficient proprietary interest in the name to justify his conveyance of the entire trade name for use by a new and entirely distinct musical group."

The Court of Appeals likewise approved this court's finding that the subject trade name had not been abandoned by the plaintiffs, notwithstanding their cessation of performances together as a group, and that defendants' use of the name created a likelihood of confusion for the public and constituted trade name infringement.

Plaintiffs are now before this court on a motion for summary judgment on the merits. Plaintiffs assert that there remains for determination no genuine issue of material fact and that they are entitled to judgment as a matter of law, whereas defendants Miccolis and Garland insist that defendant Miccolis' lack of an ownership interest in the trade name is still open to question, and that new evidence as to whether or not plaintiffs' recordings are still being bought and played must be taken in order to update this court's 1976 finding that the plaintiffs have not abandoned their trade name. Defendant Norby Walter Association asserts that summary judgment would be improper as to it inasmuch as it denies having "promoted" the second Buckingham group, and inasmuch as this court has as yet heard little evidence on this issue.

In accordance with Rule 65 of the Federal Rules of Civil Procedure, "any evidence received upon an application for a preliminary injunction which would be admissible upon the trial on the merits becomes part of the record on the trial and need not be repeated upon the trial."

Since plaintiffs have made no request for an update of damages, defendants' liability for damages, if any, will be fixed as of the date of this court's previous findings, and further evidence on the issue of plaintiffs' abandonment of the name since that time is irrelevant. Nor is such evidence necessary to ensure the continued propriety of an injunctive order. The finding of this court made at the conclusion of the hearing on the application for preliminary injunction shall constitute the court's finding of liability against defendants Miccolis and Garland as to certain counts of the complaint. Defendant Norby Walters Association is entitled to a hearing on the issue of its liability, and all parties are entitled to a hearing on the issues of damages and an accounting.

Plaintiffs' motion for summary judgment as to liability against defendants Miccolis and Garland is granted as to Count I and as to that part of Count II which is brought under Ch. 140 Ill.Rev.Stats. § 20. Count IV is dismissed as inapplicable. Since Counts V and VI seek the same relief to which it has been determined plaintiffs are entitled under Counts I and II, it is unnecessary to grant judgment as to these remaining counts.

The prayer for damages under Count III is denied.

Pursuant to 15 U.S.C. § 1119, this court has the authority, "in any action involving a registered mark," to order the cancellation of the registration of "any party to the action." Simmonds Aerocessories Ltd. v. Elastic Stop. Simmonds Aerocessories Ltd. v. Elastic Stop Nut Corp. of America, 257 F.2d 485, 491, 118 USPQ 187, 191 (3d Cir., 1958); Durox Company v. Duran Paint Manufacturing Co., Inc., 320 F.2d 882, 138 USPQ 353 (4th Cir. 1963) ; D.M. & Antique Import Corp. v. Royal Saxe Corp., 311 F.Supp. 1261, 166 USPQ 302 (S.D. N.Y. 1970). Accordingly, it is hereby ordered that the registration of the mark "The Buckinghams" held by Dennis Miccolis with the U.S. Patent and Trademark Office be cancelled.

Cause set for hearing on liability as to defendant Norby Walters Association and damages as to all defendants on November 4, 1977 at 10 a.m.

The Clerk of the Court is directed to certify a copy of the order of cancellation to the Commissioner, U.S. Patent and Trademark Office.

---

*Giammarese*, 1966 U.S. Dist. LEXIS 137270, looks into the rights of the original band members of the group, The Buckinghams (mostly known for their ironically titled hit, "Kind of a Drag").

In the following case, *Noone v. Banner Talent Assocs.*, 398 F. Supp. 260 (1975), famous lead singer Peter Noone of the band Herman's Hermits ("Mrs. Brown You've Got a Lovely Daughter," "I'm Henry the Eighth, I am," etc.) discusses whether Noone is allowed to tour with a new group in England as "Herman's Hermits." Peter Noone then brought an action in the U.S. to enjoin defendants from using the name in this country.

Noone v. Banner Talent Associates, Inc
United States District Court for the Southern District of New York
August 1, 1975
No. 75 Civ. 1546
398 F. Supp. 260

METZNER, District Judge:

Defendants Karl Anthony Green, Derek Leckenby and Jan Barry Whitwam (the individual defendants) move to dismiss the complaint for improper service and resulting lack of in personam jurisdiction, for lack of standing, for lack of subject matter jurisdiction, for failure to state a claim upon which relief can be granted, and on grounds of equity and comity. Defendant Banner Talent Associates, Inc. (Banner) joins in the motion to dismiss.

This case has already been before the court on plaintiff's motion for a preliminary injunction which was denied after an evidentiary hearing.

The individual defendants, together with plaintiff Peter Blair Noone, were the original members of an English musical rock 'n roll group known as "Herman's Hermits." Plaintiff was the lead singer of the group at the time, and held himself out and was identified as "Herman" by the public. The group achieved a world-wide reputation, made numerous million-selling records and albums, and frequent television, stage and concert appearances.

In 1969 Noone, apparently deciding that he needed greater personal exposure, caused himself to be separately billed, styling the group "Peter Noone and Herman's Hermits." The group's last record release was under this name.

In 1971 Noone left the group to pursue his individual career. The individual defendants stayed together, performing under the name "The Hermits." The four were together again, briefly, in 1973 for an American concert tour, where they were billed as "Herman's Hermits featuring Peter Noone."

In late 1973, the individual defendants, with another member, started an American tour without Noone, billing themselves as "Herman's Hermits." All of their engagements were booked by defendant Banner, a nonexclusive booking agent. Sometime thereafter, following an alleged request by Noone for the individual defendants to cease the use of the name, Noone organized a group to perform in England, billed as "Herman's Hermits." The individual defendants have brought an action in England to enjoin Noone from the use of the name in that country. Shortly thereafter, Noone brought the instant action to enjoin the individual defendants and Banner from using the name in this country. The complaint alleges two counts: one based on Section 43(a) of the Lanham Act, 15

U.S.C. § 1125(a), and the other a claim under the common law for unfair competition.

The question of service and personal jurisdiction was raised at the time of the evidentiary hearing on the motion for a preliminary injunction. After hearing the evidence, I found that service was proper and the court had personal jurisdiction of the defendants.

The individual defendants are all citizens of Great Britain. The plaintiff is also a British subject. The individual defendants argue that Section 43(a) of the Lanham Act cannot be used by a foreign plaintiff against foreign defendants. This is a question of first impression.

Section 43(a) of the Lanham Act, 15 U.S.C. § 1125(a), states in pertinent part:

"§ 1125. False designations of origin and false descriptions forbidden

(a) Any person who shall . . . use in connection with any goods or services . . . a false designation of origin, or any false description or representation . . . and shall cause such goods or services to enter into commerce, and any person who shall with knowledge of the falsity . . . cause or procure the same to be . . . used in commerce . . . shall be liable to a civil action . . . by any person who believes that he is or is likely to be damaged by the use of any such false description or representation." (Emphasis added.)

By its express terms, therefore, the section does not limit its applicability to nationals of the United States. "In general, foreigners can claim the same rights and are subject to the same duties as citizens" under the trademark laws. 4 Callman, Unfair Competition, Trademarks and Monopolies § 100.1(a), at 844 (3d Ed. 1970).

Courts have held that foreign plaintiffs have standing to sue United States nationals under Section 43(a), e. g., Scotch Whiskey Association v. Barton Distilling Company, 338 F. Supp. 595 (N.D.Ill.1971), aff'd, 489 F.2d 809 (7th Cir. 1973); Menendez v. Faber, Coe & Gregg, Inc., 345 F. Supp. 527 (S.D.N.Y. 1972), modified on other grounds , 485 F.2d 1355 (2d Cir. 1973), and that "the general provisions of the Lanham Act may be invoked against foreign citizens who infringe United States trade-marks in this country . . . ." Id. at 558-59.

Defendants argue that the doctrine of American Automobile Association v. Spiegel, 205 F.2d 771 (2d Cir.), cert. denied, 346 U.S. 887, 74 S. Ct. 138, 98 L. Ed. 391 (1953) precludes an action wholly between foreign parties. That opinion, however, merely found that Section 44 of the Lanham Act did not establish a federal law of unfair competition outside the scope of the statutory provisions of the Lanham Act. In the instant case, it is conduct under Section 43(a) that is alleged.

I should point out that although plaintiff frames his claim for relief pursuant to Section 43(a), I would find that the facts would clearly support a claim for relief pursuant to Section 44(b).

The trade name here, "Herman's Hermits," is being used in this country and has a secondary meaning in this country, apart from any that it may have in England. The gist of an action under Section 43(a) is false designation. See Colligan v. Activities Club of New York, Ltd., 442 F.2d 686, 691-92 (2d Cir.), cert. denied, 404 U.S. 1004, 92 S. Ct. 559, 30 L. Ed. 2d 557 (1971); Norman M. Morris Corporation v. Weinstein, 466 F.2d 137, 141-42 (5th Cir. 1972). Therefore, I find that plaintiff may sue the individual defendants under Section 43(a) based on the alleged misuse of the trade name within the jurisdiction of this court.

As to the motion to dismiss for failure to state a claim upon which relief may be granted, plaintiff in effect alleges that the use of the name "Herman's Hermits" is a false description in that "Herman" is not a member of the group. Section 43(a) provides relief against the type of unfair competition that is analogous to misappropriation of trade names. Geisel v. Poynter Products, Inc., 283 F. Supp. 261 (S.D.N.Y.1968). See National Lampoon, Inc. v. American Broadcasting Companies, Inc., 376 F. Supp. 733 (S.D.N.Y.1974); Rich v. RCA Corporation, 390 F. Supp. 530 (S.D.N.Y.1975). If the name "Herman's Hermits" has acquired a sufficient secondary meaning to imply, even now, that plaintiff is the lead singer of the group, then the use of the word "Herman's" would be misleading and give rise to an action under Section 43(a) as a false description. The motion to dismiss this claim is denied.

Similarly, the motion to dismiss the claim for unfair competition is denied. Once a substantial claim under the trademark laws is established, a claim for unfair competition is properly before the court. 28 U.S.C. § 1338(b).

Defendant Banner moves to dismiss on the ground that Section 43(a) was never intended to cover the activities of a booking agent. The section clearly states that it extends to any person who knowingly causes a false representation to be used in commerce. The booking agent here, even if nonexclusive, makes a profit from the booking of the individual defendants. If it causes the booking of the defendants as "Herman's Hermits" knowing that designation to be false, it would be liable under the Act.

Defendants claim that because Noone used the designation in England without their participation, he is guilty of "unclean hands" in bringing this action. The fact that plaintiff uses a name that was at one time admittedly attributable to him personally, and that he claims is his to use, has none of the illegal taint required to invoke this defense. See 4 Callman, Unfair Competition, Trademarks and Monopolies, § 87.1(b) (3d Ed. 1970).

Finally, the action in the British courts is irrelevant to the determination here. Determination of trademark rights within this country is not affected by the determination of rights in the mark in a foreign jurisdiction, especially since there is no registry, and each court is dealing with its own secondary meanings. Vanity Fair Mills, Inc. v. The T. Eaton Company, Ltd., 234 F.2d 633 (2d Cir.), cert. denied, 352 U.S. 871, 77 S. Ct. 96, 1 L. Ed. 2d 76 (1956).

Accordingly, the motion is in all respects denied.
So ordered.

Benson v. Paul Winley Record Sales Corp.
United States District Court for the Southern District of New York
June 20, 1978
No. 78 Civ. 2341
452 F. Supp. 516

OPINION AND ORDER

OWEN, District Judge

Guitarist George Benson is an internationally acclaimed jazz musician. After twenty-seven years of effort, he is today the top jazz guitarist in America. Three of his most recent records — with musicians under his direction — have sold over one million copies, and one is the largest-selling jazz album in record history. Years ago, when an unknown, Benson was hired as one of several members of a jazz combo to record music composed and directed by others. Benson, as a mere member of the group, played what was asked of him, controlling neither the musical style, nor the contents, nor the production of the record thereafter released.

Defendants Paul Winley — the composer at this old recording session — and Paul Winley Sales Corporation have now remixed and marketed this material as a collection, and titled it "George Benson, Erotic Moods." The front cover of the record jacket features a large, recent photograph of Benson and prominently displays his name alone in bold letters. Beneath the title is the caption, "X Rated LP." Defendants have altered the contents of the original recording, accenting Benson's guitar track, and have "over-dubbed" the sexually suggestive moaning of a woman on one selection called "Sweet Taste of Love." Defendants have also used Benson's name and picture in publicity for the album. One advertisement features the record jacket and the phrase "XXX Rated new LP and single" (emphasis supplied). Benson moves for a preliminary injunction restraining defendants from manufacturing and selling the album as it is now packaged and advertised.

To merit injunctive relief, it suffices for plaintiff to make a clear showing of probable success on the merits and possible irreparable injury. Sonesta International Hotels Corp. v. Wellington Associates, 483 F.2d 247, 250 (2d Cir. 1973). Both requirements are met. First, defendants' jacket design and album advertisements are false descriptions and representations in violation of § 43(a) of the Lanham Act, 15 U.S.C. § 1125(a). This provision extends to misrepresentations in advertising as well as labeling of products and services in commerce. Yameta Co. v. Capitol Records, Inc., 279 F. Supp. 582, 586 (S.D.N.Y.), vacated on other grounds, 393 F.2d 91 (2d Cir. 1968). To demonstrate probability of success on the merits in an action under § 43(a), plaintiff need merely show the likelihood of consumer deception. Rich v. RCA Corp., 390 F. Supp. 530, 531 (S.D.N.Y. 1975). Defendants have more than likely misled the public — as they doubtless intended — into believing that their album contains recent recordings by George Benson as principal performer. The prominent use of Benson's name and picture on the album and in the advertisements creates the false impression that Benson was responsible for the contents of the album. The recent jacket photograph and the promotion claims of "new" material deceptively portray the album as a current release. Defendants nowhere indicate that the performances are from five to more than twelve years old, and that Benson was a mere player.

Secondly, defendants' misrepresentations can cause irreparable injury to Benson's professional and personal reputation. "Erotic Moods," while of quality, is much less sophisticated in style than that which has engendered Benson's fame. People induced to buy the album, lured by the expectation of enjoying Benson's unique flavor, may be disappointed in the style and contents, and thus be deterred from purchasing future releases with Benson as star performer. The public may further associate Benson with the blatant sexual appeal of the "Erotic Moods" album and mistakenly believe that Benson endorses "X Rated" material. Thus defendants, attempting to capitalize upon Benson's phenomenal success, have deceitfully packaged and advertised a product that is anathema to Benson, and a threat to his professional standing and personal stature.

CBS, Inc. v. Gusto Records, Inc., 403 F. Supp. 447 (M.D. Tenn. 1974) furnishes considerable guidance although it is clearly distinguishable. There the court declined to enjoin the selling of an album bearing a current likeness of plaintiff Charlie Rich, but containing songs just as they had been recorded by Rich ten to fifteen years before his current success. The court, however, ordered that a decal be affixed to each album to clarify its contents, thus alleviating any harm that might be caused by defendant's violation of § 43(a) of the Lanham Act. The deception is much greater here. Rich in fact was the principal performer in the older recordings and exercised technical and stylistic control over the production of his work. Benson, however, is made to appear as the central and controlling artist when in fact he was not. An explanatory label placed on each "Erotic Moods" album would be inadequate to give Benson the relief to which he is entitled since both the record jackets and the labels on the records themselves contain extensive false information.

Plaintiff's motion for a preliminary injunction is granted.

So Ordered.

Third Story Music, Inc. v. Waits
Court of Appeal of California, Second Appellate District, Division Four
December 28, 1995, Decided
No. B084531.
41 Cal. App. 4th 798

EPSTEIN, Acting P. J.

This case involves a dispute between a company which owned the rights to the musical output of singer/songwriter Tom [801] Waits from 1972 to 1983 and the party which purchased those rights. The issue is whether a promise to market music, or to refrain from doing so, at the election of the promisor is subject to the implied covenant of good faith and fair dealing where substantial consideration has been paid by the promisor. We conclude that the implied convenant does not apply.

### FACTUAL AND PROCEDURAL SUMMARY

According to the complaint, Waits agreed to render his services as a recording artist and songwriter exclusively to Third Story Productions (predecessor in interest to plaintiff and appellant Third Story Music, Inc.) from 1972 to 1983, pursuant to written agreements dated July 1, 1972, and July 1, 1977. Third Story Productions transferred its rights in Waits's music to Asylum Records (predecessor in interest to defendant/respondent Warner Communications, Inc.) on August 31, 1972, and to Elektra/Asylum Records (currently a division of Warner Communications, Inc.) pursuant to an agreement dated June 15, 1977. Under these agreements, TSM was to produce master recordings featuring performances by Waits. Warner obtained from TSM the worldwide right to "manufacture, sell, distribute and advertise records or other reproductions (visual or nonvisual) embodying such recordings, to lease, license, convey or otherwise use or dispose of the recordings by any method now or hereafter known, in any field of use, to release records under any trademarks, trade names or labels, to perform the records or other reproductions publicly and to permit the public performance thereof by radio broadcast, television or any other method now or hereafter known, all upon such terms and conditions as we may approve, and to permit others to do any or all of the foregoing . . .." This clause of the agreements also specifically stated that Warner "may at our election refrain from any or all of the foregoing."

TSM was to receive as a royalty a percentage of the amount earned by Warner from its exploitation of the music. In addition, Warner was required to pay TSM a specific dollar amount as an advance on royalties.

So far as can be ascertained from the record, the parties operated under these agreements without controversy until 1993. At that time, an affiliate of TSM known as Bizarre/Straight Records sought to compile and market an album of previously released Waits compositions, including four which were the subject of the TSM/Warner agreement: On the Nickel, Jitterbug Boy, Invitation to the Blues, and Ruby's Arms. Bizarre/Straight presented a licensing proposal to Warner through its agent Warner Special Products. During negotiations, Bizarre/Straight and TSM learned that Warner had no objection to the deal, but that it would not be made final unless Waits personally approved the licensing request. For reasons unknown, but which TSM claims have to do with Waits's desire to maximize profit on music created after his association with TSM, Waits refused consent. TSM brought suit for contract damages based on breach of the implied covenant of good faith and fair dealing, claiming that Warner "has created an impediment to [TSM] receiving material benefits under the [parties'] agreements and has wrongfully interjected that requirement [the requirement of Waits's approval] into an unknown number of potentially lucrative licensing arrangements, in so doing preventing at least the issuance of the four licenses described above, and other licenses, which TSM will ascertain through discovery."

Warner demurred to the complaint, alleging that the clause in the agreement permitting it to "at [its] election refrain" from doing anything to profitably exploit the music is controlling and precludes application of any implied covenant. The demurrer was sustained on those grounds. TSM contends on appeal, and argued below, that when a party to a contract is given this type of discretionary power, that power must be exercised in good faith, and that permitting the artist to decide whether a particular licensing arrangement was or was not acceptable did not represent a good faith exercise.

## DISCUSSION
### I.

When an agreement expressly gives to one party absolute discretion over whether or not to perform, when should the implied covenant of good faith and fair dealing be applied to limit its discretion? Both sides rely on different language in the recent Supreme Court decision in Carma Developers (Cal.), Inc. v. Marathon Development California, Inc. (1992) 2 Cal. 4th 342 [6 Cal. Rptr. 2d 467, 826 P.2d 710] to answer that question. In Carma, the parties had entered into a lease agreement which stated that if the tenant procured a potential sublessee and asked the landlord for consent to sublease, the landlord had the right to terminate the lease, enter into negotiations with the prospective sublessee, and appropriate for itself all profits from the new arrangement. In the passage relied on by TSM, the court recognized that "[t]he covenant of good faith finds particular application in situations where one party is invested with a discretionary power affecting the rights of another." (2 Cal. 4th at p. 372.) The court expressed the view that "[s]uch power must be exercised in good faith." (Ibid.)

At the same time, the Carma court upheld the right of the landlord to freely exercise its discretion to terminate the lease in order to claim for itself—and deprive the tenant of—all profit from the expected sublease. In this regard, the court stated: "We are aware of no reported case in which a court has held the covenant of good faith may be read to prohibit a party from doing that which is expressly permitted by an agreement. On the contrary, as a general matter, implied terms should never be read to vary express terms. [Citations.] 'The general rule [regarding the covenant of good faith] is plainly subject to the exception that the parties may, by express provisions of the contract, grant the right to engage in the very acts and conduct which would otherwise have been forbidden by an implied covenant of good faith and fair dealing. . .. [P] This is in accord with the general principle that, in interpreting a contract "an implication . . . should not be made when the contrary is indicated in clear and express words." 3 Corbin, Contracts, § 564, p. 298 (1960). . .. [P] As to acts and conduct authorized by the express provisions of the contract, no covenant of good faith and fair dealing can be implied which forbids such acts and conduct. And if defendants were given the right to do what they did by the express provisions of the contract there can be no breach.' " (2 Cal. 4th at p. 374, quoting VTR, Incorporated v. Goodyear Tire & Rubber Company (S.D.N.Y. 1969) 303 F. Supp. 773, 777-778.)

In reaching its holding, the court cited with approval three cases in which discretionary powers were upheld despite claims that they were not exercised in good faith: Gerdlund v. Electronic Dispensers International (1987) 190 Cal. App. 3d 263 [235 Cal. Rptr. 279]; Brandt v. Lockheed Missiles & Space Co. (1984) 154 Cal. App. 3d 1124 [201 Cal. Rptr. 746]; and Balfour, Guthrie & Co. v. Gourmet Farms (1980) 108 Cal. App. 3d 181 [166 Cal. Rptr. 422]. (2 Cal. 4th at pp. 374-376.)

In situations such as the present one, where a discretionary power is expressly given by the contractual language, the quoted passages from Carma set up an apparent inconsistency between the principle that the covenant of good faith should be applied to restrict exercise of a discretionary power and the principle that an implied covenant must never vary the express terms of the parties' agreement. We attempt to reconcile the two.

## II.

We first emphasize a long-established rule concerning implied covenants. To be imposed " '(1) the implication must arise from the language used or it must be indispensable to effectuate the intention of the parties; (2) it must appear from the language used that it was so clearly within the contemplation of the parties that they deemed it unnecessary to express it; (3) implied covenants can only be justified on the grounds of legal necessity; (4) a promise can be implied only where it can be rightfully assumed that it would have been made if attention had been called to it; (5) there can be no implied covenant where the subject is completely covered by the contract.' " ( Lippman v. Sears, Roebuck & Co. (1955) 44 Cal. 2d 136, 142 [280 P.2d 775]; City of Glendale v. Superior Court (1993) 18 Cal. App. 4th 1768, 1778 [23 Cal. Rptr. 2d 305].)

With this in mind, we review the authorities cited in Carma for the proposition that a discretionary power must be exercised in good faith. In Perdue v. Crocker National Bank (1985) 38 Cal. 3d 913 [216 Cal. Rptr. 345, 702 P.2d 503], a bank was given discretion to set nonsufficient fund (NSF) charges to be paid by the customer. The contention was made that since the charges were subject to the bank's sole discretion, the contract lacked mutuality and was, in fact, illusory. (See Automatic Vending Co. v. Wisdom (1960) 182 Cal. App. 2d 354, 357 [6 Cal. Rptr. 31] [" 'An agreement that provides that the price to be paid, or other performance to be rendered, shall be left to the will and discretion of one of the parties is not enforceable' "].) By its ruling that " '[u]nder California law, an open term in a contract must be filled in by the party having discretion within the standard of good faith and fair dealing,' " the court in Perdue was able to impose an objective standard and save an otherwise illusory agreement. (38 Cal. 3d at p. 924, quoting Lazar v. Hertz Corp. (1983) 143 Cal. App. 3d 128, 141 [191 Cal. Rptr.  [805]  849].) Interjection of the implied covenant was " 'indispensable to effectuate the intention of the parties' " and was " 'justified [by] legal necessity.' " ( Lippman v. Sears, Roebuck & Co., supra, 44 Cal. 2d at p. 142.)

The same resolution was reached in Cal. Lettuce Growers v. Union Sugar Co. (1955) 45 Cal. 2d 474 [289 P.2d 785, 49 A.L.R.2d 496], where it was alleged that a contract permitting the buyer of sugar beets to set the price to be paid was illusory. The court implied an obligation to set the price fairly in accordance with the covenant of good faith and fair dealing, thus protecting the enforceability of the agreement. ( Id. at p. 484.)

In the same vein, covenants to use "good faith" or "best efforts" to generate profits for the licensor are routinely implied where the licensor grants exclusive promotional or licensing rights in exchange for a percentage of profits or royalties, but the licensee does not expressly promise to do anything. (See, e.g., Zilg v. Prentice-Hall, Inc. (2d Cir. 1983) 717 F.2d 671, 679-681 [43 A.L.R4th

1163] [discussing the difference between "best efforts" and "good faith"].) As Justice Cardozo put it in one of the earliest cases involving this type of arrangement, Wood v. Lucy, Lady Duff- Gordon (1917) 222 N.Y. 88 [118 N.E. 214], "It is true that [the licensee] does not promise in so many words that he will use reasonable efforts to place the [licensor's] indorsements and market her designs. We think, however, that such a promise is fairly to be implied. The law has outgrown its primitive stage of formalism when the precise word was the sovereign talisman, and every slip was fatal. It takes a broader view today. A promise may be lacking, and yet the whole writing may be 'instinct with an obligation,' imperfectly expressed. [Citations.] If that is so, there is a contract." (222 N.Y. at pp. 90-91 [118 N.Ed. at p. 214.)

In each of these cases, the courts were forced to resolve contradictory expressions of intent from the parties: the intent to give one party total discretion over its performance and the intent to have a mutually binding agreement. In that situation, imposing the duty of good faith creates a binding contract where, despite the clear intent of the parties, one would not otherwise exist. Faced with that choice, courts prefer to imply a covenant at odds with the express language of the contract rather than literally enforce a discretionary language clause and thereby render the agreement unenforceable. As was said in the most recent edition of Corbin's treatise on contracts: "The complaint that a promise is illusory often comes in rather poor grace from the addressee of the allegedly illusory promise, particularly where the addressor is ready and willing to carry out the expression of intention. For this reason, courts are quite properly prone to examine the context to conclude that the escape hatch was intended to be taken only 'in good faith' or in the 'exercise of a reasonable discretion' or upon some other condition not wholly within the control of the promisor. In which case, the conclusion is that the promise is not illusory." (1 Corbin, Contracts, supra, § 1.17, p. 49.) "The tendency of the law is to avoid the finding that no contract arose due to an illusory promise when it appears that the parties intended a contract. . ... An implied obligation to use good faith is enough to avoid the finding of an illusory promise." (2 Corbin, Contracts, supra, § 5.28 at pp. 149-150.)

The need to reconcile contradictory expressions of intent was also the underlying consideration in April Enterprises, Inc. v. KTTV (1983) 147 Cal. App. 3d 805 [195 Cal. Rptr. 421], cited by TSM. The contract at issue there contained an express provision allowing one party to erase tapes of a television show produced by the other after broadcast. At the same time, another provision gave the producer the right to sell the old shows in syndication. The producer brought suit for breach of contract and breach of implied covenant after it discovered some of the tapes had been erased. On appeal from a judgment dismissing the complaint without leave to amend, the court acknowledged "[t]he traditional rule" that "a covenant of fair dealing will not be implied to vary the terms of an unambiguous contract." (147 Cal. App. 3d at p. 816.) Nevertheless, the court reversed because of the possibility that the contradictory terms could be reconciled by construing the erasure clause to be limited by the implied covenant of good faith and fair dealing. The court noted, "[i]n the case of a contradictory and ambiguous contract . . . the implied covenant may be applied to aid in construction." (Ibid.)

The court in April Enterprises used the implied covenant to interpret an ambiguous discretionary power. As we have seen, the implied covenant of good faith is also applied to contradict an express contractual grant of discretion when necessary to protect an agreement which otherwise would be rendered illusory and unenforceable. Does a different result ensue where the contract is unambiguous, otherwise supported by adequate consideration, and the implied covenant is not needed to effectuate the parties' expressed desire for a binding agreement? We believe it does, and the cases cited by the court in Carma illustrate this point.

In Balfour, Guthrie & Co. v. Gourmet Farms, supra, a grain producer and a broker contracted for the purchase of grain at a price to be set in the future based on whatever the market was charging when the price was set. The broker paid a specified amount up front and had discretion to set the final price at any time after a missed margin call. Margin calls could be made if the value of the grain dropped a certain percentage below the amount paid up front. After the value dropped, and the producer missed a margin call, the broker set the price in a falling market. The producer contended this violated the covenant of good faith and "deprive[d] [it] of the fruits of its contract." (108 Cal. App. 3d at pp. 183-184.) Relying on the principle that "[a]cts in accord with the terms of one's contract cannot without more be equated with bad faith," the court concluded that the broker could exercise the discretion given by the contract to support its own commercial interest at the expense of the producers. ( Id. at pp. 190-191.)

In Brandt v. Lockheed Missiles & Space Co., supra, the employment contract at issue provided that when an employee's invention was deemed of sufficient value to apply for a patent and the patent application was granted, the employee would in all cases receive a total award of $ 600. In addition, the agreement said the employer "may, but is not obligated" to grant to any employee an additional "Special Invention Award." In response to two employees' claims that failure to make an adequate Special Invention Award in their case violated the covenant of good faith, the court held: "Few principles of our law are better settled, than that '[t]he language of a contract is to govern its interpretation, if the language is clear and explicit. . ..' [Citations.] [P] Here the language of the parties' contract of employment, i.e., the patent plan, could not be more clear and explicit. It says Lockheed's Invention Awards Committee 'may, but is not obligated to grant a Special Invention Award,' and that its decision on such matters 'shall be final and conclusive.' Lockheed had fully respected the patent plan's language; it may not reasonably be said that in doing so it violated 'a duty of good faith and fair dealing.' " (154 Cal. App. 3d at pp. 1129-1130.)

In Gerdlund v. Electronic Dispensers International, supra, 190 Cal. App. 3d 263, a party's right to exercise an option to terminate a sales representative agreement was at issue. The contract stated "[n]otice of termination may be given at any time and for any reason" on 30 days' notice. The appellate court reversed the trial court's use of the covenant of good faith to impose a requirement of cause for termination on the ground that "[n]o obligation can be implied . . . which would result in the obliteration of a right expressly given under a written contract. . . ." (190 Cal. App. 3d at pp. 268, 277.) The 30-day notice requirement supplied sufficient consideration. (See R.J. Cardinal Co. v. Ritchie (1963) 218 Cal. App. 2d 124, 143 [32 Cal. Rptr. 545] ["A contract may contain a valid provision giving one or either of the parties thereto an option to terminate it within a certain time or on specified conditions. [Citations.] . . . [P] . . . [A] provision for termination by one or either party after notice for a fixed period is enforceable and does not render the contract illusory."])

In each of these cases, as in Carma, one of the parties was expressly given a discretionary power but regardless of how such power was exercised, the agreement would have been supported by adequate consideration. There was no tension between the parties' express agreement and their intention to be bound, and no necessity to impose an implied covenant to create mutuality. The conclusion to be drawn is that courts are not at liberty to imply a covenant directly at odds with a contract's express grant of discretionary power except in those relatively rare instances when reading the provision literally would, contrary to the parties' clear intention, result in an unenforceable, illusory agreement. In all other situations where the contract is unambiguous, the express language is to govern, and "[n]o obligation can be implied . . . which would result in the obliteration of a right expressly given under a written contract." ( Gerdlund v. Electronic Dispensers International, supra, 190 Cal. App. 3d at pp. 277-278.)

## III.

We turn to the question of whether it is necessary in this case to imply a covenant of good faith to protect the enforceability of the contract, or otherwise to effectuate the clear and obvious intent of the parties.

The TSM/Warner agreement states that Warner may market the Waits recordings, or "at [its] election" refrain from all marketing efforts. Read literally, as the trial court did and respondent would have us do, this is a textbook example of an illusory promise. At the same time, there can be no question that the parties intended to enter into an enforceable contract with binding promises on both sides. Were this the only consideration given by Warner, a promise to use good faith would necessarily be implied under the authorities discussed.

The illusory promise was not, however, the only consideration given by the licensee. Under paragraph 33 of the 1977 agreement and paragraph 34 of the 1972 agreement, Warner promised to pay TSM a guaranteed minimum amount no matter what efforts were undertaken. It follows that, whether or not an implied covenant is read into the agreement, the agreement would be supported by consideration and would be binding.

As we see it, Warner bargained for and obtained all rights to Waits's 1972 to 1983 musical output, and paid legally adequate consideration. That it chose not to grant a license in a particular instance cannot be the basis for complaint on the part of TSM as long as Warner made the agreed minimum payments and paid royalties when it did exploit the work. "The courts cannot make better agreements for parties than they themselves have been satisfied to enter into or rewrite contracts because they operate harshly or inequitably. It is not enough to say that without the proposed implied covenant, the contract would be improvident or unwise or would operate unjustly. Parties have the right to make such agreements. The law refuses to read into contracts anything by way of implication except upon grounds of obvious necessity." ( Walnut Creek Pipe Distributors, Inc. v. Gates Rubber Co. (1964) 228 Cal. App. 2d 810, 815 [39 Cal. Rptr. 767].) TSM was free to accept or reject the bargain offered and cannot look to the courts to amend the terms that prove unsatisfactory.

## IV.

In its complaint, TSM asserted four causes of action against Warner—breach of contract, conspiracy, rescission, and declaratory relief. All were based on the existence of a duty of good faith in exercising the discretion given to the licensee. As we agree with the trial court that no such duty existed, demurrer was properly sustained to all four causes of action.

DISPOSITION

The judgment is affirmed.

————————

Famous "gravel-voiced" singer Tom Waits is sued by his former music producer, for, essentially, not participating in a project proposed by music producer pursuant to agreements that the parties had operated under for a number of years. The court found for Tom Waits and his record company since there could be no implied covenant by the court to change a clear contractual provision. That is, a clause in the disputed contract, which gave record company absolute discretion as to whether to perform could not be contradicted.

516 Music Industry Contracts

The following case, *Elvis Presley Enterprises Inc. v. Capece,* 141 F.3d 188 (5th Cir. 1998), is the famous "The Velvet Elvis" case  where the court held that "the Velvet Elvis" bar (in Houston—been there—nothing special) infringed on plaintiff's marks.

Elvis Presley Enters. v. Capece
United States Court of Appeals for the Fifth Circuit
May 7, 1998, Decided
No. 97-20096
141 F.3d 188

KING, Circuit Judge:

Plaintiff-appellant Elvis Presley Enterprises, Inc. appeals the district court's judgment that defendants-appellees' service mark, "The Velvet Elvis," does not infringe or dilute its federal and common-law trademarks and does not violate its right of publicity in Elvis Presley's name. See Elvis Presley Enters. v. Capece, 950 F. Supp. 783 (S.D. Tex. 1996). Because the district court failed to consider the impact of defendants-appellees' advertising practices on their use of the service mark and misapplied the doctrine of parody in its determination that "The Velvet Elvis" mark did not infringe Elvis Presley Enterprises, Inc.'s marks, we reverse the district court's judgment on the trademark infringement claims and remand the case for entry of an injunction enjoining the use of the infringing mark.

## I. BACKGROUND

Plaintiff-appellant Elvis Presley Enterprises, Inc. (EPE) is the assignee and registrant of all trademarks, copyrights, and publicity rights belonging to the Elvis Presley estate. EPE has at least seventeen federal trademark registrations, as well as common-law trademarks, for "Elvis Presley" or "Elvis" and other registrations for his likeness. However, none of these marks is registered for use in the restaurant and tavern business. Prior to trial, EPE announced plans to open a Memphis nightclub as part of a possible worldwide chain. The Memphis nightclub opened subsequent to trial. EPE licenses a wide variety of products and operates Graceland, Elvis's home, as a tourist attraction with adjacent retail stores and restaurants. Over 700,000 visitors per year come from all fifty states and from around the world to visit Graceland. Merchandise sales have brought in over $ 20 million in revenue over a five-year period and account for the largest portion of EPE's revenue.

In April 1991, defendant-appellee Barry Capece, operating through the limited partnership Beers 'R' Us, opened a nightclub on Kipling Street in Houston, Texas called "The Velvet Elvis." On August 28, 1991, Capece filed a federal service mark application for "The Velvet Elvis" for restaurant and tavern services with the United States Patent and Trademark Office (PTO). In December

1992, the service mark was published in the Official Gazette of the United States Patent and Trademark Office as required by 15 U.S.C. § 1062(a). EPE was aware of this publication, but did not file an opposition to the mark's registration within thirty days under 15 U.S.C. § 1063. Accordingly, the PTO issued a service mark registration to Capece for use of "The Velvet Elvis" mark on March 9, 1993. The Kipling Street nightclub closed in July 1993 for business reasons.

After the Kipling Street location's closing, Capece began soliciting investors to reopen the nightclub at a new location. The new nightclub, to be located on Richmond Avenue, would have the same name, "The Velvet Elvis," but it would be run by a new limited partnership, Velvet, Ltd. Audley, Inc. is the general partner of Velvet, Ltd., and Capece is the sole shareholder of Audley, Inc. Capece began renovating the new location in January 1994. In July 1994, EPE contacted Capece by letter, threatening him with legal action if the bar opened with "Elvis" in its name. The Richmond Avenue location opened in August 1994 under the name "The Velvet Elvis."

The Defendants' bar serves a wide variety of food and liquor, including premium scotches and bourbons. The menu items range from appetizers to full entrees. Live music is regularly featured at the bar, and the bar claims to be the first cigar bar in Houston. Its decor includes velvet paintings of celebrities and female nudes, including ones of Elvis and a bare-chested Mona Lisa. Other "eclectic" decorations include lava lamps, cheap ceramic sculptures, beaded curtains, and vinyl furniture. Playboy centerfolds cover the men's room walls.

In addition to the velvet painting of Elvis, the bar's menu and decor include other Elvis references. The menu includes "Love Me Blenders," a type of frozen drink; peanut butter and banana sandwiches, a favorite of Elvis's; and "Your Football Hound Dog," a hotdog. The menu bears the caption "The King of Dive Bars," and one menu publicized "Oscar at The Elvis," an Academy Awards charity benefit to be held at the bar. Numerous magazine photographs of Elvis, a statuette of Elvis playing the guitar, and a bust of Elvis were also among the decorations. By the time of trial, many of these decorations had been removed from the Defendants' bar and replaced with non-Elvis items.

Pictures and references to Elvis Presley appeared in advertising both for the Kipling Street location and for the Richmond Avenue location from the date it opened through early 1995, and some ads emphasized the "Elvis" portion of the name by "boldly displaying the 'Elvis' portion of 'The Velvet Elvis' insignia with an almost unnoticeable 'Velvet' appearing alongside in smaller script." Elvis Presley Enters. v. Capece, 950 F. Supp. 783, 789 (S.D. Tex. 1996). The Defendants made direct references to Elvis and Graceland in advertisements with phrases such as "The King Lives," "Viva la Elvis," "Hunka-Hunka Happy Hour," and "Elvis has not left the building." Advertisements also included a crown logo above the "V" in "The Velvet Elvis" mark. Advertised promotional events at the Defendants' bar have included parties commemorating Elvis's birth and death and appearances by Elvis impersonators and Elvis Presley's drummer. Some advertisements publicizing the opening of the Richmond Avenue location included direct references to Elvis and used the tag-line "the legend continues" without using "The Velvet Elvis" mark.

In April 1995, EPE filed suit against the Defendants, alleging claims for federal and common-law unfair competition and trademark infringement, federal trademark dilution, and violation of its state-law rights of publicity in Elvis Presley's name and likeness. EPE sought injunctive relief, costs, attorneys' fees, and an order to the Commissioner of Patents and Trademarks to cancel Capece's registration for "The Velvet Elvis." The case was tried to the district court, which ruled in favor of EPE on its claims of trademark infringement and unfair competition relating to the Defendants' advertising practices, but not those claims relating to their use of "The Velvet Elvis" service mark. Id. at 796-97. In addition, the court ruled in favor of EPE on its right of publicity claim in relation to the use of Elvis's name and likeness, but again not in relation to the use of "The Velvet Elvis" service mark. Id. at 801-02. As to the claims upon which EPE succeeded, the district court granted injunctive relief barring the use, in connection with the promotion or advertising of the bar, of "the image or likeness of Elvis Presley, phrases that are inextricably linked to the identity of Elvis, or from displaying the 'Elvis' portion of their service mark in print larger than that used for its counterpart 'Velvet.'" Id. at 803. Upon all other claims, the district court ruled in favor of the Defendants and denied all other relief. Id. EPE now appeals.

## II. DISCUSSION

EPE has appealed that portion of the district court's judgment denying relief on its trademark infringement claims, its federal dilution claim, and its right of publicity claim based only upon the Defendants' use of "The Velvet Elvis" mark and the district court's denial of an accounting of profits and attorneys' fees. Because it ruled in favor of the Defendants, the district court did not reach their defenses of laches or acquiescence. The Defendants reassert these defenses on appeal as alternative bases for affirming the district court's judgment. We consider each issue in turn.

### A. Trademark Infringement

The district court clearly stated EPE's claim:

[EPE] claims the inclusion of its "Elvis" trademark in the service mark "The Velvet Elvis" coupled with Defendants' use of the image and likeness of Elvis Presley in advertising, promoting, and rendering bar services creates confusion as to whether EPE licensed, approved, sponsored, endorsed or is otherwise affiliated with "The Velvet Elvis," constituting unfair competition and trademark infringement under the common law and Lanham Act.

950 F. Supp. at 789. The district court also correctly stated the generally applicable law in this circuit to a trademark infringement claim. Id. at 789-91. First, we will summarize this applicable law and then examine the district court's decision.

### 1. Applicable law

For EPE to prevail on its trademark infringement claim, it must show that the Defendants' use of "The Velvet Elvis" mark and image, likeness, and other referents to Elvis Presley creates a likelihood of confusion in the minds of potential consumers as to the source, affiliation, or sponsorship of the Defendants' bar. See Society of Fin. Exam'rs v. National Ass'n of Certified Fraud Exam'rs, Inc., 41 F.3d 223, 227 (5th Cir.), cert. denied, 515 U.S. 1103, 132 L. Ed. 2d 255, 115 S. Ct. 2247 (1995); Oreck Corp. v. U.S. Floor Sys., Inc., 803 F.2d 166, 170 (5th Cir. 1986); see also 15 U.S.C. §§ 1114(1), 1125(a)(1)(A). Liability for trademark infringement hinges upon whether a likelihood of confusion exists between the marks at issue. See Society of Fin. Exam'rs, 41 F.3d at 227. Likelihood of confusion is synonymous with a probability of confusion, which is more than a mere possibility of confusion. See Blue Bell Bio-Med. v. Cin-Bad, Inc., 864 F.2d 1253, 1260 (5th Cir. 1989); see also 3 J. THOMAS MCCARTHY, MCCARTHY ON TRADEMARKS AND UNFAIR COMPETITION § 23:3 (4th ed. 1997). A determination of a likelihood of confusion under federal law is the same as the determination of a likelihood of confusion under Texas law for a trademark infringement claim. See Zapata Corp. v. Zapata Trading Int'l, Inc., 841 S.W.2d 45, 47 (Tex. App.—Houston [14th Dist.] 1992, no writ) (applying Texas law to a trademark infringement claim); see also Blue Bell Bio-Med., 864 F.2d at 1261 (citing Chevron Chem. Co. v. Voluntary Purchasing Groups, Inc., 659 F.2d 695, 706 (5th Cir. Unit A Oct. 1981) (applying Texas law to an unfair trade practices claim)).

In determining whether a likelihood of confusion exists, this court considers the following nonexhaustive list of factors: (1) the type of trademark allegedly infringed, (2) the similarity between the two marks, (3) the similarity of the products or services, (4) the identity of the retail outlets and purchasers, (5) the identity of the advertising media used, (6) the defendant's intent, and (7) any evidence of actual confusion. See Conan Properties, Inc. v. Conans Pizza, Inc., 752 F.2d 145, 149 (5th Cir. 1985). No one factor is dispositive, and a finding of a likelihood of confusion does not even require a positive finding on a majority of these "digits of confusion." Id. at 150; see also Society of Fin. Exam'rs, 41 F.3d at 228 & n.15. In addition to the listed factors, a court is free to consider other relevant factors in determining whether a likelihood of confusion exists. See

Armco, Inc. v. Armco Burglar Alarm Co., 693 F.2d 1155, 1160-61 (5th Cir. 1982). Parody is one such other relevant factor that a court may consider in a likelihood-of-confusion analysis. See Dr. Seuss Enters. v. Penguin Books USA, Inc., 109 F.3d 1394, 1405 (9th Cir.), cert. dismissed, 138 L. Ed. 2d 1057, 118 S. Ct. 27 (1997); Nike, Inc. v. "Just Did It" Enters., 6 F.3d 1225, 1231 (7th Cir. 1993) (holding that parody is not an affirmative defense to trademark infringement but that it can be an additional factor in a likelihood-of-confusion analysis); Jordache Enters. v. Hogg Wyld, Ltd., 828 F.2d 1482, 1486 (10th Cir. 1987) (considering parody as a factor in determining whether a likelihood of confusion exists).

Neither the trademark and service mark registrations of EPE or the service mark registration of Capece disposes of EPE's trademark infringement claim. Proof of registration of a service mark or trademark is only prima facie evidence of the registrant's exclusive right to use the mark in commerce for the services specified in the registration. 15 U.S.C. § 1115(a). However, such proof does "not preclude another person from proving any legal or equitable defense or defect . . . which might have been asserted if such mark had not been registered." Id. A registration only becomes conclusive evidence of a registrant's exclusive right to use a mark after five consecutive years of continuous use in commerce, subject to a few enumerated defenses. Id. §§ 1065, 1115(b). "The Velvet Elvis" mark has not become incontestable, but Capece's registration of the mark constitutes prima facie evidence of the mark's validity and that there is no likelihood of confusion with previously registered marks. See id. § 1115(a). EPE's registration of the Elvis and Elvis Presley marks establishes that it is entitled to protection from infringement by junior users, thereby meeting the threshold requirement that the plaintiff must possess a protectible mark, which must be satisfied before infringement can be actionable. Id. §§ 1052(d), 1057, 1115(a); see also Soweco, Inc. v. Shell Oil Co., 617 F.2d 1178, 1184 (5th Cir. 1980).

2. The decision below

After correctly summarizing the applicable law, the district court then proceeded to consider EPE's trademark infringement and unfair competition claims. In doing so, the court explicitly isolated its consideration of "The Velvet Elvis" mark and the bar's decor from any consideration of the Defendants' advertising and promotional practices. Elvis Presley Enters., 950 F. Supp. at 791, 797.

a. Service mark and the bar's decor

Beginning with the bar's decor and "The Velvet Elvis" mark, the district court considered each of the digits of confusion in turn. First, on the type of mark, the district court found that EPE has strong marks, but that the "Defendants' use of the service mark 'The Velvet Elvis' when combined with the bar's gaudy decor forms an integral part of Defendants' parody of the faddish, eclectic bars of the sixties." Id. at 792. The district court found that the mark "symbolizes tacky,'cheesy,' velvet art, including, but not limited to velvet Elvis paintings" and that "the image of Elvis, conjured up by way of velvet paintings, has transcended into an iconoclastic form of art that has a specific meaning in our culture, which surpasses the identity of the man represented in the painting." Id. Despite EPE's strong marks which would normally be accorded broad protection, the bar's parody of "faddish, eclectic bars of the sixties" led the district court to find that the name and decor of the bar would not mislead consumers and that this digit weighed against a likelihood of confusion. Id. at 793.

Second, on the similarity of the marks, the district court found that "The Velvet Elvis" has a meaning independent from Elvis Presley. Specifically, the district court concluded that "The Velvet Elvis" "is symbolic of a faddish art style" that "has no specific connection with the singer other than the coincidence of its use to portray him." Id. The district court noted that "'the proper test is whether the average consumer, upon encountering the allegedly infringing mark in the isolated circumstances of the marketplace . . . would be likely to confuse or associate the defendant or his services with the plaintiff.'" Id. (quoting American Auto. Ass'n v. AAA Ins. Agency, 618 F. Supp. 787, 792 (W.D. Tex. 1985)). Because of the dissimilarity in the meanings of the Defendants' and EPE's marks, the district court found that this digit of confusion weighed against a likelihood of confusion. Id.

Third, on the similarity of the products and services, the district court noted that, at the time of trial, there was some overlap between the parties' services, but that the services were not directly competitive because they served different clienteles and had different purposes. Id. at 794. While noting that EPE's plan to open a chain of Elvis Presley nightclubs might weigh in favor of a likelihood of confusion, the district court found that "the relative clarity of 'The Velvet Elvis'' parodic purpose" made it dissimilar from any business that EPE currently operates or has plans to operate. The district court thus concluded that this digit weighed against a likelihood of confusion. Id.

Fourth, on the identity of the retail outlets and purchasers, the district court found that the majority of EPE's customers are "middle-aged white women" and that the Defendants' customers are generally "young professionals, ranging in age from early twenties to late thirties." Id. at 794. In the district court's analysis, this disparity between the customers weighed against a likelihood of confusion. Id. (relying upon Amstar Corp. v. Domino's Pizza, Inc., 615 F.2d 252, 262 (5th Cir. 1980)).

Fifth, on the identity of the advertising media, the district court found that this digit of confusion was irrelevant to the determination of a likelihood of confusion because the parties operate in different geographic markets and because EPE admits that it rarely advertises because of the strength of its marks and Elvis's image. 618 F. Supp. at 795.

Sixth, on the Defendants' intent, the district court found that the Defendants intended to parody "a time or concept from the sixties—the Las Vegas lounge scene, the velvet painting craze and perhaps indirectly, the country's fascination with Elvis." Id. The district court noted that the references to Elvis are indirect, but that the "use of his name is an essential part of the parody because the term, 'velvet Elvis,' has become a synonym for garish, passe black velvet art." Id. The district court found that the Defendants' intent weighed against a likelihood of confusion because the "clarity" of the Defendants' parody showed that they did not intend to confuse the public.

Seventh, on actual confusion, the district court found that EPE failed to show any actual confusion because "each witness acknowledged that once inside 'The Velvet Elvis' and given an opportunity to look around, each had no doubt that the bar was not associated or in any way affiliated with EPE." Id. at 796. Additionally, the district court considered the fact that the Defendants' bar had been in operation at the Richmond Avenue location without any complaints or inquiries about the affiliation of the bar with EPE. Id. Relying upon this evidence, the district found that this digit of confusion weighed against a likelihood of confusion.

Having found none of the digits of confusion weighing in favor of a likelihood of confusion, the district court found no likelihood of confusion in relation to the bar's decor or "The Velvet Elvis" mark, and therefore found that the use of the Defendants' mark caused no infringement.

b. The Defendants' advertising practices

The district court next turned to the Defendants' advertising practices and found that their advertising scheme would leave the ordinary customer with

the distinct impression that the bar's purpose was to pay tribute to Elvis Presley or to promote the sale of EPE related products and services. Consequently, use of this [advertising scheme] can only indicate a marketing scheme based on the tremendous drawing power of the Presley name and its ability to attract consumer interest and attention.

Id. at 797. Further, the district court noted that the advertising, without the backdrop of the parody, "will cause confusion, leading customers to wonder if they might find [Elvis] memorabilia" in the bar and that the Defendants' emphasis of the "Elvis" portion of the mark over the "Velvet" portion focusses attention on Elvis and "creates a definite risk that consumers will identify the bar with Presley or EPE." Id. Additionally, the district court found that the Defendants' advertising caused actual confusion. Based upon the above findings the district court found that the Defendants' advertising practices, including the actual configuration of the mark emphasizing "Elvis," constituted trademark infringement and unfair competition. Id.

Despite the facts that the Defendants had discontinued the activity that the district court found to be infringing and that Capece stated that they would not resume the activity, the district court believed that "there [was] a definite possibility that ads including the image or likeness of Elvis Presley, references to Elvis, or his name disproportionately displayed may be used in connection with 'The Velvet Elvis' again." Id. at 803. Even after acknowledging that the cessation of activity might make an injunction unavailable, the court issued an injunction barring the use in the Defendants' advertising of "the image and likeness of Elvis Presley, phrases that are inextricably linked to the identity of Elvis, or from displaying the 'Elvis' portion of their service mark in print larger than that used for its counterpart 'Velvet.'" Id.

### 3. Standard of review

We review questions of law de novo and questions of fact for clear error. Joslyn Mfg. Co. v. Koppers Co., 40 F.3d 750, 753 (5th Cir. 1994). Likelihood of confusion is a question of fact reviewed for clear error. Society of Fin. Exam'rs, 41 F.3d at 225; Blue Bell Bio-Med., 864 F.2d at 1260. However, "the 'clearly erroneous' standard of review does not insulate factual findings premised upon an erroneous view of controlling legal principles." Johnson v. Hospital Corp. of Am., 95 F.3d 383, 395 (5th Cir. 1996) (citing Johnson v. Uncle Ben's, Inc., 628 F.2d 419, 422 (5th Cir. 1980), vacated on other grounds, 451 U.S. 902, 101 S. Ct. 1967, 68 L. Ed. 2d 290 (1981)); see also In re Auclair, 961 F.2d 65, 69 n.7 (5th Cir. 1992) ("Factual findings made under an erroneous view of the law are not binding on the appellate court." (citing 1 STEVEN ALAN CHILDRESS & MARTHA S. DAVIS, FEDERAL STANDARDS OF REVIEW § 2.16, at 2-116 (2d ed. 1992))). When a likelihood-of-confusion factual finding is "inextricably bound up" in, or infected by, a district court's erroneous view of the law, we may conduct a de novo review of the fully-developed record before us. See Anheuser-Busch, Inc. v. Balducci Publications, 28 F.3d 769, 773 (8th Cir. 1994) (applying de novo review where the district court misapplied the First Amendment in relation to parody in its likelihood-of-confusion determination); see also Roto-Rooter Corp. v. O'Neal, 513 F.2d 44, 46-47 (5th Cir. 1975) (reviewing the district court's fact-finding on a likelihood of confusion de novo where it applied the incorrect legal standard).

EPE argues that the district court erroneously applied parody to its likelihood-of-confusion analysis and that this error permeated its entire analysis, infecting nearly all of its findings of fact. Within EPE's discussion of the digits of confusion, it also argues that the district court erred in isolating its consideration of the Defendants' advertising from its consideration of whether "The Velvet Elvis" mark infringes EPE's marks. If the district court erred as EPE argues, then we would review the likelihood-of-confusion finding de novo, rather than for clear error. We will consider the district court's isolation of the advertising evidence from its analysis first.

a. Isolated consideration of advertising

The use of a mark in advertising is highly probative of whether the mark creates a likelihood of confusion in relation to another mark. "Evidence of the context in which a mark is used on labels, packages, or in advertising material directed to the goods is probative of the reaction of prospective purchasers to the mark." In re Abcor Dev. Corp., 588 F.2d 811, 814 (C.C.P.A. 1978). Courts consider marks in the context that a customer perceives them in the marketplace, which includes their presentation in advertisements. See The Sports Auth., Inc. v. Prime Hospitality Corp., 89 F.3d 955, 962 (2d Cir. 1996) (considering the appearance of the mark in advertising in determining similarity of marks); Nikon Inc. v. Ikon Corp., 987 F.2d 91, 94-95 (2d Cir. 1993) (same); Oreck Corp., 803 F.2d at 171 (considering the presentation of the marks in advertising in determining the similarity of the marks and the defendant's intent); Sun Banks of Fla., Inc. v. Sun Fed. Sav. & Loan Ass'n, 651 F.2d 311, 318 (5th Cir. 1981) (considering the presentation of the marks in advertising in determining the similarity of the marks); National Ass'n of Blue Shield Plans v. United Bankers Life Ins. Co., 362 F.2d 374, 378 (5th Cir. 1966) (comparing marks as used in advertising in newspapers and on television where the black and white format did not allow for color distinctions); see also Sun-Maid Raisin Growers v. Sunaid Food Prods., Inc., 356 F.2d 467, 469 (5th Cir. 1966) ("It is the labels that the prospective purchaser sees. The trademarks cannot be isolated from the labels on which they appear.").

In the case of a service mark, advertising is of even greater relevance because the mark cannot be actually affixed to the service, as a trademark is to the goods. Many prospective purchasers first encounter the mark in advertising, rather than on the product; therefore, the service mark cannot be isolated from the advertising in which it appears. See RESTATEMENT (THIRD) OF UNFAIR COMPETITION § 21(a)(i) (1995) (stating that "the overall impression created by the [marks] as they are used in marketing the respective goods and services" is relevant to how similar two marks are (emphasis added)). The Lanham Act itself makes advertising relevant to a service mark infringement claim. In order to infringe another's mark, the infringing mark must be used in commerce. 15 U.S.C. § 1114. By definition, a service mark is used in commerce "when it is used or displayed in the sale or advertising of services." Id. § 1127 (emphasis added). In summary, advertisements used by the alleged infringer, which incorporate the allegedly infringing mark, are relevant in determining whether a mark has been infringed. Advertisements are therefore relevant to the likelihood-of-confusion analysis.

In addition, the context of the presentation of a mark, including advertising, is relevant to the meaning that the mark conveys. McGregor-Doniger Inc. v. Drizzle Inc., 599 F.2d 1126, 1133 (2d Cir. 1979) ("'The setting in which a designation is used affects its appearance and colors the impression conveyed by it.'" (brackets in original) (quoting RESTATEMENT OF TORTS § 729 cmt. b, at 593 (1938))). The Supreme Court has said that "the protection of trade-marks is the law's recognition of the psychological function of symbols." Mishawaka Rubber & Woolen Mfg. Co. v. S.S. Kresge Co., 316 U.S. 203, 205, 86 L. Ed. 1381, 62 S. Ct. 1022 (1942). To understand a symbol's psychological function, one must consider it in the context in which it is used and not in a vacuum. See American Heritage Life Ins. Co. v. Heritage Life Ins. Co., 494 F.2d 3, 11 & n.7 (5th Cir. 1974) ("Words are chameleons, which reflect the color of their environment."); 2 JEROME GILSON, TRADEMARK PROTECTION AND PRACTICE § 5.09[1], at 5-137 n.1 (Jeffrey M. Samuels ed., 1997) (noting that advertising is used by the holders of marks to "establish[] a sufficient aura of desirability to induce the public to purchase" their products and services). Courts have recognized this fact in determining whether a mark has developed a secondary meaning as an indicator of source independent from its everyday meaning, entitling the mark to protection under the Lanham Act. See, e.g., G. Heileman Brewing Co. v. Anheuser-Busch, Inc., 873 F.2d 985, 994-95 (7th Cir. 1989); American Heritage Life Ins. Co, 494 F.2d at 12; Volkswagenwerk Aktiengesellschaft v. Rickard, 492 F.2d 474, 478 (5th Cir. 1974). In an extreme example of a word taking on meaning from the context of its use, the Court of Customs and Patent Appeals found that the word "stain" connoted a "a state of relative cleanliness"—a meaning contrary to its normal meaning—when used in connection with a cleaning product, making marks that included "stain" and "clean" similar despite the aural and optical dissimilarity of the marks. See Procter & Gamble Co. v. Conway, 57 C.C.P.A. 865, 419 F.2d 1332, 1335-36 (C.C.P.A. 1970) (finding that "Mister Stain" infringed "Mr. Clean").

In this case, we are dealing with a service mark, "The Velvet Elvis," which the Defendants have used at their business location and extensively in advertising. To consider only the Defendants' use of the mark at their business location would ignore highly probative evidence of the meaning of the mark as the public encounters it in commerce and of the Defendants' intent in using the mark. By placing the mark in an Elvis context and in configuring the mark to highlight the "Elvis" portion of the mark, the Defendants have placed the mark in a context that does not alone connote tacky, cheesy art as the district court found. This contrary context of the mark has the ability to alter the psychological impact of the mark and must be considered in determining whether the Defendants' mark creates a likelihood of confusion in relation to EPE's marks. In failing to consider the Defendants' presentation of "The Velvet Elvis" mark to the public in advertising in determining whether the Defendants' use of their mark created a likelihood of confusion, the district court failed to consider the mark as perceived by the public. In addition, by isolating the advertising, the district court failed to consider how the Defendants configured the mark in emphasizing the "Elvis" portion of the name, which is highly probative of the impression they intended to convey.

The fact that the Defendants ceased many of the problematic advertising practices after receiving the cease and desist letter and shortly before EPE filed suit does not make the advertising any less relevant to the question of whether the Defendants' use of the "The Velvet Elvis" mark infringes EPE's marks. The cessation of infringing activity does not affect the determination of liability, but it may make an injunction unnecessary. See M-F-G Corp. v. Emra Corp., 817 F.2d 410, 411 (7th Cir. 1987); see also Blisscraft v. United Plastics Co., 294 F.2d 694, 702 (2d Cir. 1961) (finding it necessary to fully consider the liability issue and issue an injunction despite cessation of infringing use); Esquire, Inc. v. Esquire Slipper Mfg. Co., 243 F.2d 540, 542, 546 (1st Cir. 1957) (reversing a decision dismissing an action based upon the defendant's promise to cease infringing conduct because the plaintiff was entitled to an enforceable judgment). In this case, the district court found "a definite possibility," Elvis Presley Enters., 950 F. Supp. at 803, that the Defendants would resume their infringing advertising practices and therefore granted injunctive relief in spite of the Defendants professed intent to discontinue infringing activities. Ceasing the infringing activity does not allow an infringing party to escape liability. See Spring Mills, Inc. v. Ultracashmere House, Ltd., 689 F.2d 1127, 1133 (2d Cir. 1982).

b. Parody

As noted earlier, parody is not a defense to trademark infringement, but rather another factor to be considered, which weighs against a finding of a likelihood of confusion. See Dr. Seuss Enters., 109 F.3d at 1405; 4 MCCARTHY, supra, § 31-153, at 31-222 to 31-223. As a leading treatise has stated,

Some parodies will constitute an infringement, some will not. But the cry of "parody!" does not magically fend off otherwise legitimate claims of trademark infringement or dilution. There are confusing parodies and non-confusing parodies. All they have in common is an attempt at humor through the use of someone else's trademark. A non-infringing parody is merely amusing, not confusing.

4 id. § 31:153, at 31-223 (emphasis added); cf. Dallas Cowboys Cheerleaders, Inc. v. Scoreboard Posters, Inc., 600 F.2d 1184, 1188 (5th Cir. 1979) (noting that parody is relevant to a fair-use defense to copyright infringement but does not establish the defense). Therefore, while not a defense, parody is relevant to a determination of a likelihood of confusion and

can even weigh heavily enough to overcome a majority of the digits of confusion weighing in favor of a likelihood of confusion.

This court has yet to consider parody in relation to trademark law. However, recently in Campbell v. Acuff-Rose Music, Inc., 510 U.S. 569, 127 L. Ed. 2d 500, 114 S. Ct. 1164 (1994), the Supreme Court considered parody in the copyright context, which is relevant to the treatment of parody in the trademark context. See Balducci Publications, 28 F.3d at 776; 4 MCCARTHY, supra, § 31:153, at 31-222; Gary Myers, Trademark Parody: Lessons from the Copyright Decision in Campbell v. Acuff-Rose Music, Inc., LAW & CONTEMP. PROBS., Spring 1996, at 181. The Campbell Court noted that the heart of any parodist's claim to quote from existing material, is the use of some elements of a prior author's composition to create a new one that, at least in part, comments on that author's works. If, on the contrary, the commentary has no critical bearing on the substance or style of the original composition, which the alleged infringer merely uses to get attention or to avoid the drudgery in working up something fresh, the claim to fairness in borrowing from another's work diminishes accordingly (if it does not vanish), and other factors, like the extent of its commerciality, loom larger. Parody needs to mimic an original to make its point, and so has some claim to use the creation of its victim's (or collective victims') imagination, whereas satire can stand on its own two feet and so requires justification for the very act of borrowing.

510 U.S. at 580-81 (emphasis added and citations and footnotes omitted) (considering parody in relation to the fair-use defense to copyright infringement). From the Supreme Court's statements, it is clear that a parody derives its need and justification to mimic the original from its targeting of the original for comment or ridicule. Id. at 588 ("When parody takes aim at a particular original work, the parody must be able to 'conjure up' at least enough of that original to make the object of its critical wit recognizable."). If the original is not a target of the parody, the need to "conjure up" the original decreases as the parody's aim moves away from the original.

This same need to conjure up the original exists when a parody targets a trademark or service mark. In the case of the standard likelihood-of-confusion analysis, a successful parody of the original mark weighs against a likelihood of confusion because, even though it portrays the original, it also sends the message that it is not the original and is a parody, thereby lessening any potential confusion. See Cliffs Notes, Inc. v. Bantam Doubleday Dell Publ'g Group, Inc., 886 F.2d 490, 494 (2d Cir. 1989) ("A parody must convey two simultaneous—and contradictory—messages: that it is the original, but also that it is not the original and is instead a parody."); see also Anheuser-Busch, Inc. v. L & L Wings, Inc., 962 F.2d 316, 321 (4th Cir. 1992); 4 MCCARTHY, supra, § 31:155, at 31-235 ("'The joke itself reinforces the public's association of the mark with the plaintiff.'" (quoting Robert C. Denicola, Trademarks as Speech:

Constitutional Implications of the Emerging Rationales for the Protection of Trade Symbols, 1982 WIS. L. REV. 158, 188)). Therefore, a parody of a mark needs to mimic the original mark and from this necessity arises the justification for the mimicry, but this necessity wanes when the original mark is not the target of the parody.

In this case, the district court found that "The Velvet Elvis" mark, when combined with the bar's gaudy decor, was "an integral part of Defendants' parody of the faddish, eclectic bars of the sixties." Elvis Presley Enters., 950 F. Supp. at 792. The intent was to parody "a time or concept from the sixties—the Las Vegas lounge scene, the velvet painting craze and perhaps indirectly, the country's fascination with Elvis." Id. at 795 (emphasis added). In his testimony, Capece stated that the Defendants "were trying to make fun of the Hardrock Cafes, the Planet Hollywoods, or some of the places that were more pretentious" and that the Defendants could successfully perform their parody without using Elvis Presley's name. This testimony and the district court's analysis both indicate that neither Elvis Presley nor EPE's marks were a target of the Defendants' parody.

The Defendants argue that a parody of society can still parody a celebrity, see Cardtoons, L.C. v. Major League Baseball Players Ass'n, 95 F.3d 959, 972 (10th Cir. 1996) (noting that "a parody of a celebrity does not merely lampoon the celebrity, but exposes the weakness of the idea or value that the celebrity symbolizes in society"), but in Cardtoons, the parody of society was through the parody of the celebrity. Here, we have a direct parody of society that does not even attempt to parody the celebrity—Elvis Presley.

The Defendants' parody of the faddish bars of the sixties does not require the use of EPE's marks because it does not target Elvis Presley; therefore, the necessity to use the marks significantly decreases and does not justify the use. Capece himself conceded that the Defendants could have performed their parody without using Elvis's name. Without the necessity to use Elvis's name, parody does not weigh against a likelihood of confusion in relation to EPE's marks. It is simply irrelevant. As an irrelevant factor, parody does not weigh against or in favor of a likelihood of confusion, and the district court erred in relying upon parody in its determination of the likelihood of confusion.

In its likelihood-of-confusion analysis, the district court made determinations on five of the seven digits of confusion which either ignored relevant advertising evidence or relied upon the Defendants' parody of the sixties lounge scene. These errors have permeated the district court's findings of fact on the likelihood of confusion and on each of those digits of confusion. Therefore, we will review the likelihood-of-confusion determination and those infected findings on the digits of confusion de novo based upon the well-developed record. See Balducci Publications, 28 F.3d 769 at 773; Roto-Rooter Corp., 513 F.2d at 46-47.

4. Likelihood of confusion

In our de novo consideration of the likelihood of confusion, we will accept the district court's findings that the identity of retail outlets and purchasers weighs against a likelihood of confusion and that the identity of advertising media is irrelevant. Neither finding is challenged by the parties nor implicates the district court's errors in isolating the Defendants' advertising practices from the analysis or in its application of parody; therefore, we leave those findings undisturbed. This acceptance leaves the following digits of confusion for our consideration: (1) the type of mark, (2) the similarity of marks, (3) the similarity of products and services, (4) the Defendants' intent, and (5) actual confusion. We consider each digit of confusion in turn and then weigh them to determine whether a likelihood of confusion exists.

a. Type of trademark

The type of trademark refers to the strength of the mark. In looking at the strength of the mark, the focus is the senior user's mark. See RESTATEMENT, supra, § 21(d) & cmt. i; 3 MCCARTHY, supra, § 23:19. The stronger the mark, the greater the protection it receives because the greater the likelihood that consumers will confuse the junior user's use with that of the senior user. RESTATEMENT, supra, § 21 cmt. i; see also Amstar Corp., 615 F.2d at 259.

The Defendants conceded that EPE's marks have "worldwide fame and almost instantaneous recognition," leading the district court to find that EPE's marks are strong. Elvis Presley Enters, 950 F. Supp. at 792. The Defendants do not dispute this on appeal. Rather, the Defendants argue that "The Velvet Elvis" has a different meaning than EPE's marks and that EPE has not shown distinctiveness outside the entertainment industry. However, these issues are more appropriately considered in relation to other digits of confusion. EPE's marks are very strong and therefore strongly weigh in favor of a likelihood of confusion.

b. Similarity of marks

The similarity of the marks in question is determined by comparing the marks' appearance, sound, and meaning. See Jordache Enters., 828 F.2d at 1484; RESTATEMENT, supra, § 21(a); 3 MCCARTHY, supra, § 23:21. "Even if prospective purchasers recognize that the two designations are distinct, confusion may result if purchasers are likely to assume that the similarities in the designations indicate a connection between the two users. The relevant inquiry is whether, under the circumstances of the use," the marks are sufficiently similar that prospective purchasers are likely to believe that the two users are somehow associated. RESTATEMENT, supra, § 21 cmt. c. However, different meanings of otherwise similar marks may overcome a likelihood of confusion that would otherwise result. See 3 MCCARTHY, supra, §§ 23:26, :28; see also Long John Distilleries, Ltd. v. Sazerac Co., 57 C.C.P.A. 1286, 426 F.2d

1406, 1407 (C.C.P.A. 1970) (finding the marks, "Long John" and "Friar John," to have obvious meanings that are in no way suggestive of one another). "In determining the meaning and connotation which the trademark projects, it is proper to look to the context of use, such as material on labels, packaging, advertising and the like." 3 MCCARTHY, supra, § 23:26, at 23-61 (citing In re Nationwide Indus., Inc., 1988 TTAB LEXIS 19, 6 U.S.P.Q.2D (BNA) 1882 (T.T.A.B. 1988)); see also Hormel Foods Corp. v. Jim Henson Prods., Inc., 73 F.3d 497, 503-04 (2d Cir. 1996) (noting the relevance of the placement of the mark next to other dissimilar symbols); discussion supra Part II.A.3.a.

The district court found that "The Velvet Elvis" mark is "symbolic of a faddish art style that belongs to the culture that created it" and that the mark "has no specific connection with [Elvis] other than the coincidence of its use to portray him." Elvis Presley Enters., 950 F. Supp. at 793. The district court made this finding without considering the context into which the Defendants placed their mark. The Defendants used "The Velvet Elvis" mark in advertising that included (1) the image of Elvis Presley; (2) direct references to Graceland and Elvis Presley with phrases such as "The King Lives," "Viva la Elvis," and "Elvis has not left the building"; and (3) the "Elvis" portion of the mark boldly displayed with "an almost unnoticeable 'Velvet' appearing alongside in smaller script." Id. at 789. On one of their menus, the Defendants also advertised "Oscar at The Elvis," an Academy Awards charity benefit to be held at the bar. The context of the Defendants' advertising for the first nine months of operation of the Richmond Avenue location has imbued "The Velvet Elvis" mark with a meaning that directly evokes Elvis Presley, despite any independent meaning the mark might have. Cf. id. at 797 (noting that the Defendants' advertisements in which "Elvis" is emphasized "create a definite risk that consumers will identify the bar with Presley or EPE" and that advertisements using Elvis's image cause confusion). The Defendants' mark's connection to Elvis is enhanced by the inclusion of "Elvis" in the mark and the Defendants' decision to emphasize the "Elvis" portion of the mark, leaving the "Velvet" portion almost unnoticeable. See Lone Star Steakhouse & Saloon, Inc. v. Alpha of Va., Inc., 43 F.3d 922, 936 (4th Cir. 1995) (giving greater weight to the dominant or "salient portions" of a mark); Oreck Corp., 803 F.2d at 171 (focussing on "attention-getting" feature in comparing marks); 3 MCCARTHY, supra, § 23:44 (noting that it is proper to give greater effect to the dominant feature of a mark in the comparison). The Defendants' use of the mark outside this suggestive context where the faddish art style connotation might predominate does not counteract the Defendants' deliberate association with Elvis in their advertising. The connotation of the marks are similar, and this digit of confusion therefore weighs in favor of a likelihood of confusion.

c. Similarity of products and services

"The greater the similarity between products and services, the greater the likelihood of confusion." Exxon Corp. v. Texas Motor Exch. of Houston, Inc., 628 F.2d 500, 505 (5th Cir. 1980). Direct competition between the parties' services or products is not required in order to find a likelihood of confusion. Professional Golfers Ass'n of Am. v. Bankers Life & Cas. Co., 514 F.2d 665, 669-70 (5th Cir. 1975); see also 3 MCCARTHY, supra, §§ 24:13-:14.

One such relationship where this is true exists when the sponsor or maker of one business or product might naturally be assumed to be the maker or sponsor of another business product. . . . The deceived customer buys the infringer's product in the belief that it originates with the trademark owner or that it is in some way affiliated with the owner.

World Carpets, Inc. v. Dick Littrell's New World Carpets, 438 F.2d 482, 488 (5th Cir. 1971), cited in Professional Golfers Ass'n, 514 F.2d at 670. When products or services are noncompeting, the confusion at issue is one of sponsorship, affiliation, or connection. See Kentucky Fried Chicken Corp. v. Diversified Packaging Corp., 549 F.2d 368, 388 (5th Cir. 1977); 3 MCCARTHY, supra, §§ 24:3, :6.

The danger of affiliation or sponsorship confusion increases when the junior user's services are in a market that is one into which the senior user would naturally expand. See RESTATEMENT, supra, § 21(e) & cmt. j. The actual intent of the senior user to expand is not particularly probative of whether the junior user's market is one into which the senior user would naturally expand. Id. cmt. j.; 3 MCCARTHY, supra, § 24:19. Consumer perception is the controlling factor. See Dreyfus Fund Inc. v. Royal Bank of Can., 525 F. Supp. 1108, 1119-20 (S.D.N.Y. 1981) (noting that consumer perception controls over the actual intent of the senior user); 3 MCCARTHY, supra, § 24:19. "If consumers believe, even though falsely, that the natural tendency of producers of the type of goods marketed by the prior user is to expand into the market for the type of goods marketed by the subsequent user, confusion may be likely." RESTATEMENT, supra, § 21 cmt. j.

While we recognize that EPE has plans to open a worldwide chain of Elvis Presley restaurants and has opened its Memphis restaurant since the district court's decision, our proper focus is on (1) whether the products and services of EPE and the Defendants are similar enough to cause confusion as to source or affiliation or (2) whether the Defendants' bar is in a market into which EPE would naturally be perceived to expand. The Velvet Elvis serves food, cigars, and alcohol; provides live music; and sells t-shirts and hats. EPE licenses its marks on a wide variety of products, including t-shirts and hats, and the Defendants concede that EPE's marks are particularly strong in the music, television, and movie industries. EPE also operates family-oriented restaurants and an ice cream parlor at Graceland. Despite the breadth of EPE's licensed products, these products and services may not be similar enough to weigh in favor of a likelihood of confusion, but it is a question that we need not reach.

The pervasiveness of EPE's marks across the spectrum of products and the success and proliferation of entertainment and music-themed restaurants like Planet Hollywood and Hard Rock Cafe—which Capece testified inspired their parody—support a likelihood of confusion. Cf. Armco, 693 F.2d at 1161 ("Diversification makes it more likely that a potential customer would associate the nondiversified company's services with the diversified company, even though the two companies do not actually compete."). These restaurants have led the way, and an Elvis Presley restaurant would be a natural next step due to the public's strong familiarity with such restaurants and with Elvis. Given that EPE licenses so many products and is a strong presence in the entertainment business and that Planet Hollywood and Hard Rock Cafe have shown the success and popularity of entertainment and music-themed restaurants, the restaurant and bar business with live music is a natural area of expansion for EPE, and this digit of confusion weighs in favor of a likelihood of confusion.

d. The Defendants' intent

Proof of an intent to confuse the public is not necessary to a finding of a likelihood of confusion. Fuji Photo Film Co. v. Shinohara Shoji Kabushiki Kaisha, 754 F.2d 591, 597 (5th Cir. 1985) (noting that "'while evil intent may evidence unfair competition and deception, lack of guile is immaterial'" (brackets in original) (quoting Communications Satellite Corp. v. Comcet, Inc., 429 F.2d 1245, 1249 (4th Cir. 1970)); RESTATEMENT, supra, § 22 cmt. b; 3 MCCARTHY, supra, § 23:107. If a mark was adopted with the intent to confuse the public, that alone may be sufficient to justify an inference of a likelihood of confusion. Amstar Corp., 615 F.2d at 263; RESTATEMENT, supra, § 22 cmt. c. A good-faith intent to parody, however, is not an intent to confuse. Nike, 6 F.3d at 1231 (citing Jordache Enters., 828 F.2d 1482 at 1486). If the defendant acted in good faith, then this digit of confusion becomes a nonfactor in the likelihood-of-confusion analysis, rather than weighing in favor of a likelihood of confusion. See Fuji Photo, 754 F.2d at 597-98. However, an innocent intent in adopting a mark does not immunize an intent to confuse in the actual use of the mark. Cf. RESTATEMENT, supra, § 22 cmt. c ("Even if an actor believes in good faith that the copying of another's designation is justified, an inference that confusion is likely may arise from other circumstances that suggest an intent to confuse, such as a failure to take reasonable steps to minimize the risk of confusion.").

The district court found that the Defendants' subjective intent was an intent to parody, rather than an intent to confuse. Based upon this finding, the Defendants' intent would not support a finding of a likelihood of confusion. However, the Defendants' advertisements using the image of Elvis, referencing Elvis, and emphasizing the word "Elvis" in the mark are other circumstances that support an intent to confuse. See Elvis Presley Enters., 950 F. Supp. at 797 (noting that "use of this type of advertisement can only indicate a marketing scheme based on the tremendous drawing power of the Presley name and its ability to attract consumer interest and attention" (emphasis added)). These circumstances increase the risk of confusion and are more than just "a failure to take reasonable steps to minimize the risk of confusion." See RESTATEMENT, supra, § 22 cmt. c. The district court found that Capece's subjective intent in adopting the mark was an intent to parody, but in determining a defendant's intent, evidence of the defendant's actions is highly probative and should be considered. See Oreck Corp., 803 F.2d 166 at 173 ("[The defendant's] actions speak louder than its words . . . ."); 3 MCCARTHY, supra, § 23:113, at 23-216 to 23-217. The Defendants' use of "The Velvet Elvis" mark in their advertising evidences an intent to market the bar by relying upon the drawing power of Elvis, as found by the district court. See Elvis Presley Enters., 950 F. Supp. at 797. Therefore, the facts under this digit of confusion weigh in favor of a likelihood of confusion.

### e. Actual confusion

Evidence of actual confusion is not necessary to a finding of a likelihood of confusion, but "it is nevertheless the best evidence of a likelihood of confusion." Amstar Corp., 615 F.2d at 263. Actual confusion that is later dissipated by further inspection of the goods, services, or premises, as well as post-sale confusion, is relevant to a determination of a likelihood of confusion. See 3 MCCARTHY, supra, §§ 23:6-:7. "Infringement can be based upon confusion that creates initial consumer interest, even though no actual sale is finally completed as a result of the confusion." 3 id. § 23:6; see also Dr. Seuss Enters., 109 F.3d at 1405 (noting that no sale must be completed to show actual confusion); Mobil Oil Co. v. Pegasus Petroleum Corp., 818 F.2d 254, 259 (2d Cir. 1987) (finding liability for initial-interest confusion). Initial-interest confusion gives the junior user credibility during the early stages of a transaction and can possibly bar the senior user from consideration by the consumer once the confusion is dissipated. Id.; 3 MCCARTHY, supra, § 23:6.

EPE presented witnesses who testified that they initially thought the Defendants' bar was a place that was associated with Elvis Presley and that it might have Elvis merchandise for sale. The witnesses all testified that, upon entering and looking around the bar, they had no doubt that EPE was not affiliated with it in any way. Despite the confusion being dissipated, this initial-interest confusion is beneficial to the Defendants because it brings patrons in the door; indeed, it brought at least one of EPE's witnesses into the bar. Once in the door, the confusion has succeeded because some patrons may stay, despite realizing that the bar has no relationship with EPE. This initial-interest confusion is even more significant because the Defendants' bar sometimes charges a cover charge for entry, which allows the Defendants to benefit from initial-interest confusion before it can be dissipated by entry into the bar. Additionally, the finding by the district court that the Defendants' advertising practices caused actual confusion shows that actual confusion occurred when consumers first observed the mark in commerce. See Elvis Presley Enters., 950 F. Supp. at 797 (noting that EPE also established actual confusion in relation to advertisements with "The Velvet Elvis" mark in a context connoting Elvis Presley).

An absence of, or minimal, actual confusion, however, over an extended period of time of concurrent sales weighs against a likelihood of confusion. 615 F.2d at 263 (finding no likelihood of confusion based upon concurrent sales over fifteen years with minimal instances of confusion); see also Oreck Corp., 803 F.2d at 173 (finding no likelihood of confusion based upon concurrent sales over seventeen months with no evidence of actual confusion); RESTATEMENT, supra, § 23(2) & cmt. d. In this case, the lack of complaints is relevant but should have less weight than the district court gave it. Approximately one year after the Richmond location opened, EPE's suit against the Defendants was reported in the press, and this lessens the weight of the lack of complaints because there would be no reason to complain to EPE if one knows EPE is aware of the possible infringer and has begun legal action. In the instant case, the lack of complaints is over a thirteen-month period, which is shorter than the periods in Oreck Corp. (seventeen months) and Amstar Corp. (fifteen years), and actual confusion has been shown by the evidence of initial-interest confusion unlike in Oreck Corp.

Based upon the above facts, this digit of confusion weighs in favor of a likelihood of confusion, and this finding is supported by the district court's finding of actual confusion in relation to the Defendants' advertising practices.

f. Weighing the digits of confusion

After considering the Defendants' advertising practices and dropping parody from the analysis, all five digits of confusion that we considered de novo weigh in favor of a likelihood of confusion, and only the identity of retail outlets and purchasers weighs against a likelihood of confusion. Giving each digit of confusion its due weight, we find that a likelihood of confusion exists between EPE's marks and the Defendants' use of "The Velvet Elvis" mark. Therefore, the Defendants have infringed EPE's marks with the use of their service mark, "The Velvet Elvis."

B. Defenses

The Defendants argue that EPE is barred from seeking relief for their use of "The Velvet Elvis" mark by the defenses of laches or acquiescence. They claim that EPE should have known about their use of "The Velvet Elvis" mark in August 1991 when Capece applied for federal registration of the mark because it uses the services of a trademark search firm to aid it in defending its marks. The Defendants contend that EPE rested on its rights by failing to object when it received actual notice of their conduct by the December 1992 publication of the mark in the PTO's Official Gazette and by failing to protest the Defendants' use until July 1994 when over $ 100,000 had been invested in the Richmond Avenue location and customer loyalty had been built up by the use of the mark at the Kipling Street location.

"Laches is commonly defined as an inexcusable delay that results in prejudice to the defendant." Conan Properties, 752 F.2d at 153. A defense of laches has three elements: "(1) delay in asserting a right or claim; (2) that the delay was inexcusable; [and] (3) that undue prejudice resulted from the delay." Armco, 693 F.2d at 1161. The period for laches begins when the plaintiff knew or should have known of the infringement. Id. at 1161-62. Any acts after receiving a cease and desist letter are at the defendant's own risk because it is on notice of the plaintiff's objection to such acts. See Conan Properties, 752 F.2d at 151-52. Noninfringing use of a mark is not relevant to a defense of laches. See Mead Johnson & Co. v. Baby's Formula Serv., Inc., 402 F.2d 19, 22 (5th Cir. 1968) (finding long years of noninfringing use of mark would not establish laches as to a later infringing use).

EPE knew of the Defendants' use of "The Velvet Elvis" mark when it was published in the PTO's Official Gazette in December 1992. The Defendants have not shown that EPE should have known at an earlier time nor shown why employing a search service should have given EPE that knowledge earlier. After the Kipling Street location's closing, no infringing use of the mark was occurring because the mark was not being used in commerce, and the Richmond Avenue location's opening is not relevant to the laches period because it occurred after the Defendants' receipt of the cease and desist letter. Therefore, the period relevant for the application of laches is eight months, beginning in December 1992 and running until July 1993 when the Kipling Street location closed. We do not find that eight months was an inexcusable delay.

Additionally, even if we assume eight months to be an inexcusable delay or that the relevant period of delay should include the period the Richmond Avenue location was open until suit was filed in April 1995, no undue prejudice has been shown as a result of the delay in this case. Capece has conceded that he did not purchase the signs for the Richmond Avenue location until after he received the cease and desist letter from EPE and that he did not need to use Elvis's name in order to parody his intended target of the "faddish, eclectic bars of the sixties." Changing the name of the bar would not have destroyed the investment of capital in the nightclub. Additionally, the short period of delay here would not justify finding prejudice on the Defendants' claims of customer goodwill from the earlier location.

"Acquiescence involves the plaintiff's implicit or explicit assurances to the defendant which induce[] reliance by the defendant." Conan Properties, 752 F.2d at 153. Other than EPE's silence, the Defendants identify no assurances made by EPE to the Defendants upon which they could have relied. The period of silence relevant to acquiescence would not include any time after the cease and desist letter was sent because EPE explicitly communicated its objection, nor would it include the time while no nightclub was open because permission cannot be inferred from silence in the absence of infringing activity. Cf. Mead Johnson & Co., 402 F.2d 19 at 22. The eight months of silence does not rise to the level of an assurance upon which the Defendants could reasonably rely or by which they could claim to have been induced into reliance.

### III. REMEDIES

EPE appeals the district court's denial of an accounting of profits from the Defendants and its denial of attorneys' fees. Both of these claims were not properly preserved below and are therefore waived. "'It is a well-settled rule that a joint pretrial order signed by both parties supersedes all pleadings and governs the issues and evidence to be presented at trial.'" McGehee v. Certainteed Corp., 101 F.3d 1078, 1080 (5th Cir. 1996) (quoting Branch-Hines v. Hebert, 939 F.2d 1311, 1319 (5th Cir. 1991)). The claims, issues, and evidence are narrowed by the pretrial order, thereby narrowing the trial to expedite the proceeding. See Flannery v. Carroll, 676 F.2d 126, 129 (5th Cir. 1982); see also Branch-Hines, 939 F.2d at 1319 (finding that the pretrial order asserted the plaintiff's full range of damages); Morales v. Turman, 535 F.2d 864, 867 n.7 (5th Cir. 1976) (noting that a pretrial order can be relied upon to indicate the nature of the relief requested), rev'd on other grounds, 430 U.S. 322, 51 L. Ed. 2d 368, 97 S. Ct. 1189 (1977). Once the pretrial order is entered, it controls the course and scope of the proceedings under Federal Rule of Civil Procedure 16(e), and if a claim or issue is omitted from the order, it is waived, even if it appeared in the complaint. See Valley Ranch Dev. Co. v. FDIC, 960 F.2d 550, 554 (5th Cir. 1992) (citing Flannery, 676 F.2d at 129-30).

In the Joint Pre-Trial Order signed by the parties' counsel, EPE's demand for an accounting of profits is not mentioned, but the Joint Pre-Trial Order does mention EPE's demands for injunctive relief, damages, and attorneys' fees under the Lanham Act, 15 U.S.C. § 1117(a). Section 1117(a) also provides for the remedy of an accounting of profits and lists it separately from damages. Therefore, EPE's listing of injunctive relief, damages, and attorneys' fees under the Lanham Act in the Joint Pre-Trial Order does not act to preserve its claim for an accounting of profits, and the issue therefore was waived.

Likewise, EPE has waived its claim for attorneys' fees under the Texas right of publicity statute, TEX. PROP. CODE ANN. § 26.013(4) (Vernon Supp. 1998), because EPE never references the Texas statute in its request for attorneys' fees. All references to attorneys' fees in the Joint Pre-Trial Order request attorneys' fees under the Lanham Act, 15 U.S.C. §§ 1051-1127, explicitly or by referencing the Lanham Act's standard for their award. The first request for attorneys' fees under the Texas statute occurs in EPE's brief on appeal; as the availability of attorneys' fees under the Texas statute was never placed before the district court, we will not consider it on appeal.

While an accounting of profits and attorneys' fees are not available to EPE, EPE is entitled to an injunction enjoining the Defendants' use of "The Velvet Elvis" mark based upon the Defendants' infringement of EPE's marks by their use of that mark. See 15 U.S.C. § 1116. We find that enjoining only the activities that have associated the mark with Elvis Presley will not provide EPE with the proper relief. Defendants' advertising practices over many months imbued "The Velvet Elvis" mark with a meaning directly related to Elvis Presley, which cannot now be erased by altering the context of the mark's use. Because the Defendants have imbued the mark with an infringing meaning, use alone in the future would continue the infringement of EPE's marks. On remand, the district court shall enter the appropriate injunction enjoining the Defendants' use of "The Velvet Elvis" mark and grant any other appropriate relief. All injunctive relief entered should cover not only the Defendants and those acting in concert with them but also their successors and assigns.

## IV. CONCLUSION

For the foregoing reasons, we REVERSE the district court's judgment and REMAND this case to the district court to enter judgment for EPE and for further proceedings consistent with this opinion. EPE's motion for this court to take judicial notice of an action of the PTO, which was carried with the appeal, is dismissed as moot.

## ARTIST-AGENT AGREEMENT

This Agreement ("Agreement"), dated and effective as of August 15, 2015, by and between John Doe Inc., ("Agent"), with offices 3333 Tulip Road, Houston, Texas 77777, and Joshua Doe Inc., f/s/o Joshua Doe with offices at 1111 N Orchid Lane, Houston, Texas 77777 ("Artist").

Whereas, the Artist wishes to have an agent represent him or her in marketing certain rights enumerated herein; and

Whereas, the Agent wishes to represent the Artist;

Now, therefore, in consideration of the forgoing premises and the mutual convenience hereinafter set forth and other valuable consideration, the parties hereto agree as follows:

1. Agency. The Artist appoints the agent to act as his or her exclusive representative, pertaining to Artist's Music Projects, Radio Broadcast Projects, Music Content Projects and Music Project Acquisitions.

The Agent agrees to use his or her best efforts in submitting the Artist's work for the purpose of securing assignment for the Artist. The Agent shall negotiate the terms of any assignment that is offered, but the Artist shall have the right to reject any assignment if he or she finds the terms thereof unacceptable.

2. Promotional Materials. The Artist shall provide the Agent with such samples of work as are from time to time necessary for the purpose of securing assignments. These samples shall remain the property of the Artist and be returned within thirty (30) days of termination of this Agreement. The agent shall take reasonable efforts to protect the work from loss or damage, but shall be liable for such loss or damage only if caused by the Agent's negligence. Promotional expenses, including but not limited to promotional mailings and paid advertising, shall be paid One Hundred Percent (100%) by the Artist. The Artist shall bear the expense of shipping, insurance and similar marketing expenses.

3. Term. The term of this Agreement shall commence on the date hereof, and continue for a period of Twenty-Four (24) months hereafter (the "Initial Term"), unless otherwise extended or terminated in writing by both Parties and in accordance with Provision 9 "Termination".

4. Commissions. Artist shall pay Agent, as and when received by Artist or on Artist's behalf, a sum equal to ten percent (10%) as an Agent Commission of any and all gross monies or other considerations which Artist may earn as an Author, participant with Recording Artists, Songwriters and Music Publishers, in perpetuity, from the exploitation of all Master Recordings embodying Artist's performance, which were recorded during the Term and from the exploitation of Musical Compositions which were commercially exploited during the Term. Agent shall not be entitled to any Agent Commission hereunder after the Term on any other Master Recordings created post term, embodying Artist's performances or any other Musical Compositions. A Master Recording shall be deemed "Recorded" during a particular period of time if it was substantially completed during such period. All Agent Commission payments shall be due within ten (10) days of receipt of any and all gross monies or other considerations that Artist may earn. Late payments shall be accompanied by the interest calculated at the rate of five percent (5%) per month thereafter.

5. Auditing. Agent or his representatives shall have the right, upon at least a fifteen (15) day notice, to inspect Artist's financial accounting, books, and records and all other documents and material in Artist's possession or control with respect to the subject matter of this Agreement. Agent shall have free and full access thereto for such purposes. Agent may make such an examination for a particular statement within three (3) years from the date said statement is rendered by Agent. Agent may make those examinations during Artist's usual business hours, and at the place where Artist keeps the books and records to be examined.

6. Termination. This agreement may be terminated and the services to be rendered hereunder, without liability on thirty (30) days prior written notice to the other Party.

7. Assignment. In light of the unique services to be performed by the Artist hereunder, it is acknowledged and agreed that any purported or attempted assignment or transfer by the Agent of this Agreement or any of its duties, rights or obligations hereunder, without prior written consent of Artist, shall be ineffective and void.

8. Arbitration. Any disputes in excess of $1,000.00 arising out of this Agreement shall be submitted to binding arbitration before the Joint Ethics Committee or a mutually agreed upon arbitrator pursuant to the rules of the American Arbitration Association. The Arbitrator's award shall be final and judgment may be entered in any Court having jurisdiction thereof. The Agent shall pay all arbitration and court costs, reasonable attorney's fees, and legal interest on any award of judgment in favor of the Artist.

9. Notices. All notices shall be given to the parties at their respective addresses set forth above.

10. Independent Contractor. This Agreement shall not give rise to a partnership or joint venture, and shall be construed to create a principal and agent or employer and employee relationship, between the parties. All activities by the Agent under the terms of this Agreement shall be carried on by the Agent as an independent contractor and neither the Artist nor any employee of the Artist shall, for any purpose, be considered an agent for, or employee of, the Agent. The Agent shall be solely liable for the payment of all applicable Federal, State and local income and other taxes, worker's compensation, disability benefits, and all such additional legal requirements of like nature applicable to the Agent and any monies paid by Agent.

11. Governing law. This Agreement shall be governed by the laws of the State of Texas, without regard to the conflict of laws rules thereof, applicable to agreements made and to be wholly performed therein. The Parties agree to submit themselves to the jurisdiction of the Federal or State Courts located in Harris County, Houston, Texas in any action which may rise out of this agreement and said Courts shall have exclusive jurisdiction over all disputes pertaining to this Agreement and all matters related thereto.

In witness whereof, the parties have signed this Agreement as of the date set forth above.

_____          _____
Artist                                    Agent

Questions and Discussion

1. In *Motown Record Corp. v. Brockert*, 207 Cal. Rptr. 574 (1984), the court documents a constant phenomenon—what happens to the record company's attempts to enjoin a rising star, Teena Marie, based on existing contracts, when she blows up (i.e., becomes extremely popular seemingly overnight)? "How Ya Keep 'em. Down on the Farm (After They've Seen Paree)?" Remember, the record company is the one seeking injunctive relief here. Discuss this case.

2. *Third Story Music, Inc. v. Waits*, 41 Cal. App. 4th 798 (1995), dealt with an express clause that was deemed to be illusory. The court would not use the implied covenant of good faith and fair dealing to sanctify this clause. This dog won't hunt. Discuss this case.

3. In *Benson v. Paul Winley Record Sales Corp.*, 452 F. Supp. 516 (1978), the fabulously talented guitarist and singer, George Benson, was granted a preliminary injunction enjoining defendants, a record sales corporation, and a record shop, from their re-mixed and marketed "X-rated" album of Benson's old songs. Discuss this case.

4. In *Elvis Presley Enters. v. Capace*, 141 F.3d 188 (1998), the court found "The Velvet Elvis" bar's use of the image and likeness of Elvis Presley in advertising and promoting the bar created confusion as to whether plaintiff licensed or endorsed "The Velvet Elvis" night club. Discuss this case.

5. Look at the enclosed "Artist-Agent Agreement"—discuss it from the eyes of both the artist and agent. Remember, it's best for all parties if it's a "win-win" situation.

6. Look at section "2. Promotional Materials" in the "Artist-Agent Agreement." What could you add to strengthen the advocacy of the artist's best interests? What could you add to strengthen the advocacy of the agent's best interests?

# Chapter 10
# Performance, Merchandising, and Touring Agreements

Performance, Merchandising, and Touring agreements each have their own specific agreement. Connected to these contracts is the "Merchandise Licensing Agreement." Performance and Touring Agreements are the home of the ubiquitous booking agent. A part of the performance contract is the "rider," which specifies the performer's requests or demands that a performers needs to carry out the show. The rider includes both technical and hospitality requirements. Although this may be more urban legend than anything else, Chuck Berry demands $25,000 in cash and a vintage Cadillac convertible. He expects that the promoter will hire local musicians who know his music sufficiently enough that they can jump in after the first few chords. This is a strictly non-negotiable contract: Chuck Berry travels solo with his guitar!

(Other rider urban legends: It seems every rapper/hip hop artist requests Hennessy cognac and Grey Goose vodka.)

Other than Chuck Berry, most riders are negotiable. The technical rider usually calls for baseline equipment but can include lighting, fax machines, particular instruments, additional rigging, etc. These are points that should be discussed with the performer's tour manager.

(More urban legends: Drake asks for Nivea Chapstick; Madonna requests 20 international phone lines; Gnarls Barkley stipulates one pack of Magnum condoms plus the ubiquitous Hennessy and Grey Goose; Mariah Carey, 20 white kittens and 100 doves; and our favorite (which I'm sure is tongue-in-cheek), Marilyn Manson's rider requests "a bald-headed toothless hooker.")

Most performance contracts call for 50% payment up front when the contract is signed, and the rest is paid with a cashier's check or money order on the night of the concert, before the performance begins. Sometimes, for whatever reason, the performer has a change of heart and wants cash money before performing. Don't let this happen to you; it's a nightmare! But know this, you'll never book that artist again!

"The bottom line is that performing is usually the engine that will begin building a community around your music" (George Howard, "Getting Signed! (Boston, 2014)).

You must also pay for security and in many cases book the venue, which calls for another contract. Some venues routinely demand more security precautions if the artist is a rapper. Look into the janitorial engineers and stage hands—if they're unionized, work this detail out in advance. For many good reasons, never cross a picket line! How can you get extra money from the record company? Should you hire the local drive time D.J. in your artist's particular musical genre? How about nonprofit radio stations? Can you get tie-ins with certain products? (Grey Goose?) Charge for tables for various product sellers. Get as much as you can from the merchandising of the artist. Try to get beverage and food credits. Also note that you must pay for room and board. Remember, "it takes a village to raise a child"—or stage a performance!

Michael Coppel Promotions Pty. v. Bolton
United States District Court for the Southern District of New York
November 10, 1997, Decided; November 12, 1997, Filed
97 Civ. 2646 (DC)
982 F. Supp. 950

MEMORANDUM DECISION

CHIN, D.J.

This is a breach of contract action filed by Michael Coppel Promotions Pty. Limited ("MCP"), an Australian corporation engaged in the business of marketing and promoting concerts, against Michael Bolton ("Bolton"), the pop singer, and MBO Tours, a corporation used by Bolton to arrange concert tours. In essence, MCP claims that defendants "unjustifiably repudiated" a 1996 concert agreement when Bolton abruptly cancelled an eight-concert tour of Australian cities just two weeks before the tour was scheduled to begin. (Am. Compl. P 1).

Defendants move to dismiss the complaint pursuant to Rule 12(b)(6). They contend that plaintiff has failed to state a claim for the following reasons: (1) MCP's telefax of April 22, 1996 constitutes a counteroffer extinguishing its prior offer; (2) defendants expressly made written acceptance and payment of an advance the preconditions for an enforceable contract; and (3) the complaint fails to sufficiently allege the existence of an oral contract.

For the reasons set forth below, defendants' motion is denied.

## BACKGROUND

Plaintiff's Amended Complaint alleges that in early March of 1996 representatives of the parties "orally agreed [to] the material terms" of a concert agreement. (Am. Compl. P 2). Under the terms of this alleged contract, Bolton promised to perform eight concerts in various Australian cities between May 14-28, 1996 (the "Australian Tour"). (See id. PP 1, 25). In return, Bolton would be paid "the greater of $ 1,200,000 or 85% of the net door receipts of ticket sales." (Id. PP 3, 25). With the apparent consent of defendants' booking agent and in accordance with the "prevailing custom and usage in the concert promotion and touring business," MCP immediately commenced ticket sales for six of the eight tour dates and engaged in extensive promotional activities. (Id. PP 13, 27-30).

The parties continued to exchange telefaxes and telephone calls regarding various issues relating to the tour. In separate telephone conversations in March of 1996, Podell of ICM allegedly requested that MCP delay ticket sales for one week due to problems with the Korean tour, and then assured MCP that ticket sales could begin on March 29, 1996.

On or about April 16, 1997 ICM sent MCP a short form of the alleged concert agreement (the "Short Form"). Approximately one week later, MCP received from ICM a contract rider (the "Rider"). Plaintiff alleges that the Short Form and Rider "fairly and accurately reflected the material terms" of the previous oral agreement, but also contained conflicting new terms, such as those concerning to which institution Bolton's advance should be paid. (Id. PP 18-20).

During the week of April 22, 1996, plaintiff learned that the Korean tour had been cancelled. Shortly thereafter, Podell called Coppel to suggest that MCP cancel the Australian Tour. Coppel refused, citing the expenses already incurred and the likelihood of a last-minute surge in ticket sales. (Id. P 34).

On or about April 26, 1996 Podell cancelled the Australian Tour on behalf of Bolton and MBO, citing poor ticket sales. Plaintiff alleges that defendants backed out of the agreement "either because Bolton did not wish to endure the embarrassment of playing to less than capacity crowds if ticket sales did not improve at the Australian venues, or because the cancellation of the Korean tour dates had decreased the potential profitability of his Southeast Asian tour plans, or both." (Id. P 37).

## DISCUSSION

### A. Applicable Standard

In reviewing a motion to dismiss, this Court must accept the factual allegations set forth in the complaint as true, and draw all reasonable inferences in favor of the plaintiff. See Bernheim v. Litt, 79 F.3d 318, 321 (2d Cir. 1996). A complaint may not be dismissed under Rule 12(b)(6) unless it "appears beyond doubt that the plaintiff can prove no set of facts in support of his claim which would entitle him to relief." Id. (quoting Conley v. Gibson, 355 U.S. 41, 45-46, 2 L. Ed. 2d 80, 78 S. Ct. 99 (1957)). In other words, the issue before the Court "is not whether a plaintiff will ultimately prevail but whether the claimant is entitled to offer evidence to support the claims." Villager Pond, Inc. v. Town of Darien, 56 F.3d 375, 378 (2d Cir. 1995), cert. denied, 136 L. Ed. 2d 14, U.S. , 117 S. Ct. 50 (1996).

### B. Defendants' Motion to Dismiss

Accepting as true the factual allegations set forth in the complaint and drawing all reasonable inferences in plaintiff's favor, I hold that plaintiff has stated a claim upon which relief may be granted.

1. The April 22, 1996 Telefax

Defendants insist that no agreement, oral or written, was ever reached, and that continued negotiations reflect the unresolved state of affairs. Defendants argue that Coppel's April 22, 1996 telefax to Nash (Am. Compl., Ex. C) represents a "counteroffer" that "extinguished" defendants' initial "offer." (Defs. Mem. at 7-9).

In the fax, Coppel states:

I've received three different sets of instructions for the transfer of the deposit, nominating variously: Chase Manhattan (fax dated 16 April), Barclays' Bank PLS, London (in all versions of the contract received to date), Chemical Bank, New York (fax dated 19 April. Even if I assume that the most recent instruction is the routing information actually required I cannot comply with your instruction to transfer funds directly to the artist's account — these funds should be held by I.C.M. pending the performance of the contract, which is the way I have always operated.

. . .

Clause 4. A. My offer specified that I would be responsible for "hotel accommodation (room rate only) — please delete the words "inclusive of breakfast." B. Peter — frankly I have a problem with the tour party increasing to 42 persons — for the previous Australian tour the touring party was 29 persons.

. . .

Clause 13. Noted that sponsorship arrangements have been approved and agreed, and in this regard it is requested that the sponsorship terms agreed be attached as an addendum to the contract.

This document constitutes a counteroffer only if no enforceable oral agreement previously had been reached in March of 1996. At this early stage in the proceeding, I cannot conclude as a matter of law that no oral agreement was reached in March or that MCP's April 22, 1996 fax constituted a counteroffer. The fax is consistent with either plaintiff's or defendant's theory of the case. It can be construed either as a counteroffer or merely as evidence of ongoing negotiations as to ancillary details, representing only Coppel's request for clarification of the wire transfer procedure and his objection to the enlargement of Bolton's entourage. (Defs. Mem. at 5-6). The fax may tend to show, as defendants claim, that agreement as to material terms had not yet been reached; on the other hand, the document does not undermine plaintiff's principal argument that agreement had been reached as to the major terms and that only secondary issues remained.

Moreover, whether this document constitutes a counteroffer cannot be resolved on a motion to dismiss where, as here, the issue is bound inextricably with the fact question of whether an oral agreement has been reached. As the Second Circuit has made clear, "the issue of whether (and when) the parties intended to be bound is a factual issue that should [be] submitted to the jury." International Minerals & Resources, S.A. v. Pappas, 96 F.3d 586, 593 (2d Cir. 1996). Thus, the April 22, 1996 fax does not bar plaintiff's suit.

2. Conditions Precedent to an Enforceable Contract

Defendants also insist that plaintiff failed to comply with two conditions precedent to the formation of the concert agreement: written acceptance of the contract and payment of an advance. They point to the Rider (Am. Compl., Ex. A) as evidence that both conditions were "explicitly made prerequisite to formation" of a binding contract. (Defs. Mem. at 10).

Under New York law, where parties unequivocally indicate a desire not to be bound by an agreement "until it is reduced to writing and signed by both of them, they are not so bound . . . until it has been written out and signed." Scheck v. Francis, 26 N.Y.2d 466, 469-70, 311 N.Y.S.2d 841, 843, 260 N.E.2d 493 (1970); see also BMH Realty Ltd. v. 399 East 72nd Street Owners, Inc., 221 A.D.2d 165, 633 N.Y.S.2d 141 (1st Dep't 1995).

In this case, however, the Rider does not constitute unambiguous evidence of the parties' intent not to be bound by an oral agreement. Assuming, as I must, that an oral contract was reached in March 1996, the unsigned Rider received one month later does not conclusively prove that the conditions set forth therein were raised during formation of the alleged oral contract. Furthermore, because the Rider was unilaterally issued by defendants and was never signed by either party, this Court cannot conclude that the parties ever agreed to payment of an advance and written codification of the terms of the agreement as conditions precedent. At this point, defendants have failed to show that these conditions were clearly established "at the time of contracting." Consarc Corp. v. Marine Midland Bank, 996 F.2d 568, 576 (2d Cir. 1993); see Oppenheimer & Co. v. Oppenheim, Appel, Dixon & Co., 86 N.Y.2d 685, 688, 636 N.Y.S.2d 734, 735, 660 N.E.2d 415 (1995) (parties' expression not to be bound orally unequivocal where they had executed letter agreement indicating there would be no valid sublease unless certain conditions were met).

Plaintiff's claim of partial performance of the alleged oral contract further militates against dismissal of the complaint. MCP alleges that it relied on defendants' repeated representations and assurances for a full month, expending considerable time and money performing its contractual obligations. (See Am. Compl. PP 39-41). As the Second Circuit has noted, "partial performance is an unmistakable signal that one party believes there is a contract; and the party who accepts performance signals, by that act, that it also understands a contract to be in effect." R.G. Group, Inc., v. Horn & Hardart Co.,

751 F.2d 69, 75 (2d Cir. 1984). In light of defendants' failure to show that either party signalled its desire not to be bound by an oral contract alone, this Court may not ignore plaintiffs' allegations of partial performance.

In short, "simply because the parties contemplate memorializing their agreement in a formal document does not prevent [an] agreement from coming into effect before written documents are drawn up." International Minerals, 96 F.3d at 593. Because the Rider does not clearly demonstrate "whether or not the parties intended to be bound prior to the formal execution of the suggested . . . agreement," defendants' motion to dismiss on the basis of the Rider is denied. Buschman v. Diamond Shamrock Corp., 35 A.D.2d 926, 316 N.Y.S.2d 590, 591 (1st Dep't 1970)

3. The Sufficiency of MCP's Allegations

Finally, defendants contend that plaintiff has failed to particularize the terms of the alleged oral agreement. Under New York law, an agreement is enforceable if a meeting of the minds has occurred as to the contract's "material terms." Four Seasons Hotels Ltd. v. Vinnik, 127 A.D.2d 310, 317, 515 N.Y.S.2d 1, 6 (1st Dep't 1987). So long as such agreement has been achieved, subsequent discussions thereafter over related or tangential matters does not render the contract inchoate or invalid. See id.; see also Teachers Ins. & Annuity Assoc. of Am. v. Tribune Co., 670 F. Supp. 491, 498 (S.D.N.Y. 1987) (describing two varieties of enforceable contracts — the first where complete agreement as to "major terms" has been reached, and the second where the parties have expressed a "binding preliminary commitment" to negotiate in good faith).

Plaintiff has more than adequately stated a claim for breach of contract. MCP alleges that the parties reached a binding oral concert agreement in March of 1996. And although defendants contend that plaintiff fails to specify the terms of the oral contract in the complaint (Defs. Mem. at 6-7, 15-16), plaintiff has in fact specifically described such terms — Bolton would perform eight concerts at various Australian venues, and was in turn promised specific compensation: the greater of $ 1,200,000 or 85% of net proceeds from ticket sales. (Am. Compl. PP 3, 25). MCP further alleges that industry practice permits the promotion of concerts once initial agreement has been achieved as to material terms, even though additional details remain to be finalized. While defendants assert that concert agreements customarily require a meeting of the minds on "many significant particulars" (Defs. Mem. at 16), they fail to specify any other material terms required of a binding contract as a matter of industry practice, but as to which no agreement was had in this case.

In sum, MCP has pled a viable claim for breach of contract. Accordingly, plaintiff is entitled to offer evidence in support of its action.

CONCLUSION

Defendants' motion to dismiss is denied.

SO ORDERED.

Kass v. Young
Court of Appeal of California, First Appellate District, Division Three
February 14, 1977
Civ. No. 38186
67 Cal. App. 3d 100

Plaintiff Kass appeals from an order vacating a default judgment in a class action and vacating the default of defendant Neil Young insofar as it relates to a class action, but allowing the default to remain against appellant Young to the extent that defendant as an individual is concerned (judgment to be subject to proof of damages as to plaintiff's individual rights). Appellant Young cross-appeals from the order allowing the limited default to remain. Both sides agree that the case appears to be one of first impression as to the effect of default in an alleged class action.

The complaint alleges that Kass was one of about 14,000 patrons at a "rock" concert on March 31, 1973, at the Oakland Coliseum. Defendant Young was the star performer. He terminated the concert by abruptly walking off the stage. The purchasers of tickets "did not receive the consideration of a full concert performance for which they had paid." Damages are alleged to be about $ 98,000, including ticket prices, transportation and parking expenses. It is alleged that the entire class of patrons is affected exactly as is plaintiff.

Summons and complaint were served personally on Young on September 30, 1973. His default was entered on November 12, 1973.

At the hearing, Kass testified that about 14,000 were present; that Young walked out in the middle of a song; that everyone stood for a long time clapping and yelling, but Young did not return. Counsel for Kass presented three ticket stubs, one of which was Kass's; he proposed $ 91,000 as the amount of damages, calculated by multiplying 14,000 by the median price of $ 6.50 (tickets were $ 7.50, $ 6.50 and $ 5.50, but there was no evidence of the number sold of each category); he waived (for the whole class presumably) the parking fee item; by silence, he waived (for the class) punitive damages which had been prayed for, based on alleged malice. Read into the record were newspaper accounts which reported that the "jarring" walkoff, a "rip off," a "temper tantrum" occurred about an hour after the concert started, and reported that Young had said he couldn't go on because of repressive action of the security guards. Although at the hearing nothing was made definite about the subject of proof of membership in the class, there was a suggestion by counsel that refunds would be made to those who had retained ticket stubs.

The judge (not the judge from whose order the present appeals are taken) rendered judgment on June 26, 1974, awarding to plaintiff Kass, on behalf of himself and of all others who purchased tickets for the concert, the sum of $ 91,000; 40 percent of the recovery was awarded to plaintiff's attorney; the whole amount collected was to be deposited in the attorney's trust account; payment was to be made to those who proved to the satisfaction of counsel that they were members of the class (no method of determining the amount to be paid to each is stated; presumably each would be reimbursed his or her actual outlay); the balance unclaimed, after a reasonable time (which was not defined), would be disposed of by the court. There was no provision for notice even by publication.

On October 10, 1974, Young moved to vacate the default and the default judgment. One of the grounds was that the default and the judgment were jurisdictionally defective in that no notice had been given to the alleged class and that no class had been certified. On this ground the vacating order was made and the proposed answer of Young was permitted to be filed. (The answer alleges that Young had substantially completed his performance when he was forced to leave the stage by unnerving disturbance among the audience.)

### I. Vacating of the Default Judgment

It was proper to set aside the default judgment because of a jurisdictional deficiency, namely, that there had been no certification of the asserted class and no provision for notice to the asserted class.

A default judgment which is in excess of jurisdiction may be set aside at any time either by motion or an independent action in equity. (Sullivan v. Sullivan, 256 Cal.App.2d 301 [64 Cal.Rptr. 82].) Although, as was said at the outset, a case involving default judgment in a class action has not been found, it is to be inferred from the cases relating to the necessity for certification and for notice in class actions that the procedures which have been decreed to be mandatory establish these procedures as jurisdictional; wherefore, default judgment rendered without compliance with them is subject to vacation. In Home Sav. & Loan Assn. v. Superior Court, 42 Cal.App.3d 1006 [117 Cal.Rptr. 485], a peremptory writ of prohibition was issued restraining the trial court from proceeding to trial on the substantive merits of the cause without prior adjudication of the suitability of the lawsuit as a class action, determination of the composition of the class, and appropriate notification to its members. Although the court in that case did not refer to the failure to meet the prescribed procedures as a jurisdictional defect in so many words, nevertheless the facts that it issued a writ which normally at least is employed only to restrain a lower tribunal from exceeding its jurisdiction ( Abelleira v. District Court of Appeal, 17 Cal.2d 280 [109 P.2d 942, 132 A.L.R. 715]; 5 Witkin, Cal.

Procedure (2d ed. 1971) Extraordinary Writs, § 39, p. 3813), and that the court in Home Sav. & Loan Assn. based its decision in part on the constitutional requirement of due process of law (at pp. 1012, 1014) give evidence that the court did not regard the trial court's failure as mere procedural error.

But if Home Sav. & Loan Assn. be not authority for the proposition that the mandatory procedures are truly jurisdictional, we do not hesitate to declare them so. The strong language about the necessity of these procedures and the careful explanations of the reasons for that necessity appearing not only in Home Sav. & Loan Assn. but also in the City of San Jose v. Superior Court, 12 Cal.3d 447 [115 Cal.Rptr. 797, 525 P.2d 701]; Vasquez v. Superior Court, 4 Cal.3d 800, 820, 821 [94 Cal.Rptr. 796, 484 P.2d 964, 53 A.L.R.3d 513]; Blue Chip Stamps v. Superior Court, 18 Cal.3d 381, 385, 386 [134 Cal.Rptr. 393, 556 P.2d 755], are persuasive of the jurisdictional nature of prejudgment adjudication of the suitability of the action as a class action, determination of the composition, and appropriate notification. The elaborate and scholarly reasoning exhibited in those decisions need not be repeated here, but a few words may be said about the application of the principles established by those authorities to the present case. First, as to the parties: without determination of the proper class and of appropriate notice, the defendant would be subject not only to judgment in the purported class action but also to suits by individuals acting alone or in other asserted classes. (Home Sav. & Loan Assn. v. Superior Court, supra, at p. 1012.) To be sure, defendant Young chose not to answer the complaint; but a party in default is not made subject to unlimited effects of his default. Relief may not be given beyond that prayed for (Code Civ. Proc., § 580); damages except when fixed by contract must be proved (Code Civ. Proc., § 585; Liberty Loan Corp. of North Park v. Petersen, 24 Cal.App.3d 915 [101 Cal.Rptr. 395]); substantial amendment to the pleading after default is not permitted without second service of process (Leo v. Dunlap, 260 Cal.App.2d 24 [66 Cal.Rptr. 888]). In a purported class action, the defaulting defendant should be entitled to have the court either on motion of plaintiff's counsel or on its own motion decide the appropriateness of the class action so that if it truly be suitable and if the necessary notice be given to potential plaintiffs, there will be but a single binding judgment against him. As to potential plaintiffs, the prejudgment procedures are so connected with due process as to be jurisdictional. These persons are entitled to the best practical notice under the circumstances, advising them that they may be excluded from the class if they so request and that they will be bound by the judgment, whether favorable or not, if they do not request exclusion. (Home Sav. & Loan Assn. v. Superior Court, supra, at pp. 1012, 1013; American Pipe & Construction Co. v. Utah, 414 U.S. 538, 545-549 [38 L.Ed.2d 713, 722-724, 94 S.Ct. 756].)

Then there is a consideration of damages in this particular case relating to the potential plaintiffs which is rather unique. The representative plaintiff has simply assumed that all 14,000 patrons of the concert were equally damaged and that their damages amounted to the price of the average ticket. It may be that many of the patrons or "fans" of the performer who had entertained them for an hour did not regard themselves cheated or that some may have sympathized with his antagonism toward a number of the security guards. In the absence of notice, the single plaintiff has been able to enlist 14,000 persons, willing or not, and wherever they may be, to join his cause. In Weaver v. Pasadena Tournament of Roses, 32 Cal.2d 833, 835 [198 P.2d 514], four appellants "'on behalf of themselves and all others similarly situated'" brought an action for damages, seeking $ 100 for each person (it was estimated there were 1,850) who had been promised that upon standing in line at the box office, he could purchase two tickets to the Rose Bowl. The box office was closed early and tickets were withdrawn from sale and distributed to favored parties. The trial court held that this was not a proper representative action; there was but a large number of individuals, each of whom may or may not have, or care to assert, a claim against defendants. Appellants' complaint, said the court, as we do now, can be regarded as no more than an invitation to such persons as may be interested in joining with them in their action.

Nor are the interests of the litigants the only ones to be considered in the prejudgment determination. The representative plaintiff must show that substantial benefit will result both to the litigants and to the court. (Blue Chip Stamp v. Superior Court, supra, 18 Cal.3d at p. 385; City of San Jose v. Superior Court, supra, 12 Cal.3d at pp. 458-460; Collins v. Rocha, 7 Cal.3d 232, 238 [102 Cal.Rptr. 1, 497 P.2d 225]; Vasquez v. Superior Court, supra, 4 Cal.3d at p. 811.) The resources of the judicial system may be called upon by one or more persons, under Code of Civil Procedure, section 382, when the parties are numerous and it is impracticable to bring them all before the court, for the benefit of all.

Plaintiff-appellant contends that, although ordinarily class action issues should be resolved before trial, the defendant has admitted the allegations relating to class by failing to answer. In support of this proposition, plaintiff cites Hypolite v. Carleson, supra, 52 Cal.App.3d 566. Hypolite was described by its author as "not a typical case." (At p. 582.) The defendant expressly admitted the pertinent class action allegations in his answer. (At p. 583.) Although the class action issues of the case were not decided until after trial, appeal, reversal and remand, the facts were such that by reason of uncomplicated identification of the parties from existing records, the class action issues were as readily resolved as they could have been at the earlier and proper time. (At p. 582.) Plaintiff-appellant also argues that notice to the class was provided by the judgment itself by the mandate "that any unclaimed monies remaining in the trust account of counsel is to be disposed of by proper application to this Court for further orders." This is by no means provision for notice. Besides, there was no certification of the class. Certification is essential and in this case it is completely lacking.

Finally, there is the matter of necessary showing that the jurisdictional amount required for suit in the superior court be made (Home Sav. & Loan Assn. v. Superior Court, supra, at p. 1014) if the action be not sustained in its representative grade.

The order setting aside the default judgment must be affirmed.

## II. Vacating the Default

Plaintiff-appellant contends that it was error to set aside the default, which is a ministerial act, simply because this is a class action and that the plaintiff asserting his representative status need not give the defaulting defendant additional time to answer by withholding default until a class is ascertained. Defendant-appellant Young contends that the default as to the class was properly vacated but it was error to allow the default to stand as to the individual plaintiff because there can be but one judgment, and that if plaintiff were to proceed as an individual, his claim would fall within the jurisdiction of the municipal court. We agree with plaintiff-appellant that the default should not have been set aside at all. Although service of summons was the subject of controversy, the judge, after hearing the motion to vacate, concluded that defendant had flouted the process of the court. (There was evidence that Young tore up the summons and complaint.) The default, in our opinion, is an indivisible thing. The defendant has chosen not to reply. To set the default aside would, as plaintiff-appellant says, give to the defendant time in addition to that specified in the summons. Courts, out of respect to their own dignity, cannot permit parties to choose, without peril to themselves, to ignore the court's own process. It has been held that an action which is described in the pleadings as a class action remains such an action unless and until the court decides that it is one which is unsuitable for prosecution as a class action. ( Kahan v. Rosensteil, 424 F.2d 161, 169; Gaddis v. Wyman, 304 F.Supp. 713, 715.)

Ordinarily, if a default were allowed to remain, the vacating of a default judgment would be meaningless, because the plaintiff would be entitled at once to a renewed judgment. (Cumberpatch v. Nolan, 125 Cal.App.2d 205 [270 P.2d 540, 271 P.2d 519].) But in the case of an asserted class action, there still must be decided, following default, as a jurisdictional matter, the suitability of the lawsuit as a class action as set forth under heading I. This is so because the rights of other persons, potential plaintiffs, must be canvassed, which is not so in the ordinary action; because the defendant, although deprived of his right to respond on the merits to the cause of action as stated in the complaint, is entitled to protection against two or more judgments of which but one would be rendered in the instant case; and because the courts must, for the benefit of all litigants, protect themselves from the unnecessary multiplication of lawsuits on the one hand and from being used almost purposelessly save for the compensation of counsel. The order vacating the default is reversed. The default will remain. The order allowing the filing of the purported answer by defendant is reversed.

### III. Further Proceedings

So far as the individual plaintiff is concerned, his case may proceed following determination of the propriety of the class action. Perhaps it will have to be removed to the municipal court. If the cause proceeds as a class action, there will, of course, be but one judgment.

As was said at the outset, case law on the subject of defaults in class actions seems to be nonexistent. In our opinion, the defendant has lost his rights to defend on the merits of the action if the condition for class action be fulfilled. But the trial court, by reason of its authorities cited under heading I, must decide upon the suitability of the cause as a class action: whether it is manageable as such, whether the true purpose of a class action will be served, who the members of the class shall be, and if a class be certified, what notice shall be given. To be sure, in making inquiry into these matters, the court's scrutiny necessarily will come close into taking into account the merits of the case itself. But the court will observe a distinction, narrow though it may be, between the two subjects. The court will be concerned with such questions as: potential recovery to the individuals making up the asserted class; whether this recovery would be small in comparison with the time and expense consumed in distribution ( Blue Chip Stamp v. Superior Court, supra, 18 Cal.3d at p. 386); whether the court's resources would really be employed for the benefit of the 14,000 or mainly for the class action attorney (at p. 386; City of San Jose v. Superior Court, supra, 12 Cal.3d at p. 462); whether the action would have a beneficial deterrent effect; what likelihood there is that individual patrons would be able to prove or would care to assert their participation at the concert and any resulting damages. These and other questions the court must answer in order to decide whether the lawsuit is to proceed as a class action.

The order vacating the default judgment is affirmed. The order setting aside the default and permitting the filing of defendant's answer is reversed. The cause is remanded for further proceedings in accordance with the views expressed herein. Costs on appeal to be borne one-half by each party.

Bowes v. Cincinnati Riverfront Coliseum, Inc.
Court of Appeals of Ohio, First Appellate District, Hamilton County
August 24, 1983, Decided
Nos. C-830013, C-830073
12 Ohio App. 3d 12

Multitudinous causes (specifically fifty distinct appeals) came on to be heard upon the appeals, the transcripts of the docket, journal entries and original papers from the Court of Common Pleas of Hamilton County, evidence in connection with Civ. R. 56 motions, the briefs, the assignments of error and oral arguments of counsel. All the appeals herein (including appeals from decisions on cross-claims) were consolidated into a single appellate number, viz. C-830008. Subsequent to the oral arguments and submission of all fifty appeals, various parties compromised and agreed that their appellate proceedings be dismissed, and this court has therefore ordered those cases dismissed pursuant to App. R. 28. The cause not dismissed is composed of appellate case numbers C-830013 and C-830073, being case number A-7911085 in the Hamilton County Court of Common Pleas.

On December 3, 1979, The Who rock group performed at a concert at Cincinnati Riverfront Coliseum. Patrons and would-be patrons died while entering the Coliseum. These cases seek damages for the alleged wrongful deaths and personal injuries.The caption herein delineates the defendants, but we shall nevertheless additionally identify them. The defendants are: the Cincinnati Riverfront Coliseum, Inc. ("Coliseum"), locale of the rock performance; Brian E. Heekin, who was on December 3, 1979, a shareholder, director, the President and chief operating officer of the Coliseum, taking an active part in its day-to-day operations; the city of Cincinnati; The Who, and its four partners individually, as well as William George Curbishley, the group's personal manager who was present at the Coliseum on the evening of the instant incident; Electric Factory Concerts, local promoter of The Who on December 3, 1979; Tidal Wave Promotions, Inc., which was responsible for providing the touring facilities for The Who; nine directors of the Coliseum and Dalpepper Enterprises, Ltd., technical employer of The Who for performances outside the United Kingdom. Defendants seasonably filed motions seeking full or partial summary judgment on issues of liability. On December 23, 1982, the trial court entered "Orders On Motions For Summary Judgment." This entry in pertinent portions follows:

"All defendants in the 'Coliseum Litigation,' under the related case numbers named above, have submitted motions for either partial summary judgment, to dismiss punitive damage claims against them, and/or complete summary judgment to dismiss the total claim against them. Plaintiffs in these cases have also filed a consolidated motion for summary judgment seeking to strike the defense of assumption of risk. This Court having considered the motions, supporting memoranda, memoranda in opposition, reply memoranda, and supplemental memoranda, together with exhibits, depositions, affidavits, interrogatories, and the pleadings, now rules as follows, and accordingly

"ORDERS:

"1. Defendant Cincinnati Riverfront Coliseum, Inc.'s motion for partial summary judgment seeking to dismiss the punitive damage claims is granted;

"2. Defendants' The Who, Roger Daltry [sic], Kenny Jones, John Entwhistle, Peter Townshend, Tidal Wave Promotions, Inc., William Curbishley, and Dalpepper Enterprises, Ltd. motion for partial summary judgment on punitive damages is granted, and their motion seeking dismissal of all claims is overruled;

"3. Defendant Electric Factory Concerts' motion for partial summary judgment on punitive damages is granted, and their motion seeking dismissal of all claims is overruled;

"4. Defendants' George E. Heekin, Charles L. Heekin, Albert E. Heekin, III, Philip G. Smith, James J. Rammacher, Robert H. Castellini, Lawrence H. Kyte, Jr., William O. DeWitt, Jr., and William O. DeWitt, Sr., directors of CRC, Inc., motion for summary judgment seeking dismissal of all claims against them is granted, and they are hereby dismissed;

"5. Defendant Brian Heekin's motion for summary judgment seeking dismissal of all claims against him is granted, and he is hereby dismissed;

"6. Defendant the City of Cincinnati's motion for summary judgment seeking dismissal of all claims by plaintiffs against it is granted, and all crossclaims against it are dismissed except those of Cincinnati Riverfront Coliseum, Inc.;

"7. Plaintiffs' motion for partial summary judgment seeking to strike the defense of assumption of risk is overruled. * * *"

Thus, it is apparent that the trial court rendered favorable partial summary judgments for certain of the defendants on the plaintiffs' claims for wanton and reckless misconduct which plaintiffs wished to pursue in order to secure punitive damages. Also, the trial court, through its holdings on the defendants' motions for summary judgment, dismissed as defendants the city of Cincinnati (except as to the Coliseum's crossclaim against the city), the board of directors of Cincinnati Riverfront Coliseum, Inc. and Brian Heekin, who while also a member of the board, was additionally singled out by plaintiffs as an independent target of the actions because of his admitted role as operating officer of the Coliseum.

These appeals ensued, and five assignments of error are advanced, the first of which states:

"The trial court erred in rendering summary judgments in cases which are both factually and legally complex."

The issue said to be thus presented for our review is:

"In cases which are procedurally, factually, and legally complex, it is inappropriate for the trial court summarily to dispose of all or any part of the plaintiffs' claims without a full development of the evidence at trial."

Hence, plaintiffs would have us write a rule that Civ. R. 56 providing for summary judgments does not apply to factually and legally complex cases. We do have an unusually voluminous record containing, of course, matters which were before the trial court, and we are willing to assume, arguendo, that the matters sub judice are "factually and legally complex." Civ. R. 56 provides for the manner in which motions for summary judgments are to be considered and mandates the standards to be used in deciding such motions. The rule does not exclude "factually and legally complex" cases from resolution by summary judgment when appropriate. Such cases are not inappropriate for summary judgment. Assignment one is of no avail.

We pass over assignment two for subsequent examination.

## II.

The third assignment of error is:

"The trial court erred in rendering summary judgment in favor of the City of Cincinnati."

Plaintiffs contend that the city of Cincinnati was negligent and that it is not protected by the doctrine of municipal immunity (sometimes referred to as sovereign or governmental immunity) as held below, that the city violated R.C. 723.01 in permitting the accumulation of such a crowd on December 3, 1979, as amounted to a nuisance; and that the city is liable under Section 1983, Title 42, U.S. Code, for a violation of the civil rights of the patrons on December 3, in that the city failed legislatively or administratively to prohibit festival seating at the Coliseum or to take affirmative steps adequately and effectively to obviate certain hazards.

We agree that the trial court did err in granting summary judgment in favor of the city vis-a-vis the claimed negligence or wrongful acts or omissions of its agents or employees. Plaintiffs argue that this result is mandated by Haverlack v.. Portage Homes, Inc. (1982), 2 Ohio St. 3d 26, and King v.. Williams (1983), 5 Ohio St. 3d 137. We reverse this portion of the summary judgment in favor of the city upon the authority of Haverlack and King, supra, but particularly upon Enghauser Mfg. Co. v.. Eriksson Engineering Ltd. (1983), 6 Ohio St. 3d 31, the syllabus of which holds:

"1.The judicially created doctrine of municipal immunity is, within certain limits, abolished, thereby rendering municipal corporations subject to suit for damages by individuals injured by the negligence or wrongful acts or omissions of their agents or employees whether such agents and employees are engaged in proprietary or governmental functions. (Dayton v.. Pease, 4 Ohio St. 80, and its progeny overruled; Haverlack v.. Portage Homes, Inc., 2 Ohio St. 3d 26, followed and extended.)

"2. Under this decision abolishing municipal immunity, no tort action will lie against a municipal corporation for those acts or omissions involving the exercise of a legislative or judicial function or the exercise of an executive or planning function involving the making of a basic policy decision which is characterized by the exercise of a high degree of official judgment or discretion. However, once the decision has been made to engage in a certain activity or function, municipalities will be held liable, the same as private corporations and persons, for the negligence of their employees and agents in the performance of the activities."

In Enghauser the Supreme Court emphasized that so far as municipal government is concerned, the rule is liability — the exception is immunity. None of the exceptions to municipal liability delineated in Enghauser exists here.

We agree with the trial court in its holding that there is no genuine issue as to any material fact raised in the plaintiffs' complaint on either the nuisance theory or the contention that the city violated the civil rights of plaintiffs or plaintiffs' decedents contrary to Section 1983, Title 42, U.S. Code. Thus, assignment of error three is reversed in part and affirmed in part as indicated.

The fourth assignment of error claims that:

"The trial court erred in rendering summary judgment in favor of the board of directors of Riverfront Coliseum."

Presented thereby for appellate review is whether the actions of the Coliseum directors as directors, with particular respect to the December 3, 1979 incident, constitute triable issues of fact. The summary judgment in their favor, if it stands, of course removes them from this Coliseum litigation.

This assignment presents an extremely troublesome issue. The plaintiffs rely heavily upon R.C. 1701.59, necessarily the version which was in effect on the date of The Who concert in 1979. That section was revised in 1980 and 1981. The appropriate R.C. 1701.59 did provide, inter alia, that "all the authority of a corporation shall be exercised by its directors." Although admitting its general relevance, we believe we must consider more than this general statutory provision to decide whether summary judgment in favor of the directors should have been granted. For instance, the present R.C. 1701.59, portions of which became effective in 1980 and 1981, provides as follows:

"(B) A director shall perform his duties as a director, including his duties as a member of any committee of the directors upon which he may serve, in good faith, in a manner he reasonably believes to be in the best interest of the corporation, and with the care that an ordinarily prudent person in a like position would use under similar circumstances." (Emphasis added.)

It cannot facilely be ascertained that the present R.C. 1701.59(B), supra, directly applies to the relationship between corporate directors and third persons, such as the plaintiffs here. The legislature may have intended the enactment to apply principally to the relationship between directors and their corporation. Regardless, we ascribe some significance to R.C. 1701.59, old and new, vis-a-vis the appeals sub judice. The present section (B), above, in its requirement that directors shall perform their duties as directors with the care that an ordinarily prudent person in a like position would use under similar circumstances certainly is entitled to some consideration as a guide to the public policy of the state even though (B), as now constituted, was not enacted until a few months after December 1979.

Unquestionably, the directors delegated to Brian Heekin and other members of an operating team for the Coliseum many responsibilities, which, under law, they were justified in doing. There is evidence that Brian Heekin and his "team" were experienced. On the other hand, as plaintiffs argue, the directors as a board did not make or participate in any decisions or undertake any assignments pertinent to concerts generally, or crowd control, seating policies, or security measures specifically. The directors' own brief acknowledges this abdication. We are confronted with the question of whether under all the circumstances the directors were lawfully justified in delegating to others to the extent that they did. We examine this mindful that we are reviewing a Civ. R. 56 resolution by the trial court which decided that the moving parties (the directors) were and are entitled to judgment in their favor as a matter of law and thereby dismissing all plaintiffs' claims against them individually. We quote the following from Civ. R. 56(C):

"* * *A summary judgment shall not be rendered unless it appears from such evidence or stipulation and only therefrom, that reasonable minds can come to but one conclusion and that conclusion is adverse to the party [the plaintiffs below] against whom the motion for summary judgment is made, such party being entitled to have the evidence or stipulation construed most strongly in his favor. * * *"

We have used the wording "under all the circumstances." In the context of this Coliseum litigation, the phrase connotes, inter alia, that the directors were fully aware of the public nature of the Coliseum's business. In his deposition William O. DeWitt, Jr. testified:

"Q. What was the business of the Cincinnati Riverfront Coliseum from its inception?

"A. The business of the Coliseum was to lease the facility to various-entertainment-sports tenants to collect revenues therefrom and hopefully pay the debt service that was on the facility and create a profit."

This complete awareness of the public nature of the Coliseum's actual and intended operation was typical of all six directors deposed.

On and prior to December 3, 1979, the directors of the Coliseum also knew of the festival seating and crowd control problems. For instance, immediately following the Elton John concert on August 3, 1976, then City Manager William V. Donaldson commissioned a "Public Safety Study Team — Riverfront Coliseum" (hereinafter "PSST") whose chairperson was James D. Jester, Superintendent of the Highway Maintenance Division of the city of Cincinnati. The purpose of PSST was to have representatives of the different city agencies meet with Coliseum officials in an attempt to address and correct crowd problems at Coliseum events which had at that time — in 1976 — already occurred a number of times. The directors of the Coliseum were aware of the festival seating problems and the formation of PSST and the reason why the city manager established PSST.

It is emphasized that the record sub judice shows that the directors were aware of patron safety problems at the Coliseum. In view of this knowledge, the direct question confronting this court then is whether the trial court ruled correctly in holding as a matter of law that there is no genuine issue of material fact as to whether the directors acted with legal responsibility or whether they did absolutely nothing, or not enough. To affirm what was decided below we would have to be convinced that reasonable minds could come to but one conclusion and that conclusion would be adverse to the plaintiffs. We are unable so to conclude. Ultimate personal liability of the directors is not presently before us;    rather, we find that using the tests of Civ. R. 56, as we must, the directors of the Coliseum should not have been dismissed from the Coliseum litigation. Therefore, the fourth assignment is well-taken.

That the trial court erred in rendering summary judgment in favor of Brian Heekin and dismissing him from the cases is the challenge of assignment of error five. The appellants' interpretation of the issue thus presented for review and arguments follows:

"The record in this case presents factual issues concerning the personal liability of Brian Heekin, as a Coliseum officer and director, for The Who concert tragedy."

Not surprisingly, the plaintiffs assert that if the decision of the trial court that the directors were entitled to summary judgment and dismissal is reversed, "then the reversal of the summary judgment for Brian Heekin must automatically follow." In a word, the plaintiffs are correct in this contention. Brian Heekin was a director himself, shareholder, and the President of the Cincinnati Riverfront Coliseum. As the chief operating officer he was manifestly the Coliseum's headman with untrammeled sanction from the board; the power was concentrated in him and he exercised it authoritatively.

Under Ohio law, corporate officers may be held personally liable in tort. In Schaefer v.. D. & J. Produce (1978), 62 Ohio App. 2d 53 [16 O.O.3d 108], motion to certify overruled (Nov. 3, 1978), the Court of Appeals for Erie County was confronted with a case involving personal injuries and ensuing death as a result of a vehicle accident which occurred when a truck owned by defendant D & J Produce, Inc. failed to stop at a stop sign and collided with the vehicle driven by plaintiff's decedent. Plaintiff contended that the offending vehicle had a defective braking system, no operative hand brake, and no operative horn or other audible signal. Plaintiff also contended that it was the duty of two officers of D & J Produce to inspect and maintain the vehicle in a safe operating condition and further contended that the two officers dispatched the truck driver in a vehicle they knew or should have known was not in a safe operating condition. The trial court dismissed the two officers pursuant to a Civ. R. 56 motion, but the court of appeals reversed, holding that the summary judgment was improperly granted in favor of the two officers who therefore remained as defendants. In the third paragraph of the syllabus, which is faithful to the law of the case, it is stated:

"A corporate officer is individually liable for injuries to a third party when the corporation owes a duty of care to the third person, the corporation delegates that duty to the officer, the officer breaches that duty through personal fault (whether by malfeasance, misfeasance, or nonfeasance), and the third person is injured as a proximate result of the officer's breach of that duty."

We find assignment of error five well-taken.

### III.

We return to consider the second assignment of error. It alleges that:

"The trial court erred in rendering partial summary judgment in favor of all defendants on the plaintiffs' claim for wanton and reckless misconduct."

In other words, the appellants' remonstration in this assignment attacks the granting of partial motions for summary judgment in favor of certain of the defendants on the issue of punitive damages. As already referenced in this decision, the issue of recoverability of punitive damages from the city, from the directors or Brian Heekin is not before us in this appeal.

Fortunately, the Supreme Court has recently considered the issue raised by this assignment, viz., what facts are sufficient to raise a jury question of punitive damages. Actually, the assignment narrows the issue for us considerably since the challenge therein is to the granting of a summary judgment favoring certain defendants and finding as a matter of law that punitive damages are not recoverable from them. The case referred to is Detling v.. Chockley (1982), 70 Ohio St. 2d 134 [24 O.O.3d 239], and it is most valuable in resolving this assignment. We quote below from the unanimous opinion extensively although regretting the consumption of space thus involved in view of the already lengthy scope of this decision.

"The rationale for allowing punitive damages has been recognized in Ohio as that of punishing the offending party and setting him up as an example to others that they might be deterred from similar conduct: 'The principle of permitting damages, in certain cases, to go beyond naked compensation, is for example, and the punishment of the guilty party for the wicked, corrupt, and malignant motive and design, which prompted him to the wrongful act,' Simpson v.. McCaffrey (1844), 13 Ohio 508, 522. See, also, Rayner v.. Kinney (1863), 14 Ohio St. 283, 286-287; Smith v.. Pittsburg, Ft. W. & C. Ry. Co. (1872), 23 Ohio St. 10, 18; Railroad Co. v.. Hutchins (1881), 37 Ohio St. 282, 294. This form of civil punishment may be imposed even though the defendant may have been punished criminally for the same wrong. Roberts v.. Mason, supra, paragraph one of the syllabus.

"The operative concept in Ohio which permits the awarding of punitive damages is, in addition to fraud or insult, malice, Leichtamer v.. American Motors Corp. (1981), 67 Ohio St. 2d 456, 471. Early reported cases defined malice only by comparison to juxtaposed synonyms: 'wrongful intention,' Rayner v.. Kinney, supra, at page 287; 'fraud, malice and other willful wrong,' Smith v.. Pittsburg, Ft. W. & C. Ry. Co., supra, at page 18; 'wrongful act [that] was wanton or otherwise aggravated * * * willful, wanton or malicious,' Railroad Co. v.. Hutchins, supra, at page 294. More recent cases, however, have analyzed the malice requirement in terms of express or actual malice, Mauk v.. Brundage (1903), 68 Ohio St. 89, and legal or implied malice, Flandermeyer v.. Cooper (1912), 85 Ohio St. 327.

"Actual malice is required for a question of punitive damages to be submitted to a jury. Smithhisler v.. Dutter (1952), 157 Ohio St. 454 [47 O.O. 334], paragraph one of the syllabus; Pickle v.. Swinehart (1960), 170 Ohio St. 441 [11 O.O.2d 199], paragraph two of the syllabus. Actual malice is '"'that state of mind under which a person's conduct is characterized by hatred or ill will, a spirit of revenge, retaliation, or a determination to vent his feelings upon other persons.'"' Columbus Finance v.. Howard (1975), 42 Ohio St. 2d 178, 184 [71 O.O.2d 174]. The court recognized, however, 'that it is rarely possible to prove actual malice otherwise than by conduct and surrounding circumstances. One who has committed an act would scarcely admit that he was malicious about it, and so, necessarily, malice can be inferred from conduct.' Davis v.. Tunison (1959), 168 Ohio St. 471, 475 [7 O.O.2d 296].

"As pointed out by the court in Pickle v.. Swinehart, supra, paragraph one of the syllabus, '[t]he terms "legal malice" and "actual malice" are not synonymous.' 'Hatred, ill will or actual malice towards the injured party is not a necessary ingredient of legal malice as applied to torts, nor is it necessary that the act complained of proceed from a spiteful, malignant or revengeful disposition. If it be wrongful, unlawful and intentional and the natural and probable result of the act is to accomplish the injury complained of, malice is implied,' Flandermeyer v.. Cooper, supra, paragraph three of the syllabus.

"Additionally, concepts of recklessness, wantonness, willfulness and grossness are inferred from the conduct and surrounding circumstances to support an award of punitive damages in tort actions. Columbus Finance v.. Howard, supra, at page 184; Rubeck v.. Huffman (1978), 54 Ohio St. 2d 20, 23 [8 O.O.3d 11]. '* * * [T]he conduct of a party may be either "wanton" or "reckless" and still not have been actuated by malice or ill will. And in the concept in which "wanton" is most frequently encountered — in the field of negligence * * * it is not necessary that there be ill will toward the person injured.' Rogers v.. Barbera (1960), 170 Ohio St. 241, 244-245 [10 O.O.2d 248].

"Evidence of actual malice, therefore, must be present before a jury question of punitive damage is raised; actual malice may take either the form of the defendant's express ill will, hatred or spirit of revenge, or the form of reckless, wilful or wanton behavior which can be inferred from surrounding circumstances. * * *" Id. at 136-138.

Following this state's law on punitive damages and the standards of Civ. R. 56 mandated for resolution of motions for summary judgment, we hold as follows with respect to the involved defendants: We reverse the decisions below granting those partial summary judgments which dismissed punitive damage claims against the Coliseum, The Who and its four general partners, William Curbishley and Electric Factory Concerts. Initially we dispose of the punitive damage issue as to Tidal Wave Promotions, Inc. and Dalpepper Enterprises, Ltd.

Regarding Tidal Wave Promotions, Inc. ("Tidal Wave"), it negotiated a contract dated October 17, 1979, with the local promoter of The Who concert on December 3, 1979. One of the contract's provisions established a sound check for "approximately 6:00 p.m." on the night of the incident. On the face of it, there is nothing improper with scheduling a sound check for 6:00 p.m. What is material in the sequence of events is whether The Who's tardy arrival, a fact demonstrated in the record, was causally related to the tragedy. there is no indication that Tidal Wave's involvement extended beyond the contract referenced above. For example, there is no evidence that a Tidal Wave employee or agent was present on the scene. Finding no genuine issue of material fact as to Tidal Wave's participation which would amount to reckless, wilful or wanton behavior, we affirm the trial court's dismissal of Tidal Wave as to punitive damage liability.

We affirm also as to Dalpepper Enterprises, Ltd. because we find nothing in the record which would amount to a genuine issue of material fact of any such involvement in The Who concert as would amount to reckless, wilful or wanton behavior. It was properly dismissed below as to punitive damage liability.

So far as the Coliseum's liability for punitive damages is concerned, the record is replete with an awareness by its officers and employees of the safety problems presented by large and uncontrolled crowds at rock concerts at the Coliseum prior to December 3, 1979. See depositions of Richard D. Morgan, Director of Operations at the Coliseum, Cincinnati Police Lt. Dale Menkhaus, and Brian Heekin. Moreover, the record contains communications sent by past rock concert patrons to Coliseum officials sounding danger signals for similar future events if solutions to the problems were not implemented. The letters were answered by the Coliseum's Director of Public Relations, John Patrick Tafaro. This correspondence is included as exhibits attached to his deposition. Therefore, a jury question of punitive damages is raised, and the dismissal of the Coliseum as to such damages was erroneous.

What about the possibility of punitive damage recoverability from The Who, including the general partners Daltrey, Townshend, Entwhistle and Jones? The group arrived late for a sound check. See deposition of Lt. Dale Menkhaus. There is a genuine issue of material fact as to whether there is a causal connection between that development and the tardy opening of the Coliseum doors and the ensuing deaths and injuries. Thus, the trial court erred by dismissing claims for punitive damages against The Who.

As personal manager for The Who, William Curbishley was on the scene on December 3, 1979, and had the responsibility for contacts between The Who and others implicated in the concert. According to one of The Who partners, Roger Daltrey, Curbishley had the authority, so far as The Who was concerned, to approve festival seating. In his deposed testimony Daltrey also recognized the possibility that Curbishley might have had authority on December 3, 1979 to decide how many entrance doors would be open and when. A jury question as to punitive damages exists for Curbishley.

Lastly, the motion of defendant Electric Factory Concerts ("EFC") for partial summary judgment on punitive damages was erroneously granted. EFC, a partnership, is a promoter of various events, maintains an office in the Coliseum, and was the promoter of the concert at the Coliseum on December 3, 1979. On October 17, 1979, EFC and the Coliseum executed a written instrument termed "Permit" by which the Coliseum granted permission to EFC to use and occupy its arena on December 3, 1979, from 8:00 p.m. until 11:00 p.m. Under the provisions of the "Permit," the Coliseum reserved many prerogatives to itself, but also awarded certain functions to EFC — and some authority they shared. For instance, provision 4(d) of the "Permit" provided:

"Permittee [EFC] shall have in attendance, at Permittee's cost, a prescribed number of security and safety personnel, the exact number and suitability to be determined by the Coliseum and, if necessary, such determination shall be made after Coliseum's consultation with the City Police and Fire Department."

The "Permit" strikingly evidences the meaningful promotional role of EFC in The Who show on the subject date.

Charles A. Levy, who went by the name of "Cal" Levy, was general manager and office manager for EFC at the time of the 1979 disaster. Levy was present at the Coliseum on December 3 at the concert in his capacity of general manager and actively oversaw the entire panorama for his employer EFC. The deposition in the matter sub judice tends to demonstrate that Levy was a key person in the determination of when the doors would open on the night of the concert. For instance, Richard D. Morgan of the Coliseum officialdom stated the following in his deposition:

"Q. [By attorney] What did you say to Cal Levy, though?

"A. [Morgan] I didn't really say anything to Cal Levy when we went down. Dale Menkhaus [Cincinnati Police Lieutenant] and I then left our office, walked out through the office and walked downstairs, ran into Cal Levy looking for Larry Magid. I said to Dale, 'Let's go down and tell Magid how important' — I said, 'The boss of the Electric Factory, Larry Magid, is here. Let's go downstairs and tell him how important you feel the early opening of the doors is.' He said —

"Q. You agreed with him about the opening of the doors early, didn't you?

"A. I would have liked to have seen the doors open early, yes sir. But we went downstairs.

"Q. You would have liked to see them open at 6:30?

"A. Yes, sir. Went downstairs. They have a little dressing room which they use as an office, Electric Factory, and we went in there, and I said, 'Cal, is Larry Magid here?'

"He said, 'No, he is up eating.' And about that — so Dale said something like, 'Jesus, it would be nice if we could get those doors open earlier,' or 'at 6:30,' something like that. Did you want me to continue?

"Q. Please go ahead.

"A. Cal kind of grabbed Menkhaus by the shoulder like that (demonstrating) and said, 'Dale, you know how the act is. You know they'd freak out.'

"Q. What was that a reference to?

"A. 'Freaking out' in the rock show means that the act would get all upset, perturbed.

"Q. By what?

"A. By someone being in there and seeing them doing their sound check or something like that, by the public seeing them on stage doing their sound check and that they would get all bent out of shape or might cause some additional problems.

"Q. There is nothing about that sound check that requires that it occur after 6:30, is there?

"A. Say that again.

"Q. There is nothing about the carrying out of sound check that requires that it not occur until after 6:30?

"A. If everything was ready, it probably would have occurred at 4:30.

"Q. If Mr. Levy had it ready at 6:00, there would be reason why it didn't occur at 6:30, is that right?

"A. If it was ready, you could have it done, yes, sir.

"Q. Provided they showed up to do it?

"A. Yes, sir."

As heretofore expressed, there remain genuine issues of material fact as to whether the claims against EFC for punitive damages are meritorious.

Resultantly, assignment two is sustained in part and overruled in part. With respect to this assignment, the summary adjudication below in favor of Tidal Wave and Dalpepper Enterprises was proper; the other summary adjudications were not.

IV.

After the trial court in its December 23, 1982 order dismissed the city, the Coliseum directors and Heekin, certain cross-appeals were filed. In other words, the Coliseum, its board members, Heekin, the entire The Who (Daltrey, Townshend, Entwhistle, Jones, Curbishley, Tidal Wave and Dalpepper) and EFC wanted to protest the dismissal of the city. Thus, there are a number of appeals challenging that dismissal. Furthermore, the city became restive when the trial court dismissed members of the Coliseum board and Heekin, and it (city) cross-appealed arguing the following (from the city's brief):

"If the City of Cincinnati, Brian Heekin and the board of directors of Cincinnati Riverfront Coliseum once again become co-defendants in the Hamilton County Court of Common Pleas the City of Cincinnati should be able to pursue its cross-claim for indemnity and contribution against Brian Heekin and the board of directors of Cincinnati Riverfront Coliseum."

We hold that the cross-appeals remonstrating against dismissal of the city are well-taken, but as explicated above in some detail the dismissal is cogent only on the theory of possible negligence and not on nuisance or a civil rights violation. Furthermore, the city's cross-appeals as to the board and Brian Heekin similarly are well-taken. We note parenthetically that it is somewhat puzzling as to why the Coliseum cross-appealed against the city since the trial court's order of December 23, 1982 did not dismiss the Coliseum's cross-claim against the city although it dismissed all other cross-claims against the city. Regardless of the apparent needlessness of the cross-appeal by the Coliseum, its circumscribed cross-claim against the city is viable. Thus, the various assignments of error which attend the cross-appeals are sustained. (Incidentally, these particular assignments, located randomly throughout the myriad briefs, are somewhat depthlessly presented.)

**V.**

In summary, our holdings with respect to the liability of the various parties follow. These recapitulations below are to be credited only as they correspond to elucidative subject matter in this decision proper.

1. We reverse the order of the trial court dismissing punitive damage claims against the Cincinnati Riverfront Coliseum, Inc.

2. We reverse a similar order dismissing punitive damage claims against The Who, Daltrey, Jones, Entwhistle, Townshend and Curbishley.

3. We affirm the order below dismissing punitive damage claims against Tidal Wave Promotions, Inc. and Dalpepper Enterprises, Ltd.

4. We reverse the order below dismissing punitive damage claims against Electric Factory Concerts.

5. We reverse the order of the trial court dismissing all claims against members of the board of directors of the Coliseum and its President, Brian Heekin.

6. We reverse the dismissal of all claims by plaintiffs against the city of Cincinnati insofar as they sound in negligence.

7. We affirm the dismissal of all claims by plaintiffs against the city insofar as they sound in nuisance or a violation of civil rights.

8. We reverse the trial court's dismissal of all cross-claims against the city except as in 9, infra.

9. We affirm that portion of the trial court's order which preserves the claim of the Coliseum against the city.

10. The city's cross-claims for possible indemnification and/or contribution against the board of directors individually and Brian Heekin remain viable.

Judgment accordingly.

**MERCHANDISING LICENSE AGREEMENT**

This Agreement ("Agreement"), dated and effective as of August 15, 2015, by and between John Doe Inc., ("Licensor"), with offices 3333 Tulip Road, Houston, Texas 77777, and Joshua Doe Inc., with offices at 1111 N Orchid Lane, Houston, Texas 77777 ("Licensee").

## RECITALS

1. Licensor is the owner of the name and trademark "John Doe" (the "Trademark"), which is displayed on Schedule "C" annexed hereto.

2.   Licensee will manufacture the items set forth on Schedule A annexed hereto (the "Product").

3.   Licensee desires to sell the Product under the Trademark pursuant to the terms hereof (such Product being sold under the Trademark is referred to as the "Licensed Goods").

4.   Licensor is willing to grant a license to Licensee, to utilize the Trademark pursuant to the terms hereof.

NOW, THEREFORE, the Parties hereto agree as follows:

1.      Grant of License.

(a) During the Term (as defined in Section 2 below) of this Agreement, Licensor hereby grants to Licensee, and Licensee hereby accepts from Licensor, the exclusive right and license (the "License") to sell, manufacture, distribute, advertise and market the Licensed Goods anywhere in the territory set forth on Schedule B annexed hereto (the "Territory"), utilizing the Trademark, upon the terms set forth herein.

(b) Sales of the Licensed Goods shall be made only through those distributors and retail outlets that are compatible with the standards of the Trademark and through internet sales on the Web. Licensor and Licensee acknowledge and agree that certain retailers and distributors have previously sold such Licensed Goods and that such retailers and distributors, without limitation, meet the standards of this provision. Licensee acknowledges that the ownership of all right, title and interest in the Trademark **is and remains solely vested in Licensor**. During the Term of this Agreement, Licensee shall use the Trademark **ONLY** in connection with the marketing, and sale in the Territory of the Licensed Goods and not in connection with any other service, product or business or in any other country or geographic area.

(c) Provided Licensee is not in Default (as defined in Section 5 below) Licensor will not grant to any third party (or use itself) the contractual product exploitation right during the Term (as defined below in this Agreement) to use the Trademark in connection with the marketing and sale of the contractual product in the Territory of the Licensed Goods.  Licensor retains (i) all rights to use and license the use of the Trademark outside the Territory, and (ii) all rights to use and license the use of the Trademark in the Territory in connection with services, products and activities other than the specifically identified Licensed Goods.

(d) Effective Dates:

Contract Date - October 1, 2015
Date to Present Collection – shall commence October 1, 2015
Date for Delivery of Goods – shall commence October 15, 2015

2. Term.

(a) The initial term of this Agreement shall commence on the date hereof, and continue for a period of Twenty-Four (24) months hereafter (the "Initial Term"), unless otherwise extended or terminated in accordance with this Section.

(b) In the event that the Licensee is not in default at the end of the Initial Term, Licensee shall have the right to renew this Agreement for 2 years so long as Licensee's gross sales have been at least One Hundred Thousand Dollars ($100,000.00) in the second year of the Initial Term.

(c) Licensor and Licensee may otherwise elect to extend the Agreement upon written acceptance and mutual consent.

(d) Licensee shall give Licensor notice of its desire to renew within ninety (90) days prior to the expiration of the existing Term.

3. Royalty.

(a) In consideration for the License hereby granted, Licensee shall pay to Licensor, and Licensor shall accept from Licensee, for the twenty-four (24) month Initial Term, and for each year of the renewal period, if applicable, royalty payments (the "Royalty Payments"), as follows:

Initial Two (2) Year Term

Royalty Payments of the Net Sales each year, as follows:

A Quarterly Royalty Payment of Ten Percent (10.0%) shall issue to John Doe, Inc., for Net Sales of $1.00 to $999,999.99;

A Quarterly Royalty Payment of Fifteen Percent (15%) shall issue to John Doe, for Net Sales of $1,000,000.00 to $2,499,999.99;

A Quarterly Royalty Payment of Twenty Percent (20%) shall issue to John Doe, for Net Sales of $2,500,000.00 to $3,999,999.99,

A Quarterly Royalty Payment of Twenty Percent (25%) shall issue to John Doe, for Net Sales of $4,000,000.00 or more,

Renewal Two (2) Year Term

Royalty Payments of the Net Sales each year, as follows:

A Quarterly Royalty Payment of Ten Percent (10.0%) shall issue to John Doe, Inc., for Net Sales of $1.00 to $999,999.99;

A Quarterly Royalty Payment of Fifteen Percent (15%) shall issue to John Doe, for Net Sales of $1,000,000.00 to $2,499,999.99;

A Quarterly Royalty Payment of Twenty Percent (20%) shall issue to John Doe, for Net Sales of $2,500,000.00 to $3,999,999.99,

A Quarterly Royalty Payment of Twenty Percent (25%) shall issue to John Doe, for Net Sales of $4,000,000.00 or more,

For purposes hereof, a "quarter" shall mean a three (3) month period ending March 31, June 30, September 30 and December 31.

(b) Royalty payments hereunder shall be made within thirty (30) days after the end of each quarter during the Term. Licensee shall furnish to Licensor a detailed statement reflecting the Net Sales of Licensed Goods in such quarter (along with such specifications and details as Licensor may reasonably request) for such period and the year to date, together with payment for any Royalty Payment shown to be due pursuant to such statement. Licensee shall maintain such books and records as are necessary to determine the amounts due to Licensor hereunder and Licensor (or its duly authorized representative) will be permitted, no more than one (1) time in any calendar year (retroactive for not less than four (4) years), upon no less than fourteen (14) days written notice to Licensee, to inspect such books and records (an "Inspection") during normal business hours at Licensee's offices. If there is a five percent (5%) or greater shortage in the proper sums remitted to Licensor (a "Shortfall"), Licensee shall, in addition to immediately repaying such Shortfall to Licensor, immediately pay over to Licensor the cost of such inspection (including, without limitation, reasonable outside third party expenses, but not including attorneys fees or travel expenses) and Licensee's failure to do so shall be deemed a material breach hereof and shall constitute a "Default" as set forth in Section 4 hereof. In addition, if the result of an Inspection reveals a Shortfall on more than one occasion, the occurrence of such Shortfall shall be deemed a material breach of this Agreement constituting a "Default" as set forth in Section 4 hereof and Licensee shall not have thirty (30) days to cure such Default.

(c) The term "Net Sales" shall mean the gross sales of the Licensed Goods actually shipped to customers, less only returns, delivery charges, markdowns and allowances. There shall be no deduction from Net Sales for uncollected or uncollectible accounts or for taxes, fees, assessments, impositions, payments, or expenses of any kind (whether imposed on Licensee or otherwise) which may be incurred, paid or withheld in connection with Net Sales, or the manufacture, sale, distribution or exploitation of the Licensed Goods. If any sale is made other than at arm's length, Net Sales shall be based on the price for a corresponding sale at arm's length. There shall be no barter of the Licensed Goods without the express prior written consent of Licensor.

(d) Licensee shall provide a display of the John Doe Collection (or Sub-Brands) products listed on Schedule "A" at Licensee's showrooms and Third-Party Sublicensees and Retailers, paid by **Joshua Doe Inc.**

### 4. Advertising and Promotions

Licensee shall spend Two Percent (2%) of Annual Net Sales for Advertising and Promotions of the products under the License Agreement, upon approval of Licensor and Licensee, of which mutual consent shall not be unreasonably withheld by either Party. Expenditures shall include but are not limited to, advertising or promotions on the "JohnDoe" website, print ads, radio ads, billboards, and television ads for Woman's or Men's clothing fashion shows, as well as promotional Give-A-Ways on any television shows John Doe may host, or appear as a guest.

Licensee shall provide Licensor invoice copies of any expenditure related to Advertising and Promotions on a quarterly basis.

### 5. Default.

Licensor may, at any time (with written notice to Licensee), terminate this Agreement (effective immediately) in the event that Licensee shall materially fail to perform or shall breach any of its material obligations under this Agreement (including, without limitation, the sale of any Licensed Goods outside the Territory, the sale of any item not constituting Licensed Goods which bears the Trademark, or failure to pay any Royalty when due), and such failure or breach is not cured with ten (10) days, following written notice of such failure to perform in compliance with this Agreement. The failure to perform or the breach of such obligations shall be deemed a "General Default" and is referred to as a "Default." It is expressly understood and agreed that upon the occurrence of any event (such as an Act of God or other force majeure event) which, in the absence of any fault by Licensee, makes the performance of Licensee's duties hereunder impossible (however, not to exceed ninety (90) days), Licensee shall not be deemed to be in breach of any of the provisions of this Agreement for the length of time that such performance is impossible; provided; however, that Licensee shall, at all times, remain responsible for the prompt performance of its duties hereunder not made impossible by such occurrence.

6. Quality Control

(a) Licensee acknowledges that the goodwill and reputation associated with the Trademark will be damaged if Licensed Goods are sold which do not meet Licensor's standards required by this Agreement and Licensor shall have the right to the prior written approval of the manner in which the Trademark is utilized in connection with the Licensed Goods, their sale and promotion, which approval shall not be unreasonably withheld or delayed. Licensee and Licensor shall each conduct its business in a manner which shall not bring discredit upon the Trademark or cause Licensor's ownership of the Trademark or Licensee's use of the Trademark to be impaired, reduced or otherwise adversely affected. Licensee will comply with all applicable laws, regulations and decisions of competent authorities pertaining to its business.

(b) Licensee shall (i) upon seven (7) calendar days notice to Licensee by Licensor, permit Licensor access at all times to any facilities at which the Licensed Goods are designed, manufactured, packaged or distributed for the purpose of assuring that such quality control standards are maintained as required by this Agreement, (ii) be responsible for monitoring such quality on a day-to-day basis and for promptly reporting any material deficiencies to Licensor, and (iii) prior to manufacture and sale, submit to Licensor for approval, current and proposed designs for the Licensed Goods, representative samples of the Licensed Goods, and representative samples of labels, packaging, advertisements, catalogues, brochures, mailings, displays, and other advertising or promotional materials bearing the Trademark and used in connection with the Licensed Goods, all in accordance with the terms of this Agreement. Licensor may from time to time, at its own expense, investigate, evaluate and otherwise monitor the Licensed Goods to ensure that the quality control standards set forth in this Section 6 are being met. All labels, packaging, advertisements, brochures, catalogues, displays and other advertising and promotional materials shall continue to be the same quality, design, pattern and composition as are approved by Licensor, in its reasonable discretion, from time to time. All submissions shall be deemed approved by Licensor unless notice of objection is provided to Licensee no later than ten (10) business days after such submission to the Licensor. Licensee has the right to manufacture Licensed Products outside the Territory.

(c) Whenever Licensee uses the Trademark in advertising or in any other manner in connection with the Licensed Goods, Licensee shall, at Licensor's option, clearly indicate Licensor's ownership of the Trademark in a manner approved by Licensor.

(d) Licensee acknowledges that the purpose of the inspections conducted and quality control standards prescribed by Licensor in the Agreement, is to maintain the reputation and the goodwill of the Trademark, and to maintain and improve the image and integrity of the Trademark and the public's perception and awareness of the Trademark.

(e) Licensee shall submit to Licensor for approval, a finished pre-production sample of every style/model that is being proposed for the John Doe Collection, or Sub-Brands (if the style is available in multiple colors, only one color is necessary for submittal of pre-production sample garment, with fabric swatches of each of the other colors being proposed in the style/model), prior to presenting the sample or fabric swatch to any retailer. Upon approval of fabric swatch or pre-production sample, Licensee will submit to Licensor, one (1) top of production samples (if the style/model is available in multiple colors, only one (1) color is necessary for submittal of top of production samples). All submissions shall remain property of Licensor, and are deemed approved by Licensor unless notice of objection is provided to Licensee no later than ten (10) days after such submission to the Licensor.

(f) With regard to all sample submissions, notwithstanding the foregoing, Licensee may in the alternative provide Licensor in a timely manner with a sufficiently detailed photographic representation by email of the Licensed Goods, packaging and or materials as further described above.

(g) During the Term and any sell off period, Licensee shall have the right to sell merchantable seconds to the usual channels for such products.

7. <u>Indemnification and Insurance.</u>

(a) Licensee will indemnify, defend and hold harmless Licensor and its officers, directors, shareholders, agents, employees, representatives, associates, affiliates, attorneys, successors, and assigns, from and against any and all losses, costs, damages, liabilities and expenses whatsoever, including reasonable attorney's fees, relating to or arising directly or indirectly out of the conduct or operation of Licensee's business or sale of the Licensed Goods by Licensee, its subsidiaries, agents or employees, other than as permitted by this Agreement, or Licensee's breach of any provision of this Agreement. Licensee's obligations hereunder shall survive termination of this Agreement.

(b) During the Term of this Agreement, Licensee shall maintain at its own expense the following Insurance coverages: comprehensive general liability insurance, media liability insurance and errors & ommissions (E & O) insurance, including product liability coverage, with limits for premises and products liability in an amount of not less than Two Million Dollars and 00/100 Cents ($2,000,000.00), combined single limit for each coverage. Maintenance of such Insurance coverage shall not relieve Licensee of any responsibility under this agreement for any liabilities in excess of such insurance limits. Licensee shall furnish or cause to be furnished to Licensor on the date hereof a Certificate of such Insurance which certificate shall name Licensor as an additional named Insured and provide that the Insurer, will give Licensor at least thirty (30) days prior written notice of any impending cancellation, renewal, non-renewal, expiration, or reduction in coverage of the insurance.

(c) Licensor will indemnify, defend and hold harmless Licensee and its officers, directors, shareholders, agents, employees, representatives, associates, affiliates, attorneys, successors, and assigns, from and against any and all losses, costs, damages, liabilities and expenses whatsoever, including reasonable attorney's fees, relating to or arising directly or indirectly out of the conduct or operation of Licensor's business by Licensor, its subsidiaries, agents or employees, other than as permitted by this Agreement, any claim that Licensee's use of the Trademark in accordance with this Agreement infringes any third party's intellectual property or other rights, or Licensor's breach of any provision of this Agreement. Licensor's obligations hereunder shall survive termination of this Agreement.

8. <u>Effect of Termination</u>

(a) Upon the termination or expiration of this Agreement for whatever reason, except as otherwise provided in this Agreement:

(i) The License of the Trademark to Licensee and all of Licensee's rights under this Agreement shall immediately cease;

(ii) Licensee shall (a) immediately cease all use of the Trademark and all materials bearing the Trademark, (b) immediately cease to represent or advertise that it is in any way connected with Licensor, and (c) not adopt or use any similar marks, including, but not limited to, any marks that sound similar to the Trademark of that may have the effect of confusing the public with respect to the Trademark; and

(iii) If such termination results from a Default hereunder by either party, then the non-defaulting party shall have such rights against the defaulting party as are provided at law or in equity.

(b) Upon the termination or expiration of this Agreement, and provided that the termination was not the result of Licensee's Default, Licensee shall have the right, for a period of One Hundred and Eighty (180) days following termination or expiration of this Agreement, to sell all of its then inventory of Licensed Goods, pursuant to all of the terms hereof, including the payment and reporting obligations contained herein. Such sales shall be included in Net Sales. At the expiration of such 180-day period, Licensee shall cease any further sale of the Licensed Goods or use of the Trademark, and shall remove each label and/or imprint containing the Trademark from such Licensed Goods before disposing of them, and return each label and/or imprint to Licensor, within Ten (10) days of termination or expiration, of this Agreement.

9. <u>Certain Representations and Covenants of Licensee and Licensor; Licensor Indemnity</u>

(a). Licensee and Licensor each hereby represent and warrants to the other that they have all necessary Corporate power and authority to enter into and to execute this Agreement, and that this Agreement represents the legal, valid and binding obligation of, and enforceable against, the respective parties in accordance with its terms.

(b) Licensee hereby covenants and agrees with Licensor that if, during the term, Licensee anticipates a change of ownership of 50% or more of the common stock of Licensee, then Licensee shall provide Licensor with sixty

(60) days' written notice thereof. Upon such notice, Licensor shall have the right, at its sole option, to immediately terminate this Agreement, and Licensee shall remain responsible for the immediate payment, of all sums due to Licensor hereunder.

(c) Licensor hereby represents and warrants that Licensor is the owner of the Trademark, and that Licensor has the full authority to grant Licensee the rights described herein. Licensor shall maintain the registration of the Trademark throughout the Term. However, Licensor reserves the right to assign its Trademark to a third party.

(d) Licensee will indemnify, defend and hold harmless Licensor and its officers, directors, shareholders, agents, employees, representatives, associates, affiliates, successors, and assigns, from and against any and all losses, costs, damages, liabilities and expenses whatsoever, including reasonable attorney's fees, relating to or arising directly or a dispute concerning the rights licensed to the Licensee under this Agreement or Licensee's breach of any provision of this Agreement. Licensee's obligations hereunder shall survive termination of this Agreement for any reason.

(e) Licensor shall hold Licensee and its affiliates harmless from and shall indemnify each of them against any losses, liabilities, damages and expenses (including interest, penalties and reasonable attorneys' fees and expenses) that any of them may incur or become obligated to pay, or for which any of them may become liable or be compelled to pay in any action, claim or proceeding against any of them, by reason of any acts, whether or omission or commission, by Licensor or anyone acting on its behalf arising out of or related to this Agreement, including, without limitation, those arising out of or related to the Licensee's use of the Licensed Trademarks in accordance with this Agreement of Licensor's representations and warranties under this Agreement. The provisions of and Licensor's obligations under this Section 9 shall survive the expiration or sooner termination of this Agreement.

10. Assignment: Sublicensing.

Licensee may not, directly or indirectly, assign, transfer, or sublicense to any third party or to any independent party all or any part of its rights or duties under this Agreement, without Licensor's prior written approval **(NO EXCEPTIONS)**. Licensor may freely assign or transfer all or part of its rights and obligations under this Agreement, Licensee's rights and obligations shall survive any such assignment or transfer, by Licensor.

11. <u>Notice.</u>

Any notice or consent required to be given under this Agreement shall be in writing, and shall be deemed given if personally delivered or sent by courier:

<u>If to Licensor</u>:
John Doe Inc.
3333 Tulip Road
Houston, Texas 77777

<u>If to Licensee</u>:
Joshua Doe Inc.,
1111 N Orchid Lane
Houston, Texas 77777

or to such other addresses as each party may designate in writing, from time to time.

12. <u>Arbitration.</u>  Except with respect to any party electing to bring an action for specific performance or otherwise seeking injunctive relief (as to which the parties hereto consent to the jurisdiction of the State and Federal Courts, State of Texas, County of Harris, Houston, Texas, and any dispute among the parties hereto as to any matter covered by this Agreement shall be submitted to and settled by arbitration in Harris County, Texas, in accordance with the Commercial arbitration Rules of the American Arbitration Association. Judgment upon the award entered will be accepted by all Parties and may be entered in any court having jurisdiction. The costs of the Arbitration (other than legal fees) shall be paid by the losing party, each party shall bear its own fees and other expenses.

13. <u>Independent Contractor.</u> Nothing contained herein shall be deemed to constitute this Agreement as a joint venture, partnership or an employment agreement. It is fully understood and agreed that in the course of carrying out this Agreement, Licensee will be acting as an Independent Contractor for all purpose, including employment, labor and tax purposes. Licensee understands it has no authority to bind Licensor, and is not entitled to any benefits to employees arising out of their status as employees of Licensor.

14. <u>Entire Agreement.</u> This Agreement supersedes any and all prior agreements, written or oral, regarding the rendering of services by Licensee to Licensor and constitutes the entire agreement between Licensor and Licensee

with respect to the subject matter hereof. This Agreement may not be altered, modifies or amended except in writing, executed by Licensor and Licensee.

15. <u>Nonwaiver.</u> Failure of either party to enforce any of the provisions of the Agreement, or any rights with respect thereto or the failure to exercise any election provided for herein, shall in no way be considered to be a waiver of such provisions, rights or elections, or in any way affect the validity of this Agreement.

16. <u>Release.</u> Except as otherwise provided in this Agreement, Licensee, on its own behalf, and on behalf of its employers, employees, affiliates, attorneys, agents, successors, assigns and parent companies hereby releases, discharges and agrees to hold harmless John Doe Inc., and each of their respective affiliates, and all of their respective officers, employees, directors, agents, attorneys and assigns from any and all claims whatsoever arising from the Licensed Goods manufactured and distributed by Licensee, or for any fees or damages whatsoever resulting from the manufacturing and distribution of Licensed Goods which Licensee now has or hereinafter may have, in accordance with the terms of this Agreement. "Notwithstanding the foregoing, the foregoing release and indemnity shall not apply to any losses or claims that arise from Licensor's breach of the Agreement or any claim that Licensee's use of the Trademark in accordance with this Agreement infringes any third party's intellectual property or other distribution rights; in such circumstances, Licensor shall defend and indemnify Licensee."

17. <u>Limited Liability.</u> In the event of any dispute between Licensor and Licensee in connection with this Agreement, each party warrants and represents that it will seek remedies against the other party only, and neither party will bring or commence any action or proceeding whatsoever against any officer, director, agent, representative, or member of the other party in an individual capacity. If any court or arbitrator of competent jurisdiction shall agree to hear an action or proceeding brought by either party against any officer, director, agent, representative or member of the other party in an individual capacity, then the aforementioned officer, director, agent, representative or member against whom such action or proceeding has been commenced may use this paragraph as a full and complete defense to any such action or proceeding, and the party instituting such action or proceeding shall be liable for any costs and attorneys' fees incurred by the officer, director, agent, representative or member defending such action or proceeding.

18. <u>Governing Law.</u> This Agreement shall be governed by the laws of the State of Texas, without regard to the conflict of laws rules thereof, applicable to agreements made and to be wholly performed therein. Joshua

Doe Inc., agree to submit themselves to the jurisdiction of the Federal or State Courts located in Harris County, Houston, Texas in any action which may rise out of this agreement and said Courts shall have executive jurisdiction over all disputes pertaining to this Agreement and all matters related thereto.

19. <u>Miscellaneous.</u>

(a) This Agreement shall be binding upon and inure to the benefit of the Parties and their respective successors and permitted assigns.

(b) The invalidity of any provision of this Agreement will not affect the validity of the remaining provisions, and this Agreement will be construed as if such invalid provisions had been omitted.

20. <u>Representations & Warranties:</u> Each Party hereby represents and warrants that it has been advised of its right to retain independent legal counsel in connection with the negotiation and execution of this Agreement, and that they have either retained and have been represented by such legal counsel, or have knowingly and voluntarily waived their right to such legal counsel and desire to enter into this Agreement without the benefit of legal representation.

IN WITNESS WHEREOF, the Parties hereto have executed this Agreement on the date and year first above written.

**This Agreement is non-binding, until executed by all Parties.**

Joshua Doe Inc.,                                                John Doe Inc.


By:_____                    By:_____
Joshua Doe                                                      Mr. John Doe
Title:  President/CEO                                       Title: President/CEO

SCHEDULE "A"

<u>Products</u>
Men's Shirts

And products as specifically identified, approved and mutually agreed upon, in writing, by Licensor

SCHEDULE "B"
Territory

United States and Canada

SCHEDULE "C"

# John Doe, Inc.

All packaging as specifically identified, approved in writing, by Licensor

Questions and Discussion

1. In *Kass v. Young*, 136 Cal. Rptr. 469 (1977), an angry fan at a Neil Young concert wanted his money back. It was claimed that Neil terminated the concert by abruptly walking off the stage. [I saw him live with Booker T. & the M.G.'s with my now deceased 14-year-old son in 1993—I never saw a more gracious, generous performer who nodded to Steve Cropper when they played "(Sittin' on) the Dock of Bay"—co-written by Steve Cropper and Otis Redding, W.T.C.] This case actually involved a default judgment against Neil Young. The class action default judgment was set aside because there had been no class certification. The cause was remanded. Neil claims he walked off because of security issues. Should that make a difference?

2. In *Bowes v. Cincinnati Riverfront Coliseum, Inc.*, 465 N.E.2d 904 (Ohio App. 1983), the court looked at the tragedy at Cincinnati's Riverfront Stadium when, at the Who concert, patrons and would-be patrons were killed while entering the stadium. Summary judgment was upheld for the nuisance and civil rights claims. The court reversed summary judgment for claims of negligence or wrongful acts or omissions. The court reversed the order dismissing plaintiffs' punitive damage claim against The Who. What do you think of this?

3. Look at the Merchandising License Agreement (licensee and licensor). Please confirm if this agreement authorizes third party distribution rights.

# Chapter 11
# Film and Television Music

Music for film and television cannot only be lucrative but can also have a synergistic effect on the musician's career—for example, Joe Cocker's rendition of that old standard, "Bye Bye Blackbird," in the movie Sleepless in Seattle. The music in soundtracks can generally be divided into songs and scores. "Soundtracks are not, of course, limited to motion pictures. This discussion also relates to the creation and exploitation of music for television, video, laser discs, computer games, and CD-ROM interactive programs, not to mention music on chips inserted into toys" (Schulenburg, Legal Aspects of the Music Industry 328). The agreement will specify the duties of the music supervisor, the composer, and the film producer. Also noted will be Loan-Out Agreements, Exclusivity, Grant of Rights, Retention of Rights, Credit, and Income (Id., at 328-350). "The producer of the film hires both the music supervisor and the composer to create the soundtrack. The supervisor receives a fee for the services rendered, usually a set fee, which is part of the film's budget" (Id., at 350). "Not all music is created just for the soundtrack. There is frequently a need for source music" (Id., at 353), soundtrack albums, synchronization licenses, performance fees, and mechanical fees (Id., at 354-280) (see also Chapter 6, "Music," Mark Litwak, Contracts for the Film & Television Industry 206-29 (Beverly Hills, 3d. ed., 2012)).

In the following case, *Agee v. Paramount Communications, Inc.*, 59 F. 3d 317 (2d Cir. 1995), the court held that commercial entities could not reproduce sound recordings on soundtracks of audiovisual works, whether or not the reproduction involved synchronization.

Agee v. Paramount Communs., Inc.
United States Court of Appeals for the Second Circuit
February 24, 1995, Argued; June 26, 1995, Decided
Docket No. 94-7670
59 F.3d 317

JON O. NEWMAN, Chief Judge:

The primary issue presented by this appeal is whether incorporating a copyrighted sound recording into the soundtrack of a taped commercial television production infringes the copyright owner's exclusive right of reproduction under the Copyright Act of 1976, 17 U.S.C. §§ 106 and 114(b) (1993). We hold that it does.

Plaintiff-appellant Michael L. Agee appeals from the June 3, 1994, judgment of the District Court for the Southern District of New York (Constance Baker Motley, Judge) granting summary judgment against him on his copyright claim against defendants-appellees Paramount Communications, Inc., Paramount Pictures, and Paramount Television Group ("Paramount") and the owners of 129 television stations ("TV stations"), and dismissing his Lanham Act and unfair competition claims for failure to state a cause of action. See 853 F. Supp. 778 (S.D.N.Y. 1994). Paramount copied portions of Agee's sound recording to make the audio track of a segment of a television program, and transmitted the program to the TV stations, which in turn made their own copies for transmission to the viewing public.

We conclude that Paramount violated Agee's exclusive right of reproduction when it copied his sound recording on tape as part of the television program's soundtrack. However, we find that the copies of the program, including the duplicated portions of Agee's work, made by the TV stations are protected by the statute's "ephemeral recording" exemption, see 17 U.S.C. § 112. We agree with the dismissal of Agee's Lanham Act and unfair competition claims. We therefore affirm in part, reverse in part, and remand.

## Background

Plaintiff-appellant Michael L. Agee, a California resident, is proprietor of L&H Records, a music recording studio located in California. Through L&H Records, Agee owns copyrights in two sound recordings, "Laurel and Hardy's Music Box" ("Music Box") and "Laurel and Hardy's Music Box: Volume II" ("Music Box-Two"). Agee does not own the copyright in the musical compositions embodied in these sound recordings.

Defendant-appellee Paramount Communications, Inc. is a Delaware corporation whose principal place of business is California. Defendants-appellees Paramount Pictures and Paramount Television Group are divisions of Paramount. Paramount Pictures produces the daily, half-hour news magazine television program Hard Copy and transmits it to independently owned and operated television stations for broadcast nationwide.

Paramount copied portions of three songs from Agee's "Music Box-Two," entitled "Ku-Ku," "Cops," and "The Donkey's Ears," to make the audio track of a four-minute segment of its Hard Copy feature called "Caught on Tape." After duplicating parts of the recording, Paramount created an audiovisual work that timed or "synchronized" portions of the duplicated recording to visual images showing two young men engaged in an unsuccessful burglary attempt.

Paramount recorded the "Caught on Tape" feature on February 15, 1993, and integrated it into the Hard Copy program for satellite transmission to the TV stations for airing the next day. Portions of the feature, including Agee's recording, were also included in the opening and closing credits of the program. In addition, Paramount produced and transmitted to the TV stations a promotional commercial excerpted from the program, again including Agee's copyrighted work. The TV stations made their own copies of the program and the commercial and broadcast them to the public. Paramount neither sought nor obtained a license from Agee for the use of his recording, nor did it refer to him in the program's credits.

On September 10, 1993, Agee brought a copyright infringement action against Paramount and the TV stations for the unauthorized copying and synchronization of the songs from his sound recording, creation of a derivative work, and distribution or publication of that work to the public. Agee also alleged that defendants had engaged in unfair competition and that Paramount's use of his recording violated section 43(a) of the Lanham Act.

Agee moved by order to show cause for a temporary restraining order on November 19, 1993, seeking a preliminary injunction prohibiting the TV stations from rebroadcasting and Paramount from retransmitting the tape. The temporary restraining order was granted and then dissolved on the same day upon defense counsel's oral representation that the program would not be broadcast again. Thereafter, and prior to any discovery, Paramount and the TV stations moved for dismissal of the complaint and, alternatively, for summary judgment.

The District Court granted defendants' motion, dismissing Agee's state law and Lanham Act claims, and granting summary judgment on the copyright infringement claim after concluding that defendants had not infringed any of Agee's exclusive rights under the Copyright Act, which include the right to (1) reproduce the sound recording, (2) prepare a derivative work based upon the sound recording, and (3) distribute copies of the sound recording to the public. See 17 U.S.C. §§ 106, 114(b) (1993).

With respect to the exclusive right to reproduce a copyrighted sound recording, the District Court held that although the synchronization or "synch" right (i.e., the right to use recorded music in synchronization with visual images on the soundtrack of a television program or motion picture) had been held to be a subset of a music publisher's right to reproduce his work, see, e.g., Angel Music, Inc. v. ABC Sports, Inc., 631 F. Supp. 429, 433 n.4 (S.D.N.Y. 1986), such a synch right was not part of the sound recording copyright owner's exclusive reproduction right, which was more limited. See 853 F. Supp. at 786-87. Rather, the Copyright Act proscribed only the "unauthorized sale or public distribution" of phonorecords or audiovisual works containing Agee's sound recordings, "which did not happen in this case." Id. at 787.

In addition, the District Court concluded that Paramount had not violated Agee's exclusive right to prepare derivative works from his recording because there was "no evidence that the sounds in [Agee's] recording were remixed, or that additional lyrics or musical variations were added, or that defendant took his recording and transformed it into a new original work." Id. at 788-89.

The District Court also held that Paramount's "transmission" of Hard Copy, together with Agee's sound recording, to the TV stations and the TV stations' transmission of the program to the public did not amount to "distributions" of copies of Agee's recording to the public, but were simply public "performances" of that recording. Because sound recording copyright owners do not have exclusive performance rights, see 17 U.S.C. § 114(a), these transmissions did not infringe Agee's rights. 853 F. Supp. at 789.

Additionally, the District Court noted that the TV stations' copies of the program were protected under the "ephemeral recording" exemption, 17 U.S.C. § 112, which permits "transmitting organizations" with the right to transmit any work to make a single copy of a particular program embodying the work if certain prerequisites are satisfied. 853 F. Supp. at 789-90.

Finally, the District Court found that Agee had failed to state a cause of action under either the Lanham Act or unfair competition law. Agee's complaint did not allege that Paramount had misrepresented the source of the music used in the "Caught On Tape" segment or that it possessed a copyright in Agee's sound recordings. Rather, Agee's Lanham Act claim arose "from the same basic facts which support his failed copyright claim — defendants' alleged unauthorized use of his sound recording in their television program without paying him a royalty or recognizing him in the credits to the program." Id. at 791. As to the unfair competition claim, the District Court found that Agee had failed to plead facts or introduce evidence that his record sales or licensing revenues had been affected by defendants' use of his sound recording. Id.

This appeal followed.

**Discussion**

Paramount's duplication and transmission of Agee's sound recording as part of the soundtrack of Hard Copy, and the TV stations' subsequent duplication and transmission of that program to the viewing public, are far removed from the record piracy that prompted Congress to enact legislation protecting sound recording copyright owners. That legislation is in some respects quite limited, denying owners of copyrights in sound recordings certain exclusive rights that are available to music publishers or to owners of copyrights in the underlying musical compositions.

Nevertheless, applying de novo review, see Longo v. Shore & Reich, Ltd., 25 F.3d 94, 96 (2d Cir. 1994), we conclude that Paramount's use of Agee's sound recording infringed his exclusive right to reproduce his work, notwithstanding the fact that the Hard Copy program containing his recording was broadcast only once and was not distributed to the public for sale or rental. However, we find no violation of Agee's exclusive right to distribute copies of his sound recording to the public. Moreover, although Paramount might have infringed Agee's exclusive right to prepare derivative works, we need not resolve that question because such an infringement would not expand Paramount's liability or alter our conclusion that the TV stations' duplication and broadcast of Agee's work was protected by the ephemeral recording exemption.

A. Copyright Claim

Statutory Background. Section 106 of the Copyright Act of 1976 gives owners of copyrights in most works the exclusive right to reproduce the copyrighted work in copies or phonorecords, to prepare derivative works based upon the copyrighted work, to distribute copies or phonorecords of the copyrighted work to the public by sale or other transfer of ownership, or by rental, lease, or lending, to perform the work publicly, and to display the work publicly. 17 U.S.C. § 106. However, with respect to copyrights in sound recordings, which the Act defines as "works that result from the fixation of a series of musical, spoken, or other sounds," id. § 101, the Act confers more limited rights. Only the rights of reproduction, preparation of derivative works, and distribution of copies are conferred, and a performance right is explicitly not conferred. Id. § 114(a). Moreover, the rights that are conferred are more limited than in the case of other works.

The reproduction right is limited to the right "to duplicate the sound recording in the form of phonorecords, or of copies of motion pictures and other audiovisual works, that directly or indirectly recapture the actual sounds fixed in the recording." Id. § 114(b) (emphasis added). The derivative work right is limited to the right "to prepare a derivative work in which the actual sounds fixed in the sound recording are rearranged, remixed, or otherwise altered in sequence or quality." Id.

Also pertinent to our inquiry in this case is the exemption that section 114 extends to broadcasters for "ephemeral recordings." Specifically, it is not an infringement for a "transmitting organization entitled to transmit to the public a performance or display of a work, under a license or transfer of the copyright or under the limitations on exclusive rights in sound recordings specified by section 114(a), to make no more than one copy or phonorecord of a particular transmission program embodying the performance or display." Id. § 112(a).

To be eligible for this exemption, a "transmitting organization" must satisfy three conditions: (1) the copy must be used solely by the transmitting organization that made it, and no further copies can be reproduced from it; (2) the copy must be used "solely for the transmitting organization's own transmissions within its local service area, or for purposes of archival preservation or security"; and (3) unless preserved exclusively for archival purposes, the copy must be destroyed within six months from the date the program was first transmitted to the public.

1. Reproduction Right. Congress's primary intention in granting sound recording copyright owners the exclusive right of reproduction was to prevent the unauthorized duplication of sound recordings that was causing substantial losses in the recording industry. See United States v. Taxe, 380 F. Supp. 1010, 1014 (C.D. Cal. 1974) ("The legislative history of the [Sound Recording Amendment of 1971] indicates that its intent was to put record 'pirates' out of business."), aff'd, 540 F.2d 961 (9th Cir. 1976), cert. denied, 429 U.S. 1040, 50 L. Ed. 2d 751, 97 S. Ct. 737 (1977). Indeed, the impetus behind the Sound Recording Amendment, which was largely incorporated into the Copyright Act, was the perceived need to prevent "widespread unauthorized reproduction of phonograph records and tapes." H.R. Rep. No. 487, 92nd Cong., 1st Sess. at 1 (1971) ("House Report").

Nevertheless, as amicus Register of Copyrights observes, the statutory language pertaining to the sound recording reproduction right is broad enough to include a synch right, which would require a producer to obtain authorization from the owner of a sound recording before reproducing that recording in the soundtrack of an audiovisual work. See 17 U.S.C. § 114(b).

In addition, the legislative history indicates that Congress intended to proscribe the unauthorized duplication of sound recordings in the soundtrack of audiovisual works. See House Report at 106 (infringement of copyright owner's reproduction right takes place "whenever all or any substantial portion of the actual sounds that go to make up a copyrighted sound recording are reproduced in phonorecords . . . by reproducing them in the soundtrack or audio portion of a motion picture or other audiovisual work"). It thus appears that although the sound recording legislation was enacted primarily to combat piracy, that legislation, in its terms and its intent, is broad enough to cover some forms of reproduction even in situations where copies are not distributed to the public. The District Court considered a synch right to be an extension of the reproduction right defined by section 114(b). 853 F. Supp. at 787. We disagree. A synchronization of previously recorded sounds onto the soundtrack of an audiovisual work is simply an example of the reproduction right explicitly granted by section 114(b) to the owner of rights in a sound recording.

Moreover, the Copyright Act specifically permits certain entities to reproduce sound recordings in soundtracks, provided that copies of the programs containing those recordings are not distributed to the public. For example, Congress provided in section 114(b) that noncommercial broadcasting entities have the right to include sound recordings in educational radio and television broadcasts, and may distribute and transmit copies or phonorecords as long as "copies or phonorecords of said programs are not commercially distributed by or through public broadcasting entities to the general public." 17 U.S.C. § 114(b). The plain implication of section 114(b) is that commercial entities like Paramount may not reproduce sound recordings on soundtracks of audiovisual works, whether or not the reproduction involves synchronization.

Paramount acknowledges that its use of Agee's sound recordings in conjunction with visual images was technically a "reproduction," but argues that the pre-recording of the Hard Copy soundtrack with Agee's recorded sounds was purely "incidental" to a single, tape-delayed television performance — the technological equivalent of a live broadcast. Paramount observes that it could have played Agee's recording, in synchronization with the video tape, as part of a live performance of Hard Copy without infringing Agee's reproduction right. Just as recording a television program for later viewing permits a home viewer to shift the effective time of the performance, see Sony Corp. v. Universal City Studios, 464 U.S. 417, 429, 78 L. Ed. 2d 574, 104 S. Ct. 774 (1984), duplicating Agee's recording onto the soundtrack of an audiovisual work merely permitted Paramount to shift the time of the recording's broadcast to viewers. Paramount asserts that no copies of the program containing Agee's recording were made for distribution or sale.

In Sony, the Supreme Court held that consumers were not infringing copyrights in broadcast programs when taping television shows for later viewing. Id. at 447-55. In concluding that this recording was a fair use of the copyright, the Court noted that the work was transmitted free of charge over the broadcast airwaves, and the copy was a "time-shifting" one. Id. at 449. No evidence indicated that a consumer had published or otherwise attempted to profit from a time-shifting copy. Id. The nature of a televised copyrighted audiovisual work and the fact that time-shifting merely enabled viewers to view at a later time works that they had previously been invited to watch rebutted the presumption that reproducing a copyrighted work in its entirety was unfair.

Id. at 449-50. In addition, the Court held that time-shifting reproductions had no demonstrable effect upon the potential market for, or the value of, a copyrighted work, and that time-shifting yielded societal benefits by expanding public access to broadcast television programs. Id. at 454.

We need not decide in this case whether all copying of sound recordings, including commercial copying solely for time-shifting purposes, infringes the copyright owner's exclusive right of reproduction, because Paramount's duplication and synchronization of Agee's sound recording were designed to achieve more than a time-shifted performance of that recording. Paramount derived independent commercial value from copying Agee's sound recording because that reproduction not only shifted the timing of performance but actually enhanced the performance by ensuring that there would be no mistakes in the synchronized program broadcast to viewers. Reproducing Agee's recording in the soundtrack of Hard Copy also enabled Paramount to preserve the program intact for possible distribution or re-broadcast at a later date.

Indeed, Paramount's characterization of its reproduction as merely a time-shifted performance is belied by the additional copies and uses Paramount made of the taped synchronization. In addition to copying Agee's sound recording as part of its synchronization of the recording with the "Caught On Tape" segment, Paramount incorporated a portion of the "Caught On Tape" segment, including Agee's copyrighted work, into a promotion of the next day's program and also prepared a commercial that contained a portion of the segment along with Agee's recording. Although Paramount has not distributed copies of Hard Copy to the public or impaired the market for Agee's sound recording in any obvious sense, its uses of its taped program suggest the value to Paramount, apart from time-shifting, of reproducing Agee's work.

In short, Paramount purchased Agee's sound recording but made no attempt to obtain a license for its reproduction in the soundtrack of its program. It therefore infringed Agee's sound recording at the moment it put portions of his recording on tape to make a segment of Hard Copy. Its incorporation of the sound recording without permission violated Agee's reproduction right.

2. Derivative Works. Agee contends that Paramount also infringed his exclusive right to prepare derivative works based upon his sound recording. Under the Copyright Act, a "derivative work" is defined as a work based upon one or more preexisting works, such as a translation, musical arrangement, dramatization, fictionalization, motion picture version, sound recording, art reproduction, abridgement, condensation, or any other form in which a work may be recast, transformed, or adapted. See 17 U.S.C. § 101.

In the case of sound recordings, the Copyright Act imposes additional requirements before such a "transformation" of a preexisting work is sufficient to create a derivative work. See id. § 114(b); House Report at 106. Under section 114(b), the use of a sound recording qualifies as a derivative work only if "the actual sounds fixed in the sound recording are rearranged, remixed, or otherwise altered in sequence or quality." 17 U.S.C. § 114(b). Thus, before the Hard Copy episode could be considered a derivative work of Agee's sound recording, it must be found that Paramount altered Agee's recording in a manner that "rearranged, remixed or altered in sequence or quality" the actual sounds in the recording. To the extent Agee contends that the mere synchronization of his sound recording with visual images created an infringing derivative work, we disagree. Although a few cases may exist where a motion picture or television program is "based upon" a preexisting musical composition or sound recording, sound recordings are most often used in audiovisual works for background or performance, as in this case. Moreover, even if the mere transfer of Agee's recording to the soundtrack of an audiovisual work in itself amounted to a "transformation," such synchronization would not rearrange, remix or alter the actual sounds of the recording.

However, Agee also alleges that Paramount edited his recordings, incorporating sound effects and narration with Agee's recordings in the soundtrack. Agee claims that "defendants altered the expression embodied in Agee's recording by abridging and condensing it, reordering it, [and] adding various sound effects." At oral argument, appellant contended that Paramount reordered and interspersed the actual sounds of the songs on his recording. The District Court concluded that although the soundtrack of Hard Copy added sound effects to Agee's recording, these additions did not alter the recording itself, but were designed only to "highlight" the visual images on the program. See 853 F. Supp. at 788.

Although the interspersing and abridgement of a sound recording may not, strictly speaking, involve sampling or amount to the traditional creation of a derivative work, such use of a recording appears to fall within the language of section 114(b), perhaps constituting a rearrangement or alteration in sequence. We need not determine the extent to which the recording was altered, however, because the finding that Paramount created a derivative work is unnecessary to a finding of infringement in light of Paramount's reproduction of Agee's recording, see Twin Peaks Productions, Inc. v. Publications International, Ltd., 996 F.2d 1366, 1373 (2d Cir. 1993), and, as discussed below, would not affect our analysis with respect to the TV stations.

3. Distribution Right. Agee contends that Paramount infringed his exclusive right to distribute his sound recording when it transmitted Hard Copy, including his work, by satellite to the TV stations because such a transmission constituted a distribution of one or more copies of his recording "to the public" under 17 U.S.C. § 106(3). His contention is meritless.

The Copyright Act provides no definition of "distribution." As Agee observes, however, at least one court has concluded that the distribution right is essentially synonymous with the exclusive right of "publication" referred to in the 1909 Copyright Act. See Ford Motor Co. v. Summit Motor Products, Inc., 930 F.2d 277, 299 (3d Cir. 1991). See also House Report at 102 ("Clause (3) of section 106 established the exclusive right of publication."). The 1976 Act defines "publication" as "the distribution of copies or phonorecords of a work to the public by sale or other transfer of ownership, or by rental, lease, or lending." 17 U.S.C. § 101. In addition, "the offering to distribute copies or phonorecords to a group of persons for purposes of further distribution, public performance, or public display, constitutes "publication." Id.

We find no basis for concluding that Paramount's transmission of Agee's recording to viewers via the TV stations, rather than directly, was a "distribution." In a slightly different context, a number of courts have held that "transmissions by a cable network or service to local cable companies who in turn transmit to individual cable subscribers constitute 'public performances' by the network under [the Copyright Act]." Coleman v. ESPN, Inc., 764 F. Supp. 290, 294 (S.D.N.Y. 1991); see also David v. Showtime/The Movie Channel, Inc., 697 F. Supp. 752, 759 n.3 (S.D.N.Y. 1988) (transmission to cable operator by cable programmer is public performance under Copyright Act); WGN Continental Broadcasting Co. v. United Video, Inc., 693 F.2d 622, 625 (7th Cir. 1982).

Treating such satellite transmissions as public performances protects music publishers and owners of copyrights in musical compositions, who have exclusive performance rights under the Copyright Act; otherwise, producers and networks could avoid liability by relying on local stations to perform a copyrighted work. See David v. Showtime/The Movie Channel, Inc., 697 F. Supp. at 759 ("Congress apparently did not anticipate the eventual proliferation of organizations such as SMC who 'broadcast' their programs to the public indirectly, through local cable companies who pass the signal along to their individual customers."). By contrast, in transmitting Hard Copy, along with Agee's recording, to the TV stations for transmission to the public, Paramount was not attempting to evade liability for performing Agee's copyrighted work because Paramount itself had the right to perform that work.

It is clear that merely transmitting a sound recording to the public on the airwaves does not constitute a "distribution"; otherwise, sound recording copyright owners would have the performance rights expressly denied to them under the statute. For this reason, distribution is generally thought to require transmission of a "material object" in which the sound recording is fixed: a work that is of "more than transitory duration." See 17 U.S.C. § 101 (defining "copy"); David Nimmer & Melville B. Nimmer, 2 Nimmer on Copyright, § 8.11[A] (1993) (distribution right is right "publicly to sell, give away, rent or lend any material embodiment of copyrighted work). See also House Report at 138 ("any form or dissemination in which a material object does not change hands — performances or displays on television, for example — is not a publication no matter how many people are exposed").

Although we are unwilling to say that disseminations must always be in physical form to constitute "distributions," see, e.g., Playboy Enterprises, Inc. v. Frena, 839 F. Supp. 1552 (M.D. Fla. 1993) (unauthorized uploading of copyrighted images onto computer bulletin board with knowledge that images would be downloaded by other bulletin board subscribers), in the broadcasting context, the distinction between material and non-material embodiments, and the fact that Paramount, like most television and radio broadcasting networks, transmitted its program for broadcast to the public, are relevant factors in determining whether Paramount engaged in broadcasting rather than distribution. We conclude that Paramount's transmission of Agee's recording constituted a performance of that recording and not a distribution.

4. Ephemeral Recording Exemption. The District Court found the ephemeral recording exemption, see 17 U.S.C. § 112(a), applicable to both Paramount and the TV stations. This exemption permits "transmitting organizations," defined as broadcasting networks or local broadcasters, see House Report at 102, to make a single copy of a copyrighted work to facilitate their broadcast, provided certain prerequisites are met. Paramount now concedes that it is ineligible for this exemption because it is a program supplier rather than a broadcaster, and thus is not a "transmitting organization" under the statute. However, appellees contend that the exemption applies to the TV stations and thus protects the TV stations' copying and broadcast of Agee's recording.

There is no dispute that the TV stations are "transmitting organizations" for purposes of section 112(a). The TV stations also appear to have complied with the preconditions for invoking the ephemeral recording exemption, see 17 U.S.C. § 112(a), because they made a single copy of the program containing Agee's sound recording, used this copy solely for their own transmission in their service area, and, pursuant to their contract with Paramount, had to destroy their tape or return it to Paramount.

Agee contends, however, that the TV stations are not entitled to the ephemeral recording exemption because they copied and broadcast an unauthorized reproduction or derivative work containing Agee's sound recording. This contention is arguably supported by the language of section 112(a), which allows transmitting organizations to make a copy of a copyrighted work only if they are "entitled to transmit to the public a performance or display of a work, under a license or transfer of the copyright or under the limitations on exclusive rights in sound recordings specified by section 114(a)." Id. § 112(a). According to Agee, because the Hard Copy program was "tainted" by Paramount's unauthorized use of his work, the TV stations could not copy or perform the program without first obtaining Agee's permission. See House Report at 102 ("unless all [limitations on the scope of the ephemeral recording privilege] are met the making of an 'ephemeral recording' becomes fully actionable as an infringement").

We reject this argument, despite its surface plausibility and despite the fact that Paramount reproduced, and perhaps also prepared a derivative work based upon, Agee's recording. Because Agee has no exclusive performance rights, see 17 U.S.C. § 114(a), the TV stations were entitled to broadcast his recording without his consent. Nothing in the statute would prohibit the TV stations from also broadcasting a reproduction of Agee's sound recording since, like Paramount's transmission of its program to the TV stations, such a broadcast would still constitute a "performance." Had the TV stations themselves purchased Agee's sound recording, copied it, and then broadcast the recording to the public using the copy, they would have been at most liable for the duplication and not for the broadcast. The fact that Paramount, rather than the TV stations, reproduced Agee's recording does not alter the result.

The TV stations also would have been entitled to perform a derivative work that Paramount had created using Agee's sound recording. The statute states only that sound recording copyright owners have the exclusive right to "prepare" derivative works, see 17 U.S.C. § 114(b); it says nothing about the right to perform such works. Although some performances might create a derivative work (e.g., an improvised performance that recasts or remixes a sound recording), in this case, it was Paramount who prepared the work, with the TV stations merely broadcasting that work to the public.

Because the TV stations had the right to broadcast Agee's reproduced or altered sound recording "under the limitations on exclusive rights in sound recordings specified by section 114(a)," the stations are protected by the ephemeral recording exemption.

B. Lanham Act and Unfair Competition Claims.

Agee's Lanham Act and unfair competition claims require relatively little discussion. To state a claim for damages under the Lanham Act, Agee must allege a false representation of the source of his sound recording and actual confusion by consumers as to the source. See PPX Enterprises, Inc. v. Auto Fidelity Enterprises, Inc., 818 F.2d 266, 271 (2d Cir. 1987). Agee alleges that by failing to attribute the recording to him in the credits of Hard Copy, and by playing his recording while the credits were being shown, Paramount misrepresented the source of the recording or at least suggested that it owned a copyright in the recording.

However, Agee has alleged no facts suggesting that appellees "deliberately engaged in a deceptive commercial practice" designed to deceive the public as to the source of the product. Resource Developers, Inc. v. Statue of Liberty-Ellis Island Foundation, Inc., 926 F.2d 134, 140 (2d Cir. 1991). There is no allegation that appellees intentionally used Agee's sound recording to deceive the public, nor is there any factual allegation that the public was in any way confused as to the source of the sound recording as a result of Paramount's failure to attribute that recording to Agee.

As the District Court found, Agee based his Lanham Act claim entirely on the fact that appellees made unauthorized use of his sound recording without paying him a royalty or recognizing him in the credits to the program. See *Merchant v. Lymon*, 828 F. Supp. 1048, 1060 (S.D.N.Y. 1993) (extending Lanham Act to cover "circumstances where an artist has not been properly credited for his ownership would simply transform every copyright action into a Lanham Act action as well"). Consequently, dismissal of the Lanham Act claim for failure to state a cause of action was appropriate.

Similarly, Agee's state law unfair competition claim is baseless. Although Agee alleges that appellees' use of his sound recording has caused a "diminution of good will" by connecting his sound recording to "criminal activities" or associating it with Hard Copy, Agee has failed to plead facts indicating that his record sales or licensing revenues have in any way been affected by Paramount's use of the recording. There is no reasonable ground for believing that Agee has suffered economic losses as a result of appellees' actions, or that consumers think less of the recording.

### Conclusion

For the reasons set forth above, we affirm the dismissal of Agee's Lanham Act and state law claims as well as the grant of summary judgment in favor of the TV stations. With respect to Agee's claim of copyright infringement, we reverse the grant of summary judgment in favor of Paramount, and, because no genuine issues of material fact exist with respect to that claim, direct the entry of summary judgment for the plaintiff on the issue of Paramount's liability for copyright infringement, and we remand for determination of appropriate relief.

Broadcast Music, Inc. v. Columbia Broadcasting System, Inc.
Supreme Court of the United States
January 15, 1979, Argued; April 17, 1979, Decided
No. 77-1578
441 U.S. 1

MR. JUSTICE WHITE delivered the opinion of the Court.

This case involves an action under the antitrust and copyright laws brought by respondent Columbia Broadcasting System, Inc. (CBS), against petitioners, American Society of Composers, Authors and Publishers (ASCAP) and Broadcast Music, Inc. (BMI), and their members and affiliates. The basic question presented is whether the issuance by ASCAP and BMI to CBS of blanket licenses to copyrighted musical compositions at fees negotiated by them is price fixing per se unlawful under the antitrust laws.

I.

CBS operates one of three national commercial television networks, supplying programs to approximately 200 affiliated stations and telecasting approximately 7,500 network programs per year. Many, but not all, of these programs make use of copyrighted music recorded on the soundtrack. CBS also owns television and radio stations in various cities. It is "'the giant of the world in the use of music rights,'" the "'No. 1 outlet in the history of entertainment.'"

Since 1897, the copyright laws have vested in the owner of a copyrighted musical composition the exclusive right to perform the work publicly for profit, but the legal right is not self-enforcing. In 1914, Victor Herbert and a handful of other composers organized ASCAP because those who performed copyrighted music for profit were so numerous and widespread, and most performances so fleeting, that as a practical matter it was impossible for the many individual copyright owners to negotiate with and license the users and to detect unauthorized uses. "ASCAP was organized as a 'clearing-house' for copyright owners and users to solve these problems" associated with the licensing of music. 400 F.Supp. 737, 741 (SDNY 1975). As ASCAP operates today, its 22,000 members grant it nonexclusive rights to license nondramatic performances of their works, and ASCAP issues licenses and distributes royalties to copyright owners in accordance with a schedule reflecting the nature and amount of the use of their music and other factors.

BMI, a nonprofit corporation owned by members of the broadcasting industry, was organized in 1939, is affiliated with or represents some 10,000 publishing companies and 20,000 authors and composers, and operates in much the same manner as ASCAP. Almost every domestic copyrighted composition is in the repertory either of ASCAP, with a total of three million compositions, or of BMI, with one million.

Both organizations operate primarily through blanket licenses, which give the licensees the right to perform any and all of the compositions owned by the members or affiliates as often as the licensees desire for a stated term. Fees for blanket licenses are ordinarily a percentage of total revenues or a flat dollar amount, and do not directly depend on the amount or type of music used. Radio and television broadcasters are the largest users of music, and almost all of them hold blanket licenses from both ASCAP and BMI. Until this litigation, CBS held blanket licenses from both organizations for its television network on a continuous basis since the late 1940's and had never attempted to secure any other form of license from either ASCAP or any of its members. Id., at 752-754.

The complaint filed by CBS charged various violations of the Sherman Act and the copyright laws. CBS argued that ASCAP and BMI are unlawful monopolies and that the blanket license is illegal price fixing, an unlawful tying arrangement, a concerted refusal to deal, and a misuse of copyrights. The District Court, though denying summary judgment to certain defendants, ruled that the practice did not fall within the per se rule. 337 F.Supp. 394, 398 (SDNY 1972). After an 8-week trial, limited to the issue of liability, the court dismissed the complaint, rejecting again the claim that the blanket license was price fixing and a per se violation of § 1 of the Sherman Act, and holding that since direct negotiation with individual copyright owners is available and feasible there is no undue restraint of trade, illegal tying, misuse of copyrights, or monopolization. 400 F.Supp., at 781-783.

Though agreeing with the District Court's factfinding and not disturbing its legal conclusions on the other antitrust theories of liability, the Court of Appeals held that the blanket license issued to television networks was a form of price fixing illegal per se under the Sherman Act. 562 F.2d 130, 140 (CA2 1977). This conclusion, without more, settled the issue of liability under the Sherman Act, established copyright misuse, and required reversal of the District Court's judgment, as well as a remand to consider the appropriate remedy.

ASCAP and BMI petitioned for certiorari, presenting the questions of the applicability of the per se rule and of whether this constitutes misuse of copyrights. CBS did not cross petition to challenge the failure to sustain its other antitrust claims. We granted certiorari because of the importance of the issues to the antitrust and copyright laws. 439 U.S. 817 (1978). Because we disagree with the Court of Appeals' conclusions with respect to the per se illegality of the blanket license, we reverse its judgment and remand the cause for further appropriate proceedings.

## II.

In construing and applying the Sherman Act's ban against contracts, conspiracies, and combinations in restraint of trade, the Court has held that certain agreements or practices are so "plainly anticompetitive," National Society of Professional Engineers v. United States, 435 U.S. 679, 692 (1978);Continental T. V., Inc. v. GTE Sylvania Inc., 433 U.S. 36, 50 (1977), and so often "lack . . . any redeeming virtue," Northern Pac. R. Co. v. United States, 356 U.S. 1, 5 (1958), that they are conclusively presumed illegal without further examination under the rule of reason generally applied in Sherman Act cases. This per se rule is a valid and useful tool of antitrust policy and enforcement. And agreements among competitors to fix prices on their individual goods or services are among those concerted activities that the Court has held to be within the per se category. But easy labels do not always supply ready answers.

A

To the Court of Appeals and CBS, the blanket license involves "price fixing" in the literal sense: the composers and publishing houses have joined together into an organization that sets its price for the blanket license it sells. But this is not a question simply of determining whether two or more potential competitors have literally "fixed" a "price." As generally used in the antitrust field, "price fixing" is a shorthand way of describing certain categories of business behavior to which the per se rule has been held applicable. The Court of Appeals' literal approach does not alone establish that this particular practice is one of those types or that it is "plainly anticompetitive" and very likely without "redeeming virtue." Literalness is overly simplistic and often overbroad. When two partners set the price of their goods or services they are literally "price fixing," but they are not per se in violation of the Sherman Act. See United States v. Addyston Pipe & Steel Co., 85 F. 271, 280 (CA6 1898), aff'd, 175 U.S. 211 (1899). Thus, it is necessary to characterize the challenged conduct as falling within or without that category of behavior to which we apply the label "per se price fixing." That will often, but not always, be a simple matter.

Consequently, as we recognized in United States v. Topco Associates, Inc., 405 U.S. 596, 607-608 (1972), "[it] is only after considerable experience with certain business relationships that courts classify them as per se violations . . . ." See White Motor Co. v. United States, 372 U.S. 253, 263 (1963). We have never examined a practice like this one before; indeed, the Court of Appeals recognized that "[in] dealing with performing rights in the music industry we confront conditions both in copyright law and in antitrust law which are sui generis." 562 F.2d, at 132. And though there has been rather intensive antitrust scrutiny of ASCAP and its blanket licenses, that experience hardly counsels that we should outlaw the blanket license as a per se restraint of trade.

B

This litigation and other cases involving ASCAP and its licensing practices have arisen out of the efforts of the creators of copyrighted musical compositions to collect for the public performance of their works, as they are entitled to do under the Copyright Act. As already indicated, ASCAP and BMI originated to make possible and to facilitate dealings between copyright owners and those who desire to use their music. Both organizations plainly involve concerted action in a large and active line of commerce, and it is not surprising that, as the District Court found, "[neither] ASCAP nor BMI is a stranger to antitrust litigation." 400 F.Supp., at 743.

The Department of Justice first investigated allegations of anticompetitive conduct by ASCAP over 50 years ago. A criminal complaint was filed in 1934, but the Government was granted a midtrial continuance and never returned to the courtroom. In separate complaints in 1941, the United States charged that the blanket license, which was then the only license offered by ASCAP and BMI, was an illegal restraint of trade and that arbitrary prices were being charged as the result of an illegal copyright pool. The Government sought to enjoin ASCAP's exclusive licensing powers and to require a different form of licensing by that organization. The case was settled by a consent decree that imposed tight restrictions on ASCAP's operations. Following complaints relating to the television industry, successful private litigation against ASCAP by movie theaters, and a Government challenge to ASCAP's arrangements with similar foreign organizations, the 1941 decree was reopened and extensively amended in 1950.

Under the amended decree, which still substantially controls the activities of ASCAP, members may grant ASCAP only nonexclusive rights to license their works for public performance. Members, therefore, retain the rights individually to license public performances, along with the rights to license the use of their compositions for other purposes. ASCAP itself is forbidden to grant any license to perform one or more specified compositions in the ASCAP repertory unless both the user and the owner have requested it in writing to do so. ASCAP is required to grant to any user making written application a nonexclusive license to perform all ASCAP compositions, either for a period of time or on a per-program basis. ASCAP may not insist on the blanket license, and the fee for the per-program license, which is to be based on the revenues for the program on which ASCAP music is played, must offer the applicant a genuine economic choice between the per-program license and the more common blanket license. If ASCAP and a putative licensee are unable to agree on a fee within 60 days, the applicant may apply to the District Court for a determination of a reasonable fee, with ASCAP having the burden of proving reasonableness.

The 1950 decree, as amended from time to time, continues in effect, and the blanket license continues to be the primary instrument through which

ASCAP conducts its business under the decree. The courts have twice construed the decree not to require ASCAP to issue licenses for selected portions of its repertory. It also remains true that the decree guarantees the legal availability of direct licensing of performance rights by ASCAP members; and the District Court found, and in this respect the Court of Appeals agreed, that there are no practical impediments preventing direct dealing by the television networks if they so desire. Historically, they have not done so. Since 1946, CBS and other television networks have taken blanket licenses from ASCAP and BMI. It was not until this suit arose that the CBS network demanded any other kind of license.

Of course, a consent judgment, even one entered at the behest of the Antitrust Division, does not immunize the defendant from liability for actions, including those contemplated by the decree, that violate the rights of nonparties. See Sam Fox Publishing Co. v. United States, 366 U.S. 683, 690 (1961), which involved this same decree. But it cannot be ignored that the Federal Executive and Judiciary have carefully scrutinized ASCAP and the challenged conduct, have imposed restrictions on various of ASCAP's practices, and, by the terms of the decree, stand ready to provide further consideration, supervision, and perhaps invalidation of asserted anticompetitive practices. In these circumstances, we have a unique indicator that the challenged practice may have redeeming competitive virtues and that the search for those values is not almost sure to be in vain. Thus, although CBS is not bound by the Antitrust Division's actions, the decree is a fact of economic and legal life in this industry, and the Court of Appeals should not have ignored it completely in analyzing the practice. See id., at 694-695. That fact alone might not remove a naked price-fixing scheme from the ambit of the per se rule, but, as discussed infra, Part III, here we are uncertain whether the practice on its face has the effect, or could have been spurred by the purpose, of restraining competition among the individual composers.

After the consent decrees, the legality of the blanket license was challenged in suits brought by certain ASCAP members against individual radio stations for copyright infringement. The stations raised as a defense that the blanket license was a form of price fixing illegal under the Sherman Act. The parties stipulated that it would be nearly impossible for each radio station to negotiate with each copyright holder separate licenses for the performance of his works on radio. Against this background, and relying heavily on the 1950 consent judgment, the Court of Appeals for the Ninth Circuit rejected claims that ASCAP was a combination in restraint of trade and that the blanket license constituted illegal price fixing. K-91, Inc. v. Gershwin Publishing Corp., 372 F.2d 1 (1967), cert. denied, 389 U.S. 1045 (1968).

The Department of Justice, with the principal responsibility for enforcing the Sherman Act and administering the consent decrees relevant to this case, agreed with the result reached by the Ninth Circuit. In a submission amicus curiae opposing one station's petition for certiorari in this Court, the Department stated that there must be "some kind of central licensing agency by which copyright holders may offer their works in a common pool to all who wish to use them." Memorandum for United States as Amicus Curiae on Pet. for Cert. in K-91, Inc. v. Gershwin Publishing Corp., O. T. 1967, No. 147, pp. 10-11. And the Department elaborated on what it thought that fact meant for the proper application of the antitrust laws in this area:

"The Sherman Act has always been discriminatingly applied in the light of economic realities. There are situations in which competitors have been permitted to form joint selling agencies or other pooled activities, subject to strict limitations under the antitrust laws to guarantee against abuse of the collective power thus created. Associated Press v. United States, 326 U.S. 1; United States v. St. Louis Terminal, 224 U.S. 383; Appalachian Coals, Inc. v. United States, 288 U.S. 344; Chicago Board of Trade v. United States, 246 U.S. 231. This case appears to us to involve such a situation. The extraordinary number of users spread across the land, the ease with which a performance may be broadcast, the sheer volume of copyrighted compositions, the enormous quantity of separate performances each year, the impracticability of negotiating individual licenses for each composition, and the ephemeral nature of each performance all combine to create unique market conditions for performance rights to recorded music." Id., at 10 (footnote omitted).

The Department concluded that, in the circumstances of that case, the blanket licenses issued by ASCAP to individual radio stations were neither a per se violation of the Sherman Act nor an unreasonable restraint of trade.

As evidenced by its amicus brief in the present case, the Department remains of that view. Furthermore, the United States disagrees with the Court of Appeals in this case and urges that the blanket licenses, which the consent decree authorizes ASCAP to issue to television networks, are not per se violations of the Sherman Act. It takes no position, however, on whether the practice is an unreasonable restraint of trade in the context of the network television industry.

Finally, we note that Congress itself, in the new Copyright Act, has chosen to employ the blanket license and similar practices. Congress created a compulsory blanket license for secondary transmissions by cable television systems and provided that "[notwithstanding] any provisions of the antitrust laws, . . . any claimants may agree among themselves as to the proportionate division of compulsory licensing fees among them, may lump their claims together and file them jointly or as a single claim, or may designate a common agent to receive payment on their behalf." 17 U. S. C. App. § 111 (d)(5)(A). And the newly created compulsory license for the use of copyrighted compositions in jukeboxes is also a blanket license, which is payable to the performing-rights societies such as ASCAP unless an individual copyright holder can prove his entitlement to a share. § 116 (c)(4). Moreover, in requiring noncommercial broadcasters to pay for their use of copyrighted music, Congress again provided that "[notwithstanding] any provision of the antitrust laws" copyright owners "may designate common agents to negotiate, agree to, pay, or receive payments." § 118(b). Though these provisions are not directly controlling, they do reflect an opinion that the blanket license, and ASCAP, are economically beneficial in at least some circumstances.

There have been District Court cases holding various ASCAP practices, including its licensing practices, to be violative of the Sherman Act, but even so, there is no nearly universal view that either the blanket or the per-program licenses issued by ASCAP at prices negotiated by it are a form of price fixing subject to automatic condemnation under the Sherman Act, rather than to a careful assessment under the rule of reason.

## III.

Of course, we are no more bound than is CBS by the views of the Department of Justice, the results in the prior lower court cases, or the opinions of various experts about the merits of the blanket license. But while we must independently examine this practice, all those factors should caution us against too easily finding blanket licensing subject to per se invalidation.

A

As a preliminary matter, we are mindful that the Court of Appeals' holding would appear to be quite difficult to contain. If, as the court held, there is a per se antitrust violation whenever ASCAP issues a blanket license to a television network for a single fee, why would it not also be automatically illegal for ASCAP to negotiate and issue blanket licenses to individual radio or television stations or to other users who perform copyrighted music for profit? Likewise, if the present network licenses issued through ASCAP on behalf of its members are per se violations, why would it not be equally illegal for the members to authorize ASCAP to issue licenses establishing various categories of uses that a network might have for copyrighted music and setting a standard fee for each described use?

Although the Court of Appeals apparently thought the blanket license could be saved in some or even many applications, it seems to us that the per se rule does not accommodate itself to such flexibility and that the observations of the Court of Appeals with respect to remedy tend to impeach the per se basis for the holding of liability.

CBS would prefer that ASCAP be authorized, indeed directed, to make all its compositions available at standard per-use rates within negotiated categories of use. 400 F.Supp., at 747 n. 7. But if this in itself or in conjunction with blanket licensing constitutes illegal price fixing by copyright owners, CBS urges that an injunction issue forbidding ASCAP to issue any blanket license or to negotiate any fee except on behalf of an individual member for the use of his own copyrighted work or works. Thus, we are called upon to determine that blanket licensing is unlawful across the board. We are quite sure, however, that the per se rule does not require any such holding.

B

In the first place, the line of commerce allegedly being restrained, the performing rights to copyrighted music, exists at all only because of the copyright laws. Those who would use copyrighted music in public performances must secure consent from the copyright owner or be liable at least for the statutory damages for each infringement and, if the conduct is willful and for the purpose of financial gain, to criminal penalties. Furthermore, nothing in the Copyright Act of 1976 indicates in the slightest that Congress intended to weaken the rights of copyright owners to control the public performance of musical compositions. Quite the contrary is true. Although the copyright laws confer no rights on copyright owners to fix prices among themselves or otherwise to violate the antitrust laws, we would not expect that any market arrangements reasonably necessary to effectuate the rights that are granted would be deemed a per se violation of the Sherman Act. Otherwise, the commerce anticipated by the Copyright Act and protected against restraint by the Sherman Act would not exist at all or would exist only as a pale reminder of what Congress envisioned.

C

More generally, in characterizing this conduct under the per se rule, our inquiry must focus on whether the effect and, here because it tends to show effect, see United States v. United States Gypsum Co., 438 U.S. 422, 436 n. 13 (1978), the purpose of the practice are to threaten the proper operation of our predominantly free-market economy — that is, whether the practice facially appears to be one that would always or almost always tend to restrict competition and decrease output, and in what portion of the market, or instead one designed to "increase economic efficiency and render markets more, rather than less, competitive." Id., at 441 n. 16; see National Society of Professional Engineers v. United States, 435 U.S., at 688;Continental T. V., Inc. v. GTE Sylvania Inc., 433 U.S., at 50 n. 16;Northern Pac. R. Co. v. United States, 356 U.S., at 4.

The blanket license, as we see it, is not a "naked [restraint] of trade with no purpose except stifling of competition," White Motor Co. v. United States, 372 U.S. 253, 263 (1963), but rather accompanies the integration of sales, monitoring, and enforcement against unauthorized copyright use. See L. Sullivan, Handbook of the Law of Antitrust § 59, p. 154 (1977). As we have already indicated, ASCAP and the blanket license developed together out of the practical situation in the marketplace: thousands of users, thousands of copyright owners, and millions of compositions. Most users want unplanned, rapid, and indemnified access to any and all of the repertory of compositions, and the owners want a reliable method of collecting for the use of their copyrights. Individual sales transactions in this industry are quite expensive, as would be individual monitoring and enforcement, especially in light of the resources of single composers. Indeed, as both the Court of Appeals and CBS recognize, the costs are prohibitive for licenses with individual radio stations, nightclubs, and restaurants, 562 F.2d, at 140 n. 26, and it was in that milieu that the blanket license arose.

A middleman with a blanket license was an obvious necessity if the thousands of individual negotiations, a virtual impossibility, were to be avoided. Also, individual fees for the use of individual compositions would presuppose an intricate schedule of fees and uses, as well as a difficult and expensive reporting problem for the user and policing task for the copyright owner. Historically, the market for public-performance rights organized itself largely around the single-fee blanket license, which gave unlimited access to the repertory and reliable protection against infringement. When ASCAP's major and user-created competitor, BMI, came on the scene, it also turned to the blanket license.

With the advent of radio and television networks, market conditions changed, and the necessity for and advantages of a blanket license for those users may be far less obvious than is the case when the potential users are individual television or radio stations, or the thousands of other individuals and organizations performing copyrighted compositions in public. But even for television network licenses, ASCAP reduces costs absolutely by creating a blanket license that is sold only a few, instead of thousands, of times, and that obviates the need for closely monitoring the networks to see that they do not use more than they pay for. ASCAP also provides the necessary resources for blanket sales and enforcement, resources unavailable to the vast majority of composers and publishing houses. Moreover, a bulk license of some type is a necessary consequence of the integration necessary to achieve these efficiencies, and a necessary consequence of an aggregate license is that its price must be established.

D

This substantial lowering of costs, which is of course potentially beneficial to both sellers and buyers, differentiates the blanket license from individual use licenses. The blanket license is composed of the individual compositions plus the aggregating service. Here, the whole is truly greater than the sum of its parts; it is, to some extent, a different product. The blanket license has certain unique characteristics: It allows the licensee immediate use of covered compositions, without the delay of prior individual negotiations, and great flexibility in the choice of musical material. Many consumers clearly prefer the characteristics and cost advantages of this marketable package, and even small performing-rights societies that have occasionally arisen to compete with ASCAP and BMI have offered blanket licenses. Thus, to the extent the blanket license is a different product, ASCAP is not really a joint sales agency offering the individual goods of many sellers, but is a separate seller offering its blanket license, of which the individual compositions are raw material. ASCAP, in short, made a market in which individual composers are inherently unable to compete fully effectively.

E

Finally, we have some doubt — enough to counsel against application of the per se rule — about the extent to which this practice threatens the "central nervous system of the economy," United States v. Socony-Vacuum Oil Co., 310 U.S. 150, 226 n. 59 (1940), that is, competitive pricing as the free market's means of allocating resources. Not all arrangements among actual or potential competitors that have an impact on price are per se violations of the Sherman Act or even unreasonable restraints. Mergers among competitors eliminate competition, including price competition, but they are not per se illegal, and many of them withstand attack under any existing antitrust standard. Joint ventures and other cooperative arrangements are also not usually unlawful, at least not as price-fixing schemes, where the agreement on price is necessary to market the product at all.

Here, the blanket-license fee is not set by competition among individual copyright owners, and it is a fee for the use of any of the compositions covered by the license. But the blanket license cannot be wholly equated with a simple horizontal arrangement among competitors. ASCAP does set the price for its blanket license, but that license is quite different from anything any individual owner could issue. The individual composers and authors have neither agreed not to sell individually in any other market nor use the blanket license to mask price fixing in such other markets. Moreover, the substantial restraints placed on ASCAP and its members by the consent decree must not be ignored. The District Court found that there was no legal, practical, or conspiratorial impediment to CBS's obtaining individual licenses; CBS, in short, had a real choice.

With this background in mind, which plainly enough indicates that over the years, and in the face of available alternatives, the blanket license has provided an acceptable mechanism for at least a large part of the market for the performing rights to copyrighted musical compositions, we cannot agree that it should automatically be declared illegal in all of its many manifestations. Rather, when attacked, it should be subjected to a more discriminating examination under the rule of reason. It may not ultimately survive that attack, but that is not the issue before us today.

## IV.

As we have noted, n. 27, supra, the enigmatic remarks of the Court of Appeals with respect to remedy appear to have departed from the court's strict, per se approach and to have invited a more careful analysis. But this left the general import of its judgment that the licensing practices of ASCAP and BMI under the consent decree are per se violations of the Sherman Act. We reverse that judgment, and the copyright misuse judgment dependent upon it, see n. 9, supra, and remand for further proceedings to consider any unresolved issues that CBS may have properly brought to the Court of Appeals. Of course, this will include an assessment under the rule of reason of the blanket license as employed in the television industry, if that issue was preserved by CBS in the Court of Appeals.

The judgment of the Court of Appeals is reversed, and the cases are remanded to that court for further proceedings consistent with this opinion.

It is so ordered.

CBS v. Am. Soc'y of Composers
United States Court of Appeals for the Second Circuit
November 20, 1979, Argued; April 3, 1980, Decided
No. 120, Docket 75-7600
620 F.2d 930

This is the fourth round of litigation in a lawsuit brought by Columbia Broadcasting System, Inc. (CBS) against the American Society of Composers, Authors and Publishers (ASCAP), Broadcast Music, Inc. (BMI), and their members and affiliates. The lawsuit seeks injunctive relief to prevent ASCAP and BMI from using a blanket license to convey to television networks non-dramatic performing rights, that is, the right to "perform" copyrighted music by transmitting it to the networks' television audiences. The blanket license permits the licensee to use any music in the repertory of the licensor, as often as desired, for a one-time license fee. The license lasts for a stated term, usually but not necessarily one year. Payment is set at either a flat sum or a percentage of the network's revenue. Alternatively to barring use of the blanket license, the CBS suit seeks modification to require that ASCAP and BMI charge pre-determined amounts for each time copyrighted music is used on the air. The blanket license in its present form is alleged to be an agreement unreasonably restraining trade in violation of § 1 of the Sherman Act, 15 U.S.C. § 1.

The lawsuit was filed in 1969. Round one was an eight-week bench trial in 1973 in the District Court for the Southern District of New York (Morris Lasker, Judge). In a comprehensive opinion, replete with detailed findings, Judge Lasker found that CBS had failed to prove its allegations and ordered the complaint dismissed. Columbia Broadcasting System, Inc. v. American Society of Composers, 400 F. Supp. 737 (S.D.N.Y.1975). Round two was the prior appeal to this Court. In an opinion by Judge Gurfein, the Court ruled that the blanket license was an illegal price-fixing device, a per se violation of § 1. The matter was remanded to the District Court for formulation of an appropriate remedy. Columbia Broadcasting System, Inc. v. American Society of Composers, Authors and Publishers, 562 F.2d 130 (2d Cir. 1977). Judge Moore disagreed with the conclusion that the blanket license was price-fixing, but concurred in the decision to remand so that a "practical method" of "per use licensing" might be developed. Id. at 141. Round three occurred when the Supreme Court reviewed the decision of this Court. Writing for an eight-member majority, Justice White concluded that the blanket license was not a per se violation of § 1 and remanded the case to this Court for further proceedings, including an assessment of the blanket license under the rule of reason. Broadcast Music,

Inc. v. Columbia Broadcasting System, Inc., 441 U.S. 1, 99 S. Ct. 1551, 60 L. Ed. 2d 1 (1979). Justice Stevens dissented, agreeing with the majority that the blanket license was not a per se violation of § 1 but concluding that the record and certain of Judge Lasker's findings established a § 1 violation under the rule of reason. Id. at 25, 99 S. Ct. at 1565.

The matter is now before a panel of this Court that includes only Judge Moore from the prior panel. Additional briefs have been submitted in response to the Court's framing of specific issues, 607 F.2d 543, and extensive oral argument was heard. We now affirm the decision of the District Court.

### Facts

The three prior opinions, especially Judge Lasker's, have so fully set forth the facts that only the bare essentials need be again recounted. ASCAP has a membership of approximately 6,000 music publishing companies and 16,000 composers. BMI, a non-profit corporation, is affiliated with approximately 6,000 music publishing companies and 20,000 composers. Composers of virtually all music copyrighted in the United States have granted to either ASCAP or BMI the non-exclusive right to license users to perform their compositions. The repertory of ASCAP has more than three million compositions, and the repertory of BMI has more than one million compositions. CBS and the other two major television networks, NBC and ABC, have held blanket licenses from both ASCAP and BMI for many years. CBS first obtained its blanket license from ASCAP in 1946. At that time ASCAP held exclusive rights to the music of its members, and the blanket license it offered to broadcasters was the only device whereby they could obtain performing rights to copyrighted music.

As a matter of legal entitlement, licensing arrangements were significantly changed in 1950 when a consent decree, first entered in 1941 to settle Government litigation against ASCAP, was reopened and substantially modified. The amended consent decree permits ASCAP to obtain only non-exclusive rights from its member-composers and enjoins ASCAP from limiting, restricting, or interfering with the right of any member to issue directly to any user a non-exclusive license for performing rights. The composers thus retain the legal right to bypass ASCAP and license performing rights directly to CBS. The amended decree also requires ASCAP to offer to any broadcaster either the blanket license, or, as an alternative, a per program license. Both types of licenses permit the user to perform any music in the ASCAP repertory; for the per program license the user pays only with respect to programs on which copyrighted music is performed, whereas, with the blanket license, the user pays a one-time fee for the duration of the license. The decree also provides that in the event of disputes concerning the amount of license fees, the District

Court for the Southern District of New York is authorized to determine a reasonable fee.

Similar, though not identical provisions govern the licensing of performing rights by BMI. For purposes of this litigation, the significant fact, stipulated to by the parties, is that CBS could obtain non-exclusive licenses for performing rights directly from copyright owners affiliated with BMI with the same ease or difficulty as it could obtain such rights from copyright owners who are members of ASCAP.

As a matter of factual occurrence, CBS has never made any attempt to obtain performing rights directly from a copyright owner.

Beyond these facts concerning licensing arrangements and opportunities, some understanding is required of the facts concerning CBS's use of music. Two types of classification are involved: one concerns the function of the music, and the second concerns the circumstances under which the selection of music is made. CBS, like all broadcasters, uses music as theme, background, or feature. Theme music is played at the start or conclusion of a program and serves to enhance the identification of the program. Background music accompanies some of the action on the screen. Feature music is a principal focus of audience attention, such as a popular song sung on a variety show.

Music on network television is selected in one of three ways. Most of it, as much as 90%, is selected by production companies, or "packagers," which produce television programs and sell them to the networks. The music on these programs is almost always theme and background music, much of it composed specially for the production company. Typically the company employs a composer to write theme and background music, acquires the copyright from him, and assigns it to its own music publishing subsidiary. Such music is called "inside" music. In some instances the packager decides to use music that has already been composed, so-called "outside" music. In these instances the packager must acquire from the copyright owner the right to record the music on the soundtrack of the program's film or tape. This right is known as a "synch" right, the music often being carefully fitted to synchronize with the action on the screen. Acquisition of the synch right, however, does not carry with it the separate right to perform the music on the air. That performing right could be acquired by the packager when he acquires the synch right, and reassigned to the network; however, the industry practice has been that the network automatically acquires the performing right for all music used on packaged programs under the network's blanket license for the performing rights to all ASCAP music, and the packager therefore has no need to acquire a performing right for reassignment to the network.

A small portion of network music is selected by the network itself, in those few instances when the network is producing its own programs. A still smaller portion is selected by the person or group performing the music, in those very few instances where music is spontaneously used. Examples are a football half-time show or a late night talk show on which a guest sings an unscheduled song.

## Discussion

Our starting point for determining whether the blanket license violates § 1 is the decision of the Supreme Court remanding the case to us. That decision obliges us to make "an assessment under the rule of reason of the blanket license as employed in the television industry." 441 U.S. at 24-25, 99 S. Ct. at 1565. Since the parties are agreed that the relevant market is the licensing of performing rights to the television networks, we assume our consideration should be similarly confined to the blanket license as employed by the television networks. A rule of reason analysis requires a determination of whether an agreement is on balance an unreasonable restraint of trade, that is, whether its anti-competitive effects outweigh its pro-competitive effects. National Society of Professional Engineers v. United States, 435 U.S. 679, 98 S. Ct. 1355, 55 L. Ed. 2d 637 (1978); Continental T.V., Inc. v. GTE Sylvania, Inc., 433 U.S. 36, 97 S. Ct. 2549, 53 L. Ed. 2d 568 (1977); Chicago Board of Trade v. United States, 246 U.S. 231, 38 S. Ct. 242, 62 L. Ed. 683 (1918). In this case, however, we are met with the threshold contention of the defendants that the balancing of pro- and anti-competitive effects need not be undertaken because Judge Lasker's findings of fact demonstrate that the blanket license has no anticompetitive effect at all.

Before examining that contention, we must consider whether it is open to us under the Supreme Court's remand. It is possible to read the penultimate paragraph of Justice White's opinion the one directing us to make a rule of reason assessment as if the Supreme Court had concluded that the blanket license is a restraint of trade and was requesting further consideration only as to whether its restraining effect was unreasonable, i. e., not outweighed by pro-competitive advantages. Our reading of the entire opinion, however, persuades us that no such initial conclusion was reached. In the first place, the safer course is to read judicial opinions as deciding only what they purport to decide. That may not always be only the narrow holding, for courts, especially appellate courts, have an entirely legitimate function of elucidating principles of law, fairly raised by litigation, even if the resulting pronouncements are not absolutely required for the precise decision reached. Appellate guidance is not valueless because it is dictum. But appellate courts, endeavoring to rule beyond the precise holding of a case, normally make that intention unmistakably clear. In this instance, the Supreme Court's opinion purports to decide only whether the blanket license is a per se violation of § 1, that is, a practice with such a high likelihood of having unjustifiable anti-competitive effects that it is condemned under the antitrust laws without the need to assess its effect in a particular case. See Northern Pacific R. Co. v. United States, 356 U.S. 1, 5, 78 S. Ct. 514,

518, 2 L. Ed. 2d 545 (1958). Once the Supreme Court decided that the blanket license is not a per se violation of § 1, we believe it made no decision concerning the effect of the license in the network television industry at issue in this case, thereby leaving open the question of whether the license has any anti-competitive effect at all. Secondly, Justice White's opinion contains a specific observation that strongly supports our view of the decision's reach. The opinion declares that the majority is "uncertain whether the practice on its face has the effect . . . of restraining competition among the individual composers." 441 U.S. at 13, 99 S. Ct. at 1559. That observation leaves for consideration whether the practice could have a restraining effect as applied to the particular circumstances prevailing in the industry. To that possibility we now turn, but in doing so, we examine the record and Judge Lasker's findings to see whether the blanket license, on its face and as applied, is a restraint at all.

There can be no dispute with the observation of Justice Stevens, in his dissenting opinion, that "there is no price competition between separate musical compositions." 441 U.S. at 32, 99 S. Ct. at 1568-69. The blanket license is the only device by which performing rights are licensed to the networks, and, under a blanket license, no selector of music to be performed on a network considers what the price of using one song would be compared to the price of using any other song. No price considerations affect the choice among songs because the network holds a blanket license to perform all songs.

The absence of price competition among songs, however, does not mean that the blanket license is a restraint upon any potential competition. For price competition to exist there must be at least one buyer interested in purchasing a product from two or more sellers. In this case, there is no evidence that CBS has ever attempted to purchase performing rights to any song from the copyright owners, either the composers or the music publishing companies to which they may have assigned their copyrights. If the opportunity to purchase performing rights to individual songs is fully available, then it is customer preference for the blanket license, and not the license itself, that causes the lack of price competition among songs. Of course, even customer preference cannot save some practices from illegality under the antitrust law. If competing sellers fix the prices of their products, they violate § 1 no matter how much a buyer may prefer accepting their fixed price to negotiating with each for a lower price. But a practice that is not a per se violation, and this blanket license has authoritatively been found not to be such, does not restrain trade when the complaining customer elects to use it in preference to realistically available marketing alternatives.

Trade is restrained, frequently in an unreasonable manner, when rights to use individual copyrights or patents may be obtained only by payment for a pool of such rights, United States v. Paramount Pictures, Inc., 334 U.S. 131, 68 S. Ct. 915, 92 L. Ed. 1260 (1948) (copyrighted motion pictures); Alden-Rochelle, Inc. v.

ASCAP, 80 F. Supp. 888 (S.D.N.Y.1948) (copyrighted music); Zenith Radio Corp. v. Hazeltine Research, Inc., 395 U.S. 100, 89 S. Ct. 1562, 23 L. Ed. 2d 129 (1969) (patents), but the opportunity to acquire a pool of rights does not restrain trade if an alternative opportunity to acquire individual rights is fully available. Automatic Radio Manufacturing Co. v. Hazeltine Research, Inc., 339 U.S. 827, 70 S. Ct. 894, 94 L. Ed. 1312 (1950) (patents); Standard Oil Co. v. United States, 283 U.S. 235, 51 S. Ct. 429, 75 L. Ed. 999 (1931) (same).

CBS challenges this approach on the ground that some alternatives can always be imagined that would satisfy the market needs of an antitrust plaintiff. As CBS argues, the blanket license cannot possibly be saved from illegality under § 1 simply because CBS has the alternative of hiring composers to fill its needs for music. CBS is right. An antitrust plaintiff is not obliged to pursue any imaginable alternative, regardless of cost or efficiency, before it can complain that a practice has restrained competition. But in this case the defendants do not suggest that CBS should do anything more extraordinary than offer to buy from competing sellers. We agree with the defendants that if that opportunity is fully available, and if copyright owners retain unimpaired independence to set competitive prices for individual licenses to a licensee willing to deal with them, the blanket license is not a restraint of trade.

In fact, if there is a realistic opportunity to obtain performance rights from individual copyright holders, then the remedy CBS seeks in this case modification of the blanket license into an option to use all songs plus a charge for each use of any one song would be a clear instance of unjustified price-fixing in violation of § 1. If ASCAP were to make a per use charge for each song, it would have to determine a price to be charged. Whether or not that price varied for each song, the determination of any price for use of a song by a membership organization of competing songwriters would be classic price-fixing. See 441 U.S. at 17 n. 27, 99 S. Ct. at 1561 n. 27. If licensing directly from individual copyright owners were not feasible, then it would be arguable that per use pricing by ASCAP might be that rare instance when price-fixing does not necessarily violate § 1. But CBS's proposed remedy cannot possibly avoid the strictures of § 1 if direct licensing is feasible. We therefore turn to an examination of the feasibility of direct licensing.

It could be argued that the best evidence against the feasibility of direct licensing is the fact that CBS has brought this lawsuit at great expense to avoid taking the blanket license. That surely suggests that the blanket license is not something for which CBS has a preference. But that argument ignores the principle that "the purpose of the Sherman Act is to protect competition, not competitors." Checker Motors Corp. v. Chrysler Corp., 283 F. Supp. 876, 885 (S.D.N.Y.1968) (Mansfield, J.), aff'd, 405 F.2d 319 (2d Cir.), cert. denied, 394 U.S. 999, 89 S. Ct. 1595, 22 L. Ed. 2d 777 (1969). If the market for selling performing rights to the television networks would be competitive among copyright owners whenever any network chose to deal with them, the antitrust laws are satisfied even though one network has reasons of its own for forgoing that competitive market in preference to the blanket license. The defendants suggest that CBS's preference for the blanket license derives from its unwillingness to seek competitive prices from individual copyright owners while its network competitors enjoy the advantages of obtaining their performing rights under their blanket licenses. In defendants' view, CBS is bringing this lawsuit, not because competition among songwriters has been restrained, but because CBS wants protection from the prospect of its competitors' continuing with blanket licenses. We need not determine whether defendants' speculation is correct, but we agree that the issue is whether competition among copyright owners is realistically feasible, regardless of whether CBS may have some business reason of its own for preferring not to enter an available competitive market.

The entire trial in the District Court concerned primarily the issue of whether direct licensing was feasible. Judge Lasker placed the burden of proof upon CBS, as the plaintiff, to prove that it was not, for he concluded that there was no restraint of trade if direct licensing was feasible. After carefully analyzing the evidence CBS offered, Judge Lasker concluded that "CBS has failed to prove the factual predicate of its claims the non-availability of alternatives to the blanket license . . . ." 400 F. Supp. at 780-81. That ultimate finding is abundantly supported by subsidiary findings and by the record, which completely refute all of CBS's allegations of barriers to direct licensing.

CBS maintained that the existing market structure created by the blanket license effectively prevented it from seeking direct licensing because any money spent to acquire performance rights from individual copyright owners would be wasted once CBS had already paid ASCAP and BMI for performance rights to all music. However, nothing prevented CBS from attempting to obtain from the copyright owners performance rights for some interval following expiration of the term of the blanket license.

CBS also contended that there existed no machinery to handle the numerous transactions that would be required to obtain performance rights directly. The record establishes that such machinery is entirely feasible; indeed a single agency now serves as the broker for the thousands of transactions in which copyright owners sell television synch rights and motion picture performance rights. Nevertheless, the claim is pressed that it would take some amount of time and money to establish a similar mechanism for the individual brokering of network television performance rights. We note that Justice Stevens relied on this circumstance to conclude that "real and significant," albeit not "insurmountable" barriers to direct licensing existed. 441 U.S. at 35, 99 S. Ct. at 1570. With deference, we conclude that the evidence and Judge Lasker's analysis of it demonstrate that neither the time nor the expense of creating machinery for direct licensing establishes a barrier of which CBS can complain. It must be recalled that CBS has obtained its performance rights by blanket licenses ever since the late 1940's. Having transacted business in that fashion for that length of time, CBS cannot expect the antitrust laws to assure it that a changeover to direct licensing can be accomplished instantly or at no expense. Moreover, Judge Lasker found that the changeover could be begun very rapidly with CBS meeting its music needs as the machinery for direct licensing was put into place. When Justice Stevens refers to the machinery being created within a year, 441 U.S. at 35, 99 S. Ct. at 1570, he is citing the outer limit testified to by a CBS witness, 400 F. Supp. at 764, whereas Judge Lasker found that "the relatively modest machinery required could be developed during a reasonable planning period." Id. at 765. And when Justice Stevens refers to an expenditure of millions of dollars by CBS, he does not mean the cost of creating direct licensing machinery, but only the payment CBS will make during the final term of its blanket license. But that is an expense for which it bargained and for which it has received considerable value.

Next, CBS argued that individual copyright owners would be reluctant to deal directly with CBS in the licensing of performance rights. At trial this was the so-called "disinclination" issue. Wholly apart from the record, we have some difficulty even contemplating the feared situation of individual songwriters displaying reluctance to arrange to have their songs performed on a national television network, especially one owned by "the giant of the world in the use of music rights." Id. at 771. But we need not rely on an intuitive rejection of this CBS claim. Judge Lasker found, after hearing substantial evidence from composers and music publishers, that if CBS were to seek direct licensing, "copyright proprietors would wait at CBS' door." Id. at 779.

Finally, CBS alleged a barrier to direct licensing based upon what was called the music-in-the-can problem. CBS apprehended that, without a blanket license, it would be subject to demands for unconscionably high fees from the owners of copyrighted music already recorded on the soundtracks of taped programs and feature films in CBS's inventory. Judge Lasker properly rejected this claim both on the facts and the law. As a matter of fact, he found, based on the testimony, that "hold-ups" were not realistically to be feared, that synch rights were regularly obtained at fair prices after the recording had been accomplished, that copyright proprietors would not wish to incur CBS's disfavor by attempting a "holdup," and that the whole claim was undercut by the turnover in the CBS inventory. Id. at 775-78. Apart from the lack of factual support for the argument, Judge Lasker also correctly rejected it on the ground that it is not a consequence of the blanket license. If CBS would be vulnerable to a "hold-up" when it tries to acquire performance rights for music on a feature film it wishes to rerun, that is a consequence of CBS's failure to acquire rerun performance rights at the time it acquired the film. At that time CBS accepted the risk that it would one day have to purchase performance rights for reruns, either as part of the purchase price for a blanket license or at a separate price for a license obtained directly from the copyright owner.

Pervading these assessments of each of the CBS contentions of alleged barriers to direct licensing is one indisputable fact that perhaps overshadows all others. If CBS were to forgo the blanket license, seek direct licenses, and then discover, contrary to the facts found by Judge Lasker, that a competitive market among copyright owners was not a feasible alternative to the blanket license, it would be entitled, under the consent decree, to assure itself of continued performing rights by immediately obtaining a renewed blanket license. Indeed, Paragraph IX of the ASCAP decree permits CBS to use any music covered by a license application, without payment of fee, subject to whatever fees are subsequently negotiated or determined to be reasonable by the court if negotiations fail. Id. at 743 n. 3. In short, the District Court has found that CBS can feasibly obtain individual licenses from competing copyright owners and that it incurs no risk in endeavoring to do so. There is no basis in the record for concluding that these findings by the District Court are clearly erroneous.

Of course, the fact that CBS has failed to prove that the blanket license restrains competition among copyright owners does not guarantee that such competition will occur if CBS or the other networks elect to forgo their blanket licenses in the future. Uncertainty is created not only by the normal risks of predicting the future but also by the special circumstances currently governing the selection of music for network television programs. As previously mentioned, approximately 90% of this music is selected by the program packagers. If CBS forgoes its blanket license, we cannot predict indeed, the record gives us no adequate basis for making a prediction as to how performance rights for this 90% will be purchased. Perhaps CBS will inform the packagers that it will buy programs only when performance rights have been acquired by the production company. That would create an incentive for the packagers to consider price of performance rights for individual songs in selecting music, especially outside theme or feature music. But the packagers might decline to buy performance rights, preferring to sell their programs to other networks that continue to hold blanket licenses. To the extent that happened, CBS, if it wanted a program for which performance rights had not been purchased, would have to purchase the rights for music already selected and recorded, in which event no meaningful price competition among copyright owners would occur. Or it may happen that packagers will be so anxious to sell their programs to CBS that they will acquire performance rights, even though that might not be their initial preference.

Another situation for which prediction is hazardous concerns the CBS-produced programs that use music spontaneously selected by the performers. The blanket license, among its other virtues, assures CBS of the right to air such programs, regardless of what music the performers elect to play. Without a blanket license, CBS would have to purchase performance rights after the program was aired, or negotiate with ASCAP for some modified form of program license to secure the right to perform any music in the ASCAP repertory only on designated programs where music is spontaneously selected, or forgo the telecasting of such programs.

We mention these alternatives (and there are surely others) not to express any judgment upon them, but simply to point out the difficulty of determining what the market for performance rights will look like if CBS elects to forgo the blanket license. Neither the District Court nor we can predict that perfect competition will ensue. But what the District Court has found, and what we affirm, is that CBS has failed to prove that the existence of the blanket license has restrained competition. Since the blanket license is not a per se unlawful arrangement, its restraining effect must be proved before § 1 liability can be found. When, after a full trial, such proof is lacking, the challenge to the blanket license is properly dismissed.

Affirmed.

---

This suit was initiated to enjoin the music licensing organizations, ASCAP and BMI, from using a blanket license to convey non-dramatic performing rights on TV networks. The bottom line is that a blanket license, costing a one-time license fee and lasting for a stated period (usually, but not necessarily, one year), was not a per se violation of the antitrust laws.

Nat'l Cable TV Ass'n v. Broad. Music, Inc.
United States District Court for the District of Columbia
August 16, 1991, Decided; August 16, 1991, Filed
Civil Action Nos. 90-0209 (JHG), 90-0262 (JHG)
772 F. Supp. 614

MEMORANDUM OPINION AND ORDER
JOYCE HENS GREEN, UNITED STATES DISTRICT JUDGE
In these consolidated cases, plaintiffs, two cable television program services and trade associations representing cable program services and cable television system operators, assert antitrust claims against the defendant, Broadcast Music, Inc. ("BMI"), in connection with music performing rights licenses issued by BMI. BMI, in turn, along with several affiliates, counterclaims against the two program service plaintiffs for copyright infringement. These matters were heard by the Court in a bench trial comprising three weeks of live testimony, several additional hours of videotaped witnesses, as well as thousands of documentary and videotape exhibits. Based on the findings of fact and conclusions of law set forth below, the Court enters judgment against plaintiffs and for defendant and counterclaim plaintiffs.

## I. BACKGROUND

This suit was brought by the National Cable Television Association, Inc. ("NCTA"), Community Antenna Television Association, Inc. ("CATA"), Black Entertainment Television, Inc. ("BET"), and The Disney Channel ("TDC") against Broadcast Music, Inc. ("BMI"). Collectively, plaintiffs represent the different components of the cable television industry. NCTA is the principal trade association of the cable television industry, whose members consist of cable program services and cable system operators. CATA is also a trade association for the cable television industry whose members include cable system operators and cable program services as well; its membership overlaps with NCTA's. TDC operates a pay cable television program service that, inter alia, acquires, markets, and transmits cable programming. BET [617] operates a basic cable television program service that, like TDC, also acquires, produces, markets, and transmits programming.

Defendant and counterclaim-plaintiff BMI is a nonprofit corporation formed in 1939 by radio broadcasters that is a music performing rights licensing organization within the meaning of the Copyright Act, 17 U.S.C. § 116(e)(3). Along with its major competitor, the American Society of Composers, Authors and Publishers ("ASCAP"), and other smaller entities, most notably the Society of European Stage Authors and Composers, Inc. ("SESAC"), BMI licenses the performing rights in the copyrighted musical compositions of its affiliated composers, songwriters, and music publishers. BMI has more than 110,000 affiliates and its repertory comprises over two million copyrighted musical compositions. Pursuant to form affiliation agreements, BMI affiliates grant to BMI the non-exclusive right to license the performing rights in their existing and future copyrighted musical compositions and to sue on their behalf for infringement of those rights. In return, BMI monitors the use of affiliates' music and pays them royalties.

### A. Historical Background

Music performing rights societies were formed as a means of dealing with the difficulties of composers in obtaining compensation for the use of their music and in enforcing their copyrights. "Those who performed copyrighted music for profit were so numerous and widespread, and most performances so fleeting, that as a practical matter it was impossible for the many individual copyright owners to negotiate with and license the users and detect unauthorized uses." Broadcast Music, Inc. v. Columbia Broadcasting System, Inc. ("BMI v. CBS"), 441 U.S. 1, 4-5, 99 S. Ct. 1551, 1554-55, 60 L. Ed. 2d 1 (1979).

At issue here is the legality of what is known as "blanket licensing," the practice of BMI (as well as ASCAP and SESAC) whereby the licensee obtains the right to unlimited use of all the compositions in the BMI repertory for a specific period for a specific fee, the latter usually based on a percentage of the licensee's gross revenue. Thus, the license fee does not directly depend on the amount or type of music used, or the way in which the music is used.

Blanket licensing has been the subject of antitrust litigation for nearly sixty years, beginning with a criminal complaint filed against ASCAP in 1934. In 1941, the United States brought suit against ASCAP's blanket licensing — at that time, exclusive licensing — charging that it was an illegal restraint of trade and that ASCAP constituted an illegal copyright pool. As a result of the litigation, a consent decree was imposed in 1941. United States v. ASCAP, 1940-43 Trade Cas. (CCH) para. 56,104 (S.D.N.Y. 1941). The consent decree was substantially amended in 1950, largely as a result of complaints by the emerging television industry and a successful challenge by motion picture theaters. J1 ( United States v. ASCAP, 1950-51 Trade Cas. (CCH) para. 62,594 (S.D.N.Y. 1950)). The amended consent decree allows ASCAP to obtain only nonexclusive performing rights [618] from its members, and requires ASCAP to grant any user a nonexclusive license to perform all ASCAP compositions either for a specific period or on a per-program basis. Furthermore, ASCAP may not demand that a user obtain a blanket license. BMI has been similarly subject to the constraints of a consent decree. See United States v. BMI, 1940-43 Trade Cas. (CCH) para. 59,096 (E.D. Wis. 1941); J2 ( United States v. BMI, 1966 Trade Cas. (CCH) para. 71,941 (S.D.N.Y.)). The consent decrees do differ in some material respects. Most significantly, ASCAP's decree provides for a "rate court": if ASCAP and an applicant for a license disagree as to a fee, the applicant may petition the rate court (the United States District Court for the Southern District of New York) for a determination of a reasonable fee. ASCAP must then grant a license at the court-determined rate. BMI has no such rate court, nor any other compulsory licensing mechanism. See generally BMI v. CBS, 441 U.S. at 11-12 & n. 20, 99 S. Ct. at 1558 & n. 20. BMI has asked the U.S. Department of Justice for an amendment to its consent decree to provide for a rate court, but its request was denied. See J3, J4.

Apart from the consent decrees entered into with the United States, BMI's and ASCAP's blanket licenses have suffered but ultimately survived a number of antitrust challenges by private litigants. See Columbia Broadcasting System, Inc. v. American Society of Composers, Authors and Publishers, 400 F. Supp. 737 (S.D.N.Y. 1975), rev'd, 562 F.2d 130 (2d Cir. 1977), rev'd sub nom. Broadcast Music, Inc. v. Columbia Broadcasting System, Inc., 441 U.S. 1, 99 S. Ct. 1551, 60 L. Ed. 2d 1 (1979) ("BMI v. CBS"), on remand 620 F.2d 930 (2d Cir. 1980) ("CBS Remand"), cert. denied, 450 U.S. 970, 67 L. Ed. 2d 621, 101 S. Ct. 1491 (1981); Buffalo Broadcasting Co. v. American Society of Composers, Authors and Publishers, 546 F. Supp. 274 (S.D.N.Y. 1982), rev'd, 744 F.2d 917 (2d Cir. 1984), cert. denied, 469 U.S. 1211, 84 L. Ed. 2d 329, 105 S. Ct. 1181 (1985). In BMI v. CBS, the Supreme Court held that the issuance by ASCAP and BMI to CBS of blanket licenses at negotiated fees is not a per se restraint of trade in violation of the Sherman Act, and remanded to the Court of Appeals to assess the practice under the "rule of reason." The Second Circuit accordingly examined whether, on the record presented, the blanket license, on its face and as applied, was a restraint on trade. Upholding the district court's finding that proof of a restraining effect was lacking, the court concluded that the blanket license did not violate § 1 of the Sherman Act. 620 F.2d at 938-39. In Buffalo Broadcasting, a challenge brought by local television stations to ASCAP's blanket license, the Second Circuit reversed the district court's determination that the blanket license was an unreasonable restraint on trade in that context, holding that it was not such a restraint where there were realistically available alternatives.

B. The Cable Industry and Music Use

To understand the contentions in this litigation requires, in addition to historical background, an examination of the different components of the cable television industry and how it acquires and uses copyrighted music.

1. Structure of the Cable Industry

There are two tiers of the cable industry represented in this action: cable program services (also referred to herein as programmers) and cable system operators. The cable program services represented here are: First, TDC, a pay cable program service, which means that it usually does not carry commercial advertisements. Its services (programming) are sold to subscribers by cable system operators for a monthly fee (in addition to the basic cable fee subscribers pay to cable system operators for basic cable services). Like all pay cable program services, TDC's sources of revenue include a share of the cable operators' monthly charges, i.e. subscription fees charged by system operators to home viewers for the pay service. The second cable programmer represented here is BET, which is a basic cable program service. Basic cable program services do transmit commercial advertisements as part of their programming. Basic cable programming is sold by cable system operators to subscribers as part of the subscription fee for receipt of a package of cable television services — in other words, without additional charge. Basic cable program services obtain their revenue from advertisements and from a certain portion of the subscription fees paid by the cable system operators for carrying the basic services' programming.

The other component of the cable industry represented here consists of cable system operators. They transmit programming from four principal sources: broadcast television stations, distant broadcast television stations furnished via satellite (known as superstations), local origination programming (programming produced by the system operators), and basic and pay cable program services. Cable system operators obtain their revenues from their share of subscription fees as well as from the leasing of access to their systems for programming and advertising from local origination programming and basic cable services. Many of the thousands of local system operators are part of larger multiple system operators ("MSOs").

Cable television transmission is accomplished as follows. Cable program services transmit programming regionally or nationally via satellite or overland microwave. The programming reaches viewers (subscribers) in one of two ways. The majority of cable television appears on the screen via satellite transmission from the program services to cable television system "head-ends" owned by cable system operators. The system operators then retransmit the programming to subscribers on the same lines (wire or fiber optic cable) through which they transmit broadcast television and their own (local origination) programming. A very small percentage of subscribers receive the cable program services directly on their own home dish antennas (and pay fees directly to the program services). These two methods of transmission are used by both pay cable services and basic cable services.

2. Program Production and Music Licensing

Virtually every type of programming shown on cable television uses music in some manner. Such music is of three types: theme music, used either to introduce or close a program; background music, used to complement the visual action; and feature music, music that is the principal focus of a program, e.g., in a music variety show. J.S. para. 40; Tr. at 1734-36. See generally Buffalo Broadcasting, 546 F. Supp. at 281; CBS Remand, 620 F.2d at 933.

To use music as either theme, background, or feature in programming, producers must obtain the rights from the composers and publishers of the music. Producers either engage a composer to write original music for the program (arrangements known as "composer for hire" agreements), or obtain a license to preexisting music from a music publisher or its agent. The music composer or the composer's agent negotiates the price of a bundle of music rights; mechanical rights (the right to make a mechanical reproduction of the music), print rights (the right to publish the sheet music), grand performance rights (the right to hold dramatic performances of music such as operas and musicals), and, most relevant here, synchronization rights, the right to record or synchronize the music with the visual image or other aural aspects of the program. These rights are granted (usually as a package) to the producer for a negotiated fee.

The one right that is not granted to producers (other than producers of motion pictures for theatrical performance) is the non-dramatic performing right (hereinafter "performing right"), that is, the right to publicly perform the music. The performing rights to music owned by BMI affiliates are generally licensed through BMI and not to the producer but to the ultimate "performer," such as a broadcast or cable television entity. This distinction means that while the price of all other music rights is negotiated directly between the producer and the composer and entails the granting of those rights from the latter to the former, performing rights most often are separately obtained from BMI — usually through the blanket license at issue here.

3. Programming

Two main types of programming are carried by cable program services: original programming and syndicated programming. Original programming is that produced by the cable service itself or by independent producers specifically for the service. Most cable program services, including TDC and BET, transmit some original programming. These programs range from full-length movies to regular programs to promotional announcements and commercials. Approximately 25% of TDC's programming consists of such original materials. With regard to this component of programming, then, the program service acts as a producer and thus selects the music content.

Syndicated programming includes any pre-recorded theatrical motion picture, videotape, or other recorded work (such as broadcast television series and music videos) offered for sale or license by third-party distributors, producers, or syndicators. This previously produced programming comprises the majority of programming carried by cable program services such as plaintiffs TDC and BET. Several of plaintiffs' witnesses testified that the quantity and quality of the syndicated programming they transmit is critical to effective competition with other cable program services.

What plaintiffs are challenging here is the blanket licensing system that is applied to syndicated programming on cable television, and, in particular, the time in the process when music performing rights are acquired. Virtually all syndicated programming contains copyrighted music, a large percentage of which is in the BMI repertory. The music is selected by the producer of the syndicated program and synchronized in the program soundtrack at the time the program is created. Accordingly, when the syndicated program is sold or licensed to the cable program services, the music is "in the can," i.e. indelibly part of the program. That means that cable program services do not play any role in the selection of or negotiation over the bundle of music rights described above concerning syndicated programming.

Most standard form agreements entered into between syndicators (or other preexisting program producers) and cable program services provide that the programmers cannot alter any aspect of the syndicated product. E.g., P 50D para. 7 (TDC agreement with MGM/UA Telecommunications, Inc., Jan 15, 1990) ("You will not authorize any third party to, nor will you yourselves, cut, edit, delete from, add to, or alter the Film without our consent."); P 51E para. 11 (BET agreement with Columbia Pictures Television, Aug. 28, 1985, for a television series) ("BET shall telecast each episode in its entirety. . . ."). These contracts also contain representations and warranties that the copyright rights attached to the programs elements have been obtained by the producer or distributor, and the latter thereby indemnify the licensee against any claims based thereon — except for music performing rights. E.g., P 50D para. 7 ("We warrant that we own or control all rights (except . . . nondramatic musical performing rights) in the Film . . . ."); P 51E para. 7(b) (Contractor represents and warrants that "the Series licensed herein do not, and that the exercise by BET . . . of the rights herein granted will not [] infringe upon the common law rights, or the copyright, or the literary, dramatic, music or motion picture rights of any person . . . ."). As for music performing rights, the agreements provide that the music performing rights controlled by a music performing rights society must be paid for by the acquirer of the programming. E.g. P 50D para. 7; 51E para. 9.

The relationship between cable program services and system operators is governed by similar contractual terms. System operators, usually at the MSO level, enter into affiliation agreements with programmers for the right to exhibit that service's programming. These agreements generally prohibit system operators from editing, deleting, or altering any of the programming content.

E.g., P 53C para. 6(b) (TDC-Adelphia Communications, 1983); P 53 E para. 6(b) (TDC-Cablevision Industries, Inc., 1983); P 54G para. 4(c) (BET-American Television & Communications Corp., 1989); P 54 L para. 4(c) (BET-Falcon Cablevision, 1989). See generally Tr. at 426-27; 682-83; 747-751; Whalen V.Tr. (J16) at 24-28. The agreements also have standard-representations and warranties indemnifying the system operators against any claims of infringement concerning the program elements in programming, but in most instances, these provisions do not include music performing rights. E.g. P 53C para. 8(a); P 53A Art. 8.01; P 54G para. 8(d)(ii); P 54L para. 8(d)(ii). It is evident that without music performing rights, cable television cannot lawfully transmit programming containing copyrighted music.

In addition to original and syndicated programming carried by the cable program services, cable system operators also transmit their own programming (local origination programming), as well as public access programming. Local origination programming carried by cable system operators represents only a fraction of the total programming operators offer. It consists primarily of local news shows, talk shows, and other programs that use little or no music. Like cable program services' original programming, system operators' control of local origination programming is such that they can select the music they use and can acquire the applicable music performing rights independent of BMI.

The salient fact derived from this structure, according to plaintiffs, is that cable program services (and cable operators) have no control over the music in the vast majority of the programming they transmit as part of their service. The prevailing industry practice is that music performing rights are not conveyed and must be obtained from the copyright holder or his or her agent in order to perform the music in the program. In addition, cable program services do not obtain the right to alter or delete the music in syndicated programming. As a result, under the copyright laws, cable program services cannot lawfully transmit any syndicated programming containing music from the BMI repertory without a license from BMI. Without the licenses, then, syndicated programming would be commercially valueless to cable program services.

The gravamen of plaintiffs' argument is that cable program services are forced to obtain the blanket license from BMI in order to transmit syndicated programming, the mainstay of their program offering. Cable system operators as well must have some sort of license to transmit copyrighted music. Interestingly, as to non-cable program service programming, these matters are taken care of in different ways. Broadcast television networks and local stations (whose programming is often transmitted by cable operators) have licenses governing music performing rights. Furthermore, by statute, cable system operators receive compulsory blanket licenses at fees set by the Copyright Royalty Tribunal for distant broadcast (superstation) transmissions. 17 U.S.C.A. § 111(d) (West Supp. 1991). As for the remaining two types of programming, local origination and cable program services (or networks), licensing is unresolved, and it is the failure of BMI and the cable industry to reach agreement on the issue that led to this litigation. The focus of plaintiffs' challenge is BMI's demand for a blanket license for syndicated programming on cable television; they do not challenge the license with respect to local origination programming or programming made expressly for first exhibition on cable television.

### C. Music Licensing History of the Cable Industry

To understand the posture of this case, and the contour of the Court's inquiry, a review of the history of music licensing in the cable industry is helpful. Until December 31, 1989, licenses granted by BMI to cable program services were "through to the viewer," covering both the services' satellite and microwave transmission to system operators and home dish owners, and the retransmission of the programming by system operators to subscribers. Under this licensing regime, cable system operators did not need their own licenses for BMI music contained in programming obtained from cable programmers because their performances of that music were covered by the programmers' licenses.

During the 1980s, the cable industry expanded and matured. For example, from 1985 to 1990 subscriptions grew from 32 million to approximately 53 million households; between 1984 and 1989 total cable television subscriptions rose by 35.5%, and the average revenues per subscriber increased from $ 19.87 to $ 26.36. U.S. General Accounting Office, Telecommunications: Follow-Up National Survey of Cable Television Rates and Services (Report to the Chairman, Subcommittee on Telecommunications and Finance, Committee on Energy and Commerce, House of Representatives GAO/RCED-90-199, June 13, 1990), at 57, 59 (D 596). As of the mid-1980s, BMI had entered into blanket license agreements with five major pay cable program services (including TDC), three basic cable program services owned and operated by MTV Networks, Inc., and a variety of smaller cable networks. The fees for these licenses were either flat dollar sums or, in the case of some pay cable program services, calculated at the rate of $ 0.12 per subscriber, never amounting to more than 0.3% of the pay cable services' revenues. The majority of cable programming services (and all cable operators) are unlicensed at this time.

BMI characterizes these license fees as "start-up" rates. BMI's Vice President and General Counsel, Marvin Berenson, testified that BMI believed that these rates were not keeping up with the types of revenues the cable industry is garnering. Tr. at 2284-85. BMI accordingly sought higher fees. During 1988 and 1989, BMI offered through-to-the-viewer blanket licenses to BET and three other cable program services at a fee equivalent to one percent of each service's annual revenues.

A more important point of contention between the cable industry and BMI that hampered their ability to reach agreement was what BMI offered as an "alternate method of licensing": dual or split licensing. Under this approach, cable program services and cable system operators would have to obtain separate music performing rights licenses for the transmission of programming containing BMI music. (The system operator's license would also cover the system operator's non-program service programming). In other words, a license would be required for both the transmission of the cable programming from the programmer to the system operator, and from the system operator to subscribers. The rationale for this splitting of fees was twofold: Primarily, BMI was attempting to capture a share of the greater earnings in the cable industry, that obtained by operators. E.g., Tr. at 2334-35, 2349. And, it was attempting to obtain compensation for what it argues are the two separate public performances that occur in cable transmissions: from the cable programmer to the system operator, and from the system operator to the subscribing public. E.g., Whalen V.Tr. (J16) at 98-99.

BMI first introduced the approach in December 1989. It is undisputed that BMI actively sought to institute this new form of licensing and that it would prefer to license the cable industry in that manner thenceforth. E.g., P 178 at 4 (BMI President's Report, Apr. 2, 1990). As the Director of Legal Affairs of The Disney Channel recalled from a meeting with BMI in January 1990, BMI was adamant on this point and intended to obtain such licenses from all cable programmers. Whalen V.Tr. (J16) at 62-63. HBO had a similar experience, as reflected in notes of a meeting between BMI attorneys and HBO, where the former intimated to the latter that BMI would not be giving through-to-the-viewer licenses. P 9L at 8. BMI also threatened to sue programmers for infringement unless they acceded to BMI's demands. E.g., P 4H (BMI letter to Arts & Entertainment Cable Network, Feb. 2, 1989); P 6E at 2 (BMI letter to CBN The Family Channel, Mar. 21, 1989). At the same time, in early 1989, BMI proposed to the NCTA licensing committee a blanket license fee for system operators, at a fee of one percent of revenues, to cover their transmission of local originator and public access programming, as well as programming from unlicensed cable services. J.S. para. 84. NCTA refused.

BMI's Berenson testified that both this type of license, as well as a through-to-the-viewer license at a 1% rate, were sought from programmers. Tr. at 2334-35, 2472. Specifically, through-to-the-viewer licenses would be offered if they "encompassed the [624] entire revenue stream." Id. at 2469. BMI notes that it asked TDC, for example, to make a counterproposal, id. at 2472, but TDC never did so. Id.; Whalen V.Tr. (316) at 107. BMI, for its part, refused to go to arbitration to settle these disputes. P 6E at 2.

In any event, the program services balked at these demands, refusing to pay above 0.25% of their revenue for a through-to-the-viewer license, Tr. at

2328-29, and rejecting the split licensing approach entirely. It was clear that BMI was seeking substantial increases in license fees, no matter the type of license. E.g., Tr. at 2471. After the negotiations broke down, BMI sent letters to several program services indicating that unless license agreements were entered into, BMI would sue for infringement of their affiliates' copyrights for the programmers' unauthorized performance of BMI music.

BMI subsequently instituted a number of copyright infringement actions against unlicensed program services. These included cases against Rainbow Programming, Lifetime Television, and the Christian Broadcasting Network. In an antitrust case brought against it, BMI counterclaimed for infringement, as it has done here. The most significant action BMI brought was against Home Box Office ("HBO") and Manhattan Cable Television, Inc. ("HBO case") in December 1989 after the failure of HBO to agree to the terms of renewing HBO's license on either a dual or through-to-the-viewer basis. In that suit, BMI claimed copyright infringement and sought an injunction preventing HBO from continuing to transmit programming containing BMI music. The suit was settled a year later, well after the instant litigation began.

BMI never sued BET, although it did send the programming service a "cease and desist letter" indicating that unless BET successfully negotiated a license, BMI would sue for infringement. P 3M; Tr. at 764. BET and other programmers did offer to have the appropriate fee determined by a neutral third party and to pay interim license fees while the final license terms were decided, but BMI was not interested. Tr. at 765, 767, 769, 2306; P 6E at 2. TDC's through-to-the-viewer license agreement with BMI expired on December 31, 1989. During negotiations for renewal in later 1989 and early 1990, BMI pushed for a split license arrangement, but did offer to consider a proposal for a through-to-the-viewer license, although at a substantially increased fee. On January 30, 1990, TDC and the other plaintiffs instituted this action.

## II. THE ANTITRUST CLAIM

Section 1 of the Sherman Act forbids "every contract, combination . . . or conspiracy in restraint of trade or commerce." 15 U.S.C. § 1. Despite the literal wording, however, the statute prohibits only unreasonable restraints of trade. Standard Oil Co. v. United States, 221 U.S. 1, 31 S. Ct. 502, 55 L. Ed. 619 (1911). Thus, plaintiffs must show that a restraint exists; once such a showing is made, a "rule of reason" analysis is conducted to determine if the restraint is unreasonable and therefore unlawful. This inquiry encompasses "all of the circumstances of the case" Business Electronics Corp. v. Sharp Electronics Corp., 485 U.S. 717, 723, 108 S. Ct. 1515, 1519, 99 L. Ed. 2d 808 (1988), and entails weighing the anticompetitive effects of the challenged practice against its procompetitive effects — its impact on competitive conditions. National Society of Professional Engineers v. United States, 435 U.S. 679, 691, 98 S. Ct. 1355, 1365, 55 L. Ed. 2d 637 (1978); Continental T.V., Inc. v. GTE Sylvania, Inc., 433 U.S. 36, 49 n. 15, 97 S. Ct. 2549, 2557 n. 15, 53 L. Ed. 2d 568 (1977). As expressed by Justice Brandeis in a frequently quoted passage,

To determine that question the court must ordinarily consider the facts peculiar to the business to which the restraint is applied; its condition before and after the restraint was imposed; the nature of the restraint and its effect, actual or probable. The history of the restraint, the evil believed to exist, the reason for adopting the particular remedy, the purpose or end sought to be attained, are all relevant facts.

Chicago Board of Trade v. United States, 246 U.S. 231, 238, 38 S. Ct. 242, 244, 62 L. Ed. 683 (1918).

Portraying the blanket license as a facial restraint on competition, plaintiffs urge the Court to apply a full rule of reason analysis to BMI's blanket licensing of music in syndicated programming and the dual licensing proposed by BMI in the negotiations that led to this lawsuit. Defendant, on the other hand, insists that the Court follow the shorter path traversed by the Second Circuit in both CBS Remand and Buffalo Broadcasting and ultimately end its journey at an earlier point, by determining that the blanket license constitutes no restraint at all. BMI is confident that the Court will find, as the Second Circuit did in those two contexts, that no restraint exists because there are "realistically available alternatives" to the blanket license. See CBS Remand, 620 F.2d at 936; Buffalo Broadcasting, 744 F.2d at 925, 933; see also F.E.L. Publications, Ltd. v. Catholic Bishop of Chicago, 214 U.S.P.Q. (BNA) 409, 415 (7th Cir. 1982).

It is true that virtually any agreement or contract may restrain trade; "read literally, § 1 would outlaw the entire body of private contract law." Professional Engineers, 435 U.S. at 688, 98 S. Ct. at 1363. And while "trade is restrained . . . where rights to use individual copyrights or patents may be obtained only by payment for a pool of such rights," CBS Remand, 620 F.2d at 935-36, here there is no explicit agreement or contract restraining the sale of music performing rights or otherwise prohibiting their sale outside of the blanket license. As explained supra, the music performing rights granted by the music's composers and publishers to BMI are nonexclusive. Composers and publishers explicitly retain the right to license users directly. Plaintiffs, moreover, do not allege any tacit conspiracy on the part of defendant or its affiliates to deny the granting of those rights by the affiliates to the cable industry. Rather, they assume that the existence of BMI (the pooling of these rights) by itself automatically constitutes a restraint.

Plaintiffs also imply that the Supreme Court virtually declared that the blanket license is a restraint. The opinion does not so hold. That was not the question before the Court; what it considered, and rejected, was the legal proposition that the blanket license was per se illegal under the antitrust laws.

That conclusion might be read, in light of the remand to the Second Circuit to conduct a rule of reason analysis, to encompass a subsidiary finding that the blanket license was a restraint because it should be examined under that rubric. However, the opinion is vague on this point, its holding does not depend on such an assumption, and conclusions about implicit findings in Supreme Court opinions cannot be lightly reached. Indeed, were the Court to engage in delving for implication, there is language in the opinion suggesting that the blanket license is not a restraint. For example, the Supreme Court noted that "ASCAP is not really a joint sales agency offering the individual goods of many sellers, but is a separate seller offering its blanket license, of which the individual compositions are raw material." 441 U.S. at 22, 99 S. Ct. at 1564. The Court further observed that "the individual composers and authors have neither agreed not to sell individually in any other market nor use the blanket license to mask price fixing in other such markets," id. at 23-24, 99 S. Ct. at 1564, implying that their actions do not constitute a restraint on the music-licensing market. 33 Indeed, in a later gloss on its holding, the Supreme Court noted that "there was no limit of any kind placed on the volume that might be sold in the entire market and each individual remained free to sell his own music without restraint." National Collegiate Athletic Association v. Board of Regents ("NCAA"), 468 U.S. 85, 114, 104 S. Ct. 2948, 2967, 82 L. Ed. 2d 70 (1984).

The cases plaintiffs rely on for their contention that a restraint exists (and that the Court should therefore immediately turn to a rule of reason inquiry) do not support their cause. In fact, the significant Supreme Court cases employing or expounding this doctrine arose out of agreements that were unmistakable restraints; the focus was on whether the particular restraints involved were lawful. In Continental T.V., the Court concluded that a limit on the number of franchises granted for any given area and a requirement that each franchisee sell the respondent's products only from the locations at which he was franchised — vertical restrictions contained in franchise contracts — should be examined under the rule of reason. 433 U.S. at 59, 97 S. Ct. at 2562. In Professional Engineers, the Code of Ethics provision at issue affirmatively forbade competitive bidding for engineering services, thereby preventing engineers from soliciting and submitting price information to prospective clients until after the client had chosen an engineer. 435 U.S. at 683-84, 98 S. Ct. at 1361. And in NCAA, the object of the Court's scrutiny was a college athletic association's plan for televising college football that constituted horizontal price fixing and an output limitation on its face. "There can be no doubt that the challenged practices of the NCAA constitute a restraint of trade in the sense that they limit members' freedom to negotiate and enter into their own contracts." 468 U.S. at 98, 104 S. Ct. at 2958-59; see also id. at 99, 104 S. Ct. at 2959. In FTC v. Superior Court Trial Lawyers Association, 493 U.S. 411, 110 S. Ct. 768, 107 L. Ed. 2d 851 (1990), a boycott by court-appointed lawyers — a facial prohibition on trade — was found to be a per se restraint. In Arizona v. Maricopa County Medical Society, 457 U.S. 332, 102 S. Ct. 2466, 73 L. Ed. 2d 48 (1982), the court considered whether horizontal agreements among doctors fixing maximum prices — a clear restraint — should be subject to the per se rule or a rule of reason inquiry. Indeed, the Supreme Court used the blanket license examined in BMI v. CBS as a means of distinguishing the practice challenged in Maricopa County. In contrast to the medical services there, "the 'blanket license' was entirely different from the product that any one composer was able to sell by himself. Although there was little competition among individual composers for their separate compositions, the blanket-license arrangement did not place any restraint on the right of any individual copyright owner to sell his own compositions separately to any buyer at any price." 457 U.S. at 355, 102 S. Ct. at 2479 (footnotes omitted). That those cases invoked the rule of reason (or rejected it) has no bearing on the threshold question here, where there is no facial restraint.

This Court refuses to assume that a restraint exists and, accordingly, examines whether the blanket license is, in the first instance, a restraint at all. Plaintiffs claim that BMI's blanket license, by its very nature, is a de facto restraint of trade as applied to syndicated cable television programming with regard to both the programmers' transmission to cable operators and the cable operators' transmissions to subscribers. They highlight facts stipulated to or adduced at trial that purportedly lead to this conclusion: that BMI offers its repertory on an "all or nothing" basis, that the fees for the licenses do not reflect the quantity or quality of the compositions used, and that the fee "is not set by competition among individual copyright owners." See BMI v. CBS, 441 U.S. at 23, 99 S. Ct. at 1564. Plaintiffs also emphasize that all other rights pertaining to music use in syndicated programming are conveyed at the time of production and are done so in a competitive marketplace where negotiations as to these right are characterized by price competition. In other words, plaintiffs assert that in a world without the blanket license, music performing rights would be negotiated in the same competitive setting, via producer source licensing. In particular, the fact that syndicated programming, which the record establishes is critical to the commercial viability of both cable programmers and operators (especially from major studios), involves music "in the can," and the agreements between programmers and the producers or distributors of syndicated programming prohibit the deletion of the music contained therein, restrains plaintiffs from obtaining performing rights by any means other than blanket licenses. Because BMI's practices leave them with no choice they violate the antitrust laws.

This superficially appealing argument does not survive a close scrutiny of the record evidence. Ironically, plaintiffs, in presenting the facts as proving their lack of choice, in essence are urging the Court to determine whether a choice exists. This brings the Court to the analysis plaintiffs claim is incorrect and should be bypassed, that employed by the Second Circuit in CBS Remand and especially Buffalo Broadcasting, where the Court emphasized that the important question was whether "there are no realistically available alternatives" to the blanket license. 744 F.2d at 933.

Although not binding on this Court, and although based on a significantly different trial record, the Buffalo Broadcasting decision is instructive and warrants brief review. That case, it may be recalled, was a challenge by local broadcast television stations to blanket licenses for music performing rights. According to the Second Circuit, the appropriate inquiry was "whether the plaintiff had proved that it lacked a realistic opportunity to obtain performance rights from individual copyright holders." Id. at 926. The trial court there had considered three alternatives — per program licenses, direct licenses, and source licenses — and had found each wanting. The Court of Appeals found the trial court's conclusions wrong as a matter of law. As to per program licenses, the court of appeals declared that transactions costs (e.g., tracking down individual composers) and the burdens involved in monitoring had not been shown to be excessive in an objective sense. Id. at 926-27. As to direct licensing, the court found that plaintiff had failed to prove that it lacked sufficient market power to have the realistic opportunity to secure such licenses, particularly because no evidence was offered that the local television stations had attempted to obtain such licenses and because they were able to obtain direct licenses for their own local programming. Id. at 929. Finally, as to source licensing, the court found that plaintiff had not proved the inability to obtain licenses from producers of syndicated programming who "could, if so inclined, convey music performing rights." Id. In this regard, the court observed that "notably absent from all of the correspondence" concerning offers by the local television stations to obtain music performing rights from producers "tendered by plaintiffs is the customary indicator of a buyer's seriousness in attempting to make a purchase — an offer of money." Id. at 930-31. The court thus concluded that plaintiffs had not presented "evidence that the blanket license is functioning to restrain willing buyers and sellers from negotiating for the licensing of performing rights to individual compositions at a reasonable price." Id. at 932.

Of course, the fact that local broadcast television stations did not prevail in their antitrust case challenge to the blanket license does not mean that plaintiffs here necessarily fail in their parallel quest. Antitrust questions are always fact-specific. The plaintiffs before this Court are different, especially because they represent two distinct sets of players in the market (programmers and system operators). The evidence presented at trial is not the same as that in Buffalo Broadcasting. That being said, however, plaintiffs here have failed to carry their burden. It is clear from the record that there are realistic alternatives available — that plaintiffs, especially the cable programmers, do have a choice when it comes to obtaining music performing rights for the syndicated programming they transmit. These options are examined in turn below, first with regard to cable programmers, then with regard to cable system operators.

A. Alternatives Available to Cable Program Services

1. Source Licensing

Much of the time at trial was devoted to "supplier source licensing" or source licensing. In fact, this is the relief plaintiffs seek — to have music performing rights bargained for at the time producers select music for their syndicated product. They claim that suppliers of syndicated programming do not have the performing rights to convey, and that even if they do, the existing practice is not to pass on those rights because of the disincentive created by the blanket license.

a. Preexisting Music

Several form and actual synchronization licenses governing rights to preexisting music issued to producers of motion pictures (a significant segment of syndicated programming acquired by cable services) were introduced into evidence that contain clauses limiting the music performing rights to U.S. theatrical exhibition. These licenses typically provide that television performance of the motion picture by anyone not licensed for such performing rights by ASCAP or Bill is subject to clearance of the performing right either from publisher or ASCAP or BMI or from any other licensor acting for or on behalf of publisher, and requires an additional license fee therefor. See, e.g., P 39D para. 6 (Blackwood Music Inc. form). Similarly, a form pay/cable synchronization license used by the music publisher, the Goodman Group, for non-theatric release syndicated programs states that it does not permit any use other than synchronization or recording, "it being understood that performing rights licenses must be secured from any performing rights society or other entity having the legal right to issue such licenses as the owner of such rights." P 4011 para. 3. It has clearly been the practice in the industry not to convey performance rights along with synchronization rights. Tr. at 391, 637-40; Rider V.Tr. (P 375A) at 35-36. Nonetheless, publishers do offer licenses for preexisting music that obligate the publisher to issue separate music performing rights licenses to cover unlicensed television exhibition. Tr. at 563-72; see D 667 para. 8(a), D 985 para. 2(b)(i). These contingent direct licenses, known as "back-up" licenses, commonly provide for a mandatory performance license to be granted to any television exhibitor unlicensed by BMI, the fee therefor to be negotiated between the producer and exhibitor (or by arbitration). For example, a synchronization and performance license for the composition "You Are My Sunshine," granted by the publisher to Walt Disney Studios, provides:

With respect to the exhibition of said motion picture in the United States . . . if any television exhibitor is not licensed to perform the musical composition by a blanket license issued by the performing rights society (if any) having the performing rights thereto . . . Publisher shall, or shall cause said performing rights society to, license such television exhibitor . . . for a reasonable performance fee to be negotiated . . . or . . . such fee shall be determined by a neutral arbitrator . . . .

D 667 para. 8(a). An identical clause is present in a form used by Warner Brothers — one of the largest studios producing syndicated programming. See D 646 para. 9(a). Indeed, synchronization licenses with these or similar clauses were recently entered into between the Disney Studio and the music publishing company EMI. Boris V.Tr. (D 1111A) at 45-46; see D 1109, D 1110. Form licenses containing contingent direct licensing clauses are also used by music publishers, including Disney's Wonderland Music company. Tr. at 162. The second-largest music publisher in the world, Warner/Chapell, has used these forms since 1974. See D 14 para. 5(c).

Despite these contractual provisions to the contrary, plaintiffs rely on the existence of a "uniform expectation" that music performing rights will be licensed through BMI blanket licenses issued to cable programmers. Tr. at 366-67; 105; 1866-67. They also cite certain recent form agreements that explicitly require the licensee to obtain a separate music performing rights license, such as synchronization license forms for broadcast television used by ABKCO Music Inc., P 40A para. 3, and EMI Blackwood Music, Inc., P 40H para. 6. In any event, they argue that contingent direct licenses are the exception, rather than the rule.

Whatever the historic practice in the industry may have been, however, and whether it is a fact that only a minority of licenses for preexisting music provide for such rights, the evidence conclusively established that such licenses exist, in both standardized blank forms and in actual agreements. Furthermore, there was no evidence provided that any cable entities had attempted to utilize the contingent direct license clause. Indeed, there was evidence that no cable television programmer had ever contacted Wonderland Music, a large music publisher, concerning the clause in their form licenses. Borgeson Dep. at 37-38.

The economic realities of the industry further belie plaintiffs' claims. It is stipulated that the negotiation of synchronization and theatric performing rights licenses for preexisting music in syndicated films and programs is characterized by price competition. J.S. para. 115. In determining license fees for the right to use preexisting music, the music publisher usually obtains from the producer information on the intended use of the music (e.g., theme or background). The resulting fee proposal is then subject to negotiation, and the producer in most instances con reject the offer if the fee is believed to be too high. Tr. at 1097-99, 1165-67. Producers, moreover, commonly solicit quotations for several different preexisting compositions from different publishers, so that the producer can select the composition after receiving proposed fee rates. Tr. at 1098-99; 1833-34. Therefore, to survive in this competitive marketplace, publishers would grant contingent direct licenses to producers if they were demanded — even where current contracts do not allow for such licensing. Tr. at 1841.

Plaintiffs also point to the contractual arrangements between composers and their publishing companies as providing proof of the impediments that exist with regard to preexisting music in syndicated programming. These "songwriter agreements" govern the publisher's administration of the copyrighted compositions in the publisher's catalog, including the rights acquired by the publisher from the composer. These agreements vary both within a catalog and among publishers, but plaintiffs offered evidence of songwriter agreements with music publishing companies that prohibit the publisher from giving direct licensing without the composer's consent and that require composers' performing rights royalties to be licensed and received through BMI. See Tr. at 1863-65, 1908-10; P para. 45A 4(J); P 45J para. 5.01; P para. 45L 4(k); P para. 45HH 4(k). Plaintiffs did not show, however, that composers would not give their permission for such licenses. Further, these contractual provisions are not necessarily immutable. For example, songwriter Richard Sherman testified that, if pressed, he would grant his performing rights to the producer. Tr. at 2014. As with the other contract language discussed in this case, this language is amenable to change in response to market forces such as demand and in response to the right price.

b. Original Music

Plaintiffs also sought to prove that producers of programming containing "original music" (music specifically created for that programming) were unable to obtain the performance rights from the composer and publisher, and thus are precluded from granting licenses for performing rights even if requested to do so. The majority of music in syndicated programming is original music. Rights to original music are generally governed in the industry by "work-for-hire" agreements. These are producer-generated standard form contracts, in which the only term that is negotiated is the price. Tr. at 319-20, 1743-44, 1943-47. Pursuant to these contracts, the composer usually receives an initial ("up-front") fee and, sometimes, agrees to a further compensation formula that would permit him or her to retain the right to receive royalties from public performance of the work and for any market sales of the music that may occur.

The parties stipulated that work-for-hire agreements typically transfer from the composer to the producer "nearly all rights" to the original music. Plaintiffs introduced evidence showing that these agreements often do not grant the producer the right to perform or to authorize others to perform the music nontheatrically, without the producer obtaining express consent or an additional license from the composer. They then attempt to transform this evidence into the factual conclusion that music performing rights are not included in such agreements. Such a determination, however, would require viewing the evidence through an opaque screen.

Plaintiffs largely rely on the standard work-for-hire agreements formulated before or during the early the 1980s. These form agreements contain language identical or substantially similar to the following excerpt:

To assure the Artist of participation in the revenue which may be derived from performances of the Compositions . . . Producer will, and it does hereby, transfer and assign the world-wide Performing Rights . . . in and to the Compositions to the Artist and a publisher of the Producer's choice. . . .

P 35E, Exh. A para. 3 (1987 agreement between Patrick Williams and Twentieth Century Fox); see also P 33F, Sched. B para. 3 (1980); P 33A, Sched. A para. 3 (1990); P 35 A, Exh. A para. 3 (1982). These clauses result in the composer receiving compensation for nontheatric public performances of the music only from BMI (or ASCAP or SESAC). Further, composers testified that they understood these types of contracts to mean that producers would not or could not assign music performing rights to any third party. Tr. at 1792-94; 1982-83; 2012-13.

Yet other (and generally more recent) work-for-hire standard forms do provide for the transfer from the composer to the producers of all rights to the original music. One example of such forms provides as follows:

Notwithstanding any provisions to the contrary contained herein, if at any time any television network, television station or other company ('Television Entity') . . . does not or may not hold a non-dramatic performing license from ASCAP, BMI . . . or if a Television Entity so require, [Producer] shall automatically have the exclusive right to license to each such Television Entity the non-dramatic performing rights in and to the Music for use in connection with the Show.

D 243 § 3 (standard Disney Studio form). See also D 404 (Warner Bros); D 314 (Universal); D 205 (MGM); D 651 (Twentieth Century Fox); P 37A Exh. B para. 1(d)(i) (1990 agreement between Michael Kamen and Pathe Entertainment, Inc.); P 30A para. 9(b)(vii) (standard United Artists motion picture form); P 34G para. 8(b)(vii). Similar to the above-quoted "automatic performance rights license" is the "grant of rights" clause, such as that in a form used by the Paramount Picture Corporation for composer-for-hire agreements:

It is specifically understood and agreed that included in the ownership of all rights of [Paramount] in and to the Compositions is the specific and irrevocable right under any and all circumstances, in perpetuity, to perform publicly for profit, or otherwise, and to authorize others to do so. . . .

P 33A Sched. A para. 2; see also, e.g., P 32F para. 4 (1989 agreement); D 783 para. 8(c)(vii) (Pathe Entertainment, Inc. form); D 990 Exh. A para. 4 (Orion form).

Again, plaintiffs rely on the historic, prevailing practice in the industry and on what they claim has been the specific, uniform intent in virtually all these instances that compensation for music performing rights on cable television will be determined and distributed by BMI (or ASCAP or SESAC, as the case may be). Great significance is attached to the fact that current forms do not render music performing rights the subject of negotiation — they are subsumed into negotiations over the whole package. Plaintiffs also attempted, through their industry expert, to dismiss the clauses as giving merely "technical" rights. Tr. at 549, 561. Yet a witness for plaintiffs from TDC admitted that it could obtain such rights from the Disney Studio. Tr. at 157-58. Plaintiffs also argued that these clauses are meaningless because the contracts still provide for compensation for public performance rights to be received in the first instance through the performing rights society. But nothing is proven by the observation that these are merely back-up provisions.

Plaintiffs' assertions that there are no known instances of producers authorizing unlicensed exhibitors to perform music under one of these provisions, and that BMI composers are "generally unaware" of the existence of these clauses, carry little weight. For no evidence was offered that any cable entity ever attempted to obtain such rights through that mechanism. See Borgeson Dep. at 41-42; Breen Dep. at 57-58.

Economic realities of this segment of the music market are that there is, as the parties stipulated, intense competition among composers to be hired to write original music for such programming. Thus, producers are able to select, on the basis of quality and price, from among numerous composers to create music for their motion pictures or other syndicated programming. But plaintiffs dismiss this competition as not entirely relevant because, they claim, there is no price competition among composers regarding the licensing of cable television performing rights to that music. See Buffalo Broadcasting, 744 F.2d at 932. Again, that observation deserves little weight where there has been no opportunity for such competition to arise because it has not been pursued by the cable industry.

Finally, very few cable programmers ever attempted to obtain source licensing for syndicated programming. The Senior Vice President for Programming at TDC testified that TDC had never asked suppliers of programming to obtain performing rights. Rider V.Tr. (P 375A) at 37; see also Tr. at 136-37. Those that did — BET, HBO and The Family Channel — did not offer any additional money to obtain the performance rights. Tr. at 731-32; Isakoff V.Tr. (P 376A) at 73-74. A fact further undermining their position is that, notwithstanding their failure to offer additional compensation, source licensing was obtained in several instances. The Family Channel obtained source licensing clauses in a number of syndicated programming contracts acquired from 1987 through 1990. Isakoff V.Tr. (P 376A) at 63-64; see D 286, D 299, D 376, D 379, D

385. HBO has obtained source licensing clauses in approximately 300 agreements concerning syndicated programming since 1984. Cooke V.Tr. (P 377A) at 13-15. Plaintiffs therefore can show no restraint created by blanket licensing impeding that alternative with regard to licensing that type of music in syndicated programming.

2. Direct Licensing

With regard to direct licensing, it bears repeating that the blanket license is a non-exclusive arrangement. In other words, plaintiffs could choose to obtain licenses directly from the composers and publishers of the musical works contained in syndicated programming. Therefore, the question is not whether "direct licensing" is an option, but whether it is realistically available. There are hundreds of individual compositions that would have to be cleared with each individual copyright proprietor. And there was testimony to the effect that ascertaining the identity of and then reaching the appropriate copyright proprietors was difficult and costly. Tr. at 439-40; 688-89; 1078-79; Isakoff V.Tr. (P 376A) at 43-44. But even were that feasible, it was clear that for syndicated programming, although the programs are obviously selected and known, the musical content is not specified. Attempts by Home Box Office to obtain direct licensing for all its programming were only partially successful.

Plaintiffs insist that so long as the blanket license exists, direct licensing will not be economically feasible because copyright proprietors will want at least as much remuneration as they would obtain from distributions they receive through the blanket licensing system. HBO's strategy for obtaining direct licenses began with ascertaining what BMI had been paying the copyright proprietors. Clark HBO Dep. at 556-62. Those publishers who were willing to negotiate with HBO demanded at a minimum the same amount as their BMI distributions, and at times, much more. In other words, the blanket license serves as a pricing floor. Tr. at 1844; Boris V.Tr. (D 1111A) at 103-09; P 47T, P 47U, P AA-P DD (HBO-EMI correspondence); P 47FF-P 47II (Famous Music-BMI-HBO correspondence).

BMI points out that the sheer magnitude of the task does not make it impossible, if for no other reason than the fact that its licensing agreements with publishers (as well as composers) are nonexclusive. Furthermore, they emphasize the stipulated fact that few cable program services have attempted to obtain direct licenses for the music in their syndicated programming; in particular, neither plaintiff programming service here (TDC and BET) made any efforts in that direction. J.S. para. 126. The Court agrees that the dearth of any evidence in this regard renders plaintiffs' contentions largely speculative.

As for HBO's efforts, they too do not form a sound basis for any conclusions as to the feasibility of direct licensing. HBO did not begin its direct licensing campaign until after BMI had filed the infringement suit against it, which calls into question the results obtained. Some testimony indicated that publishers found HBO's offers to be deficient, both in the amount of money offered, Pinkus HBO Dep. at 53-54, and in the specific information conveyed, such as the number of potential exhibitors, that would enable a price to be determined. Ryan HBO Dep. at 85.

Publishers, moreover, have issued such licenses when asked. J.S. paras. 95, 132. Four publishers testified that they would grant direct licenses, for the right price. Tr. at 1184; 1844; 1901-03; Boris V.Tr. (D 1111A) at 14-16. For example, the music publisher EMI will give quotes for performing rights when approached for synchronization rights by unlicensed entities. D 840 (EMI-NBC direct license, 1990); D 843 (EMI letter to ASCAP concerning ESPN direct license); D 857 (Colgems EMI-ESPN direct license, 1990).

Finally, the laws of supply and demand would dictate that direct licenses would be granted if they were demanded. See Tr. at 2106-07. The lack of a mechanism or mechanisms for dealing with the negotiations and monitoring of such rights is not necessarily an impediment, either. Defendant's economic expert testified persuasively that the required intermediaries would arise. Tr. at 2124. The fact that the market for synchronization rights is brokered largely by one institution (the Harry Fox [634] Agency) bolsters this contention. See J.S. para. 94.

Accordingly, the Court concludes that, although clearly neither the easiest nor most convenient method, direct licenses for music in syndicated programming is a realistically available alternative to the blanket license for cable program services.

3. Per Program Licenses

Another alternative offered as evidence of the lack of restraint is the "per-program" license. Such a license is a modified form of a blanket license, providing unlimited access to the entire BMI repertory for a fee based only on programs using BMI music. Plaintiffs label this option the "disappearing alternative." Although not as accessible as source licensing, it too, the Court concludes, exists as a realistic alternative.

Plaintiffs argue that the practical unavailability of per program licenses is apparent from BMI insistence that it is not required under its consent decree to offer such licenses to cable services and operators. Apart from the shaky legal ground for BMI 's position on this issue, the fact is that BMI has offered such licenses to every cable programmer that asked for one. E.g., Tr. at 818-19; 2285, 2369-70; D 573 (offer to the Family Channel); D 575 (offer to Lifetime cable network).

Even so, plaintiffs insist that it is not a realistic option because BMI's offers for per-program licenses were at a rate of 4.5% of revenue multiplied by the fraction of the services' schedule containing BMI-repertory music — in other words, four and a half times the offered blanket license rate. Representatives of cable services testified that such a rate was so costly as to render it a meaningless alternative, e.g., Tr. at 829-30, or so costly that they believed it was not a serious offer. Id. at 761 Whalen V.Tr. (J16) at 65-67. Plaintiffs' reliance on this evidence is misplaced.

As with their approach to other kinds of licensing, plaintiffs failed to show that they made any serious efforts to obtain per program licenses. Indeed, there was an absence of evidence that cable services to whom BMI offered per program licenses ever considered that option. None ever counterproposed; certainly neither BET nor TDC indicated that they were willing to contemplate this type of licensing. Tr. at 760-61; Whalen V.Tr. (J16) at 97-98. This failure to engage in negotiation — the robust and focused give-and-take of the competitive marketplace — cannot shore up their claims of unavailability. As the Supreme Court observed, a complaint that an offeror's fee demand "is so high as to preclude agreement fails to acknowledge that an initially high asking price does not preclude bargaining." Stewart v. Abend, 495 U.S. 207, 110 S. Ct. 1750, 1764, 109 L. Ed. 2d 184, 14 U.S.P.Q.2D (BNA) 1614 (1990). It cannot be said that a quoted price is too high when it cannot be ascertained what the actual price would have been had any bargaining occurred or, better, an agreement reached.

In sum, cable program services do have realistically available alternatives to the BMI blanket license and, therefore, the latter does not constitute a restraint of trade within the meaning of § 1 of the Sherman Act.

### B. Alternatives Available to Cable System Operators

Many of the arguments plaintiffs advanced with respect to the licensing alternatives available to cable program services were also raised with respect to cable system operators, albeit with more force, because operators are, simply put, in a different position. They are further down the line in the set of transactions and transmissions that bring cable programs to the public. System operators, unlike program services, do not participate in the selection of or negotiation over syndicated programming. They have no relationship with producers or syndicators. Further, they transmit up to several dozen different cable program services, each with up to hundreds of syndicated programs containing BMI music — amounting in some cases to tens of thousands of compositions every month. See, e.g., Tr. at 439-40.

It is not only their distance from syndicated program production and the magnitude of the programming they carry that distinguishes cable operators in this context; it is also their contractual relationships with the cable programmers whose programming they transmit. Cable system operators are contractually bound to transmit cable services' programming simultaneously on receipt from the satellite, and without interruption or editing. E.g., P 53C para. 6(b); P 54G para. 4(c). Moreover, they have little advance notice (from a month or two to ten days or less) of the programming content, much less the music therein. See Tr. at 422, 437-38; 682, 686-88; Whalen V.Tr. (J16) at 19-23; Rider V.Tr. (P375A) at 40-41, 81. Also, they may not refuse to carry programming because they have not obtained music performing rights from the programmer. Clearly, these circumstances render direct licensing of cable operators cumbersome and, the Court finds, unrealistic.

Source licensing, at first blush, also would not appear to be ultimately possible, as the market now exists, because system operators simply do not interact with program producers or syndicators. However, it was demonstrated that source licensing is available to cable system operators in the sense that they could obtain clearance for these rights from their sources, the cable programming services. Plaintiffs argued that the representations and warranties in affiliation agreements concerning music performing rights are not equivalent to source licensing unless the cable network has the authority to convey the rights. But that merely begs the question of this litigation, one that has been answered affirmatively — whether the cable programmers can indeed obtain licensing from their sources.

Defendants also attacked the portrayal of system operators as helpless victims in the music performing rights market. Many system operators are vertically integrated with programming services and, in any event, most are parts of "MSOs" — they are multiple-system operators. The trial testimony of two MSO executives, Robert Miron and Julian Brodsky, revealed that MSOs are indeed vertically integrated in that they own interests in various cable programming services. E.g., Tr. at 462-63. The top fifty MSOs account for more than 90% of the nation's cable television subscribers. D 852 (FCC Report No. 90-276, July 31, 1990) at 5106. The stipulated facts illustrate the complex ownership relations among these various components of the cable industry. For example, Time Warner Inc. has a subsidiary, the MSO American Television and Communications Corporation, which owns the HBO and Cinemax Cable program services. HBO, in turn, owns an interest in BET. Time Warner Inc. also owns programming producers such as Warner Bros., Inc. and Lorimar Television, and also owns several music publishers, including Warner/Chapell Music and Warner-Tamerlane Publishing Co. and Lorimar Music Bee Corp. — the last two being affiliates of BMI. J.S. paras. 31, 33. Thus, in addition to their economic ties with programmers, MSOs often own music publishers and production companies. J.S. para. 32.

However, even if the cable operators owned by these MSOs would be able to obtain music performing rights with relative ease, or indemnification or warranties therefor, from their affiliated programming services, that does not establish that all system operators would have this opportunity realistically available to them. In other words, those cable system operators without such affiliations do not benefit from this potential advantage. More significantly, the economic concentration of the most powerful MSOs does not give them special access to the programming services with which they are not affiliated — in most cases, the majority of the programming services they carry. See Tr. at 403-10; 1059.

However, all that being said, it is also indisputable that cable system operators are themselves monopsonies — with perhaps half a dozen exceptions, cable system operators are the only purchasers and, more importantly, the only transmitters of programming in their geographic areas. (Most cable systems obtain exclusive franchises from municipalities or other local governments to transmit cable television in their territories. J.S. para. 29.) Were cable operators faced with the prospect, they would attempt to obtain licensing through an intermediary — most likely, the programmers whose fare they carry, see Tr. at 2124, and, given that they are usually the sole conduits for the cable programming system in a given area, and in consideration of their aggregated power, it is entirely plausible that programmers would accommodate them. E.g., Hirsch HBO Tr. at 315-16.

While direct licensing is not a realistic option, and while it is a closer question than with regard to programming services, it is nonetheless clear that source licensing is realistically available to cable system operators. The blanket license does not, therefore, represent a restraint of trade with regard to cable system operators.

### C. Other Alleged Constraints

Even if the above-described alternatives do exist, plaintiffs insist they are ultimately illusory because, as a practical matter, the existence of the blanket license and the industry practices that have grown up around it, serve as insurmountable obstacles to obtaining performing rights licenses through other avenues. It is recognized that program producers customarily do not discuss with BMI publishers the acquisition of the right to perform the preexisting music on cable entities. These obstacles, which plaintiffs claim bar competitive trade (as to source licensing in particular), can be grouped into three broad categories: (1) the disincentives created by the existence of the blanket license; (2) the lopsided bargaining power of BMI, particularly concerning negotiations over syndicated programming because the music therein is "in the can;" and (3) the beneficial economic relationship between producers and publishing companies.

### 1. Existence of the Blanket License

The existence of the blanket license, plaintiffs assert, creates a series of disincentives that discourage source licensing. They contend that the major distributors of syndicated product are all aware that music performing rights are treated differently from other rights, and know that because cable networks will not be able to secure source licensing from other syndicators, there is no risk of losing cable customers to other competitors if they do not offer such licenses. Thus, plaintiffs give no weight to the stipulated fact that there is competition among syndicators to sell programming, and defendant's expert's testimony to that effect. In other words, it is argued that the lack of a genuine risk of losing a sale of programming over music performing rights arrangements proves that source licensing is not a "realistic alternative" to the blanket license. This proffer suffers from the same deficiencies that weakened plaintiffs' claims about the availability of alternatives: without showing that any cable programmer ever asked a producer to include music performing rights in a license, their proof is only speculative. Further, it ignores the characteristics of supply and demand. It may be that the general competitive nature of the industry does not reflect intense competition as to this particular right, but as defendant's economic expert convincingly testified, if cable performing rights were demanded, the syndication market would provide them to avoid the risk of losing sales. Tr. at 2112-13.

2. Bargaining Power and "Music in the Can"

It is undisputed that cable networks compete with each other, with broadcast television networks, and others for the rights to carry desirable syndicated programming. It is also evident that cable programmers such as TDC and BET must obtain desirable syndicated programming to compete in their market. Bruce Rider, Senior Vice President of Programming for TDC, testified that TDC always competed with others for programming and that it is a "seller's market." Rider V.Tr. (P 375A) at 24; see also Tr. at 830. Thus, plaintiffs claims, distributors will decline to license programs to cable program services if the requested terms are inconvenient, such as a demand for music performing rights. Accordingly, to stay competitive, the argument continues, plaintiffs have no choice but to stay within the status quo — take the blanket license.

More persuasive to common sense, however, is the fact that music in syndicated programming is "in the can" and thus cable entities have no bargaining power with regard to the performing rights. Cable networks and operators do not select or negotiate for music contained in the programs; that transaction occurs at the point of production. Further, licensees of syndicated programming generally cannot edit, delete, or otherwise alter the content of the programming they obtain from syndicators without their express permission. In order to transmit syndicated programming, cable networks (and system operators) have no choice but to transmit whatever music is in the syndicated programming they have obtained. Music performing rights proprietors (whether the composer and publisher for direct licensing, or the producer for source licensing), then, can extract a higher price than might otherwise be warranted because once the acquirer of the programming has obtained the programming (including all rights but music performing rights), the acquirer is forced to take it or leave it, and once the programming is purchased, the acquirer must pay whatever price is asked in order to transmit.

BMI blames plaintiffs for their apparent quandary because they could have sought source licensing for music performing rights, but did not. "A programmer choosing to rely on the expected future availability of the blanket license when buying programming, instead of seeking source licenses at that time, cannot now be heard to attack the blanket license." Defendant's Post-trial Memorandum of Law at 48.

Second, the programmers' market position in relation to producers and syndicators is not as lopsided as plaintiffs suggest. Cable programmers have substantial market power vis-a-vis producers as the buyers of their programming. The motion picture production and sales industry is highly competitive, J.S. para. 101, and their sales to cable programmers generate substantial revenues for producers. Tr. at 594, 597; Cooke V.Tr. (P 377A) at 34-35, 41-43; Isakoff V.Tr. (P 376A) at 70. It is reasonable to conclude that, given the importance of cable to programming producers, producers would change their practices and provide source licensing if this important segment of their purchasers seriously demanded it.

As to the hold-up situation, defendant proffered testimony from music publishers that they do not exert their apparently superior bargaining power when approached by an unlicensed programmer who has already purchased programming containing their music. BMI analogized the situation to negotiations of synchronization rights license for music already "in the can," such as where a producer's five-year synchronization rights expire and the programming involved continues to be distributed. Polygram Island Music Group's Vice-President of Business Affairs Jeffrey Brabec testified that the need to maintain good relations with producers will check any abuse of his bargaining power in that situation. Similar testimony was offered by Helene Blue, the managing director of the music publisher the Goodman Group, concerning a synchronization license fee accepted by BET for the music performing rights to the music in episodes of the syndicated series "Frank's Place." The license agreed to by BET was only slightly higher than the original (expired) license. Tr. at 1887-93; D 1101 compare D 1103. The publisher's testimony is buttressed by the fact that publishers work in a highly competitive market, J.S. para. 91, and would not want to engage in any negotiating that would be perceived as coercive because the resulting ill-will would spill over to their other transactions in the business. Tr. at 1841. Also important in this regard is that publishers desire and are mandated to obtain as much exposure for the compositions in their catalogs as possible. See J.S. paras. 92, 93.

Finally, it bears noting that the Second Circuit rejected this same argument when the television network CBS argued that direct licensing was impeded by such bargaining power. CBS had claimed that "it would be subject to demands for unconscionably high fees from the owners of copyrighted music already recorded on the soundtracks of taped programs and feature film in CBS's inventory." CBS Remand, 620 F.2d at 938. As in this case, however, the trial record revealed that synchronization rights were regularly obtained at reasonable prices after the fact, and that copyright proprietors were not willing to risk their good will in the industry by engaging in "hold ups." In addition to the factual deficit in CBS' claim — the same deficit as here — the Second Circuit also observed that as a legal matter the alleged imbalance of bargaining power was not the result of the blanket license.

If CBS would be vulnerable to a 'hold-up' when it tries to acquire performance rights for music on a feature film it wishes to rerun, that is a consequence of CBS's failure to acquire rerun performance rights at the time it acquired the film. At that time CBS accepted the risk that it would one day have to purchase performance rights for reruns, either as part of the purchase price for a blanket license or at a separate price for a license obtained directly from the copyright owner.

Id. Those considerations are equally appropriate with regard to the cable industry's challenge in this lawsuit. Especially in light of the fact that the cable programmers could obtain source licenses if they so desired, the perceived inequity is of their own making. And direct licenses are indeed feasible in this context, where the programmer does choose the programming, and has hundreds, if not more, options from which to choose.

Plaintiffs also tried to show that in general terms, BMI has inflated market power because of its monopoly position with regard to the pooled rights in its repertory. They proffered the testimony of cable programming executives to the effect that BMI extracts prices not based on the value of the rights conveyed, but based on a determination by the licensee programmers of their ability to pay and their willingness to do so in circumstances where they perceive they have no practical alternative. Tr. at 110-13. They point to BMI's concession that it did not consider the cable network's ability to take advantage of alternatives when formulating the fees proposed in late 1989 and early 1990 (1% of revenues, split licensing). In other words, plaintiffs assert that defendant itself believed it had the ability to extract a monopolistic price, or at least a price substantially greater than had been demanded previously. See Preston HBO Dep. at 154-55 (BMI never considered possibility of direct license to be a constraint); Preston Dep. at 70-72 (BMI does not feel constrained by ASCAP's fees); Tr. at 2471. What the parties perceived may be relevant in determining what a reasonable license fee would be, see ASCAP v. Showtime/The Movie Channel, Inc., 912 F.2d 563, 572, 585-86 , 16 U.S.P.Q.2D (BNA) 1026 (S.D.N.Y. 1989), aff'd, 912 F.2d 563, 570-71, 16 U.S.P.Q.2D (BNA) 1026 (2d Cir. 1990) ("Showtime"), but this Court does not sit as a rate court, this Court must decide an antitrust case on the record evidence. What matters is objective availability, objective price, objective market power.

Another aspect of market power that is relevant to the Court's examination is the market power of the purchaser, not just the seller. For the seller to have undue market power requires its converse — that the purchasers have little market power. The evidence showed that plaintiffs cannot claim to have little market power in relation to BMI. First, of course, the Court has already determined that plaintiffs do indeed have a choice of licensing options, which means that they can exert power in the marketplace by refusing unfavorable terms offered by BMI. Second, even assuming that plaintiffs have little or no choice, and that they are constrained by the current structure of the market and current practices in the industry (a position already rejected), plaintiffs themselves have considerable economic power in this marketplace. Cable program services as a group represent a large force in the entertainment industry and a source of enormous potential revenue for BMI. As the industry matured in the 1980s, particularly after regulation in 1984, the number of cable program services and, more importantly, the number of subscribers thereto, rose substantially — as did revenues. E.g., U.S. General Accounting Office, Telecommunications: Follow-Up National Survey of Cable Television Rates and Services (Report to the Chairman, Subcommittee on Telecommunications and Finance, Committee on Energy and Commerce, House of Representatives GAO/RCED-90-199, June 13, 199C, at 25, 56-61 (D 596); Tr. at 472-73; D 1038 attachment (Newhouse Broadcasting Corporation's subscriber and advertising revenues from 1983 to 1989). At present, there are approximately 80 such services (15 pay, 65 basic), J.S. para. 36, serving over 80 million subscribers. See O.S. As mentioned earlier, an examination of the Ownership Stipulation reveals an intricate web of ownership relationships among cable companies; indeed, ownership is concentrated and overlapping. To cite but one example, the pay programmers HBO and Cinemax together account for over 23 million subscribers; both are owned by Time Warner Inc., which also has ownership interests in, inter alia, BET and the Turner Broadcasting System. Finally, cable programmers have a national trade association, the NCTA.

That much and more is true for cable system operators. With only a few exceptions, Tr. at 453-55, operators are granted exclusive franchises to deliver cable television to certain territories. J.S. para. 29. And, the vast majority of cable operators belong to MSOs. Finally, on a national level, they are specifically represented by the NCTA Music Licensing Committee, the purpose of which is to address licensing issues of concern to the system operator members of NCTA as well as CATA. J.S. paras. 2, 3.

These facts present a very different scenario than that in Broadcast Music, Inc. v. Moor-law, Inc., 527 F. Supp. 758 (D. Del. 1981), aff'd mem., 691 F.2d 490 (3d Cir. 1982), where the district court found that the plaintiffs there (small establishments such as bars that provide live music), were overwhelmed by the market power of BMI: "where there is no corresponding power on the buyer's side. Unlike the television network market where buyers like CBS can exercise some monopsony power of their own, the buyers [here] are weak and diffuse." 527 F. Supp. at 764. Interestingly, the ASCAP rate court concluded in Showtime that cable companies did not have substantial bargaining leverage in the market as compared to ASCAP, especially in contrast to national broadcast networks (CBS Remand) and local broadcast television stations (Buffalo Broadcasting). "CBS is, of course, one of a small handful of national networks, with the advantage of a very high public profile, substantially greater revenues than the individual cable companies, and a parent that controls a large business in music publication." Showtime, 912 F.2d at 584; cf. CBS Remand, 620 F.2d at 937-38. As for local television stations, the Magistrate Judge found they had "the bargaining advantage of negotiating Jointly through their All-Industry Committee" and the "further advantage that by virtue of their number they represent a much larger source of revenue to ASCAP and a much more difficult industry to police for copyright infringement. These circumstances also suggest that they may be able to negotiate on more equal terms with ASCAP than could the individual cable program suppliers." Id. (citations omitted). The facts adduced at this trial showed that the cable industry is not so diffuse, it is nationally organized, and it represents — both in the aggregate and on the individual programming service or system operator or MSO level — a significant source of revenue (and, given the unlicensed status of most of the industry, potential revenue) to BMI and therefore has considerable leverage in any negotiations on this subject.

3. Producers' Ties to Publishing Companies

The final impediment plaintiffs identified at trial is the economic disincentive stemming from the fact that producers often receive the publisher's share of music performing royalties resulting from the transmission of their syndicating programming. Here the parties differ on the significance of the monies involved. Defendant points to the Second Circuit's disparagement of this argument on the ground that the distributions by BMI of $ 0.50 to $ 0.85 for half-hour individual airplays were insignificant when compared to the returns on syndicated program sales, 744 F.2d at 931. As explained previously, half of every dollar of royalties distributed by BMI goes to the composer (the "writer's share") and half goes to the publisher. Producers of syndicated programming often own or control a publishing entity that becomes the publisher of the original music in their programs and thereby obtain the publisher's share of the royalties. See Tr. at 322-24, 388; 1116-18. Plaintiffs argued, then, that because producers of syndicated programming receive "substantial" economic benefits from these distributions at little cost, they have a vested interest in maintaining the blanket licensing status quo.

Defendant elicited testimony undermining this theory, however. TDC's Vice President and Counsel admitted that the Disney Studio does not consider royalties it receives from its wholly-owned publishers to be a factor in whether to issue source licensing for its syndicated programming. Tr. at 146, 149. Even plaintiffs' economic expert conceded that BMI royalty distributions are only a "minor factor" to producers considering source licensing. Tr. at 606. In any event, not all producers own or control publishing companies (20th Century Fox does not own any, Tr. at 202, 599-600) and these producers certainly have no economic interest in the publisher's share of BMI royalties. Finally, the amount of such royalties, even in the aggregate, is minuscule in comparison to the dollar figures involved in syndicated programming transactions. TDC's publisher affiliate, Wonderland Music, earned BMI royalties from cable in the low six figures. J.S. schedule B. In contrast, Disney Studios recently entered into a $ 500 million deal with just one pay cable programming service. Tr. at 605-06. It is stipulated that the largest earner of cable television royalties from BMI in 1989 received royalties in the low six-figure range, with most of the publishers in the same context earning less than $ 100,000. Although hardly pennies, these amounts pale in comparison to the millions or hundreds of millions producers of syndicated programming can earn for one film or series. As the Second Circuit observed, "those royalties are a small fraction of their syndication revenue." Buffalo Broadcasting, 744 F.2d at 931. Common sense indicates that this economic link between producers and music performing rights royalties is relatively insignificant and not a barrier to source licensing.

D. Rules of Reason Inquiry

Even had the Court agreed with plaintiffs that the blanket license does constitute a restraint on trade, it would survive scrutiny under the rule of reason analysis that such a conclusion would require.

At bottom, the rule of reason asks whether the challenged restraint enhances competition. "It focuses directly on the challenged restraint's impact on competitive conditions," Professional Engineers, 435 U.S. at 688, 98 S. Ct. at 1363, and thus entails "analyzing the facts peculiar to the business, the history of the restraint, and the reasons why it was imposed." Id. at 692, 98 S. Ct. at 1365. The history, reasons, and workings of the music licensing industry have already been extensively discussed, supra. Accordingly, the Court turns to the blanket license's effects on competition, weighing the anticompetitive effects against the offsetting procompetitive benefits. See BMI v. CBS, 441 U.S. at 24, 99 S. Ct. at 1565.

Plaintiffs asserted at trial that the anticompetitive effects of the blanket license are legion, but the actual effects identified are alleged to be (1) the reduction or nonexistence of price competition among composers for cable television music performing rights; (2) BMI's inflated market power and concomitant ability to increase prices above competitive levels; and (3) the shifting of the competitive market from the producer level (where other music and creative rights are negotiated) to the cable programmer and operator level where there is no price competition. The relevant market, it is stated, is that where the selection of music occurs; thus, plaintiffs contend the analysis should be whether the blanket license engenders competition among BMI affiliates. In sum, then, plaintiffs are arguing that the blanket license unlawfully eliminates price competition for music performing rights in syndicated programming. 6

Rule of reason jurisprudence teaches that "restrictions on price and output are the paradigmatic examples of restraint of trade that the Sherman Act was intended to prohibit." NCAA, 468 U.S. at 107-08, 104 S. Ct. at 2963. In the NCAA case, the agreement at issue had "significant potential for anticompetitive effects," 468 U.S. at 104, 104 S. Ct. at 2962, because individual competitors lose their freedom to compete. Price is higher and output lower than they would otherwise be, and both are unresponsive to consumer preference." Id. at 106-07, 104 S. Ct. at 2963 (footnotes omitted). As to the product there — the right to broadcast college football games on television — the Court observed that "many telecasts that would occur in a competitive market are foreclosed." Id. at 108, 104 S. Ct. at 2964. An examination of price and output factors in the case before this Court reveals no such compelling illegalities.

As to price, plaintiffs did not offer concrete evidence as to how the price of these rights is inflated beyond what it would be. While it is understood that there is no price competition between individual composers or compositions, see CBS Remand, 620 F.2d at 935, that alone is not conclusive. Plaintiffs did not show that the price of music performing rights in syndicated programs would be lowered, or be more competitive, if the blanket license did not exist. Instead, they offered the testimony of their economic expert, Professor Benston, that the blanket license is a classic monopoly or monopsony and therefore anticompetitive. Tr. at 1206-08. In this regard, it should be noted that this was not brought as a monopoly case under section 2 of the Sherman Act. Further, that price competition does not exist does not mean that the blanket license is the cause. With the availability of the direct and source licensing, this is a situation where price competition could exist — where there are buyers interested in purchasing a product available from two or more sellers. See CBS Remand, 620 F.2d at 935.

Plaintiffs believe that BMI's pricing is blatantly illegal. They query whether in a competitive market a BMI composer could obtain three times the performing royalties than his or her ASCAP counterpart receives, or three or four times than is received from broadcast television. This question is interesting, for as their only substantive data on price it indicates a different definition of the relevant market, the one recently identified by the ASCAP rate court in determining a reasonable cable license fee: "If we are to talk of competitive pricing, we must start with the premise that the relevant market is one for aggregative performance licenses, not the market for the services of individual composers and musicians." Showtime, 912 F.2d at 591 (Magistrate Judge's opinion). Plaintiffs' comparison between the BMI fees broadcast television licenses and earlier cable and broadcast licenses (including ASCAP rate court determinations), on the one hand, and the one percent fee demands that encouraged this litigation, on the other, are not indicative of anticompetitive pricing. Earlier fees are, of course, going to be at lower levels. Those fees, which were explicitly interim fees, do not represent the appropriate benchmark. Furthermore, the Showtime decision covered fees for a four-year period from 1984.

More importantly, that BMI sought certain fee levels does not make it an antitrust violator. An asking price is a bargaining position. There was testimony that this price was simply the opening volley in the negotiation game. For example, the one percent demand to BET was not "frozen in stone," as BMI made clear. P 3M. It is unquestioned that BMI hoped to triple its license revenues, Tr. at 2377-79, but that is even a laudable attempt to increase profits. Its proposed license fee may be "absurdly high," Brenner HBO Dep. at 44-45, but a high demand is a recognized tactic in the competitive marketplace. Furthermore, in view of the fact that price competition could occur because, to name one option, source licensing of music rights is available, it is hard to find support for plaintiffs' argument. Lastly, as to price, the Court echoes the remark in BMI v. CBS that "not all arrangements among actual or potential competitors that have an impact on price are per se violations or even restraints." 441 U.S. at 23, 99 S. Ct. at 1564 (emphasis supplied).

If negotiation occurred at the point plaintiffs want it — at the source, when producers negotiate the other sticks in the bundle of music rights they acquire in composer-for-hire music or in preexisting music — it is difficult to conclude that there would be more price competition than exists with the blanket license. As stipulated by the parties, there is tremendous competition among composers for such contracts, as there is among proprietors of preexisting music, resulting in widely varying prices for synchronization and other rights. As the Second Circuit observed in Buffalo Broadcasting,

With this degree of price competition for music on syndicated programs already in place, it is entirely a matter of speculation whether replacement of the blanket license with source licensing would add any significant increment to price competition at the point where the syndicators decide which music to use.

744 F.2d at 932-33. That prices are not competitive does not imply anticompetitive behavior. In any event, on this record, the Court cannot determine whether price competition among compositions would be promoted

by the elimination of the blanket license. What is apparent, however, is that price competition is not significantly restrained by the blanket license.

Plaintiffs attempted to show that the lack of price competitiveness is a result of, or can be inferred from, the market power of BMI. It is undeniable that BMI is a formidable presence in the music performing rights market, and is certainly perceived to be extremely powerful. But even assuming BMI has monopoly power and uses that power to extract fees, that alone does not constitute anticompetitive behavior in violation of § 1. "An excessive price alone does not establish a violation of the antitrust laws, because imposition of a high price is not, in and of itself, an anticompetitive act." Williamsburg Wax Museum, Inc. v. Historic Figures, Inc., 258 App. D.C. 124, 810 F.2d 243, 252 (D.C. Cir. 1987). As the Second Circuit explained in United States Football League v. National Football League, 842 F.2d 1335 (2d Cir. 1988): "Prices not based on superior efficiency do not injure competitors but rather invite competitive entry . . . . 'Setting a high price may be a use of monopoly power, but it is not in itself anticompetitive.'" 842 F.2d at 1361 (citations omitted) (quoting Berkey Photo Inc. v. Eastman Kodak Co., 603 F.2d 263, 294 (2d Cir. 1979), cert. denied, 444 U.S. 1093, 100 S. Ct. 1061, 62 L. Ed. 2d 783 (1980)); see also Olympia Equipment Leasing Co. v. Western Union Telephone Co., 797 F.2d 370, 375 (7th Cir. 1986) ("a firm with lawful monopoly power has no general duty to help its competitors by holding a price umbrella over their heads"), cert. denied, 480 U.S. 934, 107 S. Ct. 1574, 94 L. Ed. 2d 765 (1987); Showtime, 912 F.2d at 587 n. 31 (Magistrate Judge's opinion). Simply put, the fact that BMI has more market power than it would in a hypothetical, more competitive market for music performing rights does not necessarily make its pricing strategy anticompetitive. Cf. id., 912 F.2d at 570 (that plaintiffs in CBS Remand and Buffalo Broadcasting failed "to prove an antitrust violation does not mean that the Magistrate [Judge] lacked evidence sufficient to support a finding that ASCAP enjoys more market power than it would have in a freely competitive market.") (Second Circuit Opinion).

Moreover, there was no evidence that output was, or is, in any way impeded by the blanket license. Indeed, ample evidence was presented that the blanket license increases output. As explained by defendant's economic expert, the blanket license encourages the use of music by eliminating marginal costs once the music is purchased. Tr. at 2077-78. For example, a composition can be simultaneously consumed by many users. Having to price individual performances or individual compositions would create additional costs, thereby decreasing the total amount of music used.

The Supreme Court focused on this competitively beneficial characteristic of the blanket license, declaring that "Broadcast Music squarely holds that a joint selling arrangement may be so efficient that it will increase sellers' aggregate output and thus be procompetitive." NCAA, 468 U.S. at 103, 104 S. Ct. at 2961 (citing BMI v. CBS, 441 U.S. at 18-23, 99 S. Ct. at 1561-64). The availability of a package product that no individual could offer enhanced the total volume of music sold . . . . there was no limit of any kind placed on the volume that might be sold in the entire market and each individual remained free to sell his own music without restraint." Id. 468 U.S. at 114, 104 S. Ct. at 2967.

Another procompetitive effect is the tremendous efficiency of the blanket license, which, ultimately, reduces costs to buyers and maximizes output. This beneficial economic effect arises from the elimination of potentially thousands of transactions that would otherwise have to occur, in negotiating licenses, monitoring of use, sales, and enforcement of copyrights. "Individual sales transactions in this industry are quite expensive, as would be individual monitoring and enforcement, especially in light of the resources of single composers." BMI v. CBS, 441 U.S. at 20, 99 S. Ct. at 1563. Even outside the context in which blanket licensing arose — to compensate composers for spontaneous, live use of music in a multitude of settings — it "reduces costs absolutely by creating a [product] that is sold only a few, instead of thousands of times, and that obviates the need for closely monitoring the [programmers] to see that they do not use more than they pay for. [It] also provides the necessary resources for blanket sales and enforcement, resources unavailable to the vast majority of composers and publishing houses." Id. at 21, 99 S. Ct. at 1563 (emphasis supplied, footnotes omitted). Here, evidence was adduced indicating that the blanket license eliminated these costs for composers and publishers because without it, they would need to retain additional personnel to perform the functions performed by BMI (and ASCAP and SESAC): negotiating, monitoring, auditing, and bookkeeping. E.g., Boris V.Tr. (D1111A) at 116-17. Without the benefits of the aggregating function of the blanket license, output would be reduced because individual composers and publishers would not be financially able to accomplish these ends.

As plaintiffs point out, however, transactional efficiencies would not be eliminated were the blanket license replaced by source licensing (but not other alternatives). Producers already negotiate and enter into contracts and licenses with composers and publishers for the acquisition of all the other rights in music; music performing rights would just be part of that same process and therefore no substantial additional transaction costs would be incurred. Defendant admits that if a "complete rights buy-out" were to take place at the source, i.e. when producers license their syndicated programming, these costs would not increase, because the rights would be granted directly (eliminating negotiation costs) and indemnification could be provided at that point. See, e.g., Tr. at 2241-42. In other words, there would be direct royalty distributions, a state of affairs plaintiffs insist is far mors efficient than using BMI, whose administrative costs generally range between 15 and 20% of their collections. See J.S. para. 24. Indeed, the monitoring conducted by BMI primarily serves as a means of determining the proper distribution of fees (rather than as a copyright enforcement mechanism). J.S. paras. 21-22. Plaintiffs also claim that there is already a system in place that would permit the payment for music performing rights based on the success of the production, akin to the "residuals" system used for soundtrack royalties (e.g., P 29A para. 7) and videocassette rollover options (e.g., P 39D para. 8(a)). Producers do, at times, pay other creative artists 'back-end' compensation — residuals — based on future releases or receipts. Tr. at 398-400; 1128. This arrangement has been used for music performing rights for commercials, Boris V.Tr. (D 1111A) at 97-98, and for music rights for videocassettes and soundtracks, id. at 99. Plaintiffs conclude from these facts that the BMI blanket license is costly in comparison to producer source licensing because it creates the need for an elaborate structure for determining who should get paid, a structure that is totally unnecessary in a source licensing marketplace.

But the source licensing scenario is not as rosy as plaintiffs paint it. Plaintiffs' own industry expert explained that up-front buyouts are not preferred by creative artists because it is difficult to predict the commercial success of programming. Tr. at 634-36. Given the resulting difficulty of valuing future performances, composers predictably do not like that type of system. Tr. at 634, 1750-52, 1951-52. As for a residuals system, although preferable to up-front buy-outs, Tr. at 1954, it arose out of a talent guild system that turned out to be unworkable (it worked as a cartel, limiting entry and output) and of questionable legality. Tr. at 2117-20. Absent a guild or similar arrangement, up-front buyouts suffer from some of the inefficiencies of direct licensing, especially as regards monitoring. As defendant's economist explained, individual composers and publishers would have to monitor constantly to ensure that the user does not exceed the scope of the license or underreport the number of performances — there is a disincentive for the producer to comply with the license terms so as to lessen their liability for royalties. Tr. at 2242. Finally, "back-end" profit participation agreements, which some prominent composers have obtained, share many of the same disadvantages, and plaintiffs' expert testified that those type of agreements for other creative artists generate revenue only in the rarest of circumstances. Tr. at 617-21.

That source licensing may be less restrictive — in the sense that it is more efficient and therefore more procompetitive in certain respects than the blanket license — does not make the blanket license unlawfully anticompetitive, especially with the other factors remaining in the balance, such as transactions that would still have to take place (negotiations over price, enforcement), and in light of the conclusion that blanket licensing is not the only realistic alternative available to plaintiffs.

We must be mindful that we are not dealing here with a conventional product (or conventional market), but intellectual property, the rights to which are governed by statute. The policies of the copyright laws must also be considered. Although the copyright law does not shield intellectual property from antitrust analysis, it does shape the inquiry because it is relevant to the market at issue. As noted by Magistrate Judge Dolinger, one major benefit conferred by the blanket license on licensees is that it "represents, in effect, an insurance policy against copyright liability for the full range of the cable company's acquired programming. " Showtime, 912 F.2d at 592 (Magistrate Judge's Opinion). While the maximization of music use is not the issue here, the efficiency of the blanket license in promoting the goals of the copyright laws is obvious. It protects copyright holders from infringements and provides them compensation. See F.E.L. Publications, 214 U.S.P.Q. at 414.

Part of the reason plaintiffs could not offer convincing evidence stems from the conceptual difficulty in analyzing the competitiveness in the market of a unique product. As noted by the Supreme Court, the product at issue here, the blanket license, is more than the sum of its parts, the licenses to individual compositions. It is "a package product that no individual could offer." NCAA, 468 U.S. at 114, 104 S. Ct. at 2967. Even viewing the product as individual compositions, however, music performing rights fit only awkwardly within the mold of a regular market where price is the key determining factor in selection. Musical compositions are strikingly unique; their value reflects not only the perceived quality of the music but also the reputation of the composer, the popularity of the composition (if preexisting), historical circumstances, and other factors. The testimony revealed that price is simply not the most critical attribute in selection or purchase. E.g., Tr. at 303 (describing process of music selection and synchronization into program soundtracks); Tr. at 1098 (a Walt Disney Studio Vice President testified, "We may get quotations for five songs for the same use, and it's only after they've gone through the final phase of editing and dubbing, and possibly in some cases previewing the picture to see how it plays, that they'll decide on the final song selection.").

E. Split Licensing

The split blanket license, plaintiffs contend, fails the rule of reason test and, in any event, violates BMI's consent decree. See J2 Art. IX(A). The controversy over the split licensing proposal deserves separate treatment, because it is quite apart from the general challenge to blanket licensing for syndicated programming. At the outset, it should be noted that the issue is not as crystallized as plaintiffs claim; they insist that BMI was demanding the split license and not accepting any other alternative. As indicated earlier, that is not the case. Thus, the assessment must be of what amounts to a licensing proposal that represents one option, a fact that immediately removes much of the anticompetitive tinge that might otherwise color the split license.

As to whether a split-licensing scheme would run afoul of the antitrust laws, that question has already been answered in the negative. Plaintiffs' thesis that if cable system operators must secure licenses separate from the cable programmers they will have no alternative but to take a blanket license from BMI was simply not proven. To recapitulate, cable system operators do have realistically available alternatives. While direct licensing is not among the options, cable system operators have the ability to obtain source licensing and per program licensing. The onus of the effort involved would no doubt lead to demands for source licensing from their immediate suppliers, the cable programmers (indeed, cable operators have consistently sought indemnifications from cable program systems for this purpose).

Even were the split license a restraint — and even were there no realistically available alternatives — the split license would survive rule of reason scrutiny. Plaintiffs claim that copyright holders would be shielded from competition as to system operators because the latter have no control over the selection or use of the syndicated programs and no ability to choose among competing programs. But that is a matter between the programmers and the operators; and it was proven at trial that system operators do in fact have choice as to the programming, most notably in the clauses that permit them to edit programming for standards and practices. And, the system operators have formidable power in the market, as is evident from the vertical integration and concentration of economic power and, more importantly, the aggregated bargaining strength they can exert through their nationwide trade association, plaintiff NCTA. Furthermore, the split blanket license would have procompetitive effects in the same manner that the blanket license does for radio stations, bars, and similar sites (see Moorlaw), where the public performers of the music are unaware of what music will be played and there exists a large number of musical compositions that may be played. A blanket license for system operators would also be transactionally efficient since, as cannot be disputed, system operators need music performing rights licenses for their local origination and public access programming and the two types of licenses could be negotiated at the same time. See J.S. para. 81; Tr. at 987-89. Contrary to plaintiffs' assertion that the split license proposal demonstrates BMI's determination to cartelize the music performing rights market (i.e., an intention to act anticompetitively), it was instead an understandable, if not reasonable, response to the unlicensed status of the greater part of the cable industry, to the failure of almost seven years of negotiations with the NCTA, see J.S. paras. 81-85; Tr. at 501-02; 948-49, 952-53 — and to the resulting infringements of its affiliates' copyrights.

That a split license would not violate the antitrust laws, however, does not dispose of a separate (though related) concern: whether it violates BMI's consent decree, entered into in 1966 as settlement of an antitrust suit brought by the U.S. Justice Department. Although barely mentioned at trial, plaintiffs addressed this issue in their post-trial memoranda. They note that Art. II(4) of BMI's original (1941) consent decree required BMI to grant through-to-the-viewer licenses to radio networks, and that the 1966 decree, in Art. IX(A), broadened the provision to include television networks as well (television having been in its infancy in the early 1940s). Because cable television did not exist in 1966, and because the apparent intent of the Art. IX(A) proscription was to curb the inordinate power of BMI over down-the-line receivers of network programming , plaintiffs argue that cable system operators, as entities similar to local television network affiliates, are or should be protected by that provision.

Plaintiffs' arguments are given more force by a recent court decision. In United States v. ASCAP (In the Matter of the Application of Turner Broadcasting System, et al.), No. Civ. 13-95 (WCC) (S.D.N.Y.), Memorandum and Order July 11, 1991 ("Application of Turner"), a decision that issued after the instant case was tried and submitted, United States Magistrate Judge Dolinger ruled that ASCAP's consent decree (J1) requires it to issue a through-to-the-viewer blanket license to cable program services covering not only the programmers' transmission to cable system operators but also the transmission by cable system operators to subscribers. ASCAP, like BMI here, had asserted the right to extract licenses from both cable programmers and operators.

At issue there was the following language from the 1950 decree, which orders ASCAP to issue music performing rights licenses on request:

To a radio broadcasting network, telecasting network or wired music service . . . on terms which authorize the simultaneous and so-called delayed performance by broadcasting or telecasting . . . of the ASCAP repertory by any, some or all of the stations in the United States affiliated with such radio network or television network . . . and do not require a separate license for each station or subscriber for such performances . . . .

J1 Art. V(A). It was undisputed that this provision requires ASCAP to provide through-to-the-viewer licenses to broadcast television stations. But ASCAP claimed that cable television is not within the terms of the decree and, in any event, is so differently structured (both in terms of technology and financial arrangements) from broadcast television that even a broad reading of the provision would not warrant extending its protections to the cable industry.

The Magistrate Judge rejected these arguments. After an exhaustive examination of the history and development of the decree, including the various parties' intentions, and the general antidiscrimination provisions of the decree (see Art. IV(C)), and using traditional tools for the construction of contracts, the Magistrate Judge agreed with the plaintiff cable programmers that, as they are the functional equivalent of broadcast television networks, and the decree was not unambiguous as to the reach of that provision, they are covered by Art. V(A).

In reaching this conclusion, the Magistrate Judge determined that one of the purposes of the consent decree was to "disinfect" ASCAP as a potential combination in restraint of trade, in violation of the antitrust laws. Mem. & Order at 24. He observed that ASCAP had become a government target "because of its potential ability to control a significant portion of the market for music used in non-dramatic public performances, whether on radio or other settings" Id. at 27. The original 1941 decree thus "balanced the playing field to a degree and spared the local stations from facing the unenviable choice of either paying whatever ASCAP demanded or foregoing network programming." Id. at 28. "The Decree was designed to limit ASCAP's ability, by pooling copyrights for large amounts of music used in radio broadcasting, to extract unreasonable fees for performance of music." Id. The 1950 Decree "extended the specific protections of the 1941 Decree — including both the requirement for one license to cover the public performance of network programming . . . to all forms of mass communication known at the time that might utilize significant amounts of ASCAP music." Id. at 30. He characterized the 1950 amendments to the decree as an "effort at inclusiveness," and further noted that "on its face the [1950] Decree appears to apply to television programming transmitted to the public irrespective of the technology used to make the transmission . . . [and] also any financial arrangement between the original packager of programming identified with the packager and the entity that transmits that packaged programming to television viewers." Id. at 30-31. "The solution adopted by the Decree rests on the fact that the packager has greater ability to negotiate on equal terms with ASCAP than does the affiliated telecaster." Id. at 31.

The two technological differences were dismissed as irrelevant. As for transmission via cable or fiber-optics rather than over-the-air signals, the opinion notes, inter alia, that most broadcast programming is received via cable. And as for the fact that cable system operators carry dozens of channels whereas local broadcast television stations only carry one network, he observed that it does not make cable any less a part of the business of transmitting television programming into viewers' homes. As for differing financial structures — principally, the different economic posture of the cable industry and the fact that, unlike broadcast television, cable programmers do not pay system operators to transmit their programming — the Magistrate Judge gave them little weight. He found that the virtual monopoly of cable operating systems in their locales did not affect interpretation of Art. V(A), nor did the concentration of ownership among system operators, finding that there was no inevitability to the number of cable system operators in a given area and that cable and broadcast television compete directly for audience, programming, and advertising and that ownership was not an issue in the decree. Id. at 54-55, 59-60. As to the differing revenue collection methods, he stated that the original decree was not concerned with sources of income for the networks; "what mattered was that the networks controlled the assembling of a significant body of programming and transmitted it to a separate entity — the local station—for rebroadcast." Id. at 58.

In sum, then, the Magistrate Judge took a functional approach to decree appropriation. "In their relationship with the local system operators — which is the only relationship currently at issue in this proceeding — the program suppliers play the same role as the networks in distributing programming to local cablecasters for transmission under their name to a local television audience. It is this division of function that led the drafters of the 1950 Decree to apply the 'licensing at the source' requirement to television . . . ." Id. at 60. Accordingly, he concluded that cable programmers are "telecasting networks" within the meaning of Art. V(A) and are therefore entitled to through-to-the viewer licenses.

Although the parties in this case have not fully briefed the significance of the Application of Turner decision with regard to BMI's split license, the question whether BMI's consent decree permits it to impose split licensing is nonetheless properly before this Court. As noted above, plaintiffs here did argue the issue of BMI's consent decree (raising substantially the same arguments as the applicants in that case), and the short response by defendant to Magistrate Judge Dolinger's decision points to the identical arguments they advanced to justify their dual licensing approach.

The applicable provision in the BMI decree reads:

Defendant shall not license the public performance of any musical composition or compositions except on a basis whereby, insofar as network broadcasting by a regularly constituted network is concerned, the issuance of a single license, authorizing and fixing a single license fee for such performance by network broadcasting, shall permit the simultaneous broadcasting of such performance by all stations on the network which shall broadcast such performance, without requiring separate licenses for such several stations for such performance.

J2 Art. IX(A). When this decree was entered into, cable television did not exist, and therefore the lack of any mention of it is not relevant. Nor are the terms "network broadcasting" or "regularly constituted network" defined. Nonetheless, the Court concludes that this provision applies with equal force to the cable television industry. It is clearly within the spirit of the decree to so read Art. IX(A). And it is also common sense. Although it was earlier concluded that cable system operators do have realistic alternatives to the blanket license available to them, the question was much closer as to them than as to the cable program services, most notably because their actual options are fewer (direct licensing is clearly unrealistic) and because of their place in the sequence of events that leads to the ultimate transmission of programming to the viewer. Their relative power in the marketplace may be considerable, but so is BMI's when it comes to license the vast array of programming carried by system operators. These concerns, while insufficient to constitute an antitrust violation, are plainly the concerns that prompted the through-to-the-viewer provision for radio and television networks. Finally, the functional analysis of the rate court is persuasive. The split blanket license offered by BMI as one alternative is, therefore, unlawful because it violates BMI's consent decree.

\* \* \* \* \*

In sum, the complaints will be denied and dismissed.

## III. THE COUNTERCLAIM

Defendant BMI, as well as a number of its affiliated music publishers (hereinafter "publisher counterclaim-plaintiffs"), have asserted copyright infringement claims against plaintiffs (counterclaim-defendants) TDC and BET for the unlicensed use of their music. As the copyright proprietors, these entities have standing to sue for the infringement of their rights under the Copyright Act. 17 U.S.C. § 501.

It is undisputed that these cable programmers transmitted programming with the specific compositions listed. Indeed, TDC and BET do not dispute that those transmissions received via satellite home dishes are public performances. Yet, counterclaim-defendants assert that in transmitting their signals to cable system operators they have not "publicly performed" the music contained therein within the meaning of the Copyright Act. E.g., Isakoff V.Tr. (P376A) at 55.

To "perform" a work under the Act means "to recite, render, play, dance, or act it, either directly or by means of any device or process." 17 U.S.C. § 101. The Act states that to perform "publicly" means to perform "at a place open to the public" or to "transmit or otherwise communicate a performance . . . to the public, by means of any device or process, whether the members of the public capable of receiving the performance or display receive it in the same place or in separate places and at the same time or at different times." Id.

Plaintiffs argue there is no support in the Act or its legislative history for ruling that cable programmers' transmissions to cable system operators are public performances. They point to the House Report accompanying the Act, which they claim establishes that a certain occurrence may be a performance, such as any act by which a performance is "transmitted, repeated, or made to recur," but that such a performance "would not be actionable as an infringement unless it were done 'publicly' as defined in section 101." H.R. Rep. No. 1476, 94th Cong., 2d Sess. 63, reprinted in 1976 U.S. Code Cong. & Admin. News 5659, 5676-77. To permit liability for infringement for any transmission that may facilitate the public performance of a copyrighted work, but is only directed to a private facility, they claim, is counterintuitive. Such an approach would be duplicative and would force every entity playing a role in bringing a copyrighted work to the public to compensate copyright proprietors.

Plaintiffs' argument proves too much and too little. Not every entity playing a role in transmission is liable; only those transmitting "by means of any device or process" would be. Further, their reading ignores the language and the intent of the Copyright Act. The identical argument has been rejected previously for those reasons. In David v. Showtime/The Movie Channel, Inc., 697 F. Supp. 752 (S.D.N.Y. 1988), the issue before the court was whether the transmission of copyrighted material by a cable programming service (SMC) to an intermediary — cable system operators — for ultimate transmission to the public falls within the scope of the Copyright Act. After examining the legislative history, the court concluded that the term "public performance" was meant to be read broadly, along with all the elements of the Act. Id. at 758-59. That court's reading and its reasoning are thorough and persuasive.

Congress intended the definitions of 'public' and 'performance' to encompass each step in the process by which a protected work wends its way to its audience. Moreover, it would strain logic to conclude that Congress would have intended the degree of copyright protection to turn on the mere method by which television signals are transmitted to the public. . . . Whether SMC intended to route the protected work to the public's living rooms through a local cable company or through a transmitter atop a mountain . . . . SMC would be transmitting the copyright holder's works to the public and benefitting by those acts.

Id. at 759. Accord Coleman v. ESPN, Inc., 764 F. Supp. 290, 20 U.S.P.Q.2D (BNA) 1513 (S.D.N.Y. 1991); Broadcast Music, Inc. v. Hearst/ABC Viacom Entertainment Systems, 746 F. Supp. 320, 328-29 (S.D.N.Y. 1990) (Hearst/ABC). This Court agrees with the David court and holds that transmission by cable programmers of programming containing copyrighted music constitutes public performance of that music, and that they are therefore liable for infringement for performing those works without authorization.

Plaintiffs insist that, even if they are infringers, they cannot be liable because BMI engaged in copyright misuse. Copyright misuse is an affirmative, equitable defense to infringement that has grown out of the recognized doctrine of patent misuse. Defendant responds that the doctrine of copyright misuse does not exist.

The patent misuse doctrine denies a patent holder the right to collect for infringement where the holder uses its right to violate the antitrust laws or otherwise abuses the monopoly power granted it by the patent. See, e.g., Zenith Radio Corp. v. Hazeltine Research, Inc., 395 U.S. 100, 139, 89 S. Ct. 1562, 1585, 23 L. Ed. 2d 129 (1969). The policies underpinning this doctrine would seem to apply with equal force to the copyright laws, and so the Fourth Circuit has held. In Lasercomb America, Inc. v. Reynolds, 911 F.2d 970, 15 U.S.P.Q.2D (BNA) 1846

(4th Cir. 1990), the copyright misuse defense was allowed to be raised in an attempt to bar the holder of a copyright in computer software from obtaining infringement relief. Other courts, as well, have recognized the doctrine. E.g., United Telephone Co. v. Johnson Publishing Co., 855 F.2d 604, 612 (8th Cir. 1988); Supermarket of Homes, Inc. v. San Fernando Valley Board of Realtors, 786 F.2d 1400, 1408 (9th Cir. 1986); F.E.L. Publications, 214 U.S.P.Q. at 413 & n. 9; Mitchell Bros. Film Group v. Cinema Adult Theater, 604 F.2d 852, 865 (5th Cir. 1979), cert. denied, 445 U.S. 917, 63 L. Ed. 2d 601, 100 S. Ct. 1277 (1980); Coleman, 764 F. Supp. 290, 20 U.S.P.Q.2D (BNA) 1513 ; Moor-Law, 527 F. Supp. at 772-73. Indeed, in a copyright infringement action brought by BMI, the district court denied BMI's motion to dismiss the affirmative defense of copyright misuse, holding that it cognizable. Hearst/ABC, 746 F. Supp. at 328.

That this Court recognizes the equitable defense of copyright misuse, however, does not help plaintiffs. Plaintiffs' burden in this regard is too great. First of all, their failure to show violation of the antitrust laws makes it more difficult to conclude that BMI and the publisher counterclaim plaintiffs have misused their copyrights. While such a violation is not a prerequisite to showing misuse, see, e.g., Lasercomb, 911 F.2d at 978, its absence means that plaintiffs must otherwise show that BMI somehow illegally extended its monopoly or otherwise violated the public policy underlying copyright law. No such showing was made here. Cf. Moor-Law, 527 F. Supp. at 773 (relevant issue is whether contested feature of licensing is a product of the convenience of the parties or of an effort by the copyright holder to extend its monopoly unlawfully). Plaintiffs point to BMI's market power as the aggregate licensor of its thousands of members and the purported anticompetitive effects resulting therefrom. But, as discussed, any anticompetitive effects that the blanket license may engender are outweighed by the beneficial effects of that system — effects that promote, rather than hinder, the important public purposes of the Copyright Act: the compensation of copyright proprietors for the public performances of their works.

Lastly, plaintiffs maintain that BMI and the publisher counterclaim-plaintiffs should be estopped from asserting infringement because they have "unclean hands," i.e., because of their purportedly anticompetitive behavior. The doctrine of equitable estoppel denies a party's right to assert a claim because of that party's act or omission. Unclean hands calls for the denial of an otherwise meritorious claim where the claimant has acted so improperly as to make punishment of the claimant outweigh the defendant's unlawful conduct. See generally Hearst/ABC, 746 F. Supp. at 329-30; Coleman, 764 F. Supp. 290, 20 U.S.P.Q.2D (BNA) 1513 . As noted by the Hearst/ABC, court, unclean hands is recognized "only rarely" in copyright cases, where the copyright holder's "transgression is of serious proportions and relates directly to the subject matter of the infringement action" 746 F. Supp. at 329 (quoting 3 Nimmer on Copyright § 13.09[B] at 13-145 (1988)).

Plaintiffs/counterclaim defendants rely for this proposition on the case of Tempo Music, Inc. v. Myers, 407 F.2d 503 (4th Cir. 1969). There, the defendant successfully raised these affirmative defenses to an infringement action by an ASCAP member because ASCAP had refused to provide a list of its repertory to the defendant, who then had inadvertently infringed the plaintiff's copyright. In other words, the defendant there had attempted not to infringe, but the illegal actions of plaintiff's agent — ASCAP's consent decree requires it to provide repertory lists — had forced defendant to do so.

For plaintiffs/counterclaim defendants here to succeed with the defenses of equitable estoppel and unclean hands, then, requires them to show at least the responsibility of BMI for their infringements, as well as unlawful conduct by BMI. Plaintiffs advance three assertions in this regard: (1) BMI's exorbitant fee demands to BET for a blanket license and to TDC " only" for a split license; (2) BMI's alleged violation of the antitrust laws and of articles VIII(A) and IX(A) of its consent decree; and (3) BMI's conduct that purportedly precluded any other licensing thereby forcing plaintiffs either to take the blanket license or infringe.

Had these assertions been proven, it might have been possible to conclude that counterclaim plaintiffs assisted in bringing about TDC's and BET's unlicensed status and, perhaps, their infringements. But the evidence at trial does not permit such findings. It is clear that the asking price was only an initial demand to which plaintiffs did not fully respond and that split licensing was not the only alternative offered. BMI would violate its consent decree if it absolutely insisted on split licensing, but it has not done so. Its attempt could be characterized as a good-faith, if misguided, new approach. No preclusion of other licensing options having been demonstrated, nor antitrust violation or otherwise unlawful anticompetitive behavior shown, these defenses are valueless.

Defendants TDC and BET infringed counterclaim-plaintiffs' copyrights. There remains, however, the question of damages. Defendant-counterclaim plaintiffs requested statutory damages, see 17 U.S.C. § 504(c), and, on the basis that plaintiffs willfully infringed, they ask the Court to enhance those damages to the statutory maximum of $ 100,000 per work infringed, see id. 504(c)(2). Willfulness in this context is established where the infringer knows that his or her action constitutes infringement. Fitzgerald Publishing Co. v. Baylor Publishing Co., 807 F.2d 1110, 1115 (2d Cir. 1986). The willfulness of TDC's and BET's infringement here is obvious. Syndicated programming carried (and scheduled to be carried) by both services admittedly includes music from the BMI repertory. J.S. para. 44. TDC's license expired on December 31, 1989, but it continued transmitting programming, id. para. 77, Tr. at 142; and BET has never had a BMI license. J.S. para. 79.

It is appropriate, therefore, that statutory damages be awarded, but in a sum, at $ 45,000 per work, less than the maximum requested. Accordingly, statutory damages are $ 1,980,000 against TDC for the forty-four compositions infringed, and $ 225,000 against BET for the five compositions infringed.

## IV. CONCLUSION

Accordingly, as set forth in the findings of fact and conclusions of law recited above, it is hereby

ORDERED that the complaints are denied and dismissed. It is

FURTHER ORDERED that the defendant-counterplaintiffs' prayers are granted and a separate judgment has issued this date. It is

FURTHER ORDERED that the parties exert their best efforts to resolve the question of attorney's fees under 17 U.S.C. § 505. In the event that they are unable to reach prompt agreement, the issue shall be briefed as follows: defendant-counterclaim plaintiffs' motion shall be filed no later than September 16, 1991; plaintiffs' opposition, no later than October 7; the reply, if any, no later than October 14.

JUDGMENT - August 16, 1991, Filed

In accordance with the Memorandum Opinion and Order issued this date, judgment is hereby entered for defendant-counterclaim plaintiffs in the following amounts, plus interest from the date of judgment: $ 1,980,000 against plaintiff-counterclaim defendant The Disney Channel, and $ 225,000 against plaintiff-counterclaim defendant Black Entertainment Television, Inc.

Waits v. Frito-Lay, Inc.
United States Court of Appeals for the Ninth Circuit
December 3, 1991; August 5, 1992, Filed
No. 90-55981
978 F.2d 1093

OPINION

BOOCHEVER, Circuit Judge:

Defendants Frito-Lay, Inc., and Tracy-Locke, Inc., appeal a jury verdict and award of $ 2.6 million in compensatory damages, punitive damages, and attorney's fees, in favor of singer Tom Waits. Waits sued the snack food manufacturer and its advertising agency for voice misappropriation and false endorsement following the broadcast of a radio commercial for SalsaRio Doritos which featured a vocal performance imitating Waits' raspy singing voice. On appeal, the defendants mount attacks on nearly all aspects of the judgment.

In challenging the judgment on Waits' voice misappropriation claim, the defendants first contend that our decision in Midler v. Ford Motor Co., 849 F.2d 460 (9th Cir. 1988), cert. denied, 112 S.Ct. 1513, 1514 (1992), recognizing voice misappropriation as a California tort, is no longer good law. Next, they contend that the district court erred in instructing the jury on the elements of voice misappropriation. Finally, the defendants urge us to vacate portions of the jury's damage award, arguing that several types of compensatory damages as well as punitive damages are unavailable as a matter of law, and in any event lack evidentiary support.

In challenging the judgment on Waits' false endorsement claim under section 43(a) of the Lanham Act, the defendants contend that Waits lacks standing to sue because he is not in competition with the defendants. They also argue that Waits did not establish his claim at trial, and that damages and attorney's fees were improperly awarded.

Because it is duplicative, we vacate the award of damages under the Lanham Act. We affirm in all other respects.

## BACKGROUND

Tom Waits is a professional singer, songwriter, and actor of some renown. Waits has a raspy, gravelly singing voice, described by one fan as "like how you'd sound if you drank a quart of bourbon, smoked a pack of cigarettes and swallowed a pack of razor blades. . . . Late at night. After not sleeping for three days." Since the early 1970s, when his professional singing career began, Waits has recorded more than 17 albums and has toured extensively, playing to sold-out audiences throughout the United States, Canada, Europe, Japan and Australia. Regarded as a "prestige artist" rather than a musical superstar, Waits has achieved both commercial and critical success in his musical career. In 1987, Waits received Rolling Stone magazine's Critic's Award for Best Live Performance, chosen over other noted performers such as Bruce Springsteen, U2, David Bowie, and Madonna. SPIN magazine listed him in its March 1990 issue as one of the ten most interesting recording artists of the last five years. Waits has appeared and performed on such television programs as "Saturday Night Live" and "Late Night with David Letterman," and has been the subject of numerous magazine and newspaper articles appearing in such publications as Time, Newsweek, and the Wall Street Journal. Tom Waits does not, however, do commercials. He has maintained this policy consistently during the past ten years, rejecting numerous lucrative offers to endorse major products. Moreover, Waits' policy is a public one: in magazine, radio, and newspaper interviews he has expressed his philosophy that musical artists should not do commercials because it detracts from their artistic integrity.

Frito-Lay, Inc. is in the business of manufacturing, distributing, and selling prepared and packaged food products, including Doritos brand corn chips. Tracy-Locke, Inc. is an advertising agency which counts Frito-Lay among its clients. In developing an advertising campaign to introduce a new Frito-Lay product, SalsaRio Doritos, Tracy-Locke found inspiration in a 1976 Waits song, "Step Right Up." Ironically, this song is a jazzy parody of commercial hucksterism, and consists of a succession of humorous advertising pitches. The commercial the ad agency wrote echoed the rhyming word play of the Waits song. In its presentation of the script to Frito-Lay, Tracy-Locke had the copywriter sing a preliminary rendition of the commercial and then played Waits' recorded rendition of "Step Right Up" to demonstrate the feeling the commercial would capture. Frito-Lay approved the overall concept and the script.

The story of Tracy-Locke's search for a lead singer for the commercial suggests that nothing would do but a singer who could not only capture the feeling of "Step Right Up" but also imitate Tom Waits' voice. The initial efforts of the ad agency's creative team, using a respected professional singer with a deep bluesy voice, met with disapproval from executives at both Tracy-Locke and Frito-Lay. Tracy-Locke then auditioned a number of other singers who could sing in a gravelly style.

Stephen Carter was among those who auditioned. A recording engineer who was acquainted with Carter's work had recommended him to Tracy-Locke as someone who did a good Tom Waits imitation. Carter was a professional musician from Dallas and a Tom Waits fan. Over ten years of performing Waits songs as part of his band's repertoire, he had consciously perfected an imitation of Waits' voice. When Carter auditioned, members of the Tracy-Locke creative team "did a double take" over Carter's near-perfect imitation of Waits, and remarked to him how much he sounded like Waits. In fact, the commercial's musical director warned Carter that he probably wouldn't get the job because he sounded too much like Waits, which could pose legal problems. Carter, however, did get the job.

At the recording session for the commercial David Brenner, Tracy-Locke's executive producer, became concerned about the legal implications of Carter's skill in imitating Waits, and attempted to get Carter to "back off" his Waits imitation. Neither the client nor the members of the creative team, however, liked the result. After the session, Carter remarked to Brenner that Waits would be unhappy with the commercial because of his publicly avowed policy against doing commercial endorsements and his disapproval of artists who did. Brenner acknowledged he was aware of this, telling Carter that he had previously approached Waits to do a Diet Coke commercial and "you never heard anybody say no so fast in your life." Brenner conveyed to Robert Grossman, Tracy-Locke's managing vice president and the executive on the Frito-Lay account, his concerns that the commercial was too close to Waits' voice. As a precaution, Brenner made an alternate version of the commercial with another singer.

On the day the commercial was due for release to radio stations across the country, Grossman had a ten-minute long-distance telephone consultation with Tracy-Locke's attorney, asking him whether there would be legal problems with a commercial that sought to capture the same feeling as Waits' music. The attorney noted that there was a "high profile" risk of a lawsuit in view of recent case law recognizing the protectability of a distinctive voice. Based on what Grossman had told him, however, the attorney did not think such a suit would have merit, because a singer's style of music is not protected. Grossman then presented both the Carter tape and the alternate version to Frito-Lay, noting the legal risks involved in the Carter version. He recommended the Carter version, however, and noted that Tracy-Locke would indemnify Frito-Lay in the event of a lawsuit. Frito-Lay chose the Carter version.

The commercial was broadcast in September and October 1988 on over 250 radio stations located in 61 markets nationwide, including Los Angeles, San Francisco, and Chicago. Waits heard it during his appearance on a Los Angeles radio program, and was shocked. He realized "immediately that whoever was going to hear this and obviously identify the voice would also identify that [Tom Waits] in fact had agreed to do a commercial for Doritos."

In November 1988, Waits sued Tracy-Locke and Frito-Lay, alleging claims for voice misappropriation under California law and false endorsement under the Lanham Act. The case was tried before a jury in April and May 1990. The jury found in Waits' favor, awarding him $ 375,000 compensatory damages and $ 2 million punitive damages for voice misappropriation, and $ 100,000 damages for violation of the Lanham Act. The court awarded Waits attorneys' fees under the Lanham Act. This timely appeal followed.

## DISCUSSION
### I. Voice Misappropriation

In Midler v. Ford Motor Co., 849 F.2d 460, 463 (9th Cir. 1988), cert. denied, 112 S. Ct. 1513, 1514 (1992), we held that "when a distinctive voice of a professional singer is widely known and is deliberately imitated in order to sell a product, the sellers have appropriated what is not theirs and have committed a tort in California." The Midler tort is a species of violation of the "right of publicity," the right of a person whose identity has commercial value - most often a celebrity - to control the commercial use of that identity. See Motschenbacher v. R.J. Reynolds Tobacco Co., 498 F.2d 821, 824-25 (9th Cir. 1974). See generally J. T. McCarthy, The Rights of Publicity and Privacy (1987) (hereafter Publicity and Privacy). We recognized in Midler that when voice is a sufficient indicia of a celebrity's identity, the right of publicity protects against its imitation for commercial purposes without the celebrity's consent. See Midler, 849 F.2d at 463.

The jury found that the defendants had violated Waits' right of publicity by broadcasting a commercial which featured a deliberate imitation of Waits' voice. In doing so, the jury determined that Waits has a distinctive voice which is widely known. On appeal, the defendants attack the legal underpinnings of voice misappropriation, arguing that Midler is no longer an accurate statement of California law. They also find fault with the court's formulation of the elements of voice misappropriation in its instructions to the jury. Finally, they attack both the compensatory and punitive damages awarded by the jury as legally inappropriate and unsupported by the evidence. We address each contention in turn.

#### A. Continuing Viability of Midler

As a threshold matter, the defendants ask us to rethink Midler, and to reject it as an inaccurate statement of California law. Midler, according to the defendants, has been "impliedly overruled" by the Supreme Court's decision in Bonito Boats, Inc. v. Thunder Craft Boats, Inc., 489 U.S. 141 (1989). Additionally, they argue that the Midler tort is preempted by the federal Copyright Act. We review these questions of law de novo. See Kruso v. International Tel. & Tel. Corp., 872 F.2d 1416, 1421 (9th Cir. 1989), cert. denied, 496 U.S. 937 (1990).

Bonito Boats involved a Florida statute giving perpetual patent-like protection to boat hull designs already on the market, a class of manufactured articles expressly excluded from federal patent protection. The Court ruled that the Florida statute was preempted by federal patent law because it directly conflicted with the comprehensive federal patent scheme. In reaching this conclusion, the Court cited its earlier decisions in Sears Roebuck & Co. v. Stiffel Co., 376 U.S. 225 (1964), and Compco Corp. v. Day-Brite Lighting, 376 U.S. 234 (1964), for the proposition that "publicly known design and utilitarian ideas which were unprotected by patent occupied much the same position as the subject matter of an expired patent," i.e., they are expressly unprotected. Bonito Boats, 489 U.S. at 152.

The defendants seize upon this citation to Sears and Compco as a reaffirmation of the sweeping preemption principles for which these cases were once read to stand. They argue that Midler was wrongly decided because it ignores these two decisions, an omission that the defendants say indicates an erroneous assumption that Sears and Compco have been "relegated to the constitutional junkyard." Thus, the defendants go on to reason, earlier cases that rejected entertainers' challenges to imitations of their performances based on federal copyright preemption, were correctly decided because they relied on Sears and Compco. See Sinatra v. Goodyear Tire & Rubber Co., 435 F.2d 711, 716-18 (9th Cir. 1970), cert. denied, 402 U.S. 906 (1971); Booth v. Colgate-Palmolive Co., 362 F. Supp. 343, 348 (S.D.N.Y. 1973); Davis v. Trans World Airlines, 297 F. Supp. 1145, 1147 (C.D. Cal. 1969). This reasoning suffers from a number of flaws.

Bonito Boats itself cautions against reading Sears and Compco for a "broad pre-emptive principle" and cites subsequent Supreme Court decisions retreating from such a sweeping interpretation. "The Patent and Copyright Clauses do not, by their own force or by negative implication, deprive the States of the power to adopt rules for the promotion of intellectual creation." Bonito Boats, 489 U.S. at 165 (citing Goldstein v. California, 412 U.S. 546, 552-61 (1973) and Kewanee Oil Co. v. Bicron Corp., 416 U.S. 470, 478-79 (1974)). Instead, the Court reaffirmed the right of states to "place limited regulations on the use of unpatented designs in order to prevent consumer confusion as to source." Id. Bonito Boats thus cannot be read as endorsing or resurrecting the broad reading of Compco and Sears urged by the defendants, under which Waits' state tort claim arguably would be preempted.

Moreover, the Court itself recognized the authority of states to protect entertainers' "right of publicity" in Zacchini v. Scripps-Howard Broadcasting Co., 433 U.S. 562 (1977). In Zacchini, the Court endorsed a state right-of-publicity law as in harmony with federal patent and copyright law, holding that an unconsented-to television news broadcast of a commercial entertainer's performance was not protected by the First Amendment. Id. at 573, 576-78. The cases Frito asserts were "rightly decided" all predate Zacchini and other Supreme Court precedent narrowing Sears and Compco's sweeping preemption principles. In sum, our holding in Midler, upon which Waits' voice misappropriation claim rests, has not been eroded by subsequent authority.

The defendants ask that we rethink Midler anyway, arguing as the defendants did there that voice misappropriation is preempted by section 114 of the Copyright Act. Under this provision, a state cause of action escapes Copyright Act preemption if its subject matter "does not come within the subject matter of copyright . . . including works or authorship not fixed in any tangible medium of expression." 17 U.S.C. § 301(b)(1). We rejected copyright preemption in Midler because voice is not a subject matter of copyright: "A voice is not copyrightable. The sounds are not 'fixed.' " Midler, 849 F.2d at 462. As a three-judge panel, we are not at liberty to reconsider this conclusion, and even if we were, we would decline to disturb it.

Waits' claim, like Bette Midler's, is for infringement of voice, not for infringement of a copyrightable subject such as sound recording or musical composition. Moreover, the legislative history of section 114 indicates the express intent of Congress that "the evolving common law rights of 'privacy,' 'publicity,' and trade secrets . . . remain unaffected [by the preemption provision] as long as the causes of action contain elements, such as an invasion of personal rights . . . that are different in kind from copyright infringement." H. R. Rep. No. 1476, 94th Cong., 2d Sess. 132, reprinted in 1976 U.S.C.C.A.N. 5659, 5748. Waits' voice misappropriation claim is one for invasion of a personal property right: his right of publicity to control the use of his identity as embodied in his voice. See Midler, 849 F.2d at 462-63 ("What is put forward as protectable here is more personal than any work of authorship. . . . A voice is as distinctive and personal as a face.") The trial's focus was on the elements of voice misappropriation, as formulated in Midler: whether the defendants had deliberately imitated Waits' voice rather than simply his style and whether Waits' voice was sufficiently distinctive and widely known to give him a protectable right in its use. These elements are "different in kind" from those in a copyright infringement case challenging the unauthorized use of a song or recording. Waits' voice misappropriation claim, therefore, is not preempted by federal copyright law.

B. Jury Instructions

The defendants next contend that the district court committed prejudicial error by rejecting their proposed jury instructions on three elements of the Midler tort: the deliberate misappropriation for commercial purposes of (1) a voice, that is (2) distinctive and (3) widely known. We consider jury instructions as a whole to determine if they are misleading or inadequate. United States v. Beltran-Rios, 878 F.2d 1208, 1214 (9th Cir. 1989). We review challenges to the formulation of jury instructions for abuse of discretion. Id. Whether a jury instruction misstates the elements that must be proved at trial, however, is a question of law which we review de novo. United States v. Spillone, 879 F.2d 514, 525 (9th Cir. 1989), cert. denied, 111 S.Ct. 173, 210 (1990).

(1) "Voice" vs. "Style"

The defendants argued at trial that although they had consciously copied Tom Waits' style in creating the Doritos commercial, they had not deliberately imitated his voice. They accordingly proposed a jury instruction which distinguished in detail between voice, which is protected under Midler, and style, which is not. court rejected this instruction. Instead, its instructions on voice misappropriation track closely the elements of the tort as they are formulated in Midler. The court's instruction directed the jury to decide whether Waits' voice is distinctive, whether his voice is widely known, and whether the defendants had deliberately imitated his voice.

The defendants argue that their proposed "style" instruction was crucial because of the deliberate stylistic similarities between the Doritos commercial and "Step Right Up" and because in instructing the jury on Waits' Lanham Act claim, the court told the jury that it could consider Waits' singing style, songwriting style, and manner of presentation. In failing to give their proposed instruction, the defendants contend, the court misled the jury into believing that it could also consider the defendants' admitted imitation of Waits' style in determining liability for voice misappropriation.

We disagree because, read as a whole, the instructions were not misleading. In charging the jury, the court repeatedly noted that two claims were presented for determination and gave separate instructions on each claim. The court's voice misappropriation instructions limited the jury's consideration to voice, and in no way implied that it could consider style. Indeed, in addressing the jury in closing argument, Waits' attorney agreed with the defendants that style was not protected. Moreover, the court included an additional instruction that effectively narrowed the jury's focus to Waits' voice and indicated that style imitation alone was insufficient for tort liability. For the defendants to be liable for voice misappropriation, the court stated, the imitation had to be so good that "people who were familiar with plaintiff's voice who heard the commercial believed plaintiff performed it. In this connection it is not enough that they were reminded of plaintiff or thought the singer sounded like plaintiff . . . ." (Emphasis added.) Even if the jury were initially confused about whether the defendants could be liable simply for imitating Waits' style, this instruction would have disabused them of this notion.

(2) Definition of "Distinctive"

The defendants next argue that the court's instruction concerning the meaning of "distinctive" was an unfair and inaccurate statement of the law because it confuses the "distinctiveness" of a voice with its identifiability or recognizability. The instruction given states in part: "A voice is distinctive if it is distinguishable from the voices of other singers. . . . if it has particular qualities or characteristics that identify it with a particular singer." At trial the defendants' experts testified that identifiability depends, not on distinctiveness, but on the listener's expections; that distinctiveness and recognizability are not the same thing; and that recognizability is enhanced by style similarity. The defendants argue that these theories were inadequately dealt with by the court's instruction and that because anyone's voice is identifiable by someone, it was error for the court not to make clear the difference between distinctiveness and identifiability. We disagree.

The defendants' technical argument that distinctiveness is a separate concept from identifiability, while supported by their experts' testimony, has no basis in law. Identifiability is properly considered in evaluating distinctiveness, for it is a central element of a right of publicity claim. See Publicity and Privacy § 3.4[A] & n.1 (citing cases). Our Midler holding is premised on the fact that a person is as identifiable by voice as by any other indicia of identity previously recognized as protectable. Although we did not define "distinctiveness" in Midler, we stated: "A voice is as distinctive and personal as a face. The human voice is one of the most palpable ways identity is manifested. We are all aware that a friend is at once known by a few words on the phone. . . . These observations hold true of singing . . . ." Midler v. Ford, 849 F.2d at 463 (emphasis added). See also Motschenbacher, 498 F.2d at 826-27 (rejecting trial court's ruling that because plaintiff's face was not recognizable in advertisement photograph, his identity had not been misappropriated, and finding that plaintiff was identifiable from distinctive decorations on race car).

The court's "distinctiveness" instruction informed the jury that it could consider the recordings of Waits' voice introduced into evidence and the testimony of expert and other witnesses. The court thus invited members of the jury to use their common sense in determining whether Waits has a distinctive enough voice to warrant protection, and to consider as well what the experts had to say. This was entirely appropriate. See Publicity and Privacy, § 3.4[C] (jury must use "common sense . . . guided by the weight of the evidence" in determining minimum threshold of identifiability in right of publicity actions). The court was not required to formulate instructions endorsing expert opinions which lacked legal foundation. Finally, we are unpersuaded by the defendants' argument that the court's instruction would have allowed the jury to hold them liable for imitation of a voice that was identifiable by only a small number of people, inasmuch as Midler also requires that the plaintiff's voice be "widely known."

(3) Definition of "Widely Known"

The defendants next object to the district court's instruction concerning the element of "widely known" on the ground that it was too vague to guide the jury in making a factual determination of the issue. The court instructed the jury: "A professional singer's voice is widely known if it is known to a large number of people throughout a relatively large geographic area." (Emphasis added.) The court rejected an instruction proposed by the defendants, which reflected their contention at trial that Tom Waits is a singer known only to music insiders and to a small but loyal group of fans: "A singer is not widely known if he is only recognized by his own fans, or fans of a particular sort of music, or a small segment of the population."

The legal underpinnings of this proposed instruction are questionable. The defendants assert that because Waits has not achieved the level of celebrity Bette Midler has, he is not well known under the Midler standard. We reject this crabbed interpretation of Midler. The defendants' proposed instruction would have excluded from legal protection the voices of many popular singers who fall short of superstardom. "Well known" is a relative term, and differences in the extent of celebrity are adequately reflected in the amount of damages recoverable. See Mostenbacher, 498 F.2d at 824 n.11 ("Generally, the greater the fame or notoriety of the identity appropriated, the greater will be the extent of the economic injury suffered."). Moreover, even were these instructions inadequate in some regard the error would be harmless, for we agree with the district court that the "great weight of evidence produced at trial indicates that Tom Waits is very widely known."

In sum, we find no error in the instructions given to the jury on Waits' voice misappropriation claim.

### C. Compensatory Damage Award

The jury awarded Waits the following compensatory damages for voice misappropriation: $ 100,000 for the fair market value of his services; $ 200,000 for injury to his peace, happiness and feelings; and $ 75,000 for injury to his goodwill, professional standing and future publicity value. The defendants contest the latter two awards, disputing both the availability of such damages in a voice misappropriation action and the sufficiency of the evidence supporting the awards.

#### 1. Injury to Peace, Happiness and Feelings

The defendants argue that in right of publicity actions, only damages to compensate for economic injury are available. We disagree. Although the injury stemming from violation of the right of publicity "may be largely, or even wholly, of an economic or material nature," we have recognized that "it is quite possible that the appropriation of the identity of a celebrity may induce humiliation, embarrassment, and mental distress." Motschenbacher, 498 F.2d at 824 & n.11. Contrary to the defendants' assertions, Midler neither discussed nor limited the damages recoverable in a voice misappropriation action. Midler makes reference to the market value of Midler's voice solely to support its conclusion that her voice has economic value and, therefore, is a protectable property right. See 849 F.2d at 463.

In assessing the propriety of mental distress damages, our focus is properly directed to the nature of the infringement and its embarrassing impact on the plaintiff. Publicity and Privacy § 4.2A. Often the objectionable nature of the use will cause mental distress. Id. § 4.2B, C, [D] (discussing cases). In Grant v. Esquire, Inc., 367 F. Supp. 876 (S.D.N.Y. 1973), for example, the court found that the mere use of a celebrity's identity could cause embarrassment for which mental distress damages would be available. The case involved a suit by Cary Grant against Esquire magazine for publishing a photograph in which Grant's head was superimposed on a clothing model's torso. Like Waits, Grant had taken a public position against reaping commercial profits from the publicity value of his identity. Id. at 880. The court, after finding that Grant had a protectable right of publicity, noted that "if the jury decides in plaintiff Grant's favor he will of course be entitled to recover for any lacerations to his feelings that he may be able to establish" in addition to the fair market value of use of his identity. Id. at 881. Given the evidence that the commercial use of his voice was particularly offensive to Waits, we conclude that Waits' prayer for mental distress damages was properly submitted to the jury.

The defendants argue, however, that merely taking offense is an insufficient basis for awarding mental distress damages, and that under California law the evidence was insufficient to support the award. In California, mental distress damages may be recovered for "shame, humiliation, embarrassment, [and] anger." Young v. Bank of America, 141 Cal. App. 3d 108, 114 (1983); see also Moore v. Greene, 431 F.2d 584, 591 & n.3 (9th Cir. 1970) (damages available for anxiety, humiliation and indignity). Waits testified that when he heard the Doritos commercial, "this corn chip sermon," he was shocked and very angry. These feelings "grew and grew over a period of a couple of days" because of his strong public opposition to doing commercials. Waits testified, "It embarrassed me. I had to call all my friends, that if they hear this thing, please be informed this is not me. I was on the phone for days. I also had people calling me saying, Gee, Tom, I heard the new Doritos ad." Added to this evidence of Waits' shock, anger, and embarrassment is the strong inference that, because of his outspoken public stance against doing commercial endorsements, the Doritos commercial humiliated Waits by making him an apparent hypocrite. This evidence was sufficient both to allow the jury to consider mental distress damages and to support their eventual award.

2. Injury to Goodwill and Future Publicity Value

The defendants next argue that reputational damages are available only in defamation actions and that since Waits did not allege or prove defamation, they were unavailable here. Further, they argue, there was no evidence to support the award of such damages because Waits did not show that his career had suffered. Again, we reject these contentions.

We have no doubt, in light of general tort liability principles, that where the misappropriation of identity causes injury to reputation, compensation for such injury is appropriate. See Cal. Civ. Code § 3333 (West 1970) (available damages are those "which will compensate for all of the detriment" caused by defendant's tortious conduct). Reputational damages, moreover, have been awarded in right of publicity cases. See Clark v. Celeb Publishing, Inc., 530 F. Supp. 979, 984 (S.D.N.Y. 1981) (applying California law); Hirsch v. S.C. Johnson & Son, Inc., 90 Wis. 2d 379, 280 N.W.2d 129, 138 (1979). The central issue is not whether these damages were available, but whether the evidence was sufficient to establish injury to Waits' reputation. As we noted above, the jury could have inferred from the evidence that the commercial created a public impression that Waits was a hypocrite for endorsing Doritos. Moreover, it also could have inferred damage to his artistic reputation, for Waits had testified that "part of my character and personality and image that I have cultivated is that I do not endorse products." Finally, from the testimony of Waits' expert witness, the jury could have inferred that if Waits ever wanted to do a commercial in the future, the fee he could command would be lowered by $ 50,000 to $ 150,000 because of the Doritos commercial. This evidence was sufficient to support the jury's award of $ 75,000 for injury to Waits' goodwill and future publicity value.

D. Punitive Damage Award

The jury awarded Waits a total of $ 2 million in punitive damages for voice misappropriation: $ 1.5 million against Tracy-Locke and $ 500,000 against Frito-Lay. The defendants ask that we vacate this award, arguing that punitive damages are unavailable as a matter of law, and alternatively, that the evidence was insufficient to support their award.

In California, exemplary or punitive damages are available "where it is proven by clear and convincing evidence that the defendant has been guilty of oppression, fraud, or malice." Cal. Civ. Code § 3294(a) (West Supp. 1992). The statute defines "malice" in pertinent part as "despicable conduct which is carried on by the defendant with a willful and conscious disregard of the rights or safety of others." Id. § 3294(c)(1) (emphasis added). The defendants contend that because Midler was so recently decided and so imprecise in the scope of its holding, they could not have been aware of the rights they were infringing upon in broadcasting the commercial. Thus, they reason, their conduct was not in "conscious disregard" of Waits' property right in his voice.

Where an issue is one of first impression or where a right has not been clearly established, punitive damages are generally unavailable. See, e.g., Morgan Guar. Trust Co. v. American Sav. & Loan Ass'n, 804 F.2d 1487, 1500 (9th

Cir. 1986), cert. denied, 482 U.S. 929 (1987); Bartling v. Glendale Adventist Medical Center, 229 Cal. Rptr. 360, 364 (Cal. Ct. App. 1986). The right of a well-known professional singer to control the commercial use of a distinctive voice, however, was not an "issue of first impression" in this case. The right had been established clearly by Midler. The evidence was unequivocal that, although Midler was decided just three months before the conduct at issue, Tracy-Locke personnel responsible for making the Doritos commercial were familiar with the Midler decision. Tracy-Locke was concerned enough that the commercial could result in voice misappropriation liability that it cautioned Frito-Lay of the legal risks in choosing the Carter version. At the same time, however, Tracy-Locke stated its readiness to indemnify Frito-Lay against damages. Frito-Lay, reassured by the indemnification, chose to proceed with the Carter version. In going forward with the commercial, the defendants knowingly took a calculated risk, thereby consciously disregarding the effect of these actions on Waits' legally recognized rights.

The defendants argue, however, that although they may have been aware that legal risks were involved, they had a good faith belief that Waits' rights would not be infringed because they read the legal precedents differently. This argument leaves us unpersuaded. Good faith cannot be manufactured by looking to the law of other jurisdictions to define the rights of California residents. Midler could not be more clear that, in California at least, a well-known singer with a distinctive voice has a property right in that voice. Waits is a California resident, a fact of which Tracy-Locke personnel were aware. The defendants made a conscious decision to broadcast a vocal performance imitating Waits in markets across the country, including San Francisco and Los Angeles. This evidence is sufficient to raise at least a prima facie showing that defendants acted in conscious disregard of rights recognized in California.

Even if punitive damages are available, the defendants argue, the award must be vacated because it is not supported by clear and convincing evidence, as required by California law. Cal. Civ. Code § 3294(a). Clear and convincing evidence means evidence sufficient to support a finding of "high probability." Mock v. Michigan Millers Mutual Ins. Co., 5 Cal. Rptr. 2d 594, 610 (Cal. Ct. App. 1992). On appeal, we must determine whether, viewing the evidence in the light most favorable to Waits, any rational jury could have found a high probability that the defendants acted with malice, i.e., despicably and with willful and conscious disregard of Waits' rights. See Transgo, Inc. v. Ajac Transmission Parts Corp., 768 F.2d 1001, 1013-14 (9th Cir. 1985) (evidence supports civil jury verdict if there is "such relevant evidence as a reasonable mind might accept as adequate to support a conclusion"), cert. denied, 474 U.S. 1059 (1986); cf. United States v. Juvenile Male, 864 F.2d 641, 647 (9th Cir. 1988) (evidence supports criminal conviction if, viewed in light most favorable to prosecution, any rational jury could find elements of crime beyond a reasonable doubt).

The evidence the jury heard included testimony that Carter, the Waits impersonator, told Brenner that Waits had a policy against doing commercials and would not like this one. Brenner knew of Waits' policy because he had tried unsuccessfully to hire him for another commercial. In the face of Brenner's warnings that the commercial sounded too much like Waits and presented serious legal concerns, Grossman called a lawyer. Although the lawyer thought the scenario Grossman painted him did not present a colorable legal problem, Grossman had not told the lawyer that the commercial featured a voice that sounded like Waits - only that the "feeling" of the music was the same. Grossman urged Frito-Lay to choose the Carter version over one that did not sound like Waits. Moreover, at the same time Grossman disclosed the legal risk involved with the Carter version, he stated that Tracy-Locke would indemnify Frito-Lay in the event of a lawsuit. The responsible Frito-Lay executive, who was also familiar with Waits and his background, chose to go with the Carter version. The effect of their actions on Waits, according to his testimony, was to tarnish the artistic integrity which he had striven to achieve.

We believe that, viewed most favorably to Waits, this evidence was adequate to support a finding of high probability that Tracy-Locke and Frito-Lay acted with malice. Despicability reflects a moral judgment, "conscious disregard" a state of mind. A rational jury could have found the defendants' conduct despicable because they knowingly impugned Waits' integrity in the public eye. A rational jury also could have found that the defendants, in spite of their awareness of Waits' legal right to control the commercial use of his voice, acted in conscious disregard of that right by broadcasting the commercial. We therefore affirm the award of punitive damages.

## II. Lanham Act Claim

Section 43(a) of the Lanham Act, 15 U.S.C. § 1125(a), prohibits the use of false designations of origin, false descriptions, and false representations in the advertising and sale of goods and services. Smith v. Montoro, 648 F.2d 602, 603 (9th Cir. 1981). Waits' claim under section 43(a) is premised on the theory that by using an imitation of his distinctive voice in an admitted parody of a Tom Waits song, the defendants misrepresented his association with and endorsement of SalsaRio Doritos. The jury found in Waits' favor and awarded him $ 100,000 in damages. The district court also awarded him attorney's fees under section 35 of the Lanham Act. On appeal, the defendants argue that Waits lacks standing to bring a Lanham Act claim, that Waits' false endorsement claim fails on its merits, that the damage award is duplicative, and that attorneys' fees are improper. Before we address these contentions, however, we turn to the threshold issue of whether false endorsement claims are properly cognizable under section 43(a) of the Lanham Act, a question of first impression in this circuit.

A. False Endorsement

At the time of the broadcast of the Doritos commercial, section 43(a) provided in pertinent part:

Any person who shall affix, apply, or annex, or use in connection with any goods or services . . . a false designation of origin, or any false designation or representation . . . shall be liable to a civil action . . . by any person who believes that he is or is likely to be damaged by the use of any such false designation or representation.

15 U.S.C. § 1125 note (Amendments) (1988). Courts in other jurisdictions have interpreted this language as authorizing claims for false endorsement. E.g., Better Business Bureau v. Medical Directors, Inc., 681 F.2d 397 (5th Cir. 1982); Jackson v. MPI Home Video, 694 F. Supp. 483 (N.D. Ill. 1988); Wildlife Internationale, Inc. v. Clements, 591 F. Supp. 1542 (S.D. Oh. 1984); Geisel v. Poynter Prods., Inc., 283 F. Supp. 261, 267 (S.D.N.Y. 1968). Moreover, courts have recognized false endorsement claims brought by plaintiffs, including celebrities, for the unauthorized imitation of their distinctive attributes, where those attributes amount to an unregistered commercial "trademark." See Dallas Cowboys Cheerleaders, Inc. v. Pussycat Cinema, Ltd., 604 F.2d 200, 205 (2d Cir. 1979) (recognizing claim under § 43(a) because uniform worn by star of X-rated movie confusingly similar to plaintiffs' trademark uniforms, falsely creating impression that plaintiffs "sponsored or otherwise approved the use" of the uniform); Allen v. Men's World Outlet, Inc., 679 F. Supp. 360, 368 (S.D.N.Y. 1988) (celebrity states a claim under § 43(a) by showing that advertisement featuring photograph of a look-alike falsely represented that advertised products were associated with him); Allen v. National Video, Inc., 610 F. Supp. 612, 625-26 (S.D.N.Y. 1985) (recognizing celebrity's false endorsement claim under § 43(a) because celebrity has commercial investment in name and face tantamount to interests of a trademark holder in distinctive mark); see also Lahr v. Adell Chemical Co., 300 F.2d 256, 258 (1st Cir. 1962) (imitation of unique voice actionable as common law unfair competition); cf. Sinatra v. Goodyear Tire & Rubber Co.., 435 F.2d 711, 716 (9th Cir. 1970) (rejecting common law unfair competition claim because plaintiff's voice not sufficiently unique to be protectable), cert. denied, 402 U.S. 906 (1971).

The persuasiveness of this case law as to the cognizability of Waits' Lanham Act claim is reinforced by the 1988 Lanham Act amendments. See Trademark Law Revision Act of 1988, Pub. L. 100-667, § 35, 102 Stat. 3946. The legislative history states that the amendments to section 43(a) codify previous judicial interpretation given this provision. S. Rep. No. 515, 100th Cong., 2d Sess., at 40, reprinted in 1988 U.S.C.C.A.N. 5577, 5603. Although these amendments did not take effect until November 1989, approximately a year after the broadcast of the defendants' Doritos commercial, as a codification of prior case law and in the absence of controlling precedent to the contrary, they properly inform our interpretation of the previous version of section 43(a). Specifically, we read the amended language to codify case law interpreting section 43(a) to encompass false endorsement claims. Section 43(a) now expressly prohibits, inter alia, the use of any symbol or device which is likely to deceive consumers as to the association, sponsorship, or approval of goods or services by another person. Moreover, the legislative history of the 1988 amendments also makes clear that in retaining the statute's original terms "symbol or device" in the definition of "trademark," Congress approved the broad judicial interpretation of these terms to include distinctive sounds and physical appearance. See S. Rep. No. 101-515 at 44, 1988 U.S.C.C.A.N. at 5607. In light of persuasive judicial authority and the subsequent congressional approval of that authority, we conclude that false endorsement claims, including those premised on the unauthorized imitation of an entertainer's distinctive voice, are cognizable under section 43(a).

### B. Standing

According to the defendants, however, Waits lacks standing to sue for false endorsement. They assert that because he is not in competition with the defendants, he cannot sue under the Lanham Act. Common sense contradicts this argument, for the purported endorser who is commercially damaged by the false endorsement will rarely if ever be a competitor, and yet is the party best situated to enforce the Lanham Act's prohibition on such conduct. Our circuit precedent, however, throws into question whether such a plaintiff must be a competitor of the defendant's in order to sue under section 43(a).

In Smith v. Montoro, 648 F.2d 602 (9th Cir. 1981), we declined to restrict standing under the Lanham Act to competitors. The plaintiff in Smith, an actor who had played a starring role in a movie, sued a film distributor when it replaced his name with another actor's name in the movie's credits and advertising. Id. at 603. We characterized the section 43(a) claim there as a "reverse passing off" claim, because the plaintiff's "mark" - his name - had been removed and another's substituted. We analogized this conduct to trademark infringement, because the injury involved was "of the same economic nature." See id. at 606-07 (quoting Truck Equipment Serv. Co. v. Fruehauf Corp., 536 F.2d 1210, 1216 (8th Cir.), cert. denied, 429 U.S. 861 (1976)). Like trademark infringement, the film distributor's conduct was "an attempt to misappropriate or profit from [the plaintiff's] talents and workmanship." Id. at 607 (citations omitted).

To have standing under the Lanham Act, we declared, "the plaintiff need not be in actual competition with the alleged wrongdoer." Smith, 648 F.2d at 607. Rather, the "dispositive question" in determining standing is whether the plaintiff "has a reasonable interest to be protected against false advertising." Id. at 608 (quoting 1 R. Callman, Unfair Competition, Trademarks and Monopolies, § 18.2(b), at 625 (3d ed. 1967) and citing New West Corp. v. NYM Co. of Calif., Inc., 595 F.2d 1194, 1198 (9th Cir. 1979)). We concluded that, like a trademark holder, an actor has a "reasonable interest" in having his work product properly identified with his name, and therefore the plaintiff had standing under section 43(a). See id.

On the other hand, in Halicki v. United Artists Communications, Inc., 812 F.2d 1213 (9th Cir. 1987), we dismissed the plaintiff's claim because he had failed to show competitive injury. The plaintiff, a movie producer, had entered into a contract with a film distributor under which the plaintiff's movie would be advertised with a "PG" rating. Instead, it was advertised with an "R" rating, thus curtailing its market among young audiences. Id. at 1213. The gravamen of the complaint was that the defendant had misrepresented the film's content in advertising it. We rejected the plaintiff's contention that to state a claim under the Lanham Act, all he need do was "show that the defendants made a false representation about his film and that he was injured by the representation." Id. at 1214. Rather, the plaintiff must also show that type of injury sustained is one the Lanham Act is intended to prevent.

We noted that an express purpose of the Lanham Act is to protect commercial parties against unfair competition. Id. Thus, we held that "to be actionable, [the defendant's] conduct must not only be unfair but must in some discernible way be competitive." Id. The misrepresentation as to the film's rating, we concluded, while possibly actionable as breach of contract, was not actionable under the Lanham Act inasmuch as the plaintiff had not been injured by a competitor. Id. at 1214-15. This result, we stated, accords with congressional intent, for if such a limitation were not in place the Lanham Act would become a "federal statute creating the tort of misrepresentation." Id. at 1214.

To interpret Halicki as suggested by the defendants, for the broad proposition that only competitors have standing under section 43(a) regardless of the type of claim asserted, would create an impermissible conflict with Smith, where we held that actual competition is unnecessary. See Smith, 648 F.2d at 607-08. Where circuit precedent appears in conflict, we must attempt to reconcile it; if we cannot do so consideration en banc is appropriate. See Atonio v. Wards Cove Packing Co., 810 F.2d 1477, 1478-79 (9th Cir. 1987) (en banc). We find that Smith and Halicki may be reconciled, and we begin with the basic principle both embody: that standing under section 43(a) exists where the interest asserted by the plaintiff is a commercial interest protected by the Lanham Act.

Its drafters wrote the purposes of the Lanham Act, two of which are relevant here, into the statute itself: to make "actionable the deceptive and misleading use of marks in . . . commerce" and "to protect persons engaged in . . . commerce against unfair competition." 15 U.S.C. § 1127 (1988). Section 43(a) reflects both of these purposes, providing two bases of liability: (1) false representations concerning the origin, association, or endorsement of goods or services through the wrongful use of another's distinctive mark, name, trade dress, or other device ("false association"), and (2) false representations in advertising concerning the qualities of goods or services ("false advertising"). See, e.g., 2 J. Thomas McCarthy, Trademarks and Unfair Competition §§ 27:2-27:4, at 344-68 (2d ed. 1984) (discussing two prongs of section 43(a)); U-Haul Int'l, Inc. v. Jartran, Inc., 681 F.2d 1159, 1160 (9th Cir. 1982) (discussing trademark infringement and false comparative advertising as two distinct causes of action under § 43(a)); Spring Mills, Inc. v. Ultracashmere House, Ltd., 532 F. Supp. 1203, 1220 (S.D.N.Y.) (discussing false association and false advertising), rev'd on other grounds, 689 F.2d 1127 (2d Cir. 1982). Halicki and Smith are distinguishable, because they involve different prongs of section 43(a) liability and implicate distinct interests. Cf. Halicki, 812 F.2d at 1214 (distinguishing Smith on the basis of type of claim asserted).

We have recognized that simple claims of false representations in advertising are actionable under section 43(a) when brought by competitors of the wrongdoer, even though they do not involve misuse of a trademark. See U-Haul, 681 F.2d at 1160-61. The plaintiff's claim in Halicki was exclusively such a "false advertising" claim, for it sought redress for a simple misrepresentation as to a product's quality, the content of a movie. We were at pains to point out that the plaintiff's injury was not related to the Lanham Act's purpose of preventing the "deceptive and misleading use of marks," 15 U.S.C. § 1127, declaring that the statute's purposes with regard to the use of trademarks were irrelevant to his claim. See Halicki, 812 F.2d at 1214. Rather, where the misrepresentation simply concerns a product's qualities, it is actionable under section 43(a) only insofar the Lanham Act's other purpose of preventing "unfair competition" is served. See U-Haul, 681 F.2d at 1162 (noting congressional intent to allow false advertising suits by competitors "to stop the kind of unfair competition that consists of lying about goods or services"). In such cases, Halicki counsels that a discernibly competitive injury must be alleged. We take an example close to Halicki's facts, assuming for purposes of this hypothetical only that producers may rate their own films. If a film's distributor wrongfully indicates that a film is "PG"-rated when in reality it should be "R"-rated, a competitor with a PG-rated film would have standing: the misrated film theoretically draws young audiences away from the competitor's film because of the misrepresentation concerning the suitability of its content. In Halicki, however, the plaintiff lacked a discernibly competitive interest: he and the distributor were not independent actors in the marketplace, but rather had a contractual relationship in which the distributor agreed to act in the marketplace on the plaintiff's behalf. The interests asserted, therefore, were solely contractual and not within the zone of interests protected by the Lanham Act.

The plaintiff's claim in Smith, on the other hand, was a type of false association claim stemming from the misuse of a mark, for it alleged the wrongful removal of the plaintiff's name and the wrongful substitution of another's name. Smith teaches that where such a claim is presented, the plaintiff need not be a competitor, for the Lanham Act also grants a cause of action to certain noncompetitors who have been injured commercially by the "deceptive and misleading use of marks." See 15 U.S.C. § 1127; see also Dallas Cowboys Cheerleaders, Inc. v. Pussycat Cinema, Ltd., 467 F. Supp. 366, 374 (S.D.N.Y. 1979) (owner of a mark has right to exploit mark commercially by having consumers associate mark only with owner's goods or services, regardless of whether misappropriator deals in competing or noncompeting goods or services). Those with standing to bring such a claim include parties with a commercial interest in the product wrongfully identified with another's mark, as in Smith, or with a commercial interest in the misused mark. See Dovenmuehle v. Gilldorn Mortgage Midwest Corp., 871 F.2d 697, 700-01 (7th Cir. 1989) (only those with present commercial interest in trade name have standing to sue for its wrongful use under § 43(a)); Berni Int'l Gourmet Restaurants of America, Inc., 838 F.2d 642, 648 (2d Cir. 1988) (plaintiff must have commercial or ownership interest in mark to have standing under § 43(a)); cf. Mishawaka Rubber & Woolen Mfg. Co. v. S.S. Kresge Co., 316 U.S. 203, 205 (1942) ("If another poaches upon the commercial magnetism of the symbol he has created, the owner can obtain legal redress.").

A false endorsement claim based on the unauthorized use of a celebrity's identity is a type of false association claim, for it alleges the misuse of a trademark, i.e., a symbol or device such as a visual likeness, vocal imitation, or other uniquely distinguishing characteristic, which is likely to confuse consumers as to the plaintiff's sponsorship or approval of the product. Standing, therefore, does not require "actual competition" in the traditional sense; it extends to a purported endorser who has an economic interest akin to that of a trademark holder in controlling the commercial exploitation of his or her identity. See Allen v. National Home Video, 610 F. Supp. at 625, 628 (celebrity's interest in the marketing value of his identity is similar to that of a trademark holder, and its misuse through evocation of celebrity's persona that creates likelihood of consumer confusion as to celebrity's endorsement is actionable under Lanham Act). Moreover, the wrongful appropriator is in a sense a competitor of the celebrity, even when the celebrity has chosen to disassociate himself or herself from advertising products as has Waits. They compete with respect to the use of the celebrity's name or identity. They are both utilizing or marketing that personal property for commercial purposes. Accordingly, we hold that a celebrity whose endorsement of a product is implied through the imitation of a distinctive attribute of the celebrity's identity, has standing to sue for false endorsement under section 43(a) of the Lanham Act. Tom Waits, therefore, need not be a competitor in the traditional sense to sue under the Lanham Act for the imitation of his voice on the theory that its use falsely associated him with Doritos as an endorser. Rather, his standing was sufficiently established by the likelihood that the wrongful use of his professional trademark, his unique voice, would injure him commercially.

### C. Merits

The defendants next argue that Waits' false endorsement claim must fail on its merits because the Doritos commercial "did not represent that . . . [Waits] sponsored or endorsed their product." We disagree. The court correctly instructed the jury that in considering Waits' Lanham Act claim, it must determine whether "ordinary consumers . . . would be confused as to whether Tom Waits sang on the commercial . . . and whether he sponsors or endorses SalsaRio Doritos." The jury was told that in making this determination, it should consider the totality of the evidence, including the distinctiveness of Waits' voice and style, the evidence of actual confusion as to whether Waits actually sang on the commercial, and the defendants' intent to imitate Waits' voice. See generally, Clamp Mfg. Co. v. Enco Mfg. Co., 870 F.2d 512, 517 (9th Cir.) (discussing factors to be considered in determining likelihood of confusion, including strength of mark, similarity of marks, evidence of actual confusion, marketing channels used, and intent in selecting marks), cert. denied, 493 U.S. 872 (1989).

At trial, the jury listened to numerous Tom Waits recordings, and to a recording of the Doritos commercial in which the Tom Waits impersonator delivered this "hip" endorsement of SalsaRio Doritos: "It's buffo, boffo, bravo, gung-ho, tally-ho, but never mellow. . . . try' em, buy 'em, get 'em, got 'em." The jury also heard evidence, relevant to the likelihood of consumer confusion, that the Doritos commercial was targeted to an audience which overlapped with Waits' audience, males between the ages of 18 to 35 who listened to the radio. Finally, there was evidence of actual consumer confusion: the testimony of numerous witnesses that they actually believed it was Tom Waits singing the words of endorsement.

This evidence was sufficient to support the jury's finding that consumers were likely to be misled by the commercial into believing that Waits endorsed

SalsaRio Doritos. See Allen v. Men's World Outlet, 679 F. Supp. at 368-69 (likelihood of consumer confusion established where advertiser intentionally used a look-alike of well-known celebrity and where audience to whom commercial was directed intersected with celebrity's audience); Allen v. National Home Video, 610 F. Supp. at 626-27 & n.8 (use of celebrity look-alike in pose of product spokesperson sufficient to indicate endorsement). The jury's verdict on Waits' Lanham Act claim must therefore stand.

### D. Damages

The defendants urge us to vacate the damage award on Waits' Lanham Act claim as duplicative of those damages awarded for voice misappropriation representing the fair market value of Waits' services. Waits does not contest this point. Standing by the representations he made to the jury at trial that he was not seeking a double recovery, he asserts on appeal that he "does not oppose a reduction of the final judgment in the amount of $ 100,000 based on the overlapping Lanham Act award."

In instructing the jury on Waits' Lanham Act claim, the court stated that it could award damages for the fair market value of Waits' services. The jury awarded Waits $ 100,000 on this claim. It also awarded Waits $ 100,000 for the fair market value of his services on his voice misappropriation claim. The damages awarded under the Lanham Act, therefore, are duplicative. Accordingly, we vacate this portion of the judgment.

### E. Attorneys' Fees

Section 35 of the Lanham Act authorizes attorneys' fee awards for prevailing plaintiffs in "exceptional cases." 15 U.S.C. § 1117. Exceptional cases include those in which the defendants' conduct is "malicious, fraudulent, deliberate, or wilful." Sealy, Inc. v. Easy Living, Inc., 743 F.2d 1378, 1384 (9th Cir. 1984) (citing S. Rep. No. 1400, 93rd Cong., 2d Sess. (1974), reprinted in 1974 U.S.C.C.A.N. 7132); see Transgo, 768 F.2d at 1026. We review attorneys' fee awards under the Lanham Act for abuse of discretion. Transgo, 768 F.2d at 1026.

In awarding punitive damages on Waits' voice misappropriation claim, the jury specifically found that the defendants had acted with oppression, fraud, or malice. That finding qualifies this case as an exceptional one within the meaning of section 35. The district court was therefore within its discretion in awarding Waits reasonable attorneys' fees.

## CONCLUSION

Waits' voice misappropriation claim and his Lanham Act claim are legally sufficient. The court did not err in instructing the jury on elements of voice misappropriation. The jury's verdict on each claim is supported by substantial evidence, as are its damage awards. Its award of damages on Waits' Lanham Act claim, however, is duplicative of damages awarded for voice misappropriation; accordingly we vacate it. Finally, the court did not abuse its discretion in awarding attorneys' fees under the Lanham Act.

Waits is awarded his costs on appeal.

AFFIRMED in part and VACATED in part.

---

In a book by one of the co-authors, the case of Tom Waits is used as an example of the courts protecting "the 'persona' of the artist against false implication of endorsement generally resulting from the use of look-alikes or sound-alikes" (Walter Champion, Intellectual Property in the Sports and Entertainment Industries 151 (ABC-CLIO, 2014)). In Waits v. Frito-Lay, Inc., 978 F.2d 1093, 1107 (11th Cir. 1992), the court affirms judgment for plaintiff Tom Waits and his distinct gravelly, throaty voice on a false implied endorsement claim for use in a snack food commercial by a singer who purposefully imitated Tom Waits' peculiar singing style while praising Frito-Lay chips (Id., 151).

Newton v. Thomason
United States Court of Appeals for the Ninth Circuit
March 9, 1994; April 28, 1994, Filed
Nos. 93-55002, 93-55376, No. 93-55379
22 F.3d 1455

OPINION
PREGERSON, Circuit Judge:

Wood Newton ("Newton") appeals the district court's summary judgment in favor of television producers Harry Thomason and Linda-Bloodworth Thomason, Burt Reynolds, and Mozark Productions, Inc. (collectively "Appellees"), in Newton's misappropriation and unfair competition action. Newton alleges that the Appellees appropriated his name for a character in the television show "Evening Shade" in violation of the common law right of publicity, various state statutes, and the Lanham Act, 15 U.S.C. § 1125(a). Newton and his attorney Michael Childress ("Childress") together appeal the award of sanctions against Childress. Appellees cross-appeal the denial of their request for attorneys' fees. We have jurisdiction over both the appeal and the cross-appeal under 28 U.S.C. § 1291. On the appeal, we affirm in part and reverse in part. On the cross-appeal, we reverse and remand in part.

**BACKGROUND**

Appellant Newton is a country music songwriter and performer. In the country/western music industry, he is recognized by the name "Wood Newton." The main character in the television series "Evening Shade" [hereinafter the TV Series], is also named "Wood Newton." Prior to the television show, which started airing in September 1990, Newton was the only person with that name in the entertainment field.

Newton filed a complaint in the Northern District of Illinois, alleging that Appellees misappropriated his name and likeness and engaged in unfair competition in violation of state and federal law. The Illinois court transferred the case to the Central District of California, under 28 U.S.C. § 1404(a). Appellees moved for summary judgment the following grounds: (1) Newton consented to use of his name; (2) Appellees did not "pirate" Newton's name and identity for commercial gain; and (3) There was no likelihood of confusion between Newton and the TV Series character.

On the issue of consent, Appellees presented evidence that Newton consented in writing and by his conduct. Their evidence showed that by May or

June 1990, Newton knew that Appellees planned to use Wood Newton as one of the TV Series' character names because his sister sent him a newspaper article about the TV Series. On July 18, 1990, Newton wrote, in a letter to Harry Thomason ("Thomason") and Linda Bloodworth-Thomason ("Bloodworth"), "I've been reading about your new show . . . . I want you to know I'm flattered that you are using my name, everyone who I've talked to about it thinks it's exciting and so do I." He went on to explain the origins of his name. Newton admitted that he did not expect Thomason to think he objected to the use of his name after reading this letter. Both before and after the first broadcast in September, Newton spoke with Thomason and sent several more letters without ever objecting to or even mentioning the use of his name; he spoke only about the use of his songs.

In their moving papers, Appellees contended that Newton in fact actively encouraged them to use his name because he hoped to sell them a theme song for the TV Series. Newton wrote the July 18th letter in response to an article explaining that Appellees were looking for a theme song for the TV Series. He enclosed tapes of his music with the letter, stating "I would love to have the chance to write some music or songs for the show . . . ." Newton admitted that he intentionally failed to disclose his objections to the use of his name because he wanted to sell a song and hoped to get special consideration. Appellees used two of Newton's songs in the TV Series but rejected his proposed theme song. After Newton learned, in December 1990, that Appellees had decided not to buy his submitted theme song, he for the first time investigated his legal rights and objected to the use of his name.

To oppose Appellees' summary judgment motion, Newton submitted a declaration denying that the April 26, 1990 conversation took place and stating that, although he never objected, he also never consented to the use of his name. He explained that he did not object in part because he had mixed feelings about the idea: he wanted to see the actual use of his name and the compensation Appellees would provide him. His other alleged reasons for not objecting were that he did not even know until June or July 1990 that Appellees were going to use his name in the TV Series, and did not know until December that he had a legal right to object. He also stated that he never intended the July 18, 1990 letter to constitute consent or authorization to use his name. As evidence that Appellees never believed they had received consent, Newton presented a letter from MTM, Inc., dated October 2, 1990, which stated that "we should get a release from Wood Newton to use his name. . . ." CBS drafted an agreement that granted it the right to use Newton's name, but Newton refused to sign it.

Second, on the issue of commercial exploitation of Newton's name and identity, Appellees presented evidence that they never used the name "Wood Newton" to advertise or promote the TV Series or to sell any products or services. In newspaper announcements, for example, they merely mentioned the name "Wood Newton" as Burt Reynolds's character name.

Third, on the issue of likelihood of confusion, Appellees and Newton each described the similarities and differences between Newton and the TV Series character. Newton is a forty-five year old country music songwriter and performer. He grew up in a small Arkansas town and played high school football for a team coached by Thomason. His deceased father was named Obb Newton; Obb owned a local hardware store. Newton has been married for twenty years and has no children. He once moved from his hometown to a big city and currently lives in a different small town. The fictional Wood Newton character is a high school football coach and former pro football star who is married to a prominent attorney and has three children. He lives in a small Southern town that is modeled after Newton's (and Thomason's) hometown. His deceased father has the same name and occupation as did Newton's deceased father. At the root of his character are a dry sarcastic wit, a passion for the song "Blueberry Hill," and a lack of talent on the football team he coaches. In his declaration, Newton stated that people who he met for the first time asked him whether he took his name from Burt Reynolds's character.

Based on the submitted evidence, the district court granted summary judgment in favor of Appellees. The district court also sanctioned Newton's attorney Childress in the amount of $ 10,000 for filing Newton's complaint in the Illinois district court and denied Appellees' motion for attorneys' fees. Newton and Childress appeal and Appellees cross-appeal.

## ANALYSIS

### 1. Newton's Appeal of Summary Judgment

We review de novo the district court's grant of summary judgment. Smith v. Noonan, 992 F.2d 987, 989 (9th Cir. 1993). Viewing the evidence in the light most favorable to Newton, as the nonmoving party, we must determine whether there are any genuine issues of material fact and whether the district court correctly applied the relevant substantive law. Botefur v. City of Eagle Point, 7 F.3d 152, 154 (9th Cir. 1993).

### A. Applicable State and Federal Law

Because the case was transferred under 28 U.S.C. § 1404(a) from the Northern District of Illinois, we apply the choice-of-law rules of Illinois. Muldoon v. Tropitone Furniture Co., 1 F.3d 964, 965 (9th Cir. 1993) (citing Van Dusen v. Barrack, 376 U.S. 612, 642, 11 L. Ed. 2d 945, 84 S. Ct. 805 (1964), for the requirement that the transferee court follow the choice of law rules of the transferor court).

Illinois choice of law requires that we apply California law to Newton's state tort law right of publicity and unfair competition claims. Illinois uses the "most significant contacts" test to determine the applicable law in a tort case. Muldoon, 1 F.3d at 966 (citing Ingersoll v. Klein, 46 Ill. 2d 42, 262 N.E.2d 593, 596 (1970)). This test balances four factors: (1) the place where the injury occurred; (2) the place where the conduct occurred; (3) the parties' domicile, nationality, place of incorporation and place of business; and (4) the place where the parties' relationship is centered. Anabaldi v. Sunbeam Corp., 651 F. Supp. 1343, 1344 (N.D. Ill. 1987) (quoting Ingersoll, 262 N.E.2d at 596). [1460] In this case, the injury (broadcasting and advertising the TV Series with Newton's name) occurred nationally. (Answer, p. 4). The conduct by Appellees (making the TV Series) occurred in California. Newton is domiciled in Tennessee, Thomason and Bloodworth are domiciled in California, and Burt Reynolds is domiciled in Florida. Among the corporate defendants, Mozark Productions, Inc. and MTM Enterprises, Inc. are California corporations, and CBS, Inc. is a New York corporation. The parties' relationship was centered in California: Newton communicated with Appellees by letters and phone calls to California, making California the place "where their spheres of activity intersected." Anabaldi, 651 F. Supp. at 1345. Based on this test, the Illinois district court would have been required to apply California law to Newton's state tort claims, and we therefore do the same.

As to Newton's federal claim under the Lanham Act, we must decide whether to apply the law of our circuit or the law of the Seventh Circuit. Had the case remained in Illinois, the federal district court there would have been required to apply Seventh Circuit law. But our circuit has not decided whether, in cases involving transfer of a federal claim, the transferee court is required to apply precedent that binds the transferor court. In resolving this issue, we are persuaded by the approach taken by the D.C. Circuit in In re Korean Air Lines Disaster, 265 U.S. App. D.C. 39, 829 F.2d 1171 (D.C. Cir. 1987), aff'd on other grounds sub nom. Chan v. Korean Air Lines, Ltd., 490 U.S. 122, 104 L. Ed. 2d 113, 109 S. Ct. 1676 (1989). There, in resolving an identical question under 28 U.S.C. § 1407, the D.C. Circuit correctly pointed out that "binding precedent for all [courts] is set only by the Supreme Court, and for the district courts within a circuit, only by the court of appeals for that circuit [in the absence of Supreme Court authority]." In re Korean Air Lines Disaster, 829 F.2d at 1176 (holding that "the law of a transferor forum on a federal question . . . does not have stare decisis effect in a transferee forum situated in another circuit"). Accord Eckstein v. Balcor Film Investors, 8 F.3d 1121, 1126 (7th Cir. 1993) (after a transfer of a federal claim under 28 U.S.C. § 1404(a), transferee court normally should use its own judgment about the meaning of federal law), cert. denied, 127 L. Ed. 2d 78, 114 S. Ct. 883 (1994). We therefore hold that, when reviewing federal claims, a transferee court in this circuit is bound only by our circuit's precedent. Accordingly, we will apply our law to interpret the Lanham Act claim.

### B. Newton's State Law Misappropriation Claims

Newton contends that summary judgment was improper because there are genuine issues of material fact on two elements of his common law right of publicity claim and his statutory appropriation claim. First, he challenges the district court's finding that he undisputedly consented to the use of his name in the TV Series. Second, he argues that a genuine issue of material fact exists on whether Appellees used his name for a commercial purpose.

Viewing the evidence in the light most favorable to Newton, we still disagree with him that consent is a disputed issue. Even though, as Appellees conceded, Newton did not consent orally to the use of his name, we doubt that any fair-minded jury could find non-consent based on Newton's July 18, 1990 letter and subsequent conduct. In the letter, Newton said he was flattered that Appellees were using his name: "Everyone I've talked to thinks it's exciting and so do I." By his own deposition testimony, Newton admitted that he did not expect Thomason to believe he objected to the use of his name. Appellees went ahead with the TV Series and committed themselves to using Newton's name. Newton spoke with Thomason on several occasions in the ensuing months and never even hinted that he objected to the use of his name. He did not object until December 1990, when Appellees rejected his proposed theme song, even though he knew by May or June 1990 that they planned to use his name. Nor does the fact that a lawyer, out of caution, requested a writing from Newton stating, "I consent" mean that Appellees did not believe they had Newton's consent - recall that even Newton did not expect them to believe he objected. Although Newton never uttered the words "I consent," it is obvious that he did consent. There is no material issue of fact regarding consent.

An additional defect in Newton's state law misappropriation claims was his failure to offer sufficient evidence, in response to the motion for summary judgment, to support his general allegation that Appellees used his name for a commercial purpose. See Fed. R. Civ. P. 56(e) (party opposing summary judgment must set forth specific facts showing a genuine issue for trial and may not rest upon allegations in pleading). We recognize that California courts have liberally defined commercial purpose to include more than traditional, direct advertising. E.g., Eastwood v. Superior Court, 149 Cal. App. 3d 409, 421-22, 198 Cal. Rptr. 342 (1983) (Eastwood sufficiently alleged commercial exploitation where the National Enquirer printed his picture on the magazine cover with a sexy story title to attract consumers' attention and provide a commercial advantage over competitor publications.).

Nonetheless, commercial purpose means more than merely using a person's name as part of a cast of characters in a television program advertisement that highlights the program's general plot. In this case, Appellees did no more than use the name "Wood Newton" in the text of newspaper articles announcing Burt Reynolds's debut as a character in the TV Series. Nothing indicated that Reynolds's character name was the same as Newton's name or that the fictional character in the TV Series in any way resembled Newton. Based on the evidence before the court on summary judgment, it is clear that any commercial advantage that Appellees gained by these advertisements was totally unrelated to Newton's notoriety as a country/western music performer. See T.J. Hooker v. Columbia Pictures Indus., 551 F. Supp. 1060, 1062 (N.D. Ill. 1982) (no evidence that defendants adopted plaintiff's name for a television police drama to avail themselves of his reputation as an extraordinary woodcarver). We affirm summary judgment on Newton's state law misappropriation claims.

### C. Newton's Unfair Competition Claim Under The Lanham Act

Newton contends that a genuine issue of material fact exists on the likelihood of confusion between Newton and the TV Series character. We disagree. Mere possibility that a consumer may be misled by Appellees' use of the name "Wood Newton" is not enough to establish a cause of action for unfair competition. In opposition to the motion for summary judgment, Newton failed to offer proof of a likelihood that customers may be confused as to the source or endorsement for the TV Series.

We arrive at our conclusion by applying the following factors relevant to a determination of likelihood of confusion: "(1) strength of the plaintiff's mark; (2) relatedness of the goods; (3) similarity of the marks; (4) evidence of actual confusion; (5) marketing channels used; (6) likely degree of purchaser care; (7) defendant's intent in selecting the mark; (8) likelihood of expansion of the product lines." White v. Samsung Electronics America, Inc., 971 F.2d 1395, 1400 (9th Cir. 1992) (citing AMF, Inc. v. Sleekcraft Boats, 599 F.2d 341, 348-49 (9th Cir. 1979)), cert. denied, 113 S. Ct. 2443.

Applying these factors, none of the evidence before the court on summary judgment supports a finding of likelihood of confusion in this case. First, "in cases involving confusion over endorsement by a celebrity plaintiff, 'mark' means the celebrity's persona[, and] . . . the 'strength' of the mark refers to the level of recognition the celebrity enjoys among members of society." White, 971 F.2d at 1400 (citations omitted). Newton's work is limited to writing songs for country/western music and performing in certain Southern states. By his own declaration, he showed only that his name is known and recognized within the country/western music industry. Newton in no way showed name recognition broad enough to cover those viewers in all sections of the country to whom Appellees direct the TV Series and its advertisements. In the overall scheme of things, given the limited appeal of his work and considering the evidence before the court on summary judgment, Newton's "mark" is not strong.

Second, for evaluating the relatedness of the goods, Newton's "goods" are "the reasons for or source of [his] fame." Id. Newton's fame is based on country/western music songwriting and performing. These are completely unrelated to the TV Series, which is Appellees' "goods."

The third factor is the similarity of the marks. Both parties agree that Newton's name is identical to the fictional character's name. Still, Newton's "persona" is very different from that of the fictional character, as discussed supra. Newton responds that the differences between himself and the fictional character actually add to the confusion. In fact, the differences only underscore the improbability that viewers may believe that Newton endorses the TV Series or is in any way associated with the TV Series or the fictional character.

Fourth, there was no relevant evidence of actual confusion before the court on summary judgment. In his declaration, Newton stated that people who he met for the first time asked him whether he took his eccentric name from the Burt Reynolds character. Even if we assume that viewers erroneously believe that Newton appropriated his name from the TV Series, their confusion is irrelevant to his unfair competition claim. As Appellees correctly point out, such proof does not show that any of Newton's fans has actually been confused about whether he is affiliated with the TV Series or whether the TV Series is based on his name or life. To establish unfair competition, Newton should have presented evidence that confusion by consumers impairs his reputation and career as a professional country/western songwriter and performer. He presented no such evidence.

Fifth, the evidence before the court on summary judgment shows that the marketing channels used by Newton and Appellees are different. Newton markets his musical talents by advertising live and tape-recorded performances; most live performances occur in Southern states. Appellees, on the other hand, market the TV Series on a nationwide television network and in newspapers around the country, making it available to every television viewer and many newspaper readers in the country.

The sixth factor is the likely degree of purchaser care. Although viewers of the TV Series may not be particularly careful in determining who endorses the program, we doubt that they would actually believe that a fictional character's name represents the endorser's name. In this case, viewers are likely to perceive the fictional character as no more than a fictional character.

The seventh factor is defendant's intent in selecting the mark. To raise an inference of a likelihood of confusion, Newton must show that, in selecting his name, Appellees "intended to profit by confusing consumers." Toho Co. v.

Sears, Roebuck & Co., 645 F.2d 788, 791 n.2 (9th Cir. 1981) (emphasis in original). Newton presented no evidence that Appellees intended to profit by confusing viewers into believing that Newton, the songwriter and performer, was affiliated with the TV Series.

Eighth, there is no likelihood that Appellees will expand into Newton's market. Appellees' TV Series does not compete with Newton's music. The fact that the TV Series concerns life in a small Southern town does not persuade us, as Newton urges, that its viewers are interested in country/western music or that Newton will lose fans due to the program's success.

2. Appeal by Newton and Childress Of Sanctions Order

We review for abuse of discretion the district court's order imposing sanctions under Fed. R. Civ. P. 11. Cooter & Gell v. Hartmarx Corp., 496 U.S. 384, 405, 110 L. Ed. 2d 359, 110 S. Ct. 2447 (1990); United States v. Borneo, Inc., 971 F.2d 244, 248 (9th Cir. 1992). A district court abuses its discretion in imposing sanctions when it bases its decision "on an erroneous view of the law or on a clearly erroneous assessment of the evidence." Cooter & Gell, 496 U.S. at 405.

Rule 11 requires that an attorney sign a pleading, motion, or other paper, only if, "to the best of [the attorney's] knowledge, information and belief formed after reasonable inquiry[,] it is well grounded in fact and is warranted by existing law or a good faith argument for the extension, modification, or reversal of existing law, and . . . is not interposed for any improper purpose, such as to harass or to cause unnecessary delay or needless increase in the cost of litigation." Fed. R. Civ. P. 11. "The central purpose of Rule 11 is to deter baseless filings." Borneo, Inc., 971 F.2d at 254 (citing Cooter & Gell, 496 U.S. at 393). A court may not impose sanctions where the attorney "conducted a reasonable inquiry and . . . determined that any papers filed with the court are well-grounded in fact, legally tenable, and not interposed for some improper purpose." Id. (reversing sanctions where claim was legally tenable); Greenberg v. Sala, 822 F.2d 882, 886-87 (9th Cir. 1987) (reversing sanctions where factual errors did not render plaintiff's complaint factually frivolous); Zaldivar v. City of Los Angeles, 780 F.2d 823, 834-35 (9th Cir. 1986) (reversing sanctions where successive filings did not amount to harassment), abrogated on other grounds, 496 U.S. 384, 110 L. Ed. 2d 359, 110 S. Ct. 2447 (1990).

We conclude that the district court abused its discretion by sanctioning Newton's attorney Childress in the amount of $ 10,000 for an "unnecessary and frivolous" choice of venue. In its Order, the district court explained that Childress had no good faith justification for filing the lawsuit in Illinois because, even though venue was proper, Newton's suit was only tenuously connected to Illinois. Admittedly, only one expert witness resides in Illinois, and no parties live or have their principle place of business in Illinois. However, as each Appellee conceded in the Answer to Newton's Complaint, the injury (broadcasting the TV Series) occurred in all districts, including the Northern District of Illinois, making venue proper in any district where a defendant may be found. Attorneys are not under an affirmative obligation to file an action in the most convenient forum; their only obligation is to file in a proper forum.

We hold that filing in an inconvenient but proper forum is not a legitimate ground for Rule 11 sanctions. The choice of an inconvenient forum is sanctionable only where the choice is made for an "improper purpose" such as harassment. We reject Appellees' attempt to characterize the Illinois filing as harassment: To constitute harassment, conduct "must do more than in fact bother, annoy or vex the complaining party. Harassment under Rule 11 focuses upon the improper purpose of the signer, objectively tested, rather than the consequences of the signer's act, subjectively viewed by the signer's opponent." Zaldivar, 780 F.2d at 831-32 (emphasis added). Because there is no evidence of improper purpose, we reverse the sanctions order.

3. Appellees' Cross-Appeal

Appellees contend, in relevant part, that the district court erred by failing to grant their motion for attorneys' fees under Cal. Civil Code § 3344(a) or the Lanham Act. Because the same issues underpin all of Newton's claims, Appellees seek an award of all attorneys' fees incurred to defend the case (a total of $ 140,297.00).

Section 35 of the Lanham Act permits a court to award reasonable attorney fees to the prevailing party only "in exceptional cases." 15 U.S.C. § 1117(a). We disagree that this is an "exceptional case" warranting an award under the Lanham Act.

Cal. Civil Code § 3344(a) provides that "the prevailing party in any action under this section shall also be entitled to attorneys' fees and costs." We remand to the district court to determine a proper fee award under Cal. Civil Code § 3344(a).

AFFIRMED as to summary judgment; REVERSED as to sanctions order; REMANDED as to attorney fee award.

Muller v. Walt Disney Prods.
United States District Court for the Southern District of New York
January 17, 1994, Decided ; January 24, 1994, Docketed
93 Civ. 0427 (GLG), 93 Civ. 6175 (GLG)
876 F. Supp. 502

## MEMORANDUM DECISION

The cases before us in this motion arose from a 1939 contract between Leopold Stokowski, then the conductor of the Philadelphia Orchestra, and Walt Disney Productions, entered into for the purpose of making the beautiful music that accompanied the movie "Fantasia." Somewhat surprisingly, "Fantasia" was not a financial success upon its initial release. However, "Fantasia's" fall 1991 release on videocassette and laser disc has been profitable, to the tune of $ 190 million, according to Stokowski's estate. This event turned relations between Disney and various participants in the making of "Fantasia" discordant, leading to several different lawsuits, including those before us today. The instant motion to dismiss by Muller, the Executor under the Last Will and Testament of Leopold Stokowski, concerns claims by Disney for indemnification and a setoff from Stokowski's estate against possible judgments on behalf of the Philadelphia Orchestra Association and the publisher of Igor Stravinsky's "The Rite of Spring."

## PROCEDURAL HISTORY

In May 1992, the Philadelphia Orchestra Association (hereafter the "Association") filed suit against Disney in the Eastern District of Pennsylvania. See The Philadelphia Orchestra Ass'n v. The Walt Disney Co., No. 92 Civ. 2634 (E.D. Pa.) (McGlynn, J.) On December 30, 1992 Disney filed suit against Muller, also in the Eastern District of Pennsylvania, seeking a declaration that Stokowski's estate has no rights in connection with the sale and distribution of "Fantasia," and that Stokowski's estate must indemnify Disney for any sums adjudged against Disney in the Association's lawsuit. See The Walt Disney Co. v. Muller, No. 92 Civ. 7440 (E.D. Pa.) (McGlynn, J.).

In January 1993, Muller sued Disney in the Southern District of New York. See [504] Muller v. Disney, No. 93 Civ. 0427 (S.D.N.Y.) (Goettel, J.). The apparent reason Muller sued in this district is that Stokowski's will was probated in the Westchester County Surrogate's Court. (While he died in England in 1977, Stokowski lived out his life as a domiciliary of Scarsdale, New York.) Muller's Amended Complaint seeks, inter alia, fifty percent of Disney's profits from home sales of "Fantasia." Disney filed a motion in this court in February 1993 seeking to transfer Muller v. Disney to the Eastern District of Pennsylvania, or in the alternative, to stay the action pending resolution of Disney v. Muller. On May 26, 1993, we denied Disney's motion. See Muller v. The Walt Disney Productions, 822 F. Supp. 1033 (S.D.N.Y. 1993). On July 20, 1993, Judge McGlynn granted Muller's motion to transfer Disney v. Muller to this district.

The other related lawsuit against Disney is Boosey & Hawkes Music Publishers, Ltd. v. The Walt Disney Co., No. 93 Civ. 0373 (S.D.N.Y.) (Conboy, J.), in which the publishers of Igor Stravinsky's "The Rite of Spring," which was featured in "Fantasia," are seeking damages on the grounds that a 1939 license did not grant Disney the right to exploit "The Rite of Spring" on videocassette.

## FACTS

Muller's motion seeks to dismiss various Disney claims for failure to state a claim under which relief can be granted, and as time barred. The first object of Muller's motion is Disney's claim, embodied in Count II of the complaint in Disney v. Muller, and the first counterclaim in Muller v. Disney, that Stokowski's estate must indemnify Disney against sums awarded to the Association because Stokowski was contractually obligated to deliver to Disney an agreement between the Orchestra and Disney providing that the Orchestra and its members would retain no rights in connection with "Fantasia." Disney's second counterclaim in Muller v. Disney seeks, on the same grounds, to set off any sums awarded to the Association against any sums awarded to Stokowski's estate.

The basis for this claim is a contract dated January 18, 1939 between Leopold Stokowski and Walt Disney Productions, engaging Stokowski's services in arranging, conducting, and consulting on the music for the motion picture "Fantasia." Clause 6 provides in part:

You [Stokowski] agree to use your best efforts, at your own expense, to obligate the Philadelphia Symphony Orchestra Association, Inc. to do said recording. You further agree to furnish us [Disney] with a written commitment executed by the properly constituted and empowered authority, granting us the right to use the said Philadelphia Symphony Orchestra, its name and the music rendered by it hereunder for the purposes herein provided and contemplated in this contract.

The second object of Muller's motion to dismiss is Disney's claim, set forth in the second and third counterclaims in Muller v. Disney, that since the Association and Stravinsky's publisher are after the same videocassette and laser disc profits that Stokowski's estate is pursuing, any award in favor of the Association or Stravinsky's publisher must be set off against any award for Stokowski's estate. Disney points out that both the Association and Stokowski's estate seek to split the profits with Disney "fifty-fifty," and that all three suits against Disney seek a sum equal to any unjust enrichment by Disney. A setoff, Disney argues, is the proper mechanism for avoiding inconsistent judgments.

## DISCUSSION

### 1. Choice of Law

The initial question is which state's laws we must apply. The well-established rule is that a federal court sitting in diversity follows the choice of law rules of the state in which it is located. Klaxon Co. v. Stentor Electric Mfg. Co., 313 U.S. 487, 85 L. Ed. 1477, 61 S. Ct. 1020 (1941). Since Muller began his action against Disney in New York, we apply New York's choice of law rules. However, since Disney began its action against Muller in the Eastern District of Pennsylvania, and the action was subsequently transferred to our district pursuant to 28 U.S.C. 1404(a) after a motion by Muller, we must apply Pennsylvania's choice of law rules in Disney's action. Van Dusen v. Barrack, 376 U.S. 612, 11 L. Ed. 2d 945, 84 S. Ct. 805 (1964).

New York courts apply a "paramount interest" test to choice of law disputes involving contract issues. Hutner v. Greene, 734 F.2d 896, 899 (2d Cir. 1984). "Under such a test, 'the law of the jurisdiction having the greatest interest in the litigation will be applied and ... the facts or contacts which obtain significance in defining State interests are those which relate to the purpose of the particular law in conflict.'" Id. (citations omitted). Pennsylvania courts apply a combination of "interest analysis" and the "significant relationship" approach of the Restatement Second of Conflicts of Law to choice of law disputes involving contract issues. Melville v. American Home Assurance Co., 584 F.2d 1306, 1311 (3d Cir. 1978). This approach "takes into account both the grouping of contacts with the various concerned jurisdictions and the interests and policies that may validly be asserted by each jurisdiction." Id.

Under these similar approaches, the most likely candidates to supply the governing law in this case are California and Pennsylvania. The central issue is the relationship between Stokowski and Disney, as embodied in the 1939 contract. The contract was executed in California, and performed largely in Pennsylvania. At the time the contract was signed, as well as at the present, Disney had its principal place of business in Burbank, California. Stokowski, we were informed at oral argument, lived in many different places around the United States during this period, including California and Pennsylvania. We need not choose between California and Pennsylvania for purposes of this motion, since under either state's laws, the outcome is the same.

### 2. Indemnification

We begin with a brief discussion of ripeness. Whether a question is ripe for adjudication "turns on 'the fitness of the issues for judicial decision' and 'the hardship to the parties of withholding court consideration.'" Pacific Gas and

Electric Co. v. State Energy Resources Conservation and Development Comm'n, 461 U.S. 190, 201, 75 L. Ed. 2d 752, 103 S. Ct. 1713 (1983) (quoting Abbott Laboratories v. Gardner, 387 U.S. 136, 149, 18 L. Ed. 2d 681, 87 S. Ct. 1507 (1967)). Since Disney has not yet, and may never, incur the liability to the Association for which it seeks indemnification, the possibility of unripeness must be considered.

Indeed, in another case in this district in which the defendant raised a counterclaim demanding that the plaintiff provide indemnification or contribution against a claim asserted by a nonparty, the counterclaim was dismissed as unripe. See Allied Roofers Supply Corp. v. Jervin Construction, Inc., 675 F. Supp. 130, 133 (S.D.N.Y. 1987). However, the result in that case rested largely on the fact that the issue of indemnification could not be determined without knowing more about the nonparty claim. Id. In the instant case, by contrast, we already have all the information we need to adjudicate Disney's demands for indemnification. Following Disney's pleadings, the issue turns on our interpretation of the 1939 contract between Disney and Stokowski, and the general relationship between Disney and Stokowski. The exact nature of the liability between Disney and the Association will not add anything that is necessary to our determination today. Therefore, we find that Disney's claims for indemnification are ripe for adjudication.

In deciding whether Disney's claims for indemnification and a setoff should be dismissed pursuant to Federal Rule of Civil Procedure 12(b)(6), we accept all factual allegations in Disney's pleadings as true, and draw all reasonable inferences in the favor of Disney. Frazier v. Coughlin, 850 F.2d 129, 129 (2d Cir. 1988). We can only dismiss where "it appears beyond doubt that plaintiff can prove no set of facts in support of his claim which would entitled him to relief." Conley v. Gibson, 355 U.S. 41, 45, 2 L. Ed. 2d 80, 78 S. Ct. 99 (1957).

The first issue is whether Stokowski's 1939 contract with Disney created an express duty to indemnify. Disney's pleadings suggest such a claim, although in their motion papers they argue only for the existence of an implied duty to indemnify. Nevertheless, we will briefly consider the express terms of the contract.

Clause 6, in which Stokowski agrees to furnish a written commitment "granting [Disney] the right to use the said Philadelphia Symphony Orchestra, its name and the music rendered by it hereunder for the purposes herein provided and contemplated in this contract," contains nothing which even remotely suggests an express duty to indemnify. Furthermore, the statement in clause 7 providing that "you [Stokowski] agree to hold us harmless from and against any and all liability for or on account of the payment of any salary to musicians" shows that the parties knew how to create an express indemnification provision. Since they did not create such a provision with respect to Stokowski's agreement to deliver a contract between the Orchestra and Disney, the only reasonable conclusion is that they did not intend to do so.

Disney has argued, however, that clause 6 of the contract created an implied duty on the part of Stokowski to indemnify Disney. Disney argues that since Stokowski had a contractual duty to deliver a contract between Disney and the Orchestra, and since it was foreseeable that if he did not obtain the requisite approvals from the Orchestra Disney could be obliged to pay damages for unauthorized use, therefore Stokowski has an implied duty to indemnify Disney against any such damages.

California law recognizes two varieties of implied indemnification, both rooted in equitable considerations. Implied indemnification can arise by "contractual language not specifically dealing with indemnification or by the equities of the particular case." E.L. White, Inc. v. City of Huntington Beach, 21 Cal. 3d 497, 506-07, 579 P.2d 505, 507, 146 Cal. Rptr. 614, 619 (Cal. 1978) (en banc).

The doctrine of comparative equitable indemnity is applied to multiple tortfeasors and is designed to apportion loss among tortfeasors in proportion to their relative culpability ?. Implied contractual indemnity is applied to contract parties and is designed to apportion loss among contract parties based on the concept that one who enters a contract agrees to perform the work carefully and to discharge foreseeable damages resulting from that breach.

Smoketree-Lake Murray Ltd. v. Mills Concrete Construction Co., 234 Cal. App. 3d 1724, 1736, 286 Cal. Rptr. 435, 441 (Cal. Ct. App. 1991) (citations omitted). In this case, Disney argues that Stokowski's allegedly implied duty to indemnify is contractual. Although there is apparently some dispute in California concerning the continued validity of the theory of implied contractual indemnity, see Seamen's Bank for Savings v. Superior Court, 190 Cal. App. 3d 1485, 1493, 236 Cal. Rptr. 31, 36 (Cal. Ct. App. 1987), this is not relevant to our decision, since we do not find the doctrine applicable to the facts as alleged by Disney.

A case often cited by courts employing a theory of implied contractual indemnity is Ryan Stevedoring Co. v. Pan-Atlantic S.S. Corp., 350 U.S. 124, 100 L. Ed. 133, 76 S. Ct. 232 (1956) (superseded by statute). See Peoples' Democratic Republic of Yemen v. Goodpasture, Inc., 782 F.2d 346, 351 (2d Cir. 1986); Bear Creek Planning Committee v. Title Insurance & Trust Co., 164 Cal. App. 3d 1227, 1237, 211 Cal. Rptr. 172, 178 (Cal. Ct. App. 1985); San Francisco Unified School District v. California Building Maintenance Co., 162 Cal. App. 2d 434, 447-48, 328 P.2d 785, 793-94 (Cal. Ct. App. 1958). In Ryan, the Supreme Court found that a stevedoring contractor was obliged to indemnify a shipowner against damages suffered by a longshoreman as a result of the stevedoring contractor's improper stowage of cargo. The Supreme Court declared that "competency and safety of stowage" are "of the essence of petitioner's stevedoring contract." 350 U.S. at 133.

Disney's pleadings lend no support to the conclusion that there was anything special about the contractual relationship between Stokowski and Disney that would warrant implying a contract for indemnification against the Orchestra's claims that Disney has violated their rights. Certainly, delivering an airtight agreement between the Orchestra and Disney was not the "essence" of the contractual relationship between Disney and Stokowski. Stokowski was a conductor, not a lawyer. Nor do Disney's pleadings lend any support to the argument that a claim by the Orchestra for a share of videocassette and laser disc sales was a reasonably foreseeable result of Stokowski's alleged failure to deliver an airtight agreement between the Orchestra and Disney. In short, Disney has made no allegations about the contractual relationship between Stokowski and Disney that could support a finding of implied contractual indemnity.

The result is the same under Pennsylvania law. Pennsylvania courts have repeatedly stated that the right of indemnity "enures to a person who, without active fault on his own part, has been compelled, by reason of some legal obligation, to pay damages occasioned by the initial negligence of another, and for which he himself is only secondarily liable." Vattimo v. Lower Bucks Hospital, Inc., 502 Pa. 241, 250-51, 465 A.2d 1231, 1236 (Pa. 1983) (quoting Builders Supply Co. v. McCabe, 366 Pa. 322, 77 A.2d 368 (Pa. 1951)). This is a tort-based theory of implied indemnification, which is clearly inapposite in this case, since Disney has not alleged that Stokowski was negligent towards the Orchestra.

The parties have not presented us with any cases in Pennsylvania which apply an implied contract theory of indemnification. Disney has cited Borough of Wilkinsburg v. Trumbull-Denton Joint Venture, 390 Pa. Super. 580, 568 A.2d 1325 (Pa. Super. Ct.), appeal denied, 526 Pa. 626, 584 A.2d 310 (Pa. 1990), but this is an insurance case revolving around subrogation, rather than indemnification. If an implied contract theory of indemnification does exist in Pennsylvania, it would not apply to this case for the reasons stated in connection with the law of California.

Muller also argues that Disney's claim for implied indemnification is time-barred. We do not reach this issue, since we find that Disney has not properly pled a claim for implied indemnification.

In sum, we find that Disney has failed to state a claim for either express or implied indemnification.

3. Setoff

Disney argues that it is entitled to a counterclaim "in the nature of a set-off" of any sums adjudged against it in the Association's suit, or in Stravinsky's publisher's suit, against any sums adjudged against it in Stokowski's estate's suit. Disney grounds this argument in arguments about fairness, rather than in any specific caselaw. Disney argues that all three suits are after the same money - the profits from the videocassette and laser disc sales of "Fantasia" - and that the only way to avoid inconsistent judgments is through a setoff. Stokowski's estate argues that the three suits are based on separate contracts and thus a judgment in one should not affect a judgment in another. Disney responds by pointing out that the suits have non-contractual claims as well, such as unjust enrichment, which are all after the same pot of profits from videocassette and laser disc sales of "Fantasia."

While we are not unsympathetic to Disney's desire to avoid inconsistent judgments in the three afore-mentioned suits, we do not think that a counterclaim for a setoff is the proper legal mechanism.

The common law doctrine of setoff allows parties that owe mutual debts to each other to assert the amounts owed, subtract one from the other, and pay only the balance. Darr v. Muratore, 8 F.3d 854, 1993 WL 433726 (1st Cir. 1993); Matter of Bevill Bresler & Schulman Asset Management, 896 F.2d 54, 57 (3d Cir. 1990); Kruger v. Wells Fargo Bank, 11 Cal. 3d 352, 362, 521 P.2d 441, 447, 113 Cal. Rptr. 449, 455 (Cal. 1974). In Pennsylvania, a setoff is similarly described as "a counter-claim demand which defendant holds against plaintiff, arising out of a transaction extrinsic of plaintiff's cause of action." M.N.C. Corp. v. Mount Lebanon Medical Center, Inc., 510 Pa. 490, 495, 509 A.2d 1256, 1259 (Pa. 1986) (citation omitted); accord Hill v. Port Authority Transit System of Allegheny County, 137 Pa. Commw. 132, 140, 585 A.2d 1129, 1133 (Pa. Commw. Ct. 1991), aff'd, 531 Pa. 457, 613 A.2d 1206 (Pa. 1992).

Regardless of the exact wording, the doctrine of setoff requires that the two parties involved have mutual demands or debts. In the instant case, Disney is seeking to offset demands by three separate parties against it. We know of no cases applying the doctrine of setoff in such a situation. The doctrine of setoff was formulated for the convenience of two opposing parties owing mutual debts, and in order to avoid unnecessarily bankrupting a party. It is not a mechanism for avoiding inconsistent judgments among three or more parties.

### CONCLUSION

Summing up, we found (i) that Disney's pleadings cannot support their claim that Stokowski's estate must indemnify Disney for possible sums adjudged against Disney in the Philadelphia Orchestra Association's lawsuit; and (ii) that Disney's claims that sums adjudged against it in the Association's lawsuit and in the lawsuit of Stravinsky's publisher should be set off against sums adjudged against it in Stokowski'S estate's lawsuit do not state a valid cause of action. We therefore grant Muller's motion to dismiss Disney's counterclaims in Muller v. Disney and count II of Disney's complaint in Disney v. Muller.

SO ORDERED.

---

*Muller*, of course, deals with Conductor Leopold Stokowski's contribution to Walt Disney's movie, Fantasia, by Leopold's estate. There are other lawsuits by the Orchestra Association and publishers of Igor Starvinsky's Right of Spring. The impetus of this lawsuit is Fantasia's release on videocassette and laser disc in the Fall of 1991, which was very profitable to the tune of $190 million. Here, the court holds that the estate of Stokowski does not have to indemnify Disney nor does it have to set-off against the Stravinsky and Association suits against the Estate's lawsuit.

In the following case of *Cream Records, Inc. v. Jos. Schlitz Brewing Co.*, 754 F.2d 826 (9th Cir. 1985), the court looks into Schlitz malt liquor's infringment on the "The Theme from Shaft." "To avoid unjust enrichment of Benton [the advertiser] as a result of its unlawful use of Cream's copyrighted music, the district court must assess a separate award of damages against Benton by making a reasonable approximation of the portion of Benton's profits due to the infringing music" (at 829).

Cream Records, Inc. v. Jos. Schlitz Brewing Co.
United States Court of Appeals for the Ninth Circuit
November 8, 1983, Argued and Submitted; February 25, 1985, Decided
No. 83-5713
754 F.2d 826

Appellant Cream sued appellees alleging that music in a TV commercial prepared by Benton and Bowles to advertise Schlitz beer infringed appellant's copyright on a popular rhythm and blues composition, "The Theme from Shaft."

The jury found infringement. By agreement of the parties the issue of damages was submitted to the court which awarded Cream a total of $17,000. Cream appealed.

## DAMAGES

Schlitz applied to Cream for a one-year license to use the Shaft theme music in its commercial. Cream quoted a fee of $100,000. (Cream conceded at trial, and the district court found, that the market value of such a license was $80,000.) After Schlitz failed to take a license, another manufacturer approached Cream for a license but withdrew when the Schlitz commercial was aired. There was testimony that use of a well-known popular song in a commercial destroys its value to other advertisers for that purpose.

The district court awarded Cream $12,000 in damages for loss of the license fee. The court reasoned that the value of a license for use of the entire song for a year was $80,000, that only a small portion of the song was actually used in the Schlitz commercial, and the reasonable value of a license for use of that portion was 15% of the value of a license to use the entire song.

The only evidence before the court was that unauthorized use of the Shaft theme music in Schlitz's commercial ended Cream's opportunity to license the music for this purpose. There was no evidence that Schlitz sought, or Cream was willing to grant, a license for use of less than the entire copyrighted work, that a license limited to the portion used in the commercial would have had less value, or that use limited to this portion would have had a less devastating effect upon Cream's opportunity to license to another. Since defendants' unauthorized use destroyed the value of the copyrighted work for this purpose, plaintiff was entitled to recover that value as damages. 3 Nimmer, The Law of Copyright, § 14.02 at 14-6 (1984).

**PROFITS**

17 U.S.C. § 504(b) (1982) provides that, in addition to actual damages suffered as a result of the infringement, the copyright owner is entitled to recover "any profits of the infringer that are attributable to the infringement and are not taken into account in computing the actual damages." The statute also defines and allocates the burden of proof, providing, "in establishing the infringer's profits, the copyright owner is required to present proof only of the infringer's gross revenue, and the infringer is required to prove his or her deductible expenses and the elements of profit attributable to factors other than the copyrighted work."

Schlitz. Cream offered proof that Schlitz's profit on malt liquor for the period during which the infringing commercial was broadcast was $4.876 million. Cream sought to recover $66,800 as the portion of Schlitz's profit attributable to the infringement, arguing that the expenditure for the infringing commercial constituted 13.7% of Schlitz's advertising budget for the year, the infringing music was responsible for 10% of the commercial's advertising power, and, therefore, 1.37% of the profit on malt liquor were attributable to the infringement.

The district court concluded that the infringement "was minimal," consisting principally of a ten-note ostinato, and that the infringing material did not add substantially to the value of the commercial. The court also concluded, however, that the commercial was successful, that "it sold some beer," and "that the music had a portion of that." The court continued, "So I have to find some profit of the defendants which is allocable to the infringement, but, as I say, I think it's miniscule. I have interpolated as best I can. They made a profit of $5 million. One-tenth of 1 percent is $5,000, so I will add that. . . ."

Cream argues that since it established Schlitz's total profits from the sale of malt liquor, the burden was placed on Schlitz to prove any portion of the profits not attributable to the infringement, and since the defendants put on no evidence, Cream was entitled to recover the part of Schlitz's profits it sought. The court's lesser award, Cream argues, was wholly arbitrary, and supported by no evidence in the record.

Defendants respond that Cream failed to establish that any part of the profits from the sale of malt liquor were attributable to the commercial, much less to its infringing portion, and was therefore entitled to no share of the profits at all. One of the court's formal findings, prepared by defendants, might be read as stating that no causal connection had been shown between the infringement and defendants' profits. It is clear from the court's statements, including those quoted above, however, that the court concluded from the jury's verdict and from the evidence that some of the profits from malt liquor sales were in fact attributable to the use of plaintiff's copyrighted music in the commercial. The court determined the share of the profits attributable to the infringing material as best it could and awarded Cream 1/10th of 1% of those profits. Defendants have not cross-appealed the judgment, and may not challenge the determination of causation upon which it rests.

We also reject Cream's contention. Although the statute imposes upon the infringer the burden of showing "the elements of profit attributable to factors other than the copyrighted work," 17 U.S.C. § 504(b), nonetheless where it is clear, as it is in this case, that not all of the profits are attributable to the infringing material, the copyright owner is not entitled to recover all of those profits merely because the infringer fails to establish with certainty the portion attributable to the non-infringing elements. "In cases such as this where an infringer's profits are not entirely due to [829] the infringement, and the evidence suggests some division which may rationally be used as a springboard it is the duty of the court to make some apportionment." Orgel v. Clark Boardman Co., 301 F.2d 119, 121 (2d Cir. 1962). As Learned Hand said in Sheldon v. Metro-Goldwyn Pictures Corp., 106 F.2d 45, 51, 42 U.S.P.Q. (BNA) 540 (2d Cir. 1939), aff'd, 309 U.S. 390, 84 L. Ed. 825, 60 S. Ct. 681 (1940):

But we are resolved to avoid the one certainly unjust course of giving the plaintiffs everything, because the defendants cannot with certainty compute their own share. In cases where plaintiffs fail to prove their damages exactly, we often make the best estimate we can, even though it is really no more than a guess (Pieczonka v. Pullman Co., 2 Cir., 102 F.2d 432, 434), and under the guise of resolving all doubts against the defendants we will not deny the one fact that stands undoubted.

By claiming only 1.37% of Schlitz's malt liquor profits, Cream recognizes the impropriety of awarding Cream all of Schlitz's profits on a record that reflects beyond argument that most of these profits were attributable to elements other than the infringement. As to the amount of profits attributable to the infringing material, "what is required is . . . only a reasonable approximation," Sheldon v. Metro-Goldwyn Pictures Corp., 309 U.S. at 408; see also Twentieth Century-Fox Film Corp. v. Stonesifer, 140 F.2d 579, 583-84 (9th Cir. 1944); MCA, Inc. v. Wilson, 677 F.2d 180, 186 (2d Cir. 1981), and Cream's calculation is in the end no less speculative than that of the court. The disparity between the amount sought by Cream and the amount awarded by the court appears to rest not so much upon a difference in methods of calculation as upon a disagreement as to the extent to which the commercial infringed upon the copyright and the importance of the copyrighted material to the effectiveness of the commercial. These were determinations for the district court to make.

The parties agreed that the issue of damages and profits would be tried to the court. The jury's verdict did not expressly determine the degree to which the commercial infringed upon Cream's copyright. The court's factual findings, though perhaps unfavorable to Cream, do not conflict with the general verdict. Cf. Blake v. Hall, 668 F.2d 52, 54 (1st Cir. 1981).

Benton. Cream claimed all of Benton's profit from the TV commercial; the district court awarded none at all. In announcing its judgment the court initially overlooked the claim against Benton. When alerted to the omission the court said, "I will somehow incorporate that into the profit that I awarded with respect to the company. I can't conceive of an award of more than the amount I gave. You can find Benton and Bowles' profit in there by reducing the amount of profit of the beer company."

Obviously it would be improper to assume the profits of the advertising company would be subsumed in the profits of the firm hiring it, if that was the court's intention. Indeed, the profits of the advertising firm were necessarily excluded from the award against the hiring company, since, under § 504(b), Schlitz must be allowed to deduct the monies paid to the advertising firm in calculating its profits.

To avoid unjust enrichment of Benton as a result of its unlawful use of Cream's copyrighted music, the district court must assess a separate award of damages against Benton by making a reasonable approximation of the portion of Benton's profits due to the use of the infringing music.

Plaintiff is awarded costs on appeal including reasonable attorney's fees in an amount to be determined by the district court.

Reversed and remanded for proceedings not inconsistent with this opinion.

———————

### Combined Synchronization and Master Use License Agreement

This Combined Synchronization and Master Use License Agreement ("License") is made and entered into this _____ day of _____, 2015, by and between ("Artist") and _____ ("Company").

**1. Picture:** The "Picture" is the motion picture being produced by the Company and tentatively entitled "_____".

**2. Territory and Term:** The Territory of this license is throughout the universe. The Term of this license is in perpetuity.

**3. Composition:** The "Composition" is entitled "_____" written by (Artist Name).

**4. Master:** The "Master" is the master recording of the Composition embodying the performance of the Artist.

**5. Grant of Rights:** Artist hereby irrevocably licenses and grants to Company the following perpetual and nonexclusive rights and licenses:

**a)** to record, arrange, dub, reproduce, perform, and synchronize the Composition and the Master, or any portion thereof, in the soundtrack of or in timed relation with the Picture;

**b)** to make copies of the Picture embodying the Composition and the Master, and to distribute, and to license and authorize others to distribute, such copies throughout the world in any medium or forum, whether now known or hereinafter created;

**c)** to utilize the Composition and the Master, or any portion thereof, for the purpose of advertising and promoting the Picture.

**6. Representations and Warranties:** Each party represents and warrants to the other that:

a) It is a corporation duly organized, validly existing and in good standing under the laws of its State of incorporation and has the corporate power and authority to execute, deliver and perform its obligation hereunder;

b) The execution, delivery and performance by such party of this Agreement do not and will not violate or result in any breach of any material contractual obligation of such party or require the consent, approval or authorization of any third party; and

c) This Agreement has been duly executed and delivered by such party and constitutes the legal valid and binding obligation of such party enforceable against such party in accordance with its terms, except as enforceability may be limited by applicable bankruptcy, insolvency or other similar laws affecting the enforcement of creditors' rights generally.

**7. Limitations:** The rights granted herein expressly do not include the right to record, arrange, reproduce, perform, distribute, or otherwise use or exploit either the Composition or the Master in any manner separately or independently of the production or marketing of the Picture. All rights not explicitly granted to the Company in this license are reserved exclusively by the Artist. Any use of either the Composition or the Master in a soundtrack album derived from the Picture shall be subject to a separate written agreement to be negotiated in good faith between the parties.

**8. Consideration:** In Consideration for the rights granted herein, the Company agrees to pay the Artist the sum of _____ United States dollars upon the execution of this agreement.

**9. Copy:** The Company shall provide the Artist with one (1) finished copy of the Picture in DVD or digital format.

**10. Credit:** Artist shall receive credit in the Picture in substantially the format:
Words and music by (Artist Name)
Performed by (Artist Name)
Copyright © 2008 (Artist Name)
Size and placement of the credit in the Picture shall be at the sole discretion of the Company.

**11. Cue sheet:** The Company agrees to prepare an accurate music cue sheet for the Picture and file the cue sheet with the Artist's performing rights society, with a copy provided to the Artist, within thirty (30) days after the completion of the Picture.

**12. Artist's Warranty:** Artist hereby represents and warrants that he is the author of the Composition, the owner of all rights granted herein, and has the full legal right, power and authority to grant this license.

**13. Attorney Review:** Artist represents and warrants that Artist has been advised of their right to retain Independent Legal Counsel, in connection with the negotiation and execution of this Agreement, and that Artist has either retained and has been represented by such Legal Counsel, or have knowingly and voluntarily waived Artist's right to such Legal Counsel, and desire to enter into this Agreement without the benefit of Legal Counsel.

Assignment: The rights granted herein shall insure to the benefit of the Company, its licensees, successors and assigns.

_____        _____
(Producer)                              Date

(address)_____
_____
_____


_____        _____
(Composer/Performer)                    Date

(address)_____
_____
_____

Questions and Discussion

1.  What are synchronization rights? Why are they so important?

2.  In *Agee*, Paramount created an audiovisual for Hard Copy that synchronized portions of a copyrighted recording to visual images showing two young men engaged in an unsuccessful burglary attempt. The court holds that this taped TV production infringes the copyright owner's exclusive right to reproduction under the Copyright Act. What if the two men were African Americans and the police officers were white, would that strengthen the court's decision?

3.  *Waits v. Frito-Lay* is a sound-alike case involving the use of Tom Waits' distinctive voice in a Frito-Lay TV ad. The ad gives the impression of his voice was purposeful. Does that make a difference, legally?

# Chapter 12
# Music in Cyberspace

"Cyberspace is the universe of information that is available from computer networks and is the connective tissue of society-at-large." (Walter Champion, Intellectual Property Law in the Sports and Entertainment Industries 193 (2014)). The question is, how is the artist going to get paid for the use of their intellectual property? "Intellectual property is of course old school, and the printed book (whatever that is) horse and buggy, but the information superhighway changes everything. These changes decide what we "must mark, appreciate; understand, and learn how to use those changes so as to deter and effectively pursue Internet copyright violators" (Id.).

"Between iTunes, Vcast, TiVo, PSP, Windows Media, cellular phones, public Wi-Fi, and available broadband internet access, the consumer is already well on the way towards multiplatform on-demand access to worldwide content" (Id., quoting Patrick Turner, "Digital Video Copyright Protection with File-Based Content," 16 Media L. & Pol. 165 (Summ. 2007)). "And let's not forget mobile entertainment and ringtones. The music business was significantly changed through the advent of digital technology. In the late 1980s, there was digital sampling to illegal Internet downloads accompanied by home copying, which was first done via blank cassettes and then by CD 'rippers' and "burners and file sharing over peer-to-peer exchange technologies" (Champion, Intellectual Property in the Sports and Entertainment Industries 193-94). "[T]he explosion of inexpensive high-quality cameras, microphones, musical instruments, sound-recording equipment, and personal-computer based editing systems. . . [coupled with] the demoralization of the means of distribution—the Internet broadband access, computer-based burning and printing of CDs and DVDs., . . and user-driven web applications such as YouTube, Flickr, and RSS . . . permit the distribution of video and other content to potentially huge audiences" (Id., at 194, quoting Erik Johnson, "Rethinking Sharing Licenses Entertainment Media, " 26 Cardozo Arts & Ent. L.J. 391, 393 (2008)).

"Digital media is the new frontier of music licensing" (Darren Wilsie and Daylle Deanna Schwartz, The Musician's Guide to Licensing Music 213 (N.Y. 2010)).

"It's obvious to say that the greatest need for music content nowadays is the web. . . web designers, new Web broadcasters, advertisers, corporations and new media teams are . . . examples of the growing music customers" (*Id.*, at 214, quoting Larry Mills, V.P., Pump Audio).

A&M Records v. Napster, Inc.
United States Court of Appeals for the Ninth Circuit
October 2, 2000; February 12, 2001, Filed
No. 00-16401, No. 00-16403
239 F.3d 1004

AMENDED OPINION

BEEZER, Circuit Judge:

Plaintiffs are engaged in the commercial recording, distribution and sale of copyrighted musical compositions and sound recordings. The complaint alleges that Napster, Inc. ("Napster") is a contributory and vicarious copyright infringer. On July 26, 2000, the district court granted plaintiffs' motion for a preliminary injunction. The injunction was slightly modified by written opinion on August 10, 2000. A&M Records, Inc. v. Napster, Inc., 114 F. Supp. 2d 896 (N.D. Cal. 2000). The district court preliminarily enjoined Napster "from engaging in, or facilitating others in copying, downloading, uploading, transmitting, or distributing plaintiffs' copyrighted musical compositions and sound recordings, protected by either federal or state law, without express permission of the rights owner." Id. at 927. Federal Rule of Civil Procedure 65(c) requires successful plaintiffs to post a bond for damages incurred by the enjoined party in the event that the injunction was wrongfully issued. The district court set bond in this case at $ 5 million.

We entered a temporary stay of the preliminary injunction pending resolution of this appeal. We have jurisdiction pursuant to 28 U.S.C. § 1292(a)(1). We affirm in part, reverse in part and remand.

I.

We have examined the papers submitted in support of and in response to the injunction application and it appears that Napster has designed and operates a system which permits the transmission and retention of sound recordings employing digital technology.

In 1987, the Moving Picture Experts Group set a standard file format for the storage of audio recordings in a digital format called MPEG-3, abbreviated as "MP3." Digital MP3 files are created through a process colloquially called" ripping." Ripping software allows a computer owner to copy an audio compact disk ("audio CD") directly onto a computer's hard drive by compressing the audio information on the CD into the MP3 format. The MP3's compressed format allows for rapid transmission of digital audio files from one computer to another by electronic mail or any other file transfer protocol.

Napster facilitates the transmission of MP3 files between and among its users. Through a process commonly called "peer-to-peer" file sharing, Napster allows its users to: (1) make MP3 music files stored on individual computer hard drives available for copying by other Napster users; (2) search for MP3 music files stored on other users' computers; and (3) transfer exact copies of the contents of other users' MP3 files from one computer to another via the Internet. These functions are made possible by Napster's MusicShare software, available free of charge from Napster's Internet site, and Napster's network servers and server-side software. Napster provides technical support for the indexing and searching of MP3 files, as well as for its other functions, including a "chat room," where users can meet to discuss music, and a directory where participating artists can provide information about their music.

### A. Accessing the System

In order to copy MP3 files through the Napster system, a user must first access Napster's Internet site and download the MusicShare software to his individual computer. See http://www.Napster.com. Once the software is installed, the user can access the Napster system. A first-time user is required to register with the Napster system by creating a "user name" and password.

### B. Listing Available Files

If a registered user wants to list available files stored in his computer's hard drive on Napster for others to access, he must first create a "user library" directory on his computer's hard drive. The user then saves his MP3 files in the library directory, using self-designated file names. He next must log into the Napster system using his user name and password. His MusicShare software then searches his user library and verifies that the available files are properly formatted. If in the correct MP3 format, the names of the MP3 files will be uploaded from the user's computer to the Napster servers. The content of the MP3 files remains stored in the user's computer.

Once uploaded to the Napster servers, the user's MP3 file names are stored in a server-side "library" under the user's name and become part of a "collective directory "of files available for transfer during the time the user is logged onto the Napster system. The collective directory is fluid; it tracks users who are connected in real time, displaying only file names that are immediately accessible.

C. Searching For Available Files

Napster allows a user to locate other users' MP3 files in two ways: through Napster's search function and through its "hotlist" function.

Software located on the Napster servers maintains a" search index" of Napster's collective directory. To search the files available from Napster users currently connected to the net-work servers, the individual user accesses a form in the MusicShare software stored in his computer and enters either the name of a song or an artist as the object of the search. The form is then transmitted to a Napster server and automatically compared to the MP3 file names listed in the server's search index. Napster's server compiles a list of all MP3 file names pulled from the search index which include the same search terms entered on the search form and transmits the list to the searching user. The Napster server does not search the contents of any MP3 file; rather, the search is limited to "a text search of the file names indexed in a particular cluster. Those file names may contain typographical errors or otherwise inaccurate descriptions of the content of the files since they are designated by other users." Napster, 114 F. Supp. 2d at 906.

To use the "hotlist" function, the Napster user creates a list of other users' names from whom he has obtained MP3 files in the past. When logged onto Napster's servers, the system alerts the user if any user on his list (a "hotlisted user") is also logged onto the system. If so, the user can access an index of all MP3 file names in a particular hotlisted user's library and request a file in the library by selecting the file name. The contents of the hotlisted user's MP3 file are not stored on the Napster system.

D. Transferring Copies of an MP3 file

To transfer a copy of the contents of a requested MP3 file, the Napster server software obtains the Internet address of the requesting user and the Internet address of the" host user" (the user with the available files). See generally Brookfield Communications, Inc. v. West Coast Entm't Corp., 174 F.3d 1036, 1044 (9th Cir. 1999) (describing, in detail, the structure of the Internet). The Napster servers then communicate the host user's Internet address to the requesting user. The requesting user's computer uses this information to establish a connection with the host user and downloads a copy of the contents of the MP3 file from one computer to the other over the Internet, "peer-to-peer." A downloaded MP3 file can be played directly from the user's hard drive using Napster's Music-Share program or other software. The file may also be transferred back onto an audio CD if the user has access to equipment designed for that purpose. In both cases, the quality of the original sound recording is slightly diminished by transfer to the MP3 format.

This architecture is described in some detail to promote an understanding of transmission mechanics as opposed to the content of the transmissions. The content is the subject of our copyright infringement analysis.

## II.

We review a grant or denial of a preliminary injunction for abuse of discretion. Gorbach v. Reno, 219 F.3d 1087, 1091 (9th Cir. 2000) (en banc). Application of erroneous legal principles represents an abuse of discretion by the district court. Rucker v. Davis, 237 F.3d 1113, 2001 WL 55724, at *4 (9th Cir. 2001) (en banc). If the district court is claimed to have relied on an erroneous legal premise in reaching its decision to grant or deny a preliminary injunction, we will review the underlying issue of law de novo. Id. at *4 (citing Does 1-5 v. Chandler, 83 F.3d 1150, 1152 (9th Cir. 1996)).

On review, we are required to determine, "whether the court employed the appropriate legal standards governing the issuance of a preliminary injunction and whether the district court correctly apprehended the law with respect to the underlying issues in the case." Id. "As long as the district court got the law right, 'it will not be reversed simply because the appellate court would have arrived at a different result if it had applied the law to the facts of the case.'" Gregorio T. v. Wilson, 59 F.3d 1002, 1004 (9th Cir. 1995) (quoting Sports Form, Inc. v. United Press, Int'l, 686 F.2d 750, 752 (9th Cir. 1982)).

Preliminary injunctive relief is available to a party who demonstrates either: (1) a combination of probable success on the merits and the possibility of irreparable harm; or (2) that serious questions are raised and the balance of hardships tips in its favor. Prudential Real Estate Affiliates, Inc. v. PPR Realty, Inc., 204 F.3d 867, 874 (9th Cir. 2000)." These two formulations represent two points on a sliding scale in which the required degree of irreparable harm increases as the probability of success decreases." Id.

## III.

Plaintiffs claim Napster users are engaged in the wholesale reproduction and distribution of copyrighted works, all constituting direct infringement. The district court agreed. We note that the district court's conclusion that plaintiffs have presented a prima facie case of direct infringement by Napster users is not presently appealed by Napster. We only need briefly address the threshold requirements.

A. Infringement

Plaintiffs must satisfy two requirements to present a prima facie case of direct infringement: (1) they must show ownership of the allegedly infringed material and (2) they must demonstrate that the alleged infringers violate at least one exclusive right granted to copyright holders under 17 U.S.C. § 106. See 17 U.S.C. § 501(a) (infringement occurs when alleged infringer engages in activity listed in § 106); see also Baxter v. MCA, Inc., 812 F.2d 421, 423 (9th Cir. 1987); see, e.g., S.O.S., Inc. v. Payday, Inc., 886 F.2d 1081, 1085 n.3 (9th Cir. 1989) ("The word 'copying' is shorthand for the infringing of any of the copyright owner's five exclusive rights. . . ."). Plaintiffs have sufficiently demonstrated ownership. The record supports the district court's determination that "as much as eighty-seven percent of the files available on Napster may be copyrighted and more than seventy percent may be owned or administered by plaintiffs." Napster, 114 F. Supp. 2d at 911.

The district court further determined that plaintiffs' exclusive rights under § 106 were violated:" here the evidence establishes that a majority of Napster users use the service to download and upload copyrighted music. . . . And by doing that, it constitutes—the uses constitute direct infringement of plaintiffs' musical compositions, recordings." A&M Records, Inc. v. Napster, Inc., Nos. 99-5183, 00-0074, 2000 WL 1009483, at *1 (N. D. Cal. July 26, 2000) (transcript of proceedings). The district court also noted that "it is pretty much acknowledged . . . by Napster that this is infringement." Id. We agree that plaintiffs have shown that Napster users infringe at least two of the copyright holders' exclusive rights: the rights of reproduction, § 106(1); and distribution, 4229 § 106(3). Napster users who upload file names to the search index for others to copy violate plaintiffs' distribution rights. Napster users who download files containing copyrighted music violate plaintiffs' reproduction rights.

Napster asserts an affirmative defense to the charge that its users directly infringe plaintiffs' copyrighted musical compositions and sound recordings.

B. Fair Use

Napster contends that its users do not directly infringe plaintiffs' copyrights because the users are engaged in fair use of the material. See 17 U.S.C. § 107 ("The fair use of a copyrighted work … is not an infringement of copyright."). Napster identifies three specific alleged fair uses: sampling, where users make temporary copies of a work before purchasing; space-shifting, where users access a sound recording through the Napster system that they already own in audio CD format; and permissive distribution of recordings by both new and established artists.

The district court considered factors listed in 17 U.S.C. § 107, which guide a court's fair use determination. These factors are: (1) the purpose and character of the use; (2) the nature of the copyrighted work; (3) the "amount and substantiality of the portion used" in relation to the work as a whole; and (4) the effect of the use upon the potential market for the work or the value of the work. See 17 U.S.C. § 107. The district court first conducted a general analysis of Napster system uses under § 107, and then applied its reasoning to the alleged fair uses identified by Napster. The district court concluded that Napster users are not fair users. We agree. We first address the court's overall fair use analysis.

1. Purpose and Character of the Use

This factor focuses on whether the new work merely replaces the object of the original creation or instead adds a further purpose or different character. In other words, this factor asks "whether and to what extent the new work is 'transformative. '"See Campbell v. Acuff-Rose Music, Inc., 510 U.S. 569, 579, 127 L. Ed. 2d 500, 114 S. Ct. 1164 (1994).

The district court first concluded that downloading MP3 files does not transform the copyrighted work. Napster, 114 F. Supp. 2d at 912. This conclusion is supportable. Courts have been reluctant to find fair use when an original work is merely retransmitted in a different medium. See, e.g., Infinity Broadcast Corp. v. Kirkwood, 150 F.3d 104, 108 (2d Cir. 1994) (concluding that retransmission of radio broadcast over telephone lines is not transformative); UMG Recordings, Inc. v. MP3. com, Inc., 92 F. Supp. 2d 349, 351 (S.D.N.Y.) (finding that reproduction of audio CD into MP3 format does not "transform" the work), certification denied, 2000 U.S. Dist. LEXIS 7439, 2000 WL 710056 (S.D.N.Y. June 1, 2000) ("Defendant's copyright infringement was clear, and the mere fact that it was clothed in the exotic webbing of the Internet does not disguise its illegality.").

This "purpose and character "element also requires the district court to determine whether the allegedly infringing use is commercial or noncommercial. See Campbell, 510 U.S. at 584-85. A commercial use weighs against a finding of fair use but is not conclusive on the issue. Id. The district court determined that Napster users engage in commercial use of the copyrighted materials largely because (1) "a host user sending a file cannot be said to engage in a personal use when distributing that file to an anonymous requester "and (2) "Napster users get for free something they would ordinarily have to buy." Napster, 114 F. Supp. 2d at 912. The district court's findings are not clearly erroneous.

Direct economic benefit is not required to demonstrate a commercial use. Rather, repeated and exploitative copying of copyrighted works, even if the copies are not offered for sale, may constitute a commercial use. See Worldwide Church of God v. Philadelphia Church of God, 227 F.3d 1110, 1118

(9th Cir. 2000) (stating that church that copied religious text for its members "unquestionably profited" from the unauthorized "distribution and use of [the text] without having to account to the copyright holder"); American Geophysical Union v. Texaco, Inc., 60 F.3d 913, 922 (2d Cir. 1994) (finding that researchers at for-profit laboratory gained indirect economic advantage by photocopying copyrighted scholarly articles). In the record before us, commercial use is demonstrated by a showing that repeated and exploitative unauthorized copies of copyrighted works were made to save the expense of purchasing authorized copies. See Worldwide Church, 227 F.3d at 1117-18; Sega Enters. Ltd. v. MAPHIA, 857 F. Supp. 679, 687 (N.D. Cal. 1994) (finding commercial use when individuals downloaded copies of video games "to avoid having to buy video game cartridges"); see also American Geophysical, 60 F.3d at 922. Plaintiffs made such a showing before the district court.

We also note that the definition of a financially motivated transaction for the purposes of criminal copyright actions includes trading infringing copies of a work for other items, "including the receipt of other copyrighted works." See No Electronic Theft Act ("NET Act"), Pub. L. No. 105-147, 18 U.S.C. § 101 (defining "Financial Gain").

2. The Nature of the Use

Works that are creative in nature are "closer to the core of intended copyright protection" than are more fact-based works. See Campbell, 510 U.S. at 586. The district court determined that plaintiffs' "copyrighted musical compositions and sound recordings are creative in nature . . .which cuts against a finding of fair use under the second factor." Napster, 114 F. Supp. 2d at 913. We find no error in the district court's conclusion.

3. The Portion Used

"While 'wholesale copying does not preclude fair use per se, 'copying an entire work 'militates against a finding of fair use.'" Worldwide Church, 227 F.3d at 1118 (quoting Hustler Magazine, Inc. v. Moral Majority, Inc., 796 F.2d 1148, 1155 (9th Cir. 1986)). The district court determined that Napster users engage in "wholesale copying" of copyrighted work because file transfer necessarily "involves copying the entirety of the copyrighted work." Napster, 114 F. Supp. 2d at 913. We agree. We note, however, that under certain circumstances, a court will conclude that a use is fair even when the protected work is copied in its entirety. See, e.g., Sony Corp. v. Universal City Studios, Inc., 464 U.S. 417, 449-50, 78 L. Ed. 2d 574, 104 S. Ct. 774 (1984) (acknowledging that fair use of time-shifting necessarily involved making a full copy of a protected work).

4. Effect of Use on Market

"Fair use, when properly applied, is limited to copying by others which does not materially impair the marketability of the work which is copied." Harper & Row Publishers, Inc. v. Nation Enters., 471 U.S. 539, 566-67, 85 L. Ed. 2d 588, 105 S. Ct. 2218 (1985)."The importance of this [fourth] factor will vary, not only with the amount of harm, but also with the relative strength of the showing on the other factors." Campbell, 510 U.S. at 591 n.21. The proof required to demonstrate present or future market harm varies with the purpose and character of the use:

A challenge to a noncommercial use of a copy-righted work requires proof either that the particular use is harmful, or that if it should become wide-spread, it would adversely affect the potential market for the copyrighted work. … If the intended use is for commercial gain, that likelihood [of market harm] may be presumed. But if it is for a noncommercial purpose, the likelihood must be demonstrated.

Sony, 464 U.S. at 451 (emphases added).

Addressing this factor, the district court concluded that Napster harms the market in "at least" two ways: it reduces audio CD sales among college students and it "raises barriers to plaintiffs' entry into the market for the digital downloading of music." Napster, 114 F. Supp. 2d at 913. The district court relied on evidence plaintiffs submitted to show that Napster use harms the market for their copyrighted musical compositions and sound recordings. In a separate memorandum and order regarding the parties' objections to the expert reports, the district court examined each report, finding some more appropriate and probative than others. A&M Records, Inc. v. Napster, Inc., 114 F. Supp. 2d 896, 2000 WL 1170106 (N.D. Cal. 2000). Notably, plaintiffs' expert, Dr. E. Deborah Jay, conducted a survey (the "Jay Report") using a random sample of college and university students to track their reasons for using Napster and the impact Napster had on their music purchases. Id. at *2. The court recognized that the Jay Report focused on just one segment of the Napster user population and found "evidence of lost sales attributable to college use to be probative of irreparable harm for purposes of the preliminary injunction motion." 114 F. Supp. 2d at 923, Id. at *3.

Plaintiffs also offered a study conducted by Michael Fine, Chief Executive Officer of Soundscan, (the "Fine Report") to determine the effect of online sharing of MP3 files in order to show irreparable harm. Fine found that online file sharing had resulted in a loss of "album" sales within college markets. After reviewing defendant's objections to the Fine Report and expressing some concerns regarding the methodology and findings, the district court refused to exclude the Fine Report insofar as plaintiffs offered it to show irreparable harm. Id. at *6.

Plaintiffs' expert Dr. David J. Teece studied several issues ("Teece Report"), including whether plaintiffs had suffered or were likely to suffer harm in their existing and planned businesses due to Napster use. Id. Napster objected that the report had not undergone peer review. The district court noted that such reports generally are not subject to such scrutiny and overruled defendant's objections. Id.

As for defendant's experts, plaintiffs objected to the report of Dr. Peter S. Fader, in which the expert concluded that Napster is beneficial to the music industry because MP3 music file-sharing stimulates more audio CD sales than it displaces. Id. at *7. The district court found problems in Dr. Fader's minimal role in overseeing the administration of the survey and the lack of objective data in his report. The court decided the generality of the report rendered it "of dubious reliability and value." The court did not exclude the report, however, but chose "not to rely on Fader's findings in determining the issues of fair use and irreparable harm." 114 F. Supp. 2d at 912, Id. at *8.

The district court cited both the Jay and Fine Reports in support of its finding that Napster use harms the market for plaintiffs' copyrighted musical compositions and sound recordings by reducing CD sales among college students. The district court cited the Teece Report to show the harm Napster use caused in raising barriers to plaintiffs' entry into the market for digital downloading of music. Napster, 114 F. Supp. 2d at 910. The district court's careful consideration of defendant's objections to these reports and decision to rely on the reports for specific issues demonstrates a proper exercise of discretion in addition to a correct application of the fair use doctrine. Defendant has failed to show any basis for disturbing the district court's findings.

We, therefore, conclude that the district court made sound findings related to Napster's deleterious effect on the present and future digital download market. Moreover, lack of harm to an established market cannot deprive the copyright holder of the right to develop alternative markets for the works. See L.A. Times v. Free Republic, 2000 U.S. Dist. LEXIS 5669, 54 U.S.P.Q.2D (BNA) 1453, 1469-71 (C.D. Cal. 2000) (stating that online market for plaintiff newspapers' articles was harmed because plaintiffs demonstrated that "[defendants] are attempting to exploit the market for viewing their articles online"); see also UMG Recordings, 92 F. Supp. 2d at 352 (" Any allegedly positive impact of defendant's activities on plaintiffs' prior market in no way frees defendant to usurp a further market that directly derives from reproduction of the plaintiffs' copyrighted works."). Here, similar to L.A. Times and UMG Recordings, the record supports the district court's finding that the "record company plaintiffs have already expended considerable funds and effort to commence Internet sales and licensing for digital downloads." 114 F. Supp. 2d at 915. Having digital downloads available for free on the Napster system necessarily harms the copyright holders' attempts to charge for the same downloads.

Judge Patel did not abuse her discretion in reaching the above fair use conclusions, nor were the findings of fact with respect to fair use considerations clearly erroneous. We next address Napster's identified uses of sampling and space-shifting.

5. Identified Uses

Napster maintains that its identified uses of sampling and space-shifting were wrongly excluded as fair uses by the district court.

a. Sampling

Napster contends that its users download MP3 files to "sample" the music in order to decide whether to purchase the recording. Napster argues that the district court: (1) erred in concluding that sampling is a commercial use because it conflated a noncommercial use with a personal use; (2) erred in determining that sampling adversely affects the market for plaintiffs' copyrighted music, a requirement if the use is non-commercial; and (3) erroneously concluded that sampling is not a fair use because it determined that samplers may also engage in other infringing activity.

The district court determined that sampling remains a commercial use even if some users eventually purchase the music. We find no error in the district court's determination. Plaintiffs have established that they are likely to succeed in proving that even authorized temporary downloading of individual songs for sampling purposes is commercial in nature. See Napster, 114 F. Supp. 2d at 913. The record supports a finding that free promotional downloads are highly regulated by the record company plaintiffs and that the companies collect royalties for song samples available on retail Internet sites. Id. Evidence relied on by the district court demonstrates that the free downloads provided by the record companies consist of thirty-to-sixty second samples or are full songs programmed to "time out," that is, exist only for a short time on the downloader's computer. Id. at 913-14. In comparison, Napster users download a full, free and permanent copy of the recording. Id. at 914-15. The determination by the district court as to the commercial purpose and character of sampling is not clearly erroneous.

The district court further found that both the market for audio CDs and market for online distribution are adversely affected by Napster's service. As stated in our discussion of the district court's general fair use analysis: the court did not abuse its discretion when it found that, overall, Napster has an adverse impact on the audio CD and digital download markets. Contrary to Napster's assertion that the district court failed to specifically address the market impact of sampling, the district court determined that "even if the type of sampling supposedly done on Napster were a non-commercial use, plaintiffs have demonstrated a substantial likelihood that it would adversely affect the potential market for their copy-righted works if it became widespread." Napster, 114 F. Supp. 2d at 914. The record supports the district court's preliminary determinations that: (1) the more music that sampling users download, the less likely they are to eventually purchase the recordings on audio CD; and (2) even if the audio CD market is not harmed, Napster has adverse effects on the developing digital download market.

Napster further argues that the district court erred in rejecting its evidence that the users' downloading of" samples" increases or tends to increase audio CD sales. The district court, however, correctly noted that "any potential enhancement of plaintiffs' sales . . . would not tip the fair use analysis conclusively in favor of defendant." Id. at 914. We agree that increased sales of copyrighted material attributable to unauthorized use should not deprive the copyright holder of the right to license the material. See Campbell, 510 U.S. at 591 n.21 ("Even favorable evidence, without more, is no guarantee of fairness. Judge Leval gives the example of the film producer's appropriation of a composer's previously unknown song that turns the song into a commercial success; the boon to the song does not make the film's simple copying fair."); see also L.A. Times, 54 U.S.P.Q.2D (BNA) at 1471-72. Nor does positive impact in one market, here the audio CD market, deprive the copyright holder of the right to develop identified alternative markets, here the digital download market. See 54 U.S.P.Q.2D (BNA) at 1469-71. [1019]

We find no error in the district court's factual findings or abuse of discretion in the court's conclusion that plaintiffs will likely prevail in establishing that sampling does not constitute a fair use.

b. Space-Shifting

Napster also maintains that space-shifting is a fair use. Space-shifting occurs when a Napster user downloads MP3 music files in order to listen to music he already owns on audio CD. See 114 F. Supp. 2d at 915-16. Napster asserts that we have already held that space-shifting of musical compositions and sound recordings is a fair use. See Recording Indus. Ass'n of Am. v. Diamond Multimedia Sys., Inc., 180 F.3d 1072, 1079 (9th Cir. 1999) ("Rio [a portable MP3 player] merely makes copies in order to render portable, or 'space-shift, 'those files that already reside on a user's hard drive. . . . Such copying is a paradigmatic noncommercial personal use."). See also generally Sony, 464 U.S. at 423 (holding that" time-shifting," where a video tape recorder owner records a television show for later viewing, is a fair use).

We conclude that the district court did not err when it refused to apply the "shifting" analyses of Sony and Diamond. Both Diamond and Sony are inapposite because the methods of shifting in these cases did not also simultaneously involve distribution of the copyrighted material to the general public; the time or space-shifting of copyrighted material exposed the material only to the original user. In Diamond, for example, the copyrighted music was transferred from the user's computer hard drive to the user's portable MP3 player. So too Sony, where "the majority of VCR purchasers . . . did not distribute taped television broadcasts, but merely enjoyed them at home." Napster, 114 F. Supp. 2d at 913. Conversely, it is obvious that once a user lists a copy of music he already owns on the Napster system in order to access the music from another location, the song becomes "available to millions of other individuals," not just the original CD owner. See UMG Recordings, 92 F. Supp. 2d at 351-52 (finding spaceshifting of MP3 files not a fair use even when previous ownership is demonstrated before a download is allowed); cf. Religious Tech. Ctr. v. Lerma, 1996 U.S. Dist. LEXIS 15454, No. 95-1107 A, 1996 WL 633131, at *6 (E. D. Va. Oct. 4, 1996) (suggesting that storing copyrighted material on computer disk for later review is not a fair use).

### c. Other Uses

Permissive reproduction by either independent or established artists is the final fair use claim made by Napster. The district court noted that plaintiffs did not seek to enjoin this and any other noninfringing use of the Napster system, including: chat rooms, message boards and Napster's New Artist Program. Napster, 114 F. Supp. 2d at 917. Plaintiffs do not challenge these uses on appeal.

We find no error in the district court's determination that plaintiffs will likely succeed in establishing that Napster users do not have a fair use defense. Accordingly, we next address whether Napster is secondarily liable for the direct infringement under two doctrines of copyright law: contributory copyright infringement and vicarious copyright infringement.

## IV.

We first address plaintiffs' claim that Napster is liable for contributory copyright infringement. Traditionally, "one who, with knowledge of the infringing activity, induces, causes or materially contributes to the infringing conduct of another, may be held liable as a 'contributory' infringer." Gershwin Publ'g Corp. v. Columbia Artists Mgmt., Inc., 443 F.2d 1159, 1162 (2d Cir. 1971); see also Fonovisa, Inc. v. Cherry Auction, Inc., 76 F.3d 259, 264 (9th Cir. 1996). Put differently, liability exists if the defendant engages in "personal conduct that encourages or assists the infringement." Matthew Bender & Co. v. West Publ'g Co., 158 F.3d 693, 706 (2d Cir. 1998).

The district court determined that plaintiffs in all likelihood would establish Napster's liability as a contributory infringer. The district court did not err; Napster, by its conduct, knowingly encourages and assists the infringement of plaintiffs' copyrights.

### A. Knowledge

Contributory liability requires that the secondary infringer "know or have reason to know" of direct infringement. Cable/ Home Communication Corp. Network Prods., Inc., 902 F.2d 829, 845 & 846 n. 29 (11th Cir. 1990); Religious Tech. Ctr. v. Netcom On-Line Communication Servs., Inc., 907 F. Supp. 1361, 1373-74 (N. D. Cal. 1995) (framing issue as" whether Netcom knew or should have known of" the infringing activities). The district court found that Napster had both actual and constructive knowledge that its users exchanged copyrighted music. The district court also concluded that the law does not require knowledge of "specific acts of infringement" and rejected Napster's contention that because the company cannot distinguish infringing from noninfringing files, it does not "know" of the direct infringement. 114 F. Supp. 2d at 917.

It is apparent from the record that Napster has knowledge, both actual and constructive, of direct infringement. Napster claims that it is nevertheless protected from contributory liability by the teaching of Sony Corp. v. Universal City Studios, Inc., 464 U.S. 417, 78 L. Ed. 2d 574, 104 S. Ct. 774 (1984). We disagree. We observe that Napster's actual, specific knowledge of direct infringement renders Sony's holding of limited assistance to Napster. We are compelled to make a clear distinction between the architecture of the Napster system and Napster's conduct in relation to the operational capacity of the system.

The Sony Court refused to hold the manufacturer and retailers of video tape recorders liable for contributory infringement despite evidence that such machines could be and were used to infringe plaintiffs' copyrighted television shows. Sony stated that if liability "is to be imposed on petitioners in this case, it must rest on the fact that they have sold equipment with constructive knowledge of the fact that their customers may use that equipment to make unauthorized copies of copy-righted material." Id. at 439 (emphasis added). The Sony Court declined to impute the requisite level of knowledge where the defendants made and sold equipment capable of both infringing and "substantial noninfringing uses." Id. at 442 (adopting a modified "staple article of commerce" doctrine from patent law). See also Universal City Studios, Inc. v. Sony Corp., 480 F. Supp. 429, 459 (C. D. Cal. 1979) ("This court agrees with defendants that their knowledge was insufficient to make them contributory infringers."), rev'd, 659 F.2d 963 (9th Cir. 1981), rev'd, 464 U.S. 417, 78 L. Ed. 2d 574, 104 S. Ct. 774 (1984); Alfred C. Yen, Internet Service Provider Liability for Subscriber Copyright Infringement, Enterprise Liability, and the First Amendment, 88 Geo. L.J. 1833, 1874 & 1893 n. 210 (2000) (suggesting that, after Sony, most Internet service providers lack "the requisite level of knowledge" for the imposition of contributory liability).

We are bound to follow Sony, and will not impute the requisite level of knowledge to Napster merely because peer-to-peer file sharing technology may be used to infringe plaintiffs' copyrights. See 464 U.S. at 436 (rejecting argument that merely supplying the "'means' to accomplish an infringing activity" leads to imposition of liability). We depart from the reasoning of the district court that Napster failed to demonstrate that its system is capable of commercially significant noninfringing uses. See Napster, 114 F. Supp. 2d at 916, 917-18. The district court improperly confined the use analysis to current uses, ignoring the system's capabilities. See generally Sony, 464 U.S. at 442-43 (framing inquiry as whether the video tape recorder is "capable of commercially significant noninfringing uses") (emphasis added). Consequently, the district court placed undue weight on the proportion of current infringing use as compared to current and future noninfringing use. See generally Vault Corp. v. Quaid Software Ltd., 847 F.2d 255, 264-67 (5th Cir. 1997) (single noninfringing use implicated Sony). Nonetheless, whether we might arrive at a different result is not the issue here. See Sports Form, Inc. v. United Press Int'l, Inc., 686 F.2d 750, 752 (9th Cir. 1982). The instant appeal occurs at an early point in the proceedings and "the fully developed factual record may be materially different from that initially before the district court. ..." Id. at 753. Regardless of the number of Napster's infringing versus noninfringing uses, the evidentiary record here supported the district court's finding that plaintiffs would likely prevail in establishing that Napster knew or had reason to know of its users' infringement of plaintiffs' copyrights.

This analysis is similar to that of Religious Technology Center v. Netcom On-Line Communication Services, Inc., which suggests that in an online context, evidence of actual knowledge of specific acts of infringement is required to hold a computer system operator liable for contributory copyright infringement. 907 F. Supp. at 1371. Netcom considered the potential contributory copyright liability of a computer bulletin board operator whose system supported the posting of infringing material. Id. at 1374. The court, in denying Netcom's motion for summary judgment of noninfringement and plaintiff's motion for judgment on the pleadings, found that a disputed issue of fact existed as to whether the operator had sufficient knowledge of infringing activity. Id. at 1374-75.

The court determined that for the operator to have sufficient knowledge, the copyright holder must "provide the necessary documentation to show there is likely infringement." 907 F. Supp. at 1374; cf. Cubby, Inc. v. Compuserve, Inc., 776 F. Supp. 135, 141 (S.D.N.Y. 1991) (recognizing that online service provider does not and cannot examine every hyperlink for potentially defamatory material). If such documentation was provided, the court reasoned that Netcom would be liable for contributory infringement because its failure to remove the material "and thereby stop an infringing copy from being distributed worldwide constitutes substantial participation" in distribution of copyrighted material. Id.

We agree that if a computer system operator learns of specific infringing material available on his system and fails to purge such material from the system, the operator knows of and contributes to direct infringement. See Netcom, 907 F. Supp. at 1374. Conversely, absent any specific information which identifies infringing activity, a computer system operator cannot be liable for contributory infringement merely because the structure of the system allows for the exchange of copyrighted material. See Sony, 464 U.S. at 436, 442-43. To enjoin simply because a computer network allows for infringing use would, in our opinion, violate Sony and potentially restrict activity unrelated to infringing use.

We nevertheless conclude that sufficient knowledge exists to impose contributory liability when linked to demonstrated infringing use of the Napster system. See Napster, 114 F. Supp. 2d at 919 ("Religious Technology Center would not mandate a determination that Napster, Inc. lacks the knowledge requisite to contributory infringement."). The record supports the district court's finding that Napster has actual knowledge that specific infringing material is available using its system, that it could block access to the system by suppliers of the infringing material, and that it failed to remove the material. See Napster, 114 F. Supp. 2d at 918, 920-21.

### B. Material Contribution

Under the facts as found by the district court, Napster materially contributes to the infringing activity. Relying on Fonovisa, the district court concluded that "without the support services defendant provides, Napster users could not find and download the music they want with the ease of which defendant boasts." Napster, 114 F. Supp. 2d at 919-20 ("Napster is an integrated service designed to enable users to locate and download MP3 music files."). We agree that Napster provides "the site and facilities" for direct infringement. See Fonovisa, 76 F.3d at 264; cf. Netcom, 907 F. Supp. at 1372 ("Netcom will be liable for contributory infringement since its failure to cancel [a user's] infringing message and thereby stop an infringing copy from being distributed world-wide constitutes substantial participation."). The district court correctly applied the reasoning in Fonovisa, and properly found that Napster materially contributes to direct infringement.

We affirm the district court's conclusion that plaintiffs have demonstrated a likelihood of success on the merits of the contributory copyright infringement claim. We will address the scope of the injunction in part VIII of this opinion.

### V.

We turn to the question whether Napster engages in vicarious copyright infringement. Vicarious copyright liability is an "outgrowth" of respondeat superior. Fonovisa, 76 F.3d at 262. In the context of copyright law, vicarious liability extends beyond an employer/employee relationship to cases in which a defendant "has the right and ability to supervise the infringing activity and also has a direct financial interest in such activities." Id. (quoting Gershwin, 443 F.2d at 1162); see also Polygram Int'l Publ'g, Inc. v. Nevada/TIG, Inc., 855 F. Supp.

1314, 1325-26 (D. Mass. 1994) (describing vicarious liability as a form of risk allocation).

Before moving into this discussion, we note that Sony's "staple article of commerce" analysis has no application to Napster's potential liability for vicarious copyright infringement. See Sony, 464 U.S. at 434-435; see generally 3 Melville B. Nimmer & David Nimmer, Nimmer On Copyright §§ 12.04[A][2] & [A][2][b] (2000) (confining Sony to contributory infringement analysis: "Contributory infringement itself is of two types —personal conduct that forms part of or furthers the infringement and contribution of machinery or goods that provide the means to infringe"). 617 PLI/Pat 455, 528 (Sept. 2, 2000) (indicating that the "staple article of commerce" doctrine "provides a defense only to contributory infringement, not to vicarious infringement"). The issues of Sony's liability under the "doctrines of 'direct infringement' and 'vicarious liability'" "were not before the Supreme Court, although the Court recognized that the "lines between direct infringement, contributory infringement, and vicarious liability are not clearly drawn." Id. at 435 n. 17. Consequently, when the Sony Court used the term "vicarious liability," it did so broadly and outside of a technical analysis of the doctrine of vicarious copyright infringement. Id. at 435 ("Vicarious liability is imposed in virtually all areas of the law, and the concept of contributory infringement is merely a species of the broader problem of identifying the circumstances in which it is just to hold one individual accountable for the actions of another."); see also Black's Law Dictionary 927 (7th ed. 1999) (defining "vicarious liability" in a manner similar to the definition used in Sony).

A. Financial Benefit

The district court determined that plaintiffs had demonstrated they would likely succeed in establishing that Napster has a direct financial interest in the infringing activity. Napster, 114 F. Supp. 2d at 921-22. We agree. Financial benefit exists where the availability of infringing material "acts as a 'draw' for customers." Fonovisa, 76 F.3d at 263-64 (stating that financial benefit may be shown "where infringing performances enhance the attractiveness of a venue"). Ample evidence supports the district court's finding that Napster's future revenue is directly dependent upon "increases in user-base." More users register with the Napster system as the "quality and quantity of available music increases." 114 F. Supp. 2d at 902. We conclude that the district court did not err in determining that Napster financially benefits from the availability of protected works on its system.

## B. Supervision

The district court determined that Napster has the right and ability to supervise its users' conduct. Napster, 114 F. Supp. 2d at 920-21 (finding that Napster's representations to the court regarding "its improved methods of blocking users about whom rights holders complain ... is tantamount to an admission that defendant can, and sometimes does, police its service"). We agree in part.

The ability to block infringers' access to a particular environment for any reason whatsoever is evidence of the right and ability to supervise. See Fonovisa, 76 F.3d at 262 ("Cherry Auction had the right to terminate vendors for any reason whatsoever and through that right had the ability to control the activities of vendors on the premises."); cf. Netcom, 907 F. Supp. at 1375-76 (indicating that plaintiff raised a genuine issue of fact regarding ability to supervise by presenting evidence that an electronic bulletin board service can suspend subscriber's accounts). Here, plaintiffs have demonstrated that Napster retains the right to control access to its system. Napster has an express reservation of rights policy, stating on its website that it expressly reserves the "right to refuse service and terminate accounts in [its] discretion, including, but not limited to, if Napster believes that user conduct violates applicable law ... or for any reason in Napster's sole discretion, with or without cause."

To escape imposition of vicarious liability, the reserved right to police must be exercised to its fullest extent. Turning a blind eye to detectable acts of infringement for the sake of profit gives rise to liability. See, e.g., Fonovisa, 76 F.3d at 261 (" There is no dispute for the purposes of this appeal that Cherry Auction and its operators were aware that vendors in their swap meets were selling counterfeit recordings."); see also Gershwin, 443 F.2d at 1161-62 (citing Shapiro, Bernstein & Co. v. H.L. Green Co., 316 F.2d 304 (2d Cir. 1963), for the proposition that "failure to police the conduct of the primary infringer" leads to imposition of vicarious liability for copyright infringement).

The district court correctly determined that Napster had the right and ability to police its system and failed to exercise that right to prevent the exchange of copyrighted material. The district court, however, failed to recognize that the boundaries of the premises that Napster "controls and patrols" are limited. See, e.g., Fonovisa, 76 F.3d at 262-63 (in addition to having the right to exclude vendors, defendant "controlled and patrolled" the premises); see also Polygram, 855 F. Supp. at 1328-29 (in addition to having the contractual right to remove exhibitors, trade show operator reserved the right to police during the show and had its "employees walk the  aisles to ensure 'rules compliance'"). Put differently, Napster's reserved "right and ability" to police is cabined by the system's current architecture. As shown by the record, the Napster system does not "read" the content of indexed files, other than to check that they are in the proper MP3 format.

Napster, however, has the ability to locate infringing material listed on its search indices, and the right to terminate users' access to the system. The file name indices, therefore, are within the "premises" that Napster has the ability to police. We recognize that the files are user-named and may not match copyrighted material exactly (for example, the artist or song could be spelled wrong). For Napster to function effectively, however, file names must reasonably or roughly correspond to the material contained in the files, otherwise no user could ever locate any desired music. As a practical matter, Napster, its users and the record company plaintiffs have equal access to infringing material by employing Napster's "search function."

Our review of the record requires us to accept the district court's conclusion that plaintiffs have demonstrated a likelihood of success on the merits of the vicarious copyright infringement claim. Napster's failure to police the system's "premises," combined with a showing that Napster financially benefits from the continuing availability of infringing files on its system, leads to the imposition of vicarious liability. We address the scope of the injunction in part VIII of this opinion.

## VI.

We next address whether Napster has asserted defenses which would preclude the entry of a preliminary injunction.

Napster alleges that two statutes insulate it from liability. First, Napster asserts that its users engage in actions protected by § 1008 of the Audio Home Recording Act of 1992, 17 U.S.C. § 1008. Second, Napster argues that its liability for contributory and vicarious infringement is limited by the Digital Millennium Copyright Act, 17 U.S.C. § 512. We address the application of each statute in turn.

### A. Audio Home Recording Act

The statute states in part:

No action may be brought under this title alleging infringement of copyright based on the manufacture, importation, or distribution of a digital audio recording device, a digital audio recording medium, an analog recording device, or an analog recording medium, or based on the noncommercial use by a consumer of such a device or medium for making digital musical recordings or analog musical recordings.

17 U.S.C. § 1008 (emphases added). Napster contends that MP3 file exchange is the type of "noncommercial use" protected from infringement

actions by the statute. Napster asserts it cannot be secondarily liable for users' nonactionable exchange of copyrighted musical recordings.

The district court rejected Napster's argument, stating that the Audio Home Recording Act is "irrelevant" to the action because: (1) plaintiffs did not bring claims under the Audio Home Recording Act; and (2) the Audio Home Recording Act does not cover the downloading of MP3 files. Napster, 114 F. Supp. 2d at 916 n. 19.

We agree with the district court that the Audio Home Recording Act does not cover the downloading of MP3 files to computer hard drives. First, "under the plain meaning of the Act's definition of digital audio recording devices, computers (and their hard drives) are not digital audio recording devices because their 'primary purpose' is not to make digital audio copied recordings." Recording Indus. Ass'n of Am. v. Diamond Multimedia Sys., Inc., 180 F.3d 1072, 1078 (9th Cir. 1999). Second, notwithstanding Napster's claim that computers are "digital audio recording devices," computers do not make "digital music recordings" as defined by the Audio Home Recording Act. Id. at 1077 (citing S. Rep. 102-294) ("There are simply no grounds in either the plain language of the definition or in the legislative history for interpreting the term 'digital musical recording' to include songs fixed on computer hard drives.").

B. Digital Millennium Copyright Act

Napster also interposes a statutory limitation on liability by asserting the protections of the "safe harbor "from copyright infringement suits for "Internet service providers" contained in the Digital Millennium Copyright Act, 17 U.S.C. § 512. See Napster, 114 F. Supp. 2d at 919 n. 24. The district court did not give this statutory limitation any weight favoring a denial of temporary injunctive relief. The court concluded that Napster "has failed to persuade this court that subsection 512(d) shelters contributory infringers." Id.

We need not accept a blanket conclusion that § 512 of the Digital Millennium Copyright Act will never protect secondary infringers. See S. Rep. 105-190, at 40 (1998) ("The limitations in subsections (a) through (d) protect qualifying service providers from liability for all monetary relief for direct, vicarious, and contributory infringement."), reprinted in Melville B. Nimmer & David Nimmer, Nimmer on Copyright: Congressional Committee Reports on the Digital Millennium Copyright Act and Concurrent Amendments (2000); see also Charles S. Wright, Actual Versus Legal Control: Reading Vicarious Liability for Copyright Infringement Into the Digital Millennium Copyright Act of 1998, 75 Wash. L. Rev. 1005, 1028-31 (July 2000) ("The committee reports leave no doubt that Congress intended to provide some relief from vicarious liability").

We do not agree that Napster's potential liability for contributory and vicarious infringement renders the Digital Millennium Copyright Act inapplicable per se. We instead recognize that this issue will be more fully developed at trial. At this stage of the litigation, plaintiffs raise serious questions regarding Napster's ability to obtain shelter under § 512, and plaintiffs also demonstrate that the balance of hardships tips in their favor. See Prudential Real Estate, 204 F.3d at 874; see also Micro Star v. Formgen, Inc. 154 F.3d 1107, 1109 (9th Cir. 1998) ("A party seeking a preliminary injunction must show . . . 'that serious questions going to the merits were raised and the balance of hardships tips sharply in its favor.'").

Plaintiffs have raised and continue to raise significant questions under this statute, including: (1) whether Napster is an Internet service provider as defined by 17 U.S.C. § 512(d); (2) whether copyright owners must give a service provider "official" notice of infringing activity in order for it to have 4252 knowledge or awareness of infringing activity on its system; and (3) whether Napster complies with § 512(i), which requires a service provider to timely establish a detailed copyright compliance policy. See A&M Records, Inc. v. Napster, Inc., No. 99-05183, 2000 WL 573136 (N. D. Cal. May 12, 2000) (denying summary judgment to Napster under a different subsection of the Digital Millennium Copyright Act, § 512(a)).

The district court considered ample evidence to support its determination that the balance of hardships tips in plaintiffs' favor:

Any destruction of Napster, Inc. by a preliminary injunction is speculative compared to the statistical evidence of massive, unauthorized downloading and uploading of plaintiffs' copyrighted works—as many as 10,000 files per second by defendant's own admission. See Kessler Dec. P29. The court has every reason to believe that, without a preliminary injunction, these numbers will mushroom as Napster users, and newcomers attracted by the publicity, scramble to obtain as much free music as possible before trial.

114 F. Supp. 2d at 926.

## VII.

Napster contends that even if the district court's preliminary determinations that it is liable for facilitating copyright infringement are correct, the district court improperly rejected valid affirmative defenses of waiver, implied license and copyright misuse. We address the defenses in turn.

### A. Waiver

"Waiver is the intentional relinquishment of a known right with knowledge of its existence and the intent to relinquish it." United States v. King Features Entm't, Inc., 843 F.2d 394, 399 (9th Cir. 1988). In copyright, waiver or abandonment of copyright "occurs only if there is an intent by the copyright proprietor to surrender rights in his work." 4 Melville B. Nimmer & David Nimmer, Nimmer On Copyright P 13.06 (2000); see also Micro Star v. Formgen, Inc., 154 F.3d 1107, 1114 (9th Cir. 1998) (discussing abandonment).

Napster argues that the district court erred in not finding that plaintiffs knowingly provided consumers with technology designed to copy and distribute MP3 files over the Internet and, thus, waived any legal authority to exercise exclusive control over creation and distribution of MP3 files. The district court, however, was not convinced "that the record companies created the monster that is now devouring their intellectual property rights." Napster, 114 F. Supp. 2d at 924. We find no error in the district court's finding that "in hastening the proliferation of MP3 files, plaintiffs did nothing more than seek partners for their commercial downloading ventures and develop music players for files they planned to sell over the Internet." Id.

### B. Implied License

Napster also argues that plaintiffs granted the company an implied license by encouraging MP3 file exchange over the Internet. Courts have found implied licenses only in" narrow" circumstances where one party "created a work at [the other's] request and handed it over, intending that [the other] copy and distribute it." SmithKline Beecham Consumer Healthcare, L.P. v. Watson Pharms., Inc., 211 F.3d 21, 25 (2d Cir. 2000) (quoting Effects Assocs., Inc. v. Cohen, 908 F.2d 555, 558 (9th Cir. 1990)), cert. denied, 121 S. Ct. 173 (2000). The district court observed that no evidence exists to support this defense: "indeed, the RIAA gave defendant express notice that it objected to the availability of its members' copy-righted music on Napster." Napster, 114 F. Supp. 2d at 924-25. The record supports this conclusion.

### C. Misuse

The defense of copyright misuse forbids a copyright holder from "securing an exclusive right or limited monopoly not granted by the Copyright Office." Lasercomb Am., Inc. v. Reynolds, 911 F.2d 970, 977-79 (4th Cir. 1990), quoted in Practice Mgmt. Info. Corp. v. American Med. Ass'n, 121 F.3d 516, 520 (9th Cir.), amended by 133 F.3d 1140 (9th Cir. 1997). Napster alleges that online distribution is not within the copyright monopoly. According to Napster, plaintiffs have colluded to "use their copyrights to extend their control to online distributions."

We find no error in the district court's preliminary rejection of this affirmative defense. The misuse defense prevents copyright holders from leveraging their limited monopoly to allow them control of areas outside the monopoly. See Laser-comb, 911 F.2d at 976-77; see also Religious Tech. Ctr. v.

Lerma, 1996 U.S. Dist. LEXIS 15454, No. 95-1107 A, 1996 WL 633131, at *11 (E.D. Va. Oct. 4, 1996) (listing circumstances which indicate improper leverage). There is no evidence here that plaintiffs seek to control areas outside of their grant of monopoly. Rather, plaintiffs seek to control reproduction and distribution of their copyrighted works, exclusive rights of copyright holders. 17 U.S.C. § 106; see also, e.g., UMG Recordings, 92 F. Supp. 2d at 351 ("A [copyright holder's] 'exclusive' rights, derived from the Constitution and the Copyright Act, include the right, within broad limits, to curb the development of such a derivative market by refusing to license a copyrighted work or by doing so only on terms the copyright owner finds acceptable."). That the copyrighted works are transmitted in another medium—MP3 format rather than audio CD— has no bearing on our analysis. See id. at 351 (finding that reproduction of audio CD into MP3 format does not "transform" the work).

## VIII.

The district court correctly recognized that a preliminary injunction against Napster's participation in copyright infringement is not only warranted but required. We believe, however, that the scope of the injunction needs modification in light of our opinion. Specifically, we reiterate that contributory liability may potentially be imposed only to the extent that Napster: (1) receives reasonable knowledge of specific infringing files with copyrighted musical compositions and sound recordings; (2) knows or should know that such files are available on the Napster system; and (3) fails to act to prevent viral distribution of the works. See Netcom, 907 F. Supp. at 1374-75. The mere existence of the Napster system, absent actual notice and Napster's demonstrated failure to remove the offending material, is insufficient to impose contributory liability. See Sony, 464 U.S. at 442-43.

Conversely, Napster may be vicariously liable when it fails to affirmatively use its ability to patrol its system and preclude access to potentially infringing files listed in its search index. Napster has both the ability to use its search function to identify infringing musical recordings and the right to bar participation of users who engage in the transmission of infringing files.

The preliminary injunction which we stayed is overbroad because it places on Napster the entire burden of ensuring that no "copying, downloading, uploading, transmitting, or distributing" of plaintiffs' works occur on the system. As stated, we place the burden on plaintiffs to provide notice to Napster of copyrighted works and files containing such works available on the Napster system before Napster has the duty to disable access to the offending content. Napster, however, also bears the burden of policing the system within the limits of the system. Here, we recognize that this is not an exact science in that the files are user named. In crafting the injunction on remand, the district court should recognize that Napster's system does not currently appear to allow Napster access to users' MP3 files.

Based on our decision to remand, Napster's additional arguments on appeal going to the scope of the injunction need not be addressed. We, however, briefly address Napster's First Amendment argument so that it is not reasserted on remand. Napster contends that the present injunction violates the First Amendment because it is broader than necessary. The company asserts two distinct free speech rights: (1) its right to publish a "directory" (here, the search index) and (2) its users' right to exchange information. We note that First Amendment concerns in copyright are allayed by the presence of the fair use doctrine. See 17 U.S.C. § 107; see generally Nihon Keizai Shimbun v. Comline Business Data, Inc., 166 F.3d 65, 74 (2d Cir. 1999); Netcom, 923 F. Supp. at 1258 (stating that the Copyright Act balances First Amendment concerns with the rights of copyright holders). There was a preliminary determination here that Napster users are not fair users. Uses of copyrighted material that are not fair uses are rightfully enjoined. See Dr. Seuss Enters. v. Penguin Books USA, Inc., 109 F.3d 1394, 1403 (9th Cir. 1997) (rejecting defendants' claim that injunction would constitute a prior restraint in violation of the First Amendment).

## IX.

We address Napster's remaining arguments: (1) that the court erred in setting a $ 5 million bond, and (2) that the district court should have imposed a constructive royalty payment structure in lieu of an injunction.

### A. Bond

Napster argues that the $ 5 million bond is insufficient because the company's value is between $ 1.5 and $ 2 billion. We review objections to the amount of a bond for abuse of discretion. Walczak v. EPL Prolong, Inc., 198 F.3d 725 (9th Cir. 1999).

We are reluctant to dramatically raise bond amounts on appeal. See GoTo. com, Inc. v. The Walt Disney Co., 202 F.3d 1199, 1211 (9th Cir. 2000); see also Fed. R. Civ. P. 65(c). The district court considered competing evidence of Napster's value and the deleterious effect that any injunction would have upon the Napster system. We cannot say that Judge Patel abused her discretion when she fixed the penal sum required for the bond.

B. Royalties

Napster contends that the district court should have imposed a monetary penalty by way of a compulsory royalty in place of an injunction. We are asked to do what the district court refused.

Napster tells us that "where great public injury would be worked by an injunction, the courts might... award damages or a continuing royalty instead of an injunction in such special circumstances." Abend v. MCA, Inc., 863 F.2d 1465, 1479 (9th Cir. 1988) (quoting 3 Melville B. Nimmer & David Nimmer, Nimmer On Copyright § 14.06[B](1988)), aff'd, 495 U.S. 207 (1990). We are at a total loss to find any" special circumstances" simply because this case requires us to apply well-established doctrines of copyright law to a new technology. Neither do we agree with Napster that an injunction would cause "great public injury." Further, we narrowly construe any suggestion that compulsory royalties are appropriate in this context because Congress has arguably limited the application of compulsory royalties to specific circumstances, none of which are present here. See 17 U.S.C. § 115.

The Copyright Act provides for various sanctions for infringers. See, e.g., 17 U.S.C. §§ 502 (injunctions); 504 (damages); and 506 (criminal penalties); see also 18 U.S.C. § 2319A (criminal penalties for the unauthorized fixation of and trafficking in sound recordings and music videos of live musical performances). These statutory sanctions represent a more than adequate legislative solution to the problem created by copyright infringement.

Imposing a compulsory royalty payment schedule would give Napster an "easy out" of this case. If such royalties were imposed, Napster would avoid penalties for any future violation of an injunction, statutory copyright damages and any possible criminal penalties for continuing infringement. The royalty structure would also grant Napster the luxury of either choosing to continue and pay royalties or shut down. On the other hand, the wronged parties would be forced to do business with a company that profits from the wrongful use of intellectual properties. Plaintiffs would lose the power to control their intellectual property: they could not make a business decision not to license their property to Napster, and, in the event they planned to do business with Napster, compulsory royalties would take away the copyright holders' ability to negotiate the terms of any contractual arrangement.

## X.

We affirm in part, reverse in part and remand.

We direct that the preliminary injunction fashioned by the district court prior to this appeal shall remain stayed until it is modified by the district court to conform to the requirements of this opinion. We order a partial remand of this case on the date of the filing of this opinion for the limited purpose of permitting the district court to proceed with the settlement and entry of the modified preliminary injunction.

Even though the preliminary injunction requires modification, appellees have substantially and primarily prevailed on appeal. Appellees shall recover their statutory costs on appeal. See Fed. R. App. P. 39(a)(4) ("if a judgment is affirmed in part, reversed in part, modified, or vacated, costs are taxed only as the court orders.").

AFFIRMED IN PART, REVERSED IN PART AND REMANDED.

UMG Recordings, Inc. v. MP3.com, Inc.
United States District Court for the Southern District of New York
August 23, 2000, Decided
00 Civ. 472 (JSR)
109 F. Supp. 2d 223

JED S. RAKOFF, U.S.D.J.

By order dated July 31, 2000, the Court denied plaintiff's motion to have the statutory damages in this case computed on a "per song" rather than "per-CD" basis. Here is why.

Under the Copyright Act, "the copyright owner may elect, at any time before final judgment is rendered, to recover, instead of actual damages and profits, an award of statutory damages for all infringements involved in the action, with respect to any one work, for which any one infringer is liable individually, or for which any two or more infringers are liable jointly and severally, in a sum of not less than $ 750 or more than $ 30,000 as the court considers just." 17 U.S.C. § 504(c)(1). In other words, for the purpose of computing statutory damages, the relevant unit is not the number of infringements but the number of infringed "works." See Twin Peaks Prods. Inc. v. Publications Int'l, Ltd., 996 F.2d 1366, 1381 (2d Cir. 1993). Unfortunately, the Copyright Act does not define the term "work." But in their Complaint in this case, as well as in their successful motion for summary judgment on the issue of liability, plaintiffs focused on defendant's unlawful copying of plaintiffs' CDs, implying that each such CD was the relevant "work" unit for purposes of this case.

In their instant motion, however, plaintiffs argue that the relevant "work" unit for purposes of computing statutory damages is each individual, copyrighted song on each such CD, as opposed to each copyrighted CD as a whole. This argument immediately encounters the objection that the very subsection of the Copyright Act that authorizes the award of statutory damages, § 504(c)(1), expressly states that: "For the purposes of this subsection, all parts of a compilation or derivative work constitute one work." As stated in the applicable House Report, section 504(c)(1) "makes clear . . . that, although they are regarded as independent works for other purposes, 'all the parts of a compilation or derivative work constitute one work'" for the purposes of determining an award of statutory damages. See H.R. Rep. No. 1476, 94th Cong., 2d Sess. 162, reprinted in 1976 U.S.C.C.A.N. 5659, 5778. Accord, e.g., ASA Music Prods. v. Thomsun Electronics, 1998 U.S. Dist. LEXIS 22362, 49 U.S.P.Q.2D (BNA) 1545, 1552, 1998 WL 988195 (S.D.N.Y. 1998); RSO Records, Inc. v. Peri,

596 F. Supp. 849, 862 n. 16 (S.D.N.Y. 1984); Stokes Seeds Ltd. v. Geo. W. Park Seed Co., Inc., 783 F. Supp. 104, 107-08 (W.D.N.Y. 1991).

Plaintiffs concede that each CD that defendant copied is a "compilation" under § 504(c)(1), see Pls. R. Mem. at 1. They nonetheless argue that because each song on each CD has an "independent economic value," statutory damages should be awarded for each song. See Gamma Audio & Video, Inc. v. Ean-Chea, 11 F.3d 1106, 1117 (1st Cir. 1993). They suggest that such a conclusion is implicit in Twin Peaks, supra, in which the Second Circuit held that eight separately written television episodes of a widely known series constituted eight different works for purposes of awarding statutory damages, see 996 F.2d at 1381, and they further emphasize that in this very case the defendant listed individual songs, encouraged users to create their own playlists without regard to a given CD album, and measured the traffic on its service according to the number of "hits" received for each individual song-title. See Goodman Aff., Exhs. 2 and 3.

But none of this is relevant in the face of the unequivocal statutory language and plaintiffs' own assertion that what the defendant actually copied were the complete CDs. Nor has the Second Circuit ever adopted the "independent economic value" test. In Twin Peaks, in fact, the Second Circuit did not even discuss the independent economic value, vel non, of the copyrighted television episodes.

More generally, it is hard to see the appropriateness of an "independent economic value" test to statutory damages — as opposed to actual damages, for which every copyright holder remains free to sue on a "per-song" rather than "per-CD" basis. If such a test were applied, the result would be to make a total mockery of Congress' express mandate that all parts of a compilation must be treated as a single "work" for purposes of computing statutory damages, since, as the House Report expressly recognizes, the copyrighted parts of a compilation will often constitute "independent works for other purposes." H.R. Rep. No. 1476, 94th Cong., 2d Sess. 162, reprinted in 1976 U.S.C.C.A.N. 5659, 5778.

When Congress speaks, the courts must listen: so our constitution mandates. When, as here, Congress' statement is clear, to disregard that message would be nothing less than an unconstitutional arrogation of power by the judiciary. The Court declines plaintiffs' invitation to tread that treacherous path.

-------------------

In *UMG Recordings*, plaintiff moved to have statutory damages in its copyright case on a "per song" rather than "per-CD" basis. The court didn't buy it, on the basis that it was contrary to express statutory language that considers all parts of compilation or derivative work as one "work" when it comes to the calculation of damages.

In the following case, *New Kids on the Block v. News Am. Publig. Inc*, 971 F.2d 302 (9th Cir. 1992), the New Kids sued newspapers that had used plaintiff's group's names to conduct polls. The newspapers' granting of summary judgment was affirmed on the basis that they were entitled to the defense of a fair use for trademark infringement because they used the name for identification, not endorsement. Defendants also had a complete defense to misappropriation claims under Cal. Civ. Code Section 3344(d), because they used the group's name in connection with a true news account.

New Kids on the Block v. News Am. Publ'g, Inc.
United States Court of Appeals for the Ninth Circuit
December 4, 1991; July 24, 1992, Filed
No. 90-56219, No. 90-56258
971 F.2d 302

OPINION

KOZINSKI, Circuit Judge.

The individual plaintiffs perform professionally as The New Kids on the Block, reputedly one of today's hottest musical acts. This case requires us to weigh their rights in that name against the rights of others to use it in identifying the New Kids as the subjects of public opinion polls.

Background

No longer are entertainers limited to their craft in marketing themselves to the public. This is the age of the multi-media publicity blitzkrieg: Trading on their popularity, many entertainers hawk posters, T-shirts, badges, coffee mugs and the like - handsomely supplementing their incomes while boosting their public images. The New Kids are no exception; the record in this case indicates there are more than 500 products or services bearing the New Kids trademark. Among these are services taking advantage of a recent development in telecommunications: 900 area code numbers, where the caller is charged a fee, a portion of which is paid to the call recipient. Fans can call various New Kids 900 numbers to listen to the New Kids talk about themselves, to listen to other fans talk about the New Kids, or to leave messages for the New Kids and other fans.

The defendants, two newspapers of national circulation, conducted separate polls of their readers seeking an answer to a pressing question: Which one of the New Kids is the most popular? USA Today's announcement contained a picture of the New Kids and asked, "Who's the best on the block?" The announcement listed a 900 number for voting, noted that "any USA Today profits from this phone line will go to charity," and closed with the following:

New Kids on the Block are pop's hottest group. Which of the five is your fave? Or are they a turn off? . . . Each call costs 50 cents. Results in Friday's Life section.

The Star's announcement, under a picture of the New Kids, went to the heart of the matter: "Now which kid is the sexiest?" The announcement, which appeared in the middle of a page containing a story on a New Kids concert, also stated:

Which of the New Kids on the Block would you most like to move next door? * wants to know which cool New Kid is the hottest with our readers.

Readers were directed to a 900 number to register their votes; each call cost 95 cents per minute.

Fearing that the two newspapers were undermining their hegemony over their fans, the New Kids filed a shotgun complaint in federal court raising no fewer than ten claims: (1) common law trademark infringement; (2) Lanham Act false advertising; (3) Lanham Act false designation of origin; (4) Lanham Act unfair competition; (5) state trade name infringement; (6) state false advertising; (7) state unfair competition; (8) commercial misappropriation; (9) common-law misappropriation; and (10) intentional interference with prospective economic advantage. The two papers raised the First Amendment as a defense, on the theory that the polls were part and parcel of their "news-gathering activities." The district court granted summary judgment for defendants. 745 F. Supp. 1540 (C.D. Cal. 1990).

## Discussion

While the district court granted summary judgment on First Amendment grounds, we are free to affirm on any ground fairly presented by the record. Jackson v. Southern Cal. Gas Co., 881 F.2d 638, 643 (9th Cir. 1989); Pelleport Inv., Inc. v. Budco Quality Theatres, Inc., 741 F.2d 273, 278 (9th Cir. 1984). Indeed, where we are able to resolve the case on nonconstitutional grounds, we ordinarily must avoid reaching the constitutional issue. In re Snyder, 472 U.S. 634, 642-43, 86 L. Ed. 2d 504, 105 S. Ct. 2874 (1985); Schweiker v. Hogan, 457 U.S. 569, 585, 73 L. Ed. 2d 227, 102 S. Ct. 2597 (1982). Therefore, we consider first whether the New Kids have stated viable claims on their various causes of action.

### I.

A. Since at least the middle ages, trademarks have served primarily to identify the source of goods and services, "to facilitate the tracing of 'false' or defective wares and the punishment of the offending craftsman." F. Schechter, The Historical Foundations of the Law Relating to Trade-marks 47 (1925). The law has protected trademarks since the early seventeenth century, and the primary focus of trademark law has been misappropriation - the problem of one producer's placing his rival's mark on his own goods. See, e.g., Southern v. How, 79 Eng. Rep. 1243 (K.B. 1618). The law of trademark infringement was imported from England into our legal system with its primary goal the prevention of unfair competition through misappropriated marks. See, e.g., Taylor v. Carpenter, 23 F. Cas. 742 (C.C.D. Mass. 1844) (Story, J.). Although an initial attempt at federal regulation was declared unconstitutional, see the Trade-Mark Cases, 100 U.S. 82, 25 L. Ed. 550 (1879), trademarks have been covered by a comprehensive federal statutory scheme since the passage of the Lanham Act in 1946.

Throughout the development of trademark law, the purpose of trademarks remained constant and limited: Identification of the manufacturer or sponsor of a good or the provider of a service. And the wrong protected against was traditionally equally limited: Preventing producers from free-riding on their rivals' marks. Justice Story outlined the classic scenario a century and a half ago when he described a case of "unmitigated and designed infringement of the rights of the plaintiffs, for the purpose of defrauding the public and taking from the plaintiffs the fair earnings of their skill, labor and enterprise." Taylor, 23 F. Cas. at 744. The core protection of the Lanham Act remains faithful to this conception. See 15 U.S.C. § 1114 (prohibiting unauthorized use in commerce of registered marks). Indeed, this area of the law is generally referred to as "unfair competition" - unfair because, by using a rival's mark, the infringer capitalizes on the investment of time, money and resources of his competitor; unfair also because, by doing so, he obtains the consumer's hard-earned dollar through something akin to fraud. See Paul Heald, Federal Intellectual Property Law and the Economics of Preemption, 76 Iowa L. Rev. 959, 1002-03 (1991).

A trademark is a limited property right in a particular word, phrase or symbol. And although English is a language rich in imagery, we need not belabor the point that some words, phrases or symbols better convey their intended meanings than others. See San Francisco Arts & Athletics, Inc. v. U.S.O.C., 483 U.S. 522, 569, 97 L. Ed. 2d 427, 107 S. Ct. 2971 (1987) (Brennan, J., dissenting) ("[A] jacket reading 'I Strongly Resent the Draft' would not have conveyed Cohen's message."). Indeed, the primary cost of recognizing property rights in trademarks is the removal of words from (or perhaps non-entrance into) our language. Thus, the holder of a trademark will be denied protection if it is (or becomes) generic, i.e., if it does not relate exclusively to the trademark owner's product. See, e.g., Kellogg Co. v. National Biscuit Co., 305 U.S. 111, 83 L. Ed. 73, 59 S. Ct. 109 (1938) ("shredded wheat"); Eastern Air Lines, Inc. v. New York Air Lines, Inc., 559 F. Supp. 1270 (S.D.N.Y. 1983) ("air-shuttle" to describe hourly plane service). This requirement allays fears that producers will deplete the stock of useful words by asserting exclusive rights in them. When a trademark comes to describe a class of goods rather than an individual product, the courts will hold as a matter of law that use of that mark does not imply sponsorship or endorsement of the product by the original holder.

A related problem arises when a trademark also describes a person, a place or an attribute of a product. If the trademark holder were allowed exclusive rights in such use, the language would be depleted in much the same way as if generic words were protectable . Thus trademark law recognizes a defense where the mark is used only "to describe the goods or services of [a] party, or their geographic origin." 15 U.S.C. § 1115(b)(4). "The 'fair-use' defense, in essence, forbids a trademark registrant to appropriate a descriptive term for his exclusive use and so prevent others from accurately describing a characteristic of their goods." Soweco, Inc. v. Shell Oil Co., 617 F.2d 1178, 1185 (5th Cir. 1980). Once again, the courts will hold as a matter of law that the original producer does not sponsor or endorse another product that uses his mark in a descriptive manner. See, e.g., Schmid Laboratories v. Youngs Drug Products Corp., 482 F. Supp. 14 (D.N.J. 1979) ("ribbed" condoms).

With many well-known trademarks, such as Jell-O, Scotch tape and Kleenex, there are equally informative non-trademark words describing the products (gelatin, cellophane tape and facial tissue). But sometimes there is no descriptive substitute, and a problem closely related to genericity and descriptiveness is presented when many goods and services are effectively identifiable only by their trademarks. For example, one might refer to "the two-time world champions" or "the professional basketball team from Chicago," but it's far simpler (and more likely to be understood) to refer to the Chicago Bulls. In such cases, use of the trademark does not imply sponsorship or endorsement of the product because the mark is used only to describe the thing, rather than to identify its source.

Indeed, it is often virtually impossible to refer to a particular product for purposes of comparison, criticism, point of reference or any other such purpose without using the mark. For example, reference to a large automobile manufacturer based in Michigan would not differentiate among the Big Three; reference to a large Japanese manufacturer of home electronics would narrow the field to a dozen or more companies. Much useful social and commercial discourse would be all but impossible if speakers were under threat of an infringement lawsuit every time they made reference to a person, company or product by using its trademark.

A good example of this is Volkswagenwerk Aktiengesellschaft v. Church, 411 F.2d 350 (9th Cir. 1969), where we held that Volkswagen could not prevent an automobile repair shop from using its mark. We recognized that in "advertising [the repair of Volkswagens, it] would be difficult, if not impossible, for [Church] to avoid altogether the use of the word 'Volkswagen' or its abbreviation 'VW,' which are the normal terms which, to the public at large, signify appellant's cars." Id. at 352. Church did not suggest to customers that he was part of the Volkswagen organization or that his repair shop was sponsored or authorized by VW; he merely used the words "Volkswagen" and "VW" to convey information about the types of cars he repaired. Therefore, his use of the Volkswagen trademark was not an infringing use.

The First Circuit confronted a similar problem when the holder of the trademark "Boston Marathon" tried to stop a television station from using the name:

The words "Boston Marathon" . . . do more than call attention to Channel 5's program; they also describe the event that Channel 5 will broadcast. Common sense suggests (consistent with the record here) that a viewer who sees those words flash upon the screen will believe simply that Channel 5 will show, or is showing, or has shown, the marathon, not that Channel 5 has some special approval from the [trademark holder] to do so. In technical trademark jargon, the use of words for descriptive purposes is called a "fair use," and the law usually permits it even if the words themselves also constitute a trademark.

WCVB-TV v. Boston Athletic Ass'n, 926 F.2d 42, 46 (1st Cir. 1991). Similarly, competitors may use a rival's trademark in advertising and other channels of communication if the use is not false or misleading. See, e.g., Smith v. Chanel, Inc., 402 F.2d 562 (9th Cir. 1968) (maker of imitation perfume may use original's trademark in promoting product).

Cases like these are best understood as involving a non-trademark use of a mark - a use to which the infringement laws simply do not apply, just as videotaping television shows for private home use does not implicate the copyright holder's exclusive right to reproduction. See Sony Corp. v. Universal City Studios, Inc., 464 U.S. 417, 447-51, 78 L. Ed. 2d 574, 104 S. Ct. 774 (1984). Indeed, we may generalize a class of cases where the use of the trademark does not attempt to capitalize on consumer confusion or to appropriate the cachet of one product for a different one. Such nominative use of a mark - where the only word reasonably available to describe a particular thing is pressed into service - lies outside the strictures of trademark law: Because it does not implicate the source-identification function that is the purpose of trademark, it does not constitute unfair competition; such use is fair because it does not imply sponsorship or endorsement by the trademark holder. "When the mark is used in a way that does not deceive the public we see no such sanctity in the word as to prevent its being used to tell the truth." Prestonettes, Inc. v. Coty, 264 U.S. 359, 368, 68 L. Ed. 731, 44 S. Ct. 350 (1924) (Holmes, J.).

To be sure, this is not the classic fair use case where the defendant has used the plaintiff's mark to describe the defendant's own product. Here, the New Kids trademark is used to refer to the New Kids themselves. We therefore do not purport to alter the test applicable in the paradigmatic fair use case. If the defendant's use of the plaintiff's trademark refers to something other than the plaintiff's product, the traditional fair use inquiry will continue to govern. But, where the defendant uses a trademark to describe the plaintiff's product, rather than its own, we hold that a commercial user is entitled to a nominative fair use defense provided he meets the following three requirements: First, the product or service in question must be one not readily identifiable without use of the trademark; second, only so much of the mark or marks may be used as is reasonably necessary to identify the product or service; and third, the user must do nothing that would, in conjunction with the mark, suggest sponsorship or endorsement by the trademark holder.

B. The New Kids do not claim there was anything false or misleading about the newspapers' use of their mark. Rather, the first seven causes of action, while purporting to state different claims, all hinge on one key factual allegation: that the newspapers' use of the New Kids name in conducting the unauthorized polls somehow implied that the New Kids were sponsoring the polls. It is no more reasonably possible, however, to refer to the New Kids as an entity than it is to refer to the Chicago Bulls, Volkswagens or the Boston Marathon without using the trademark. Indeed, how could someone not conversant with the proper names of the individual New Kids talk about the group at all? While plaintiffs' trademark certainly deserves protection against copycats and those who falsely claim that the New Kids have endorsed or sponsored them, such protection does not extend to rendering newspaper articles, conversations, polls and comparative advertising impossible. The first nominative use requirement is therefore met.

Also met are the second and third requirements. Both The Star and USA Today reference the New Kids only to the extent necessary to identify them as the subject of the polls; they do not use the New Kids' distinctive logo or anything else that isn't needed to make the announcements intelligible to readers. Finally, nothing in the announcements suggests joint sponsorship or endorsement by the New Kids. The USA Today announcement implies quite the contrary by asking whether the New Kids might be "a turn off." The Star's poll is more effusive but says nothing that expressly or by fair implication connotes endorsement or joint sponsorship on the part of the New Kids.

The New Kids argue that, even if the newspapers are entitled to a nominative fair use defense for the announcements, they are not entitled to it for the polls themselves, which were money-making enterprises separate and apart from the newspapers' reporting businesses. According to plaintiffs, defendants could have minimized the intrusion into their rights by using an 800 number or asking readers to call in on normal telephone lines which would not have resulted in a profit to the newspapers based on the conduct of the polls themselves.

The New Kids see this as a crucial difference, distinguishing this case from Volkswagenwerk, WCBV-TV and other nominative use cases. The New Kids' argument in support of this distinction is not entirely implausible: They point out that their fans, like everyone else, have limited resources. Thus a dollar spent calling the newspapers' 900 lines to express loyalty to the New Kids may well be a dollar not spent on New Kids products and services, including the New Kids' own 900 numbers. In short, plaintiffs argue that a nominative fair use defense is inapplicable where the use in question competes directly with that of the trademark holder.

We reject this argument. While the New Kids have a limited property right in their name, that right does not entitle them to control their fans' use of their own money. Where, as here, the use does not imply sponsorship or endorsement, the fact that it is carried on for profit and in competition with the trademark holder's business is beside the point. See, e.g., Universal City Studios, Inc. v. Ideal Publishing Corp., 195 U.S.P.Q. 761 (S.D.N.Y. 1977) (magazine's use of TV program's trademark "Hardy Boys" in connection with photographs of show's stars not infringing). Voting for their favorite New Kid may be, as plaintiffs point out, a way for fans to articulate their loyalty to the group, and this may diminish the resources available for products and services they sponsor. But the trademark laws do not give the New Kids the right to channel their fans' enthusiasm (and dollars) only into items licensed or authorized by them. See International Order of Job's Daughters v. Lindeburg & Co., 633 F.2d 912 (9th Cir. 1990) (no infringement where unauthorized jewelry maker produced rings and pins bearing fraternal organization's trademark). The New Kids could not use the trademark laws to prevent the publication of an unauthorized group biography or to censor all parodies or satires which use their name. We fail to see a material difference between these examples and the use here.

Summary judgment was proper as to the first seven causes of action because they all hinge on a theory of implied endorsement; there was none here as the uses in question were purely nominative.

## II.

The New Kids raise three additional claims that merit brief attention.

A. The New Kids claim that USA Today's and The Star's use of their name amounted to both commercial and common law misappropriation under California law. Although there are subtle differences between these two causes of action, all that's material here is a key similarity between them: H The papers have a complete defense to both claims if they used the New Kids name "in connection with any news, public affairs, or sports broadcast or account" which was true in all material respects. See Cal. Civ. Code § 3344(d); Eastwood v. Superior Ct., 149 Cal. App. 3d 409, 421 & 426, 198 Cal. Rptr. 342 (1983) (extending the section 3344(d) defense to common law misappropriation claims); see also Leidholdt v. L.F.P. Inc., 860 F.2d 890, 895 (9th Cir. 1988), cert. denied, 489 U.S. 1080, 103 L. Ed. 2d 837, 109 S. Ct. 1532 (1989); Maheu v. CBS, Inc., 201 Cal. App. 3d 662, 676-77, 247 Cal. Rptr. 304, 7 U.S.P.Q.2D (BNA) 1238 (1988).

In this case, USA Today's and The Star's use of the New Kids' name was "in connection with" news accounts: The Star ran concurrent articles on the New Kids along with its 900-number poll, while USA Today promised a subsequent story on the popularity of various members of the singing group. Both papers also have an established track record of polling their readers and then reporting the poll results as part of a later news story. The New Kids' misappropriation claims are barred by California Civil Code section 3344(d).

B. The New Kids' remaining claim is for intentional interference with prospective economic advantage, but they ignore the maxim that all's fair in love, war and the free market. Plaintiffs' case rests on the assumption that the polls operated to siphon off the New Kids' fans or divert their resources away from "official" New Kids products. Even were we to accept this premise, no tort claim has been made out: "So long as the plaintiff's contractual relations are merely contemplated or potential, it is considered to be in the interest of the public that any competitor should be free to divert them to himself by all fair and reasonable means. . . . In short, it is no tort to beat a business rival to prospective customers." A-Mark Coin Co. v. General Mills, Inc., 148 Cal. App. 3d 312, 323, 195 Cal. Rptr. 859 (1983); see B. Witkin, 5 Summary of California Law § 669 at 766 (1988) ("one competitor may induce customers of the other to do business with him"). Because we have already determined that the newspapers' use of the mark was "fair and reasonable," the New Kids do not have a tort claim based on the fact that they may have lost some business to a competitor.

Conclusion

The district court's judgment is

AFFIRMED.

---

## MASTER TRACK LICENSE

THIS AGREEMENT is made and entered into as of this \_\_\_ day of _____, 20\_\_\_\_by and between _____ (hereinafter referred to as "Licensee") and between _____ (hereinafter referred to as "Licensor").

It is the desire of Licensee to use that certain master recording (hereinafter referred to as the "Master") embodying the performance of _____ (hereinafter referred to as the "Artist") of the musical composition _____ (hereinafter referred to as the "Composition") in episodes of _____ (hereinafter referred to as the "Program").

1. In consideration of the mutual covenants set forth herein, Licensor hereby grants to Licensee, its successors in interest, assigns and licensees the non-exclusive, irrevocable right to record, dub and synchronize the Master in whole or in part into and with the Program, advertisements and trailers thereof,

and to exhibit distribute, exploit, market and perform each Master embodied within the Program, to be used in connection with audio-visual contrivances such as video cassettes, video tapes, video records and similar compact audio-visual devices whether now known or hereafter developed (hereinafter referred to as "Videograms"). Such rights pursuant to this paragraph I (b), include:

> (i) the right to utilize such Videograms for any of the purposes, uses and performances hereinabove set forth;

> (ii) the right to sell, lease, license or otherwise make such Videograms available to the public as a device intended primarily for "home use" (as such term is commonly understood in the phonograph record industry).

2. In full consideration of the rights herein granted to Licensee, Licensee agrees to pay to Licensor the sum of _____ ($_____) Dollars for the Master licensed hereunder, which sum shall be payable within ten (10) days of first use by Licensee of the Master in the Videograms. Said ($_____) Dollars shall represent payment in full for the right to distribute or license the distribution worldwide of up to Ten Thousand (10,000) Videograms of the Program. Licensee shall have the right to distribute or license the distribution of such Videograms in unlimited quantities, worldwide, subject to additional payment to Licensor of ($_____) Dollars for each additional Ten Thousand (10,000 units (or fraction thereof) distributed above the initial Ten Thousand (10,000) units. Each such additional ($_____)Dollars payment shall be paid to Licensor not later than the end of the semi annual period (June 30 and December 31) following the month during which the first unit of said additional Ten Thousand (10,000) units (or fraction thereof) were distributed in accordance with the terms hereof.

3. Licensor represents and warrants that it has obtained any approvals and permissions required from the Artist (or any other parties) and to pay to Artist (or any other such parties) any fees (other than union "re-use" fees), if applicable, with respect thereto.

4. Licensee agrees to obtain the appropriate license from the owner or controller of the Composition embodied in the Master and pay all fees with respect thereto.

5. Licensee agrees to make any and all payments to musicians, vocalists and any other parties (other than Artist) whose performances are included in the Master, if such payments are required under the American Federation of

Musicians Labor Agreement and/or any other applicable union or guild agreements in connection with the so-called "re-use" of the Master. Subject to availability, Licensor shall promptly provide Licensee with all necessary information to enable Licensee to make such payments, including without limitation the names, addresses, social security numbers and union local numbers of such performers.

6. Nothing herein contained shall be deemed to obligate Licensee to use the Master, or to produce, exhibit, exploit or broadcast the Program, and Licensee shall have fulfilled its entire obligation by payment of the sum provided in paragraph 2.

7. In the event each or any Master is used within the Program:

> (a) Licensee agrees to include a written announcement as to the title of the Composition and the name of the Artist and Licensor just prior to the use of the Master within the Program.

> (b) Licensee agrees to further include a visual courtesy screen credit at the conclusion of the Master use within each Program and all Videogram copies indicating the title of the Composition, the Artist and Licensor's name, to appear substantially in the following manner:

> Title of Song: "_____"
> Performed by: "_____"

> (c) Any casual, inadvertent, unavoidable or unintentional failure to give such credit, due to exigencies of time or otherwise, shall not be deemed a breach hereof. Licensee shall not be liable for the acts or omissions of third persons in such connection.

8. Licensor agrees to supply Licensee, at Licensee's request, with a suitable first-rate tape copy of the Master licensed hereunder, and Licensee agrees to pay Licensor's actual costs incurred in connection with the duplication and delivery of such tape copy.

9. Subject to Licensor's ability to obtain approval from its Artist, the parties hereto, upon Licensee's request, agree to negotiate in good faith in the event that Licensee elects to exploit the Program containing the Master by any means other than the use for which the license is provided herein, including but not limited to free TV, pay TV, subscription TV, CATV and cable TV.

10. Notwithstanding anything to the contrary expressed or implied above, this license shall specifically exclude so-called soundtrack album or any other record rights.

11. Licensor hereby grants to Licensee the non-exclusive, worldwide right to use the Master in the exhibition of the Program on any commercial carriers such as airlines, ships and trains. Licensor further grants to Licensee the non-exclusive right to use the Master in connection with the Program in traditional non-theatrical markets such as educational, religious or charitable organizations, armed forces, clubs, libraries and film festivals.

12. Licensor warrants that Licensor is the exclusive owner or controller of the Master and that Licensor has the right to enter into this agreement and to grant to Licensee each and every right granted to Licensee herein.

13. Each party (the "Indemnitor") agrees to indemnify the other party (the "Indemnitee") and undertakes to hold the Indemnitee, its successors in interest, assigns, licensees, affiliates, officers, employees and agents harmless from all claims, actions, damages, liabilities, losses, costs and/or expenses, including reasonable attorneys' fees, resulting from any breach or claim of breach by the Indemnitor of any of the representations, warranties and agreements made herein by the Indemnitor. Such Indemnitee shall send written notice to the Indemnitor of any such claim and the Indemnitor shall have the right to participate in the defense of any such claim, at the sole expense of the Indemnitor. The Indemnitee shall not settle any such claim without receiving the prior written consent of the Indemnitor. Such written consent shall not be unreasonably withheld.

14. All notices hereunder shall be in writing and shall be addressed to Licensee and to Licensor at the addresses given on the first page hereof, until Licensee or Licensor shall give the other written notice of new addresses. Copies of all notices to Licensee will be sent to _____. All notices shall be sent either by certified or registered mail, return receipt requested, postage prepaid, or by telegram, charges prepaid. Service of any such written notice shall be deemed to have been effected as of the date of deposit in the mail or the date of deposit in the telegraph office, as the case may be.

15. Licensee may freely transfer and assign this license or all or any of its rights hereunder; this license shall inure to the benefit of Licensee, its successors in interest, assigns and licensees. No assignment unless consented to

by Licensor, shall relieve Licensee from liability for the performance of all the terms and conditions as set forth hereinabove.

16. This agreement constitutes the entire agreement between Licensee and Licensors and cannot be altered, modified, amended or waived, in whole or in part, except by a written instrument signed by the parties sought to be bound. Should any provision of this agreement be held to be void, invalid or inoperative, such decision shall not affect any other provision hereof, and the remainder of this agreement shall be effective as though such void, invalid or inoperative provision had not been contained herein. This agreement shall be governed by and construed in accordance with the laws of the State of

_____.

17. In no event shall Producer have fewer rights than a member of the public would have in the absence of this agreement.

If the foregoing correctly reflects the mutual understanding between the parties hereto, please so indicate by signing below.

LICENSEE: _____ LICENSOR: _____

Questions and Discussion

1. "Although *A&M Records v. Napster, Inc.* no longer reflects state-of-the-art for peer-to-peer file sharing, the case captures the technological and social trends critical to understanding the revolution taking place in music distribution. It also anticipated changes in legal doctrines of fair use and reveals the impact of computer software on the music industry. Napster's original operation ceased because of this and other legal difficulties over copyright infringement, and Roxio eventually acquired it. Thereafter, Napster was an online music store; it merged with Rhapsody in December 2011" (W. Champion, Intellectual Property Law in the Sports and Entertainment 57 (footnote omitted). Is the "ideal of Napster" dead? Should it be?

2. "Copyright infringement occurs when another person's software, music, or any other media is downloaded without their permission. This usually occurs on the Internet and is done in a purposeful manner." ". . . Napster established a website where it offered downloads of songs of all genres—new and old. A&M Records . . . accused Napster of stealing music and making it available to people Worldwide." ". . . Napster settled for $26 million to different recording companies and songwriters, and its apology and agreement to shut down the site likely saved it millions more." (Champion, Intellectual Property in the Sports and Entertainment Industries 60, footnote omitted). Did Napster go too far in making amends, or not far enough?

3. The court in *Napster* found a commercial use in the "repeated and exploitative copying" of the works, even if they were not offered for sale. Does that make sense?

4. The *Napster* court noted that file sharing by individual users is not "fair use." But, is that Napster's fault?

5. In *Metro-Goldwyn-Mayer Studios, Inc. v. Grokster, Ltd.*, 518 F. Supp. 2d 1197 (C.D. Cal. 2007), the court established that it had the power to issue a permanent injunction prohibiting this distributor of peer-to-peer file sharing software from inducing infringement by end users of its software to require the distributor to undertake sufficient efforts to minimize end user infringement. Can we ever stop all end user infringement?

6. The *New Kids* court ruled that there are three elements to satisfying a nominative fair use defense: "where the defendant uses a trademark to describe the plaintiff's product rather than its own we hold that a commercial user is entitled to nominative fair use defense provided he meets the following three requirements: First, the product or service in question must be one not readily identifiable without use of the trademark; second, only so much of the mark or marks may be used as is reasonably necessary to identify the product or service; and third, the user must do nothing that would, in conjunction with the

mark, suggest sponsorship or endorsement by the trademark holder" (at 308). Should the New Kids have decided differently in using these particular facts as a basic maneuver in emasculating the fair use defense?